The Tao of Islam

The Tao of Islam

A Sourcebook on Gender Relationships in Islamic Thought

Sachiko Murata

Foreword by
Annemarie Schimmel

STATE UNIVERSITY OF NEW YORK PRESS

Production by Ruth Fisher

Marketing by Bernadette LaManna

Published by
State University of New York Press, Albany

Printed in the United States of America

For information, address the State University of New York Press,
State University Plaza, Albany, NY 12246

Library of Congress Cataloging-in-Publication Data

Murata, Sachiko, (Date).
The Tao of Islam : a sourcebook on gender relationships in Islamic thought / Sachiko Murata : foreword by Annemarie Schimmel.
p. cm.
Includes bibliographical references and index.
ISBN 0-7914-0913-9 (alk. paper). — ISBN 0-7914-0914-7 (pbk. : alk. paper)
1. Women in Islam. 2. Islam—Doctrines. 3. Cosmology, Islamic. 4. Tao. I. Title.
BP173.4.M87 1992
297′.1978344—dc20 91-2610
CIP

10 9 8 7 6 5 4 3 2 1

CONTENTS

Foreword by Annemarie Schimmel ◆ vii
A Note on Dates and Citations from the Koran ◆ xi

Introduction ◆ 1
The Intellectual Tradition in Islam 2 / The Feminist Critique of Islam 4 / The Background of the Present Book 4 / Chinese and Islamic Thought 6 / Theological Polarity 8 / Signs of God 10 / Cosmic Correspondences 14 / Human Equilibrium 15 / The Plan of the Book 17

PART 1

1 **The Three Realities** ◆ 23
Signs in the Horizons and the Souls 23 / Qualitative Correspondence 27 / Qualitative Levels 31 / Human All-Comprehensiveness 33 / Children of the Elements 37 / The Myth of Adam's Creation 39 / Human Becoming 43 / The Cosmic and Human Books 45

PART 2: Theology

2 **Divine Duality** ◆ 49
God and the Essence 49 / Incomparability and Similarity 51 / Complementary Names 55 / God and His Vassal 57 / The One and the Two 58 / The Creation of the Many 61 / The Differentiation of the Undifferentiated 62 / Being and Knowledge 66 / Majesty and Beauty 69 / Awe and Intimacy 74 / Social Implications of Divine Duality 76

3 **The Two Hands of God** ◆ 81
Right and Left 82 / The Views of Koran Commentators 84 / Fingers and Feet 85 / The Two Hands in the *Futūḥāt al-makkiyya* 88 / The *Fuṣūṣ al-ḥikam* 91 / Mu'ayyid al-Dīn Jandī 92 / ʿAbd al-Razzāq Kāshānī 96 / Dāwūd Qayṣarī 99 / Ṣadr al-Dīn Qūnawī 101 / Saʿīd al-Dīn Farghānī 105 / Farghānī on the Two Handfuls 109

PART 3: Cosmology

4 **Heaven and Earth** ◆ 117
The Creation of the Cosmos 118 / The Tao of Heaven and Earth 121 / Heaven and Earth as Correlative Terms 123 / Similitudes 127 / Shifting Relationships 130 / The Seven Heavens 133 / The Four Elements 135 / The Virtues of the Earth 139

5 Macrocosmic Marriage ◆ 143
Fathers and Mothers 144 / Universal Marriage 147 / Triplicity 151 / The Pen and the Tablet 153 / The Intellect and the Soul 155 / Natural Children 158 / Changing Relationships 161 / The Faces of the Intellect 164 / The Two Wings of Gabriel 168

6 Human Marriage ◆ 171
Marriage in Society 171 / Man's Degree over Woman (I) 173 / Man's Degree over Woman (II) 177 / Mutual Love 181 / Women Made Lovable 183 / The *Fuṣūṣ al-ḥikam* 188 / Mutual Longing 190 / Witnessing God in Women 191 / Marriage and Creation 193 / Perfect Sexual Union 195 / The Symbolism of Grammatical Gender 196 / Spiritual Counsel 199

7 The Womb ◆ 203
Universal Worship 203 / The Mercy of Existence 206 / Nature as Wife and Mother 209 / Love for Parents 212 / The Womb as Microcosm 215 / The Womb as Nature 218

PART 4: Spiritual Psychology

8 Static Hierarchy ◆ 225
Principles of *Taʾwīl* 225 / Names of the Unseen 229 / Signs of the Microcosm 229 / Spirit 232 / Soul 236 / Intellect 238 / The Spirit's Kingdom 242 / Heaven and Earth 243

9 Dynamics of the Soul ◆ 249
Struggle on the Path to God 249 / The Soul's Evil 254 / Conflicting Character Traits 257 / The Soul's Receptivity 260 / Manliness and Chivalry 266 / Negative Masculinity 269 / Adam, Eve, and Iblis 273 / The Soul's Animals 277 / Purifying the Soul 283

10 The Heart ◆ 289
In the Koran and the Hadith 289 / Between Spirit and Soul 292 / The Heart in the School of Ibn al-ʿArabī 299 / The Birth of the Heart 304 / The Heart's Birth According to ʿIzz al-Dīn Kāshānī 306 / The Heart's Birth According to Ibn al-ʿArabī's School 311 / The Soul as Virgin Mother 313 / The Perfected Heart 314 / True Men and True Women 316

Postscript ◆ 321
Appendix I Chronological List of Authors Cited ◆ 327
Appendix II Notes on Authors Cited ◆ 329
Notes ◆ 333
Bibliography ◆ 357
Index of Koranic Verses ◆ 363
Index of Hadiths and Sayings ◆ 379
General Index ◆ 385

FOREWORD

In my presidential address during the International Congress for the History of Religion in Rome in August 1990 I summed up many discussions with and remarks of colleagues and students by stating that it is high time that the history of religion be studied not only from a typical Western vantage point but also that it take into consideration other ways of looking at concepts like religion, God, revelation, and so on. To be sure, there are a number of scholars, especially from East Asia, whose contributions to the history or phenomenology of religion are remarkable, not only in the field of their own religious traditions such as Buddhism, Confucianism or Shinto, but also in the study of other religions such as Islam. Nevertheless, our outlook seems still to be determined largely by our "biblical" background and the "classical" approach to scholarship.

Another topic that frequently came up during the discussions in Rome was the role of the feminine element in the various religious traditions. Here again, the inherited way of studying women's roles from an "external" viewpoint was considered important. But other interpretations, like the "spiritual role of the feminine" in the history of religions, were also mentioned—aspects which my late teacher and friend Professor Friedrich Heiler in Marburg discussed decades ago in his classes. It was he who liked to quote—with a certain sadness—the remark of the German Indologist Moriz Winternitz: "Women have always been the best friends of religion, but religion has generally not been a friend of women."

The truth of Winternitz's statement becomes particularly evident when it comes to the study of Islam and women's position in Islam. Islam has barely been studied from the phenomenological viewpoint in order to integrate its structures into the structures of other religions. Not a single book on the phenomenology of religion deals with Islam, which is generally considered to be uninteresting and uninspiring and to be, at best, a perfect example of a "legalist" religion. It is certainly much easier to look only at the surface and judge that the possibility of polygamy and easy divorce are negative features and to point constantly to the concept of purdah (although the overstressed application of veiling developed only after a certain period) than to try to see the more positive sides of Islam. Medieval Western remarks, according to which women have no soul in Islam, were happily taken over by scholars and even more by the general public. Very few scholars have tried to look beneath the surface and to discover structures that would surprise those who have been brought up with the traditional, negative attitude toward Islam. And unfortunately, recent events in the Islamic world have supported the convictions of the critics and the impression that women, in a militant, fundamentalist society, are an oppressed group without any rights, not able to voice their opinions or to have a say in their own religious affairs. A look at the role of women in the Turkish war of liberation in the early 1920s or at the active participation of women in the Indian independence movement and the quest for Pakistan in the 1940s can easily prove the contrary.

Given these facts it is perhaps not surprising that a new approach to gender relations in Islam comes from a Japanese woman, Sachiko Murata, who, after a thorough study of Islamic law and of the esoteric tradition of Islam, offers in this book the fruits of her investigations and reaches conclusions which may surprise many readers.

Dr. Murata rightly points out that in Islam, as in every religion, the principle of unity, which differentiates itself into duality and from there into plurality, is central; hence the title of her book, *The Tao of Islam*. One can say without exaggeration that the problem of unity and its working in creation has been a central topic of theological, and especially mystical, thought in Islam. When I was teaching at the Faculty of Islamic Theology (Ilāhiyat Fakültesi) in Ankara, Turkey, in the 1950s and tried to explain to my students Rudolf Otto's definition of the two aspects of the *Numen* (the Divine or the Totally Other), that is, the manifestation of the *mysterium tremendum* and the *mysterium fascinans*—the majestic, wrathful and the loving-kind, beautiful aspect of the One Divine Being—my students reacted with amazement: "But we have known that for centuries!" they said. "We always knew that God has a *jalāl* side and a *jamāl* side, the aspects of Powerful Majesty and Wonderful Kindness, and that these two fall together in Him as *kamāl*, perfection."

Their remark was to the point, and writing as a phenomenologist of religion I feel that there is no difficulty in naming the overpowering, masculine, *jalāl* aspect as yang and the loving-kind, beautiful, *jamāl* aspect as yin. For everyone knows that only by the togetherness of these two principles can life continue. There is no life without the systole and the diastole of the heartbeat, without inhaling and exhaling, or without the two poles between which the electric current can move. Long ago the Sufis interpreted the divine creative order *kun*, "Be!" (which is written in Arabic with the two letters *k.n.*) as pointing to the "two-colored yarn" which veils, like a fabric, the basic unity of the Divine Being. Mawlānā Jalāluddīn Rūmī in particular has described the constant interplay of the two aspects of life in powerful prose in *Fīhi mā fīhi* and alluded to it in ever so many verses in his lyrical *Dīwān* and his *Mathnawī*. And does not the mystical interpretation of the Arabic alphabet connect the first letter, the slim, straight *alif* with its numerical value of one, to the first manifestation of the Divine Unity; and the second letter, *bā*ʾ, with its numerical value of two, with the beginning of the created universe? For the Koran's first letter is the *bā*ʾ of the word *bismillāh*, "In the name of God."

Given this general tendency in Islam to organize things and mental states in dual groups and to see everything as created under this aspect, how could the masculine and the feminine sides to life not be equally important? For without their cooperation no new life can exist on earth. Not in vain did Rūmī see "mothers" everywhere: Virtually everything in the cosmos is a mother, giving birth to something higher than itself—whether it is the flintstone that "gives birth" to the spark, which in turn produces fire when it meets congenial matter, or the earth that, fertilized by the sky, produces plants as the result of the *hieros gamos*, the sacred marriage. Rūmī even described woman, in the first book of the *Mathnawī*, as someone whom one would be tempted to call "creator."

To correct the traditional misunderstanding of women's roles in Islam it would suffice to see how the Qurʾān mentions the *muslimūn wa muslimāt*, the *muʾminūn wa muʾmināt* together: the male and the female Muslims, the male and female believers. Women have the same religious duties as men (with the exception that they cannot perform these duties in a state of female impurity). The Prophet himself emphasized in a famous saying the fact that "God has made dear to me from your world perfume and women, and my spiritual consolation is in prayer"—a saying which forms the basis of Ibn al-ʿArabī's chapter on Muhammad in his *Fuṣūṣ al-ḥikam*. The role which the Prophet's first wife, the mother of his surviving children, played in his spiritual development cannot be overrated: Khadīja, the "mother of the faithful," by her loving care and understanding, gave him the strength to endure the frightening experience of the first revelation that descended upon him to shake him to his innermost heart, for she believed in his message. Later, his youngest wife, ʿĀ'isha, not only played an important political role but also was the source of many hadiths in which she informed the listeners of the Prophet's customs and sayings, thus inaugurating the list of women who studied, transmitted, and taught Hadith in the Islamic Middle Ages. One must not forget Fāṭima, the Prophet's youngest daughter, who married his cousin ʿAlī, became the mother of Ḥasan and Ḥusayn, the second and third Imams of Shia Islam, and was elevated in Shia piety to an extremely high position—be it as a kind of *mater dolorosa* whose two sons fell victim to political machinations (even though that happened decades after her death) or as intercessor or, in mystical terminology, as *umm abīhā*, "her father's mother."

One could go on and enumerate the women who played a role in the history of mystical thought and practice, and it is evident from Sufi biographies that most of the future spiritual leaders received their first religious inspiration from their pious mothers—did not the Prophet state that "Paradise lies at the feet of the mothers"?

This feminine side to Islamic life is usually overlooked, since most scholars, being male, have never lived in the company of women in a Muslim home and hence have not seen how important a role women, and especially mothers, play in their homes, be it in Turkey or in the Indo-Pakistani world. Scholars might read of some medieval Muslim queens, such as Raziya Sultana of Delhi (1236–40) and her near contemporary Shajarat al-Durr of Egypt (1246–49) or mention the names of some princesses who influenced their consorts in their political decisions and were eulogized by great poets. Or they may have heard of a few highborn ladies who excelled in poetry, calligraphy, or religious pursuits. But of the inner family life, little has been known to them. Moreover, it is all too easy to judge a foreign civilization from the viewpoint of twentieth century Western standards. Wiebke Walther, in her fine and extensive study *Die Frau in Islam* (Women in Islam), has remarked that even in Germany in some areas men still had the legal right to beat their wives in the 1880s.

There is one verse in the Qur'ān which due to its context has often been misinterpreted but which points exactly, in my understanding, to the ideal gender relation: "Your wives are a garment for you, and you are a garment for them" (2:188). A garment is, according to ancient religious ideas, the alter ego of a human being. The garment can serve as a substitute for the person, and with a new garment one gains as it were a new personality. Furthermore, it hides the body, hinders the looking at the private parts, protects the wearer. According to this interpretation, husband and wife are so to speak each other's alter ego, and each of them protects the partner's honor. This seems to show how well the yang-yin principle works in marital relationships: Husband and wife are equal in their perfect togetherness.

Many of the disrespectful sayings about women, especially among ascetics and mystics, stem from the fact that in Arabic the word for soul, *nafs*, is a feminine noun and, based on the expression in sura 12:53, it is often understood as the *nafs ammāra*, "the soul that incites to evil." Therefore the *nafs* is usually represented under the image of a stubborn, restive horse or camel, a black dog, a snake, a mouse, but also as a disobedient woman. Whoever has read medieval Arabic and Persian texts is well aware of this application of the term *nafs*, whose major external projection is *dunyā*, the "world of matter," again a feminine noun. But similar deprecative descriptions of the dangerous woman and *Frau Welt*, "Mrs. World," can also be found in medieval Christian writings and sermons, where only the virgins are extolled as they strive to emulate Mary's example. However, the concept of the "woman soul" has enriched Islamic literature. Its most famous representative is the figure of Zulaykhā, who consumed herself in her love for the paragon of beauty Yūsuf (Joseph). She was purified through long years of suffering to become, as one might say, the *nafs lawwāma*, the "blaming soul" (sura 75:2), and finally she was united with her lost beloved as *nafs muṭmaʾinna*, the "soul at peace" (sura 89:27). This development of the *nafs* through the stages mentioned in the Qurʾān has inspired not only Persian and Turkish mystics but also numberless Indo-Muslim poets. Supported by indigenous folktales in which the story always centers around a woman, they sang of the woman's wanderings through deserts and mountains in quest of her lost beloved until she is finally purified and dissolved in love. For the great mystery of the mystical path—the education of the lower faculties through submission in love—can best be expressed with the symbol of the woman soul. United with her beloved, she can reach the perfect unity of *jamāl* and *jalāl*, of yin and yang, in the all-surrounding *kamāl*, "perfection of the Divine."

These are just a few thoughts that came to me when I was reading Sachiko Murata's book. I know that some people will probably object to her sapiential approach to gender relations, as it seems to be too far away from the image they have acquired of Islam. But the texts which are translated in this book—most of them for the first time—show that her approach is perfectly valid. In fact, the numerous texts in themselves constitute a most important aspect of the book; they form an anthology of mystical wisdom in themselves and should be studied carefully by everyone interested in Islam. Even if the *ahl-i ẓāhir*, those who judge women's roles in Islam (and Islam in general) from a purely historical, sociological, or philological viewpoint, should disagree with some of Dr. Murata's conclusions, they will still discover a great number of hitherto unknown sources that may help them understand Islam somewhat better.

It seems fitting that a woman wrote this book on gender relations, just as the first true historical approach was given by a German woman, Wiebke Walther, and the first independent study of Rābiʿa, the early woman saint in Islam (d. 801 in Irak), was published (in 1928) by a British orientalist woman, Margaret Smith. Rābiʿa, who introduced the element of pure love into the early ascetic movements in Islam, was praised by generations of later writers and poets, and we may close our foreword with the lines which Jāmī (d. 1492 in Herat) quoted from the Arab poet al-Mutanabbī to honor this woman saint of Basra:

> If all women were like the one we have mentioned
> Then women would be preferred to men.
> For the feminine gender is no shame for the sun,
> Nor is the masculine gender an honor for the crescent moon!

Annemarie Schimmel
Harvard University

A NOTE ON DATES AND CITATIONS FROM THE KORAN

Dates are indicated according to both the *hijra* lunar calendar (A.H.) and the Christian era. The two dates are separated by a slash; for example, 1/622, 700/1300, 1410/1990.

Citations from the Koran are indicated, usually in parentheses or brackets, by the number of the sura (chapter) and the *āya* (verse) separated with a colon; for example, 28:88.

INTRODUCTION

Nowadays not too many people still think that Islam appeared when fierce Arab warriors charged out of the desert on camels to slaughter Christians and convert the heathens by means of the sword. But old ideas about the place of women in Islam have hardly changed. The most difficult task I have faced in years of teaching Islam is how to provide an accurate account of the role of women in face of the deep prejudices of not only my students but also my colleagues.

Several years ago I was asked to teach a course called "Feminine Spirituality in World Religions." Given my training and background, it was natural for me to spend a good deal of time focusing on the Far Eastern traditions and Islam. And given the background of the students, it was natural for them to come into class convinced, on some level of their awareness, that Eastern women, and especially Muslim women, are the most oppressed and downtrodden women on earth, and that although Islam may have something interesting to say on some level, it certainly has nothing to offer on the level of women's role in society. I found that the only way to overcome the mental obstacles in my students was to take a backdoor approach. Hence I came at Islam not from within a Western context, with all the presuppositions about sexuality and gender roles that this implies, but from the East. My introductory text in this course has been, and remains, the *I Ching*. Only if people can put aside their prejudices for a while and deal with gender relationships on a supra-mundane level can they begin to grasp the principles that infuse a worldview such as the Chinese or the Islamic.

The ultimate problem, when we speak of cross-cultural differences in the question of relationships among men and women, is that in a very real sense we have been living in different worlds. The cultural presuppositions of Westerners about what is important in life are profoundly different from the traditional views of Muslims or Japanese. This does not mean that we have to remain silent if we see injustice in another world, but it does mean that we should ask ourselves if our cultural spectacles allow us to see correctly. It also means that we should ask ourselves, granted that we are seeing correctly, if our analysis of the causes of the injustice is accurate. Comparable social conditions in our own society, with its specific worldview, may call for one solution, and in another society they may call for a different solution.

I offer no answers as to whether or not Muslim women are any more oppressed than women elsewhere. What I do maintain, however, is that generally the role of women in traditional Islam—not in any given Islamic society today—is consistent with the Islamic worldview. In the countries today where Islam is the dominant religion, the situation may be very different. It is probably fair to say that the principles that I have tried to bring out in the present book are not put into practice anywhere on the face of the earth, since there are no longer any integral Islamic societies.

Society in the contemporary Islamic world knows abuses like society anywhere else. But we need to distinguish between abuses that arise from living in accordance with the Islamic ideals and those that arise from breaking with those same ideals. In the former case, I would maintain that the "abuses" are more apparent than real and go back to our inability to grasp the principles that animate an alien civilization. In the latter case, the abuses are real.

How can abuses that do, in fact, exist be remedied? The prevalent approach seems to require that Islamic societies should follow various Western solutions. But if there is one thing that the Western solutions share in common, it is antipathy to the principles of gender relationships that are set down in the Islamic intellectual tradition. This is as much to say that all Western suggestions for the reform of Islam involve changing the principles upon which Islam is built. Islam has to be "brought into the twentieth century."

Another approach tries to revive the Islamic worldview and apply it as it is supposed to be applied. This way is also fraught with difficulties, but at least it holds up hope that people will remain faithful to their origins and roots and, what is far more important in the Islamic perspective, faithful to what God wants from them. The difficulties inherent in this approach appear in what is commonly called "Islamic fundamentalism." In most cases, the various movements that the Western media lump into this category have as great an antipathy to the Islamic intellectual tradition as the purely Western approaches.

The Intellectual Tradition in Islam

Before going any further, I need to state clearly what I mean by the Islamic "intellectual tradition," since this is the key to what I have tried to do in the present book. I have in mind a deep current in Islamic thought that goes back to the Koran and the Hadith. What differentiates this tradition from the legalistic approach of the Sharia (Islamic law) is that its representatives ask about the "why" of things, not simply the "how." In contrast, the jurists, who speak for the Sharia, are largely concerned with telling people *what* they must do. They do not ask *why* such things should be done, since they take for granted the Sharia's basic prescriptions. But no matter how important the Sharia may be for Islamic society, it is built upon principles that transcend itself (a fact of which the practitioners of the science known as *uṣūl al-fiqh* [the principles of jurisprudence] have always been acutely aware). The intellectual tradition has been concerned with exploring these principles in the deepest sense. Once the principles are brought out, they can be applied in novel ways, without breaking the spirit or the letter of the Sharia. Without knowledge of the principles, novel approaches can be advanced that observe the Sharia, but all too often these break with its spirit.

The issues raised by the modern concern with the politics of gender cannot be addressed through the Sharia, since the Sharia simply issues commandments. It does not tell us why a woman receives less in inheriting from her parents than her brother does. If someone objects, the answer of the jurists can only be that God has told us to do it this way. Nowadays, Muslim apologists also bring forth all sorts of sociological considerations with a view to answering certain Western-inspired objections. But this legal and sociological approach tells us nothing about the deeper reasons for the Islamic worldview. It is the deeper reasons that the intellectual tradition addresses.

Answers to the questions that naturally arise about gender relationships cannot be found by posing them to those who are unfamiliar with the principles and roots of Islamic thought. Throughout Islamic history, the jurists have been criticized by the great authorities of the intellectual tradition—such as Ghazālī—for their narrow-mindedness, lack of depth, and one-dimensioned approach to the problems that people face as human beings. One of the most unfortunate signs of the contemporary malaise of the Islamic world is that the intellectual authorities have all but disappeared from the scene, while the jurists have a free hand to say what they want. There are many reasons for this, not the least of them the fact that Westerners have always considered "orthodox" Islam to lie in the Sharia, in spite of the fact that some Western scholars have pointed out that the Sharia deals only with "orthopraxy," not "orthodoxy." The "sound teachings" of Islam are the concern of people who are not primarily jurists, though typically they are also experts in jurisprudence. Nor can "orthodoxy" be limited to the views of the proponents of Kalām (dogmatic theology). There are other ways to investigate the underlying teachings of Islam that have at least as much claim as Ashʿarite Kalām to "orthodoxy." Moreover, Kalām does not engage in speculation on the nature of reality in terms that can be enlightening for the question of gender relationships. Its fundamental concern is to shore up the authority of the Koran as a source of commandments. Ultimately, it has the Sharia in view, not the nature of reality itself.

In the present work I have been concerned to study the works of those intellectual authorities who have asked fundamental questions concerning the nature of gender within the matrix of ultimate reality. Most of these authorities have been classified as "Sufis." This does not mean that they are "mystics" in any pejorative sense of the term. What it does mean is that they do not limit themselves to surface readings and superficial interpretations. I have also looked at several representatives of the philosophical tradition, since the philosophers also ask the right questions. Moreover, the line between philosophy and theoretical Sufism is often exceedingly difficult to draw. Figures like Bābā Afḍal Kāshānī, Suhrawardī al-Maqtūl, or Mullā Ṣadrā use the language of philosophy but have the same vision of the inner world that infuses the Sufi approach.

Throughout the research that led to the writing of this book, I was looking for answers to questions that only these representatives of what might better be called the "sapiential tradition" had the resources to deal with. What does gender signify in the worldview of Islam? How are male and female related to the structure of the natural world? What are the theological roots of gender distinctions? Is God primarily father, or mother, or both, or neither? What is it in the nature of existence itself that manifests itself as sexual distinctions? Are these distinctions essential to the nature of reality, or peripheral? Can we ignore gender distinctions? If so, in what domains can we ignore them? If not, where and why must we observe them? What happens if we decide that we do not like the perceived result of gender distinctiveness? To what extent can we change observed gender relationships in order to build better human beings and better societies?

These questions cannot be addressed on the level of the Sharia, which simply presents human beings with a list of dos and don'ts. Nor can they be addressed by Kalām, which is locked into an approach that places God the King and Commander (a close associate of God the Father) at the top of its concerns. But they can be addressed and are addressed by the sapiential tradition, which is interested in the structure of reality as it presents itself to us.

A number of modern scholars have undertaken studies of the place of gender in the Islamic consciousness, but normally they have employed psychological models in their approach. This is fine and useful. But it hardly gives the Islamic tradition credit for being able to analyze the human psyche in its own way. The Sufis would be the first to point out that modern approaches to the human being are blind to most of reality. By the very nature of their chosen disciplines, modern scholars cannot delve into the deeper levels of the psyche with which the authorities of the sapiential tradition are concerned. Such scholars can provide us with interesting interpretations of the "unconscious" forces at work in Muslims, but they throw no direct light on the unconscious forces at work in their own psyches that have led them to pose the questions they pose. Asking the great Muslim authorities what they have to say about all this may have the advantage of providing us with an insight into the conscious and unconscious minds of everyone concerned.

The Feminist Critique of Islam

This is not the place to review the feminist critique of Islamic society and thought found in the writings of many contemporary authors, since I am not concerned directly with the same issues. But I would like to make as explicit as possible why I think that the present book has something to say to this critique.

It seems to me that feminists who have criticized various aspects of Islam or Islamic society base their positions upon a worldview radically alien to the Islamic worldview. Their critique typically takes a moral stance. They ask for reform, whether explicitly or implicitly. The reform they have in view is of the standard modern Western type. Among other things, this means that there is an abstract ideal, thought up by us or by our leader, which has to be imposed by overthrowing the old order. This reform is of the same lineage as the Western imperialism that originally appeared in the East as Christian missionary activity. The white man's burden gradually expanded its horizons—or reduced them, depending on how you look at it. Salvation was no longer touted as present in Christianity, but in science and progress. The "orientalist" perspective fits nicely, as many scholars have shown, into this blatantly triumphalistic approach to non-Western societies. Here we have the masculine impulse toward domination run wild, with catastrophic results for the world. Remember that unbridled technological expansion with its concordant ecological ills—the rape of the earth—grew up directly out of this same impulse.

Many other reformist currents in Western thought have been infused with the same will to do good for others, even if the others do not realize that good is being done for them. Certain forms of feminism seem to fit into the same line of thinking. We see new variants on the old, domineering, and negatively masculine attitude known as proselytism. In the Islamic world—or, in the Japanese world, for that matter—its appeal has been heard only by those who have lost touch with their own intellectual and spiritual universe. The spokespeople for the movement tell us that the rest will follow, as soon as their consciousness is raised. But here we certainly cannot be blamed for asking how we can tell the difference between up and down.

It is precisely at this point—in discerning the difference between up and down, right and left, backward and forward, good and evil—that Islam has the right and even the duty to call its own intellectual authorities to witness. And those of us living in the West and concerned with the issues have the duty to ask the right questions. For these are profound issues, having the most intimate bearing on what it means to be human. And that is the fundamental concern of the Islamic tradition: What is a human being? Once that is established, we can ask why there are two basic kinds of human being, male and female, and how the two interrelate. At this point, we have the right to ask if the mode of their interrelationship in any given situation is a correct one. And most importantly, we have to ask about the normative principles in terms of which we can judge the correctness of the relationship.

The Background of the Present Book

This book has a long history, as long as my own interest in Islam. As an undergraduate studying family law at Chiba University outside of Tokyo, I became fascinated—through a curious set of circumstances—with what I heard about Islamic family law, which allows a man to have four wives, while he is expected to maintain peace and harmony at the same time. Eventually, after a year working in a law firm, my curiosity overcame me, especially when an Iranian friend offered to arrange a scholarship for me at Tehran University. I went with the aim of studying Islamic law, but first I had to learn Persian. I spent three years in course work and then wrote a Ph.D. dissertation in Persian literature on the role of women in the *Haft paykar*, a poetical work by Niẓāmī (d. ca. 600/1204).

It did not take me long to realize that my preconceptions about the place of women in Islamic society—preconceptions that the Japanese learned originally from Western sources—had nothing to do with the realities of Iranian society (this was long before the "Islamic" revolution). In any case, I had no hesitations about entering the Faculty of Theology at Tehran University, where I was the first non-Muslim to enroll in the program on jurisprudence (*fiqh*). Many of my fellow classmates were mullas who had decided that they needed a degree to be successful in the new order (here I say "fellow" advisedly, since I was the first woman in the program). I was always treated with respect and courtesy by faculty and students. I had the opportunity of studying Islamic law with some of the foremost authorities in the field. I remain especially grateful to Professor Abu'l-Qāsim Gurjī, one of the most outstanding students of Ayatollah Khū'ī, who always displayed special care to make sure that I was not disadvantaged by the years of study that most of my classmates had already put into the subject.

One of my best memories of those years is the time spent studying with my private tutor, Sayyid Ḥasan Iftikhārzāda Sabziwārī, who wore the turban of the clerical class and was thoroughly trained in the traditional method, though he was pursuing a Ph.D. in Islamic philosophy at Tehran University. Well versed in the intellectual as well as juridical sciences, he guided me through some of the most difficult texts of jurisprudence and "principles of jurisprudence" (*uṣūl al-fiqh*). With his help and the general guidance of my professor, Toshihiko Izutsu, I was able to translate the tenth/sixteenth century classic on principles of jurisprudence, *Maʿālim al-uṣūl*, into Japanese.[1] Iftikhārzāda had a difficult time at first convincing his wife that he really did have a Japanese woman as a student. His wife thought for sure that he was hiding something with this outlandish story. He finally had to bring her over to visit me, making sure first that my husband would be there as well.

In all the years of working with traditional scholars such as Gurjī, Iftikhārzāda, and others, I never felt that I was being treated special because I was a woman. They debated the issues with me as they would with their mulla colleagues. Sometimes they convinced me they were right, and on occasion I would convince them that they were wrong. Most often we kept our own views, while respecting the other. On the level of knowledge, gender was not an issue. But when a man visited someone's house with his wife, certain rules had to be observed.

I finished an M.A. dissertation at the Faculty of Theology on the topic of temporary marriage (*mutʿa*) and its social relevance. The topic is a fascinating one, but this is not the place to discuss it.[2] I will only remark that I spent several years of studying the legal and social ramifications of this institution. Generally Westerners to whom I mention the topic are convinced that it is unacceptable in today's world or in any world, without questioning their own presuppositions about marriage. In my mind, this is one of the areas in which Western stereotypes prevent a sympathetic understanding of a practical and realistic social institution. In fact *mutʿa* prevents many of the social ills connected with what I would call de facto temporary marriage in the West (either through casual or other nonlegal relationships, or through serial relationships made possible by divorce). Like any institution, *mutʿa* has its own special abuses, but these go back precisely to *abuse*, not to the institution as it is set down in the Sharia.

In Iran I began serious study of the sapiential tradition in addition to my juridical studies. For years I sat in on Professor Izutsu's class on the *Fuṣūṣ al-ḥikam* of Ibn al-ʿArabī. I also attended a class that extended over several years given by Seyyed Hossein Nasr on the great Persian classic of

Ibn al-ʿArabī's school, *Sharḥ-i gulshan-i rāz*. One of my fondest memories of those years rests with the luminous teaching of Jalāl al-Dīn Humāʾī, whose very presence was enough to convince me that Islam has a profound and living spiritual tradition. When my studies at the Faculty of Theology were cut short by the revolution, I came to America where I continued my research in the intellectual tradition in earnest.

From my earliest contacts with the manifestations of classical Islamic civilization, whether in art and architecture, poetry, legal teachings, mores, cooking, and overall worldview, I felt it held some deep kinship with my own Far Eastern background. By 1977 I had decided to write a Ph.D. dissertation comparing Islamic and Confucian teachings on the family, but the revolution brought this research to an end. During these same years, I was studying the *I Ching* with Professor Izutsu, and I became familiar with the explicit philosophical underpinnings of Chinese thought.

When I joined the faculty at Stony Brook in 1983, I was asked to teach the course called "Feminine Spirituality in World Religions" mentioned above. For the first time I faced squarely the problem of dealing with deep-seated prejudices, not only in relation to Islam, but especially in relation to the question of the role of women. From the beginning I realized that I would have to approach Islam with the help of a Far Eastern perspective, or else I would face complete defeat. It was only natural that I would return to the *I Ching* when I was searching for a way to conceptualize Islamic teachings on the feminine principle without doing violence to the original texts. In fact I found that by the time we had finished studying the *I Ching* and Chinese teachings on women in general, the students' defenses were down. I made my task much easier by taking the approach that I do in this book: I looked at the principles involved in gender relationships on the level of theology, cosmology, and psychology. At that time I had at my disposal a relatively small number of texts, but these were sufficient for the few weeks I was able to devote to Islam in class. Towards the end of the discussion, when we turned toward the ideal role of women in society according to Islamic spiritual teachings, students had no difficulty appreciating the fact that Islamic gender roles were neither haphazard nor motivated primarily by political concerns.

I have written the present book on the basis of the approach employed in that class. However, I should make clear that I do not consider my methodology "comparative." I am well aware of the dangers implicit in comparative approaches that come to facile conclusions on the basis of superficial resemblances. To compare two things, we need to deal with them on the same level, but that is not my intention, nor could I do so if I wanted to. What I am trying to do is to bring out certain salient features of Islamic thought by referring to certain principles drawn from a non-Western tradition. By doing so I hope to avoid various presuppositions about the nature of reality and especially about gender relationships found in most Western studies of Islam. My hope has been that a relatively novel point of view might bring out something important in Islamic thought that has been missed by the usual approaches.

From the outset, then, it should be clear that when I speak of the Tao or yin and yang, I have in view a rather generalized understanding of these terms. I know that in actual fact, there has been a great diversity of opinions on these matters in Chinese history. I do not push my comparisons, because then I could no longer generalize on the Chinese side of things. In short, the view of the principles of Chinese thought presented here is my own, and many specialists might disagree with it.

Chinese and Islamic Thought

Chinese cosmology describes the universe in terms of yin and yang, which can be understood as the active and receptive or male and female principles of existence. Yin and yang embrace each other in harmony, and their union produces the Ten

Thousand Things, which is everything that exists. The famous symbol of Tai Chi, the "Great Ultimate" or the Tao, portrays yin and yang as constant movement and change. In any given phenomenon, the relationship between yin and yang is constantly changing. Hence the whole universe changes moment by moment, like a running river. "Change," or *I*, is the process whereby heaven and earth and everything between them are created and re-created. Yin and yang are the principles of change and the symbols for all movement in the universe. When the sun rises, the moon disappears. When spring comes, winter goes. In the words of Confucius, "Like a running river, the whole universe is flowing ceaselessly day and night." Existence means harmonious change on the basis of the Tao. If harmony between yin and yang were to be lost, the universe would cease to flow and nothing could exist.

These basic teachings of Chinese thought are familiar to most educated readers in the West. Given the popularity of the *I Ching* and the omnipresence of the yin/yang symbol, few people need to be told that Chinese thought is concerned with harmony, equilibrium, and balance between two principles of existence. In contrast, Islamic cosmology is practically unknown, since few scholars have devoted attention to the worldview behind Islamic institutions.

Much of Islamic cosmology is reminiscent of Chinese cosmology in that it is based upon a complementarity or polarity of active and receptive principles. But the Muslim sages employ terminology that is not so familiar. A bit more analysis is needed before the play of the two principles can be brought out clearly. Moreover, thought that is specifically Islamic begins with God, as does the practice that both precedes the thought and grows up organically out of it. The first of the five "pillars" of Islamic practice is the declaration with the tongue that "There is no god but God and Muhammad is His messenger." The first of the articles of faith is God. The definition of the first and most fundamental of the three principles of Islam, *tawhīd*, "the profession of Unity," is that "There is no god but God."

If duality is found in the cosmos, it must be connected somehow to the One who is beyond all duality. "Before" the existence of the universe, there was nothing but the Creator.[3] All Muslims agree that the existence of the universe depends upon this one Reality.

According to a hadith commonly cited by Sufis, the Prophet said "God was and there was nothing with Him." The great authority on hadith, al-Bukhārī, gives us the version, "God was and there was nothing other than He."[4] In the "beginning" there was only God, but He was totally nonmanifest. Nothing else existed to display the individual attributes and qualities found in the undifferentiated One. The Chinese tradition tells us that before yin and yang came into existence, there was Tai Chi or the "Great Ultimate," and it was totally undifferentiated. Confucius is reported to have said, "There is Tai Chi in Change, Change generates the two primary forces, the two primary forces generate the four images, and the four images generate the eight trigrams."[5]

Here the "two primary forces" refers to what later is consistently called yin and yang. But there are a number of opinions concerning the "four images." One view holds that these are the four states of yin and yang, that is, great or old yin, great or old yang, small or young yin and small or young yang. Another opinion holds that these are the four elements: metal, wood, water, and fire. Still another maintains that these are the four seasons, and another that they are softness, hardness, shade (yin), and brightness (yang). No matter which view is followed, the "four images" represent the primal elements of existence, which bring forth change within the realities of all things. They are permutations of yin and yang. On the next level, the "eight trigrams" represent the primordial nature of existence and are symbolized by father, mother, three sons, and three daughters.

Confucius says, "There are no greater primordial images [of things] than heaven and earth. There is nothing that has more movement and change than the four seasons."[6] Heaven represents pure yang and earth represents pure yin. The four seasons represent the four elements: metal is autumn, wood is spring, water is winter, and fire is summer.

In all of this there is a constant attention to the qualities possessed by different phenomena. The most primordial quality is that of the Tao itself. From one point of view, that quality is sheer oneness. From another point of view, it is a totally harmonious interrelationship between two tendencies that we will refer to as yin and yang. Each of these two is but a face of the Tao, and each merges and melds into the other. Yet a certain distinction can be drawn, and that is the root of the distinction that can be drawn among the four seasons, the eight trigrams, the sixty-four hexagrams, the Ten Thousand Things. The oneness of the Tao manifests itself on every level in a specific mode that gives that level its peculiar qualities. Those qualities define the identity of the level. All qualities go back to the two and the one. All qualities can be shown to have interrelationships on some level, since they manifest the same principle. It is these interrelationships and correspondences that are of particular interest to the cosmologist. Through them one grasps the unity of the whole. Without them we are left with meaningless quantity and multiplicity.

Theological Polarity

In Islamic terms, the world or cosmos (*al-ʿālam*) can be defined as "everything other than God" (*mā siwā Allāh*), without spatial or temporal qualifications. Especially in the later intellectual tradition, nothing is discussed independently from its relationship (*nisba*) with God. It is the relationship that sets up a perspective in terms of which right understanding can be achieved. But there are always two fundamental relationships, radically different, yet polar, since God is a single reality.

In one respect, God is infinitely beyond the cosmos. Here, the theological term is *tanzīh*, which means "to declare God incomparable" with everything that exists. From this point of view, God is completely inaccessible to His creatures and beyond their understanding. This is the classical position of Kalām. Many verses could be cited to show that the Koran takes this point of view, such as "Glory be to God, the Lord of Inaccessibility, above everything that they describe" (37:180), or, in simpler terms, "Nothing is like Him" (42:11). In this respect, God is an impersonal reality far beyond human concerns. He is the God of a certain form of negative theology.

Though the proponents of Kalām have often been looked upon by Western scholars as the representatives of "orthodox" Islam, this is to impose an inappropriate category upon Islamic civilization, as many other scholars have pointed out. In fact, by and large the criteria for being Muslim have been following the Sharia and acknowledging the truth of a certain basic creed. Beyond that, a variety of positions concerning the details of the creed were possible, and none could be said to be "orthodox" to the exclusion of the others. When we look at Islamic intellectual history with this point in mind, we see, in fact, that there is no question of a universally recognized "orthodox" school of thought, but rather a large number of schools that debate among themselves concerning how the basic items of the creed are to be understood. The result is a long and dynamic history of intellectual interaction.

However this may be, the point here is simply that dogmatic theologians with their almost exclusive emphasis upon God's incomparability represented only a small number of intellectuals who had relatively little influence on the community at large. Popular Islam, the philosophical tradition, and the spiritual tradition represented by the great Sufis stressed, or at least found ample room for, a second point of view that is clearly supported by many Koranic verses. The God of the theologians, as Ibn al-ʿArabī remarked, was a God whom no one could possibly love, since He was too remote and incomprehensible.[7] But the God of the Koran, the Prophet, and the spiritual authorities is a God who is supremely lovable, since He is dominated by concern for His creatures. As the Koran puts it, "He loves them, and they love Him" (5:54). God's love for creation brings about love for God in the creatures. This God of compassion and love can be grasped and understood. To use the theological term, He must be "declared similar" (*tashbīh*) in some fashion to His creation. We can rightly conceive of Him in human attributes. This is the point of view of God's immanence in all things, and it is clearly supported by such Koranic verses as "Wherever you turn, there is the face of God" (2:115) and "We are nearer to the human being than the jugular vein" (50:16). In this respect, God is a personal God.

These two basic theological perspectives form two poles between which Islamic thought takes shape. The most sophisticated of the Muslim thinkers strike a delicate balance between the two positions. Both negative and positive theology are needed to bring about a right understanding of the Divine Reality. One can gain a certain grasp of the role these two perspectives have played in Islam by seeing an analogy with the Confucian emphasis upon yang and the Taoist stress upon yin. In other words, if asked whether the Tao itself is dominated by yin or yang, a Confucianist would more likely answer yang, while a Taoist would more likely say yin. In the same way, the experts in jurisprudence and Kalām—that is, those Muslim authorities who defend the outward and legalistic teachings of Islam—lay stress upon God's incomparability. They insist that He is a wrathful God and warn constantly about hell and the divine punishment. He is a distant, dominating, and powerful ruler whose commands must be obeyed. His attributes are those of a strict and authoritarian father. In contrast, those authorities who are more concerned with Islam's spiritual dimension constantly remind the community of the prophetic saying, "God's mercy precedes His wrath." They maintain that mercy, love, and gentleness are the overriding reality of existence and that these will win out in the end. God is not primarily a stern and forbidding father, but a warm and loving mother.

Islamic thinking about God centers upon the divine names or attributes revealed in the Koran, the so-called ninety-nine names of God. Each of the two basic perspectives, incomparability and similarity, is associated with certain names or attributes. God's incomparability calls to mind such names as Mighty, Inaccessible, Great, Majestic, Compeller, Creator, Proud, High, King, Wrathful, Avenger, Slayer, Depriver, and Harmer. The tradition calls these the names of majesty (*jalāl*), or severity (*qahr*), or justice (*ʿadl*), or wrath (*ghaḍab*). In the present context, I would call them "yang names," since they place stress upon greatness, power, control, and masculinity.

In contrast, God's similarity calls to mind such names as Beautiful, Near, Merciful, Compassionate, Loving, Gentle, Forgiving, Pardoner, Life-giver, Enricher, and Bestower. These are known as the names of beauty (*jamāl*), or gentleness (*luṭf*), or bounty (*faḍl*), or mercy (*raḥma*). They are "yin names," since they place stress on submitting to the wishes of others, softness, acceptance, and receptivity.

By and large the external and legalistic approach to Islam places greater stress on the yang names. While acknowledging the yin names, the legalists interpret them in ways that place their significance in the background. In contrast, the sapiential authorities stress the yin names. The idea that "God's mercy precedes His wrath"—or "God's yin characteristics predominate over His yang characteristics"—pervades their approach to reality. The first approach stresses God's incomparability, distance, and otherness. The second stresses His similarity, nearness, and sameness.

The contrast between these two approaches to reality is reflected throughout Islamic thought and society. Those who emphasize God's remoteness and distinction tend to dwell on the world of multiplicity and difference. They stress the discreet reality of individuals, the difference between the Creator and the creature, the distinctions among things, the reality of these distinctions. In contrast, those who emphasize God's similarity, nearness, and "withness" (*maʿiyya*, from the Koranic verse, "He is with you wherever you are" [57:4]) prefer to dwell on the establishment of unity and interrelationship. Distinctions are relative and can be erased from a different point of view. Reality lies not primarily in outwardness and separation but in inwardness and sameness.

In trying to bring out the basic Taoist approach to reality, Roger T. Ames contrasts it with the dominant modes of philosophical thinking in the West. His remarks provide us with a slightly different way of encapsulating the contrast between the legalistic and sapiential approaches to Islamic teachings. The contrast he sets up is especially instructive in that, by and large, the general perception of Islam in the West would place Islamic thought in the Western tradition, that is, in the first category that Ames describes. He explains that Taoism in particular and Chinese thought in general avoid dualistic explanations and prefer looking at things in "polar" terms.

> The separateness implicit in dualistic explanations of relationships conduces to an essentialistic interpretation of the world, a world of "things" characterized by discreteness, finality, closedness, determinateness, independence, a world in which one thing is related to the "other" extrinsically. By contrast, a polar explanation of relationships gives rise to a holographic interpretation of the world, a world of "foci" characterized by interconnectedness, interdependence, openness, mutuality, indeterminateness, complementarity, correlativity, coextensiveness, a world in which continuous foci are intrinsically related to each other.[8]

Both of these approaches are found in Islamic thought. But by and large, the proponents of Kalām and jurisprudence stress the first, while the sapiential authorities stress the second. For the most part, the two perspectives have lived in peaceful coexistence, each acting as a check to the possible excesses of the other. On the whole, the dualistic approach predominates in social teachings, while the polar approach is stressed in spiritual teachings. Moreover, the sapiential tradition accepts the first approach as the valid and even necessary starting point for the second. Hence it uses the same language at the outset, which has led many scholars to miss the relational and polar nature of the thinking. If I preserve the language of duality in many places, this is simply to follow the texts themselves. But the reader will soon see that the duality is often set up as a philosophical whipping boy. Until distinction is drawn, polarity cannot be brought out. Until opposition is perceived, it cannot be overcome. The ultimate aim is always the establishment of *tawḥīd*, the unity and interrelatedness of all reality.

Signs of God

The Koran repeatedly affirms that all things are "signs" (*āyāt*) of God, which is to say that everything gives news of God's nature and reality. As a result, many Muslim thinkers, the cosmologists in particular, see everything in the universe as a reflection of the divine names and attributes. These names and attributes represent qualities, such as majesty, beauty, life, knowledge, and so on. Hence the qualitative dimension of things—to the extent that it can be differentiated from the dimension that is purely quantitative or "material" (in the sense of hylic, or simply potential)—is of primary interest. In respect of similarity, the qualities of creation give us news of the divine attributes, though in respect of incomparability, they announce that God is totally other. To the extent that they display similarity and give us knowledge of ultimate Reality, the signs of God establish qualitative analogies among created things. These analogies provide the means of discerning relationships—often quite hidden relationships that make no sense in terms of modern categories—among things and between the things and God.

In a famous saying, the Prophet explained why God created the cosmos: "God says, 'I was a hidden treasure and I desired to be known. Therefore I created the creatures so that I might be known.'"[9] Hence the world is the locus in which the Hidden Treasure is known by the creatures. Through the universe God comes to be known, and since there is nothing in the universe but created things, it is the created things themselves that give news of the Hidden Treasure. Many cosmologists employ terms like *ẓuhūr* (manifestation) and *tajallī* (self-disclosure) to explain the relationship of the world to God. Through the cosmos, God discloses Himself to His creatures. The creatures themselves are the manifestation of God's names and attributes. Their qualities are ultimately God's qualities.

We have already seen that the attributes of God are divided into two broad and complementary categories, the yang and yin names. In the view of the cosmologists, these two categories work in harmony to bring the cosmos into existence. As Rūmī puts it, referring to the two kinds of names by their dominant quality, "Severity and gentleness were married, and a world of good and evil was born from the two."[10]

Many theologians see a reference to the two kinds of divine names in the Koranic expression the "two hands of God." They take this as a symbol for the relationship between incomparability and similarity, or majesty and beauty. The Koran says that only human beings among all creatures were created with both hands of God (38:76). This is read as an allusion to the fact that, as the Prophet said, Adam was created in God's own form. Hence, human beings manifest all the names of God, both the names of severity and the names of gentleness. In contrast, the angels of mercy were created only with God's right hand, while the satans were created only with His left hand. Only a human being represents a complete image of the Divine Reality; every other thing offers an imperfect image that is dominated by one hand or the other. Only humans were created through a perfect balance of both kinds of attributes.

Since the Reality of God disclosed through the cosmos can be described by opposite and conflicting attributes, the cosmos itself can be seen as a vast collection of opposites. The two hands of God are busy shaping all that exists. Hence mercy and wrath, severity and gentleness, life giving and slaying, exalting and abasing, and all the rest of the contradictory attributes of God are displayed in existence.

One way we perceive this constant interaction of the names is through change (*ḥaraka*) and transmutation (*istiḥāla*). Chuang Tzu could say, "The existence of things is like a galloping horse. With every motion existence changes, at every second it is transformed."[11] For their part, the dominant school of Kalām, the Ashʿarites, said that nothing stands still in creation and no phenomenon remains constant in its place for two successive moments. Everything is in constant need of divine replenishment, since nothing exists on its own. Things can exist only if God gives them existence. If God were to stop giving existence to the universe for an instant, it would disappear. Hence, at each moment God re-creates the cosmos to prevent its annihilation.

The concept of the continual re-creation of the cosmos became a mainstay of Islamic cosmological thinking. Many authorities interpreted this constant change and transmutation in terms of the interplay of the diverse divine names. Thus, at each instant, the divine mercy and gentleness create all things in the universe. In other words, at each instant God reaffirms His similarity with things and His presence in the cosmos. But God is also incomparable and other. Hence, just as His mercy creates, His wrath destroys. His unique and absolute reality displays "jealousy" (*ghayra*): It does not allow any "others" (*ghayr*) to exist alongside it. At each instant, the divine gentleness brings the world into existence, and at each instant the divine severity destroys it.[12] Every succeeding moment represents a new universe, similar to the preceding universe, but also different. Each new universe represents a new self-disclosure of God. According to the cosmological axiom, "God's self-disclosure never repeats itself," since God is infinite.[13]

The cosmos is a constantly shifting and changing pattern of relationships among God's signs, which are the loci of manifestation for His names. The universe is created and maintained through the activity of opposite divine attributes that display the activity of the single Principle. Hence duality can be perceived at every level. However, if we look more closely, we should be able to see the opposing forces not as absolutely opposed, but rather as complementary or polar. Yin and yang are working together everywhere, producing transmutation and constant change.

The Koran quotes God as saying, "And of everything We created a pair" (51:49). Or again, "God Himself created the pair, male and female" (53:45). All things in the universe are paired with other things. Several of the pairs mentioned in the Koran take on special importance as the fundamental principles of creation. These include the Pen (*al-qalam*) and the Tablet (*al-lawḥ*), which are specifically Islamic symbols, and heaven and earth, which find deep parallels in the Chinese tradition and elsewhere.

The Pen and the Tablet are mentioned in a few Koranic verses and some sayings of the Prophet. Referring to itself, the Koran says, "Nay, but it is a glorious Koran, in a guarded tablet" (85:21–22). Commentators explain this tablet as an invisible spiritual reality on which the Koran—the eternal and uncreated word of God—is written. The Koran refers to the Pen in the first verses that were revealed to the Prophet: "Read out! And thy Lord is the most generous, who taught by the Pen, taught man what he knew not" (96:1–5). In another verse, God swears by the Pen: "By the Pen and what they inscribe!" (68:1). These short and rather enigmatic verses provided a great deal of food for meditation, especially since the Prophet himself added a certain amount of interesting clarification. In some hadiths he said that the Pen was God's first creation, while elsewhere he said that the first thing created by God was the Intellect (*ʿaql*). These are the loci classici for the identification that the cosmologists make between the cosmic Pen and the "First Intellect." All creatures are latent and undifferentiated in the Intellect's knowledge, just as ink is present inside the Pen. Then, by means of the Intellect, God creates the whole universe.

The qualities connected with the term Pen are clearly of the yang type, while the term Intellect adds a certain yin side to this same reality. The Muslim cosmologists, like the Chinese, never see anything as exclusively active or exclusively receptive. Everything in the cosmos has both yin and yang qualities. These can be discovered by investigating the various relationships that things establish with other things. Thus, for example, the first spiritual being is called by the name Pen because it has an active and masculine side to its nature. God created it as a means to bring the rest of the cosmos into existence. Hence the Pen has a face turned toward the universe. It writes upon the Tablet, and the cosmos comes to exist as the written words of God. In contrast, this first spiritual reality is called intellect (*ʿaql*) at least partly because it has a receptive and feminine side to its nature. Etymologically, *ʿaql* signifies tying, binding, and constricting. The Intellect has a face turned toward God through which it contemplates God and receives constant replenishment from His light. At the same time it constricts and limits the light through its own finitude as a creature.

In order to bring the universe into existence, the Pen needs a place within which to write. Without the Tablet, no duality could appear within spiritual existence, and without duality, there could be no physical universe, which depends upon twos, threes, fours, ad infinitum. Just as the Pen is called the "First Intellect," so also the Tablet is called the "Universal Soul." In relation to God, the First Intellect is receptive, dark, and yin, but in relation to the Universal Soul, it is the Pen: active, luminous, and yang. This principle has important repercussions in psychology, where spirit and soul in the human being are seen to possess the same qualities as the First Intellect and the Universal Soul.

Along with many other Muslim thinkers, Ibn al-ʿArabī describes all the realities in the cosmos as manifestations of different divine names. He finds the archetypes of the Pen and Tablet in the Koranic verse, "God governs the affair and He differentiates the signs" (13:2). The Pen manifests the divine name Governor, while the Tablet manifests the divine name Differentiator. On a lower level of existence, the spirit manifests the name Governor in relation to the body. The spirit, which is the principle of life and awareness, governs, controls, and directs the body in the same way that the Pen governs, controls, and directs the Tablet. The body in turn manifests the name Differentiator, since it displays the powers and qualities of the spirit's single reality through its innumerable functions and activities.

Without the Tablet, the Pen could not write. The Tablet takes what is undifferentiated in the Pen and manifests all its details. It allows for the articulation of the existential words of God at a spiritual level of existence. This symbolism of the divine, creative words is central to Islamic cosmological thinking, no doubt because a large number of Koranic verses allude to it. One of the most often cited supports for the idea that all things are words of God is the verse, "God's only command, when He desires a thing, is to say to it 'Be!' and it is" (36:82). Hence, say the cosmologists, each creature is a unique expression of the divine word "*Be!*" The Pen writes out these divine words on the Tablet, thus manifesting the spiritual essences of all things. The spirit of each and every thing in the cosmos is brought into existence as a unique word on the Tablet. Both Pen and Tablet, yang and yin, active and receptive, are necessary for the spiritual realities of all things to come into actuality.

The Pen has two faces. With one face it looks at God, and with the other it looks at the Tablet and everything below it. In the same way, the Tablet has two faces. With one face it looks at the Pen, and with the other it looks at the worlds that lie below it. In relation to the Pen, the Tablet is receptive and thereby manifests differentiation. But in relation to the cosmos, the Tablet is active and manifests governing control. It becomes a yang reality. In Ibn al-ʿArabī's view, when we investigate the Tablet's relationship to the cosmos more carefully, we see both creativity and receptivity, both governing and differentiating. Hence, when the Tablet is discussed by its name "Universal Soul," it is said to have two faculties, the faculty of knowing, through which it receives from the Intellect, and the faculty of acting or doing, through which it exercises control. It knows the details of the existence of all things, since these are differentiated within itself. Since it knows these details, it governs the destiny of all things, since nothing escapes from its knowledge. It acts by bestowing existence upon what it knows.

Pen and Tablet illustrate the workings of yang and yin within the spiritual or invisible world. On a lower level of existence, the spiritual world interacts with the visible world. This interaction is frequently described in terms of heaven and earth, a pair of terms constantly employed in the Koran. The cosmologist Nasafī explains that the term *heaven* refers to everything that stands above something else, while the term *earth* refers to everything that stands below something else. Thus, the terms are relative and depend upon our point of view. That which is called "earth" in respect to one thing may be called "heaven" in respect to another, just as a single reality may be yang in relation to one thing and yin in relation to another.

Heaven acts through effusing light and existence, while earth is receptive toward these effusions. However, the station of the earth has a certain priority over that of heaven. This is not to suggest that one of them comes into existence first. For there is always a heaven and an earth, an aboveness and a belowness, in creation.

Creation is that which is "other than God." Hence it is not one, God alone being one in every respect. Since creation demands multiplicity by definition, it is a locus for separation and deployment. When two things are present, one is above and one is below with respect to the relationship established by certain qualities. If we take other qualities into account, the relationship may be reversed. If earth is prior to heaven in a certain respect—even, one can say, "above" heaven—this simply means that the sufficient reason for the existence of heaven is to bestow upon the earth. Without an earth, heaven is meaningless. You cannot have an above without a below—nor, of course, can you have a below without an above. If the earth were not ready to receive effusion, there could be no heaven. Heaven and earth are defined in terms of each other, since they are polar realities. Hence the existence of the earth is a precondition for the manifestation of qualities that are concealed in heaven.

The heavenly realities are formless or

spiritual, and the earth gives them bodily forms. In the same way, the analogue of heaven within the human microcosm, the "spirit," can do nothing without a body, which acts as its vehicle and instrument. Just as God created the universe to manifest His own perfections—the Hidden Treasure—so also the spirit needs the body to bring its own potentialities into actuality. As Rūmī puts it,

> The spirit cannot function without the body, and without the spirit, the body is withered and cold.
>
> Your body is manifest and your spirit hidden: These two put all the world's business in order.[14]

Nasafī divides all existent things into three kinds: Giver of effusion, receiver of effusion, and product of the interrelationship between the two. "Heaven" is that which is above something else and gives effusion to it. It may be a spiritual or a corporeal reality. "Earth" is that which is below something else and receives effusion from it. It may belong either to the spiritual or the corporeal world. The creatures are the children of heaven and earth, the product of their interrelationship. Rūmī expresses this idea in verse:

> In the view of intellect, heaven is the man
> and earth the woman.
> Whatever the one throws down,
> the other nurtures.[15]

In this context Confucius sounds like just another Muslim cosmologist:

> Heaven is lofty and earth is low. . . . The creative directs the great beginning, and the receptive completes all things.[16]

Cosmic Correspondences

Careful reading of the Koran and the Hadith shows that Islam's basic view of men and women postulates a complementarity of functions. "And of everything We created a pair" (51:49). Neither can be complete without the other. In Islamic cosmological thinking, the universe is perceived as an equilibrium built on harmonious polar relationships between the pairs that make up all things. Moreover, all outward phenomena are reflections of inward noumena and ultimately of God. All multiplicity is reducible, in some way, to the One. All creatures of the universe are nothing but God's signs. The pairs, male and female included, must therefore tell us something about God's own Self.

One of the many cosmological sciences developed in classical Islamic civilization was astrology or "the properties of the stars" (*aḥkām al-nujūm*). For most Muslim thinkers, the object of this science was to bring out the manner in which heaven, along with the realities it contains, exercises specific influences upon the earth. Astrological investigation takes the form of discovering the qualitative correspondences between things in the upper world and the lower world. For the more perspicacious, there is no question of any direct "influence" by the stars. Rather, the relationships among heavenly bodies and between heaven and earth throw light on corresponding or analogical relationships found in this world and in the soul. The key here is analogy or correspondence. And this is established by the qualities that things manifest, all of which ultimately go back to the One. In other words, different things, at different levels of reality or in different times and places, manifest the same qualities of the Real (*al-ḥaqq*).

Closely related to the type of analogical thinking found in astrology is the *ta'wīl* or esoteric interpretation of the Koran practiced by many Sufis and also certain Shi'ite authorities. The goal of *ta'wīl* was frequently to show how Koranic verses that speak of the cosmos or recount stories of the prophets have a second level of interpretation pertaining to the inward situation of the human individual. The microcosm "corresponds" to the macrocosm. On this level, the Koran depicts the drama of the human soul in its relationship with God.

At first reading, *ta'wīls* may seem arbitrary. But this is not so if one takes into account the analogical thinking out of which the tradition arises. The keys to *ta'wīl* can best be sought in texts dealing with the correspondences between macrocosm and microcosm, texts that are often deeply embedded in Greek learning. In such texts astrology is placed in this wider context of analogical thinking.

Human Equilibrium

Cosmological thinking in Islam is intimately bound up with the Islamic worldview as a whole. In no sense is it some sort of disinterested scientific investigation of the nature of things. On the contrary, most cosmologists have been concerned with demonstrating the analogies among all levels of existence in order to show that human beings play a unique role in the universe as God's representatives or vicegerents (*khalīfa*). This in turn demands human responsibility. The legalistic perspective tends to say that human beings must answer to God because a slave has no right to disobey his master's commands. He is duty bound by the fact that he is owned. In contrast, the sapiential perspective stresses noblesse oblige: As divine representatives, human beings have no choice but to assume responsibility for themselves and their surroundings. God's presence in the world and one's self must be recognized and acknowledged, and then one must act as God would act, as God's representative must act.

Hence the sapiential tradition is constantly concerned with describing the human context in a manner that highlights the similarity with God demanded by vicegerency. In order to do this, it needs to illustrate how human qualities correspond to the divine qualities, and how the qualitative relationships among the things of the cosmos place the human being at the pinnacle of created existence, with a great burden of responsibility to match the honor. All creatures other than human beings are good, since they are creatures of God, signs of God, loci of manifestation for the qualities of God, and can be nothing other than what they are. Human beings may possess a certain natural goodness as signs of God. But, in contrast to all other things, they also may be evil if they fail to make proper use of the peculiar nobility given exclusively to them. To be fully and properly human, human beings must actualize in themselves all the good qualities naturally inherent in creation, but at the same time these must be utilized according to a normative balance and harmony. Evil appears when people break this balance or work contrary to the Tao of heaven and earth. Evil has no other entry into the world, since only human beings have the freedom to choose it. This freedom gives them a unique nobility, centrality, and all-comprehensiveness, but it also opens the door to abuse. The only creatures somewhat similar to human beings in this respect are those beings created from fire and known as the "jinn," whose special qualities will be discussed later. They are also free to say no to the Tao. The leader of the evil jinn—as opposed to the good jinn who say yes—is Iblis or Satan.

All things in the universe reflect the names and attributes of God in diverse and differentiated modes. In contrast, human beings bring all these qualities together. As a result, they act as the mediating reality in existence, the place where God interacts with the cosmos in a direct manner. For in God all these qualities are present in undifferentiated oneness, while in the cosmos they are present in differentiated manyness. Only in human beings are they present in both differentiated and undifferentiated mode.

Followers of Ibn al-ʿArabī often refer to the human reality as the Great Isthmus-nature (*al-barzakhiyyat al-kubrā*). Like an isthmus (*barzakh*), human beings stand between the two oceans—God and the cosmos. Because of the centrality and "all-comprehensiveness" (*jamʿiyya*) of the human situation, only human beings can upset the harmony and equilibrium that is naturally established between God and the cosmos. Moreover, because of their mediating situation, the fact of acting as God's representatives, only human beings can establish perfect harmony and equilibrium between God and creation.

A cosmos without humans is inconceivable, since they alone act as a locus of manifestation for God as such. Of course here we have in view not the human species as found here on earth, but the qualities that are present in that species and may be found in analogous species in other worlds: the qualities of centrality, all-comprehensiveness, isthmus-nature, vicegerency. Only in "human beings" according to this definition is the image of God reflected fully. Only in them is the Hidden Treasure displayed in its original variety and concentrated brilliance, yet at the created level. Human beings are the pivot and axis of the cosmos, around which all things turn. They must perform their function of mediating and establishing peace and harmony among all things. Yet, paradoxically, precisely because they are images of God and share in His freedom, they are free to shirk their responsibility, break the harmony, and corrupt the universe.

In short, the purpose of Islamic cosmological teachings is to express within the context of the intellectual tradition the obligations of human existence. People are obliged by their very nature to live in harmony with the Tao, or to "submit" (*islām*) to the ways of heaven and earth in order to establish harmony upon earth in general and within human society in particular. The ultimate goal of the Islamic sapiential tradition is expressed nicely by Chuang Tzu with his words, "Heaven and earth and I live together—all things and I are one."[17]

To review what has already been said, the one God is looked upon from two points of view. In respect to God's distance and incomparability, human beings and all other creatures are His absolute servants and must submit to His will. But in respect to His similarity and nearness, human beings have another role to play. Since they were created in the divine form and with God's two hands, they alone find in themselves all the qualities of God and creation. Hence they alone can be God's vicegerents in the earth.

In gaining correct knowledge of God, one needs to combine the declaration of God's incomparability with the understanding of His similarity. These are not empty concepts, however. Each of them makes demands. Fully understanding them means that certain attitudes are set up in the soul. These attitudes can be summed up by two key Koranic terms: servant (*ʿabd*) and vicegerent (*khalīfa*). We have already suggested that Islam looks upon vicegerency as the supreme human state, the goal of human life. But in order to represent God, a person must first be worthy of the mission. God does not send any beggar out on His behalf. In fact, to speak of vicegerency as the supreme human state is misleading unless one understands that vicegerency is a perfect yang attitude toward the cosmos that has as its necessary and inseparable complement a perfect yin attitude toward God. Servanthood and vicegerency are two sides of the same coin. Moreover, servanthood has a certain priority over vicegerency, just as the Intellect has a certain priority over the Pen. Though Intellect and Pen are identical, until the Intellect takes from God, the Pen cannot write. So also, until human beings submit to the will of God (*islām*) and become His servants, they cannot be His proper representatives.

How we understand God and the human self depends on the point of view. Neither God nor a human being has two essences. God is one, and the human being is one. But human beings are like two-sided mirrors. One side reflects the qualities of servanthood as manifested in all creation, and the other side reflects the qualities of Lordship as possessed by God. Human beings are both lord and servant. As Ibn al-ʿArabī puts it,

> A human being is two transcriptions: an outward transcription and an inward transcription. The outward transcription corresponds to the macrocosm in its totality, while the inward transcription corresponds to God.[18]

The outward dimension of the human being is related to servanthood, the inward dimension to lordship and vicegerency. The outward dimension reflects distance from God and therefore brings to mind His incomparability. The inward dimension reflects nearness and is connected to God's similarity. The two dimensions thus reflect the two hands of God through which human beings were created.

The whole cosmos comes into existence through the marriage of the complementary divine names, the names of beauty and majesty. The first group of names is connected more closely to God's similarity, while the second group is connected to His incomparability. God's double relationship with created things results in the polar structure of humans: spiritual and corporeal, or formless and formal. The bodily dimension of reality is connected with the limiting qualities of earth. These include hardness, heaviness, solidity, darkness, ignorance. God is totally incomparable with such attributes. The spiritual dimension of created reality is connected with the qualities of light. These include incorporeality, intangibility, luminosity, subtlety, intelligence. These are closely connected to God's similarity. God is the Light of the heavens and the earth, the Knower of all things, the Subtle. Only through sharing in His attributes can human beings possess a spiritual dimension. The spirit is inherently nearer to God than the body, and therefore relatively "similar" to Him.

But in the human being, the outward form or body is inseparable from the spirit. Spirit and body together manifest all the divine names. The dark, earthly, ignorant side of human nature is inconceivable without God's incomparability. In short, the original nature (*fiṭra*) of human beings is the reflected image of the divine reality. Spiritual perfection is to realize one's primordial and original nature, the divine reality latent in oneself.

This whole discussion cannot be epitomized better than by the words of Confucius: "One yin and one yang. This is Tao. To inherit from the Tao is good. To actualize the Tao is the primordial human nature."[19]

The Plan of the Book

My primary concern in this book is to bring out the type of thinking that has gone on among those Muslim authorities who were concerned with the underlying nature of polar relationships. In order to do this, it is not sufficient simply to say in general terms that the Muslims said such and such or thought in this way or that. Their thinking needs to be presented as nearly as possible in their own words so that we do not impose our thinking upon them. The meaning of words is intimately related to the way in which the language is used and to the context. The paraphrasing that is commonly done in books on the history of Islamic thought has the effect of losing nuances of thought and expression that are every bit as important as the "meaning" of the words.

All this has to do with what I call a "qualitative" approach. The "qualities" at issue are normally present in the very form of the discourse, in the adjectives and verbs that are employed. We cannot "go straight to the point" without missing the point. The more we can quote the actual texts, the more it may be possible to find out what is really at issue for the Muslim authorities themselves.

I pay great attention to consistency of translation. It is not merely a question of making sure that the technical terminology of Islamic philosophy or Sufism is recognized as such and preserved as key terms. In fact, the more I work with the texts, the more I realize that the "peripheral" words are just as important as the "important" words. None of these texts was written in a vacuum. The authors paid extremely close attention to the words they were employing. The words have not only a technical meaning, but also a shade or tone that colors and shapes the whole discussion. The texts I cite range over a period of about a thousand years, though most pertain to a period of four hundred years. Several schools of thought are represented here, yet they all used the same words. And they had in mind the usage of these words in the Koran, the Hadith, and other schools of thought. As soon as we change the translation to meet what seems to us to be a change of context, important correlations are lost to sight. Yet it is my thesis that the central issue in Islamic thought is relationship or correlation. If we lose the linguistic correlations, we will have a much more difficult time bringing out conceptual correlations.

The book is structured in a way that I see as largely having been imposed on me by the nature of the material. Islamic thought always begins with God. *Tawḥīd*, or the statement, "There is no god but God," is taken as the fundamental given by all Muslim thinkers. Hence it is necessary to deal with "theology" at the outset. But by theology I do not mean Kalām, since that is a particular kind of dogmatic theology that is not very helpful in the investigation of the issues with which I am concerned. I have in mind theology in the literal sense of the term: knowledge of God. This is the primary concern not only of the proponents of Kalām, but also of many Sufis and most philosophers. And it is the "sapiential" approach of the latter two groups that opens up the symbolic universe of Islamic discourse to the type of investigation that I have undertaken.

Before dealing with theology, however, I found it useful to say something more about qualitative thinking and the overall structure of what I call the "Tao of Islam." Hence in the first chapter I discuss the three great realities that make up this Tao: God, the cosmos, and the human being. I show how the sapiential tradition has seen these three realities as being inseparable. Each manifests the same "qualities" or attributes or characteristics, but in different modes. Each can be seen as a replica of the Tao, with the two fundamental principles, yin and yang, harmoniously present.

The rest of the book is concerned primarily with providing textual evidence for the claims made in the introduction and chapter 1. Hence it is divided into three sections: God, the cosmos, and spiritual psychology, or metacosm, macrocosm, and microcosm. I employ the term *spiritual psychology* in order to indicate that Islamic views on the microcosm are related to the spiritual perfection of human beings, which is the central goal of Islam according to the intellectual tradition with which I am concerned.

No attempt is made to make each of the three sections of the book deal exclusively with the topic in question. Given the nature of the material, this is impossible without serious distortion. The three major topics are interrelated on all sorts of levels, and the texts do not discuss them in isolation. The section headings merely delineate the major theme of each section, but the other two themes necessarily come up as well.

The central issue, in my view, is theological in the broadest sense of the word. How Islam pictures gender relationships depends upon its picture of the nature of reality. Absolute reality (*al-ḥaqīqat al-muṭlaqa*) is God, whom the Koran often calls the Real (*al-ḥaqq*). It is my hope that this book has something to say to the ongoing theological debate over everything implied in such terms as "God the Father" and "God the Mother," even if the issues are presented here in exclusively Islamic terms.

This book has evolved considerably since I first conceived of it. After three years of teaching "Feminine Spirituality in World Religions," I applied for a fellowship from the National Endowment for the Humanities to write a book on "the feminine principle in Islam." I received the fellowship and was able to devote the 1986–87 academic year to gathering most of the material found in the book. I am deeply grateful to NEH for this help. The more I studied the texts, however, the more it became clear to me that Islamic views on the feminine can in no way be separated from Islamic views of the masculine. The work gradually evolved into an investigation of gender relationships. But even this had to be mentioned in the subtitle, since such relationships represent only one example of a much broader phenomenon. This phenomenon is a type of polar thinking that places relationships at center stage. The goal of this thinking is to show how all things are interrelated within the context of the absolutely Real. In other words, the goal is to establish unity (*tawḥīd*), though this unity does not erase the effect of polarity. Quite the contrary, establishing unity shows how polarity is itself the primary principle through which unity manifests itself. Hence the final title of the work, *The Tao of Islam*, refers to relational thinking in Islam and the fact that polarity expresses unity. Since male and female make up one of the many relational pairs found in existence, the question of gender relationships plays an important role in the study.

In its present form the book owes a good deal to my husband, William C. Chittick. Not only have I made free use of his published and unpublished works, but years of collaboration and discussion have helped shape my own ideas—and his—about the issues discussed. He has checked the translations against the originals and devoted a good deal of time to editing the final version of the book. I owe special gratitude to Professor Izutsu, who not only taught me Arabic and then Ibn al-ʿArabī's metaphysics, but who also gave me the key to understand Islamic cosmogenesis in terms of the *I Ching*. The seed he planted in my mind years ago has finally given fruit in this book.

1

1

THE THREE REALITIES

In most of our texts, three basic realities are kept in view: God, the cosmos or macrocosm, and the human being or microcosm. We can picture these as the three angles of a triangle. What is particularly interesting is the relationships established among the angles. God at the apex and source brings the two angles at the base into existence, since both macrocosm and microcosm are derivative realities. Each angle can be studied in relation to one or both of the other two angles.

The triangular picture is made more complex by the fact that each of the three realities has two basic dimensions and can be pictured as a cross. The vertical axis represents one kind of relationship, the horizontal axis another kind. At the apex, the vertical axis is set up by the distinction between the Divine Essence and the divine attributes, while the horizontal axis reflects the relationships between complementary divine names, such as Exalter and Abaser, or Life-giver and Slayer. Parallel distinctions can be drawn in both microcosm and macrocosm. "Heaven and earth" or "spirit and body" represent the vertical axis, while interrelationships among realities at each level set up a number of horizontal axes. For the moment, it is important to bring out this basic triangular structure of the whole of reality. Later chapters will deal with internal and external relationships.

Signs in the Horizons and the Souls

The most common terms in our texts for macrocosm and microcosm are the literal Arabic translations of the Greek expressions: *al-ʿālam al-kabīr*, the "large world," and *al-ʿālam al-ṣaghīr*, the "small world." Often *larger* and *smaller* are used instead of *large* and *small*. Sometimes primacy is given to the human being. Then the macrocosm becomes the "large human being" (*al-insān al-kabīr*) and the microcosm the "small human being" (*al-insān al-ṣaghīr*).[1] The term *macrocosm* is synonymous with *world* or *cosmos*, which is usually defined as "everything other than God." When our authors use the term *macrocosm* instead of *cosmos*, they do so in order to set up a contrast with the microcosm. The microcosm is the human individual, who epitomizes all the qualities found in God and the macrocosm.

Many authors allude to the macrocosm and microcosm through the expression "the horizons and the souls" (*al-āfāq wa'l-anfus*). This expression goes back to the Koranic verse, "We shall show them Our signs upon the horizons and within their own souls, until it is clear to them that He is the Real" (41:53). These "signs" (*āyāt*) of God found both outside and inside human beings are one of the basic recurring themes of the Koran. The Book employs the term *sign* in singular or plural form 288 times in several closely related senses. A sign is any phenomenon that gives news of God. It may be a prophet, a prophetic message, a prophetic miracle, or simply the things of the natural world. It may pertain to the outer, macrocosmic realm, or the inner, microcosmic realm. "In the earth there are signs for those having sure faith, and in your souls. What, do you not see?" (51:20–21). In short, everything in the universe is a sign of God.

Dozens of Koranic verses express the idea that all natural objects are God's signs. It is important to grasp this idea as fundamental to Islamic thought, since it sets up relationships between God and the cosmos in no uncertain terms. The verses where the term is employed usually mention in addition the proper human response to God's signs: remembering, understanding, seeing, having gratitude, reflecting, using the intellect, fearing God, and so on. I cite a few examples to make this point completely clear:

> It is He who has appointed for you the stars, that by them you might be guided in the shadows of land and sea. We have distinguished the signs for a people who know. (6:97)
>
> And the good land—its vegetation comes forth by the leave of its Lord. And the corrupt—it comes forth but scantily. Even so We turn about the signs for a people who have gratitude. (7:58)
>
> In the alternation of night and day, and what God has created in the heavens and the earth—surely there are signs for a godfearing people. (10:6)
>
> And that which He has multiplied for you in the earth of diverse hues—surely in that is a sign for a people who remember. (16:13)
>
> Have they not regarded the birds, which are subjected in the air of heaven? Naught holds them but God. Surely in that are signs for a people who have faith. (16:79)
>
> And of His signs is that He shows you lightning, for fear and hope, and that He sends down out of heaven water and revives the earth after it is dead. Surely in that are signs for a people who have intellect. (30:24)
>
> God takes the souls at the time of their death, and that which has not died, in its sleep. He withholds that against which He has decreed death, but looses the other till a stated term. Surely in that are signs for a people who reflect. (39:42)

When the Koran commands people to see all things as God's signs, it is encouraging them to make use of a particular type of mental process that is not oriented toward objects, things, or data. On the contrary, the Koran tells us that we must perceive things not so much for what they are in themselves but for what they tell us of something beyond themselves. The things are likenesses, similitudes, symbols. As Lane tells us in his classic Arabic dictionary, quoting an ancient authority, the word *āya* "properly signifies any apparent thing inseparable from a thing not equally apparent, so that when one perceives the former, he knows that he perceives the other, which he cannot perceive by itself."[2] God is invisible by definition. Yet, traces and intimations of His awesome reality can be gleaned from all things, if only we meditate upon them.

Attention to the signs of God encourages a sensitivity toward the unseen dimensions of existence. The approach is hardly "scientific," since material and quantitative considerations are of no intrinsic interest, unless they too become pointers to the One (as in the Pythagorean approach of the Ikhwān al-Ṣafāʾ). This idea might be expressed by saying that the Koran discourages "scientific" thought while encouraging "poetic" thought. It asks people to look at the meaning and inner significance of things in relation to God. It warns them against imagining that the significance of phenomena is limited to their form and appearance, or to their relationships with other phenomena. Attention must be turned primarily toward those qualities of existing things that tell us of the ultimate reality beyond the things. These qualities provide intimations of God's modes of activity or of His own names and attributes.

In short, discussions of the significance of the phenomena found within microcosm and macrocosm often have nothing to do with what we would call a "scientific evaluation" of the human being and the world.

The texts are concerned rather with a qualitative appraisal of interrelationships between the realms of the visible (*al-shahāda*) and the unseen (*al-ghayb*). The unseen is a domain that is not only inaccessible to the senses at this moment, but inaccessible to them by definition, no matter what scientific instruments may be employed to search it out. However, the unseen domain of the macrocosm is not inaccessible to the corresponding realms in the microcosm. The human spirit may, under certain circumstances, perceive realities of the unseen realm.

At times the terminology employed in the texts may remind us of a scientific approach. There is frequent discussion of things in the world that can be observed, measured, and counted. But as a general rule, Muslim thinkers were not primarily interested in the things themselves. Rather, they were concerned with showing how the signs or attributes of God can be observed in different creatures and various domains of existence. When the qualities found in the outside world coincide with the qualities of the inside world, this is even more reason for pondering, reflecting, and meditating upon God's signs.

Many if not most of the Muslim cosmologists studied the outside world in order to bring out what we can learn about God from the qualities present in the visible universe. Few of the Western scholars who have looked at cosmological texts have appreciated this approach. They have been interested mainly in the "history of science," considering Islamic cosmology as a primitive form of science. This may help explain why so few Muslim scholars have taken Islamic cosmology seriously in the past century. It is usually dismissed as unscientific, or symbolic at best, though few have attempted to investigate in what manner that symbolism might be useful in the contemporary world. Most Muslim scholars, either because of a hereditary literal-mindedness deriving from the juridical tradition or an acquired literal-mindedness stemming from popular scientism, have not looked at cosmology in the way in which it has been taught by the great theoreticians. The study of Islamic cosmology can gain a great deal if we perceive it as built upon a world of images, of qualitative and not quantitative entities, of correspondences and hidden analogies.

Certainly modern science tells us that phenomena are not what they appear to be, but its methodology precludes taking help from anything beyond itself to enter into the unseen realms. From the beginning Islamic cosmological thinking has been based on the idea that things are pointers and not of any ultimate significance in themselves. Once we recognize that the qualities that things manifest rather than the things in themselves are of primary interest, then we will be able to perceive that Islamic cosmology presents us with a perspective that has no relationship with the changing viewpoints of scientific cosmology. We are dealing with a scheme of qualitative correspondences that depict the relative standing of God, the cosmos, and the human being. Whether the earth goes round the sun or vice versa is irrelevant. "Up and down" or "heaven and earth" are pairs of terms explicating a certain set of relationships that hold true regardless of changes in "scientific truth."

In *Kashf al-asrār*, a commentary on the Koran written in 520/1126, Rashīd al-Dīn Maybudī takes the verse, "We shall show them Our signs upon the horizons and within their souls," as an explicit command to meditate upon the qualities of existence. Though he does not discuss the correspondences between microcosm and macrocosm as such, his qualitative evaluation is typical. He begins by comparing the human body to a tablet, a place wherein God writes, an analogy that we often meet:

> In this verse, God says: Why do you not look into yourself and meditate upon your own structure? The Lord of the worlds has recorded many fine points of wisdom and realities of handiwork with the pen of eternal gentleness upon the tablet of this structure. Upon it He has inscribed various kinds of artistry and different varieties of ennoblement. He made the round head—the tent of intellect and the meeting place of knowledge—into a monastery of the senses. If anyone has con-

sidered this hollow structure, this compound person, to have any worth, he has done so because of the person's intellect and knowledge. The worth of a human being lies in intellect and his importance in knowledge, his perfection in intellect and his beauty in knowledge.

God created the forehead of the human being like a bar of silver. He strung the two bows of his eyebrows with pure musk. He poured the two dots of his eye's light into two cups of darkness. He made a hundred thousand red roses grow up in the garden of his two cheeks. He concealed thirty-two teeth like pearls in the oyster shell of his mouth. He sealed his mouth with glistening agate. From the beginning of his lip to the end of his throat He created twenty-nine waystations, making them the places of articulation for the twenty-nine letters. From his heart He brought a king into existence, from his breast a royal parade ground, from his aspiration a fleet-footed mount, from his thought a swift messenger. He created two taking hands and two running feet.

All the aforementioned is but the robe of creation and the beauty of the outward realm. Beyond this is the perfection and beauty of the inward realm. For a moment ponder the Lord's subtleties and kindnesses and the traces of the divine solicitude and care that have arranged this handful of earth. Look at the different kinds of honor and the special privileges of nearness that He has placed within human beings. For He created the whole cosmos, but He looked not upon a single creature with the eye of love, He sent not a single messenger to any existent thing, He sent no message to any creature. When the turn of the children of Adam arrived, He pulled them up through gentleness and caressed them through bounty and quarries of light. He made their inmost mystery the place of His own glance, He sent them messengers, He set angels over them as guardians, He placed the fire of love in their hearts, and He sent them continuous incitements to yearning and motives for desire.

The purpose of all these words and allusions is to show that a human being is a handful of earth. Whatever ennoblement and honor people have received derives from the gentleness and care of the holy Lord. When He gives, He gives because of His own generosity, not because of your worthiness. He gives because of His magnanimity, not because of your prostration. He gives through His bounty, not because of your good works. He gives because He is Lord, not because you are lord of the manor.[3]

The signs of God provide the means to know God, and this, for the sapiential tradition, is the goal of human life. In the Koran, God says, "I created jinn and mankind only to worship Me" (51:56). The Prophet's companion Ibn ʿAbbās explains that the words "to worship Me" mean "to know Me."[4] For sapiential authorities, this knowledge of God depends upon knowledge of the signs in oneself. These authors must have known that the alleged hadith, "He who knows his own soul [or "himself"] knows his Lord," is not found in the standard works, but they frequently cite it, since it expresses in the most succinct way the goal of acquiring knowledge. The saying is certainly supported by the Koranic verses that point to the signs within the microcosm as the key to understanding. Maybudī provides a poetic explanation for the necessity of knowing the signs in oneself while commenting on the Koranic verse, "And among His signs is that He created you of dust. Then lo, you are mortals, all scattered abroad" (30:20):

> God is saying, "O child of Adam! If you want to know the signs and banners of God's Oneness and recognize the marks of His Singularity, open the eye of consideration and intelligence, roam in the world of the soul, and gaze upon the root of your own creation.
>
> "You were a handful of earth, a shadowy stem fixed in the darkness of your own unknowing, bewildered in the darkness of attributes. Then the rain of lights began to fall from the heaven of mysteries: 'He poured His light down upon them.'[5] That earth turned into jasmine and that stone became a pearl. That dense stem gained value through this subtle graft. The earth became pure, the darkness became light.
>
> "Yes, it is We who adorn and paint. We adorn whom We will with Our light. We adorn the Garden with Our friends, We adorn Our friends with the heart, and We adorn the heart with Our own light. We do this so that if they do not reach the pavilions of Our inaccessibility through the carcass of their own misfortune, they will reach Us through the

ray of the good fortune of Our majesty's light."

A shaykh was asked, "What is the sign of that light?"

He replied, "Its sign is that through that light the servant knows God without finding Him, loves Him without seeing Him, turns away from being occupied with and remembering himself through being occupied with and remembering Him. He finds ease and rest in His lane, he tells secrets to His friends and asks favors from them. By day he is busy with religion's work, by night intoxicated with certainty's tidings. By day he dwells with creatures of good character, by night with the Real, fixed in sincerity."[6]

Qualitative Correspondence

To say that all natural phenomena are the signs of God is to say that everything in existence tells us something about God. The more common Koranic meaning of the word *sign*, however, is not that of a natural phenomenon, but of a divine revelation. All the prophets, from Adam down to Muhammad, were sent in order to manifest the signs of God, to deliver His messages. The great message that begins Islam in the specific historical sense, the Koran, is a collection of God's signs. The word employed for verse of the Koran is precisely this term *sign*.

The fact that the word *sign* means both natural phenomenon and divine revelation implies that the knowledge that phenomena, whether macrocosmic or microcosmic, make available to human beings corresponds to the knowledge given by the prophets in general and the Koran in particular. This is one reason that Muslims have, by and large, seen no contradiction between seeking knowledge of the natural world and receiving knowledge of the invisible world through revelation. The greatest proof of God is the way things are. The natural order is so astonishing that it can only be the result of God's own order.

The fundamental Koranic teachings about God are phrased in terms of His activities and names. In other words, if the Koran tells us through linguistic signs what God does and who He is, the whole of the cosmos says the same thing in a sign language aimed at "those who have eyes." By its very existence, creation announces the divine attributes and acts. When the various schools of the Islamic intellectual tradition attempt to summarize the Koran's teachings about the nature of God's activities and His relationship to the world, they commonly do so by mentioning and explaining God's names or attributes. Books on the "ninety-nine names of God" were written by proponents of Kalām, philosophers, and Sufis.[7]

For our purposes here, we can consider the term *name* (*ism*) of God synonymous with the term *attribute* (*ṣifa*), though some theologians distinguish between the two. It is useful, however, to draw a grammatical distinction between them, since a name is an adjective (serving as a proper noun), while an attribute is an abstract noun. For example, God is called by the name Merciful, while the corresponding attribute is mercy. His name is Just and His attribute is justice.

When Muslim thinkers look upon the signs of God on the horizons and within their own souls, they frequently express what they find in terms of divine attributes. For example, if we look at the world, we find some things that are inanimate, some that are alive, and some that are dead after having been alive. In the distinctions set up here we have signs of the divine attribute life, which manifests itself in some creatures but not in others. As Maybudī remarks in typical fashion in the passage quoted above, human beings—and all other things of this world—are but handfuls of earth. They have nothing of their own. If people, in contrast to the dust in the street, are alive, this life must derive from God's intervention. Human life can only come on loan from the divine life. Moreover, if some people were once alive and are now dead, this must be because they had their life on loan from God, who has now taken it back. Hence, by meditating upon the quality of life, we understand that God is Alive (*al-ḥayy*), and that He is also the Life-giver (*al-muḥyī*) and the Slayer (*al-mumīt*). Three of the "ninety-nine names of God" have thus been established.

It would be possible, with the help of the numerous treatises that have been written on the "names of God" and the views of various Koran commentators, Sufis, philosophers, and proponents of Kalām, to derive all the names of God from the macrocosmic and microcosmic signs. But my purpose here is simply to show that it is characteristic for many if not most of the great representatives of the Islamic intellectual tradition to perceive the qualities of things in terms of their relationship to divine attributes. On this basis, the qualitative analogies that are found among things in the cosmos and things in the soul, and between the soul and the world, become a significant if not primary mode of knowledge, since these analogies tie all things back to the Real.

As pointed out in the introduction, the mode of Koran commentary known as *ta'wīl* (esoteric hermeneutics) depends in many of its forms upon qualitative analogies among things, especially between the microcosm and the macrocosm. If one is not aware of the internal logic of these analogies and correspondences, this mode of commentary appears arbitrary. But if one has a background in the cosmological literature dealing with the relationship between the signs in the horizons and the signs in the souls, one will see that a work such as ʿAbd al-Razzāq Kāshānī's *Ta'wīl al-Qur'ān* is embedded in this tradition and draws few analogies that could be called original.

In order to introduce examples of this type of thinking, I provide below a few passages setting up analogies between microcosm and macrocosm. I quote first from the Ikhwān al-Ṣafā' or "Brethren of Purity," the famous sages of the fourth/tenth century who were thoroughly influenced by Greek philosophical texts translated into Arabic, especially works on the numerical symbolism of Pythagoras. In the following, from the treatise "On the saying of the sages that the human being is a microcosm," the Ikhwān al-Ṣafā' draw analogies between the structure of the microcosm and various structures observable in the outward world. I repeat that I quote this and other passages below merely to familiarize the reader with the type of thought processes and analogies that infuse the tradition. The information as information is not the point. What is important is the qualities perceived within phenomena and the type of relationships that are then set up. Note that the authors themselves make explicit that they are looking for likenesses (*mithālāt*) and similarities (*tashbīhāt*), that is, relationships on a qualitative level. They are not interested in the phenomena as such, but in the qualities that the phenomena manifest.

> The first sages considered this corporeal world with the vision of their eyes and witnessed the manifest dimensions of affairs with the perception of their senses. Then they reflected upon the states of the cosmos with their intellects, scrutinized the scope of the activity of its universal individuals with their insights, and took cognizance of the varieties of the cosmos's individual things with their deliberation. They did not find a single part of the cosmos more complete in structure, more perfect in form, and more similar to the totality than the human being.
>
> The human being is a totality brought together from a corporeal body and a spiritual soul. Hence the sages found likenesses for all the existent things of the corporeal world in the condition of his body's structure. These existent things include the wonderful compositions of the world's celestial spheres, its different kinds of constellations, the movements of its planets, the composition of its pillars and mothers, the diversity of its mineral substances, the various kinds of plants, and the marvelous bodily frames of its animals.

The pillars (*arkān*) or mothers (*ummahāt*) are the four elements, which combine to produce the children (*mawālīd*) or "the things that are born" (*muwalladāt*), that is, the three kingdoms: inanimate objects, plants, and animals.

> Moreover, within the human soul and the permeation of the structure of the body by its faculties they found similarities with the different kinds of spiritual creatures, such as the angels, the jinn, the human beings, the satans, the souls of other animals, and the activity of their states in the cosmos.
>
> When these affairs became clear to them

in the human form, they named this form a "small world." Here we want to mention a few of these likenesses and similarities. . . .

As we said, the human being is a totality brought together from a dark body and a spiritual soul. If one takes into account the state of the body and the marvels of the composition of the organs and the modes of the conjunction of the articulations, the body resembles a house prepared for an inhabitant. But when one takes into account the state of the soul, the wonders of its controlling powers in the structure of the bodily frame, and its faculties' permeation of the body's articulations, the soul resembles the inhabitant of the house along with his servants, wife, and children.

If one considers the human being in another respect, one finds that the structure of the body with the diversity of the shapes of its organs and the variety of the composition of its articulations is similar to the shop of an artisan. In respect of the permeation of the structure of the bodily frame by the soul's faculties, its marvelous acts in the organs of the body, and the various movements in the bodily articulations, the soul is similar to an artisan in his shop with his disciples and apprentices, as we explained in the treatise on "The practical crafts."

In another respect, if one considers the structure of the human body in respect of the multiplicity of the combinations of the strata of the bodily frame, the wonders of the composition of the bodily articulations, the many diverse organs, the branching out of the veins and their extension into the regions of the organs, the disparity of the containers in the depths of the body, and the activity of the faculties of the soul, the human being resembles a city full of bazaars with various crafts, as we explained in the treatise on "The composition of the body."

In another respect, when the human being is considered from the point of view of the soul's governing control over the states of the body, its good management, and the permeation of the structure of the body by its faculties and activities, then the human being resembles a king in a city with his soldiers, servants, and retinue.

In another respect, if one considers the state of the body and its being engendered along with the state of the soul and its configuration with the body, the body resembles the womb and the soul resembles the embryo, as we explained in the treatise on "The configuration of the particular soul and its emergence from potentiality into actuality."

In another respect, if one considers, one finds the body like a ship, the soul like the captain, works like the goods of traders, this world like the ocean, death like the shore, the next world like the city of the merchants, and God the king who gives recompense.

In another respect, if one considers, one finds the body like a horse, the soul like the rider, this world like a racecourse, and works like the race.

In another respect, if one considers, one finds the soul like a farmer, the body like the farm, works like seeds and produce, death like the reaping, and the next world like the threshing floor, as we explained in the treatise on "The wisdom in death."[8]

Elsewhere in the same treatise, the Ikhwān al-Ṣafāʾ point out similarities between the human body and the existent things of the visible world, where the four pillars or mothers combine to produce the children. The correspondences between the great and small worlds mentioned here have resonated down through the Islamic intellectual and poetical tradition to recent times. It should be kept in mind that the four elements—earth, air, water, and fire—are qualities rather than concrete substances. They are not identical with the substances that go by these names in the visible world, since the elements are noncompound or "simple" (*basīṭ, mufrad*), which is to say that they are not found in the visible world, which is made totally of compound things (*murakkabāt*). Even when our authors do not state this explicitly, they discuss the elements in order to bring out the qualities pertaining to the different elements that are found in the compound things.

Below the moon there are four pillars. These are the mothers through whom the things that are born—the animals, plants, and minerals—subsist. In the same way, within the structure of the body are found four members that make up the whole of the body: the head, the breast, the belly, and the area from the abdomen to the bottom of the feet. These four correspond to those four. This is because the head corresponds to the element fire in respect of visual rays and sensory movement.

The breast corresponds to the element air because of the breath and the breathing of air. The belly corresponds to the element water in respect of the moistures within it. The area from the abdomen to the bottom of the feet corresponds to the element earth, because it is established upon the earth, just as the other three are established above and around the earth.

These four pillars give rise to vapors from which winds, clouds, rain, animals, plants, and minerals are engendered. In the same way the four members give rise to vapors in the human body, like mucous from the nostrils, tears from the eyes, and saliva from the mouth, the winds born in the belly, and the liquids that come out, like urine, excrement, and others.

The structure of the human body is like the earth, its bones are like the mountains, its bones' marrow like the minerals, its abdomen like the ocean, its intestines like rivers, its veins like streams, its flesh like the land, its hair like plants, the places where hair grows like good soil, the places where it does not grow like briny earth, the face down to the feet like a flourishing city, the back like a ruins, the front of the face like the east, behind the back like the west, the right hand like the south, the left hand like the north, the breathing like the winds, the person's speech like the thunder, his shouts like lightning, his laughter like daylight, his weeping like rain, his despair and sorrow like the darkness of night, his sleep like death, his wakefulness like life, the days of his youth like days of spring, the days of his young manhood like the days of summer, the days of his maturity like the days of autumn, the days of his old age like the days of winter.

His movements and acts are like the movements and turning of the planets, his birth and his presence like ascendent constellations, his death and his absence like constellations that have set. . . .

Just as the sun is the head of the planets in the celestial sphere, so also among men there are kings and leaders. Just as the planets are connected to the sun and to each other, so also are people connected to kings and to each other. Just as the planets turn away from the sun through strength and increase of light, so also people turn away from kings through power to rule, robes of honor, and high degrees.

Just as Mars is related to the sun, so is the head of the army related to the king. Just as Mercury is related to the sun, so are scribes and viziers related to kings. Just as Jupiter is related to the sun, so are judges and possessors of knowledge related to the kings. . . .

Just as the moon is related to the sun, so also are rebels related to kings. That is because the moon takes light from the sun at the beginning of the month until it stands face to face with it and resembles it in light, becoming similar to it in its condition. In the same way, rebels follow the command of kings. Then they refuse to obey them and struggle against them in the kingdom.

In addition, the states of the moon are similar to the states of the things of this world, that is, animals, plants, etc., since the moon begins increasing in light and perfection at the beginning of the month until it becomes complete in the middle of the month. Then it starts to decrease and dissolve and is effaced by the end of the month. In the same way, the states of the inhabitants of this world increase in the beginning. They never cease growing and being configured until they are complete and perfect. Then they begin to decline and decrease until they dissolve and come to nothing.[9]

ʿAzīz al-Dīn Nasafī (d. ca. 695/1295) demonstrates the same type of analogical thinking within the context of a simplified and more or less popularized version of the teachings of Ibn al-ʿArabī:

When the sperm drop falls into the womb, it represents the First Substance. When the embryo has four strata, it represents the elements and the natures. When the members appear, the outward members—like the head, the hands, the stomach, the private part, and the feet—represent the seven climes. The inward members—like the lungs, the brain, the kidney, the heart, the gallbladder, the liver, and the spleen—represent the seven heavens.

The lungs are the first heaven and represent the sphere of the moon, since the moon is the lungs of the macrocosm, the intermediary between the two worlds. There are many angels in this sphere, while the angel who is in charge of temperate water and air is the leader of these angels.

The brain is the second heaven and represents the sphere of Mercury, since Mercury is the brain of the macrocosm. There are many angels in this sphere, while the angel who is in charge of learning to write, acquiring knowledge, and managing livelihood is the leader of these angels. His name is Gabriel, and Gabriel is the secondary cause of the knowledge of the people of the world.

The kidneys are the third heaven and represent the sphere of Venus, since Venus is the kidney of the macrocosm. There are many angels in this sphere, and the angel who is in charge of joy, happiness, and appetite is the leader of these angels.

The heart is the fourth heaven and represents the sphere of the sun, since the sun is the heart of the macrocosm. There are many angels in this sphere, and the angel who is in charge of life is the leader of these angels. His name is Seraphiel, and Seraphiel is the secondary cause of the life of the inhabitants of the world.

The spleen is the fifth heaven and represents the sphere of Mars, since Mars is the spleen of the macrocosm. There are many angels in this sphere, and the angel who is in charge of severity, wrath, beating, and killing is the leader of these angels.

The liver is the sixth heaven and represents the sphere of Jupiter, since Jupiter is the liver of the macrocosm. There are many angels in this sphere, and the angel who is in charge of provision is the leader of these angels. His name is Michael, and he is the secondary cause of the provision of the inhabitants of the world.

The gallbladder is the seventh heaven and represents the sphere of Saturn, for Saturn is the gallbladder of the macrocosm. There are many angels in this sphere, and the angel who is in charge of taking spirits [at death] is the leader of these angels. His name is Azrael, and he is the secondary cause of the taking of the spirits of the inhabitants of the world.

The animal spirit is the Footstool and represents the sphere of the fixed stars, since the sphere of the fixed stars is the Footstool of the macrocosm. There are many angels in this sphere.

The psychic spirit is the Throne and represents the sphere of the spheres, since the sphere of the spheres is the Throne of the macrocosm.

The intellect is the vicegerent of God.

As long as the bodily members do not grow and develop, they represent the minerals. When they grow and develop, they represent plants. When sensation and volitional movement appear, they represent animals.[10]

Qualitative Levels

Different things in the universe give news of God in diverse ways and various degrees. God is Light, and "There is no light but Light." Nevertheless, the unreal light of others is somehow similar to His light. Wherever the quality of luminosity is found, this is a trace of the divine Light. A glowing ember manifests light, as does the sun. Neither of these is true light, but all the same, the light of the sun is more intense and more real than the light of the ember.

Every divine attribute exhibits the same characteristic: It is found in varying degrees throughout creation. When we consider the cosmos as a hierarchy of the differing intensities of a specific attribute, we see that the hierarchy grows up out of the distinction between God and the cosmos. God possesses the attribute fully. In and of itself the "other"—anything in the cosmos, or the cosmos itself—has nothing of the attribute. If we can speak of the attribute as being present in the cosmos, we do so inasmuch as the attribute is borrowed from God, much as light is borrowed from the sun.

Take, for example, the distinction between Light (*nūr*) and darkness (*ẓulma*). God is sheer and utter Light, with no admixture of darkness. Light is God, Being, Reality. In contrast, darkness is utter nonexistence, utter unreality. The cosmos in itself is darkness, since "in itself"—without God's support—it does not exist. But inasmuch as the cosmos may be said to exist and act as a locus within which the signs of God are manifest, it is a mixture of light and darkness, often called "brightness" (*ḍiyā'*). What is more, the cosmos manifests brightness on an indefinite number of levels in every conceivable intensity. Each thing in the cosmos reflects light in a different degree. There is a vast if not infinite hierarchy ranging from the least luminous created thing to the most luminous. Hence, on the basis of the initial distinction between absolute light and absolute darkness, we quickly reach a spectrum ranging from the brightest to the darkest. And between the two absolutes, all qualities are relative.

Each thing is bright in relation to absolute darkness, or dark in relation to absolute Light.[11]

Many divine attributes can be analyzed in a similar way. Thus, for example, God is absolute Power, while nothingness is absolute lack of power. The cosmos is the place of a hierarchy ranging from the strongest to the weakest.

God is absolute Life, while nothingness is absolute death. The cosmos is a hierarchy ranging from the weakest degree of life—or the most intense degree of existing death—to the most intense degree of life, manifest in those angels who are everlasting. But of course, in the last analysis, "Everything is perishing but His face" (28:88) or His reality, so everything is touched by death except God Himself.

Gradation in the cosmos always has to do with qualitative distinctions. Different qualities allow for different degrees. The most fundamental gradation is that of light or its synonym, Being or existence (*wujūd*), and this is the hierarchy of existing worlds. We will return to the question of ontological hierarchy later. Here I want to stress the different degrees in which the things of the cosmos manifest various divine attributes.

The same basic attributes are found in the whole cosmos, and each thing by force of its circumstances must manifest certain attributes in some mode. Hence analogies can be established among outwardly disparate realities by the fact that they manifest the same qualities. It is these qualitative analogies that form the fundamental subject matter of the sapiential tradition with which we are concerned. Upon them is built the Tao of Islam.

It is important to grasp here that the same attributes are found (or concealed) in every domain of existence. Distinctions among domains are related to the fact that different domains reflect or manifest the divine attributes in different degrees. The Ikhwān al-Ṣafāʾ provide an early and clear explanation of this principle:

> Know, brother, that the attributes of God in which none of His creatures share and the knowledge whereby nothing else is known are that He is Beginner, Deviser, Creator, Engenderer, Powerful, Knowing, Alive, Existent, Originator, Eternal, and Active. Moreover, out of His generosity toward existence, He gives these attributes to existence in an appropriate and fitting way.
>
> Hence He effuses upon the Intellect [the first creation] that it be beginner, effectuator, alive, powerful, deviser, knowing, active, existence. Hence the Intellect acts as beginning for that which appears from it. It is active while being the object of an act. It effectuates while being effected and caused. It gives life to that which is below it just as life was given to it. It exists through the existence of the acts that emerge from it.
>
> The same thing can be said about the sharing of His attributes by the spiritual and corporeal beings. These are particular attributes that are said metaphorically (*maqāla majāziyya*) to belong to these beings. The attributes are connected (*iqtirān*) to them along with their opposites, just as existence is connected with nonexistence, knowledge with ignorance, life with death, power with incapacity, movement with rest, and light with darkness. All the existent things described by these attributes are connected to their opposites, by which God is not described. No, He is Creator of existence and nonexistence, so He alone possesses subsistence. He brings knowledge and ignorance into existence, so He possesses knowledge exclusively.
>
> So also is the existence of the acts and works of both the spiritual and the corporeal creatures. These acts and works correspond to the deposits placed within them and the traces effused upon them through the fact that some of them acquire from others. This is true to the extent that He brings all of them into existence and gives life to them. Then He is not described by the meaning of their attributes, nor are they worthy of sharing with Him in them. But they possess degrees and stations. Each of them has an attribute through which it is greater than what lies below it. Each possesses the excellence of this attribute exclusively. This attribute is an existent thing that is not hidden from those who ponder. For example, take the attribute of power in all animals, from a minnow to the human being. Every individual animal has a power whereby it is distinguished from the others. The final stage is the power of the human being over all of them, whether through a corporeal strength, or through a disposition of the soul.
>
> Then there is the knowledge that is pos-

sessed exclusively by human beings whereby they are distinguished from animals. All human beings share in this knowledge, but this is not an equal sharing, rather a sharing of incomparability, separation, exaltation in ranks, and ranking in degrees.[12] The final stage is their gnosis of God, achieved by the prophet in his own time and the sage in his time. It is effused upon them by the strength of the person's connection to that upper world which is singled out for knowledge, a world that can rightly be the teacher of everyone below it. And you should know that the human being who gives people knowledge of what they need is the vicegerent of God among them, His trustee over them.

Then there is life, which is also shared by all animals, all those described by movement from place to place. And every animal possesses movement and life. But they are not equal, since they do not exist in a single state. Some of them have short lifespans, others long lifespans, and others between the two. The one singled out for everlasting life is the one who passes from the form of humanity to the form of the angels, from what is below the sphere of the moon to what is above it.

So also is the attribute of the spiritual beings and the angels. They also share in these attributes in differing degrees. Each one of them has an apportioned part and a known limit.[13]

Human All-Comprehensiveness

Within the created world, human beings occupy a peculiar position not shared by any other creature. The nature of this position is expressed in many ways, such as the "Trust" accepted by humans but rejected by the heavens, the earth, and the mountains (33:72). In seeking to explain the ontological and cosmological roots of this unique human situation, our authors frequently contrast the manner in which qualities appear in the macrocosm and the microcosm. Though they constantly speak of similarities and correspondences, these are not seen to be matters of human convention or linguistic accidents. Rather, they are ontological realities, much more deeply embedded in the structure of the universe than those quantitative attributes that keep macrocosm and microcosm separate, such as temporal and spatial factors.

In the Sufi tradition, especially Ibn al-ʿArabī and his followers, the qualitative analogy between macrocosm and microcosm is established primarily in terms of the divine names. The macrocosm is viewed as the locus of manifestation for all the names of God, but spread out in an indefinitely vast expanse of time and space. God was a Hidden Treasure wanting to be known, so He made the Treasure manifest. Every jewel in the infinite treasury was placed within the domain of "otherness," which can be divided into two fundamental worlds, the unseen and the visible. Or, if we want to be more careful about protecting the divine incomparability, we can say that every jewel remained hidden in the Divine Treasure, but the infinite Light of God, by shining through the jewels, spread the qualities of each jewel throughout the worlds. Jāmī (d. 898/1492) has this analogy in mind in the following quatrain. He explains his meaning in the prose passage that follows:

> The entities were all colored windows
> upon which fell the rays of Being's Sun.
> In every window—red, yellow, blue—
> the light appeared in the window's color.

The light of God's Being—"And God's is the highest likeness" [16:60]—is like sensory light, while the realities and immutable entities are like different colored pieces of glass. The variegations of the self-manifestation of the Real within those realities and entities is like the diverse colors.

The colors of light show themselves according to the colors of the glass, which is light's veil. But in actual fact, light has no color. If the glass is clear and white, light appears within it as clear and white. If the glass is dark and colored, light appears dark and colored. At the same time, light in itself is one, simple, and all-encompassing. It has no color and no shape. In a similar way, the light of the Real's Being has a self-manifestation with each reality and entity. If that reality and entity should be near to simplicity, luminosity, and clarity—such as the entities of disengaged intellects and souls—Being's

> light appears in that locus of manifestation in extreme clarity, luminosity, and simplicity. If instead it is far from simplicity, like the entities of corporeal things, then Being's light will appear dense, even though, in itself, it is neither dense nor subtle.
>
> Hence it is He—exalted and holy is He—who is the true One, free of form, attribute, color, and shape at the level of unity. And it is also He who manifests Himself within the multiple loci of manifestation in diverse forms, in accordance with His names and attributes.[14]

Once the light of God brings about the manifestation of the jewels of the Hidden Treasure within the cosmos, we can discern different levels of intensity in manifestation. The further we move away from the Treasure itself, the closer we get to dispersion and darkness. The further we ascend toward the Treasure, the closer we approach Unity and luminosity.

To return to the analogy of the jewels being brought out of the Hidden Treasure, one might expand upon it as follows: The jewels are kept in a single infinite safe under lock and key. As the Treasure is revealed, they are taken out in sacks to the spiritual world, the rubies in one sack, the emeralds in another, the pearls in another. Then the sacks are opened and the jewels are poured individually into the rest of the universe, where they mix together and are covered with grime. Few indeed are those who recognize them for what they are. The analogy cannot do justice to the actual situation, of course, since the jewels we know cannot occupy more than one place at one time. But these jewels from the Hidden Treasure remain in safekeeping, while also being distributed in sacks. They remain in the sacks, while also being scattered throughout the visible universe.

The cosmos as a whole displays every jewel in the Treasure, but in a mode of indefinite deployment. In other words, every divine name finds many loci of manifestation in the universe. In contrast, the microcosm also contains every jewel, but here they are found in a mode of unity and concentration. One might say that God placed in the human being one jewel from each sack. Since all diamonds are fundamentally the same, by having one diamond in their makeup, human beings have a kinship with all diamond entities.

Most commonly our texts explain this doctrine by expanding upon the idea of the divine names, thus avoiding the drawbacks and limitations of concrete imagery. Each name represents a quality. Each name can be analyzed in terms of its scope (*saʿa*), or the degree to which it is reflected within the multiple phenomena of the universe. Some attributes are reflected in all things, some in many things, some in a few things, some in only one species.

In short, the macrocosm manifests all the names of God, but in a differentiated mode. The microcosm manifests all names, but in a relatively undifferentiated mode. On the divine level, the undifferentiation of the names is represented by the Hidden Treasure, locked and sealed. But we know that the jewels are in God, waiting to manifest their properties. It is this level of reality that is designated by the name Allah, the "all-comprehensive name" (*al-ism al-jāmiʿ*). This name refers both to God as such, without regard to the names, and to God as possessing all the names. Each name refers to Allah. Each denotes the single Essence (*al-dhāt*), other than which there is no true reality. But each denotes that Essence in terms of a specific relationship that the Essence assumes with created things. Only the name Allah denotes that reality as embracing all relationships and non-relationships.

The cosmos as a whole manifests all these names. So also does the human being. Hence Ibn al-ʿArabī calls the human being "the all-comprehensive engendered thing" (*al-kawn al-jāmiʿ*).[15] That is why, our authors tell us, the Prophet said that Adam was created in the image or form (*ṣūra*) of "Allah," not any other divine name. All this is implied in the story of Adam's creation in the Koran, where he is taught "all the names" (2:31).

But why was the human being created? This also is explained by the hadith of the Hidden Treasure. God "wanted [or "loved"] to be known," and it is human beings alone who can know God in His fullness, as comprehending all the names, since only they were created in the form of the all-comprehensive name. God's love for the type of knowledge that can be actualized only by human beings brought the world into existence. Jāmī speaks for the whole sapiential tradition when he recounts the story of the creation of Adam from the Koran (2:30–34), drawing a number of conclusions about the nature of human beings. The passage is from his *mathnawī, Silsilat al-dhahab*. Each poetical section is preceded by a short summary in prose.

> Explaining that the children of Adam do not know their own perfection and imperfection, since they were not created for themselves. On the contrary, they were created for other than themselves. He who created them created them only for Himself, not for them. He gave them only what would be proper for them in order to belong to Him. Were they to know that they were created for their Lord, they would know that God created the creatures in the most perfect form. . . .

> People always believe
> that they were created for themselves.
> Whatever appears to them as appropriate,
> they consider to be good and perfect,
> But whatever they imagine as inappropriate
> they put into the category of imperfection.
> But this belief is error itself,
> since they were created for God.
> The goal of their creation, whatever it might be, cannot be surpassed.
> In reality the human being's perfection is that which is desired from his existence by God.
> From the existence of the things God only wanted
> the manifestation of His names or attributes.
> No matter what appears in the courtyard of the cosmos,
> the goal is manifesting the property of a name.
> If we suppose that a thing did not come to exist,
> how could the property of the name be shown?
> That is why the Prophet addressed
> his Companions long ago, saying,
> "If there were to appear from you no work
> within which there was the taint of sin,
> God would create people of error
> so that they might sin and err,
> And then ask forgiveness for that sin,
> making manifest the property of the Forgiver."[16]

Here Jāmī voices one of the typically Islamic arguments in theodicy: Since God is forgiving, sins must exist, or else there would be nothing to forgive. It is His quality of forgiveness which, in the last analysis, brings about sinfulness. Aḥmad Samʿānī (d. 534/1140) gives us a more poetical rendition of the same principle (even though he writes in prose) as follows. He quotes God's hidden command to all things:

> "O tree, put up your head next to Adam's throne! O appetite for the fruit, enter into Adam's heart! O accursed one, let loose the reins of your whispering! O Eve, you show the way! O Adam, don't eat the fruit, have self-restraint! O self-restraint, don't come near Adam!"
>
> O God, God, what is all this? "We want to bring Adam down from the throne of indifference to the earth of need. We want to make manifest the secret of love."
>
> "O servant, avoid disobedience and stay away from caprice! O caprice, you take his reins! O world, you display yourself to him! O servant, you show self-restraint! O self-restraint, don't come near him!"
>
> O God, God, what is all this? "We want to make the servant plead with Us. We want to make manifest Our attribute of forgiveness."[17]

Ibn al-ʿArabī and his followers employ the same line of reasoning to argue for the necessity of that which is. Everything depends upon God's names. And God's names are not accidents, deducible by us because of the nature of phenomena. On the contrary, God's names—revealed in that self-manifestation of God known as His Word, the Koran—designate the very nature of Reality. It is we and phenomena that derive from the names, not the names that derive from our speculation. Hence sin itself, which God defines through the Sharia, is brought about by God's desire to show His mercy and forgiveness. As Ibn al-ʿArabī writes,

The power of the form in which human beings were created demands that God threaten them with punishment. But God's wisdom demands that the divine names be given their rights. The names All-forgiver, Forgiver, and their sisters have properties only because of opposition to the Sharia. If no one acted against the Sharia, these names would not receive their rights in this abode.[18]

Jāmī continues his discussion of human all-comprehensiveness by explaining why the angels objected to God's creation of Adam: Since they were limited in their configuration and knew only some of the divine names, they could not grasp God's wisdom.

Explaining that the angels were not able to grasp this meaning. Hence they loosed the tongue of criticism against Adam and gave witness that he would "do corruption in the earth and shed blood" [2:30].

It was outside the plane of the angels
for them to comprehend this subtlety.
When Adam was honored with his robe,
they had to speak with arrogance and pretension:
"O God, we call Thee glorified,
we sing Thy praises, we put things in order.
"Why dost Thou stir up a form from water and clay,
one who will work corruption and shed much blood?
"Here in Thy threshold Thou hast the most excellent.
What is the wisdom in creating the less excellent?
"When you have a rose, what good are thorns and twigs?
When you have a phoenix, why do you need a fly?"
Then God taught Adam the names,
all of them—that is, the realities of things.
In the gnostic's view, the "names of God"
are nothing but the realities of all that exists.
God taught Adam each of these names,
He let him understand the attributes of His Essence.
Then He said to the angels,
"Tell Me about these names."
They all turned away from their own arrogance.
Each one admitted its own incapacity.
"We know nothing beyond what Thou hast taught,
we grasp nothing beyond what Thou hast given.
"Our creation is Thy handiwork,
our knowledge and vision are Thy mercy.
"Whatever Thou hast shown us, we know—
whatever lies beyond that, we know not."
Then for the second time He made this call,
now to Adam: "Tell Me the names,
"Those names through which you become manifest,
since you have knowledge of all their mysteries."
At the command of God, Adam spoke,
detailing those names, one by one,
For of everything
Adam is the whole, all else the part.
Everything in the parts is found in the whole,
but the part cannot encircle the whole.
No part has a perfect grasp of the whole,
but the whole knows the situation of every part.
When the whole comes to know itself
all the parts become the objects of its knowledge.
But if the part comes to know itself
it cannot know more than itself—
Even if it should gain knowledge of itself,
it will remain ignorant of the other parts.

Explaining that the child of Adam is the whole, while all other things are like parts:

What is a child of Adam? An all-comprehensive isthmus [*barzakh*],
the form of creation and the Real found within;
An undifferentiated transcription, announcing
the Essence of the Real and His ineffable attributes;
Connected to the subtleties of the Invincibility,
comprising the realities of the Dominion;
His inward self drowned in the ocean of Oneness,
his outward self dry-lipped on the shore of separation.
Not a single attribute of God
escapes manifestation within his essence.
He is knowing, hearing, and seeing,
speaking and desiring, alive and powerful.
So too of the realities of the cosmos,
each is found embodied within him,
Whether the celestial spheres or the elements,
the minerals, the plants, or the animals.
Written within him is the form of good and evil,

kneaded into him is the habit of devil and beast.
Were he not the mirror of the Abiding Face,
why did the angels prostrate themselves to him?
He is the reflection of the beauty of the Holy Presence.
If Iblis cannot fathom this, what does it matter?
Whatever was concealed in the Hidden
Treasure God made manifest in Adam.
His existence is the final cause
of the manifestation and appearance of creation,
For knowledge was the motive for creation,
and he is the outward locus for its perfection.[19]

Children of the Elements

Everything in the cosmos manifests the names and attributes of God, while the macrocosm as a whole manifests the properties of all God's names. In the same way, everything in the human being manifests God's names and attributes, while the individual human being as a whole—at least in the case of those who are fully human and have become God's vicegerents—manifests all God's names. Hence the difference between a human being and any other individual creature goes back to human wholeness (or potentiality for such) and the partialness of everything else.

One of the most common ways in which human wholeness is illustrated is by comparing the human being to the other children of the elements: minerals, plants, and animals. In minerals, we find few divine qualities, and those only through employing imagination and metaphor. We can say that inanimate things show the effect of God's creativity and power, while precious minerals, such as gold and diamonds, stand at the pinnacle of mineral possibilities, since they manifest the divine qualities of light and beauty in the manner most appropriate to inanimate existence.

In plants certain divine attributes are clearly reflected, such as life and power, while others can be discerned without a great stretch of the imagination. For example, plants reflect the divine attribute of knowledge, since they "know" how to find nourishment and light. Many of them manifest God's bounty and generosity through their produce and fruit.

Animals have a still greater concentration of divine attributes, since they manifest in a rather clear way the "four pillars of divinity": life, knowledge, desire, and power. Traces of other attributes can also be found. But it is in the human being that the divine perfections begin to manifest themselves in full abundance and with great intensity. All the divine attributes are present, at least potentially, in all humans. And the degree to which these attributes can be actualized can be guessed only by studying the lives of the greatest exemplars of the human race, who, in the Islamic view, are the prophets and the friends of God. So also great heroes, kings, artists, poets, statesmen—all manifest in more limited domains the extent to which the divine qualities can be actualized.

The four children of the elements—minerals, plants, animals, and human beings—are ranked in a natural hierarchy on the basis of the qualities that they can manifest. A clear progression can be seen in most of these attributes by meditating upon the qualities present in the ascending degrees of the children. Knowledge, for example, increases steadily through the levels, and on the human level no limits to the degree of its actualization can be imagined.

In the early Muslim philosophical tradition, the ontological levels represented by the four children are seldom discussed explicitly in terms of divine attributes, but rather in terms taken over from Greek philosophy. In the following passage, I quote from the Ikhwān al-Ṣafā', who look at the ascending levels of macrocosmic existence, all of which are repeated in the microcosm, in terms of the qualities they manifest. An uninformed reader might see this discussion as a primitive form of evolutionism, but that would be to mix the quantitative approach of modern science with the qualitative approach of the Muslim sages. In fact, it is a question of the progression and increasing intensity of qualities on different levels of manifestation. This is a static, ever-present phenomenon, not one to be observed over vast stretches of time.

> The existent things below the sphere of the moon are of two kinds: simple and compound. The simple things are the four pillars: fire, air, water, and earth. The compound things are the things that are born from them, the engendered, corruptible things: animals, plants, and minerals. The minerals are the first to be engendered, then plants, then animals, then the human being. Each kind possesses a characteristic that it is the first to acquire. The characteristic of the four pillars is the four natures—heat, cold, wetness, and dryness—and the transmutation of some of them into others. The characteristic of plants is to take nourishment and to grow. The characteristic of animals is sensation and movement. The characteristic of human beings is rational speech (*nuṭq*), reflection (*fikr*), and deducing logical proofs. The characteristic of the angels is that they never die.
>
> Human beings may share the characteristics of all these kinds. Human beings have the four natures, which accept transmutation and change like the four pillars. They undergo generation and corruption like the minerals. They take nourishment and grow like the plants. They sense and move like the animals. And it is possible that they will never die, like the angels, as we explained in the "Treatise on Resurrection."[20]

The Sufi tradition usually formulates these same ideas in terms of divine names and attributes. In the following passage, ʿAzīz al-Dīn Nasafī explains that the children of the elements differ among themselves according to the degree in which they manifest the attributes of the "spirit" (*rūḥ*). *Spirit* is the most common term our authors use for the direct reflection of the divine Unity on the created level. The inherent qualities of the spirit include luminosity, life, intelligence, desire, power, and the rest of the divine attributes. On its own level of existence, the spirit brings together all the attributes of God into a unified, created whole. Then the attributes of spirit are differentiated and projected into the visible world through the body. Neither body nor spirit can achieve its full perfection without the other. In the last analysis, the body is merely the manifestation of the invisible qualities of the spirit within the visible world. Behind the four children stand four kinds of spirit, while the children manifest their qualities. But in fact, the four kinds of spirit are a single spirit.

A thing's constitution, literally its "mixture" (*mizāj*) of the four elements, allows the spirit to manifest itself in different intensities. A constitution near to "equilibrium" (*iʿtidāl*) is able to bring together in a balanced way loci of manifestation for most or all the divine names. A constitution far from equilibrium can manifest only a few of the names. Nasafī refers to the names here in terms of what Ibn al-ʿArabī and his followers sometimes call the "seven leaders," the seven principle names upon which the existence of the cosmos depends: life, knowledge, desire, power, hearing, sight, and speech.

> Constitutions are of two kinds: in equilibrium or not in equilibrium. The former kind is not found below the sphere of the moon. . . . Constitutions that are not in equilibrium have no more than three states: near to equilibrium, far from equilibrium, or intermediate between near and far.
>
> The mineral body and mineral spirit appear from that which is far from equilibrium. The plant body and plant spirit appear from that which is intermediate. The animal body and animal spirit appear from that which is near to equilibrium. The human being is one kind of animal.
>
> O dervish! It is this animal spirit which, by means of training and nurturing, by learning and repetition, and by spiritual struggle and invocations, rises up through the levels. At each level it takes on another name. . . . The spirit is not more than one. The body is with the spirit and the spirit with the body. The two are not separate.
>
> O dervish! Each of the individual existent things has what is necessary for itself within itself. The spirit does not come from someplace, nor does it go anyplace. The spirit is light, and the cosmos is overflowing with this light. This light is the spirit of the cosmos, and this light takes the cosmos to perfection and keeps it moving—through nature at the level of plants, through volition at the level of animals, and through the intellect at the level of the human being. Thus a poet has said,

Go, find an eye! Every speck of dust,
when you look, is a world-displaying cup.

O dervish! At one level this light is called "nature," at another level "spirit," at another level "intellect," and at another level "Non-delimited Light." All creatures of the cosmos are seeking this light. They seek for it outside of themselves, and the more they seek, the further from it they move. . . .

In the first level, life, knowledge, desire, power, hearing, sight, and speech do not exist in actuality. But as the levels ascend, gradually life, knowledge, desire, power, hearing, sight, and speech come into actualized existence. Perfection lies where the thing appears. Moreover, there is no doubt that the fruit is the subtlest and noblest level of a tree, and the fruit of the existent things is the human being. The Greatest Electuary, the Highest Elixir, the World-displaying Cup, and the Universe-displaying Mirror is the human being who possesses knowledge.

In other words, the light found in the spirit of the cosmos that is overflowing into the cosmos does not have actualized knowledge, desire, and power. Then the light ascends through the levels. As it does so, life, knowledge, desire, and power gradually come into actualized existence. That light is not separate from the locus of manifestation. It is related to it as cream is related to milk.[21]

The Myth of Adam's Creation

Islamic thought puts human beings at center stage, but not human beings "objectively considered," but rather "qualitatively recognized." Muslims should seek for knowledge in order to know God, cosmos, and self. Ultimately, the highest knowledge lies in knowing ourselves, since "He who knows his own soul, knows his Lord."[22] Knowing one's own self means, among other things, knowing what it means to be human. Hence the myth of Adam is a constant point of reference in our texts. The question of its historicity is not brought up, since that is totally irrelevant to the story's meaning. And the story's meaning is found in the qualities that are ascribed to Adam and the other characters who are mentioned in the narrative.

Najm al-Dīn Rāzī (d. 654/1256), the author of one of the great Persian prose classics of Sufism, *Mirṣād al-ʿibād*,[23] retells the story of Adam's creation with close attention to the qualities that the tradition ascribes to human beings and other creatures. In so doing, he expresses in abbreviated form many of the major topics that will be brought out in the course of this book. He explains how the divine attributes become manifest within human beings and illustrates the close relationship between the microcosm and the macrocosm. Like Jāmī in the passage quoted above, he wants to clarify the meaning of the Koranic verses that refer to human all-comprehensiveness and the fact that the most luminous of creatures, the angels, were unable to fathom human nature.

At the beginning, Rāzī looks at the two grand movements that our authors observe in the macrocosm as a whole: the descent from the Origin (*mabdaʾ*) and the ascent to the Return (*maʿād*). The whole cosmos is frequently pictured as a circle made up of two arcs (*qaws*), the Arc of Descent and the Arc of Ascent. The top of the circle corresponds to the First Intellect, while the bottom corresponds to the corporeal human body. Human beings as human beings begin ascending from the bottom point of the circle. If they reach the end of their journey, they join with the Active Intellect, which is identical in a certain mode with the First Intellect.

God said, "I am about to create a mortal from clay" [38:71]. The Prophet said, narrating the words of God, "I kneaded the clay of Adam with My two hands for forty days."[24]

You should know that when it was desired to fashion the human frame from the four elements—water, fire, wind, and earth—these were not kept in the attribute of simplicity. Rather, they were carried down through the descending degrees. The first descending degree was that of compoundness, for the element at the stage of simplicity is closer to the World of the Spirits, as was explained. When it is desired to bring the element to the station of compoundness, it must leave simplicity behind and advance to compoundness. Thereby it moves one descending degree away from

> the World of the Spirits. When it comes to the vegetal station, it must pass beyond the station of compoundness and inanimateness. Hence it falls one descending degree further from the World of the Spirits. When it leaves the vegetal realm to join with the animal realm, it goes down one more descending degree. When it reaches the human station from the animal realm, it descends one more degree. There is no degree lower than the human person. This is the "lowest of the low."

The "lowest of the low" is mentioned in the Koranic verse, "We created the human being in the most beautiful stature, then We drove him down to the lowest of the low" (95:4–5). In Rāzī's interpretation, this "driving down" has to do with increasing multiplicity, dispersion, and distance from the World of the Spirits. These qualities become more and more manifest during the movement toward the outermost realm of existence, which in modern terms is called the "material world." Elements are noncompound and invisible, belonging to a subtle domain of existence rather than the realm of density that can be seen. Minerals, plants, and animals display increasing diversity and distance from the original oneness of the elements.

But this is only to speak of the visible world, called the "Kingdom" (*mulk*). When we take the invisible world or the "Dominion" (*malakūt*) into account, the picture is different. Instead of a descent, an ascent is taking place. The elements themselves are nonmanifest, so the divine attributes are totally hidden within them. Inanimate objects display practically none of the luminous properties of the divine names. However, the "Dominion" or unseen dimension of plants is clearly ruled by the divine attribute life, and this becomes manifest in growth and reproduction. The "Dominion" of the animals adds to life such attributes as knowledge and desire. In short, although there is a descent into multiplicity, a corresponding ascent takes place through which creatures are able to manifest more and more of the divine names. This ascent reaches its peak in the human being, or rather, in perfect human beings. Rāzī continues his discussion:

> These words have to do with the elements, which, through changing states, go down through the descending degrees that mark distance from the spirits. However, if you look at the Dominion of inanimate objects, after passing through several levels it reaches the human level. Hence, this is a question of ascending degrees, not descending degrees. At each station, the Dominion moves closer to the spirits, not further from it. However, we were talking about the form of the elements, which is the Kingdom, not the Dominion of the elements. . . . Thus it is clear that the highest of the high is the human spirit, while the lowest of the low is the human frame. . . .
>
> My shaykh, the king of his age, Majd al-Dīn Baghdādī, said in a collection of his writings: "Glory be to Him who brought together the nearest of the near and the farthest of the far through His power!"
>
> The human frame belongs to the lowest of the low while the human spirit belongs to the highest of the high. The wisdom in this is that human beings have to carry the burden of the Trust—knowledge of God. Hence they have to possess the strength of both worlds to perfection. For there is nothing in the two worlds that has their strength, that it might be able to carry the burden of the Trust. They possess this strength through attributes, not through form.
>
> Since the human spirit pertains to the highest of the high, nothing in the World of the Spirits can have its strength, whether angels, satans, or anything else. In the same way the human soul pertains to the lowest of the low, so nothing in the World of the Souls can have its strength, whether beasts, predators, or anything else. . . .
>
> In the kneading of the clay of Adam, all the attributes of satans, predators, beasts, plants, and inanimate objects were actualized. However, that clay was singled out for the attribution of "My two hands." Hence each of these blameworthy attributes was a shell. Within each was placed the pearl of a divine attribute. You know that the sun's gaze turns granite into a shell that contains pearls, garnets, rubies, emeralds, turquoises, and agates.
>
> Adam was singled out for "I kneaded the clay of Adam with My two hands" for the period of "forty days," and according to one tradition, each day was equivalent to one thousand years. Consider then—for which pearl was Adam's clay the shell? And this honoring of Adam was before the spirit was blown into him. This was the good fortune of

the bodily frame, which was to be the palace of the vicegerent. For forty thousand years He labored through His own Lordship. Who knows what treasures He prepared there?

This passage expresses, among other things, the great respect that Muslims in general accord to God's creation. That human beings are made in the form of God extends to the bodily frame. Earth, in spite of all its lowliness, has a tremendous rank in the eyes of God. Rāzī deals with this issue within one context, and in later passages we will see Ibn al-ʿArabī and others bringing out the divine roots of the fact that the earth, the body, and all yin realities are eminently honorable. The general principle reverberates throughout Islamic thought and, of course, goes back to the fact that on one level the Tao of Islam demands equal respect for yang and yin.

Rāzī next provides some of the accounts that are given about God's sending the various angels to gather the earth from which Adam would be molded. In spite of all the angelic entreaty, the earth refused to come.

> The first honor that was bestowed upon the earth was that it was called to God's Presence by several messengers, but it pretended not to care. It said, "We know nothing of the mystery of these words." . . . Yes, such is the rule: The more people deny love, the higher they rise once they become lovers. Just wait, everything will be turned upside down.
>
> For a while I denied love for the idols—
> My denial threw me into days like this.
>
> In this state, all the angels were biting the fingers of wonder with the teeth of astonishment: "What kind of mystery is this? Lowly earth has been summoned to the Presence of Inaccessibility with all this honor. In spite of its perfect lowliness and despicableness, the earth keeps on pretending not to care and makes itself unapproachable. Nevertheless, the Presence of Independence, Utter Freedom, and Perfect Jealousy does not leave it. He does not summon anyone else in its place. He does not discuss this mystery with anyone else." . . .
>
> The Divine Gentlenesses and Lordly Wisdom spoke softly into the inmost mystery of the angels, "I know what you know not" [2:30]: "How should you know what business I have with this handful of earth from eternity without beginning to eternity without end? . . . Be patient for a few days while I show the handiwork of My power through this handful of earth. I will polish the rust of creation's darkness from the face of the mirror of its original nature. You will see the changing pictures of a chameleon in its mirror. The first picture will be that all will have to prostrate themselves before it."
>
> Then from the cloud of generosity the rain of love fell down on Adam's earth, making the earth into clay. He made a heart of clay within clay with the hand of power.
>
> Love's dew made clay of Adam's earth,
> throwing uproar and tumult into the world.
> Love's lancet pierced the spirit's vein—
> out fell a drop. They called it heart. . . .
>
> According to some traditions, for forty thousand years the divine power, in accordance with perfect wisdom, exercised its handiwork on the water and clay of Adam between Mecca and Ṭā'if. In his outward and inward dimensions the divine power set up mirrors corresponding to the divine attributes. Each mirror was the locus of manifestation for one of the attributes of Divinity. It is well known that one thousand and one mirrors corresponding to one thousand and one attributes were employed. . . .
>
> Strange to say, God's uncaused solicitude showed several thousand kindnesses and tendernesses to the soul and heart of Adam in the Unseen and the Visible, but none of the angels brought nigh were told the secret. None of them recognized Adam. One by one they passed by Adam. They would say, "What strange picture is this that He is painting? What kind of chameleon is He bringing out from behind the veil of the Unseen?"
>
> Beneath his lips Adam was saying, "Though you do not know me, I know you. Just wait till I lift my head from this sweet sleep. I will list your names one by one." For among the pearls that had been buried within him was the knowledge of all the names: "And He taught Adam all the names" [2:31].

Up until this point, Rāzī has explained that human beings are set apart from all other creatures because they are made in the divine form, comprehending all the attributes of God. Now he turns to the great consequence of having been created in God's form: Everything found in differentiated form in the macrocosm is found in an undifferentiated mode within the microcosm. Rāzī makes this point by telling how Iblis—Satan—attempted to discover Adam's mystery. Note the qualities attributed to Iblis as soon as he appears: deceit and having only one eye. The first quality is perhaps to be expected, the second is not so clear. It alludes to the fact that Iblis—or the microcosmic equivalent, which is the lower soul, called "the soul that commands to evil"—perceives only the "form" (*ṣūra*) of things, not their "meaning" (*maʿnā*). Iblis lacks the light of intellect (*ʿaql*), though he is clever and cunning, and hence he is unable to perceive the signs of God for what they are. He sees the immediate context of things, but cannot grasp the beginnings and ends of things. Rūmī often refers to Iblis as one eyed, as in the following:

> With both eyes, see the beginning and the end! Beware, be not one eyed, like the accursed Iblis![25]
>
> Close your Iblis-like eye for a moment. After all, how long will you gaze upon form? How long? How long?[26]

The reader will remember that—according to most authorities—Iblis was one of the jinn and not one of the angels, since he is made of fire, while they are made of light. However, his aeons of piety had brought him into their proximity, so he mixed freely with them.

> However much the angels examined Adam, they did not come to know what sort of all-comprehensive reality he was. But Iblis the deceitful was once walking around Adam. Gazing upon him with his one squint eye, he saw that Adam's mouth was open. He said, "Just wait. Now I have found a way to undo the knot of our problem. I will enter this hole and see what sort of place this is."
>
> When Iblis went in and traveled around Adam's makeup, he found it to be a small world. He found there a representation of everything that he found in the large world. He found the head like the heaven with seven strata. Just as the seven planets are in the seven heavens, so also he found that in the seven strata of the head are seven human faculties: imagination, intuition, reflection, memory, recollection, governing, and *sensus communis*. Just as there are angels in the heaven, there were in the head the sense of sight, hearing, smell, and taste. Iblis found his body to be like the earth: Just as in the earth are found trees, plants, flowing streams, and mountains, so there are found corresponding things in the body. The longer hair, such as the hair on the head, is like trees, while the shorter hair, such as the hair on the body, is like plants. There are veins like running streams and bones like mountains.
>
> Just as in the macrocosm there are four seasons—spring, autumn, summer, and winter—so in Adam, who is the microcosm, there are the four natures: heat, cold, wetness, and dryness, prepared within four things—yellow bile, black bile, phlegm, and blood.

There is no need to continue with the details of Iblis's investigation, since the text is readily available and in any case it is similar to the passage from the Ikhwān al-Ṣafā' quoted above. It is sufficient for our purposes to recognize that the macrocosm/microcosm relationship is common in Islamic thought and that it follows upon the idea that all qualities found in these two worlds derive from the divine names. The conclusion of this section of the passage provides a preview of the last chapter of this book, which is dedicated to the heart:

> When Iblis had traveled the whole frame of Adam, he recognized the macrocosm in all the traces that he saw. However, when he reached the heart, he found it to be like a pavilion. In front of it, the breast was like the square erected before a royal palace. However much he tried to find a way into the pavilion so that he could go into the heart, he was not able to. He said to himself, "All that I have seen was easy. The difficult task is here. If I ever experience harm from this person, it will probably be from this place. If God has some special business with this frame or has prepared something within, it is probably in this place." With a hundred thousand thoughts, he turned back from the door of the heart in despair.

Iblis reports to the angels that nothing is to be feared from this hollow person, who is like the other animals, though there is one place that cannot be entered. The angels are not satisfied with Iblis's explanation, and soon they hear from God that this being of water and clay is to be His vicegerent. Their perplexity increases, but they prostrate themselves before Adam as commanded. In the final section of the chapter, Rāzī points to the tremendous station of the human body, which corresponds to the macrocosm. But, he says, the real worth of the human being derives from the divine spirit, which in truth lies outside microcosm and macrocosm and rules over both.

> All these honors pertained to Adam's frame, which is the microcosm in relation to the macrocosm. But the Presence singled out his spirit for Himself, for He said, "I blew into him of My own spirit" [15:29]. At the same time, this world, the next world, and everything within them are but a microcosm in relation to the infinitude of the World of the Spirit. So look at what honors he was given!
>
> When the two—spirit and frame—are brought together in a special order, they move on to their own perfection. Who knows what felicity and good fortune will be showered down on their head? Wretched is the person who is deprived of his own perfection and looks upon himself with the eye of disdain! He employs the preparedness [*istiʿdād*] of the human level, which is the noblest of existent things, in acquiring the objects of animal appetite, while animals are the meanest of existent things! He fails to recognize his own worth!
>
> You were brought up from the two worlds,
You were nurtured by many intermediaries.
The first in creation, the last to be enumerated
is you—take not yourself in play.[27]

Human Becoming

There are two fundamental differences between human beings and all other creatures. The first is that human beings are totalities, while other creatures are parts of a whole. Human beings manifest all the attributes of the macrocosm, while other creatures manifest some of those attributes to the exclusion of others. Human beings are made in the form of God as such, while other creatures are forms of various partial configurations of God's qualities.

The second fundamental difference is that other creatures have fixed courses from which they never swerve, courses defined by the limited qualities that they manifest. In contrast, human beings have no fixed nature since they manifest the whole. The whole is strictly indefinable, since it is identical with "no thing," no specific quality or qualities. Hence human beings, in contrast to other creatures, are mysteries. Their ultimate nature is unknown. They must undergo a process whereby they become what they are to be. The possibilities open to a given animal are defined *grosso modo* by its species, while the possibilities open to a human being are defined precisely by their indefinability. All human beings begin with the same unlimited potentiality since they are divine forms. The ultimate destiny of each is "limited" only by the divine source of the form, which is to say that human beings are defined by the fact that they open up to the Infinite.

The cosmos embraces "everything other than God," and every part of the cosmos has a proper role to play. The overall configuration of the cosmos does not change, since it is always "everything other than God," though the individual parts undergo ceaseless change. But all things other than human beings, like the cosmos as a whole, sit in specific niches and cannot be anything other than what they are. An elephant never turns into a frog. But human beings, even if they have their own specific niches from "God's point of view," are always in the process of development from their own points of view. A frog—an incomplete human being—can turn into a prince, if kissed by the spirit. The cosmos cannot become more or less of a cosmos, and a butterfly is always just that, even when it is a worm. But a human being can be more or less than human. This is the mystery of the human situation, the fact that, although people are determined by the Tao, yet they can upset the Tao. In Chinese terms, a "small human being" is not the same as a "great human being." Both are human, yet their attributes are fundamentally different. Moreover, each person undergoes transformations during his or her lifetime. One may cease being a small human being and become a great human being.

When representatives of the Islamic intellectual tradition refer to "human beings," sometimes they have in mind what we would mean by the term today. But this is true only if they are using the term loosely, in the sense that it can refer to any child of Adam and Eve. In this meaning, no distinction is drawn between those who live up to the purpose of creation and those who do not. In the passage quoted above, Jāmī says, "In reality the human being's perfection is that which is desired from his existence by God." On every level, the Islamic tradition distinguishes between those who meet the expectations of God and those who do not, or those who live up to the human role in existence and those who do not. For example, on the most basic level of general belief, the Koran distinguishes between those who have faith and those who do not: the "believers" and the "unbelievers." In all the perspectives of Islamic life and thought, people are separated into groups according to the degree to which they fulfill the purpose of life.

In the sapiential tradition, the goal of human life is frequently called "perfection" (*kamāl*). This is identified first with the station of the prophets and second, in the more philosophical perspective, with that of the great sages or, in the more Sufi approach, with the station of the "friends" of God (*awliyā'*). The most detailed and sophisticated exposition of the nature of this supreme human station is found in the writings of Ibn al-ʿArabī. His position, here as elsewhere, has dominated the sapiential tradition down to modern times.[28] It is Ibn al-ʿArabī who makes the term "perfect human being" (*al-insān al-kāmil*) central to this whole discussion. Those who do not attain to perfection, he calls "animal human beings" (*al-insān al-ḥayawān*).

Human perfection is usually identified with the station of the vicegerents of God, the first of whom was Adam, the object of God's words, "I am placing in the earth a vicegerent" (2:30). As we have already seen, the particular eminence of the human being has to do with having been taught all the names of God, or acting as a locus of manifestation for the name Allah. Hence Ibn al-ʿArabī declares that only this attribute of being a "form of God" defines a true human being.[29]

All human beings, as children of Adam, manifest the form of God. But few human beings manifest it in its full actuality, harmony, and equilibrium. In effect, those who attain to perfection bring the name Allah, and thereby all the names of God, from potentiality within themselves to actuality in the cosmos. Those who fail to reach perfection actualize the qualities of only some of the names. Thereby they join the animals and other non-human beings, who are partial reflections of God.

The process of actualizing the names begins in the womb, where the unborn infant has the possibility of developing all the perfections of human existence. But at the beginning of the stay in the womb, the embryo does not manifest any more perfections of existence than an inanimate object. In effect, the embryo begins as a mineral, as the lowest "child" of Nature. As the embryo develops, it gradually assumes the perfections of the other children. It acquires the powers of growth and assimilation connected to plants, then various faculties connected with animals, such as sensation and volitional movement. When the infant is born, it is hardly more than an animal. The rational soul—the distinguishing mark of being human in the ordinary sense of the term—does not begin to manifest itself fully until around puberty. The human being continues to actualize potentialities throughout his or her life, in varying degrees and intensities. Those destined for perfection move even beyond the qualities usually referred to as human. They actualize qualities associated with angelic beings, such as pure intelligence and acting only according to the command of God. Ultimately they ascend beyond the angels and, like the Prophet during his *miʿrāj* (night journey) enter into the

Divine Presence. Rūmī provides many poetical accounts of this rise from the inanimate to the truly human. In typical fashion, he refers to the passage from a lower state to a higher state as a "death," but a death that is really a birth into a higher realm of existence.

> I died from the mineral kingdom and became a plant; I died to vegetative nature and attained to animality.
>
> I died to animality and became a human being. So why should I fear? When did I ever become less through dying?
>
> Next time I will die to human nature, so that I may spread my wings and lift my head among the angels. . . .
>
> Once again, I will be sacrificed from angelic nature and become that which enters not the imagination.[30]

The Cosmic and Human Books

Islamic texts frequently describe the universe as the book of God. This goes back to many Koranic passages connected to writing, such as the already mentioned fact that the Koran refers both to its own verses and to the phenomena of nature as "signs." Human beings are made in God's form, and mastery of speech in all its dimensions is one of the outstanding and exceptional attributes of both God and the human being. God's speech is observed in three basic locations: the macrocosm, the microcosm, and the revealed books, the Koran in particular. The Koran employs closely related imagery to explain its own genesis and that of created things: The book is the spoken word of God, and the universe is the result of God's saying to the things "Be!"

Though from the point of view of God's incomparability we are forced to conclude that we do not know what it means to ascribe "speech" to God, we can also take the point of view of similarity. Since God is somehow similar to the creatures, a certain tentative validity will apply to the comparison between human and divine speech. We can learn something about the way God creates the world by investigating the way in which we produce language. The analogy between people and God was not created in vain. It necessarily tells us something about the third term, the macrocosm, and about the relationship of all three to the true Speaker.

Since the macrocosm can be compared to a book, it follows naturally that the same image can be used for the microcosm. Thus, for example, Ibn al-ʿArabī refers to both microcosm and macrocosm as copies or transcriptions (*nuskha*) of everything found in the Divine Presence, which is the original of both copies. "The cosmos is a divine transcription upon a form of the Real."[31] Human beings are "transcriptions of the Divine Presence,"[32] since they were created upon the form of God and reflect all the divine names. "The human being created upon the form of the All-merciful is the perfect transcription."[33]

Both macrocosm and microcosm are transcriptions of the Divine Presence, so the two are copies of each other. But since the human being is equivalent to the whole cosmos, each human being is greater than any individual part of the cosmos. "The human being is the all-comprehensive word and the transcription of the cosmos. Everything in the cosmos is a part of the human being, while the human being is not a part of anything in the cosmos."[34] It follows that human beings are transcriptions of both God and the cosmos: "The human being is a noble summary within which is gathered together the meaning of the macrocosm. God made him a transcription comprehending everything in the macrocosm and all the names of the Divine Presence."[35]

The macrocosm manifests all the names of God in the mode of indefinite deployment, differentiation, and dispersion, while the microcosm displays them in the mode of unity, undifferentiation, and concentration. Using the analogy of the book, Nasafī explains the relationship between the small and large worlds as follows:

> When God created the existent things, He called this the "cosmos" [*ʿālam*], since the existent things are a "mark" [*ʿalāma*] of His existence and His knowledge, desire, and power. O dervish! The existent things are in

one respect a mark, and in another respect a writing. In respect of being a writing, God called the cosmos a "book." Then He said, "Whoever reads this book will recognize Me and My knowledge, desire, and power."

At that time the readers were the angels. These readers were extremely tiny, while the book was extremely large. The readers could not see the edges of the book or all of its pages, since they were incapable of doing so. God saw this, and made a transcription of the cosmos, writing a summary of this book. He called the first the macrocosm and the second the microcosm, the first the large book and the second the small book. Whatever was in the large book He wrote in the small book, without increase or decrease, so that whosoever reads the small book will have read the large book.

Then God sent His vicegerent to this microcosm, the vicegerent of God being the intellect. When the intellect sat as vicegerent in the microcosm, all the angels of the microcosm prostrated themselves to it, save sensory intuition [*wahm*], which did not prostrate itself, refusing to do so. In the same way, when Adam sat as vicegerent in the macrocosm, all the angels prostrated themselves to Adam, save Iblis, who did not prostrate himself, refusing to do so.[36]

O dervish! In the microcosm, the intellect is God's vicegerent, while in the macrocosm the intelligent human being is God's vicegerent. All the macrocosm is the domain of God, while all the microcosm is the domain of God's vicegerent. When the intellect sat as vicegerent, it was addressed as follows: "Intellect, know thyself and thy own attributes and acts in order to know Me and My attributes and acts!"[37]

2

Theology

2

DIVINE DUALITY

As soon as "God" is mentioned in the context of Islamic thought, the word can be understood from two points of view. We can consider God as He is in Himself, in which case we leave aside the cosmos, which is everything other than God. From this point of view, most Muslim thinkers have come to the conclusion that God in Himself, the "Essence" (*dhāt*) of God, cannot be known. He is beyond our grasp. This comes down to the perspective of incomparability (*tanzīh*), which was discussed in the introduction.

If we mention the cosmos in the same breath with God, then we have to take into account a number of relationships that are established between God and the cosmos. These relationships are given verbal expression by the divine names. In this respect we can either say that God is completely different from His creatures, thereby once again declaring His incomparability, or we can say that a certain similarity can be discerned. Or we can take both positions at once.

In short, to speak of God—and this is unavoidable in Islam or, rather, inseparable from Islam—brings up at least two basic perspectives on the Divine Reality. Duality is inherent in speech and rational thought. We affirm God's Unity—*tawḥīd*—but in doing so we establish the reality of duality, since it is we who speak. As the Ḥanbalī Sufi Khwāja ʿAbdallāh Anṣārī (d. 481/1089) puts it,

None has affirmed the Unity of the One,
since all who affirm it deny it.
The *tawḥīd* of him who speaks of His description
is a loan, made null by the One.
His *tawḥīd* of Himself is His *tawḥīd*—
he who describes it has gone astray.[1]

There is something self-contradictory about a discourse that claims to establish the unity of the Real. The Real in His Unity effaces all duality. By declaring His Unity we affirm duality through being ourselves and speaking.

At the same time, it needs to be kept in mind that this "duality" never implies absolute separation. What is at issue is polarity, or two complementary dimensions of a single reality. If we use the term *duality*, it is because the texts commonly speak of two principles. Moreover, the more mythic and unreflective expositions of Islamic principles often discuss things as if they were truly different. In contrast, the sapiential tradition keeps the language of duality, but it understands duality strictly in terms of interrelationships and polarity.

God and the Essence

Duality, in short, pertains to the nature of human discourse about God. To conceive of God we have to grasp the limitations of our own conceptions, since, as the perspective of incomparability maintains, "None knows God but God." Hence we have two Gods: the God of my conception, and the real God, who is beyond my conception. The God of discourse pertains to my conception. The other God is understood neither by you nor by me that we might talk about Him meaningfully. No one explains this better than Ibn al-ʿArabī, as, for example, in his discussion of the "god of belief."[2]

The fact that God is unknowable follows from the basic assertion of *tawḥīd*: "There is nothing real but the Real." Given that God is absolutely and infinitely Real while the cosmos and its contents are only relatively real, the Divine Reality lies beyond the grasp of created reality. The Absolute escapes the relative. "What does dust have to do with the Lord of lords?" asks the Arabic proverb.

If we can indeed know something of God, this follows from the fact that the relatively real is, after all, real in some mode. The mode in which it is real connects it to the absolutely Real. In other words, we and the cosmos are related to God through the divine attributes that display their traces and signs in cosmic existence. We cannot know God in Himself, only God inasmuch as He reveals Himself through the cosmos.

Within the Taoist context, as soon as we name the Tao, we need to recognize the Tao beyond names, the unnameable Tao that we cannot grasp. But the Tao that we are able to name demands yin and yang, since they are inherent within its own nature. Hence we begin with a double duality: first, the Tao that can be named and the Tao that cannot be named and second, the yin and the yang that define the laws of the nameable Tao. So also in Islamic thought: The God who can be discussed forces us to acknowledge the God beyond discussion. If we insist that God is One, still, the God beyond discussion is One in an unknowable way, while the God of discussion is One in a way open to understanding.

When we leave aside the unknowable God and refer to the knowable God, we have the same two perspectives: We know that our knowledge of God is deficient, which is to say that He is incomparable. At the same time we know that we can know something about Him, which is to say that He is similar. Hence we have incomparability and similarity on two different levels. The first level establishes a distinction between God as absolutely unknowable in Himself and relatively knowable through His attributes. The second level looks at the relatively knowable attributes and then establishes a distinction between those attributes that declare Him different and those that allow a certain similarity.

For many Muslim authorities, the difference between what can be known and what cannot be known about God establishes the conceptual distinction between God and the Essence of God. There is no ontological distinction, since ultimate reality, Being, is one. Here the Chinese tradition provides us with parallel concepts in the distinction between the "Great Ultimate" and the "Chaos" or "Non-ultimate." Islamic thought makes clear that we are not dealing here with two realities, but with two different ways of looking at the relationship between God and the cosmos. In the first sense, God creates a universe and can be known through it. In the second sense, the same God is independent of the universe and has no need for it. He holds Himself back from His creatures not because He is secretive or stingy, but because they are utterly different from Him and incapable of embracing His reality. Rūmī alludes to this point in his famous line, "If you pour the ocean into a cup, how much will it hold? One day's store."[3]

Strictly speaking, the Essence as Essence has no relationships with anyone or anything. When we speak of relationships, we are discussing the Essence inasmuch as It is a God (*ilāh*). At this level of "divinity" (*ulūhiyya*), there are two basic points of view from which relationships can be discussed: From the first point of view, we discuss the relationships that God has with the cosmos. Once these relationships are established, we see that God has names and attributes that in some way conflict with other names and attributes. Then we have the second point of view, the question of relationships among the divine names themselves. In practice, however, these two perspectives are almost inseparable, since a divine attribute, by its very nature, sets up a relationship both with the cosmos and with other attributes. Both kinds of relationships are frequently expressed in terms that recall yin and yang.

The very term *relationship* or *relation* (*nisba*) is fundamental for Ibn al-ʿArabī's school of thought and commonly employed in other perspectives. Ibn al-ʿArabī uses it synonymously with the Koranic *name* (*ism*) and the preferred term of the proponents of Kalām, *attribute* (*ṣifa*).[4] Relationships have to be taken into account as soon as we conceive of two realities. And the two primary realities are God and the cosmos. As Ibn al-ʿArabī puts it,

> Once God has created the cosmos, we see that it possesses diverse levels and realities. Each of these demands a specific relationship with the Real. . . . Examples of these intelligible qualities include creation, provision, gain, loss, bringing into existence, specification, strengthening, domination, severity, gentleness.[5]

Other schools of thought also employ the term relationship. Rūmī even employs the term in his poetry. He is discussing the mystery of the perfected human heart that embraces God:

> This heart has a thousand names and attributes. Each name is another relationship, different from the others.
>
> So also, in relation to you one person is a father, but in relation to another he is a son or a brother.
>
> The numerous names of God are relational, so toward the unbeliever He is Invincible, toward us Merciful.
>
> How many there are who are angels in relation to you in your belief, but devils in relation to another!
>
> Likewise your awareness is unveiled in relation to you, but hidden in relation to others.[6]

Incomparability and Similarity

To speak of two, we have to make distinctions, and the first and most obvious distinction is that between God and the cosmos. In any case, that is where we are and that is where we begin. The fact that there is a cosmos suggests that there is something in the reality of God that brings the cosmos into existence. The existence of the cosmos depends upon the Real. But various dimensions or qualities of the cosmos depend upon specific divine attributes. As was illustrated in the first chapter, the life of things in the cosmos derives from God's life, their knowledge from His knowledge, their power from His power, their love from His love, and so on with all positive and "good" qualities. That reality which possesses fully the sum total of all the qualities upon which the cosmos depends is known as "God." But there are attributes of God to which the cosmos has no direct connection. For example, God is "independent of the worlds" (3:97), but nothing in the cosmos is independent of the worlds or of God.

The fundamental Koranic teaching about God is that He is one God, "There is no god but He." The pictures drawn of this Koranic God vary according to period and school of thought, but all Muslim thinkers draw heavily upon Koranic teachings as justification for their positions. If we look at Islamic theology as a whole, we can see two basic emphases, both of them concerned with demonstrating God's oneness. Though there is a good deal of anthropomorphic imagery in the earliest period, the position that soon gains ascendancy in Kalām or dogmatic theology is that of the divine incomparability. All references to God's eyes, hands, feet, etc., in the Koran and the Hadith were interpreted in a rational mode to exclude any similarity with what is designated by the same names among human beings. Speaking in broad generalities, one can say that most early philosophers took the same position.

Many of the Sufis were not so willing to dismiss Koranic references to God's hands and eyes as figures of speech. Ibn al-'Arabī draws on many of his predecessors to formulate a clear doctrine of similarity as a complement to the theological emphasis upon incomparability. For Ibn al-ʿArabī and his followers—which means for much of Islamic thought down to recent times—neither of these positions can be exclusive. God is similar in His incomparability, and incomparable in His similarity. Both positions must be maintained if perfect knowledge is to be achieved.[7] Ibn al-ʿArabī's best known expression of this idea is a poem found in the third chapter of his *Fuṣūṣ al-ḥikam:*

> If you speak of incomparability, you delimit,
> and if you speak of similarity, you define.
> If you speak of both, you have hit the mark—
> you are a leader and a lord in the gnostic sciences.

To see the relationship between incomparability and similarity in yin/yang terms, it is necessary to investigate the qualitative implications of the theological positions. The easiest way to do this is to show how those Koranic names of God that refer to a specific attribute of existence are connected to one or both views.

On one level, all the divine names can be understood in terms of God's incomparability. The Koran declares that "Nothing is like Him" (42:11), and this statement can be applied to any name of God. If nothing is like Him, we have no way of understanding Him, since understanding depends upon similarity and accessibility. God is omniscient and all-powerful, absolutely other than our ignorance and weakness. Everything that can properly be said about God has to be negated from the creatures. All of God's attributes belong to Him exclusively. If we use familiar words to refer to the divine Reality, this simply illustrates our own limitations and the impossibility of expressing the Unknowable in language.

From this perspective, all the divine names follow the incomparability established by the first half of the Shahāda, "There is no god but God." For example, God is the Real (*al-ḥaqq*). In other words, "There is no real but the Real." Nothing is real but God; everything other than God is unreal. The reality of a quality belongs strictly to God. If we apply the same quality to a created thing, this at best is a metaphor. God is the Knowing or the Knower (*al-ʿalīm*). "There is none that knows but the Knowing." Only God's knowledge is true knowledge, and what goes by that name in our world is in fact ignorance. God is the Just (*al-ʿadl*). "There is none just but the Just." Divine justice alone balances the scales; our version of justice is at best a pale imitation. In short, if we look at the description of God provided by the Koran from the point of view of incomparability, we see that "Everything is perishing but His face" (28:88) and everything other than God is unreal.

Though the Sufis, as remarked earlier, stress the divine similarity, they do so only after having brought out the divine incomparability. They do not disagree with the proponents of Kalām concerning incomparability, they simply refuse to accept incomparability as the only valid point of view. And when Sufis do speak of incomparability, they usually leave aside the dry, rationalistic approach of Kalām and discuss it in a poetical mode that reminds us of the divine goodness and love. Take, for example, the following passage from *Rawḥ al-arwāḥ* by Aḥmad Samʿānī. He is explaining the ultimate insignificance of ritual practices. He begins by quoting an Arabic sentence that is probably a maxim handed down from a Sufi shaykh. "Moving the finger," "standing," and "sitting" all allude to various parts of the ritual prayer (*ṣalāt*).

> Chivalrous youth! "He who seeks nearness to the King by sitting in a corner of his room moving his finger is mocking himself." The miserable wretch who stands or sits in the hut of his own misery and thinks that, because of that standing and sitting, he is doing a favor to the King of the age is the leader of the world's madmen. Placed next to the perfection of the divine beauty, all the acts of obedience and worship, good works, deeds, sayings, and states issuing from the children of Adam from the beginning of existence to the end of the age are the noise of an old woman's spindle. Beware, think not that you are doing someone a favor! Through His generosity and bounty, He called this handful of scattered and worthless dust to the court of His eternity. He spread the carpet of bold expansiveness within the palace of guidance. Otherwise, how could this meanest creature in existence and this speck of impure dust have the courage to place his foot on the edge of the carpet of the King of kings?[8]

But the Koran also speaks of God's similarity and nearness. It does not limit itself to providing a picture of divine incomparability and human insignificance. God is not only inaccessible and infinitely beyond the reach of miserable dust, He is also ever present with His servants, for the divine mercy and generosity play a decisive role.

A simple calculation of the number of divine names that occur in the Koran shows that the names that imply God's closeness to and concern for human beings, such as Merciful, Compassionate, Kind, Generous, and Forgiving, far outnumber names that speak of Him in terms of distance and transcendence. These names of proximity demand that God be concerned with the intimate details of everyday human life. God is "with you wherever you are" (57:4). He is "nearer to you than the jugular vein" (50:16). "Wherever you turn, there is the face of God" (2:115). Islamic spirituality has been concerned with this perspective from earliest times. Especially in texts that have to do with the intimate relationships between God and human beings—such as prayers and supplications—appeals to God's kindness, mercy, forgiveness, and generosity have always played a central role.[9]

To conceive of God as distant, through His greatness, power, majesty, holiness, and so on, is to understand Him as the yang element in a yin/yang relationship. We have no effect upon Him, while everything we are and everything we do derive from His activity. In contrast, to conceive of Him as loving, near, generous, and forgiving is to understand Him as receptive to our wants and needs. "When My servants ask you about Me—surely, I am near. I respond to the supplication of the supplicator when he supplicates Me" (2:186). What is God's "response" other than His reaction to our initiative? It is interesting to note that Ibn al-ʿArabī—while pointing to the divine origin of all receptivity in this world—brings this verse to prove that God Himself possesses the attribute of reception.[10] Likewise, he points out that God "responds to the supplication of the supplicator" through the attributes of munificence and generosity.[11] The names that demonstrate His giving and loving nature show His receptivity toward human concerns.

It would not be difficult to classify most of the institutionalized forms of Islam in terms of the stress they place upon incomparability or similarity.[12] The Sharia emphasizes God's overwhelming power and authority, the kingly and lordly aspects of the divine reality, the fact that human beings *must* obey His will because of the negative consequences of His wrath. Receptivity is not ignored—after all, the whole idea of reward and punishment depends upon God's reception of our acts. But the warm and maternal dimensions of love, compassion, and mercy are not placed in the forefront. For its part, Kalām places stress upon incomparability, as noted above. Most of the earlier Muslim philosophers also take this position, though once the school of Ibn al-ʿArabī begins to gain prominence, the philosophers tend to move toward a more balanced perspective, as illustrated for example by Mullā Ṣadrā. Sufism emphasizes similarity, especially in its devotional and popular dimensions.

In short, the views of God found in the Koran, the Hadith, and the major expressions of Islamic thought can be understood as a spectrum running from incomparability to similarity and including all sorts of intermediate positions. If incomparability is pushed too far, the result will be *taʿṭīl*, the heretical idea that God is totally disconnected from the world. If similarity is pushed too far, this can lead to incarnationism (*ḥulūl*) or unificationism (*ittiḥād*), the view that God and the human being are one. Both extremes have appeared on occasion and have been roundly condemned by the community at large.

But even those Muslims who place great stress upon similarity normally give priority to incomparability. They do this in order to prevent deviation from Islamic norms and rejection by the Muslim community. Moreover, the Sufis are the first to point out that human beings must take into account the limitations that rule over all created things. Because of these limitations, the divine reality takes precedence over the relative reality of created things. In order to see things as they are, human beings must first grasp their own weakness and incapacity, the nothingness of the relatively real in face of the absolutely real. Then the mode in which the relatively real manifests the absolutely real can be brought out. In practice, this means that those dimensions of Islam that stress incomparability take precedence over those that stress similarity. Since the Sharia stresses incomparability and is concerned with showing God's greatness and human insignificance, observance of the Sharia is the foundation upon which the path to God is built. Following God's commands and submitting to the divine will open up human beings to God's mercy, kindness, and generosity. First people observe the rules of the king's court; then only are they shown into his presence.

The Koran describes desirable human attributes in terms that help clarify the nature of the human response to incomparability and similarity. From the point of view that places stress upon incomparability, the dominant human qualities are yin: The human being is a servant or slave (*ʿabd*). The most desirable human quality is "submission" (*islām*) to God's will, which manifests itself as observance of His Sharia. This picture of the human situation clearly depends upon a lord or king who gives commands. Heaven rules over earth. Human beings have to follow the law in order to show the respect that the king deserves. At the same time, of course, humans have the freedom to upset the equilibrium between heaven and earth by refusing to obey heaven's commands.

From the perspective that stresses similarity, the Koran depicts the human being as God's vicegerent (*khalīfa*) who was taught the names of all things. This is the human being as form of God. The fact that human beings have been taught the names of all things shows that they possess the attributes of all things within themselves. And these attributes are none other than the attributes of God, or the "signs" of God's names. Here a yang element in human nature is brought out, since human beings stand in God's stead as rulers over the cosmos. They are still yin in relation to God, but a desirable and good yang relationship to the cosmos is made explicit. Since people carry within themselves the divine Trust, they have the power to exalt or debase, to preserve or destroy. The divine attributes are actively at work through human beings.

The fact that human beings are God's servants is the basic teaching of Islam, accepted by everyone. "I have not created jinn and men except to serve Me" (51:56) says God. Everyone must follow the Sharia, no questions asked, no disputes accepted. This is a safe and sure road. But the idea that human beings should also be God's vicegerents has been looked upon askance by some authorities, especially those who speak from the viewpoint of Kalām and jurisprudence. Although everyone agrees that human beings are God's servants, they do not agree that humans are or can be His vicegerents. Nor is there any agreement as to what is meant by the hadith—is it really a hadith?—"God created Adam in His own form." That God is yang and human beings are yin is accepted universally. But that human beings may be yang as God's representatives is sometimes viewed with suspicion. And the suspicion is justified, for this point of view opens the door to self-aggrandizement and psychological—not to mention social—disorder. What is to prevent those who see themselves as yang from considering themselves yang in relation to God? Thereby the right order is reversed. People corrupt themselves and those upon whom they have influence. This is a theme that comes out clearly in a good deal of Sufi psychology, some of which we will meet later on. It helps explain why Ibn al-ʿArabī makes servanthood the highest human quality. Perfect servanthood demands perfect effacement before that which truly is. To claim the slightest degree of lordship, as Ibn al-ʿArabī would say, is to place oneself in an exceedingly dangerous situation.

However this may be, the yin and yang of human existence can be seen in relation to the attributes of vicegerency and servanthood. Every positive human quality can be seen as the response to a divine quality. Human beings are defined vis-à-vis the divine.

As servants, they bow before God's attributes. God is king, they are slaves. God is merciful, they are objects of mercy. God is great, they are small. God is yang, they are yin. But as vicegerents, human beings manifest the divine qualities and dominate over the cosmos, which is yin in relation to their yang. They are kings and lords, the cosmos is servant and slave. They are merciful, the beings of the cosmos are receptive to their merciful activity. They are great and powerful, the cosmos is small and weak. They are vengeful, other people suffer the effects of their vengeance. "Have you not seen how God has subjected to you everything in the heavens and the earth?" asks the Koran (31:20).

Servanthood goes back to the divine incomparability, the fact that human beings are nothing in face of God. Vicegerency goes back to the divine similarity, the fact that human beings manifest nothing but the attributes of God. The totality of human beings as divine forms makes them lords over all partial reflections of the Real.

Complementary Names

Muslim thinkers classify the names of God according to many different schemes. Commonly they differentiate among names pertaining to God's Essence, those that pertain to His attributes, and those that pertain to His acts. Though the principles by which the classification is undertaken differ among different authorities and even in different works of the same author, the following, which derives from one of Ibn al-ʿArabī's schemes, is sufficient for present purposes: Names of the Essence designate God as He is in Himself. They are names that cannot properly be applied to anything other than God. An example is the name Allah. Names of the attributes give news about God's intrinsic reality, though they have no necessary connection with the created things. Examples are Alive, Knowing, Desiring, Powerful, Speaking, Hearing, and Seeing. The opposites of these names cannot be applied to God. Names of acts refer to God's relationships with creaturely things. In cases where the relationship varies according to the characteristics of the other term of the relationship, the opposites of these names can also be applied to God. Examples of these pairs of opposites are Merciful and Wrathful, Gentle and Severe, Beautiful and Majestic, Guider and Misguider, Exalter and Abaser, Forgiver and Avenger, Benefiter and Harmer, Life-giver and Slayer, Expander and Contractor.

Some names may be classified in more than one category, depending on how they are defined or considered. Hence a name of an act may also be viewed as a name of an attribute or even a name of the Essence. For example, Merciful, considered as a name of an act, has an opposite, which is Wrathful. But a sound hadith tells us that "God's mercy precedes His wrath," while the Koran states that God's mercy embraces *all* things, not just some things. Hence that which is an object of wrath may be in fact, on a deeper level, an object of mercy. In other words, mercy is more fundamental to the divine reality than wrath. Every wrathful act of God is in fact merciful, just as a father's anger toward his child may be based upon love. Rūmī expresses this idea by referring to the maternal side of the yin attributes, and then pointing out that the father is also "maternal," but in a hidden way: "Even if the mother is all mercy, observe God's mercy in the father's severity.[13]

In the case of God, there is no question of suggesting that His wrath and severity "may be" based upon love, since mercy is one of God's essential attributes, often identified, as we will see in a Chapter 7, with the Divine Being Itself. Hence Ibn al-ʿArabī and his followers distinguish between the fundamental mercy of God, called the mercy of the All-merciful (*al-raḥmān*), and the secondary mercy of God, called the mercy of the All-compassionate (*al-raḥīm*). The first permeates all things, while the second may be held back. The second manifests itself most clearly in paradise. Wrath, which is manifest most clearly in hell, can be understood as the opposite of this second kind of mercy. The first kind of mercy has no opposite. It transcends and encompasses wrath. It is present in both paradise and hell.

The relationship between contrasting names of acts is especially interesting from the point of view of our discussion. As mentioned in the introduction, these names are frequently divided into two categories known as the names of mercy and wrath, or gentleness and severity, or beauty and majesty, or bounty and justice. The contrast between these two groups is constantly kept in view by our authors. When God establishes a relationship with creatures in terms of either group, specific results are found in the cosmos. In brief, names of beauty demand that God be near to creatures and that they feel intimacy (*uns*) with Him. Names of majesty demand that He be far from them and that they feel awe (*hayba*) of Him. The first category of names pertains more to the receptive or yin side, since they are connected with such "feminine" qualities as love, beauty, and compassion. In contrast, the second category pertains more to the dominating, controlling, and forceful side of things, the yang dimension. Both sides are essential to existence, and neither side can be completely separated from the other. Beauty has its majesty, and majesty has its beauty. Wrath is certainly merciful, while mercy may not always be free from wrath. A smaller mercy now may prevent a greater mercy later.

At first sight, complementary attributes pertain to a horizontal relationship. Life-giver and Slayer, Forgiver and Avenger, Exalter and Abaser are all sets of divine names that come in the standard lists. Each pair has to do with opposite conditions found in the cosmos: Some things are alive, and they die; others are dead, and they come to life. Some people are forgiven in this life only to suffer vengeance in the next, while others suffer vengeance here and reap the benefits of forgiveness in paradise. Some are high, some are low, but relationships are fluid. What goes up must come down, and, in the divine scheme, what goes down through servanthood will certainly go up through vicegerency.

Since the creatures are ranked in degrees according to the intensity of the divine qualities reflected within them, there is both a "horizontal" qualitative relationship among creatures of the same world or domain, and a vertical relationship according to different worlds or domains. For example, bodily things may be large and small, high and low, bright and dark, right and left, and these qualities may reflect divine qualities only dimly. Human beings have internal dimensions that go far beyond the corporeal. When humans are taken into account, the horizontal relationships involve many attributes that are explicitly divine. The attributes of acts, when reflected within human beings, set up polar relationships, either within an individual or between individuals: People may be merciful and wrathful, forgiving and vengeful, generous and just, gentle and severe. As human attributes, these can change quickly into their opposites, depending on circumstances. There can be no question of absolutes here, since we are dealing with relationships.

Some relationships among human beings involve the names of attributes, those names whose opposites may not be ascribed to God. Thus we have knowledge and ignorance. But of course there is neither absolute knowledge nor absolute ignorance in any human being, so what is really being discussed is two different degrees of knowledge: more knowledge and less. So, also, we can speak of powerful and weak, but we are really discussing two different degrees of power. All the names of attributes can be examined in similar terms.

When we look at vertical relationships, we have in view different levels of existence of different worlds, whether in the macrocosm or the microcosm. The basic distinction here is between spirits and bodies. Qualitatively speaking, spirits are luminous, bodies are dark (less luminous); spirits are high, bodies are low (less high); spirits have knowledge, bodies are ignorant (have less knowledge). Discussion of worlds always calls to mind hierarchical relationships. To say "world of the spirits" is to say luminous, alive, high, subtle, knowledgeable, etc. But discussion of the spiritual world establishes these qualities in the relative sense of being "more so" than the creatures that are corporeal and stand on a lower level of existence. If corporeal things are dark, dead, low, dense, and ignorant, they are not so absolutely, only in relation to the spiritual things with which they are implicitly contrasted when the term *corporeal* is used.

To use an attribute in describing something is to conjure up a relationship. It is these relationships that must be grasped if we are to achieve a coherent picture of the Islamic cosmos and the human place within it. Theoretical discussion of these relationships can be drawn out indefinitely. But it will be much more useful for our purposes to see how some of the Muslim authorities envisage these relationships in order to describe the cosmos and the goal of human life. We will return to this task in the next chapter. First a few more words must be said about the fundamental dualities of existence.

God and His Vassal

In the intellectual tradition, to say cosmos is to say God, since the cosmos is "everything other than God." Even for Islam in general, it makes no sense to speak of the cosmos without speaking of God. God is the foundation for all meaningful thought, all conceptualization that can have a positive effect upon human becoming. Moreover, it is impossible to discuss God in positive terms without discussing the cosmos, since these "positive terms" are precisely the divine names understood in terms of similarity. Even names of incomparability can only be understood through knowledge acquired by existing in the cosmos.

This inseparability of God and the cosmos leads Ibn al-ʿArabī to differentiate between two fundamental meanings in the word *God* (*Allāh*). God in Himself—the Essence—is incomparable and therefore not the object of positive knowledge. He is "independent of the worlds." In contrast, God as named by the divine names demands the relationships established between Himself and the cosmos. Considered from this second point of view, God demands a servant in respect to which He is a God. Making use of the relationships inherent in the Arabic language, Ibn al-ʿArabī sets up a polarity between the word *god* (*ilāh*) and the past participle of the same word, the *godded over* (*maʾlūh*), which we can translate as "divine thrall." He commonly refers to other examples of the same grammatical relationship, such as Lord (*rabb*) and vassal (*marbūb*), or Creator (*khāliq*) and creature (*makhlūq*). Given Arabic's triliteral system of verbal roots, the very existence of the one word makes the existence of the other word necessary. In the same way, the very existence of one side of the polar relationship makes the other side necessary. There can be no vassal without a lord, no divine thrall without a God, no creature without a creator, no object of knowledge (*maʿlūm*) without a knower (*ʿālim*), and so on. By the same token, without these loci in which the divine activity becomes manifest, the divine names have no meaning. In short, unless we have the Divine Essence Itself in view, to speak of God is to speak of a relationship between the Real (*al-ḥaqq*) and the creature (*al-khalq*).

The primary relationship between God and the divine thrall is that of heaven and earth, or spirit and soul, or yang and yin. God is great, high, bright, creative, while the creature is small, low, dark, and receptive. From this point of view, God is yang and the cosmos is yin. As Ibn al-ʿArabī expresses it,

> That which exercises effects [*muʾaththir*] in every respect, in every state, and in every presence is God, while that which receives effects in every respect, in every state, and in every presence is the cosmos.[14]

There can be no cosmos without this yang/yin relationship. Both yin and yang are equally necessary for the Ten Thousand Things to appear:

> No result can occur—that is, nothing can come into existence—except between two things: the divine power and the possible

thing's reception of activity. Were one of these two realities lacking, no entity would become manifest for the cosmos.[15]

But Ibn al-ʿArabī does not neglect the logic of relationships. The vassal depends for its existence on the Lord. So also the Lord depends for its existence on the vassal. The influence goes both ways. Just as yang acts and yin receives, so also yin through its receptivity *acts* upon yang and yang through its activity upon yin *receives* yin's activity. The yin/yang symbol indicates this interrelationship with the white dot on the black side and the black dot on the white side. There can be no absolutes when the two sides depend on each other. God needs the vassal if He is to be a God, and the vassal needs God if it is to be a vassal.

Ibn al-ʿArabī caused a bit of scandal among some of the more exoterically minded scholars when he developed this correlativity in some detail. But this basic insight was present before him and continued to permeate the sapiential perspective. It is simply the logic of similarity, which demands that each side resemble the other. If the world is similar to God, then God must in some way be similar to the world. Ibn al-ʿArabī expresses some of these ideas as follows:

> Were the Essence to be stripped of these relationships, It would not be a god. Our entities occasioned these relationships, so through the fact that we are divine thralls we make Him a god. He is not known until we are known.[16]
>
> Since the cosmos has no subsistence except through God, and since the attribute of Divinity has no subsistence except through the cosmos, each of the two is the provision (*rizq*) of the other. . . .
>
> We are His provision,
> since He feeds upon our existence,
> just as He is the provision
> of engendered things, without doubt.
> He preserves us in engendered existence
> and we preserve the fact that He
> is a god. In these words
> there is no lie.[17];

It was such poetical expressions of these ideas that must have raised the most eyebrows. Other verses make the same point:

> Establish me, that I may establish You as a God—
> Negate not the "me," lest You disappear.[18]
>
> The spirit of the Great Existence
> is this small existence.
> If not for it, He would not say,
> "I am the Great, the Powerful."[19]
>
> He praises me, and I praise Him,
> He worships me, and I worship Him.[20]

In short, since the vassal makes the Lord a Lord, the Lord is acted upon by the vassal. Hence God is yin and the servant is yang. This mutual yin/yang relationship is set up already in the nameable Tao. It is only the unnameable Tao, the Essence Itself, which is "independent of the worlds." God as utterly and absolutely incomparable is not acted upon by anything, since there are no "others" to do the acting.

The One and the Two

To say God is to say cosmos, and vice versa. To speak of servants or vassals is to speak of Lord. According to a mathematical symbolism well known to our authors, to say one is to say two, and to say two is to say one. Each demands the other. The concept of God demands incomparability and similarity, the cosmos, polar names. The cosmos in turn demands hierarchy and the reduction of the dispersed qualities to their purest, incomparable, formless Essence. As soon as we accept the principle of similarity, duality is demanded by Unity and Unity by duality.

Ibn al-ʿArabī provides many formulations that distinguish between the Absolute Unity of the Divine Essence and the relative unity of the Divinity that embraces the polar names. Thus he contrasts the "Unity of the One" (*aḥadiyyat al-aḥad*) and the "Unity of

Manyness" (*aḥadiyyat al-kathra*): "In respect of His Self, God possesses the Unity of the One, but in respect of His names, He possesses the Unity of Manyness."[21] In speaking of the unknowable Essence, beyond all relationships, Ibn al-ʿArabī often cites the prophetic saying, "God is, and nothing is with Him":

> The Real alone is singled out for Unity. This is the Unity of the Essence, not the Unity of Manyness, which is the unity of the names. For the unity of the names makes the One two, since God, in respect of His Essence, "is, and nothing is with Him." Hence, nothing makes His Unity two but the unity of creation. Thereby the quality of making two [*shafʿ*] becomes manifest.
>
> Nothing enters engendered existence
> save doubling.
> Look—the Lord comes to be
> from the vassal![22]

Muslim discussions of the cosmos begin with two, God and the world. But in the cosmos itself, there are two principles, variously named. The qualitative evaluation of numbers by the Pythagoreans found many supporters in Islam, since the Muslims saw therein a clear expression of the necessities inherent in the concept of God and the cosmos. It should be kept in mind that in such discussions, "one" is not considered a number, any more than the Lord is thought of as a vassal. But to say one is to say two, three, and so on, ad infinitum, since one is one-half of two, one-third of three, and so forth. The dualities inherent in this approach are fundamental, since they are already implicit in one, the source of number, and explicit in two, the first of the numbers. Two corresponds to the first creation, the prototype of everything in created existence. God is one and only one, but everything other than God is two or more. The Ikhwān al-Ṣafāʾ make this point succinctly while reminding us of the three Koranic verses that speak of "two of every kind," such as God's command to Noah concerning what to place in the Ark: "Carry in it two of every kind" (11:40).

> Everything below God is "two of every kind," since He is the One, the Unique, the Everlasting, "who did not give birth and was not born" [112:3].[23]

The qualitative relationship between one and the numbers is summarized by the Ikhwān in describing the position of Pythagoras. In brief, since God is one and everything other than God is incomparable with Him, everything else must be two or more. But since all things are also similar to God in some manner, they partake of a certain oneness.

> The nature of existent things accords with the nature of numbers. If a person comes to know the numbers, their properties, nature, genera, species, and characteristics, he will then be able to know the quantity of the genera and species of existent things, the wisdom in their quantities as they are now, and why they are not more or less.
>
> God originates the cause of existent things and creates and devises the creatures. He is truly one in every respect. Hence wisdom does not allow that all things should be a single thing in every respect, nor that they should be different in every respect. On the contrary, it is necessary that all things be one through matter and many in form. In addition, wisdom does not allow that all things be dual, triple, quadruple, quintuple, sextuple, or such like. On the contrary, the wisest way and soundest arrangement is that they be as they are now in terms of numbers and measures. This is the utmost wisdom and the sound arrangement. In other words, some things are dual, some are triple, quadruple, quintuple, sextuple, etc., ad infinitum.[24]

Our interest here is in duality, even though all the other numerical relationships grow out of duality. But that is precisely the point. Yin/yang gives rise to the Ten Thousand Things by means of intermediate principles, which are represented in the I Ching by the eight trigrams and the sixty-four hexagrams. In all cases, yin/yang lies at the root, and this fundamental duality in turn manifests the Tao.

In another treatise, the Ikhwān al-Ṣafāʾ expand on the relationship between the many and the one while listing the things in the cosmos that manifest the qualities of numbers. The passage is worth quoting in its entirety, since it mentions all the dualities with which we will be concerned, along with many more that we will have no space to cover. The primacy of duality comes out clearly in the simple numerical dominance of dual principles over everything else.

> When God originated the existent things and devised the creatures, He arranged them in existence and put them into a hierarchy like the levels of the numbers emerging from one. Thereby their manyness provides evidence for His Unity, while their hierarchy and arrangement provide evidence for the sound order of His wisdom in His handiwork. And thereby their relationship to Him who is their creator and originator will be like the relationship of the numbers to the one which is before two and which is the root and origin of number, as we explained in the treatise on arithmetic.
>
> The explanation of this is as follows: God is truly one in every respect and meaning, so it is not permissible that any created and originated thing be truly one. On the contrary, it is necessary that it be a one that is multiple, dual, and paired. For God first began through a single act with a single object of that act, united in its own activity. This was the cause of causes. It was not one in reality. No, within it there was a certain duality. Hence it has been said that He brought into existence and originated dual and paired things, and He made them the principles of the existent things, the roots of the engendered things.
>
> That is why philosophers and sages spoke about matter and form. Some of them spoke about light and darkness, while others spoke about substance and accident, good and evil, affirmation and negation, confirmation and deprivation, spiritual and corporeal, Tablet and Pen, effusion and intellect, love and subdual, motion and rest, existence and nonexistence, soul and spirit, generation and corruption, this world and the next world, cause and effect, origin and return, or seizure and extension.[25]
>
> In an analogous manner, many natural things are found to be paired or opposite, like the moving and the resting, the manifest and the nonmanifest, the high and the low, the exterior and the interior, the subtle and the dense, the hot and the cold, the wet and the dry, the increasing and the decreasing, the inanimate and the growing, the speaking and the silent, the male and the female. "Two of every kind" [11:40].
>
> The constantly changing states of the existent things—the animals and the plants—are found to be similar: life and death, sleep and wakefulness, sickness and health, pain and pleasure, misery and bliss, happiness and grief, sorrow and joy, well-being and corruption, harm and benefit, good and evil, felicity and misfortune, retreat and advance.
>
> So also are the properties of affairs established by the convention of the Sharia: command and prohibition, promise and threat, awakening desire and instilling fear, obedience and disobedience, praise and blame, punishment and reward, lawful and unlawful, injunctions and rulings, right and wrong, beautiful and ugly, truthfulness and falsehood, truth and error.
>
> So also are all dual, paired, opposite affairs. In short, "Two of every kind."
>
> Know, my brother, that since wisdom did not allow that all existent affairs should be dual and paired, God made some of them triple, some quadruple, quintuple, sextuple, septuple, etc., as far as they reach. We shall mention a few of them after this chapter, God willing.
>
> And know, my brother, that all existent things are of two kinds, no less and no more: the universal and the particular, nothing else.[26]

The relationships among the numbers correspond to the relationships among the realities that structure the cosmos. The Ikhwān enumerate the basic levels of the macrocosm—employing many terms that we will discuss in later chapters—as follows:

> The relationship of the existent things to God is like the relationship of the numbers to one. The Intellect is like two, the Soul like three, Prime Matter like four, Nature like five, the Body like six, the celestial sphere like seven, the pillars [the four elements] like eight, and the children [the three kingdoms] like nine.[27]

Examples of conceptual pairs in Muslim thinking could be multiplied indefinitely. While explaining the meaning of the hadith, "God has seventy thousand veils of light and darkness," Najm al-Dīn Rāzī sums up the general picture:

> The seventy thousand worlds are all included in two worlds, which are called here "light" and "darkness." These are the Dominion [*malakūt*] and the Kingdom [*mulk*]. They are also called the "unseen" [*ghayb*] and the "visible" [*shahāda*], the "corporeal" [*jismānī*] and the "spiritual" [*rūḥānī*], the "next world" and "this world." All these pairs are the same. Only the expressions differ.[28]

The Creation of the Many

At the stage of the Great Ultimate, yin and yang are united and cannot manifest their separate properties. In the Islamic view, God is named by all His names "before" the creation of the universe. Our authors often point out that here the term *before* has a logical rather than temporal significance. At this stage the names are only virtualities. Within God they cannot be distinguished from each other, since each is identical with Him. He Himself is Alive, Knowing, Desiring, Powerful, and so on. Each name refers to the same Being, the same Reality, without any multiplicity.

As yin and yang begin to manifest their separate properties, they generate the Ten Thousand Things. Thus the Tao reveals itself in all things through yin and yang. Likewise, when God wanted to distinguish among the names and bring out their specific properties, He created the universe and the creatures so that the names and attributes could have "loci of manifestation" (*maẓhar*) for their own individual qualities. If we look at the Real in Himself without taking into consideration His relationship with the cosmos, He is not a "Lord," since there are no vassals. He can only be a "God" in virtue of the divine thrall.

Muslim cosmologists often describe the reason for creation in terms of the famous *ḥadīth qudsī* mentioned above. David is said to have asked God, "Why didst Thou create the creatures?" He replied, "I was a hidden treasure and I wanted [literally "loved"] to be known. Hence I created the creatures so that I might be known." Considered as the Essence, God was a Hidden Treasure, a closed and locked chest of jewels. These "jewels" are the perfections of existence represented by the divine names and attributes. "I was a Hidden Treasure" means that I was Alive, Knowing, Desiring, Powerful, Hearing, Seeing, Merciful, Forgiving, and so on, but all these names were nonmanifest. Without a cosmos, the names are indistinguishable. In Myself, every name is the same as every other. The Alive is identical with the Hearing and the Desiring, the Forgiving is identical with the Avenger, the Merciful is the same as the Wrathful. Ibn al-ʿArabī and his followers frequently bring out the unity of the Essence in spite of the many names by comparing It to the human soul:

> "And in your souls—what, do you not see?" [51:21]. There is nothing but a rational soul, but it is intelligent, reflecting, imagining, remembering, form-giving, nutritive, growth-producing.[29]

"I wanted to be known." In other words, since I possessed all these perfections within Myself, I wanted them to be displayed outwardly so that others could see them as well. In order for these names to be known, there has to be multiplicity, since no name is different from any other name at the level of absolute Oneness. Through multiplicity, each name can manifest its own properties as distinct from the properties of the other names.

"Hence I created the creatures that I might be known." The creatures are the receptacles, places, or loci within which God's names are displayed. Without them the Treasure would remain eternally hidden.

Many of our authors discuss the hadith of the Hidden Treasure in terms of the fundamental separation that must take place between mercy and wrath, gentleness and severity, beauty and majesty. In the first passage quoted below, Samʿānī alludes to the Hidden Treasure, while in the next two Rūmī is quite explicit:

> O dervish! He has a gentleness and a severity to perfection, a majesty and a beauty to perfection. He wanted to distribute these trea-

> sures. On one person's head He placed the crown of gentleness in the garden of bounty. On another person's liver He placed the brand of severity in the prison of justice. He melts one in the fire of majesty, He caresses another in the light of beauty.[30]

> God says, "I was a Hidden Treasure, so I wanted to be known." In other words, "I created the whole of the universe, and the goal in all of it is to make Myself manifest, sometimes through gentleness and sometimes through severity." God is not the kind of king for whom a single herald would be sufficient. If all the atoms of the universe were His heralds, they would be incapable of making Him known adequately.[31]

> "I was a Hidden Treasure, so I wanted to be known": "I was a treasure, concealed behind the curtain of the Unseen, hidden in the retreat of No-place. I wanted My beauty and majesty to be known through the veils of existence. I wanted everyone to see what sort of Water of Life and Alchemy of Happiness I am."[32]

Jāmī versifies the hadith of the Hidden Treasure as follows:

> David said to the manifesting God,
> "O Thou who art free of poverty and need,
> What is the wisdom of creating the creatures?
> This is a mystery no creature understands."
> He said, "I was a treasure, full of jewels,
> hidden from the discerning eye of every jeweler.
> "I Myself saw in Myself all those jewels
> without the intermediary of any locus of manifestation.
> "I wanted to take all those hidden jewels
> and show them outside My own Essence,
> "So that outside this sitting place of mystery
> their properties may become distinguished.
> "All may thereby find a route to existence,
> all may become aware of self and other.
> "I created a few discerning jewelers
> so that they might uncover those jewels
> "And make manifest the jewel of beauty,
> that the bazaar of love might become busy.
> "With it they will adorn the faces of the beautiful
> and increase the love of the lovers."
> The names, hidden in the Essence, could be seen
> only through the manifestation of the things.
> The names had a hidden beauty,
> but they rested in the levels of possibility.
> With one unveiled glance, that hidden Beauty
> became manifest in the loci of possibility.
> Every auspicious beauty and perfection
> scattered throughout the cosmos—
> Consider it a ray of that perfection and beauty,
> a differentiation of the level of undifferentiation.
> See, for example, the attribute of knowledge,
> disclosing itself in the loci of the ulama:
> It is the knowledge of God that has appeared
> but within the levels of delimitation.[33]

The Differentiation of the Undifferentiated

The names of God are identical with God Himself. When God said, "I was a Hidden Treasure," the names were latent within Him. They represent all the qualities possessed by Absolute Reality. But in the Real Himself, the names are not distinct from the Real. Only when the cosmos appears do the names display their distinct characteristics. In God the names are undifferentiated (*ijmāl*), while in the cosmos the properties of the names appear in differentiated form (*tafṣīl*). But undifferentiation and differentiation are already found within the Divine Reality. When Ibn al-ʿArabī calls God the "One/Many" (*al-wāḥid al-kathīr*), he means that God is One in His Essence and many in the relationships that He has with the cosmos, relationships denoted by the names. Ibn al-ʿArabī's followers commonly refer to this distinction by employing the terms *aḥadiyya* (Exclusive Unity) and *wāḥidiyya* (Inclusive Unity). *Exclusive Unity* refers to the reality of God in Himself, without regard to the cosmos, while *Inclusive Unity* refers to God envisaged as the source of the cosmos.

Differentiation becomes actualized in the cosmos, but its principle is found in Reality Itself, which is Sheer Being (*al-wujūd al-maḥḍ*). In a cosmological context, Ibn al-ʿArabī frequently discusses the relationship between undifferentiation and differentiation in terms of the two divine names, the Governor (*al-mudabbir*) and the Differentiator (*al-mufaṣṣil*), names that are alluded to by the Koranic verse, "He governs the affair, He differentiates the signs" (13:2). Governing is a yang quality of domination and control. Differentiating is a yin quality of receiving and displaying what has been received. Ibn al-ʿArabī identifies governing with God's determining the measure (*taqdīr*) of things before their creation. Each thing has specific qualities determined by the divine names that define it. In other words, each thing is defined by the reality of Being Itself. As Ibn al-ʿArabī says, "The Real described Himself as 'Governing the affair' only so that we might know that He does nothing except what is required by the wisdom of Being."[34] Differentiation is then equivalent to God's bestowal of existence upon the things.[35] It is the movement from oneness in the Hidden Treasure to manyness in the cosmos. Through existence, the things come into the engendered universe and manifest the qualities that they have borrowed from God. In the words of Ibn al-ʿArabī,

> The property of the Governor of affairs is that He makes affairs firm within the Presence of All-comprehensiveness and Witnessing and gives them that of which they are worthy. This all takes place before they come into existence in their entities. . . . Once He has made them firm, as we said, the Differentiator takes them. This name pertains exclusively to the ontological levels. The Differentiator sends down each engendered thing and affair into its own level and station. This name is like the master of ceremonies at a king's banquet.[36]

Ibn al-ʿArabī sometimes refers to the Governor and Differentiator as the first two "names of the cosmos" (*asmāʾ al-ʿālam*), or the first divine names that demand the existence of the cosmos. Hence they are the "leaders" (*imām*) of the other names.[37] The two together give birth to the "mothers of the names," the seven basic divine names: Alive, Knowing, Desiring, Powerful, Speaking, Generous, and Just. Hence these seven mothers are the daughters (*banāt*) of Governor and Differentiator.[38]

Ibn al-ʿArabī and his followers often use the term *differentiation* in a slightly different sense. We just saw that the Governor is God inasmuch as He determines the measure of the immutable entities. The Governor is Being inasmuch as It possesses certain immutable qualities that must become manifest according to specific configurations determined by Being's own reality. In an analogous way, colorless light determines within itself the properties of all the colors before they become manifest through the appropriate conditions. The colors are innate to the very nature of light. And at the level of the nonmanifest divine names or the latent colors, all realities are one, since they have no existence other than the Light of the Real.

In contrast, the work of the Differentiator is to bestow existence upon the entities, allow the colors to become manifest individually, bring the jewels out from the Hidden Treasure. In the Real, all things are one, but in manifestation, each entity has its own specific existence. Each color has its own special locus, each jewel a unique setting. In other words, through the Differentiator, multiplicity is actualized.

When we say that the Differentiator pertains to the domain of manyness, we can quickly grasp another closely related sense of the term *differentiation*. This sense comes to the fore when the term is contrasted with its opposite, *undifferentiation*. In the One, the things are undifferentiated, while in the cosmos they are differentiated. At each level of existence, a parallel relationship can be discerned. The higher level is undifferentiated in relation to the lower level.

Undifferentiation and differentiation are often considered synonymous with the terms *all-comprehensiveness* (*jamʿ*) and *dispersion* (*farq* or *tafriqa*). As in similar pairs, the relationship is taken into account, not any absolute value attached to either side. What is differentiated from one point of view may be undifferentiated from another point of view. Undifferentiation is basically yang, while differentiation displays yin qualities. Undifferentiation is the higher, more powerful, more luminous, and prior dimension of reality. But it is able to manifest itself only through differentiation, which is lower, weaker, darker, and receptive toward its activity. However, any level that we can envisage may be described as yang from one point of view and yin from another point of view. In the following, Saʿīd al-Dīn Farghānī (d. 695/1296) describes the whole cosmos—that is, all the levels of God's self-disclosure—in terms of this yang/yin relationship, showing that at each level the perspective can be changed so that yang becomes yin. Farghānī was a disciple of Ibn al-ʿArabī's stepson, Ṣadr al-Dīn Qūnawī (d. 673/1274) and the author of a major commentary on the poetry of the Egyptian Ibn al-Fāriḍ (d. 632/1235). Qūnawī and Farghānī bring the teachings of Ibn al-ʿArabī to an early peak in terms of sophisticated technical terminology.

Farghānī's discussion has in view the two "arcs" mentioned in the previous chapter: The first is the Arc of Descent, through which the universe gradually enters into multiplicity until it reaches the point of greatest differentiation in the human being. The second is the Arc of Ascent, through which human beings complete the circle. The movement goes from oneness to manyness and back to oneness. But Farghānī shows in the following that at each level of the movement we are dealing with a reality that has two aspects or "faces" (*wajh*). One face is closer to oneness, the other to manyness. One face is relatively undifferentiated, the other relatively differentiated. Each level is both yin and yang. But it is yin in one respect and yang in another respect. Everything depends upon the relationship that we have in view. Farghānī begins by speaking of the self-disclosure (*tajallī*) of the Real, the radiation of Being's Light. Even if some of the terms employed are unclear, that is not really important for the present discussion.[39] What should be completely clear is that the representatives of the sapiential tradition often describe the relationship between God and the cosmos as a set of interconnecting yang/yin relationships. The fundamental yang/yin differentiation between the absolutely Real and the relatively real repeats itself on many intermediate levels. Through each intermediary, the relationship between God and the world becomes subtler and more complex.

Self-disclosure descends and passes through the divine and engendered levels by means of undifferentiation and differentiation. Or, you can call the two "all-comprehensiveness" and "dispersion."

We have shown that the First Entification and Self-disclosure possesses true oneness, all-comprehensiveness, and undifferentiation. But this undifferentiation and all-comprehensiveness is relatively differentiated, for within it are contained the modes of Inclusive Unity.

This relative differentiation of the First Entification can be considered as all-comprehensive and undifferentiated. Then it is identical with the Second, Unitary Entification and Self-disclosure.

This all-comprehensiveness and undifferentiation of the Second Entification also possesses a dispersion and differentiation. It is the manyness of the objects of God's knowledge and the relative manyness made manifest through the divine names.

The all-comprehensiveness of this dispersion and the undifferentiation of this differentiation is the reality and existence of the Supreme Pen.

The differentiation and dispersion of the Pen is the reality of the Guarded Tablet along with the spirits, angels, and spiritualities that it comprises.

The all-comprehensiveness of this dispersion and the undifferentiation of its differentiation is the Dust Entity.

Its dispersion and differentiation is the Throne, the Footstool, and all the imaginal forms.

The all-comprehensiveness and undifferentiation of these is the Greatest Element.

The dispersion and differentiation of the Greatest Element is the pillars, the heavens, and the children, with all the forms of their genera, species, and some of their individuals.

The true all-comprehensiveness and ultimate undifferentiation of this dispersion and differentiation is the form of Adam.

His dispersion and differentiation, in respect of universals, is that which his meaning and form comprehend, which is the realities of the vicegerents and the perfect human beings. This includes every prophet and messenger. Or rather, each prophet and messenger is an all-comprehensiveness and an undifferentiation for the dispersion of those of his people who are under his scope, whether they accept him or reject him.

The form of the all-comprehensiveness of

all, the all-comprehensive unity of their universal dispersion, and the true undifferentiation of their differentiation—whether those of them who follow or those who are followed—is only the most perfect, Muhammadan form and his most all-comprehensive reality and meaning (God bless him and give him peace!).

The dispersion of this all-comprehensive unity is the realities of the vicegerents, perfect human beings, Poles, and Substitutes, as well as those in this Muhammadan community who enter under the sway of each.[40]

Here again we meet the idea that the specific reality of human beings has to do with the fact that they comprehend all conceivable realities, divine and human. In the view of Ibn al-ʿArabī and his followers, the existence of human beings is demanded by the nature of reality itself. Certain possibilities of God's self-disclosure could not be made manifest without Adam and his children. Hence the "fall" of Adam is not necessarily a negative affair. Ibn al-ʿArabī points out that God said to the angels, "I am placing within the earth a vicegerent" (2:30) long before Adam "fell" into the earth. Adam was clearly being created to serve God on the earth, not in the Garden. Hence, Ibn al-ʿArabī remarks, Adam's fall was the means whereby God bestowed honor upon him, making him His own representative. In contrast, Iblis was made to fall because of his disgrace.[41] This perspective is by no means unique to Ibn al-ʿArabī. Many authors saw Adam's disobedience as a *felix culpa*. Samʿānī often refers to this perspective in *Rawḥ al-arwāḥ*. For example, he points out that human beings were created for God, not for paradise. When Adam ate the forbidden fruit—the "wheat"—he was simply expressing his desire to busy himself with his Beloved. Adam's jealousy (*ghayra*) did not allow him to look at anything "other" (*ghayr*) than God.

By God the Tremendous! They placed the worth of paradise on Adam's palm. There was no bride more beautiful than paradise among all the existent things. It had such a beautiful face and such a perfect adornment! But the ruling power of Adam's aspiration entered from the world of the Unseen Jealousy. He weighed the worth of paradise with his hand and its value in the scales. Paradise began to shout, "I cannot put up with this brazen man!"

O chivalrous youth! If tomorrow you go to paradise and you look at it from the corner of your heart's eye, in truth, in truth, you will have fallen short of Adam's aspiration. Something that your father sold for a grain of wheat—why would you want to settle down there?[42]

O dervish! You should not believe that Adam was brought out of paradise for eating some wheat. God wanted to bring him out. He did not break any commandments. God's commandments remained pure of being broken. Tomorrow, He will bring a thousand thousand people who committed great sins into paradise. Should He take Adam out of paradise for one small act of disobedience?[43]

In continuing the passage quoted above, Farghānī treats the fall as the entrance of human beings into the world of differentiation. The fall had to occur so that the Hidden Treasure could become completely manifest. The Garden was a domain in which people lived in relative undifferentiation, so the possibilities inherent in their existence could not become manifest. The root meaning of the Arabic word for Garden, *janna*, is concealment, since, Farghānī tells us, the perfections of creation were concealed therein.

Since Adam was the possessor of a descent and a fall, he had to be a locus of manifestation comprehending all the divine names that become entified in the Second Level of the descent of the nonmanifest ontological self-disclosure. Thereby God could actualize His name-derived perfection, which is conditional upon differentiation and multiplicity. Hence Adam was an all-comprehensive root. He was an all-comprehensiveness that comprised the dispersion of all the human forms, through which the quality of "lastness" became entified. For it has been reported that the human being was the *last* existent thing to be created. That is why he was commanded to fall from the Garden. For in the Garden is the meaning of the concealment of everything and the undifferentiation of all the parts and differentiated details.

> Adam was "taught the names" [2:31]. These are entified in the Second Level, which is the level of the Real as Manifest. This level excludes the knowledge of the names of the Essence. The names of the Essence are the concomitants of the First Level—which is the level of the Real as Nonmanifest. These "names of the Essence" are the true objects named by the names that were taught to Adam, but their knowledge is possessed exclusively by the Muhammadan Presence.[44]

By entering into this world, human beings become the supreme yin reality, since they bring about the ultimate differentiation of all the divine names. The Hidden Treasure cannot be completely known until it is totally manifest. Its total manifestation depends upon the outward existence of all sorts of qualities that pertain exclusively to human beings, such as generosity and justice. Moreover, many of the divine names —the possibilities latent in the very nature of Being—cannot become manifest until the worst imaginable evils are displayed in existence. Neither vengeance nor forgiveness have meaning outside of sin, and neither can achieve its full splendor without the deepest depths of moral depravity. All this takes place in the midst of relationships between the absolutely Real and the relatively real.

Being and Knowledge

Undifferentiation can be distinguished from differentiation by the fact that the first is closer to unity and the second to multiplicity. The first is dominated by a relative oneness and the second by a relative manyness. The relatively one is yang and the relatively many, yin. The many make manifest the qualities of the one just as earth displays the nonmanifest virtues of heaven. Farghānī states the principle succinctly: "Activity [*fāʿiliyya*] pertains to oneness, and receptivity [*qābiliyya*] pertains to manyness."[45]

If we look back to the deepest root of oneness and undifferentiation, we reach the absolutely nondelimited and nonentified Reality, which is one in every respect. This is "Sheer Being" (*al-wujūd al-maḥḍ*), to which reference was made earlier in this chapter.

In Islamic thought, *wujūd* (Being or existence) is contrasted with *māhiyya* (quiddity or "whatness"). The latter is frequently employed as a synonym for such terms as reality (*ḥaqīqa*), entity (*ʿayn*), thing (*shayʾ*), and object of divine knowledge (*maʿlūm*). Different authors draw a range of distinctions among the terms. What is clear is that *wujūd* in itself is strictly indefinable and unknowable. Delimitation and definition of any sort belong specifically to the quiddity, not to *wujūd*. The quiddity of the thing can be known, but not the *wujūd* that allows it to be present in our experience or knowledge. Or, from a slightly different point of view, we can only know *wujūd* inasmuch as it is determined and defined by a thing. We cannot know *wujūd* as such, only inasmuch as its qualities are manifested by the things. In other words, we know *wujūd* through the realities inasmuch as they exist, or inasmuch as they manifest *wujūd*.

Wujūd is sometimes described as that which is nonmanifest in itself while making other things manifest. It is identical with "light," which is invisible in itself while allowing us to see other things. What we call "visible light" is but a dim reverberation of true, invisible light. We are able to see it because it is thoroughly mixed with darkness. Even on the physical level, the brighter the light, the more difficult it is to see. And there is no theoretical limit to light's brightness. In the same way, what we call *wujūd* (existence) is in fact the existing things, which are but dim reverberations of true *wujūd* (Being).

The fundamental movement in the cosmos from undifferentiation to differentiation can be taken back to the movement from Being, which is absolutely undifferentiated, to existence, which is a name applied to all the differentiated things that reflect Being. *Existence* in this sense is a synonym for *cosmos*. The word also indicates that something is found within the cosmos, as when we say that a cat exists. If we ignore all particular, defined existences, then we are left with Being, which is indefinable and unknowable. It is identical with the divine Essence.

"Existence" then is the sum total of the created things. Or, use of the word indicates that a certain created thing is found. Since the created thing is found, it is delimited and defined by the conditions within which it is found. This delimitation and definition mean that it is not pure existence, but existence in certain distinct modes that exclude the possibility of simultaneous existence in other distinct modes. Hence the existent thing is other than Being as such, which knows no limits or constraints. The thing is a mixture of existence in certain modes and nonexistence in other modes. To speak of "Sheer Being" is to indicate that the absolutely Real, in contrast to everything else, has no admixture of nonexistence. It is nothing but light, while everything else is light mixed with darkness.

In Itself, Being is absolutely undifferentiated. Farghānī sometimes expresses this idea by saying that Being is one, while everything else is two or more. Hence he employs the famous term *waḥdat al-wujūd*, the Oneness of Being, to allude to the absolute nonentification and undifferentiation of the Essence.[46] He then finds the principle of all differentiation in the divine knowledge. God, according to the Koran and the almost unanimous opinion of Muslim thinkers, knows all things, particulars as well as universals.[47] And He knows them for all eternity concurrent with His knowledge of Himself. In other words, knowledge and awareness are qualities inherent within Being, and Being knows every reality that becomes manifest through Its own reality. Light embraces consciously every degree of light and darkness.

Hence Farghānī sees existence ruled by twin principles: The Oneness of Being and the Manyness of Knowledge (*kathrat al-ʿilm*). He is providing an explanation for what Ibn al-ʿArabī means when he calls God the One/Many. God is not many in existence, only in the sense that His knowledge has many objects, for God knows all things.

Frequently our authors compare God's knowledge to human awareness: One person does not become many persons because he or she knows many things. In the same way, God's Being and Knowledge are identical. As Farghānī puts it, "Both the Oneness of Being and the Manyness of Knowledge through its objects are attributes of the Essence in respect of Its nondelimitation and nonentification."[48] There is no ontological plurality at the level of the absolutely Real. Even at the level of the relatively real, to speak of ontological plurality is either to misunderstand the actual situation or to use language in a metaphorical and inexact manner, in order to make oneself understood. In fact, there is only one Being, just as there is only one light. The multiplicity of existing things does not contradict the Oneness of Being any more than the multiplicity of colors and shapes contradicts the oneness of light.[49]

Sheer Being is one, which is to say that it is absolutely undifferentiated. Knowledge has many objects, so it is relatively differentiated. From this point of view, Being is yang and the divine knowledge is yin. Together they are the Tao. The fruit of their relationship is the cosmos.

In respect of the fact that the Oneness of Being and the Manyness of Knowledge are identical, the Real is known as the Unity of All-comprehensiveness (*aḥadiyyat al-jamʿ*). In respect of the fact that the two are discernible from each other and interrelate, the Real is known as the Divinity or the Station of All-comprehensiveness (*maqām al-jamʿ*). In Ibn al-ʿArabī's school, these different designations are said to refer to "levels" (*martaba*) or "presences" (*ḥaḍra*), which can be distinguished in theory and through their effects in the cosmos, but which have no ontological distinction. Farghānī writes,

> Before the level of Divinity we have the level of the Unity of All-Comprehensiveness, where the Oneness of Being and the Manyness of Knowledge are identical with each other. . . . Within this Presence, oneness and manyness, Being and Knowledge, entification and nonentification are all identical with each other and with the Essence, without any kind of separation or distinction.[50]

Being is one in every respect, while each thing in the cosmos can be understood to be a quiddity that has been irradiated with the light of Being. The specific thing is itself, and it exists by virtue of the ray of Being, just as the color red is a specific reality, while it exists by virtue of light. In order for the thing to come into existence, it must be receptive to the ray of Being. Hence Being is yang, since Its activity brings the thing into existence. The thing is yin, since its receptivity allows it to come into existence.

In some passages, Farghānī clarifies this discussion by reminding us that Being has certain inherent qualities, and these are designated by the divine names. Hence activity (*fiʿl*) and effectivity (*taʾthīr*) belong to Being and the names. Reception (*qabūl*) and receiving activity (*infiʿāl*) pertain to knowledge and the realities of the objects known by it. These objects are the possible things (*mumkināt*), which have no claim on existence. Until existence is given to them, they remain nonexistent objects of God's knowledge.[51]

At the level of the Divinity or the Station of All-comprehensiveness, there is no existing cosmos. But God is One and knows all things. Hence we can speak of the Oneness of Being and the Manyness of Knowledge without regard to the cosmos. In other words, yang and yin are inherent to the reality of God. In respect of Being, He is yang and in respect of knowledge He is yin. Farghānī makes this point while commenting on the following verse of the great poet Ibn al-Fāriḍ, who is speaking for the Muhammadan Reality, which is identical with the Divinity in this respect:

> It [the Essence] was bounteous
> while no preparedness took its effusion.
> It was prepared to give
> before any readiness to receive.

> In other words, at the beginning of the business of bringing the cosmos into existence, nothing but the two aforementioned realities were entified within My Essence: the Oneness of Being and the Manyness of Knowledge through its objects. There was nothing else to be found. What then had the preparedness to receive, acquire, and seek the ontological aid? Hence in respect of its Oneness of Being My own Essence bestowed aid. It effused and was active. But in respect of the manyness of knowledge through its objects, My own Essence was prepared for and receptive to that effusion and aid. Hence the business of giving existence to the cosmos and making it manifest was completed through the undifferentiated and differentiated forms of Myself.[52]

The undifferentiated form of God is Being, while the differentiated form of God is His knowledge. Within His knowledge are found all objects of knowledge. He knows all things for all eternity, so all realities, all quiddities are found within His knowledge. As Ibn al-ʿArabī puts it,

> The Real's knowledge of Himself is identical with His knowledge of the cosmos. . . . His Self never ceases to exist, so His knowledge never ceases to exist. And His knowledge of Himself is His knowledge of the cosmos, so His knowledge of the cosmos never ceases to exist. Hence He knows the cosmos in its state of nonexistence. He gives it existence according to its form in His knowledge.[53]

In all this, activity is ascribed to the One Being and receptivity to the objects of knowledge. These two are yang and yin within the divine Reality Itself. But the logical relationship here is "vertical," since Being precedes knowledge. It is possible for a thing to be without knowing anything, but it is not possible for a thing to know something without being. Hence knowledge is a quality possessed by Being, while the objects of knowledge are the concomitants of Being. In other words, Being pertains to the divine name *Allah*, which denotes absolute Reality as such. Knowledge is an attribute of Allah that follows upon Allah's reality. Hence, in the typical listing of the divine names, *the Alive* is given priority over *the Knowing*, since a thing cannot have knowledge if it is not alive. In the words of Ibn al-ʿArabī,

> Life is a precondition for the attribution of every relationship to God, whether knowledge, desire, power, speech, hearing, seeing, or perception. If the relationship of life were removed from Him, all these relationships would be removed as well. . . . For the God [*al-ilāh*] cannot be conceived of without these relationships.[54]

Majesty and Beauty

We began this chapter by showing how the very idea of God demands that we conceive of Him as He is in Himself (the Essence) and as we relate to Him (the Divinity). To distinguish between these two is to declare God's incomparability and His similarity. This leads to the fact that certain divine names are associated with the two sides. The names of Majesty have a close relationship with incomparability, while those of Beauty are more closely related to similarity. But God's names can be considered distinct from one other only in relation to created things. In God Himself they are identical with God. Hence, to speak of the divine names is to speak of God and creation, which is the most basic of yang/yin distinctions. This difference between God and the cosmos led us to connect all oneness and undifferentiation with yang and all manyness and differentiation with yin. Finally we came back to Being and knowledge, which are the roots of Oneness and manyness in the Real.

In the process of discussing these basic relationships, the distinction between the two groups of divine names known as those of majesty and beauty, or severity and gentleness, has come up on a number of occasions. This distinction needs further explanation, since it is a fundamental theme that permeates the Koran and the Hadith and sets the tone for all the discussions with which we are concerned. We will meet it repeatedly in coming chapters.

While declaring God's incomparability and asserting His similarity represent two extremes in Islamic thought, most authors of the sapiential tradition try to strike a balance between the two. In general incomparability is associated with qualities such as majesty (*jalāl*), severity (*qahr*), wrath (*ghaḍab*), justice (*ʿadl*), anger (*sakhṭ*), distance (*buʿd*), vengeance (*intiqām*), invincibility (*jabarūt*), inaccessibility (*ʿizza*), holiness (*qudus*), magnificence (*kibriyāʾ*), and so on. In the spiritual psychology developed by the Sufis, the human response to such divine qualities is designated by terms such as awe (*hayba*), fear (*khawf*), and contraction (*qabḍ*). In the same way, similarity is associated with beauty (*jamāl*), gentleness (*luṭf*), mercy (*raḥma*), bounty (*faḍl*), good-pleasure (*riḍā*), nearness (*qurb*), forgiveness (*maghfira*), pardon (*ʿafw*), love (*maḥabba*), etc. In spiritual psychology, the human response is intimacy (*uns*), hope (*rajāʾ*), and expansion (*basṭ*). This is the rough scheme that is reflected throughout Islamic thought, though many variations and permutations can be found, since relationships change according to perspective. Thus, for example, Ibn al-ʿArabī often follows the majority opinion by associating awe with majesty and intimacy with beauty, but in many passages he reverses the relationship, providing in the process a much subtler evaluation of the connection between God and human beings.[55]

As suggested earlier, the human qualities associated with the recognition of God as Majestic and Severe are the qualities of the servant (*ʿabd*). On the most basic level, the servant submits to the divine will because that is the proper attitude of the vassal before the lord, or of earth before heaven. Even people who think that they are not submitting do so in fact, since, as our poets tell us, the dust mote can do nothing else before the sun. But this second sort of submission brings no profit, since it is compulsory rather than voluntary. In short, the relationship between God and servant suggests a distance and opposition that are not overcome: The Real is high and the unreal is low, the Real is Majestic and the unreal is awe-stricken, the Real is Lord and the unreal is vassal, the Real is Magnificent and the unreal is trifling.[56]

The human qualities associated with the actualization of God's similarity are of a different sort, since they allude to the elimination of distance and difference. The vicegerent of the King represents the King by making use of His prerogatives. It goes without saying that the vicegerent has already submitted to the King. No king appoints a rebel as his representative. Once having submitted, the servant is given a robe of honor. The robe comes from the king, and the vicegerent wears it in his name.

The attributes of the vicegerent have to be viewed from two points of view. If we look at the vicegerent vis-à-vis the king, the vicegerent is the king's servant, and so he is a yin reality. But if we look at him in relationship to his charge, which is the cosmos, then he reflects the king's yang attributes. He displays the names of majesty and severity because the king is a ruler. Ibn al-ʿArabī frequently refers to this double relationship, as in the following passage:

> At root the servant was created only to belong to God and to be a servant perpetually. He was not created to be a lord. So when God clothes him in the robe of mastership and commands him to appear in it, he appears as a servant in himself and a master in the view of the observer. This is the ornament of his Lord, the robe He has placed upon him.[57]

If we look at the vicegerent in relation to the king, what distinguishes him or her from other servants is nearness to the king. God relates with this servant predominately in terms of the names of mercy and beauty.

Again, these relationships are not hard and fast. As pointed out above, mercy may be hidden in wrath and vice versa. Here I simply want to bring out the general stress of our texts and the fact that the issue of relationships is central to the type of thinking that goes on. In certain branches of Islamic learning, such as jurisprudence and Kalām, emphasis is placed on the quality of human distance from God and the resulting necessity of fear, awe, and submission. In other branches of Islamic lore, especially Sufism, stress is placed upon the quality of nearness after distance, or nearness along with distance. God is seen as primarily near and secondarily far. The goal of submission and servanthood is to reestablish the right relationships so that distance and nearness can play their proper roles. As Ibn al-ʿArabī puts it, although "He is with you wherever you are" (57:4), it is not true that we are with Him wherever He is. That is the goal. He is always near, but we have to establish nearness.[58]

From a slightly different point of view, servanthood is juxtaposed not with vicegerency but with love. Distance and incomparability demand awe, while nearness and similarity demand intimacy. Intimacy is togetherness and union, and this is achieved through love. God's love is primary, the servant's love secondary. The Sufis read the Koranic verse "He loves them and they love Him" (5:54) as expressing the actual ontological relationship. Human love can be born only from divine love.[59]

As soon as we begin talking of love, then we talk of separation and union. Within love itself, the two relationships—distance and nearness—are present. Though love is a quality connected primarily with God's beauty and gentleness, it also demands majesty and severity. Rūmī is the mouthpiece par excellence for the dialogue between gentleness and severity that takes place within the context of the servant's love for God. And since the whole universe is a servant infused with love, everything within it reflects the interplay between these two attributes. All the pairs and opposites found in creation mirror God's beauty and majesty. Annemarie Schimmel expresses Rūmī's view:

> God's twofold aspects are revealed in everything on earth: He is the Merciful and the Wrathful; His is *jamāl*, Beauty beyond all beauties, and *jalāl*, Majesty transcending all majesties.[60]

The accompanying table lists the qualitative correlations found throughout Rūmī's poetry.

Aḥmad Samʿānī contrasts servanthood and love by meditating on the implications of the Covenant of Alast. Before bringing human beings into this world, God said to them, "Am I not (*alast*) your Lord?" They all replied, "Yes, we give witness" (7:172). This covenant sets up a number of relationships. Note how Samʿānī associates love with inwardness and spirit, and servanthood with outwardness and body. The spirit is high and near to God, worthy to love Him. The body is low and far from God, worthy to serve Him. Samʿānī has God address bodies and spirits, telling them their own proper qualities. Finally the author turns to

Table 1 Correlations in Rūmī's Poetry*

GENTLENESS	SEVERITY
angels	devils
intellect	ego
paradise	hell
light	fire
Adam	Iblis
saints	unbelievers
religion	unbelief
union	separation
expansion	contraction
hope	fear
laughter	tears
joy	heartache
sweetness	bitterness, sourness
sugar	vinegar
spring	autumn
summer	winter
day	night
rose	thorn
faithfulness	cruelty
pure wine	dregs
intoxication	sobriety, thought
intoxication	winesickness

*From SPL 93.

a meditation upon a verse of the Fātiḥa, the opening chapter of the Koran that is recited in each cycle of the daily prayers: "Thee alone we serve and Thee alone we ask for help" (1:4). Service or worship (*ʿibāda*) is the attribute of the servant who obeys the commands of the king. Asking for help is the attribute of the supplicant who goes to the king's door and seeks entrance into his court. The point of some of the correspondences drawn below may be obscure. This is partly due to the fact that the original is in rhymed prose, so that there is a correlation set up in the words themselves that adds weight to the argument in Persian.

On the Day of "Am I not your Lord" a table of love was set up. Through the property of gentleness, they sat you down at the table and gave you a lawful bite from the covenant of the majesty of Lordship. With the hand of "Yes," you placed that bite in love's mouth. There is no bite more appetizing than the bite of *tawḥīd* in the mouth of love.

Beware, beware! Do not throw away this bite with the casting of dislike. If you do, you will remain forever in the affliction [*balā'*] of your "Yes" [*balā*].

The first shoot planted in the garden of your hearing was the shoot of Lordship. He watered it with gentleness until it sent down roots. Then the branch of being faithful grew up. "Those who are faithful to their covenants when they engage in a covenant" [2:177]. The leaf of good-pleasure grew. "God is pleased with them and they are pleased with Him" [5:119]. The blossom of praise and laudation bloomed. "Those who praise God in every state." The fruit of union and encounter set. "Faces on that day radiant, gazing at their Lord" [75:22–23]. He recorded the Covenant of Lordship on the tablets of the spirits with the ink of succor and the pen of the eternal gentleness. "Those—He has written in their hearts faith and confirmed them with a spirit from Him" [58:22].

To the bodily frames, He spoke of Lordship. To the spirits, He spoke of love. O frames, I am God! O hearts, I am the lover!

O frames, you belong to Me! O hearts, I belong to you!

O frames, toil! For that is what Lordship requires from servanthood. O hearts, rejoice!

Have joy in Me and sing My remembrance [*dhikr*]. For that is what is demanded by unqualified love.

O frames, stay within the realities of struggle! O hearts, stay within the gardens of witnessing!

O frames, occupy yourselves with ascetic discipline! O hearts, dwell in the rosegardens of beginningless gentleness!

O frames, keep on questioning! O hearts, keep on receiving gifts!

O frames, express your need [*niyāz*]! O hearts, pretend to be disdainful [*nāz*]!

O frames, activity belong to you! O hearts, pain belongs to you!

Since pain is something from which modern civilization teaches us to flee, it perhaps needs to be remarked here that this is the pain of separation, the pain that increases the fire of love. Rūmī, the spokesman for love, is also the champion of pain in the heart. As he puts it,

Pain is an alchemy that renovates—where is indifference when pain intervenes?

Beware, do not sigh coldly in your indifference! Seek pain! Seek pain, pain, pain![61]

Hence Samʿānī is telling us that the body has to be busy with the obligations of servanthood, such as prayer, fasting, and good works. But the heart has to busy itself with reflecting on its own situation, its own indifference, its own distance from the Beloved. It must be rejuvenated and transmuted through the pain of love. Samʿānī continues:

O frames, do not let go of obedience! O hearts, obey only Me!

O frames, occupy yourself with suffering! O hearts, sit on top of the treasure!

O frames, be like the knocker on a door! O hearts, ascend beyond the Glorious Throne!

O frames, give the body on credit! O hearts, buy and sell only for cash! Do you not see that when there is talk of the frame, promises are made? "[But as for him who feared the Station of his Lord] and forbade the soul its caprice, surely paradise shall be the refuge" [79:40–41]. But when there is talk of the heart, there is talk of ready cash. "I sit with him who remembers Me."[62] "I am with My servant's opinion of Me."[63] "He is with you wherever you are" [57:4]. O dervish! The paradise of separation is found in the paradise of union. But the paradise of union is not found in the paradise of separation.

O frames, you have a path to walk on [*madhhab*]! O hearts, you have a spring to drink from [*mashrab*]![64]

O frames, occupy yourself with ritual prayer and fasting! O hearts, busy yourself with secret whispering, supplication, pain, and melting!

O frames, travel through "Thee alone we serve"! O hearts, gaze through "Thee alone we ask for help"!

"Thee alone we serve" because we belong to Thee. "Thee alone we ask for help" because we exist through Thee.

"Thee alone we serve," remaining faithful to servanthood. "Thee alone we ask for help," gazing upon the pure goodness of Lordship.

"Thee alone we serve" because we are servants at Thy door. "Thee alone we ask for help" because we number among those Thou lovest.

"Thee alone we serve" because we are attendants. "Thee alone we ask for help" because we are lovers, and it is appropriate [for the Beloved] to extend a hand to the intoxicated lover.

"Thee alone we serve" negating belief in predestination. "Thee alone we ask for help" rejecting belief in free will.

"Thee alone we serve" through our effort. "Thee alone we ask for help" so that Thou wilt preserve us in our covenant.

"Thee alone we serve" is to bind the belt of diligence on the waist of truthfulness. "Thee alone we ask for help" is to ask for the effusion of the bounty of His Being's generosity. It is a necessary precondition that you bring your own diligence and lay it before His generosity. Perhaps the rays of His generosity's sun will shine upon your diligence. Then your diligence can become worthy of the presence of His majesty.

"Thee alone we serve" through the majesty of Thy command. "Thee alone we ask for help" through the perfection of Thy bounty.

"Thee alone we serve" because of the mightiness of Thy command. "Thee alone we ask for help" because of the treasury of Thy bounty.

"Thee alone we serve" arises from the lane of dutiful attendance. "Thee alone we ask for help" arises from the lane of aspiration.

When the servant says, "Thee alone we serve," the Real says, "Accept whatever he has brought." When the servant says, "Thee alone we ask for help," He says, "Give him whatever he wants."[65]

In their more theoretical works, the Sufis developed a complicated science of spiritual psychology by analyzing the nature of the possible and desirable relationships between human beings and God. As in the passage just quoted, close attention is paid to Koranic verses that refer to these relationships. In these theoretical works, reference is made to the different modalities of relationship as "stations" (*maqāmāt*) and "states" (*aḥwāl*). Both stations and states are inner qualities that are acquired on the path to God. The two are differentiated by the fact that stations are permanent and earned, while states are transitory and given as divine gifts. One of the most famous and basic presentations of the stations is *Manāzil al-sā'irīn* by Khwāja ʿAbdallāh Anṣārī. He describes ten categories of waystations, each of which has ten qualities. Each quality is then further subdivided into three levels. Anṣārī provides Koranic texts that mention each quality explicitly or implicitly. There are dozens of important works of this sort, and they all deserve to be studied from the point of view of the yin/yang relationships established by the qualities discussed.

In *Mashrab al-arwāḥ*, a discussion of one thousand waystations of the travelers on the path to God, Rūzbihān Baqlī (d. 606/1209) provides numerous passages relating various human and divine attributes in terms of the standard associations. In the following he juxtaposes majesty and beauty:

> The unveiling of beauty is the place where spirits are plundered through passionate affection, yearning, and love. Through it the gnostic is given the ability to travel through the attributes and to remain constant in the vision of eternity and subsistence. The gnostic says, "The station of the witnessing of beauty demands intoxication, ecstasy, and turmoil."
>
> The vision of majesty is the station in which the elect are overcome by fear, dread, veneration, and reverence. The gnostic says, "The vision of majesty distracts the spirits and upsets the bodies."[66]

Najm al-Dīn Kubrā (d. 618/1221) describes how the attributes of majesty and beauty affect the soul. He explains why majestic attributes pertain more to the outward, bodily realm, while beautiful attributes have an affinity with the inward, spiritual realm. He also points explicitly to the feminine quality of the beautiful attributes and the masculine quality of the majestic attributes. As noted above, contraction (*qabḍ*) is a response to yang qualities and expansion (*basṭ*) to yin qualities. The "others" are those who have not yet achieved worthiness to know God's mysteries, those who remain separate from Him. God keeps the mysteries from the "other" (*ghayr*) out of "jealousy" (*ghayra*), and the gnostics follow suit.

> When God's elect servants gain knowledge of His stores and hidden treasures and recognize that these will keep on increasing forever without being exhausted, they become joyful in what they have and begin seeking increase. They cling fast to dignity and avoid showing anything, out of jealousy and fear lest the mysteries become manifest to the "others." The attributes of invincibility and magnificence cover them over, while they conceal the attributes of mercy and beauty. Hence they undergo contraction in their bodies, as if they were bound in chains, because of the intensity of the dignity, the patient waiting, and the reminder. But they undergo expansion in their hearts and spirits, just as cotton expands with the blowing of the wind.
>
> Someone may ask why attributes of awe and invincibility should cover them while they conceal attributes of beauty, bounty, and mercy. We would reply: Because beauty, bounty, and mercy are beautiful and attractive women. Since they are free and curtained ladies, they remain concealed behind the veil lest the "others" be tempted by them.[67]
>
> Someone may ask why attributes of awe and invincibility are not desired. We would reply: They are desired, but the "others" will see their forms, not their meanings. Their forms are terrifying—like snakes, lions, scor-

pions, and serpents. The "others" avoid things like this, not desiring them, in contrast to the attributes of beauty. Hence in their forms, attributes of beauty are related to attributes of majesty just as women are related to men. But in respect of their meanings, the relationship is opposite.[68]

What exactly Kubrā means by this last sentence is not clear. Perhaps he has in mind the "Taoist" idea—which we will meet in detail in chapter 6—that the yin dimension of reality determines the nature of things more profoundly than the yang dimension. In the outward domain, majesty rules over beauty, but in the inward domain, yin rules over yang.

Awe and Intimacy

Sufi texts discuss many pairs of human qualities that come to exist because of differing human relationships with the divine. We have already mentioned fear and hope, contraction and expansion, and intimacy and awe. Other commonly discussed pairs are concentration and dispersion, presence and absence, intoxication and sobriety, obliteration and affirmation, concealing and disclosure, variegation and stability.[69] By investigating any of these pairs we can bring out basic Muslim attitudes toward divine/human relationships. I want to look more closely at intimacy and awe, which are commonly juxtaposed, as stated above, with beauty and majesty.

Abū Bakr al-Kalābādhī (d. 380/990) provides an early definition of intimacy in *al-Taʿarruf li madhhab al-taṣawwuf*. Explanations from the important Persian commentary on this work, *Sharḥ-i taʿarruf* by Abū Ibrāhīm Mustamlī Bukhārī (d. 434/1042-43), are added in brackets:

> {Kalābādhī placed the chapter on intimacy after the chapter on remembrance [*dhikr*] because, as we said, a person remembers God in the measure that he witnesses Him. The more one witnesses God, the more one remembers. When witnessing increases greatly, it yields intimacy. Do you not see in the visible world that the more a person is something's companion, the more he becomes intimate with it, so much so that he sees the intimacy equal to love? Just as the lover suffers pain through separation from the beloved, so also the person who is intimate with something suffers pain by being separated from it. . . .
>
> {It sometimes happens that a person fears something. If he sees that thing, his liver melts and the life is frightened out of him. But gradually he gains courage and hides his fear. Little by little, he gains intimacy with that affliction. Finally he becomes so intimate with the affliction, which used to frighten the life out of him, that separation from it would be the death of him. That affliction becomes the food of those who suffer it to such an extent that blessing becomes an affliction for them. They suffer from blessing the way others suffer from affliction. These are examples from common experience.
>
> {It has been said that when Moses was taken to meet his Lord, He commanded him to throw down his staff. Then it became a serpent. This was done so that he would become intimate with affliction and not fear the trickery of Pharoah's sorcerers. Al-Ḍaḥḥāk says that Moses had a thousand miracles in his staff. . . . The staff that was for Pharoah an affliction was for Moses an intimate. It has also been said that when Muhammad was taken on the ascent [*miʿrāj*], the wisdom in that was for him to see the affliction of the Resurrection and the chastisement of hell. Thereby he became intimate with affliction and chastisement. At the Resurrection, when everyone is struck by fear, he will be secure. Then all the people at the Resurrection will say, "Oh, my soul!" But he will say, "Oh, my community!"[70] . . .}
>
> Al-Junayd was asked about intimacy. He replied, "It is the removal of shyness while awe is still there." The "removal of shyness" means that hope should dominate over fear.
>
> Dhu'l-Nūn was asked about intimacy. He replied, "It is the lover's bold expansiveness [*inbisāṭ*][71] toward the Beloved." Its meaning is expressed in the words of God's Friend [Abraham]: "Show me how Thou bringest the dead to life" [2:260]. {The root of this is that the more love increases, the more God's kind caresses increase. The more kind caresses increase, the more intimacy is achieved. Bold expansiveness occurs in the measure of intimacy. Do you not see that if Abraham had not possessed the station of friendship, he would not have been so boldly expansive with God? No one has the courage to show

such bold expansiveness to his Lord. The dead will come to life at the Resurrection. But since Abraham had gained the station of friendship, he was bold. He asked God to show him immediately what the creatures will see tomorrow at the Resurrection. Asking for something before its proper time is bold expansiveness. If a person has not achieved the beginnings of intimacy and love, he will not be boldly expansive. Then Kalābādhī brings another example:}

Likewise, this bold expansiveness of intimacy is expressed in the words of Moses: "Show me, that I might gaze upon Thee" [7:143]. {Moses wanted to see God, but the vision of God has been promised for the Resurrection. However, since he had found intimacy, he asked to have immediately what had been deferred for later. . . . }

God's words, "Thou shalt not see Me" [7:143] are a kind of an excuse, meaning, "You cannot." {God wants to say: I do not forbid you to see Me because it is not permitted or proper. On the contrary, I forbid it because in your present attribute you do not have the ability to see Me; or, because this place where you have asked for vision is not the place of vision; or, it is not the time for vision.

{The proof of these words is that Moses' people had asked for the same thing, but they received burning as their share.[72] It was not their place to show bold expansiveness. But Moses received an excuse, since it was his place to be boldly expansive. . . . }

Ibrāhīm al-Māristānī was asked about intimacy. He replied, "It is the heart's joy in the Beloved."

Shiblī was asked about intimacy and He replied, "It is that you become alienated from yourself." {When the servant gains intimacy with God, he becomes alienated [*waḥsha*] from everything other than God. But the nearest thing to himself is himself. That is why Shiblī says that he must become alienated from himself. When he is alienated from the nearest person, then it is obvious that he is not intimate with anyone. The meaning of "becoming alienated from oneself" is that in his own self he should have no bold expansiveness toward the Beloved. He should have no desire either to attract gain or to repel loss. He should be so joyful in intimacy and so absent from himself that if the Beloved should forbid bestowal, he will not ask why. And if He should decide on affliction, he will not ask why He decided on that. For if he were to attend to these things, he would be busy with something other than the Beloved. To the extent that the lover is busy with other than the Beloved, he is separate from the Beloved. . . . }

Dhu'l-Nūn said, "The lowest station of intimacy is that though the person is thrown into the Fire, that does not make him absent from Him with whom he is intimate."

One of the Sufis said, "Intimacy means that he should be so familiar with formulae of remembrance that he remains absent from the vision of others."[73]

By the time of Hujwīrī (d. ca. 465/1072)—the author of one of the first major Sufi works in Persian, the *Kashf al-maḥjūb*—the contrasting qualities associated with intimacy and awe were clearly established. Note that he discusses two main opinions concerning the two attributes. The first set of opinions is close to the view of the proponents of Kalām, since it stresses God's incomparability, distance, and majesty. In this perspective, the preferred human attribute is awe, while intimacy is inferior, since it can be established only with creatures. The second group of opinions stresses God's similarity to human beings and the primacy of His beauty over His majesty. In this perspective, intimacy is superior. The word *witness* (*shāhid*) employed toward the beginning of the passage is a Sufi technical term that refers to the face of God that the traveler perceives in his or her heart. Ibn al-ʿArabī defines it as "the trace that witnessing leaves in the heart of the witnesser."[74]

Intimacy and awe are two states experienced by the dervishes who travel on the path to the Real. They are as follows: When the Real discloses Himself to the heart of the servant through the witness of majesty, his share in that is awe. When He discloses Himself to the servant's heart through the witness of beauty, his share in that is intimacy. The people of awe are weary in His majesty, while the people of intimacy revel in His beauty. There is a difference between a heart that is burning in the fire of love because of His majesty and a heart that is radiant in the light of witnessing because of His beauty.

Some of the shaykhs have said that awe is the degree of the gnostics, while intimacy is the degree of the disciples. The more a person steps into the Presence of the Real and declares the incomparability of His qualities, the more the authority of awe dominates over his heart and the more his nature flees from intimacy. For a person can become familiar only with his own kind. Since kinship and similarity between the servant and the Real are impossible, there can be no intimacy with Him. In the same way, He cannot be intimate with the creatures.

If intimacy is possible, it is possible with His remembrance [*dhikr*]. But His remembrance is other than He, since it is the attribute of the servant. And in love, if one gains ease with the other, this proves that one has spoken falsely and is making claims and imagining things. . . . It is related that Shiblī said, "For a long time I imagined that I was reveling in love for the Real and had intimacy with witnessing Him. Now I know that people can have intimacy only with their own kind."

Another group maintains that awe is the companion of chastisement, separation, and punishment, while intimacy is the result of union and mercy. Therefore God preserves His friends from awe and similar qualities and makes them the companion of intimacy. For without doubt love demands intimacy. Just as there cannot be love between two of the same kind, so also there cannot be intimacy. My shaykh used to say, "I wonder at those who say that intimacy with the Real is impossible, when He has said, 'When My servants ask thee about Me—surely, I am near' [2:186]. 'Surely, My servants' [15:42]. 'Say to My servants' [17:53]. 'O My servants, today no fear is on you, neither do you sorrow' [43:68]."

Without doubt a servant who sees this bounty will love Him, and when he loves Him, he will become intimate with Him. For awe toward a beloved is to be far apart, while intimacy is to be one. It is a human attribute to become intimate with the one who bestows blessings. The Real has given us so many blessings, and we have knowledge of that. It is impossible for us to speak of awe.

As for me, ʿAlī ibn ʿUthmān al-Jullābī, I say that both groups are correct with all their differences. The authority of awe rules over the soul and its caprice. It annihilates our mortal nature. But the authority of intimacy rules over the inmost mystery and nurtures knowledge. Hence, through disclosing Himself in majesty, the Real annihilates the souls of His friends. Through disclosing Himself in beauty, He causes their inmost mysteries to subsist. Hence, those who were people of annihilation placed awe first, while those who are the masters of subsistence preferred intimacy.[75]

Here we see Hujwīrī making a distinction parallel to those made later by Samʿānī: Awe is the proper attitude for the soul, while intimacy is the proper attitude for the spirit or inmost mystery. When contrasted with spirit, the soul (*nafs*) represents the lower, dark, descending, and ignorant tendency in the human being, while the spirit represents the higher, luminous, ascending, and intelligent dimension. Since the soul is dark and low, it is distant from God. Hence it is associated with the names of majesty and severity. Since the spirit is luminous and high, it is near to God. Hence it is associated with the names of beauty and gentleness. We will meet these contrasts repeatedly in coming chapters.

Many more descriptions of intimacy and awe could be cited.[76] Instead I will quote only one more text, by Najm al-Dīn Kubrā. He is describing the perfection of the spiritual master, the shaykh, who flies with the "two wings" of beauty and majesty.

> Through these two wings, the shaykh deviates from the straight path and also goes straight. . . . Sometimes the attributes of beauty disclose themselves to him, that is, bounty, mercy, gentleness, and generosity. Then he is immersed in intimacy. Sometimes the attributes of majesty disclose themselves to him, that is, power, tremendousness, magnificence, inaccessibility, chastisement, and intense assault. Then he is immersed in awe. Sometimes the attributes mix, so he witnesses both intimacy and awe. The attributes mix only when the Divine Essence discloses Itself, since the Essence is the Mother of the attributes, bringing all of them together.[77]

Social Implications of Divine Duality

It may be useful at this point to summarize the present chapter and draw some preliminary conclusions concerning the divine-human relationship as pictured in the Islamic sapiential tradition. All of Islam begins with the assertion of God's Unity (*tawḥīd*), an assertion that is expressed in the formula, "There is no god but God." But from the outset we are faced with the distinction between God and the cosmos, since God's oneness is asserted by His creatures. This in turn allows us to speak of God's utter difference and distance from the cosmos (incomparability), demanded by the fact that He is Real and the cosmos is unreal. It also allows us to speak of a certain similarity and nearness to the cosmos, demanded by the fact that the cosmos is in fact here. If it were utterly unreal, it would not exist. Since it has a semblance of reality, that semblance can come only from the Real. On this basis it is possible to speak meaningfully about relationships between God and the cosmos. These relationships are known as the divine names or attributes.

God is the primary reality, while the cosmos has a certain derivative reality. Hence God controls the cosmos utterly. God is yang and the cosmos is yin.

But God controls the cosmos in two basic modes, in accordance with the two basic relationships that can be discerned between Him and it: incomparability and similarity. The first relationship is associated with the names of majesty and severity, the second with the names of beauty and gentleness. From this point of view, God is both yang and yin.

The general perspective of the Sharia and Kalām stresses God as yang. God is Majestic and Severe. In response, human beings must cower and tremble. In other words, they have to "submit" (*islām*) to God's will and become His servants.

The general perspective of Islamic spirituality, especially certain forms of Sufism, stresses God as yin. "God's mercy precedes His wrath." He created the universe out of mercy and love. His only concern in doing so was to serve our welfare.

If God is primarily yin for many Sufis, why do they not refer to God as "She"? First, sometimes they do, as we will see in chapter 6. Second, from a certain very important point of view, the yin nature of God is situated on a lower level, within a greater yang. God is yang in relation to the cosmos because of ontological priority. Then, within the context of God's utter control of the universe—a universe that properly speaking possesses nothing of its own to control—God shows Himself as both yang and yin. Third, God's "feminine" nature entails certain dangers for human beings. If they were to count on it alone and ignore the "masculine" side of the divine character, they would most likely fall into the fire of hell—that is, distance from God. This point is fundamental to the Islamic perspective and needs some clarification.

As our authors tells us, God's love, mercy, kindness, gentleness, bounty, and beauty breed intimacy. Intimacy is characterized by "bold expansiveness," the feeling that we can say to our beloved anything we want to say and do in the beloved's presence anything we want to do. In contrast, God's wrath, severity, justice, majesty, greatness, tremendousness, and magnificence give rise to awe. When we stand in awe of the king, we are very careful to do things just right. We observe all the customs of the court, all the rules of courtesy and good manners (*adab*).

The first principle of the relationship between God and the cosmos is that realness (*ḥaqqiyya*) belongs to God, while the creatures are derivative realities. God created the cosmos to make the Hidden Treasure manifest. Only after that can He be known by the creatures, who themselves are part of the Hidden Treasure. Until the cosmos exists, there can be no "others," no knowledge by others, and no enjoyment of mercy and love by others. Once God creates the cosmos out of love and mercy, He is concerned to nurture knowledge of Himself in the others, since all reality and bliss lie in the Real, the Blissful. As long as the others remain veiled from the Real, they are in danger of dissipating the blessings that have been given to them. Through prophecy God reminds the "others" of the Real.

The greatest veil preventing human beings from seeing the Real is themselves. Instinctively they place themselves at center stage. The first and fundamental goal of prophecy is to deliver people from depending upon their own selves, since these selves have no intrinsic reality. In order for people to be delivered from relying on a false reality, they must recognize that the truly Real is utterly different from themselves. True reality belongs to God alone. They must seek for this God far from themselves, lest they attribute reality to the "other," that is, themselves. This distant God who is utterly Real and effaces our reality is King, Majestic, Incomparable, Inaccessible. In relation to Him we can only be servants. Again, the goal is to establish the right relationship between the Real and the unreal, or between the inherently Real and the conventionally real, or between God and creation.

This is the perspective of submission and servanthood. It demands observance of the Sharia. It also demands recognizing God as the supreme Yang, the overarching Authority. This perspective sees society as a framework for setting up the right relationships with God. It demands rules and regulations, good manners, and awe. There is no bold expansiveness here, only timid contraction. Human beings must know their own place and stick to it.

As we have seen, the tradition connects this dimension to the body and the soul, the lower dimensions of the human reality. The body and "the soul that commands to evil" keep us distant from God. Yet these dimensions of reality appear as truly real to most people. The soul must be transformed from its "normal" state of commanding to evil to the "normative" state of being at peace with God. This is the topic of part 4 of this work.

In the Islamic perspective, submission to God (*islām*) is the first step for every human being. It is the sine qua non of human existence.[78] Through it one maintains good behavior. It is the safe road that leads to the king's court. And one must always stay in awe of the Infinite King.

The Sufis, who speak for Islamic spirituality, say nothing different, but they also bring out the complementary perspective: Awe may be primary from a certain point of view, but intimacy can also be achieved. And once it is achieved, it is found to be more inherently real than awe. Sufis place great stress upon the gentle and merciful names of God. They constantly quote and comment on the sound hadith, "God's mercy precedes His wrath." They cite the vicegerency of Adam and the fact that the prophets manifest God's attributes on earth. They emphasize love more than service and worship. Ibn al-ʿArabī, who paid more attention to the nuances of word usage than perhaps anyone else in Islamic history, points out that the external orientation of Kalām stresses God's incomparability so much that it negates the possibility of love between human beings and God.[79]

Most Sufis stress love for God as the primary means of reaching God. Love demands intimacy, just as it demands similarity. One of intimacy's implications is "bold expansiveness." This leads to a side of Sufism that has constantly been remarked upon by Muslims and non-Muslims, that is, its tendency toward antinomianism. For the most part, this has not involved an actual disregard for the rules and regulations of the Sharia. But it has involved, on occasion, rather outlandish manifestations of "bold expansiveness."

For example, the phenomenon of "ecstatic utterances" (*shaṭḥiyyāt*) was well known, especially in early Sufism.[80] Sayings such as al-Ḥallāj's "I am the Real" or Abū Yazīd's "There is nothing in my cloak but God" fall into this category. Sufis like Rūzbihān Baqlī wrote major treatises collecting and explaining these sayings. Ulama seeking to defend God's incomparability and the sanctity of the Sharia seized upon such sayings to prove that the Sufis were blasphemers and unbelievers. The place of these ecstatic utterances in Islamic thought can be understood when they are correlated with God's similarity, mercy, and gentleness. "She" is so kind and gentle that She does not take Her lovers to task for their boldness. As Sufis often remark, the Sharia is not applicable to madmen, nor to those who are intoxicated. The Koran itself says, "Do not approach the ritual prayer while you are drunk. Wait until you know what you are saying" (4:43). The bold expansiveness of intimacy wipes away self-awareness and allows no room for knowing what you are saying.

As everyone knows, Islam set up a social order from the outset, in contrast, for example, to Christianity. Islamic social teachings are so basic to the religion that still today many people, including Muslims, are completely unaware of Islam's spiritual dimensions. The social order demands rules and regulations, fear of the king, respect for the police, acknowledgement of authority. It has to be set up on the basis of God's majesty and severity. It pays primary attention to the external realm, the realm of the body and the desires of the lower soul, the realm where God is distant from the world.

In contrast, Islamic spiritual teachings allow for intimacy, love, boldness, ecstatic expressions, and intoxication in the Beloved. All these are qualities that pertain to nearness to God. They are actualized within the spirit, the heart, the inmost mystery—not on the level of the lower soul. But this inner spirituality can be built only on the foundation of the outer realm, which includes the body and the Sharia. In other words, spirituality itself cannot govern society. Government is yang business, the realm of the Sharia. When spirituality gets too close to the social realm, bold expansiveness and antinomianism are the result, which the Muslim legal authorities rightly condemn.

In short, on the social level, Islam affirms the primacy of God as King, Majestic, Lord, Ruler. It establishes a theological patriarchy even if Muslim theologians refuse to apply the word father (or mother) to God. God is yang, while the world, human beings, and society are yin. Thereby order is established and maintained. Awe and distance are the ruling qualities.

On the spiritual level, the picture is different. In this domain many Muslim authorities affirm the primacy of God as Merciful, Beautiful, Gentle, Loving. Here they establish a spiritual matriarchy, though again such terms are not employed. God is yin and human beings are yang. Human spiritual aspiration is accepted and welcomed by God. Intimacy and nearness are the ruling qualities. This helps explain why one can easily find positive evaluations of women and the feminine dimension of things in Sufism.[81]

God's wrath and severity govern that which is distant from God, while His mercy and gentleness take under their wing that which is near. Distance is the realm of duality, multiplicity, differentiation, distinction, discernment, right and wrong, commands and prohibitions, good and evil, the Sharia. Nearness is the realm of unity, oneness, undifferentiation, sameness, loss of distinctions, union with God. These latter qualities coalesce with the divine mercy, kindness, gentleness, and love.

To the extent that human beings dwell in the world of multiplicity, they must acknowledge their receptivity and subservience to the domain of oneness. Submission to God's will and the Sharia are incumbent upon them. To the extent that they dwell in the world of unity, they are yang and God is yin, since God welcomes them into His loving arms, serving their every desire. The spirit is not so much submitted to God as one with God. This is the goal of Islamic spirituality. And this perspective places the divine mercy and compassion, the divine yin, at the pinnacle of values.

Again, this primacy of yin cannot function on the social level, since it undermines the authority of the law. If we take in isolation the Koranic statement, "Despair not of God's mercy—surely God forgives all sins" (39:53), then we can throw the Sharia out the window. In the Islamic perspective, the revealed law prevents society from degenerating into chaos. One gains liberty not by overthrowing hierarchy and constraints, but by finding liberty in its true abode, the spiritual realm. Freedom—lack of limitation and constraint, bold expansiveness—is achieved only by moving toward God, not by rebelling against Him and moving away.

A number of hadiths allude to the dangers of stressing God's yin qualities. For example, the Prophet is reported to have said to his companion Muʿādh, "He who meets God not associating anything with Him will enter the Garden." Muʿādh said,

"Shall I give this good news to the people?" The Prophet replied, "No. I fear that they will rely upon it."[82] A similar hadith has ʿUmar—whom the tradition represents as incarnating the stern qualities of the Sharia—object to the Prophet for saying something similar. "You must not do that," says ʿUmar, "for I am afraid the people will rely upon it. Let them go on doing good deeds." The Prophet replied, "Let them."[83]

ʿAṭṭār (d. 618/1221) makes the same point more explicitly in an anecdote he tells about the great Sufi shaykh, Abu'l-Ḥasan Kharraqānī (d. 425/1033):

> It is related that one night the Shaykh was busy with prayer. He heard a voice saying, "Beware, Abu'l-Ḥasan! Do you want me to tell people what I know about you so that they will stone you to death?"
>
> The Shaykh replied, "O God the Creator! Do You want me to tell the people what I know about Your mercy and what I see of Your generosity? Then no one will prostrate himself to You."
>
> A voice came, "You keep quiet, and so will I."[84]

Sufism is concerned with "maintaining the secret" (*ḥifẓ al-sirr*) for more reasons than one. The secret of God's mercy threatens the plain fact of His wrath. If "She" came out of the closet, "He" would be overthrown. But then She could not be found, for it is He who shows the way to Her door.

3

THE TWO HANDS OF GOD

In the previous chapter we had in view a basic yang/yin relationship between God and creation, or the One and the many, or Being and the potential manyness present in God's knowledge. In other words, we looked at the yang/yin relationship mainly on a vertical axis, extending from the Essence down to the world. But "horizontal" relationships of a yin/yang type also play an important role in Islamic thought, even though the horizontality is usually reduced to verticality under closer inspection. In this chapter I turn to a more detailed analysis of intra-divine relationships, including the horizontal.

The qualities associated with incomparability and similarity, or wrath and mercy, are frequently discussed as polar opposites or contraries. God's relationship with the cosmos is described in two apparently conflicting ways. It is easy for us to see wrath as the opposite of mercy, and at first glance the two seem to have little in common. But the two attributes refer to a single Essence. Both denote the same reality, and hence in the last analysis they are identical. Ibn al-ʿArabī for one is quite explicit in drawing out the fact that the divine names denote two basic realities: a specific quality in relation to the things of this world, and a single supreme reality that is not different from any other reality.[1] For example, the name Wrathful denotes God's anger in respect to certain created things, an anger that has to be clearly differentiated from mercy, since wrath manifests itself in realities such as hell, while mercy becomes manifest in realities such as paradise. At the same time, the name Wrathful also denotes God as such, the Essence that is beyond all names and includes all names, for "There is none wrathful but God." Hence it is not distinct from any other name.

The more carefully our authors attend to the divine side of the names, the more attention they pay to the sameness of the names, rather than their difference. When polar names are at issue, complementarity and reciprocity are emphasized. An interesting series of texts that bear directly on this question is found in the works of Ibn al-ʿArabī and his followers. These texts explain a Koranic passage found in the story of God's creation of Adam. God commands Iblis to prostrate himself, and Iblis refuses to do so. God says to Iblis, "What prevented you from prostrating yourself before him whom I created with My own two hands?" (38:75). The earliest commentaries on this passage are concerned mainly to emphasize incomparability: God's "two hands" are not at all like human hands. Some early authorities maintain that there is no special significance in the fact that the hands are two. But Ibn al-ʿArabī and his followers were intensely interested in every nuance of the Koranic text. They took seriously the dogma that this is the very Word of God. In their view, there is no reason for God to waste words. When He says something, He does so with one or more specific purposes in view. In respect of His incomparability, it is impossible to know what He means. But in respect of His similarity, He is teaching what can be known about Himself. Hence there must be some significance to the "two hands," especially since the expression is not a common one in the Koran. In brief, they understand the "two hands" to indicate a polar relationship in God Himself. That He should create Adam with these two hands indicates that He employed this polarity to bring the microcosm into existence. The microcosm itself, made in the image of God, must have "two hands" in the same qualitative sense that God has them, not only physically. And so also must the macrocosm, which is the microcosm's mirror image.

The more the verse of the two hands is meditated upon, the more it raises questions that could fairly be asked of those who are experts in the Koranic text: What is a "hand" of God? Why do other verses mention God's hand in the singular, while still others speak of His "hands" in the plural? Why is Adam singled out for the only Koranic mention of creation by "two hands"? (One other verse speaks of God's two hands using the same word *yad*: "His two hands are outspread; He expends how He will" [5:64], but it has no immediate connection with creativity.) Does God have right and left hands as we do? What is the meaning of the hadith that tells us that "both hands of God are right hands"? In what follows my primary concern is not necessarily to answer these questions or to analyze in detail the meaning of God's "two hands," but to illustrate how Muslim thinkers describe polar relationships.

Right and Left

Though the Koran seldom makes reference to God's two hands using the dual form of the word *yad*, it does allude to the right and left hands of both God and human beings employing other terminology, and it ascribes significantly different qualities to the two sides. The word *yamīn*, meaning right side or right hand, is employed in the Koran twenty-four times. The Arabic language employs words from the same root to indicate good luck or good fortune, and the Koran uses some of them in this meaning. It uses the word *shimāl*, left side or left hand, eleven times. This term also means ill luck or misfortune.

As is to be expected from the implications of the words, the Koran associates different qualities with right and left. In brief, the right hand is connected with good fortune and felicity, the left with the opposite qualities. The eschatological significance of the terms is especially clear in the expressions "Companions of the Right" and "Companions of the Left." These are the inhabitants of paradise and hell. A few Koranic verses can help demonstrate the qualities connected to right and left:

> The Companions of the Right (O Companions of the Right!) amidst thornless lote-trees and serried acacias, and spreading shade and outpoured waters, and fruits abounding. . . . The Companions of the Left (O Companions of the Left!) amidst burning winds and boiling water and the shadow of a smoking blaze neither cool, neither goodly. . . . (56:27–43)
>
> On that day you shall be exposed, not one secret of yours concealed. Then as for him who is given his book in his right hand, . . . he shall be in a pleasing life in a lofty Garden. . . . But as for him who is given his book in his left hand, he shall say, "Would that I not been given my book . . . ". "Take him, and fetter him, then roast him in Hell." (69:19–26).
>
> On the day when We shall call all men to their leaders, and whoso is given his book in his right hand—those shall read their book, and they shall not be wronged a single date-thread. (17:71)

Another significant use of the term *right* is in the expression "right side of the mountain," from whence Moses was called by God (19:52, 20:80, 28:30).

The hadith literature makes many significant references to right and left, and these have had a deep impact upon the way Muslims evaluate these two directions. In brief, the right is associated with cleanliness, purity, and blessedness, while the left is connected with their opposites. Following the Sunna of the Prophet, Muslims begin significant acts with the right hand or right foot. They put on their right shoe first and enter a house or a mosque with the right foot. For acts connected with impurity, such as cleaning oneself after going to the toilet, they employ the left hand. They enter a toilet with the left foot. Traditionally they eat with the right hand and are shocked if anyone picks up food with the left hand. Left-handedness is strongly discouraged.

The qualitative significance of the terms left and right is suggested by Koranic commentaries on the expression Companions of the Right and Left. Maybudī tells us that the earliest commentators had four basic opinions concerning the expression "Companions of the Right," all of them closely related:

1. At the Resurrection, the Companions of the Right will be taken to the right side into the Garden, while the Companions of the Left will be taken to the left side into the Fire.
2. Ibn ʿAbbās says that the Companions of the Right were taken out of the right side of Adam when God extracted his seed from his loins (cf. 7:172), while the Companions of the Left were taken out from Adam's left side. Reference is made to the two groups in a hadith, "God created Adam and struck him with His right hand. His seed came out on the right hand white like silver and on the left hand black like coals. God said, 'These are for the Garden, and it is no concern of Mine. These are for the Fire, and it is no concern of Mine.'"[2]
3. Al-Ḍaḥḥāk says that at the Resurrection the Companions of the Right will be given their books in their right hands, while the Companions of the Left will be given their books in their left hands.
4. Al-Ḥasan and al-Rabīʿ say that the Companions of the Right are those who were "auspicious" (*mayāmīn*) and blessed toward themselves and lived their lives in obedience to God, while the Companions of the Left were "inauspicious" (*mashāʾīm*) toward themselves and lived their lives in acts of disobedience.[3]

The theologian Fakhr al-Dīn Rāzī (d. 606/1209) adds another reason: The Companions of the Right are those who will see their light on their right hands, as indicated in Koran 57:12: "On the day when you see the believers, men and women, their light running before them and on their right hands. 'Good tidings for you today! Gardens underneath which rivers flow . . .'".[4]

The Koran refers explicitly to the right hand of God in a single verse: "The earth altogether shall be His handful (*qabḍa*) on the Day of Resurrection, and the heavens shall be rolled up in His right hand" (39:67). The latter half of the verse recalls 21:104: "On the day when We shall roll up heaven as a scroll is rolled for the writings. . . ". The Prophet is reported to have said, "God will grasp the heavens in His right hand, while the earths will be in His other hand. Then He will shake them."[5] For the most part, early Koran commentators offer no explanations for the nature of the two hands mentioned or alluded to in these verses. Ṣadr al-Dīn Qūnawī provides interesting explanations in the context of commenting on various hadiths. We will return to one of his explanations below and another in chapter 7. Both confirm the picture that we have drawn to this point: Right is associated with the auspicious and blessed, and these in turn are connected to spirituality and that which comes from God. Left is associated with the inauspicious and that which is distant from God.

These associations help explain the sense of the hadith alluded to above concerning the fact that God has "two right hands." In it, the Prophet describes how God created Adam, then held out His two hands to him while both were closed, telling him to choose one. Adam replies, "I choose the right hand of the Lord, though both hands of my Lord are right and blessed."[6] If one of God's hands were "left," it would be inauspicious. But since "God's mercy precedes His wrath," even wrath is in fact a mercy. God's "left" is in truth right. As Ibn al-ʿArabī puts it, "God has two blessed, open hands. In other words, within them is mercy. So nothing of chastisement is connected to them."[7] Moreover, it would clearly be bad manners to say that one of God's hands is inauspicious. Did not the Prophet say, "The good, all of it, is in Thy two hands, while evil does not go back to Thee"?[8] As Ṣadr al-Dīn Qūnawī remarks,

> As for the prophetic sayings that both of God's hands are right and blessed, this is true out of courtesy [*adab*]. It is also true when we verify the matter in respect of the attribution of the two hands to Him, though not in respect of their effect in that which comes into existence through them.[9]

In other words, in respect to Himself, God had two right hands, since everything He creates is part of His plan. But in respect to us, one of God's two hands is a left hand, since it is connected to misfortune and the Fire.

Many of the implications of the terms right and left are summed up by Maybudī in his discussion of Koran 50:17–18: "When the two angels meet together, sitting one on the right, and one on the left, not a word he utters, but by him is an observer ready." These are the angels that write down a person's good and evil deeds:

> It is reported that the two angels given charge of the servant sit like the servant. The one on the right writes his good deeds, while the one on the left writes his evil deeds. When the servant sleeps, one stands above his pillow, while the other watches over him from his feet. When the servant walks, one goes before him and one goes behind, both of them defending him from harm.
>
> It is said that the angel of good deeds is changed each day, another angel being sent. The wisdom in this is that tomorrow he will have many witnesses for his acts of obedience and good deeds. But the angel of evil deeds is not changed, so that only that angel will know his defects.
>
> The equivalent of this in the Koran is found in the verse, "O My servants who have been immoderate against yourselves, despair not of God's mercy—surely God forgives all sins" [39:53]. In saying "who have been immoderate" God sums everything up. He keeps the lid on and does not go into details. He says: O Gabriel, you deliver the revelation, for "they have been immoderate," and there is no need for you to know what they have done. O Muhammad, you recite the revelation, for "they have been immoderate," and there is no need for you to know what they have done. Generous Lord, compassionate King! He did not want Gabriel to know the sins of the servants and the Messenger to recite their acts of disobedience. . . .
>
> "Not a word he utters, but by him is an observer ready." The angel on the right is the angel of bounty, the angel on the left the angel of justice. Just as bounty [*faḍl*] rules over justice [*ʿadl*], so also the right-hand angel rules over the left-hand angel. O angel on the right hand! You be the commander. Write down ten good deeds for every good deed he performs. O angel on the left hand! You be the follower. Write down nothing except what the angel on the right hand tells you to write. When the servant commits an act of disobedience, the angel on the right hand says, "Wait seven days before you write it down. Perhaps he will offer an excuse and repent."
>
> What is all this? It is the result of a single decree that God issued in eternity without beginning: "My mercy precedes My wrath."[10]

The Views of Koran Commentators

Some of the earliest suggestions as to the nature of God's "two hands" through which Adam was created are found in the Shiʿite hadith literature. According to the eighth Imam, ʿAlī al-Riḍā (d. 203/818), the two hands refer to strength (*quwwa*) and power (*qudra*), two basically synonymous terms.[11] When asked about this verse, the fifth Imam, Muḥammad al-Bāqir (d. ca. 117/735), is reported to have said,

> In the speech of the Arabs, "hand" means strength [*quwwa*] and blessing [*niʿma*]. The Koran says, "Remember Our servant David, the man of might [literally "the possessor of hands"]" [38:17]. "And heaven, We built it with might ["hands"]" [51:47]. He says, "He confirmed them ["gave them a hand"] with a spirit from Him" [58:22]. It is said, "So-and-so has many hands with me," that is, he has shown me bounties and beneficence. Or, "He has shown me a white hand," that is, blessing.[12]

The early Koran commentators paid little attention to the questions posed above concerning the significance of the verse of the two hands. In *Laṭāʾif al-ishārāt*, the famous Sufi and theologian Abu'l-Qāsim Qushayrī (d. 465/1072) writes that the verse indicates that "what God deposited in Adam is not found with anyone else, so [God's] special favor (*khuṣūṣiyya*) becomes manifest within him."[13]

The Shiʿite commentator Ṭabrisī (d. 548/1153–54) holds that God mentions two hands in order to stress the ascription of Adam's creation to Himself. He says that several authorities have interpreted it to mean "I undertook his creation by Myself" and that it is similar in meaning to the passage, "of that which Our own hands [plural] wrought" (36:71). Hence it is structurally analogous to the verse "The face of Thy Lord remains" (55:27), where "face" adds nothing to the basic meaning, which is, "Thy Lord remains." Ṭabrisī also mentions that some have interpreted the two hands to refer to power and cites three lines of poetry to show that the Arabs use the expression to mean power and strength.[14]

Maybudī suggests that the meaning is that God singled Adam out for creation with two hands to "honor" (*karāma*) him among all creatures.[15] Fakhr al-Dīn Rāzī devotes most of his discussion of this verse in his "Great Commentary" to proving that God cannot be compounded of bodily parts. He mentions the three received interpretations of "hand" as power, blessing, or emphasis, but he carefully provides arguments against each without being able to explain why the term should be dual, admitting in the end, with the expression, "And God knows best," that the passage has left him puzzled.[16]

Bayḍāwī (d. ca. 700/1300) says that the two hands emphasize God's power and the fact that He created Adam without any intermediary, such as father or mother; or it alludes to the diverse activities involved in Adam's creation.[17]

Fingers and Feet

Before continuing this discussion of God's two hands, it may be useful to mention various interpretations of God's fingers and feet. A hadith tells us that "The hearts of all the children of Adam are like a single heart between two fingers of the All-merciful. He turns it wherever He desires. O God, O Turner of hearts, turn our hearts toward obeying Thee."[18] Other hadiths make similar points, and we will return to some of their implications in chapter 10. Here I cite a single text by Samʿānī that refers to the two fingers as God's bounty and justice, that is, His mercy and wrath or His gentleness and severity:

> The Lord of Inaccessibility created the Throne and placed it upon the shoulders of the angels brought nigh. He created Paradise and gave it to [the angel] Riḍwān. He created hell and gave it to [the angel] Mālik. When He created the heart of the believer, Riḍwān said, "Give it to me, for within it is found the nectar of intimacy and the wine of holiness." Mālik said, "Give it to me, for within it is found the flames of yearning and the fire of passion." The angels brought nigh said, "Give it to us, for it is the elevated throne of love and the wide plain of kindness." Others said, "Give it to us, for it is an adorned heaven, its passing thoughts like shooting stars."
>
> The Lord of Inaccessibility dismissed them all and said, "The hearts are between two of the fingers of the All-merciful." What is meant by this is bounty and justice. Sometimes the breeze of bounty blows over the heart, and it springs up joyfully. Sometimes the burning wind of severity storms against it, and it melts. It is perplexed between the two attributes, senseless between the two states.[19]

According to Koran 10:2, those who have faith will have a *qadam ṣidq* with their Lord. The literal meaning of *qadam* is foot, while the word's root carries the sense of advancement and moving forward. The term *ṣidq* means truth, truthfulness, firmness, hardness, strength. Translators of the Koran have rendered this passage in a variety of ways: "They have a sure footing with their Lord" (Pickthall, Arberry). "There is an advance of sincerity gone before them with their Lord" (Palmer). "For them is advancement in excellence with their Lord" (Muhammad Ali). "Their endeavors shall be rewarded by their Lord" (Dawood). Some of these translations try to bring out the literal sense, while others try to bring out the implied meaning, following explanations provided by commentators. Neither the translators nor most commentators have the boldness of Ibn al-ʿArabī, who takes the literal sense of the expression seriously. According to his understanding, the verse can be translated "foot of truthfulness." Moreover, he interprets this as the foot of God, not the foot of the people who have faith. This accords with his constant attempts to "give things their rights" and therefore to ascribe priority to the Real.

This is not to suggest that Ibn al-ʿArabī understands the verse to mean that God has a physical foot, simply that the qualities summed up by the term *foot* are divine qualities. He tells us that the "foot" refers to fixity or firmness or immutability (*thubūt*). Thus it alludes to the immutable entity of the servant, which is forever fixed in God's knowledge. In *Iṣṭilāḥāt al-ṣūfiyya* ("The Technical Terms of the Sufis"), Ibn al-ʿArabī defines "foot" as follows:

> The foot is that which belongs immutably to the servant in God's knowledge of him. God says, "They have a foot of truthfulness." In other words, they have a previous solicitude of their Lord toward them in the knowledge of God.[20]

In another passage he says that the Foot of Truthfulness alludes to something that God has let His servants know about before He gives it to them. Then He gives it to them, and He is truthful in His promise.[21]

In many passages Ibn al-ʿArabī juxtaposes this "foot of truthfulness" with the foot of God mentioned in several versions of a hadith where "foot" is clearly the intended meaning—though the hadith obviously needs explanation. One of these versions reads as follows:

> People will be thrown into the Fire continuously and it will keep on saying "Are there any more?" [50:30] until the Lord of the worlds places His foot within it. Then parts of it will shrink off into other parts, and it will say, "Enough, enough!"[22]

Ibn al-ʿArabī quotes a version of the hadith that puts the name "Invincible" (*al-jabbār*) in place of "Lord of the worlds." Thereby he connects the Fire with one of the names of majesty and severity. In his view, these two feet of God—the foot of truthfulness and the foot of the Invincible—allude respectively to mercy and wrath, since they are connected to the Garden and the Fire. The Foot of Truthfulness establishes and fixes the people of paradise in their gardens, while the Foot of Invincibility establishes the people of Gehenna in their places.[23]

> God ascribed the foot to the Invincible, since this name pertains to tremendousness [*ʿaẓama*], and the Fire exists through tremendousness, while the Garden exists through generosity [*karam*].[24]

God lets down His two feet on the "Footstool" (*kursī*), which is mentioned in Koran 2:254 and is understood to lie below God's Throne (*ʿarsh*). The Koran says that "The All-merciful sat upon the Throne" (20:5). Hence, Ibn al-ʿArabī tells us, the Throne knows nothing of wrath. Mercy and wrath appear as distinct qualities only within the Footstool. The Foot of Truthfulness is pure mercy, while the Foot of Invincibility is mercy mixed with wrath.[25]

In one passage, Ibn al-ʿArabī connects the two feet to God's two handfuls and to a series of contrasting attributes. He states that the complementary activity of the two feet brings the universe into existence. Without them, there would be no differentiation. Without differentiation, there could be no creation. Here Ibn al-ʿArabī also explains why God throws one handful into the Fire, another into the Garden, and then says, "It is no concern of Mine."

> The Fire is an abode of majesty, invincibility, and awe, while the Garden is an abode of beauty, intimacy, and the gentle divine descent. These two feet are the "two handfuls." One of them is for the Fire, and "it is no concern of His." The other is for the Garden, and "it is no concern of His." He is unconcerned since both handfuls go back to mercy in the end. . . .
>
> Through the two feet God gives wealth and poverty, through them "He makes to die

and makes to live" [53:44], through them He fills with inhabitants and empties of inhabitants, through them "He creates the pair, male and female" [53:45], through them He abases and exalts, gives and withholds, harms and benefits. Were it not for these two, nothing would happen in the cosmos.

Were it not for the two feet, no one in the cosmos would associate others with God [*shirk*]. For the two feet share properties in the cosmos. Each of them has both an abode in which it exercises governing control and certain people over whom it exercises governing control as God wills. . . .

God's great solicitude toward the cosmos is that He sits upon the Throne that encompasses the cosmos through His name All-merciful. "To Him will be returned the whole affair" [11:123]. That is why He is the "most merciful of those who have mercy" [7:151]. Were it not for His mercy, those in the cosmos who have mercy would have no mercy. His mercy precedes all.

The two feet consist of the polarity of the divine names, such as the First and the Last, the Manifest and the Nonmanifest. Then the like of this becomes manifest from the feet in the cosmos: the world of the unseen and the world of the visible, majesty and beauty, nearness and distance, awe and intimacy, gathering and dispersion, curtaining and disclosure, absence and presence, contraction and expansion, this world and the next world, the Garden and the Fire.[26]

In another passage, Ibn al-ʿArabī provides a similar explanation of the meaning of God's two feet:

Through the act of these two feet, there became manifest within the cosmos "two of every kind" [11:40], by the ordainment of the Inaccessible. This goes back to the existence of Nature's two active principles, the two faculties of the Soul, the two faces of the Intellect, the two letters of the divine word "Be!"

Table 2 The Two Feet of God According to Ibn al-ʿArabī in the *Futūḥāt*

FOOT OF THE INVINCIBLE	FOOT OF TRUTHFULNESS
Fire	Garden
tremendousness	generosity
mercy mixed with wrath	pure mercy
majesty	beauty
invincibility	gentle divine descent
awe	intimacy
giving poverty	giving wealth
giving death	giving life
emptying of inhabitants	filling with inhabitants
male	female
abasing	exalting
withholding	giving
harming	benefiting
associating others with God	[*tawḥīd*]
First	Last
Nonmanifest	Manifest
unseen	visible
distance	nearness
dispersion	gathering
curtaining	disclosure
absence	presence
contraction	expansion
this world	next world
coldness	heat [Nature's active principles]
action	knowledge [Soul's faculties]
toward God	toward cosmos [Intellect's faces]
incomparability	similarity

> and the two divine attributes in "Nothing is like Him"—which is one attribute—and "He is the Hearing, the Seeing" [42:11], which is the other attribute. Those who declare His incomparability do so on the basis of "Nothing is like Him." Those who declare His similarity do so on the basis of "He is the Hearing, the Seeing." Here there is an Unseen and a visible. The Unseen is incomparability, and the visible is similarity.[27]

The correspondences that Ibn al-ʿArabī mentions here can be summarized in Table 2. Note that these distinctions are by no means absolute, since the root of all qualities is the One Reality. Hence each term of a pair is somehow found in the other term, like the white and black dots in the yin/yang symbol. The least one can say is that the one side demands the other side by its very reality, since the two terms are inseparable in conception and existence.

Ibn al-ʿArabī does not explicitly place the qualities on the two sides, so the classification offered in the table can surely be modified from other points of view. For example, from one point of view this world is manifest while the next world is nonmanifest. From another point of view—reflected in the table—this world pertains to God's name Nonmanifest, since God is not manifest here. In contrast, God is manifest in the next world, especially at the Resurrection, where, the Koran tells us, everyone will meet Him.

In several passages, Ibn al-ʿArabī connects the two feet to the division of the single divine word into two kinds of word through revelation: rulings (*ḥukm*) and reports (*khabar*). Through rulings God gives commands and prohibitions, while through reports He gives news about unseen things, such as Himself, the prophets of the past, and the next world.[28] Farghānī refers to the two feet briefly in a similar context. He says that the divine command (*amr*) is one, in accordance with the Koranic verse, "Our command is but one word, like the blink of an eye" (54:50). However, when it reaches the Footstool, the one command becomes divided into commands (*amr*) and prohibitions (*nahy*), following the two feet. Commands preserve the effects of oneness in the descent from the Footstool into this world. Prohibitions preserve the effects of oneness in the ascending return from the reality of manyness to the reality of oneness.

> The affairs of the two engendered worlds are built upon these two properties: descent and ascent. These two properties go back to those two roots: oneness and manyness. The goal of creation is achieved through these two kinds: command and prohibition. That is why these have been referred to as the "two feet" upon which the person stands.[29]

The Two Hands in the Futūḥāt al-makkiyya

We return to the Koranic verse in which God says to Iblis, "What prevented you from prostrating yourself before him whom I created with My own two hands?" (38:75). Ibn al-ʿArabī frequently discusses the significance of this verse. He agrees with those commentators who see the verse as signaling a special rank for Adam.

> From the first existent thing down to the last of the children—the animals—God did not combine both His hands in anything He created except the human being, that is, in the human being's earthly and bodily configurations. He created everything else either by divine command or with one hand.[30]

> The creation of every created thing in the cosmos is attributed to a hand of God. God says, "Of that which Our hands wrought" [36:71], employing the plural form of hand. Every creative hand in the cosmos is His hand, a hand within His kingdom and under His control. Hence all of creation belongs to God. "Verily, His are the creation and the command" [7:54]. The hadith literature has mentioned that God planted the tree of Ṭūbā with His hand and created the Garden of Eden with His hand. Here the singular form of hand is employed. God uses the dual form only in the case of the creation of Adam, who is the perfect human being.[31]

In the above passage Ibn al-ᶜArabī does not tell us what these two hands are, but he does suggest that they are special or, as he writes elsewhere, that they were attributed to Adam "to give him eminence (*tashrīf*) over everyone else."[32] He expands upon the theme of "giving eminence" in several places.

> God said, "What prevented you from prostrating yourself before him whom I created with My two hands?" Thereby He gave Adam eminence. The context shows that He "touched" [*mubāshara*] His creature with His two hands—in the manner befitting His majesty.[33] That is why he called him a "mortal" [*bashar*]. "Hand" means power, and there is no eminence in that for the one to whom it is given. Hand also means blessing, and this is the same, since God's blessings and power embrace all existent things. Hence there must be something other than these two attributes that can be understood from "two hands." This something must be a quality possessed only by Adam.[34]

In some passages, Ibn al-ᶜArabī implies that the two hands refer to two kinds of names that Adam was taught, or the fact that he was given knowledge of all things, both the divine and the created.

> The divine form belongs rightly to Adam only because He was created with the two hands. Hence all the realities of the cosmos were brought together within him. And the cosmos demands the divine names. Hence the divine names were brought together within him. That is why Adam was singled out for the knowledge of "the names, all of them" [2:31], that is, all the names that turn their attention toward the cosmos. But God did not give this knowledge to the angels, though they are the higher, nobler world. God says, "He taught Adam the names, all of them." He did not say, "some of them."[35]

> If you like, the attribute of Adam is the Divine Presence. If you like, it is the fact that he brings together all the divine names. Or, if you like, it is the words of the Prophet, "God created Adam in His own form." This is Adam's attribute. God brought together His two hands in creating him, so we know that He gave him the attribute of perfection. Hence He created him perfect and all-comprehensive, which is why he receives all the divine names. He brings together the whole cosmos in respect of its realities. He is an independent world, but everything else is a part of the cosmos.[36]

> When God wanted the perfection of this human configuration, He combined in it His two hands, gave it all the realities of the cosmos, and disclosed Himself to it in all the names. Hence it gained the divine form and the form of engendered existence.[37]

When Ibn al-ᶜArabī considers the specific significance of the two hands, he sometimes maintains that they refer to incomparability and similarity, since these two perspectives define the dual nature of the human relationship to God. In other passages, he looks at the divine attributes that are connected with incomparability and similarity and cites them as the significance of the hands. In other words, he pays attention to the individual attributes that manifest these two fundamental dimensions of the human/divine relationship, attributes such as majesty and distance on one side and beauty and nearness on the other.

> When the servants of the Real witness Him, they see Him as possessing two relationships, that of incomparability and that of descent to the imagination through a kind of similarity.
>
> The relationship of incomparability is His self-disclosure in "Nothing is like Him" [42:11]. The other relationship is His self-disclosure in the Prophet's words, "Worship God as if you see Him." . . . It is also mentioned in God's words, "Wherever you turn, there is the Face of God" [2:115]—"there" being an adverb of place, while the "Face" of God is His Essence and Reality. This other relationship is also mentioned in all the hadiths and verses that have come with words, along with their meanings, that apply to created things. . . .
>
> It has been reported concerning the human configuration that "God created Adam in His own form." In the Koran God says that He created him "with His two hands," since He wanted to point out his eminence. This is shown by the context, since He tells Iblis about it after Iblis claims eminence over

Adam through his own configuration. God says, "What prevented you from prostrating yourself before him whom I created with My two hands?" Here "hands" cannot mean power, because of the dual. Nor can it mean that one hand is blessing and the other is power, since that is true of every existent thing. There would be no eminence for Adam according to that interpretation, and this would contradict the fact that His words point out Adam's eminence.

Hence it was these two relationships—the relationship of incomparability and that of similarity—that turned their attentiveness toward the creation of the human being.[38]

Ibn al-ʿArabī sometimes comments on the two "handfuls" to which reference is made in the Koranic verse cited earlier: "The earth altogether shall be His handful on the Day of Resurrection, and the heavens shall be rolled up in His right hand" (39:67). It is helpful to know that the verbal form of the same word "handful" means to grasp, while the gerund *qabḍ* becomes a technical term in Sufi psychology that we have already met, a term that is normally translated as "contraction." As was pointed out in the previous chapter, the opposite of contraction is expansion (*basṭ*). Contraction is connected to awe and to the human relationship with the names of majesty. In contrast, expansion is connected to intimacy and to the human relationship with the names of beauty. The two words are employed together as verbs in a single Koranic verse: "God contracts, and He expands, and to Him you shall be returned" (2:245). Partly on the basis of this verse, God is called by the two divine names Expander and Contractor. The first is a name of beauty, the second a name of majesty. All this is not without relevance to the type of relationship that is envisaged if the earth is "God's handful." The implication of the word's literal meaning is that the earth is contracted and constrained. Hence it stands in awe of the names of majesty. But the heavens, the same verse tells us, are "rolled up in His right hand," and by definition the right hand is blessed. Hence, if the right handful is to be the opposite of the left handful, it must be associated with expansion and the names of beauty, even if it is a "handful." So it should not be surprising that Ibn al-ʿArabī calls the two handfuls the "two worlds, that is, the world of felicity and the world of wretchedness."[39] Felicity is the attribute of the people of paradise, while wretchedness is the quality of the people of hell. This conclusion follows directly upon the hadith of the two handfuls and God's lack of concern for them. As Ibn al-ʿArabī remarks,

God brought the cosmos out as two handfuls. He brought two waystations into existence for them. He said, "These are for the Garden, and it is no concern of Mine. These are for the Fire, and it is no concern of Mine." No protester protested to Him at this point, since nothing existed beside Him. So everything is under the control of His names. One handful is under the names of His affliction [*balāʾ*], and the other handful is under the names of His bounties [*ālāʾ*].[40]

The cosmos comes into existence through the mixture of the two handfuls. Without yin and yang, nothing could exist.

He brought the cosmos into existence to make manifest the authority of His names. For power without an object of power, generosity without bestowal, a provider without someone provided for, a helper without anyone helped, and a compassionate one without any object of compassion would be realities devoid of any effects.

In this world God mixed the cosmos. He mixed the two handfuls into dough, then He separated individuals out from it. Hence this entered into that, and that entered into this—from each handful into its sister—and the situation became confused. It is here that those who have knowledge become ranked in degrees by extracting the loathsome from the good and the good from the loathsome. The ultimate end is deliverance from the mixture and the distinguishing of the two handfuls. Then the one handful will be alone in its world, and the other in its world. Thus God says, "God will distinguish the loathsome from the good, and place the loathsome one upon another, and so heap them up altogether, and put them in Gehenna" [8:37].[41]

The Fuṣūṣ al-ḥikam

In the first chapter of his most famous and influential work, the *Fuṣūṣ al-ḥikam*, Ibn al-ʿArabī offers a slightly different interpretation of the meaning of the "two hands." He points to the polar attributes of God, then says that God created the perfect human being as comprising both sets of attributes.

> God described Himself as manifest and nonmanifest. He brought the cosmos into existence as a world of the unseen and a world of the visible, so that we might perceive the nonmanifest through our unseen dimension and the manifest through our visible dimension. He described Himself through good pleasure and wrath, so He brought the cosmos into existence possessing fear and hope: We fear His wrath and we hope for His good pleasure.[42] He described Himself as beautiful and possessing majesty, so He brought us into existence having awe and intimacy.[43] And so it goes with everything which is attributed to Him and by which He is named.
>
> God called these two attributes the "two hands" through which He turned toward creating the perfect human being, who brings together the realities and individuals of the cosmos. Hence the cosmos is visible, while the vicegerent is unseen. . . .
>
> God brought His two hands together in Adam only to give him eminence. That is why He said to Iblis, "What prevented you from prostrating yourself before him whom I created with My two hands?" This refers only to the fact that he brings together the two forms, the form of the cosmos and the form of the Real, and these are the two hands of the Real. But Iblis was a part of the cosmos. He had not actualized this all-comprehensiveness. That is why Adam was a vicegerent, for if he had not had the form of both Him who made him vicegerent and that over which he had been given charge, he would not have been a vicegerent.[44]

The contrasting sets of divine attributes mentioned in this passage are shown in Table 3. Note that in the early part of this passage Ibn al-ʿArabī mentions explicitly three sets of names—(1) Nonmanifest and Manifest, (2) the Possessor of Wrath and of Good-pleasure (*riḍā*), and (3) the Majestic and the Beautiful—as displaying the properties of the two hands. In the later part of the passage he gives a rather different interpretation of the two hands by calling them (4) the form of the cosmos and the form of the Real. In the first three cases, the hands refer to polar attributes possessed by God Himself. In the last case, they refer to God and everything other than God. In short, Ibn al-ʿArabī envisages four sets of relationships. These can be explained as follows:

In the first three cases, the two hands refer to both a vertical and a horizontal relationship within God. With a little meditation these two relationships are reducible to the basic polarity, that of incomparability and similarity. The two names Nonmanifest and Manifest clearly correspond to incom-

Table 3 The Two Hands According to the *Fuṣūṣ*

QUALITIES OF GOD	
manifest	nonmanifest
good pleasure	wrath
beauty	majesty
form of cosmos	form of Real
QUALITIES OF THE COSMOS AND THE HUMAN BEING	
visible	unseen
hope	fear
intimacy	awe

parability and similarity, since it is precisely the fact that God is absolutely nonmanifest that prevents us from having knowledge of Him and comparing Him to anything else. And it is His attribute of being Manifest—"Wherever you turn, there is the Face of God" (2:115)—that allows us to declare Him similar to all things. Here we have a vertical axis within God, stretching from the names inasmuch as they manifest Him to the Essence inasmuch as It is eternally Unknown.

The next two sets of divine attributes can be read as indicating either vertical or horizontal relationships. What is more, the vertical relationship is reversible, depending on the point of view. Both sets refer to the two categories of complementary names that we have already discussed: severity and gentleness, or majesty and beauty. As a horizontal relationship, the two names indicate that God's yin and yang attributes work harmoniously together. He creates the universe with the two hands of majesty and beauty, thereby keeping it perfectly in balance. As a vertical relationship, the two can be seen first as representing the severity of distance and incomparability as opposed to the gentleness of nearness and similarity. In this sense, the yang names stand beyond the yin names, and this is the "Confucian" perspective alluded to in the introduction. However, if we apply the principle, "My mercy precedes My wrath," we have the "Taoist" perspective, which places the mercy of yin as the attribute of God in Himself, while the wrath of yang comes into play only in relationship to some of the creatures of the universe.

The fourth pairing—in which the two hands are referred to as the forms of God and the cosmos—sets up a yang/yin distinction between the Absolute and the relative, that which is truly Real and that which is metaphorically real. Neither is separable from the other, since the cosmos is the "thrall" of God and the vassal of the Lord. The cosmos is the manifestation of God's names and attributes. Both Real and cosmos are God's hands, since one is the Hidden Treasure, and the other is the manifestation of the Hidden Treasure. In the last analysis, one hand is God as Nonmanifest and the other is God as Manifest. Nothing is conceivable without both. The divine Unity demands the divine polarity. God is the One/Many (*al-wāḥid al-kathīr*).

All these divine relationships can then be seen as having their analogues on the human level. In any case, it is not my purpose to impose my own analysis on the texts. Rather, I want to illustrate how the Muslim thinkers themselves spoke of yin and yang complementarity employing their own terminology, such as receptive (*qābil*) and active (*fāʿil*), and how they themselves were perfectly aware of the way in which the relationships change with a shift of perspective. Hence I turn to some of the major authors who followed in Ibn al-ʿArabī's footsteps. The first three wrote the most influential of the more than one hundred commentaries on the *Fuṣūṣ al-ḥikam*.

Muʾayyid al-Dīn Jandī

Jandī (d. ca. 700/1300) was an important disciple of Ṣadr al-Dīn Qūnawī, who was Ibn al-ʿArabī's stepson and the most influential of his immediate followers. Qūnawī did not write a full commentary on the *Fuṣūṣ al-ḥikam*, but his relatively short treatise, *al-Fukūk* or *Fakk al-khutūm*, explains the meaning of the chapter headings of the *Fuṣūṣ* and influenced practically all the commentators. Jandī wrote the earliest detailed commentary on the *Fusūs*, and his commentary was to surpass even his master's *al-Fukūk* in influence. In its introduction, Jandī tells us how he began studying the text with Qūnawī. While Qūnawī was in the process of explaining the preface, Jandī was overcome by a spiritual state through which he came to know the meaning of the book from beginning to end. He told Qūnawī about this, who replied that he had experienced the same thing when Ibn al-ʿArabī had begun explaining the work to him.[45] By telling us this anecdote Jandī no doubt wants us to understand that his explanation of the *Fuṣūṣ* is connected to the work's spiritual origin and is not simply a transmission of Qūnawī's teachings.

Table 4 The Two Hands According to Jandī

Essence	First Entification
nonentification	entification
nondelimitation	delimitation
oneness	manyness
activity	receptivity
firstness	lastness
nonmanifestation	manifestation
wrath	good pleasure
majesty	beauty
severity	gentleness
Unseen	[visible]
[infinity]	finitude
contraction	expansion
withholding	giving
putting down	lifting up
fear	hope
contraction	expansion
awe	intimacy
subtlety	density
spirit	nature
attributes of God	attributes of the cosmos

Jandī discusses the two hands of God while commenting upon the passage from the *Fuṣūṣ al-ḥikam* quoted above. Characteristically, he develops Ibn al-ʿArabī's themes in great detail. Later commentators who borrow material from him usually abbreviate his words, and we will refrain from translating everything he has to say about this passage.

Jandī begins his discussion by going back to the deepest roots of polarity in the Real. The Divine Essence, he points out, is utterly "nondelimited" (*muṭlaq*). It is so free of limitations that we cannot limit It by saying that It is free of limitations. In other words, God's utter freedom demands that He be able to assume all constraints, while not being delimited or defined by them. This is a theme of Chapter 3 of the *Fuṣūṣ al-ḥikam*, which begins with the words, "In the view of the People of the Realities, declaring the incomparability of the Divine Side is identical with definition and delimitation."[46] If we say that God is incomparable in any restricted sense, we are claiming that He cannot be similar. This is to remain blind to one-half of the divine message. "In the same way," says Ibn al-ʿArabī, "he who declares Him similar without declaring Him incomparable has delimited and defined Him and has not known Him."[47]

Qūnawī and his followers commonly refer to God's utter nondelimitation as His "nonentification" (*lā taʿayyun*). The term indicates that He cannot be identified with any defined and determined entity.[48] As we have seen on more than one occasion, God in Himself is "no thing" (*lā shayʾ*) or no entity, since His Reality transcends and embraces all things, all entities. Hence, His Essence is "nonentified." But in respect of the fact that the Real can be called "God" in contrast to the cosmos, He is nondelimited in a sense that is opposed to delimitation. He is one specific, nondelimited reality, while the cosmos is a completely different, delimited reality. From this point of view, God is known as the First Entification or the Breath of the All-merciful. At issue is but a single Being, but the two points of view in respect of which Being can be considered allow us to distinguish between the Divine Essence (Nonentification) and God (the First Entification), or between the unnameable and nameable Taos. This is the root of all duality and polarity, as Jandī explains. In what follows, the text of the *Fuṣūṣ al-ḥikam* is printed in italics:

> *God described Himself as manifest and nonmanifest. . . . God called these two attributes the "two hands" through which He turned toward creating the perfect human being,* since he brings together the realities and individuals of the cosmos. . . .
>
> The essential nondelimitation worthy of the Essence does not stand opposed to delimitation and definition. No, this nondelimitation means that He is not delimited by the delimitation that is a nondelimitation set up in opposition to delimitation. Hence the Essence is nondelimited in respect of both delimitation and nondelimitation. For in Itself, the Essence combines both of these, while not being delimited by either. On the contrary, It is nondelimited in respect to both points of view. In this station there is no tongue, no property, no name, no attribute—only sheer stupefaction and utter muteness.
>
> Through the First Entification . . . there comes to be entified for the Nondelimited Entity an entification and a nonentification, a nondelimitation and a delimitation, a oneness and a manyness, an activity and a receptivity. Hence, through the First Entification, the essential relationships become entified. These are firstness, lastness, nonmanifestation, and manifestation.

Jandī makes here the point that was stressed at the beginning of chapter 2: In Himself, God is incomparable. But Jandī adds a subtle nuance to which I did not refer: This initial divine incomparability is so utterly absolute that it makes the Essence incomparable with incomparability. Hence nothing prevents Him from being similar. Then, inasmuch as we know God, we can perceive Him as both incomparable and similar. Note in the above the correlations Jandī draws between attributes: activity or yang corresponds to nonentification, nondelimitation, and oneness. Receptivity or yin corresponds to entification, delimitation, and manyness.

In continuing his explanation, Jandī clearly differentiates between the two basic levels of considering the Real: (1) the Entity or Essence Itself, which is incomparable with both incomparability and similarity; and (2) the First Entification, which embraces the two attributes of (a) incomparability, and (b) similarity. In the process of saying this, Jandī correlates yang and yin with the names of majesty and beauty.

> In respect of the Entity, He cannot be considered in terms of entification or nonentification. He is neither first, nor last, nor nonmanifest, nor manifest. To ascribe these relationships to Him is not more worthy and fitting than not to ascribe them.
>
> In respect of His nondelimitation, God is Nonmanifest. The [fact that He is] Nonmanifest means that through the inaccessibility of His Unseen, He cannot be encompassed. He does not enter into the finite, nor does He have a beginning. Hence He possesses majesty.
>
> In respect of His entification, He is manifest and beautiful, since all things go back to Him and support themselves through Him, for He is the origin of all entifications. . . .
>
> Hence duality becomes manifest through the First Entification in the Entity who is One through true oneness. In respect of the Presence of His Majesty, He displays severity to the entities of the "others." He is wrathful against them through the jealousy of Unity. However, in respect of the entification, He gives His good pleasure to every receptive attribute that brings about entification and every entified thing that receives the attribute. This is a good pleasure singled out specifically for the specific characteristics of the things.

As pointed out in the previous chapter, jealousy (*ghayra*) is a quality that appears in relationship to the "other" (*ghayr*).[49] The divine majesty and wrath look at the others and annihilate them, since God's incomparability does not allow anything else to exist. There is none real but the Real. Everything else is unreal, evanescent, nonexistent. However, the divine beauty, mercy, and good pleasure look at the other and affirm it. God is similar to all things and present in them. Hence He bestows upon them a certain reality. His love and concern preserve and protect the creatures. The interplay between these two attributes, these two hands of God, keeps the universe in constant movement and transmutation. At every instant wrath destroys the others, and at every instant mercy recreates them.

These two hands possess contraction and expansion, giving and withholding, lifting up and putting down. In keeping with them He brought us into existence possessing fear and hope, expansion and contraction, awe and intimacy. We have awe of His majesty and feel intimate with His beauty. *We fear His wrath and hope for His good pleasure*. Hence the properties of the duality mentioned in the two hands became manifest within us, just as the Prophet said in the hadith, "He created Adam with His two hands." . . .

For the same reason, "God kneaded the clay of Adam with His two hands for forty days." In other words, our Lord—blessed and exalted is He—disclosed Himself in His own form. In keeping with that form, He created Adam and kneaded his clay with His two blessed hands. Then, through the blessing of His universal, all-comprehensive, divine attentiveness, the clay fermented and became mature through the mystery of the unity of the essential, divine comprehension of the two hands. Finally His blessed form appeared and became manifest in Adam's clay in the "best stature" [95:4] and the most perfect balance and design. Hence all the realities—both the majestic and severe and the beautiful and gentle—became manifest within him, and through them he became perfect. Within him is the mystery of nondelimitation and delimitation, entification and nonentification. Hence he is the most perfect, the most comprehensive, and the most complete engendered thing. As locus of manifestation, he is the most excellent, the widest, and the most inclusive. . . .

God brought His two hands together in Adam . . . [otherwise] *he would not have been a vicegerent*. This is because perfection lies in the unity of comprehending all things. In addition, all perfections flow forth from the unity of comprehending these two blessed divine hands. Hence the perfections that rise up from the two hands must be brought together in Adam while being multiplied. For the all-comprehensive unitary condition results in the fact that every reality of the two hands becomes manifest in him who comprehends all things through the condition of all-comprehensiveness.

This explains why Iblis, who was part of the cosmos, was called to task for failing to prostrate himself before Adam: Incumbent upon every one of the spiritual powers and the natural powers, whether altogether or singly, are yielding, submission, obedience, and entrance under the command of him who possesses the all-comprehensiveness of the two hands. For the two hands grasp the world of subtle spirits and the world of dense nature, and Iblis dwells in one of these worlds.

Iblis's reality contradicts the reality of Adam both in reality and nature, since the reality of Adam is the manifest form of the unity of the all-comprehensiveness of everything brought together by God and the engendered world. God brought His two hands together in Adam only because humanness is a reality requiring equilibrium [*iʿtidāl*] and the perfection of bringing together both entification and nondelimitation, both manyness and oneness, and the lack of constriction by any particular entification. In contrast the reality of Iblis is the form of disequilibrium through entification and being veiled. Iblis becomes defined by the particular ego [*al-anāniyyat al-juzʾiyya*]. He is delimited by seeking exaltation, claiming eminence, manifesting self, and rising up against the reality of the One Entity. For entification conceals [*kufr*] the One Entity, veils It, and rises up against It. This reality requires a fiery separation that rises up against the other elements.

God in Himself is "no thing," since each thing has delimited and defined characteristics that make it into a thing as distinct from other things. But God is the all-comprehensive reality, the coincidence of opposites, in whom all characteristics are found. Human beings are created in God's form, so they bring together all the divine attributes. Each of them is the "all-comprehensive engendered thing." Human perfection involves actualizing all these attributes such that none dominates over any other. Ibn al-ʿArabī refers to this perfection as the "station of no station."[50] Each "station" is delimited and defined by certain attributes, but the perfect human being is free of all delimitations and definitions. This is the perfection of Adam, created with both hands. He thereby combines the perfection of nonentification, or not being any thing to the exclusion of any other thing, and entification, or possessing all attributes. In contrast, Iblis represents delimitation, definition, constriction, entification. He is "some thing," and he wants to keep that thingness as his own. "I am better than he" (38:76), says Iblis, thereby claiming eminence and specificity for himself. Hence he proves that he is an "unbeliever" (*kāfir*), that is—in the literal sense of the term—"one who conceals." What is he concealing but the nondelimitation and nonentification of the Real?[51] But the perfect human being is utter servant, completely surrendered to the Real. He makes no claims, since he has nothing of his own. And having nothing of his own is precisely his perfection, for it allows him to be "no thing," just as God is no thing. Therefore he stands in the station of no station. All this Jandī finds implied already in the fact that God created Iblis from fire.

> Fire is the form of elemental disequilibrium through entification. The entification rises up against that which is entified within it. It oversteps its bounds and conceals [*kufr*] it. In other words, it covers [*sitr*] it. But this entification has no fixity, since the light of the Entity that is entified within the veil-substance of each entification tears it away and consumes it in fire.
>
> It is appropriate for the entification to be cursed, driven away, and negated from the face of the Entity entified within it. For through and in itself the entification is a veil in one respect over Him who is entified, even if it points to Him in another respect. When people witness the fact that something else lies beyond the entification and that the entification derives from that something, they witness the Reality through the veil. But those who witness nothing but the veil-substance of the entification become veiled by it.
>
> The entification is a veil over itself. Hence it never sees the Entity that becomes veiled by it, just as the image of the viewer imprinted within the inward depths of a mirror does not become manifest upon the surface of a mirror. First the reality of the veil must be cursed away from the face of him who is veiled. That is why every entification calls for an ego through which it is veiled from others, from itself, and from the entity of the whole through which the whole subsists. . . . We alluded to this mystery in our poem,
>
> Let not the similar shapes veil you
> from Him who takes shape within them,
> while they are coverings.
> Be aware of Him when He appears in any locus
> of His manifestation, for in the actual situation
> are found display and concealment—
> Like the ocean: An ocean from all eternity,
> while the things found in time
> are waves and streams.
>
> That which is veiled through the entification seeks to be self-ruling and alone through its particular entification, since it has no entrance into universality. The divine all-comprehensive unity and the human all-comprehensive unity contradict it and negate it. This is the meaning of the fact that the Divine Presence and the human presence curse Iblis: the particularity of entification acts as a veil over the universal, fundamental Entity. But entification takes place. And this can happen only in respect of domination by one of the outwardly manifest parts of Him who is entified, or that which brings about entification. So understand!
>
> Since God brought the two forms together in Adam—the form of the Real and the form of creation—he possessed the level of the "comprehension of all-comprehensiveness" [*jamʿ al-jamʿ*]. This level corresponds to the form of God, since the Divine Reality must be the unity comprehending all necessary realities. The necessary realities demand by their very essences the comprehension of all engendered realities. It was through this all-comprehensiveness that Adam rightly possessed the vicegerency.[52]

ʿAbd al-Razzāq Kāshānī

Kāshānī (d. 736/1335) is one of the most famous members of the school of Ibn al-ʿArabī. Among his well-known works is an esoteric commentary on the Koran, from which we will have occasion to quote in later chapters. His commentary on the *Fuṣūṣ al-ḥikam* was one of the most influential. It reflects the teachings of Qūnawī and Jandī. In fact, he studied the *Fuṣūṣ* with the latter. In the following, I quote a few particularly relevant sections of his commentary on the passage discussed above:

> Having shown us the signs of His names and attributes within the cosmos, the Real placed within us the means to recognize these signs. He made us share with the cosmos in His attributes, so that we might recognize what is within it through what is within ourselves. However, it was not possible for the cosmos to receive all the Real's names and attributes. For the cosmos is distinguished from the Real by the fact that the Real is inherently Necessary while the cosmos is a possible thing. Real and cosmos are inseparable from what their own realities demand: independence and poverty. Hence the cosmos receives only those effects of the names that are appropriate to its poverty and imperfection. But through all-comprehensive unity, God combined both the Real and the cosmos within us. That is why the Shaykh divides the names and attributes into two kinds. The first kind is shared by all three: the Real, us, and the cosmos. Hence the Shaykh says, *God described Himself as manifest and nonmanifest, so He brought the cosmos into existence as a world of the unseen and a world of the visible, that we might perceive the nonmanifest through our unseen dimension and the manifest through our visible dimension.* Both the cosmos and the Real are described by the two [attributes of manifestation and nonmanifestation]. The Shaykh distinguishes between the two descriptions by making the cosmos two worlds, an unseen world and a visible world, since the cosmos does not possess all-comprehensive unity. However, he does not distinguish between the description of the Real and our description, since he attributes the unseen and the visible to us in respect of our specific all-comprehensive unity. Hence we share in God's meaning and form, but the cosmos does not.

Table 5 The Two Hands According to Kāshānī

POLAR ATTRIBUTES OF GOD	
nonmanifestation	manifestation
wrath	good pleasure
majesty	beauty
taking hand	giving hand
QUALITIES POSSESSED BY COSMOS AND HUMAN BEINGS VIS-À-VIS GOD	
God	*Cosmos and humans*
activity	receptivity
good pleasure	hope
wrath	fear
beauty	intimacy
majesty	awe
giving hand	taking hand
taking hand	giving hand
QUALITIES OF GOD VIS-À-VIS VICEGERENT	
nonmanifestation	manifestation
Giver of vicegerency	vicegerent
Lord	servant
QUALITIES OF VICEGERENT VIS-À-VIS THE COSMOS	
all-comprehensiveness	[dispersion]
lord	servant
spirit	form
unseen	visible

As for the second kind of names and attributes, here the Shaykh makes us equal to the cosmos. In contradistinction to every active attribute belonging solely to God, he specifies an attribute receptive toward activity shared by us and the cosmos. Hence he says, *He described Himself through good pleasure and wrath, and He brought the cosmos into existence possessing fear and hope*. Fear is a reception of activity and effects from the effectivity of wrath; through it we know His wrath. So also is hope in contrast to good pleasure. That is why the Shaykh says, *We fear His wrath and hope for His good pleasure*.

Then he says, *He described Himself as beautiful and possessing majesty, so He brought us into existence having awe and intimacy*. This is because awe is a reception of activity from the attribute of majesty. Through it we know His tremendousness and His majesty. In the same way, intimacy is the counterpart of beauty. Hence He made us accord with His attributes in one respect and with the attributes of the cosmos in another respect. . . .

God called these two attributes, that is, the polar qualities that He possesses, such as manifestation and nonmanifestation, good pleasure and wrath, beauty and majesty, *the "two hands" through which He turned toward creating the perfect human being*.

His words, *since he brings together the realities and individuals of the cosmos*, let us know that while the perfect human being is equal to the cosmos in his realities and individuals, he is singled out from the cosmos through the unitary all-comprehensiveness. By means of this all-comprehensiveness the individuals of the cosmos are unified. In the same way, the four elements are unified through composition, the qualities of the elements [i.e., wetness, dryness, heat, and cold] are unified through the [human] constitution, and the [human] form is unified through those powers of the cosmos known as "proportioning." Hence this form has the preparedness to receive the spirit that was blown into it.[53]

Through all this the perfect human being becomes worthy of the vicegerency. For the vicegerent must have affinities with Him who makes him a vicegerent in order that he may know His attributes and names and convey His command to the one in his charge. He must have affinities with the one in his charge in order that he may know it through its attributes and names and put the command into effect as is worthy of its individuals. Hence the vicegerent has affinities with the Real through his spirit and his all-comprehensive unity, while he shares with the cosmos through his form, the parts of his existence, and his individuals.

Therefore the vicegerent is the servant of God, the lord of the cosmos. His form, which derives from the cosmos, is visible, while his spirit is unseen. His lordship derives from his unseen dimension. That is why the Shaykh says,

Hence the cosmos is visible, while the vicegerent is unseen, since, in respect of his form, he is included in the cosmos, but in respect of his meaning, he is the vicegerent of God, the lord and sultan of the world. . . .

God brought His two hands together in Adam only to give him eminence. That is why He said to Iblis, "What prevented you from prostrating yourself before him whom I created with my two hands?" The Shaykh has mentioned that the two polar attributes are the two hands of God through which He turned toward the creation of the perfect human being. He has also given examples of polar attributes of God that share in the fact that they exercise effects, so they are polar giving hands. He has alluded to the fact that the attributes of the cosmos are polar, sharing in the fact that they receive activity. Hence they are hands that receive and take. He has made us equal in these attributes with the cosmos. Hence he now wants to establish that we have also been given eminence, since God has brought together [in us] the two hands that are polar in giving and in receiving. For God has two polar hands that give, like good pleasure and wrath, as well as polar hands that take and receive. Look at His words, "Do they not know that God is He who receives repentance from His servants and takes the free will offerings?" [9:104].

That is why He rebuked and blamed Iblis for failing to prostrate himself before Adam. For Iblis saw in Adam those attributes of the cosmos, such as fear and hope, that receive activity, but he did not see the active attributes. Moreover, Iblis did not recognize that the receptive attributes also belong to God, since they pertain to the preparedness that is effused through the Most Holy Effusion.

The Most Holy Effusion (*al-fayḍ al-aqdas*) is the state of the immutable entities as they are known by God "before" they enter into the created world. The Holy Effusion (*al-fayḍ al-muqaddas*) is then the self-disclosure of God in the cosmos whereby

He makes the immutable entities manifest. In terms more familiar to Islamic theology, one could say that the Most Holy Effusion refers to the things as they are known by God for all eternity, while the Holy Effusion refers to their actual appearance in the cosmos as creatures.[54] Hence Kāshānī is saying that the Most Holy Effusion, which is God's knowledge of the cosmos, is a receptive reality and the source of all receptivity in the cosmos. We have already met this idea in Farghānī's discussion of the Oneness of Being and the Manyness of Knowledge.

> *This refers only to the fact that he brings together the two forms, the form of the cosmos and the form of the Real, and these are the two hands of the Real.* In other words, just as the polar, giving attributes are the two hands of the Real, so also the giving hands and the receiving and taking hands are also two polar hands of God. If Adam did not possess those receptive attributes, he would not have known God through all His names, nor would he have worshiped Him by them.[55]

Dāwūd Qayṣarī

Sharaf al-Dīn Dāwūd Qayṣarī (d. 751/1350) studied the *Fuṣūṣ al-ḥikam* with Kāshānī. Thus his commentary represents the third in a direct line going back to Ibn al-ʿArabī through Kāshānī, Jandī, and Qūnawī. In explaining the above passage, Qayṣarī brings out rather clearly the different types of relationship implied in Ibn al-ʿArabī's discussion:

> *He brought the cosmos into existence possessing fear and hope: We fear His wrath and hope for His good pleasure.* Here the Shaykh mentions the concomitants of good pleasure and wrath, which are fear and hope. He did not say, "He brought us into existence possessing good pleasure and wrath," even though we are described by these two attributes. Thereby he wanted to stress his first point, which is to explain the interrelationship between the Real and the cosmos, since the two kinds of attributes—the active and the receptive toward activity—demand each other.

Here God is active, while the servants are receptive. But activity cannot exist with-

Table 6 The Two Hands According to Qayṣarī

CONTRARY ATTRIBUTES OF GOD	
beauty	majesty
gentleness	severity
mercy	inaccessibility, greatness, hiddenness
QUALITIES PERTAINING TO REAL VIS-À-VIS COSMOS	
active	receptive
good pleasure	hope
wrath	fear
beauty	intimacy
majesty	awe
CONTRARY ATTRIBUTES OF HUMAN ALL-COMPREHENSIVENESS	
right hand	left hand
form of the Real	form of the cosmos
activity	receptivity
making manifest	becoming a locus of manifestation
Lordship	servanthood

out receptivity, and vice versa. Through hope and fear we react to the divine activity, but at the same time, through our reaction the divine attributes of good pleasure and wrath gain their reality.

> *He described Himself as beautiful and possessing majesty, so He brought us into existence having awe and intimacy. And so it goes with everything which is attributed to Him and by which He is named.* By "beautiful" are meant the attributes of beauty, which are those attributes connected to gentleness and mercy. By "majesty" are meant those attributes connected to severity, inaccessibility, greatness, and hiddenness. *He brought us into existence having awe and intimacy.* This is an example which brings together both points he is making, the explanation of interrelationship [between the Real and the cosmos] and the fact that the human being was created upon His form. This can be explained as follows:
>
> "Awe" can be considered an active attribute. Thus it is said, "The sultan is awe-inspiring." In other words, people sense his tremendousness in their hearts. Awe can also be considered a receptive attribute. Thus it is said, "Awe of the sultan"—alarm and wonder—"fell into my heart." The same thing can be said concerning intimacy in respect to him who is greater in rank than you and him who is lower in rank. The first demands the reception of activity, while the second demands activity, since intimacy is the removal of alarm and awe. In the first case, the possessor of the higher level removes the alarm from you, and, in the second, you remove it from someone else. Awe derives from majesty and intimacy derives from beauty. . . .
>
> *God called these two attributes*—majesty and beauty—*the "two hands"* metaphorically, since through them the divine acts are completed and Lordship becomes manifest. In the same way, through his hands a human being is able to give and receive, and hence his acts are completed through his hands. *Through which He turned toward creating the perfect human being, since he brings together the realities and individuals of the cosmos. . . .* The human being brings together the cosmos's "realities," which are the loci of manifestation for all the attributes of beauty and majesty. These realities are the immutable entities of the cosmos. As for the "individuals," the Shaykh means the existent things found in the external realm. It is as if he is saying that since the human being brings together all the immutable entities through his own immutable entity and all the externally existent things through his own external entity, he possesses all-comprehensive unity, both in knowledge and external entity. . . .
>
> *Hence the cosmos is visible, while the vicegerent is unseen.* In other words, the cosmos is manifest while the vicegerent is nonmanifest. He applied the term *manifest* to the cosmos, even though some of it—like the world of disengaged spirits—is unseen, only figuratively, as one applies the name of the part to the whole. What he means by "cosmos" here is the spiritual and corporeal macrocosm, since it is the form of the human reality, a reality that is unseen. And since the perfect human being is a locus of manifestation for the perfections of this reality, a vicegerent, and a governor of the cosmos, he made him "unseen" in respect of his reality, which always remains in the unseen, even if the vicegerent exists in the external realm.

Here Qayṣarī points to basic Islamic teachings on the role of the vicegerent in the cosmos. In short, the integrated and realized microcosm plays an active role in relationship to the macrocosm, which is always dispersed and differentiated. The perfect human being is the "bridge" between God and the world, whereby God governs and controls the cosmos. But all this, as we saw in the previous chapter, depends upon "servanthood." Human beings can represent God in the world and govern the macrocosm on His behalf only if they have first submitted to His will and follow His command at every level of their own multi-leveled selves. Such perfected human beings have achieved an inner oneness with God. Their spiritual dimensions have been integrated into the "Divine Breath" from which they arose, their souls are willing instruments for the spirits, while their bodies are corpses in the hand of the soul (to use the Sufi analogy for the proper relationship between a disciple and his spiritual master). The "reality" of such a person is his or her innermost dimension, somehow not different from God. In virtue of that reality, the perfect human being governs everything in the macrocosm.

In continuing his interpretation of this

passage, Qayṣarī explains Ibn al-ʿArabī's understanding of the "two hands" in terms of active and receptive names of God. The "presence of a thing" as used in this passage means realm or domain and, more specifically, everything in existence defined by the accompanying attribute. Thus the "Presence of Lordship" designates the realm of God's controlling activity inasmuch as He is Lord of all worlds, while the "Presence of Servanthood" designates the cosmos inasmuch as it is controlled by God. As the Koran says, "There is nothing in the heavens and the earth which does not come to the All-merciful as a servant" (19:93).[56] The point that is especially significant here is that the relationship between God and the cosmos is described in terms of Lord/servant, which is seen as equivalent, as indicated above, with active/receptive or yang/yin.

God said to Iblis, "What prevented you from prostrating yourself before him whom I created with My two hands?" This refers only to the fact that he brings together the two forms, the form of the cosmos, the engendered realities, *and the form of the Real*, the divine realities. *And these are the two hands of the Real.* He made the cosmos the "hand of the Real" only because it is the locus of manifestation for His names and attributes. Thus he called the attributes of beauty and majesty "the two hands," as already mentioned. But here he calls the two forms "the two hands" in order to remind us that there is no difference between the two forms in reality, except in respect of [the activity of] making manifest and [the receptivity of] becoming a locus of manifestation. Moreover, since the active and receptive are in reality a single thing that becomes manifest sometimes in the form of activity and sometimes in the form of receptivity, He called them "two hands." The right hand represents the active forms connected to the Presence of Lordship. The left hand represents the receptive forms connected to the Presence of Servanthood. . . .

But Iblis was a part of the cosmos. He had not actualized this all-comprehensiveness, since he is the locus of manifestation for the name "Misguider." This name is one of the names included in the name Allah, for which Adam is the locus of manifestation. Hence Iblis did not comprehend all the names and realities.[57]

Ṣadr al-Dīn Qūnawī

Many other explanations of this passage could be quoted from commentators on the *Fuṣūṣ al-hikam*. But the above passages are sufficient to illustrate that yin/yang thinking comes naturally to the Muslim authorities who speak for intellectual Sufism. Instead of continuing with this survey of *Fuṣūṣ* commentaries, I turn to two extremely influential authors of Ibn al-ʿArabī's school who did not write commentaries on the *Fuṣūṣ*.[58]

Qūnawī explains the meaning of God's two hands in a number of works. In *Sharḥ al-ḥadīth*, he discusses the verse that tells us that the whole earth will be God's handful and the heavens will be held in His right hand. The earth is in God's left hand because "the world of the elements and everything that becomes compounded and is born from them" pertains to the left side. The Companions of the Left will be grasped by this hand in the next world, since they will not have ascended to the spiritual domain.

What dominates over the world of the elements—which is held in the mentioned handful—is opacity, darkness, and density. Therefore God attributed the wretched to it. For the wretched are dominated by the specific characteristics of composition and density. The Messenger alluded to this when he said, "The thickness of the unbeliever's skin on the Day of Resurrection will be a three-day's journey."[59] God called attention to it with His words, "No indeed, but the book of the ungodly is in Sijjīn" [83:7]. Sijjīn is the low world that is attributed to the hand known as the "handful" and the "left hand." Concerning the Companions of the Right, God says, "No indeed, the book of the lovingly kind is in the high realms" [83:18]. This is like His words, "The heavens are rolled up in His right hand" [39:67].

The secret of the fact that the lovingly kind and their book are in the high realms is that the parts of their dense configuration and their natural, constitutional faculties become transubstantiated, purified, and transmuted through sanctification and purification—which are achieved by means of knowledge, works, and adornment with praiseworthy at-

Table 7 The Two Hand(ful)s According to Ṣadr al-Dīn al-Qūnawī

right hand	left hand
heavens	earth
spirits	bodily things, Nature, elements
subtlety	density
[light]	darkness
[translucence]	opacity
[simplicity]	composition
Garden	Fire
felicitous	wretched
high world	low world
unseen	visible
angels	natural bodies
meanings (suprasensory things)	forms
nonmanifest things	manifest things
incomparability	similarity
tawḥīd	associating others with God

tributes and exalted character traits—into angelic, fixed, pure faculties and attributes inherent in their souls, which are now at peace with God [*muṭma'inna*]. God reported on this in explaining the states of souls. He says, "Prosperous is he who purifies it" [91:9]. The Messenger of God alluded to this in the words of his supplication, "O God, give my soul its godfearingness and purify it! Thou art the best who purifies it!"[60]

The state of the wretched is the opposite. Their spiritual faculties and attributes have been absorbed by their natural faculties. Thereby their spiritual substantiality comes to nothing, as if it has been transmuted and become dense. God will bring together the decomposed parts of their bodies and their natural configuration, which have been colored by the properties of their corrupt beliefs and opinions, their ruinous acts, and their blameworthy character traits while they subsisted for long years in this configuration and abode. He will recompose them in the configuration of the afterlife. Then without doubt through all this they will reach a situation that requires that the thickness of the bodily skin of one of them will be a three-days' journey—in contrast to what I indicated concerning the state of the lovingly kind.

This is why it has been reported concerning the configuration in the Garden that the inhabitants will become manifest in a single moment in numerous palaces. They will take pleasure in every group of their families and move back and forth in whatever forms suit their appetites. This takes place only because of what we mentioned: The parts of their dense configuration have been absorbed into the subtle realities of their substances and colored by their attributes. The characteristics of their souls and their spiritual faculties have dominated over the faculties of their natural constitutions. They have become like angels: They become manifest in any form they wish.[61]

In his commentary on the opening chapter of the Koran, Qūnawī mentions the two hands in the context of describing the nature of human perfection. The fundamental difference between a human being and any other engendered thing is that a human manifests all the divine names, while anything else is limited to acting as a locus of manifestation for some of the names. A human being is total, while everything else is partial. A human being stands at the center of the circle of existence, while other creatures stand at the periphery.

In explaining the meaning of the words of Koran 1:4, "Thee alone do we serve" (or "worship"), Qūnawī points out that all things serve and worship God, since, as the Koran puts it, "None is there in the heavens and the earth that comes not to the All-merciful as a servant" (19:93). But non–human beings serve only the specific name or names that act as their Lords. In contrast, human beings—at least in the case of perfect humans—serve not specific names but the universal, all-comprehensive name Allah, since God created them in the form of that name.

> The tree rooted in the Divine Presence has branches. These branches are able to carry what comes to them to the extent that each of them is permeated by a share of the mystery of the reality of Allah. This share derives from the permeation of the essences of all things by the All-holy Essence. These branches are the divine names, and the root permeates the essences of all things through the fact that the Essence's self-disclosure permeates the levels of Its names in keeping with what the level of each of these names requires. That is why we have said on more than one occasion, "In one respect each name is the same as the Named, and in another respect it is other than It."[62]

Each name, such as Alive, Knowing, Desiring, and Powerful, manifests something of the reality of Allah, the absolutely Real. To the extent that the reality of the Knowing corresponds to the absolutely Real, the Knowing discloses the Real's Essence and is identical with the Real. But to the extent that the Knowing fails to correspond to the absolutely Real, something of the Real escapes it. Each branch of the Root is thus identical with the Root and different from the Root at one and the same time. Then each branch is connected to the creatures found in the cosmos. Some creatures manifest life, some knowledge, some power, some desire, and so on, while, of course, most creatures manifest several names at once. But when a certain name dominates over the nature of a thing, that name becomes the thing's "kibla," the direction toward which the thing renders its service and worship.

> Each name of the Real causes the manifestation of one of the kinds in the cosmos, so the name is that kind's kibla. One name makes the spirits manifest, another causes the relatively simple forms to become manifest, and still another brings the natures and compound things into manifestation. Likewise each of the three children becomes manifest through a specific name. That name is designated by the level in which it becomes manifest, or rather, by the state of the locus of manifestation and its inherent, unmade preparedness.[63] After that, the name becomes the thing's kibla in its attention and worship. It knows the Real only in this respect, and the Real supports it only from this presence. The thing takes a share from the nondelimited form of the Presence to the extent of the relationship of that name to the actuality that comprehends the levels of all the names and attributes.

The "nondelimited form of the Presence" is that created thing which manifests God as such. In other words, it is the perfect human being, the "all-comprehensive engendered thing" (*al-kawn al-jāmiʿ*) discussed earlier. Allah is the "all-comprehensive name" (*al-ism al-jāmiʿ*), since the reality to which this name refers—the absolutely Real—comprehends the levels of all names and attributes. Hence the form of the all-comprehensive name, which is the perfect human being, manifests all these names and attributes. Each partial creature shares in the totality that is the perfect human being only to the extent that the name which it manifests participates in the all-comprehensive name. The Knowing manifests Allah to one degree, the Forgiving to a lesser degree, and the Avenger to a still lesser degree. Hence those creatures who manifest the Knowing correspond more closely to the Real than those who manifest the Avenger.

Having introduced the question of how different creatures manifest in different degrees the Divine Presence (the Reality designated by the name Allah), Qūnawī turns to the question of how the perfect human being manifests all the names of God. Here he interprets God's two hands as referring to the two basic dimensions of human all-comprehensiveness: the visible and the invisible, or the corporeal and the spiritual.

> As for the human being, the manifestation of his form depends upon God's turning toward him totally when He brings him into existence. It depends upon the "two hands," as God has reported. One of these two hands holds the unseen, while the other holds the visible. From the one become manifest the holy spirits, from the other Nature, bodily things, and forms. That is why human beings bring together the knowledge of all the names

and are colored by the property of their presences. They are the most comprehensive of those things that were singled out for forms and possess the attribute of manifestation. They are also the most comprehensive of those things that were singled out for the nonmanifest things—such as spirits, which possess the attribute of unseenness and hiddenness. Hence human beings are not delimited by a station that would constrict them in the way the angels are constricted. God alludes to the angels' constriction with His words, "None of us there is but has a known station" [37:164]. Nor are human beings restricted as natural bodies are restricted.

After discussing the nature of human perfection, Qūnawī turns to teachings developed in detail by Ibn al-ʿArabī, although the principles were already well known. In brief, Ibn al-ʿArabī presented a complex psychology of "sanctity" (*walāya*), the state of being a "friend" (*walī*) of God. There is not one kind of friend, but a vast number of types, conveniently summarized by the ninety-nine names of God. Each name designates a particular quality of the absolutely Real, and each quality can dominate a fully developed human personality. Then the person manifests through his or her human perfection that divine quality more than any other. The basic nature of the person is delineated by names such as Servant of the Knowing, Servant of the Forgiving, and Servant of the Majestic. Kāshānī provides a description of ninety-nine human types among the friends of God, each of whom is a servant of a specific name.[64] The accounts of the prophets whom the prophet Muhammad met during his night journey need to be understood in a similar way. Each prophet manifests certain divine qualities, qualities which in turn are manifested through the celestial spheres. Hence these prophets are associated with those spheres, but they are not "located" there. Islamic astrology is based precisely upon such qualitative correspondences between God, the macrocosm, and human beings.

Next Qūnawī turns to the manner in which the two basic dimensions of the human being designated by the term "two hands" interrelate so that three basic human types come into existence. Some people are dominated by the spiritual (the right hand), some by the corporeal (the left hand), and some establish a perfect balance between the two.

Another coming together is actualized between these spiritual and suprasensory constitutions and the natural constitutions. This coming together has diverse properties that can be classified in three kinds:

The first kind is specific to those people whose spiritual properties dominate over their natural properties. In them their natural powers are subordinate to their spiritual powers.

A second kind is specific to most people. This is the opposite of the first, since their spiritual powers and attributes are consumed by the property of their natural powers.

The third kind is specific to perfect human beings and any of the Solitaries[65] whom God wills. Their verse is, "He gave everything its creation, then guided" [20:50]. So understand, for this is a station that cannot be explained in detail!

The domination of the names in different proportions—or, the differing ways in which the two hands interrelate—brings different degrees of understanding into existence.

To return to our discussion: Because of what we mentioned, there becomes manifest in keeping with the domination the property required by the quality of the dominant level, name, or nature. Though the locus is not empty of the property of all the names, it is ascribed to the one whose ruling authority becomes manifest within it. Hence one person declares God's incomparability, one declares His similarity, one brings together incomparability and similarity, one associates others with God, one declares His unity, and so on.[66]

What we mentioned causes the branching out of incompatible opinions, diverse states, disparate waystations, goals, and attentivenesses. Those who know the levels of Being and the realities of the names will know the secret of beliefs, revealed laws, religions, and opinions in all their diverse kinds. They will know how all these combine and grow up.[67]

In short, Qūnawī tells us that the interrelationship between the two hands of God brings all correlation and polarity in the universe into existence. It establishes the fundamental created dualities, such as the unseen and the visible. It also sets up the fundamental human perceptions, such as declaring similarity and incomparability. All movement, change, and process in the universe can be traced back to the two hands.

Saᶜīd al-Dīn Farghānī

Qūnawī's student Farghānī mentions God's two hands while explaining the nature of the Breath of the All-merciful.[68] God speaks, and within His Breath become manifest the existential words that are the creatures of the universe. The Breath itself is a single breath, yet it can be considered at several levels. For example, it may be seen as identical with the Breather, as the Breather's exhalation, as the Breather's articulated speech in which many words are made distinct, or as individual words making up a coherent sentence. Each level represents one of the worlds which make up the cosmos. The All-merciful Breath is sometimes called the "First Entification," that is, the first level of reality within which "entities" and things can be discerned, the first level where we may properly speak of distinct attributes and qualities. Beyond the Breath stands the nondelimited Essence, also called the "He-ness" (*huwiyya*) or the "Unseen of the Unseen" (*ghayb al-ghayb*). Concerning It nothing positive may be affirmed, since the Real Itself is "no thing," just as the highest station of human perfection is "no station." Already in the Breath yang and yin are present as the potentialities that will bring the cosmos into existence.

> The first thing that becomes entified and manifest from the Unseen of the Unseen is the Divine, All-merciful Breath. This is one reality within which are contained the property of activity [*fiᶜl*] and effectivity [*ta'thīr*] as well as receptivity [*qabūl*] and receiving acts [*infiᶜāl*]. Or rather, within it are contained God's names, attributes, and acts. This is to say that on the first level—which is identical with His true Oneness—the knower, knowledge, and known, the agent, receptacle, and act, are all a single thing, without distinction or difference. Then on the second level the entity of the All-merciful Breath becomes entified and manifest from the Unseen of the Unseen.

The All-merciful Breath, at the highest level, refers to the potentiality of all manifestation within the Real. At this level God's "face" is turned toward creation, and hence one can speak about the relationships that will be established once creation comes to exist. Thus, for example, God is the Knowing or the Knower, and, as such, He knows all things that will come into manifestation. But as long as the things have not yet come into manifestation, He knows the things within Himself. He Himself is the only reality, since nothing else exists. Hence the Knower and the known are one, while the process of knowing—the "knowledge"—is identical with the Knower and

Table 8 The Two Hands According to Farghānī

right hand	left hand
activity	receptivity, receiving effects
effectivity	receiving effects
Necessity	possibility
Being	Knowledge
true oneness	true manyness
relative manyness	relative oneness
mercy of necessity	[wrath]
simplicity	composition
subtlety	density
heavens	earth

the known. A similar analysis can be made of many divine attributes.

At the next level, which Farghānī now describes, certain realities can be discerned as distinct from the Breath. The first of the realities that can be discerned is Being (*wujūd*), that is, the Necessary Being which is God. He is necessary because He cannot not be. As such He is contrasted with all other things, which are "possible," since they may or may not be. Being is truly one, since It alone truly is. All other things "are" to the extent they are given existence by Being, much as the sun gives light to every illuminated thing. But along with Its Oneness, Being possesses a certain relative manyness, the Manyness of Knowledge.

> In this second level the first reality and presence contained within God's inclusive unity and manifest through and distinct from the entity of the All-merciful Breath is the Presence of Being. This is called the Presence of Necessity, by way of naming a thing by its concomitant. To this Presence are ascribed true Oneness and relative manyness. Because of the true Oneness that is ascribed to it, the property of activity and effectivity and all the divine names related to this Presence [of activity] are ascribed to it and to all the loci of manifestation that are related to it.

As was mentioned at the end of the previous chapter, Being is active because It is the source and origin of all the things that stem from It. They receive Its rays, much like things receive color from light. To speak of Necessity is to speak of possibility, since the two are inseparable from each other in conception. If Necessity is connected to Being, possibility is connected to the multiple objects found in Being's knowledge. Hence we have the distinction between the Oneness of Being and the Manyness of Knowledge.

Within God's knowledge all things are known for all eternity. But they do not exist in and of themselves, any more than our ideas exist outside ourselves. When the things exist, their existence is borrowed from Being, just as light is but a ray of the sun. Once an object of God's knowledge is given existence, it shows its receptivity toward Being simply by its existence. It does not actively possess Being, since sooner or later it ceases to exist. In short, at this second level Necessity and possibility set up an active/receptive, yang/yin relationship.

> On this second level, as the counterpart of this Presence [of Being], the Presence of Knowledge connected to possible objects of knowledge becomes manifest and distinct. This is named the Presence of Possibility, by way of naming a thing by the description of that which is within it. To this Presence, in respect of the possible realities that it contains, are ascribed true manyness and relative, all-comprehending oneness. Because of the intensity of the attribution of manyness to it, its dependencies and contents are specific to reception, receiving effects, and receiving activity.

True ontological oneness is solely the attribute of God, the Necessary Being. Such oneness is eternal, absolute, and infinite. In contrast, manyness is found among the things, each of which is changing and limited. The One possesses necessarily all perfections as Its own, while each of the many things borrows certain perfections for a period of time and then relinquishes them. The One lends and the many borrow, the One gives and the many receive, heaven bestows and the earth gives birth to the Ten Thousand Things.

However, in questions of yang/yin relationships, or in matters of correlativity such as Lord and vassal, there can be no absolutes. What is active from one point of view is receptive from another. If Necessity is active toward possibility, the very fact that Necessity cannot be conceived of apart from possibility demonstrates that Necessity receives effects from possibility. At the outset Farghānī stated that Necessity is truly one and relatively many. To the true oneness pertains activity, but to the relative manyness pertains a certain receptivity. An analogous thing can be said about possibility.

> Since the Presence of Necessity has the property of relative manyness, it possesses a kind of reception through receiving the activity of the demand and request of the pre-

paredness [of created things] and complying with what is requested.

"Preparedness" (*isti*ᶜ*dād*) is the specific configuration taken by a thing's possibility that makes it receptive to existence in certain modes but not in other modes. The divine effusion of existence is one, but the things receive it according to their own specific characteristics. As Qūnawī puts it,

> The Effusion is one, but the preparednesses are diverse and disparate. This is like fire that comes to naphtha, sulfur, dry wood, and green wood. Without doubt, the first and quickest to receive ignition and manifestation in the form of fire will be the naphtha, then the sulfur, then the dry wood, then the green wood. When you look carefully at what we said, you will see that the cause of the speed of naphtha's reception of ignition before the others, then the sulfur, is nothing but the strength of the affinity between the constitution of naphtha and fire and the fact that they share in certain intrinsic qualities.[69]

In short, each possible thing within God's knowledge has a specific preparedness, or specific characteristics through which it becomes a receptacle for existence. But this preparedness is not simply passive, since there can be no absolute yin. By its very nature it demands and requests from the Real that He irradiate it with His light so that it may enter into existence.[70] Farghānī continues:

> Since the Presence of the Objects of Knowledge and Possibility has the property of relative oneness, it possesses effectivity and activity through demanding and requesting from the Presence of Necessity.

Next Farghānī considers the Breath of the All-merciful as a single unified whole. Within it Necessity and possibility are two dimensions of the same reality, the two hands of God. From this point of view, the Breath is a *barzakh* (isthmus) tying together the two sides. It is identical with the inmost reality of the perfect human being. It is the all-comprehensive reality to which reference has already been made. Here the Breath may also be viewed as the inmost reality of the macrocosm, in which case it is referred to as the "Cloud," within which, according to the Prophet, God was found "before He created the creatures."[71]

> As for the isthmus-like, undifferentiated, human presence and the differentiated, Cloud presence, these bring together the two presences in one respect and separate them in another respect. They comprise the divine attributes and the engendered realities and carry the self-disclosure of the Breath which brings together everything.
>
> Necessity is one of God's hands, open through mercy. Since this mercy pertains exclusively to the receptivities of "those who are godfearing and pay the alms tax" [7:156], this is the right hand. Hence the Presence of the Objects of Knowledge and Possibility is the other hand.

Here Farghānī's point can be understood by reference to the two basic kinds of mercy that are differentiated in Ibn al-ᶜArabī's school, to which reference was made earlier. The two are mentioned in the Koranic verse, "My mercy embraces all things, and I shall write it down for those who are godfearing and pay the alms tax, and those who indeed believe in Our signs, those who follow the Messenger" (7:156). In respect of the fact that God's mercy embraces all things, it is called the "mercy of free gift" or the "mercy of the All-merciful." But in respect of the fact that God "writes down" mercy for those who have faith, He is making it necessary for them, since He does not break His word. Hence this second mercy is called the "mercy of necessity" or the "mercy of the All-compassionate."[72] The first mercy reaches all things, even objects of wrath. It encompasses paradise and hell, and brings the cosmos into existence. It is manifest precisely through the Breath of the All-merciful. Then, within the Breath of the All-merciful, the first mercy is divided into two: mercy and wrath. This second mercy is the opposite of wrath, while the first mercy has no opposite, except nonexistence. The second mercy is the mercy of necessity that pertains to the name All-compassionate and is written for the faithful. Opposed to it, on the left hand, is the wrath that reaches the unbelievers. The locus of manifestation for the All-merciful mercy is the whole cosmos, including paradise and hell. The locus of manifestation for the All-compassionate mercy is the Garden, and that of wrath is the Fire. The mercy of necessity is related to the right hand precisely because the "Companions of the Right" are the people of paradise. In this perspective, the mercy of free gift stands beyond the opposition set up by the two hands. In another respect, it is yang, while both hands are yin in relation to it.

> The two hands are connected with the blessing of all the name-derived perfections, since they embrace both the entities and the manifestations of these perfections. Hence "both of God's hands are right and blessed." This takes into account true perfection, not relative perfection.

In other words, in respect to the full manifestation of Being, the whole cosmos is perfect, so both of God's hands are right. But in respect to the differing qualities of the two hands, certain parts of the cosmos are more perfect than other parts. The Companions of the Right are more perfect than those of the left, just as the faithful are more perfect than the unbelievers. For the Companions of the Right partake of felicity and mercy, and mercy is the "precedent attribute" of God. "God's mercy precedes His wrath," which is to say that it manifests a greater range of ontological perfections than wrath. Nevertheless, from another point of view, the unbelievers are what they must be, even if they are less perfect than the faithful and end up as Companions of the Left. Both faithful and unbelievers are necessary for the manifestation of the divine names.[73] This point will be explained in more detail below.

> Whenever the property of oneness, simplicity, and subtlety is more manifest in any of the spiritual or corporeal loci of manifestation—such as the heavens—then the relationship with the manifestation of the Presence of Necessity and the effect of its effectivity and activity are stronger. In such a case it is more appropriate for the thing to be attributed to the right hand.
>
> Whenever the property of manyness, composition, and density are more apparent within something—like the earth—then its relationship to the manifestation of the Presence of the Objects of Knowledge and Possibility and to the property of receptivity and receiving effects is more complete and stronger.

Note here that Farghānī again stresses that the properties of oneness and manyness, right and left, activity and receptivity, are relative qualities. Both are present in all phenomena, but things can nevertheless be differentiated inasmuch as some are dominated by one side and some by the other. Both hands are God's hands. Neither hand has anything negative in itself and in respect of the absolute perfection alluded to above. However, in relation to various individuals and relative perfections, the domination of the left hand over the right hand leads to wretchedness for those who experience it. The reason for this is that manyness, composition, and density are the attributes of distance from God and are connected to the divine names that affirm incomparability. Hence they are connected to wrath, and in the next world wrath is experienced as the torments of hell. In contrast, oneness, simplicity, and subtlety are the attributes of nearness to God and are connected with similarity and paradise. In both cases, whether attributes connected with similarity or incomparability are affirmed, the relationship with God is fundamental. Whichever hand is discussed, it must be connected with the Real.

> It is most appropriate, out of courtesy, to attribute the hand, without qualification, to God. Look at His words, "The earth, all of it, is His handful on the day of resurrection, and the heavens are rolled up in His right hand! Glory be to Him above what they associate" [39:67], that is, what they associate by ascribing the hand, activity, and existence to that which is independent of Him.[74]

In other words, *tawḥīd*, or the profession of God's Unity (the opposite of *shirk*, or associating others with God), can be achieved only by ascribing both hands and all the qualities that they imply to God Himself.

In brief, Farghānī understands the two hands to refer to the two basic constituent forces of existence, which are referred to from different points of view according to the attributes that dominate over them: incomparability and similarity, oneness and manyness, necessity and possibility. These are found both in the relationship between the Real and the cosmos, and in that between the unseen dimensions of the cosmos and the visible dimensions.

Farghānī on the Two Handfuls

In his commentary on Ibn al-Fāriḍ's poetry, Farghānī provides a marvelous discussion of the two handfuls that ties together most of the qualities that we have been discussing up until this point. He shows that polarity is fundamental to reality: It is demanded by the very nature of the Real, who is One in His Being and many in His knowledge. This fundamental distinction is the yang and yin of existence. From it arises all diversity.

Farghānī is commenting on the following lines of Ibn al-Fāriḍ:

> Were it not for the veil of engendered existence,
> I would speak—
> But my observance of the ruling properties
> of the loci of manifestation keeps me silent.
> For there is no vanity,
> and the creatures were not created aimlessly,
> Even if their actions
> do not follow the proper way.
> Their affairs run ahead
> according to the branding of the names.
> The wisdom that describes the Essence
> puts its property into effect.
> It turns them about in the two handfuls—
> "No concern . . . , no concern . . . ,"
> One handful is given bliss,
> the other wretchedness.[75]

Here Ibn al-Fāriḍ is discussing the fact that all things are exactly what they must be. All things follow the laws of their own natures, and these natures in turn manifest the divine names. Both mercy and wrath must have loci of manifestation, so paradise and hell must necessarily exist. But they can only exist through their inhabitants, the Companions of the Right and the Companions of the Left.

Must we then say that there is nothing but good in existence? We can say so, but only if we look at things from the point of view of the Oneness of Being without reference to the Manyness of Knowledge. However, human beings are commanded to look at things in terms of distinction and differentiation. The Sharia sets down the difference between good and evil, true and false, right and left. As long as we are human, we must observe the divine command.[76] Farghānī begins his commentary on the first of Ibn al-Fāriḍ's verses as follows:

> The poet is saying that engendered existence and its levels are a veil. This existence is delimited by the properties of manyness. It affirms the other and otherness. It sees opposition to God's commands and opposed qualities. The poet says: If this were not the case, I would have said that everything that becomes manifest in existence is good and unitary, with no evil found within it. I would have said that all paths lead to a single goal, there being no otherness or difference in the goal. However, I am obliged to observe the levels and the requirements of the loci within which the divine names become manifest. I must give to each level and to each locus of manifestation its right. This does not allow me to speak these words.

Having explained the literal significance of the verses, Farghānī turns to the distinction between the Oneness of Being and the diversity of the cosmos that results from the diversity of the divine names or the Manyness of Knowledge. What is especially interesting in this discussion is the way in which he contrasts the qualities of Being (*al-wujūd*) and engendered existence (*al-kawn*), or the Real and creation. The term *realness* (*ḥaqqiyya*) refers to all the specific qualities that pertain to the Real (*al-ḥaqq*), as opposed to those qualities that pertain to created things, "unrealness" (*buṭlān*) or "ca-

Table 9 The Two Handfuls According to Farghānī

right handful	left handful
Being	engendered existence
oneness	manyness
all-comprehensiveness	dispersion
realness	unreality
uniformity	distinction, diversity
[sameness]	otherness
equilibrium	deviation
luminosity	darkness
lifting of veils	being veiled
guidance	misguidance
compassion	severity
exalting	abasing
submission	ignorance of the Real
faith	unbelief, denial
acquiescence	refusal
observing lawful & unlawful	following caprice & appetite
[sincerity]	hypocrisy
good-pleasure of God	anger, wrath
Garden	hellfire
bliss	chastisement, punishment
felicity	wretchedness
World of the Dominion	World of the Kingdom
simplicity	[composition]
spirit, soul	elemental nature
activity, effectivity	[receptivity]
high things	low things
heavens	earth

price" (*hawā*). The opposition between the Real and the unreal or caprice is standard, going back to such Koranic verses as "The Real has come and the unreal has vanished away" (17:81); or, "Had the Real followed their caprices, the heavens and the earth and everything within them would have been corrupted" (23:71).

> In Its own Essence the One Real Being has a property, description, and characteristic that never leaves Its level. This property is oneness, all-comprehensiveness, and the uniformity of realness, purified from the contamination of the unreal, free of distinction and otherness. Engendered existence and its levels also have a characteristic, property, and quality. This is manyness, dispersion, and contamination by the unreal, or its domination over the concealed realness. . . . Within this manyness are established distinction, otherness, diversity, and strife.
>
> Nothing makes engendered existence manifest with all its characteristics, properties, and qualities except the One Being. None of the rays of the light of the One Being become manifest within the engendered levels for the sake of making manifest the name-derived perfection except in the loci of disclosure that are the engendered realities.
>
> Hence the Oneness of Being remains behind the veil of the manyness of the engendered realities. As long as any effect and property pertaining to engendered existence dominates over someone or becomes manifest within him, the Oneness of Being's all-comprehensiveness and its property of undifference will not become manifest to him, no matter what he perceives.

Though Farghānī does not mention the Manyness of Knowledge in this passage, he alludes to it by speaking of the manyness of the engendered realities. For the engendered realities are precisely the objects of God's knowledge that have been given existence and are now found in the cosmos.

> Each engendered reality, in respect of its being delimited by engendered existence and

the properties of the engendered levels, has two faces: The first face is turned toward Being, which makes manifest this reality's properties, attributes, and effects. This face demands the manifestation of the effects of Oneness, which are balance [*ʿadāla*], all-comprehensiveness, luminosity, realness, the lifting of the veils, and the reception of the effects of guidance and compassion.

The second face is turned toward its own self [*nafs*] and the concomitants of its own self. This face demands the manifestation of manyness, deviation, darkness, unreality, the domination of the property of being veiled, and the effect of misguidance and severity.

Each of these two faces has a specific property and effect.

The property of the engendered reality's face turned toward Being is submission [*islām*]; faith in God, His messengers, and the Last Day; acquiescence to commands and prohibitions; limiting oneself to the rulings of the lawful and the unlawful and the beautiful and the ugly, while distinguishing among these and the requirements of each, that is, reward and punishment as a result of being worthy of it. The property of this face includes faith that every act and word, whether beautiful or ugly, commanded or prohibited, brings about the configuration of the forms of the ascending degrees and descending degrees, the lasting bliss and the painful chastisement, of the Garden and the Fire.

Hence the property of this face is submission, faith, delimiting oneself by the rulings of the Sharia and of commands and prohibitions, and acting according to this in the heart and the bodily frame. The effect and fruit of this property are attaining to the good-pleasure of the One, Real Existence-giver and entering into His Gardens. These Gardens are the forms of that good-pleasure and the locus of manifestation for His right handful in the next world. They are a rising up in the degrees of the next world. In other words, they are the configuration of the forms of bliss, which are the houris, the palaces, and so on, in the *barzakh* and the next world.

The property of the face that is turned toward its own self and the concomitants of its own self are ignorance of the Real, denial of the realness of every religion and sharia, refusal of everything that comes from the Real through the prophets and messengers. It is the denial of all the reports given by the prophets that affirm resurrection and recompense, Garden and Fire. It is to abandon oneself to the caprice [*hawā*] of the soul and nature and to ride upon the appetite [*shahwa*]. Caprice and appetite are the domination of unreality over the hidden and concealed realness.

Hence the property of this face is unbelief, disobedience, refusal, following caprice and nature, abandoning oneself to full gratification of appetites and enjoyments, accusing of falsehood, and hypocrisy. The effect of this property is the manifestation of falling under the anger of the Real Existence-giver. One enters into His hellfire, which is the form of His anger and wrath and the locus of manifestation for His left handful. One falls into the place of being taken to account and criticized during one's reckoning. Various forms of chastisement and punishment and the things that cause them are configured in the *barzakh* and the next world. The reason for this is that every beautiful or ugly act that issues from a human being, whether it comes from the heart or the bodily frame, must have an effect and fruit, whether in this world, in the *barzakh*, or in the next world.

These then are the properties of the right hand and the left hand. All are traceable to Oneness and manyness, which in turn are connected to Being and engendered existence. Here Farghānī brings together the qualities explicit and implied in Ibn al-ʿArabī's original discussion of the verse of the two hands in the *Fuṣūṣ al-ḥikam*. Having set up these distinctions, Farghānī turns again to Ibn al-Fāriḍ's verse. He points out that people in control of intellect (*ʿaql*), which is the human faculty that discerns between truth and falsehood, observe the requirements of manyness. Intellect, it should be noted, is the microcosmic equivalent of the prophet. Just as prophets bring commands and prohibitions, so the correctly functioning human intellect discerns what is right and wrong. Here Farghānī also refers to the connection between intellect and wisdom (*ḥikma*). For, as Ibn al-ʿArabī remarks, the wise man is "he who does what is proper for what is proper as is proper,"[77] and this depends totally upon discernment and differentiation.

Human beings may be confined within the bond of the properties and levels of engendered existence and present with them. They may be aware of themselves and their own engendered existence, ascribe things to themselves, and perceive the engendered properties. Then they remain veiled from witnessing the Oneness of Being and its world and from the uniformity of realness. They have no share whatsoever in that or in the property of its world. They remain captive to the property of the world of wisdom, the manyness of its requirements, and the requirement of the two faces and properties of engendered realities. They cannot avoid these situations. And they will be held responsible for them because of the requirement of the world of wisdom. In such a situation, they will be subject to the properties of reward, punishment, calling to account, responsibility, and reckoning in this world and the next world. Both these worlds pertain to engendered existence and fall under the sway of the world of wisdom.

However, people may escape from the tie of engendered existence and the bond of the levels. They may join the vast expanse of the World of Oneness such that they are present with that Presence and gaze upon it, having realized it. They remain forgetful and negligent of engendered existence, its levels, and all the realities that it contains. They have no awareness of themselves, their existence, and all the attributes, accidents, and concomitants that are seen to pertain to themselves. They witness and see the One Real through the Real, not through themselves or through their own vision. At this point, their entities and existences are colored with the property of that world. Hence they observe no other, otherness, or anything unreal. They see all things as One Entity, without distinction or difference. Such is the state of the enraptured, "attracted ones" [*majdhūb*] and some of the "rational madmen" [*ʿuqalāʾ al-majānīn*].[78] People like this rise up empty of any thought of religious prescriptions, command and prohibition, lawful and unlawful, or any of the rulings of the Sharia. For these things are all connected to the perfection of intellect and the actuality of discerning through intellect between good and evil, profit and loss, harm and benefit, withholding and bestowing, exalting and abasing, gentleness and severity, acceptance and rejection, pleasure and pain. Once this discerning intellect disappears and is forgotten and neglected, all the prescriptions of the Sharia and the distinctions between lawful and unlawful are abolished.

When such people come back from the World of Oneness to the world of engendered existence and become aware of themselves so that their discerning intellects return, then all the religious prescriptions return. They will be held responsible for all the rulings of the Sharia, since they are present with engendered existence and its levels. Hence the properties of engendered existence apply to them.

Some people make use of the property of the World of Oneness when they are once again present with engendered existence and aware of their own engendered existence and their intellects. They apply this property to good and evil, pain and pleasure, and so on. They say, "In the World of Oneness I saw all things as a single thing. Hence for me there is no more command and prohibition, lawful and unlawful, or distinction among things. For me everything is one, with no difference between lawful and unlawful." Such people are heretics [*zindīq*] and libertines [*mubāḥī*], and their blood can be shed.

Note that here we have a great authority in the sapiential tradition, a great Sufi, telling us that people who blatantly transgress the Sharia can rightly be killed. "Bold expansiveness" has its place—in the inmost depths of the spirit, where the seeker is one with God. It must stay in its place. On the outer level, the domain of majesty and awe, the Sharia's authority stands supreme. Farghānī continues:

These considerations explain the words of the poet. The veil of engendered existence separates creation from the World of Oneness and the witnessing there of the unity of all things, religions, and creeds. The poet is aware of that veil. He is present with and perceives engendered existence and its properties. These properties are the loci of manifestation for all the requirements of the divine names. He says: I must observe the properties of the engendered loci of manifestation. In other words, I must delimit myself by the rulings of the Sharia, affirm what it affirms, and negate what it negates. If not for all this, I would speak of the realness of all things and all religions and their unity, without any admixture of unreality whatsoever. I would say that there is no calling to account and no responsibility for anything that issues from a human being. This would be based upon my witnessing of the world and property of Oneness. However, the necessity of observing the mentioned rulings keeps me quiet. It prevents me from saying this and obligates me to say the opposite, in keeping with the requirements of the world of engendered existence and wisdom and their levels.

Ibn al-Fāriḍ cannot simply declare that all things are one, since this would be to negate the requirements of the Manyness of Knowledge. However, he also cannot ignore his vision of the Oneness of Being. Since he embraces both perfections, he must express both truths. Hence he declares that the reality of the situation combines the properties of both sides. Both oneness and manyness must be affirmed. Farghānī continues speaking for Ibn al-Fāriḍ:

The fact that I bring together the two qualities of oneness and manyness along with their properties leads me to see that there is no unqualified vanity [*ʿabath muṭlaq*] or unmixed unreality in existence. Nor is there any within the creation of those creatures who dwell in unbelief, misguidance, and error. None of this is empty of a hidden realness. The Wise Existence-giver brings together the qualities of guidance and misguidance, compassion and severity, exalting and abasing, good-pleasure and wrath. When He brings anything into existence, He does so to manifest the perfections connected to the requirements of His Most Beautiful Names and Exalted Attributes. Not all existent things accord in their existence and acts with the requirements of the properties of guidance and right conduct. However, they do accord with what is required by the names Intensely Severe, Misguider, Abaser, and so on. . . .

Hence there is no vanity,
and the creatures were not created aimlessly,
Even if their actions
do not follow the proper way.

The poet means to say as follows: I have been prevented from speaking about the realness of all things and of everything that appears in existence only because it is incumbent upon me to observe and take into account the properties of the engendered loci of manifestation. Otherwise, I would have spoken about that realness. For there is no vanity—in the sense of an unmixed vanity without any realness—to be found or established in anything that appears in existence. The creatures were not brought into existence for sheer unreality. On the contrary, everything that becomes manifest in existence must have a hidden realness within it. But no one is apprised of this except God and those people whom He allows to witness the Oneness and Realness of Being and the fact that it permeates all existent things.

Even if the acts of people do not become manifest in proper forms for those who look upon these acts from the perspective of the requirements of the name Guide, this lack of correct manifestation does not detract from the fact that there is a hidden realness established within them. The realness that is the concomitant of existence without qualification permeates all the divine names and their requirements. Every divine name—such as Guide and Misguider, Compassionate and Intensely Severe—is nothing but the Real Being Itself. However, here a quality is ascribed to the Divine Presence, such as guidance and misguidance, mercy and severity, exalting and abasing. For just as God ascribes guidance to that Presence through His words, "God guides whomsoever He will to a straight path" [2:213], so also He ascribes misguidance to It through His words, "God misguides the wrongdoers" [14:27]. All ontological aid that reaches those who are guided in their guidance comes only from the presence of the name Guide and by means of this name. And all aid that reaches the misguided in their misguidance comes only from the presence of the Misguider and by means of this name. The purpose of all this is to make manifest the perfection that pertains to each of these two names. Hence no existent thing is empty of realness. However, in those who are guided the realness is manifest, while in those who are misguided it is hidden and concealed.

Their affairs run ahead
according to the branding of the names.

In other words: The Shariite and proper affairs, acts, words, and character traits of the guided flow on and become manifest from them in accordance with the requirement of the name Guide. The mark of this name's requirement is the manifestation of the effects of realness that are established within them through the ruling of the Sharia.

The improper and deviant affairs, acts, words, and character traits of the misguided flow on and become manifest from them in accordance with the requirement of the name Misguider. The mark of its requirement is the concealment of realness within them. Realness is overcome by their property of caprice and nature.

The wisdom that describes the Essence
puts its property into effect.

This wisdom describes the Essence as bringing together the two handfuls in Himself. These are the right handful, which pertains to felicity, and the left handful, which pertains to wretchedness. This wisdom puts its property into effect by engendering the two handfuls. It singles out each group for a single handful.

He turns them about in the two handfuls—
"No concern . . . , no concern . . . ."

The requirement of the configuration of this world is that the properties of the two handfuls should be mixed and blended with each other. Hence, one of its requirements is that the people of the two handfuls are turned about with this configuration. Sometimes He gives bliss to the people of the handful of wretchedness. He makes them happy through the felicity of comfort, ease, and a carefree livelihood. He chastises and afflicts the people of the felicitous handful with deprivation, trouble, and a constrained livelihood. Sometimes He does the opposite. Sometimes He gives bliss and happiness to both, sometimes he afflicts and brings hardship for both. Hence He turns them about in this abode in the two handfuls. . . .

One handful is given bliss,
the other wretchedness.

One of these two handfuls is the handful of bliss and felicity, the other the handful of chastisement and wretchedness. Each of them has formal and supra-sensory forms and loci of manifestation entified within the two planes, this world and the next world.

The World of the Kingdom [*mulk*] is the world of composition and elemental nature. It is the locus of manifestation for the left handful.

The World of the Dominion [*malakūt*] is the world of the soul and spirit and the world that renders praise with the tongue of action by manifesting the properties of activity, controlling power, and effectivity within the World of the Kingdom. It is the locus of manifestation for the right handful.

The high things and the low things, which are called the heavens and the earths, are the loci of manifestation for the two handfuls, by reason of His words, "And the earth is His handful." Their acting as loci of manifestation was singled out for the Day of Resurrection because on that day it will be completely manifest. For God says, "Surely the abode of the next world—that is life" [29:64].

Then faith and unbelief act as loci of manifestation for the two handfuls on the supra-sensory level.

Everything we have said is brought together in God's words, "All that is in the heavens and all that is in the earth glorifies God. His is the kingdom and His is the praise, and He is powerful over everything. It is He who created you. One of you is an unbeliever and one of you a person of faith. And God sees the things that you do" [64:1–2]. The perfect and perfected shaykh, Muḥyī al-Dīn ibn al-ʿArabī says, "This is the glorification of the two handfuls."[79] His words are an eloquent and perfect allusion to what we have said.[80]

3

Cosmology

4

HEAVEN AND EARTH

In God, duality is prefigured by the Essence and the Divinity and can be seen manifesting itself in the complementary divine names. But the first duality that may properly be called "ontological" appears in the distinction between God and everything other than God. Only then can we discuss two different realities as separately existent, even if, in the last analysis, the existence of the second is seen to be shadow-like and ephemeral, or even metaphorical, since it is utterly beholden to the existence of the first. This is the distinction made in Islamic philosophy between the Necessary Being, or that which cannot not be, and the possible thing, or that which may or may not exist, depending upon circumstances determined by the Necessary Being.

An ontological distinction can be drawn between God and the cosmos. In the same way ontological distinctions can be drawn among the things present within the cosmos, each of which manifests distinct and different qualities of the Real. In short, the cosmos is the locus of real duality and real multiplicity. There is no question of merely positing duality or seeing it "in principle." Rather, a great variety of pairings and relationships actually exist, and these set up dualities as real as the things themselves. The Koran itself makes the primacy of two over the other numbers explicit in such verses as, "And of everything We created a pair" (51:49).

Rashīd al-Dīn Maybudī, in explaining the literal sense of this verse, tells us that by "pair" (*zawjān*) is meant male and female among living things and the diverse kinds among inanimate things, for example, heaven and earth, sun and moon, night and day, land and sea, rough ground and smooth ground, winter and summer, light and darkness, faith and unbelief, felicity and wretchedness, sweet and bitter.[1] In bringing out the deeper sense of the verse, Maybudī sees these dual "signs" in all things as indications of God's incomparability: God created things in pairs to distinguish between His own Unity and the manyness of the others. Creation is impossible without duality, because God alone is One.

Maybudī then points to the connection between the Koran's mention of the "pairs" and the conclusion that the Koran draws in the next verse: "So flee unto God." If we were concerned with cosmology as a primitive form of science, this verse would appear irrelevant to the discussion, since it tells us nothing about the nature of the universe. But Maybudī typifies the sapiential approach to cosmological thinking by emphasizing the intimate link between two fundamental dimensions of the Tao of Islam: the phenomena of the natural world and the moral and spiritual imperatives of human life. Since the cosmos depends totally upon God for its existence and reality, the human response must be to acknowledge the actual situation by giving up self-centeredness and reliance upon created things.

> Whenever God creates a temporally engendered thing, He creates it as a pair, as two things linked to each other or opposite each other, for example, male and female, day and night, light and darkness, heaven and earth, land and sea, sun and moon, jinn and mankind, obedience and disobedience, felicity and wretchedness, guidance and misguidance, mightiness and lowliness, power and incapacity, strength and weakness, knowledge and ignorance, life and death. He created the attributes of the creatures in this manner—linked with each other or opposite each other—so that they would not be similar to the attributes of the Creator and so that His Unity and Singularity might become manifest to the creatures: His mightiness is without lowliness, His power without incapacity, His strength without weakness, His knowledge without ignorance, His life without death, His joy without sorrow, His subsistence without annihilation.
>
> God is One and Unique: One in Essence and Attributes, Unique in worthiness. He is incomparable with everyone and separate from everything. "Nothing is like Him" [42:11]. No one is like Him and He has no similar or compeer. Similarity derives from associates, and God has no associate. He is without likeness and need. The door of His withholding is closed and the door of His generosity open. He forgives sins and caresses the faulty. He makes His love apparent by caressing servants. He loves His servants, though He has no needs. His love acts between Himself and the servant without association. Hence it is appropriate for the servant, no matter what his state—whether wounded by the arrow of affliction or immersed in gentleness and bestowal—to seize hold of His generosity and seek refuge in Him, fleeing to Him from the creatures, just as He Himself has commanded: "So flee unto God!"
>
> Flight is one of the stations of the spiritual travelers, one of the waystations of love. When someone truly reaches this station, his mark is that he sees his whole self as a debt to be paid, all his words as complaint, all his works as sin. He loses hope in his own activity and finds fault in his own sincerity. If good fortune should come his way, he sees it as God's bounty and a decree of eternity without beginning, not as a result of his own effort and activity.[2]

The Creation of the Cosmos

If all things are created in pairs, "everything other than God" should also be a pair, that is, built up from two divergent but complementary realities. Several sets of pairs can be suggested as comprising all things, as we saw on page 60, where the Ikhwān al-Ṣafā᾽ were quoted as mentioning some of the terms employed to refer to the roots of all created things: form and matter, light and darkness, affirmation and negation, and so forth. If we look at the Koran, probably no set of terms is employed in a more inclusive sense than the unseen (*ghayb*) and the visible (*shahāda*), which are paired ten times, always in the divine name, "the Knower of the unseen and the visible." Most authors identify these with the two fundamental worlds of the cosmos. These are the spiritual and the corporeal worlds, also called the Dominion (*malakūt*) and the Kingdom (*mulk*), or the Command (*amr*) and the Creation (*khalq*). This is how ʿAbd al-Razzāq Kāshānī explains the meaning of the above Koranic name:

> *The Knower of the unseen*, that is, the realities of the World of the Spirits, which are His Dominion, *and the visible* [6:74], that is, the form of the World of the Bodies, which are His Kingdom.[3]

The most commonly mentioned pair in the Koran that can be interpreted as referring to the total cosmos is heaven and earth. A number of verses suggest that everything in the universe is encompassed by these two. The least that can be said is that heaven and earth are mentioned as two fundamental points of reference in this world. For example:

> It is He who in heaven is God and in earth is God. (43:84)
>
> From God nothing whatever is hidden in heaven and earth. (3:5, 14:38)

> Not so much as the weight of an ant in earth or heaven escapes from thy Lord. (10:61)
>
> My Lord knows what is said in heaven and earth. (21:4)
>
> Didst thou not know that God knows all that is in heaven and earth? Surely that is in a Book. (22:70)
>
> And not a thing is there hidden in heaven and earth but it is in a Manifest Book. (27:75)
>
> You are not able to frustrate Him either in the earth or in heaven. (29:22)

The word *heaven* (*samā'*) is employed in the Koran 120 times in the singular and 190 times in the plural, and the word *earth* (*arḍ*) is used 460 times.[4] The expression "heaven and earth" or "heavens and earth" occurs well over 200 times. The constant juxtaposition of the two terms—not to mention their conceptual interrelationship—makes it practically impossible to mention one without bringing the other to mind.

It should be noted that the basic meaning of the word *samā'* (heaven) is "the higher, or upper, or highest, or uppermost, part of anything." It is also used to mean sky, clouds, rain, and bounty. In contrast, the verbal root of the word *arḍ* (earth) means to thrive and produce; to become fruitful; to be soft when tread upon and pleasant when sat upon; to be lowly, submissive, naturally disposed to do good. The *arḍ* is "that whereon are mankind," the ground, the floor; anything that is low. In the following verse, the Koran seems to be expressing simply the literal sense of the two terms through analogy: "Your Lord, who . . . assigned to you earth for a bedding, and heaven for a building" (2:22).

When mentioning heaven (or the heavens) and earth, the Koran often adds the expression "everything between the two" (*mā baynahumā*), which can be considered as a Koranic synonym for the "Ten Thousand Things" of the Chinese tradition. "God is He that created the heavens and the earth and everything between the two in six days" (32:4, 25:59).[5]

There may be some created things that do not fit into the three categories of heaven, earth, and everything between the two, though this would depend upon how heaven and earth are defined. Some authors use the two terms as equivalent to unseen and visible, while others make heaven and earth the high and low points in the visible universe. When Ibn al-ʿArabī writes, "There is nothing in compound engendered existence except a heaven and an earth,"[6] he excludes from heaven the "simple" things, among which are the four elements and the angels, who dwell in the spiritual or invisible realm. However, by employing the terms indefinitely, he is leaving room for "the heaven and the earth" to be a broader expression. Moreover, the use of the term "heaven" in the Koran does not exclude a spiritual dimension, as Ibn al-ʿArabī is fully aware. In another context he identifies "heaven" with everything high and "earth" with everything low, thereby considering the two terms as embracing all created things:

> God said that He "did not create the heavens," that is, every high world, "and the earth," that is, every low world, "and everything" of the cosmos "between the two except through the Real" [30:8].[7]

Nasafī understands the pair heaven and earth as denoting a specific type of relationship, that of giving or "effusing" (*fayḍ*) and receiving or "accepting effusion" (*istifāḍa*). In his view, the terms can refer to any giver and receiver, while "everything between the two" refers to the result of the relationship. Understood in this sense, heaven and earth encompass everything in engendered existence, including the spiritual creatures:

> Heaven is something that is high and effuses upon a level below it. This effusing may come from the world of bodily things or from the world of spirits. Earth is something that is relatively low and accepts effusion from a level above it. This receiver of effusion may belong to the world of corporeal things or to the world of spirits. Hence a single thing may be both earth and heaven. . . . Among bodily things there may be both heaven and earth, and among spirits there may be both heaven and earth. . . .
>
> Now you have come to know that the effuser, whatever kind it may be, is heaven,

and the receiver of effusion, whatever kind it may be, is earth. Hence it has been established for you that the number of heavens and earths cannot be known to anyone. "He created seven heavens" [65:12] does not prove that there are none but these seven.

Although heaven is the effuser and earth the receiver of effusion, the level of the earth is prior to the level of heaven. Hence Eve is prior to Adam. However, there was never any time when there was no earth and no heaven, since there is always an earth and a heaven. But the level of earth is prior to the level of heaven. . . .

No existent thing is outside these three: Either effuser, or receiver of effusion, or that which appears from the two.[8]

Nasafī's insistence that the level of earth is prior to that of heaven seems to be rooted in the same logic that makes Ibn al-ʿArabī say that the "Lord" cannot be a lord without a "vassal," and the "God" depends upon the existence of the "divine thrall." Moreover, the Koranic creation myth makes clear that God first turned His attention toward the earth. After putting it in order, He differentiated the heavens:

It is He who created for you all that is in the earth, then He lifted Himself to heaven and proportioned them as seven heavens. (2:29)

What, do you disbelieve in Him who created the earth in two days? . . . And He ordained therein its provisions in four days, equal to those who ask. Then He lifted Himself to heaven when it was smoke, and said to it and to the earth, "Come willingly, or unwillingly." . . . So He determined them as seven heavens in two days. (41:9–12)

The Koran employs the word *heaven* (or *sky*) as it is commonly used in creation myths and in Far Eastern thought, never in the sense of "paradise" or what the Koran calls the "Garden" (*janna*). Sufi cosmologists usually place paradise outside the seven heavens altogether, since the Prophet visited it during his *miʿrāj* after having passed through them. According to Ibn al-ʿArabī, it is located between the eighth and the ninth heavens, that is, the Footstool and the Throne.[9]

Heaven and earth designate a vertical and static dimension of the cosmos. As such they are contrasted with the pair "this world" (*al-dunyā*) and the "next world" (*al-ākhira*), which designate a horizontal and dynamic relationship between our present situation in this life and our future situation after death. The static relationship between heaven and earth will remain in force until the Last Day, but then it will subsist in transmuted form. "On the day the earth shall be changed to other than the earth, and the heavens, and they sally forth unto God, the One, the Intensely Severe" (14:48).

The Koran's description of God's creation of heaven and earth recalls a primordial act that brings duality into existence and establishes the "pairs" as the fundamental components of existence. The Koran states explicitly that the heavens and the earth existed together in an undifferentiated state before creation.

Have not the unbelievers beheld that the heavens and the earth were a mass all sewn up, and then We unstitched them, and out of water fashioned every living thing? (21:30)

In six passages the Koran attributes to God the name, "*fāṭir* of the heavens and the earth." Translators usually render this term as "Originator" or "Creator," but the basic meaning of the root is to cleave, split, or rend. Hence the expression calls to mind the standard mythic theme of the separation of heaven and earth in order for a cosmos to come into existence. Other passages explain that it is only God's power that keeps heaven and earth apart.

And heaven—He raised it up [*rafʿ*], and set the Balance. . . . And earth—He set it down [*waḍʿ*] for all beings, therein fruits. . . . (55:7–11)

He holds back heaven lest it should fall upon the earth, save by His leave. (22:65)

What, do they not consider how the camel was created, how heaven was raised up, how the mountains were hoisted, how the earth was spread flat [*saṭḥ*]? (88:18–20)

And of His signs is that the heaven and earth stand firm by His command. (30:25)

A microcosmic equivalent of the separation of the heavens and the earth is the creation of Adam and Eve from a single soul. The two souls that derive from the primordial single soul then become the first human "pair" (*zawjān*). "Spouse" (*zawj*) in the following means literally one of the two members of a pair.

> It is He who created you from one soul and made from it its spouse that he might rest in her. (7:189)
>
> He created you of a single soul, then from it He appointed its spouse. (39:6)[10]

Typically, the Koran mentions the creation of the heavens and earth and then refers to other things that help fill up the space in between.

> Praise belongs to God, who created the heavens and the earth and appointed the darknesses and the light. (6:1)
>
> Surely your Lord is God, who created the heavens and the earth in six days. Then He sat Himself upon the Throne. He makes the night cover the day, which it pursues urgently. And [He created] the sun, the moon, and the stars. (7:54)
>
> He created the earth and the high heavens; the All-merciful sat Himself upon the Throne. To Him belongs all that is in the heavens and the earth and all that is between them, and all that is beneath the soil. (20:4–6)

The Tao of Heaven and Earth

In the Muslim view, there is nothing neutral or indifferent about heaven and earth. Creation has a purpose, and this purpose is intimately connected with the role of human beings. A Muslim cannot be Muslim and at the same time look "objectively" and "scientifically" at the cosmos, since that would imply detachment and disinterest, as if the universe were mute, without any message of moral and spiritual significance. To say that the cosmos reveals God's signs is to say that human beings must consider it in terms of the higher principles from which it derives. The Tao of heaven and earth must impinge upon the Tao of human conduct on both the individual and social levels. These two Taos are in truth one and the same Tao. There is no fundamental difference between the laws that govern nature and the laws that govern the social and moral orders.

One of the Koranic terms that is a good candidate for translating the word *Tao* into Arabic is *ḥaqq*, which means true, right, real, proper, correct (and the corresponding nominal forms). The Koran employs the word about 350 times, repeatedly stating that human beings must conform to it. A thorough explication of the range of its Koranic meanings would demand a lengthy monograph. Here I will discuss a few of the senses of the term that are immediately relevant to the present discussion.

The only reality that deserves the name *ḥaqq* in every sense is God. The opposite of *ḥaqq* is *bāṭil* (unreality or falsehood or vanity). In respect of God's incomparability, everything other than God—the whole cosmos—is false and unreal, but in respect of His similarity, all things reflect *ḥaqq* to some degree. The most direct reflections of *ḥaqq* are the prophets and the scriptures. Hence they also deserve the name *ḥaqq*. In the following, I translate *ḥaqq* as "real" in order to maintain consistency with its usage in a wide variety of contexts throughout this book, even though "truth" would often be a better translation.

> That is because God is the Real, and brings the dead to life, and is powerful over everything. (22:6)
>
> That is because God is the Real, and what they call upon apart from Him is unreal. (22:62, 31:30)
>
> That then is God, your Lord, the Real. What is there after the Real save going astray? (10:32)
>
> The Real has come and the unreal has vanished away. Surely the unreal is ever certain to vanish. (17:81)
>
> Say: "Is there any of your associates who guides to the Real?" Say: "God—He guides to the Real. Which is worthier to be followed: He who guides to the Real, or he who guides not, unless he is guided?" . . . Most of them follow only surmise, and surmise avails naught against the Real. (10:35–36)
>
> God sent forth the prophets . . . , and He

> sent down with them the Book with the Real, that it might judge between the people concerning their differences. (2:213)
>
> What We have revealed to thee of the Book is the Real, confirming what was before it. (35:31)
>
> These are the signs of the Book. And that which has been sent down to thee from thy Lord is the Real, but most people have no faith. (13:1)
>
> With the Real We have sent [the Koran] down, and with the Real it has come down. (17:105–6)
>
> O people, the Real has come to you from your Lord. Whosoever is guided is guided only to his own gain, and whosoever goes astray, it is only to his own loss. (10:108)
>
> What, is he who knows that what is sent down to thee from thy Lord is the Real, like him who is blind? Only those who have minds remember. (13:19)
>
> And a party had grieved, thinking of God thoughts that were not the Real, such as the pagans thought. . . . (3:154)
>
> O People of the Book, go not beyond the bounds in your religion, other than the Real, and follow not the caprices of a people who went astray before. . . . (5:77)

The Real brought by the prophets is the norm for human conduct in the present world. So also, it will be the norm through which human conduct will be weighed on the Day of Resurrection.

> Of those We created are a nation who guide by the Real, and by it act with justice. (7:181)
>
> Slay no soul that God has forbidden, except by the Real [i.e., by right]. (6:151, 17:33, 25:68)
>
> On that day God will give them in full their repayment in the Real, and they shall know that God is the manifest Real. (24:25)
>
> The weighing on that day is the Real. (7:8)

In short, the Koran employs the word *ḥaqq* to refer to the absolute reality that is God, the reflection of this reality that is revelation, the correct mode of activity that is the norm for human beings, and the standard by which human activity will be judged. It also employs the word *ḥaqq* in reference to the natural, created world. It insists that God's signs (or "verses") become manifest both in revelation and in the natural phenomena of the cosmos. Just as the prophets came with the Real, so also the universe was created with the Real.

> We created the heavens and the earth and everything between the two only with the Real. (15:85)
>
> Have you not seen that God created the heavens and the earth with the Real? (14:19)
>
> It is He who created the heavens and the earth with the Real. And the day He says, "Be!" and it is, His saying is the Real. (6:73)
>
> God created the heavens and the earth with the Real; surely in that is a sign for those who have faith. (29:44)
>
> It is He who made the sun a radiance, and the moon a light, and determined it by stations, that you may know the number of the years and the reckoning. God created that not save with the Real, differentiating the signs for a people who know. (10:5)
>
> We created not the heavens and earth, and everything between the two, in play. We created them only with the Real. (44:38–39)
>
> We have not created heaven and earth and everything between the two as vanity. (38:27)
>
> Had the Real followed their caprices, the heavens and the earth and everything within them would have been corrupted. (23:71)

The interrelationship of these meanings of the word Real are summed up nicely by Ibn al-ʿArabī. Having quoted a Koranic verse about creation "through the Real," he writes,

> The Real through which the cosmos was created is the Real after which we model our conduct [*taʾaddub*]. For it is the cause of the existence of the entities within the cosmos. Through it God will judge among His servants on the Day of Resurrection. According to it He sent down the revealed laws. Hence God said to His messenger David, "O David, We have appointed thee a vicegerent in the earth, so rule among people with the Real and follow not caprice" [38:26]. Although caprice is created with the Real, it is one of the things between heaven and earth, or it is the earth itself. Hence the station of right conduct [*adab*] is acting according to the Real and stopping with the Real.[11]

Human caprice or self-will (*hawā*)—an aberrant wind (*hawā'*) that does not conform to the Real but blows people's minds this way and that—upsets the balance of heaven and earth. Following caprice instead of following God's guidance is the fundamental shortcoming of human beings.

> Follow not caprice, lest you swerve. (4:135)
> Follow not their caprices, leaving the Real that has come to thee. (5:48)
> If thou followest their caprices, after the knowledge that has come to thee, then thou wilt surely be among the wrongdoers. (2:145)
> Have you seen him who has taken his caprice to be his god? (25:43)
> Who is further astray than he who follows his caprice rather than guidance from God? (28:50)
> Obey not him whose heart We have made forgetful of Our remembrance [*dhikr*], so that he follows his own caprice, and his affair has become all excess. But say: "The Real is from your Lord. Let whosoever will have faith, and let whosoever will disbelieve." (18:28–29)

The path of correct human conduct coincides with the Real and grows up out of the very nature of existence. Human beings were created to serve God and to act as vicegerents over His kingdom. Hence they accepted the Trust that was refused by the other creatures.

> I created jinn and mankind only to serve Me. (51:56)
> We offered the Trust to the heavens and the earth and the mountains, but they refused to carry it and were afraid of it. And the human being carried it. (33:72)

It is because of the trust and the vicegerency that human beings are given power over other creatures.

> Have you not seen that God has subjected to you whatsoever is in the heavens and the earth? (31:20)
> And He subjected to you the sun and the moon, constant upon their courses, and He subjected to you the night and the day, and gave you of all you asked Him. (14:33)
> Hast thou not seen that God has subjected to you all that is in the earth, and the ships to run upon the sea at His commandment? (22:65)
> He has subjected to you what is in the heavens and what is in the earth, all together, from Him. Surely in that are signs for a people who reflect. (45:13)

Human beings stand apart from heaven, earth, and the Ten Thousand Things because of their peculiar function in the cosmos. All other things follow the Real by their very natures, but humans have been given the freedom to accept or to reject the Real. This freedom makes them responsible for their choices. If they fail to live up to the Trust, they will suffer the consequences simply by the law of cause and effect. By rejecting the Tao, the normative equilibrium of the cosmos, they put themselves out of kilter with heaven and earth. What goes up must come down, and what deviates from the Real must be brought back to it. When deviation produces a distorted nature, the return to equilibrium will be experienced by the deviant as distortion and agony. The cosmos is the testing ground wherein human beings prove their own substances.

> It is He who created the heavens and the earth in six days—and His Throne was upon the water—that He might try you, which one of you is fairer in works. (11:7)

Heaven and Earth as Correlative Terms

The Real manifests itself in the heavens and the earth, appearing as the signs that human beings should ponder. The signs, whether prophetic or natural, point the way to conformity with the Real. The way in which heaven and earth—the most fundamental of created pairs—interrelate illustrates the laws that govern relationships in all domains.

The most salient feature of the heavens and the earth is the fact that they and everything within them are the property and kingdom of God, who exercises absolute control over them. The Koran makes this point in scores of verses. For example, the passage "And to God [or "to Him"] belongs the kingdom of the heavens and the earth" occurs fourteen times, sometimes along with the words, "and everything between the two" (5:17) or "everything within them" (5:120). Since all belong to God, all are His servants.

> None is there in the heavens and the earth but it comes to the All-merciful as a servant. He has indeed counted them, and He has numbered them exactly. (19:93)
>
> To God prostrate themselves all who are in the heavens, and every creature crawling on the earth. (16:49)
>
> To God prostrate themselves all who are in the heavens and the earth, willingly or unwillingly. (13:15)
>
> The seven heavens and the earth, and everyone within them, glorify Him. There is nothing that does not glorify Him in praise, but you do not understand their glorification. (17:44)

The Ikhwān al-Ṣafā᾽ make this same point employing more philosophical language:

> The whole cosmos, with its high spheres, exalted heavens, and everything within it, such as spiritual lights, natural, moving souls, faculties coursing through the corporeal pillars, and all the existent things and creatures; everything included in the heavens and the earth, from the highest of the high to the lowest of the low—all of it is a single body standing ready to receive the universal effusion from its God.[12]

ʿAbd al-Razzāq Kāshānī presents the same idea within the context of Ibn al-ʿArabī's doctrine of the Oneness of Being. He is commenting on the Koranic verse, "To Him belongs all that is in the heavens and the earth. All are obedient to Him" (2:116). In this verse, Kāshānī reads heavens and earth as referring to everything in existence, the high worlds and the low:

> *To Him belongs all that is in the heavens and the earth.* In other words, to Him belong the World of the Spirits and the World of the Bodies, which are the nonmanifest world and the manifest world. . . . *All are obedient to Him*, existent through His Being, acting through His act, nonexistent in their own essences. This is the utmost limit of obeying Him and undertaking His right, since He is Nondelimited Being, so nothing less than He exists. The entified existences are His attributes and names.[13]

Kāshānī makes a similar point in commenting on the verse, "Praise belongs to God who created the heavens and the earth and appointed the darknesses and the light" (6:1). Note how he describes heaven and earth as manifesting the complementary divine attributes encompassed by the terms *majesty* and *beauty*.

> *Praise belongs to God who created the heavens and the earth* as the manifestation of the perfections and attributes of beauty and majesty within the loci of manifestation, which are all the differentiated existent things. This is the perfection of all. Nondelimited praise belongs specifically to the Divine Essence, which comprehends all Its attributes and names in respect of origination. He brought into existence the heavens, the World of the Spirits, and the earth, the World of the Body. He configured within the World of the Body *the darknesses* of its levels, which are veils dark in their essence, and within the World of Spirits *the light* of knowledge and perception.[14]

On the one hand the heavens and earth are totally subordinate to God. God is yang, and the heavens and earth are yin. On the other hand the relationship between God and cosmos is repeated in the relationship between heaven and earth. Just as the cosmos is submitted to God, so also the earth is submitted to heaven. When the Koran employs the term *heavens* in the plural, it usually pairs it with the term *earth* and has in view the primary relationship between God and the cosmos. For example, "Do you not know that God's is the kingdom of the heavens and the earth?" (2:107). But when the Koran uses the term *heaven* in the singular, it frequently has in view the delineation of a relationship between the higher and lower domains of the cosmos as a reflection of the God/cosmos relationship. The relative qualities attributed to heaven and earth in these passages are of particular interest here, since they establish many of the terms of the Koranic yang/yin.

The heaven is the source for what God sends down to the earth and to human beings, for example, water and provisions. Qualitatively speaking, the heaven is high, active, and creative, while the earth is low, receptive, and fruitful.

> And We sent down out of heaven water blessed, and caused to grow thereby gardens and grains of harvest and tall palm trees laden with clusters of dates, a provision for the servants, and thereby We brought to life a land that was dead. (50:9–11)
>
> . . . the water that God sends down from heaven, therewith giving life to the earth after it is dead. (2:164; cf. 25:48, 29:63, 30:24)
>
> . . . the provision God sends down from heaven, and therewith brings the earth to life after it was dead. (45:5)
>
> Hast thou not seen how God has sent down out of heaven water, and in the morning the earth becomes green? (22:63)
>
> It is He who sent down out of heaven water, and thereby We have brought forth the shoot of every plant. (6:99)
>
> Hast thou not seen how God sends down out of heaven water, and therewith We bring forth fruits of diverse hues? (35:27)
>
> It is God who . . . sent down out of heaven water wherewith He brought forth fruits to be your provision. (14:32)
>
> In the earth are signs for those having sure faith; and in your selves. What, do you not see? And in heaven are your provision and that which you are promised. So, by the Lord of heaven and earth, it is as surely Real as that you have speech. (51:20–23)
>
> He who . . . sent down for you out of heaven water; and We caused to grow therewith gardens full of loveliness whose trees you could never grow. (27:60)
>
> It is He who sends down to you out of heaven water of which you drink . . . and thereby He brings forth for you crops, and olives, and palms, and vines, and all manner of fruit. (16:10)
>
> It is He who shows you His signs and sends down to you out of heaven provision. (40:13)

As the storehouse of provision, heaven is the source for everything that appears on earth. God's signs come down from heaven, whether as revelations or natural phenomena. Not only do blessings and bounty descend, but also wrath and punishment. The angels come down out of heaven, but only with the Real, only in conformity with the Tao.

> If We will, We shall send down on them out of heaven a sign, so their necks will stay humbled to it. (26:4)
>
> We sent down upon the wrongdoers punishment out of heaven for their ungodliness. (2:59)
>
> We sent down upon them punishment out of heaven for their wrongdoing. (7:162)
>
> Had there been in the earth angels walking at peace, We would have sent down upon them out of heaven an angel as Messenger. (17:95)
>
> We send not down the angels, save with the Real. (15:8)

Since God creates the heavens and the earth with the Real, everything that comes down from heaven comes down in a measure determined by the Real and known by God. Many Muslim theologians employ the word *measure* (*qadar*) in the sense of destiny or predestination, but the Koran uses the term in a broader sense. It refers both to the relationship between God and the cosmos, where everything is created in measure, and to the relationship between the two dimensions of the macrocosmic reflection of that relationship, that is, heaven and earth.

> Naught is there, but its treasuries are with Us, and We send it not down but in a known measure. And We loose the winds fertilizing, and We send down out of heaven water, and We give you to drink, and you are not its treasurers. It is We who give life, and make to die. (15:21–22)
>
> He who appointed the earth to be a cradle for you, . . . and who sent down out of heaven water in measure. And We brought to life thereby a land that was dead; even so you shall be brought forth. (43:10–11)
>
> And We sent down out of heaven water in measure and lodged it in the earth. (23:18)

Just as heaven and earth are one of the fundamental "pairs" created by God, so also everything created within the heavens and the earth duplicates this dual relationship.

> And heaven—We built it with hands, and We extend it wide. And the earth—We spread it forth. O excellent Smoothers! And of everything We have created a pair, that perhaps you may remember. (51:47–49)
>
> He . . . sent down water out of heaven, and therewith We have brought forth pairs of various growing things. (20:53)

Heaven, in short, is associated with highness, light, ascent, activity, blessing, provision, origination. Earth is associated with lowness, darkness, descent, reception, fruitfulness, actualization. The qualities associated with the two sides may be found in many sets of pairs, beginning with the complementary divine names. Thus Rūmī connects heaven and earth with a pair of divine names, Uplifter (*rāfiʿ*) and Downletter (*khāfiḍ*), and hence also with all the shifting and changing qualities of the world. Through the interaction of these two names, God keeps the cosmos separated into pairs and preserves it from dissolving back into the undifferentiation from whence it came. The realm of many shades and colors that these names produce will not be overcome by God's Unity until the next world.

> The Creator is Uplifter and Downletter. Without these two attributes, no act could be performed.
>
> Look at the letting down of earth and the lifting up of heaven: Without these two attributes, heaven could not revolve, O friend!
>
> The downletting and uplifting of this earth is of another kind: Half the year desolate, half the year green and moist.
>
> The downletting and uplifting of this circling and distressful time is of another kind: One half night, one half day.
>
> The downletting and uplifting of this mixed bodily constitution is that it is sometimes well and sometimes ill.
>
> Know that all the states of the world are like this: famine, drought, peace, war—all for putting to the test.
>
> This world flies through the air with these two wings—these two make our souls a place of fear and hope.
>
> All this is so that the world may continue to flutter like a leaf in the cold and hot winds of resurrection and death,
>
> Until the vat of our Jesus-like one-coloredness destroys the value of our vat of one hundred different dyes.
>
> For that world is like a salt desert—everyone who goes there loses his multicoloration.
>
> Look at the earth: It makes the many colored creatures into one color in the grave.
>
> This earth is the salt desert of the outward bodies, while the salt desert of meanings is something else.
>
> That salt desert of meanings is supra-formal, forever new, from eternity without beginning until eternity without end.
>
> In this world newness is the opposite of oldness—in that world newness has no opposite, no like, no number.[15]

In passages quoted above, Kāshānī demonstrated how heaven and earth display yin qualities in relation to the divine. In another passage, he shows how heaven displays yang qualities in relation to earth. He is commenting on the Koranic verse, "There is nothing that does not glorify Him in praise, but you do not understand their glorification" (17:44).

> Each thing has a characteristic that does not belong to any other thing. Each has a perfection possessed by it alone. When it has not yet actualized that perfection, it yearns for it and seeks it. When it actualizes it, it preserves and loves it. By making manifest its own characteristic, it declares God incomparable with any associate [*sharīk*]. Otherwise, it would not be unique in that characteristic. It is as if the thing says with the tongue of its state, "I declare Him one just as He made me one." By seeking its own perfection, it declares Him incomparable with the attributes of imperfection. It is as if it says, "O Perfect, make me perfect." By making its own perfection manifest, it is saying, "The Perfect Perfecter has made me perfect," and so on.
>
> Even a lioness, for example, through its care for her cub, is saying, "Be kind to me, O Kindly! Have mercy upon me, O Compassionate!" And by seeking provision she says, "O Provider!"
>
> Hence the seven heavens glorify Him through everlastingness, perfection, elevation, effectivity, bringing into existence, lordship, and by the fact that "Each day He is upon some task" [55:29]. The earth glorifies Him with constancy, fixity, creativity, provi-

sion, nurturing, kindliness, mercy, receiving obedience, showing thanks through reward, and so on.[16]

Similitudes

In many—if not most—of the Koranic passages where heaven and earth are discussed, "heaven" can be read as "sky" without any apparent problem. God sends down water from the sky. In other words, the rains come. Likewise the English word *heaven* can refer both to the sky and to a spiritual realm that is also "up," but in a different sense. The Islamic tradition reads the term in either or both senses, as appropriate to a given context.

But even if we understand a Koranic verse about rain and the earth coming to life in the most literal sense, it is difficult to interpret it in a purely naturalistic way. Certainly such verses mean that living things depend upon water, and this water is sent down from the sky by God. But the discussion concerns life. And life, in the Islamic context, is a divine attribute. As the Koran puts it, "He is the Alive, the Self-subsistent" (2:255). Hence a verse about sky and rain is also saying that through rain, God gives life—His own quality—to a lifeless world. A suprasensory, invisible attribute enters this world through visible means. Parallel remarks can be made for every divine attribute, since no attribute can be perceived in itself. Attributes can be known only inasmuch as they become manifest through things and activities. Hence Muslim intellectuals have never supposed that the Koran juxtaposes sky and earth simply to describe the physical facts of existence. All things, after all, are signs of God. The physical is the manifestation of the spiritual. The two are intimately intertwined, even if we understand them as opposites. "Things become distinguished through their opposites," as the Arabic proverb reminds us. Heaven cannot be known without earth, nor earth without heaven.

The Koran itself identifies heaven as the locus of the angels, or at least the direction from which the angels "come down" when they have occasion to appear in this world. "Upon the day that heaven is split asunder with the clouds, and the angels are sent down in majesty" (25:25). When we look at the hadith literature and the commentary tradition, the intimate relationship between the high dimension of physical reality and the spiritual or divine order of things is made explicit. For example, the Prophet used to walk outside with his head uncovered in the rain. When asked why he did so, he said, "It is newly acquainted with my Lord."[17]

The Koran itself encourages interpretation going beyond the merely phenomenal level. Not only does it often tell us that all natural phenomena are "signs" for people who reflect, it also frequently points out that its own words are similitudes or likenesses or analogies (*amthāl*). The commentators, even the more literal minded like Fakhr al-Dīn Rāzī, are quick to follow its leads. For example, in its first use of the term *heaven*, the Koran makes clear that the term is employed as a similitude.

> The likeness of [the hypocrites] is . . . as a cloudburst out of heaven in which are darkness, thunder, and lightning. They put their fingers in their ears against the thunderclaps, fearful of death; and God encompasses the unbelievers. (2:19)

Maybudī, having dealt with the literal meaning of the words, then turns to the meaning of the passage as a likeness. Though he does not state explicitly the meaning of "heaven" in the passage, by implication it is either God as the ultimate source of the Koran, or the angelic world, the Koran's more immediate source. The "hypocrites" are those who make an outward show of believing in Islam but are inwardly its enemies.

> The hypocrites are like a group of travelers caught in the desert during a severe rain on a dark night. The rain is so severe, the night so dark, the thunder so loud, and the lightning so bright that they fear that they will be hit by a thunderbolt and die.
>
> The rain is the likeness of the Koran, since it brings hearts to life, just as rain

brings the dead land to life. The darknesses are like the unbelief in which the hypocrites are stuck. The thunder is like those verses of the Koran that threaten and frighten them, while the lightning is like their giving witness to faith. In other words, when the lightning flashes, the hypocrites are able to see a short way ahead in that darkness and rain. When the lightning ceases, they are kept back. In the same way, when they give witness, they join with submission [*islām*]. But when they go back to their satans, they deny their witnessing and fall into the darkness of unbelief.

Just as lightning is not continuous and the stranded person takes no real benefit from it, so also the hypocrites take no benefit from giving witness, since it has no reality. And just as those travelers in the darkness put their fingers in their ears so as not to hear the sound of torment and thunderbolts, since it threatens them with death, so also the hypocrites put their fingers in their ears so as not to hear the verses of the Koran and the revelation, which make manifest their secret. They fear that their hearts may incline toward it, that it will bring them into submission and faith. They insist on unbelief because they are afraid that if they fall away from it they will come to submission.[18]

In repeatedly referring to its verses as likenesses, the Koran is clearly asking its readers to ponder and reflect and then to apply the lessons learned to their own situation. In using terms such as *heaven* and *earth* as likenesses, it has in view the qualities associated with the two sides in the world view of the people to whom it is addressed, and in the modified world view represented by the Koran itself. The qualitative correspondences depend largely on analogies between the microcosm and macrocosm.

I quote one more verse that the Koran presents explicitly as a likeness to illustrate how the Muslim thinkers developed the qualitative descriptions of nature found in the text:

> He sends down out of heaven water, and the wadis flow each in its measure, and the torrent carries a swelling scum. And out of that over which they kindle fire, being desirous of ornament or delightful objects, out of that rises a scum the like of it. So God strikes both the Real and the unreal. As for the scum, it vanishes as jetsam, and what profits men abides in the earth. Even so God strikes His similitudes. (13:17)

The first explanation is taken from *Laṭā'if al-ishārāt* of Qushayrī (d. 465/1072).

This verse comprises similitudes struck by God to compare the revealed Koran with water sent down from heaven. He compares hearts to wadis, and He compares the whisperings of Satan and the fancies of the soul to scum on top of water. He compares the Real to substances pure of loathsomeness, like gold, silver, copper, and so on. He compares the unreal to the scum of these substances.

Wadis are diverse in their smallness and largeness, and they carry water according to their measure, whether little or much. In the same way, hearts are diverse in their ability to carry, according to their weakness or strength.

When a flood takes place in a wadi, it purifies it. In the same way, when the Koran is memorized in hearts, it negates whisperings and caprice from them.

Water may be accompanied by that which makes it opaque, while parts of it may be freed from what sullies it. This is similar to the situation of faith and the understanding of the Koran in the hearts of the faithful when they are delivered from the insinuations of Satan and from ruinous thoughts. Hearts vary from pure to opaque.

The substances from which containers are made are delivered from loathsomeness when they are melted down. In the same way the Real becomes distinguished from the unreal. The Real remains and the unreal disappears.

It is said that the lights that shine in hearts negate the traces of discomfort, the light of certainty negates the darkness of doubt, knowledge negates the insinuations of ignorance, the light of recognition negates the trace of disavowal, the light of witnessing negates the traces of lower human nature, and the lights of concentration negate the traces of dispersion. When the lights of the realities shine, the traces of sensual gratifications turn to nothing. The lights of the rising sun of gnosis negate the darkness of the "night," which is to take the trace of "others" into account.

Moreover, the substances from which containers are made are diverse. One container is made of gold, another from zinc, and so on. So also hearts are diverse. A tradition says,

"God has containers, and they are hearts."[19] One person is a striving renouncer, another an ecstatic lover, another a fearful worshiper, another a gnostic declarer of Unity, another an abstinent worshiper, another a Sufi aspirant given over to praying all night. Their poet says,

Their colors are greatly varied and yet
they are given the same water from one pool.[20]

Rashīd al-Dīn Maybudī, writing in Persian about seventy-five years after Qushayrī, comments on the same verse as follows. The verse itself is italicized.

This verse is the sphere of the science of reality and gnosis. *He sends down out of heaven water*. In other words, He revealed from on high to the hearts and ears of the prophets and He inspired the intellects and insights of the sages. . . . *The wadis flow each in its measure*. In other words, He made the hearts see to the measure of their capacity, life, and illumination. The hearts of the prophets became bright and illumined with the light of revelation and messengerhood, and the hearts of God's friends with the lamp of wisdom and gnosis. *In its measure*, that is, each individual [sees] according to his own measure, in degrees and levels. One is higher, one in the middle, one lower. The ranking in degrees and the disparity are apparent to everyone. Concerning the prophets He says, "We preferred some of the prophets over others" [17:55]. Concerning the friends, He says, "They are degrees with God" [3:163]. One has more than prophecy through messengerhood, another has more than wisdom through prophecy, another has more than knowledge through gnosis, another has more than faith and witnessing through tasting the reality, another has the knowledge of certainty with explication, another the truth of certainty with direct vision. He gave to each person what was appropriate. He placed within each heart where there was room.

And the torrent carries a swelling scum. . . . Though those hearts are bright and lit up, they are not free of whisperings, insinuations, and minor lapses, since Satan is always sitting in ambush waiting for a way into hearts. He wants to toss in a doubt or a mistake, make up a lie, steal away something memorized. Satan even pilfered a little something from him who was the greatest in the world, the lord of the children of Adam, the pearl of the oyster of nobility, in spite of the perfection of prophecy and the fearlessness of messengerhood. For God says: "[We sent never any Messenger or Prophet before thee], but that Satan cast into his wish, when he was wishing" [22:52]. So he sought refuge in God from Satan's goading, for he said: "My Lord, I seek refuge in Thee from the goadings of Satan."[21]

And out of that over which they kindle fire, that is, out of that which they reflect upon, ponder, and deduce from; *being desirous of* a proof or an unveiling; *out of that rises a scum*. A scum is something in addition to the inspiration of God and the suggestion of the angel. [This scum is] *the like of it*, that is, like the error being cast by Satan. In other words, one person is busy in the sea of reflection with the hand of deduction bringing out the pearls of meanings from Koranic verses and hadiths. Another seeks for the realities of unveiling through pondering the attribute of inspiration. They strive and work so much in their reflection, pondering, and deduction that they pass beyond the right measure and seek increase over the inspiration of God and the suggestion of the angel. This increase is just like that which Satan has decked out fair. Both must be avoided.

As for the scum, it vanishes as jetsam. In other words, as for the error, the lapses, and the excess, they vanish through remembrance, because of His words, "The godfearing, when a visitation from Satan touches them, remember, and then see clearly" [7:201].

And what profits men . . . abides in the earth. In other words, it takes firm root in the heart. That erroneous opinion, lapse of the tongue, and excess because of Satan does not last and does not find a resting place in the heart of the person of faith. Those who have faith have the mention of God upon their tongues and His remembrance in their hearts. Satan's trouble-making cannot last when there is remembrance of God. That is why the Lord of the worlds says, "When a visitation from Satan touches them, they remember, and then see clearly" [7:201]. That which is useful for people becomes firmly rooted in the heart. It is useful because the wholesomeness of the heart and religion lie within it, since it follows the measure of the Sharia and the Reality. It is a tree whose roots are firmly grounded, whose branches are luxuriant, whose wood is fruitful. Its roots are driven into the earth of faithfulness, its branches spread in the air of contentment, and it gives the fruits of vision and encounter.

In short, this verse alludes to the fact that when the light of knowledge shines in the heart, it clears away the traces of disobedience's darkness. But these lights are diverse, and these acts of disobedience differ. The light of certainty takes away the darkness of doubt, the light of knowledge takes away the insinuations of ignorance, the light of recognition effaces the traces of disavowal, the light of witnessing takes away the traces of the darkness of lower human nature, the light of concentration lifts up the traces of dispersion. Then, beyond all of these, stands the light of professing God's Unity [*tawḥīd*]. When the sun of Unity lifts its head from the horizon of the Unseen, duality says,

Night went, O Morning, and I became one with Thee—
How long this talk of human attributes and man?[22]

ʿAbd al-Razzāq Kāshānī explains the same verse from a strictly microcosmic point of view. Heaven is the holy human spirit, water is knowledge sent down by God, and the hearts are the instruments through which human beings receive the divine knowledge. The soul is the dark, earthlike dimension of the human being, cut off from the divine light. It must be transformed through love, thereby taking on the luminous qualities of heaven and discarding the limiting qualities of earth.

He sends down out of heaven, which is the spirit of holiness, *water*, that is, knowledge. *And the wadis*, the hearts, *flow each in* the *measure* of their preparednesses. *The torrent* of knowledge *carries a scum*, that is, the loathsome, vile, and base attributes of the earth, which is the soul. *And out of that over which they kindle* the *fire* of love—out of the gnostic sciences, unveilings, realities, and meanings that stir up love—*being desirous of* the *ornament* of the soul and the soul's splendor through these things, since these are the soul's perfections; *or* [being desirous of] *delightful objects*, that is, virtuous character traits that are acquired through these perfections, since these are some of the things within which the soul takes delight; *out of that rises a scum*, loathsomeness, *the like of it*. This scum represents things like the soul's gazing upon and seeing itself, conceiving of itself as perfect or virtuous and adorned with the ornament of those attributes, its being self-satisfied with and becoming veiled, and everything else that is considered a blight of the soul and the sins of its states. *So God strikes both the Real and the unreal. As for the scum, it vanishes as jetsam*, thrown far away, annihilated through knowledge, as God says: "[He sends down on you water from heaven], to purify you thereby" [8:11]. *And what profits men*, that is, the meanings from the Real and the pure virtues, *abides in the earth*, the soul.[23]

Shifting Relationships

Along with the Koranic terms unseen and visible, or heaven and earth, some authorities employ other sets of Koranic terms, such as Dominion and Kingdom, or Command and Creation. Various authors draw the line between the two sides with

Table 10 Contrasting Qualities According to Kāshānī in *Taʾwīl al-Qurʾān*

yang	yin
heaven	earth
unseen	visible
dominion	kingdom
command	creation
high	low
bright	dark
subtle	dense
spiritual	corporeal
suprasensory	sensory

different degrees of complexity and sophistication. Normally the visible world is considered to be the same as the realm of corporeal and sensory things, while the unseen world embraces spiritual and nonsensory things. Thus Kāshānī writes,

> *It is He who created the heavens*, the spirits, *and the earth*, the body, *through the Real* [6:73], thereby putting everything in its proper place as is the requirement of His Essence.[24]
>
> *To God belongs the kingdom of the heavens*, the World of the Spirits, *and of the earth*, the World of the Bodies, *and all that is between them* [5:17], all the forms and accidents, manifest and nonmanifest.[25]

These parallel sets of terms establish a clear relationship that can be understood in terms of contrasting qualities. In general the first term represents yang qualities and the second yin. (See Table 10.)

The situation becomes more complex as soon as we follow the logic of relationships and shake loose from the idea that absolute difference can appear in the created realm. Every correlative term is limited and defined by its correlative. Hence it cannot be an absolute point of reference. The differentiations among things that make it possible to know them come only through distinction and opposition. "Things become distinguished through their opposites." As Rūmī puts it,

> The locus of manifestation for a thing is its opposite, so each opposite aids its own opposite.[26]

> No opposite can be known without its opposite. Having suffered a blow, you will know a caress.[27]

There can be no absolutes within creation, since nothing stands alone. At the very least, a thing must be subordinate to its Creator. But the Creator is not absolute in every respect, since It is delimited by the created, just as the Lord is bound by the vassal and the God by the divine thrall. Only the Essence is absolute, since It alone has no need for anything else. It is independent and self-sufficient, with or without the universe. Hence God as Essence stands beyond opposition. He has no opposites in existence. But God as possessor of the names stands opposite the cosmos. Moreover, the names of the acts He performs within the cosmos diverge. Hence these names have contraries within God, such as Beautiful and Majestic. In this respect He brings all opposites together within Himself. To quote Rūmī again,

> His description is not contained within the intellect, for He is the Coincidence of Opposites. Wonderful composition without composition! Wonderful freely acting Compelled One![28]

If we look at the attributes of God's Essence, such as life and knowledge, we see that their opposites—death and ignorance—do not exist as such. What we call death and ignorance are relative lacks of life and knowledge. Only absolute nonexistence—which, of course, does not exist—could possess absolute death and absolute ignorance.

> God's light has no opposite within existence, that through its opposite it might be made manifest.[29]

> Every light has a fire, every rose a thorn; a serpent watches over every treasure hidden in the ruins.
>
> Oh, Thy Rosegarden has no thorns! Thy pure Light has no fire! Around Thy Treasure is no serpent, no blow, no teeth![30]

In other words, absolute light is God, absolute knowledge is God, absolute power is God, absolute good is God, and so on. The absolute opposites of these qualities do not exist. Hence the whole universe is in some respect similar to God, since it reflects these names in some way. But since the corporeal things are the most distant existent things from God, the opposites of God's attributes can be attributed to them, so long as we remember that these are not absolute ascriptions. Thus, for example, God is the High (*al-ʿalī*), the heavens are high, the earth is low. God is the Light of the heavens and the earth (24:35), the heavens are luminous, the earth is dark. God is the Alive, the spiritual world is alive through the divine spirit, and the corporeal world has no life except through the spiritual domain. God is the Knower of the unseen and the invisible, the spiritual beings have knowledge of various dimensions of the two worlds, the corporeal beings have such a limited knowledge that, in effect, they are ignorant.

The ascription of attributes such as highness, light, life, and knowledge to created things pertains to a relative domain. If the First Intellect embraces the knowledge of all created things, yet it is ignorant in face of God's infinite knowledge. If heaven is high, this is to speak of its relationship with earth, since heaven is low in relation to God. The same thing can be said for other qualities that are attributed to heaven, such as bright and subtle. These are not absolute qualities, since they are possessed only in relation to earth. Hence also, earth is not low, dark, and dense in any absolute sense, only in relation to heaven. In relation to absolute nothingness earth is high, luminous, and subtle.

Since there are no absolutes within creation, things can be understood only in their relationships with God or with other things. There are two extreme poles, represented by spirit and body, light and darkness, heaven and earth, subtlety and density. Between the two poles stands a spectrum of created things that are in some ways qualitatively ambivalent. From about the time of Suhrawardī (d. 587/1191) onward, many Muslim cosmologists refer to this realm that fills the space between the spiritual world and the corporeal world as the "World of Imagination." This "imaginal" realm is neither completely corporeal nor completely spiritual. Ibn al-ʿArabī and his school develop this three world scheme in great detail.

We should not think that there are any hard and fast lines separating the three worlds. In fact, many of our authors tell us that the worlds are innumerable and that these three are merely the "general principles" (*kulliyyāt*) of the worlds.[31] There are no sharp edges in existence. As Ibn al-ʿArabī puts it, "There is nothing in existence but *barzakhs*," that is, "isthmuses" or intermediate stages of existence.[32] Everything lies between two other things and every world between two other worlds. Nothing can be known in itself, only in relationship to other things. Ibn al-ʿArabī concludes that everything in existence other than God can be called "imaginal," since each thing manifests qualities in an ambiguous sort of way. Neither absolute light (*nūr*) nor absolute darkness (*ẓulma*) can be found in the created realm, so all things are varying degrees of "brightness" (*ḍiyāʾ*), neither purely luminous nor purely dark. There is no absolute highness or lowness, so all things stand in the middle. There is no absolute subtlety or density, so everything is a mixture of the two.

By discussing three worlds instead of two, Muslim cosmologists place even greater stress upon qualitative ambiguity and the importance of taking relationships into account. The middle world is "imaginal" because, like an image in a mirror or a dream, it combines attributes of both sides and cannot be discussed in isolation without distorting its reality. It is neither a spirit nor a body, but it has certain attributes that are spiritual and certain that are bodily. It is neither luminous nor dark, but something in between. Like fire, it combines light and darkness. The whole cosmos is imaginal because it stands halfway between the absolutely Real, or Being, and the absolutely unreal, or nothingness.

The cosmic World of Imagination is subtle in relation to bodily things, but dense in relation to spiritual things. Depending on the point of view, it is luminous or dark, high or low, spiritual or corporeal, suprasensory or sensory. We have already seen that the status of the heavens is rather ambiguous. Sometimes heaven is considered identical with the spiritual world, sometimes it is seen as one of the two poles of the corporeal world. In some verses the Koran speaks of the "unseen of the heavens and the earth" (2:33, 11:123, 16:77), thereby suggesting that both heaven and earth have unseen as well as visible dimensions. Because the seven heavens are ambiguous in nature, neither completely corporeal nor completely spiritual, the cosmologists often place them in the imaginal world. The planets clearly partake of the same ambiguity. As bodies that we witness in the sky, they are visible, but as "swimmers" (*sābiḥ*) in a heavenly world inhabited by angels, they have invisible dimensions.

How then do we gain knowledge of things, if the labels we place upon them have no absolute worth? Whatever knowledge we gain will clearly be ambiguous. But ambiguous knowledge can be sufficient to describe our situation in relation to God. In effect, such a way of looking at things relativizes everything other than God, and this is one of the primary senses of "There is no god but God": There is no truth but the Truth, no real but the Real, no absolute but the Absolute. Any knowledge having any degree of certainty can only be acquired by perceiving the relationship between the Absolute and the things. Relationships are defined in terms of a vast number of qualities, and these are summarized by the divine names and attributes. Through God's names, provided in revelation by the Real Itself, human beings gain access to those qualities that provide a relatively absolute handhold on the nature of things.

The degree to which a given author attempts to sort out the various relationships among the levels of the cosmos depends upon a large number of factors, such as his own grasp of the fundamental texts, his training in various sciences, and the point he wishes to bring out. It is the last which is of particular importance for our purposes, since it helps explain why a single author will seemingly contradict himself, or explain the same Koranic verse in a variety of ways depending upon the context of the discussion. What is envisaged is the qualitative relationships, and these may change depending on the specific qualities envisaged.

The Seven Heavens

The Koran states explicitly in several verses that there are seven heavens. It also refers to the planets that "swim" in each heaven. The seven "planets"—in the Greek sense of wandering heavenly bodies—are the moon, Mercury, Venus, the sun, Mars, Jupiter, and Saturn. The heavens as such are invisible, while the planets are visible, at least to the extent that their light shines down on earth. But as we have already seen, many cosmologists place the heavens and the planets in an ambiguous realm, neither completely visible nor completely invisible.

Some of the clearest early texts that place the heavens within a relatively unseen dimension of existence are the accounts of the Prophet's ascension to God (*miʿrāj*). The Prophet tells us that he met one or more of the earlier prophets in each of the heavens. He describes corporeal and sensory events that took place in the sphere of each planet. Yet these events clearly pertain to a spiritual domain of existence. In other words, the events occurred in an ambiguous realm, neither purely corporeal nor purely spiritual. This is the realm known later as the "World of Imagination." Finally the Prophet passed beyond the heavens into a purely spiritual world and eventually into the Divine Presence, beyond all differentiation and opposition. One of the oldest of these accounts is found in the two most authoritative collections of hadith, Bukhārī and Muslim. It reads in part as follows:

> While I was lying down at al-Ḥaṭīm [a wall on the northwest side of the Kaaba] someone came to me and made a split from here to here (meaning from the pit of his chest to the hair below his navel), then took out my heart. I was next brought a gold dish full of faith, and my heart was washed, then filled up and put back. . . . I was then brought a beast smaller than a mule and larger than a donkey, which was white, was called al-Burāq, and stepped a distance equal to the range of its vision. I was mounted on it, and Gabriel went with me till he came to the lowest heaven. He asked that the gate be opened. When he was asked who he was, he replied that he was Gabriel. He was asked who was with him. He replied that it was Muhammad. He was asked whether he had been sent for. When he replied that he had been, the words were uttered, "Welcome; his coming is good," and the gate was opened.

> When I entered Adam was there, and Gabriel said, "This is your father Adam, so give him a salutation." I did so, and when he had returned my salutation he said, "Welcome to the good son and the good prophet." Gabriel then took me up till he came to the second heaven.[33]

So the account continues. Muhammad meets John and Jesus in the second heaven, Joseph in the third, Idris (usually identified with Enoch) in the fourth, Aaron in the fifth, Moses in the sixth, and Abraham in the seventh. These prophets clearly do not exist in their earthly bodies in the visible world. They have returned to God. But they have not "gone to heaven" in the Christian sense simply because they are located in the "heavens," since, as remarked earlier, heaven in the Islamic sense is not paradise. Nor does their location within the heavens suggest that they have not reached salvation or do not dwell in the Garden. Quite the opposite. It suggests that because of their attaining to the highest stages of human perfection, they dwell with God in perfect felicity. But at the same time, they are the human embodiments of the seven degrees of the heavenly world. Each of them is an outstanding exemplar of those divine qualities that "come down from heaven" into the earth. The Koran says of the prophets, "They *are* degrees with God" (3:163), not, "They *have* degrees." As Ibn al-ʿArabī remarks, this verse suggests that each prophet plays a cosmic function far beyond any "human" role in the ordinary sense of the term.[34] Ṣadr al-Dīn Qūnawī makes these points in keeping with the teachings of Ibn al-ʿArabī's school:

> Know that every prophet and friend of God . . . is a locus of manifestation for one of the universal realities of the cosmos, the divine names pertaining to those realities, and the spirits of those realities. These spirits are the Higher Plenum[35] with all the diversity of their levels and their relationships with the high world. To this point the Prophet made allusion when he said that Adam is in the first heaven, Jesus in the second, Joseph in the third, Idris in the fourth, Aaron in the fifth, Moses in the sixth, and Abraham in the seventh.
>
> It is clear that the spirits of these prophets are not spatially located. Therefore the Prophet meant only to point to the strength of their relationships—in respect of their levels, their sciences, their states, and the levels of their communities—with that heaven. In this world, their states are the form of the properties of the levels and the heavens. It is in this connection that all the great ones among the Folk of God mention in their technical terms that some of the friends of God are "upon the heart of Gabriel," some "upon the heart of Michael," some "upon the heart of Seraphiel," and so on.[36]

Qūnawī's disciple Farghānī explains the qualitative nature of the heavens in terms of the divine names, which are the roots of all created qualities. He has been discussing the creation of the heavens and the earth from the "mass all sewn up," the undifferentiated original substance mentioned in the Koran. "To become entified" (*taʿayyun*), a technical term that we have already met, means to become determined and differentiated as a specific entity or thing, as distinct from other entities and things. Note that the relationship envisaged at first is that between God and the cosmos. Hence the cosmos's quality of receptivity is stressed.

> The sewn-up material that belongs to the heavens and the earth became entified such that the heavens became distinguished from the earth. Heaven was engendered as a subtle smoke while earth became a dense compound thing.
>
> The name Form-giver became entified to give each of the two an appropriate form. God addressed their material with His words, "[Then He lifted Himself up to heaven when it was smoke, and He said to it and the earth,] 'Come willingly, or unwillingly.' [They said, 'We come willingly']" [41:11]. In other words, come forward and receive the form determined for each of you by the name Form-giver. "Come willingly" in respect of the property of your particular existence, which has knowledge of its own good and of the perfection connected to its reception of everything that issues forth from its Universal Root. It chooses that reception and inclines toward it by its very essence, with no resistance. Or come "unwillingly," in respect of the property of your possibility and your nonexistence, which is ignorant of its own good and perfection. You will be forced, through coercion and severity, to accept to make manifest the Root of perfection.

"They said, 'We come willingly,'" because they were near the root of their innate disposition and the domination of the property of oneness and undifferentiation—which are the most specific characteristics of Being within them in this state—over the property of differentiation and manyness, which are the specific characteristics of possibility.

At this stage of existence heaven and earth are dominated by oneness rather than manyness, Necessity rather than possibility, Being rather than knowledge. Hence they were perfectly receptive to the one effusion from the One. They were naturally infused with luminosity, subtlety, nearness, and all the attributes connected to the side of the Necessary Being. They had hardly any trace of the individual self-assertion connected to manyness, dispersion, distance, darkness, and possible existence. Hence the heavens and earth were perfect "Muslims." As good servants of God, they submitted readily to His command. Then the yang power of the One exercised its effects in various modalities. Heaven, through its receptivity toward the undifferentiated power of the One, is differentiated into the seven heavens. Each heaven manifests diverse qualities that were latent in the One and designated by various divine names. Note that in each case Farghānī carefully qualifies himself in order not to make the point of view in question seem in any way exclusive of other points of view.

At this point, the property of the original movement of love, . . . in keeping with the property of the name Form-giver, permeated the sewn-up spiritual material that was actualized in the sensory level. Hence that material came into movement in respect of its central point, following a cyclic motion. It assumed the form of a first heaven in one respect and a fourth heaven in another respect in keeping with the property of the name Form-giver. It became the locus of manifestation for the attribute of life and the domination of heat. In keeping with God's noble purpose for the name that was entified within this heaven—that is, the name Alive—the name Form-giver entified a luminous locus of manifestation: the planet called the sun. The sun became as it were the governing soul of this heavenly form.

Then Form-giver entified three heavens above the form of this heaven and three below it, and it entified within each of them a governing soul: the planet specified for each heaven. That planet is the locus of manifestation for a name that is entified according to a reality whose locus of manifestation is the heaven.

Hence the fourth heaven, which is in the center of the seven heavens, is the locus of manifestation for the attribute of life. The third heaven is the locus of manifestation for desire, the second the locus of manifestation for equity and justice, the first the locus of manifestation for speech. . . . The fifth heaven is the locus of manifestation for power, the sixth for knowledge, the seventh for generosity. That is why Abraham—who is described by generosity, magnanimity, and care for the rights of guests through himself, his property, and his sons[37]—is seen in the seventh heaven.

The planet sun is the locus of manifestation for the Alive, which is all-comprehensive.[38] The manifestation of the governing property of its gatekeeper, the Life-giver, is most complete and manifest through it and in it.

The planet Venus is the locus of manifestation for the name Desiring. The manifestation of the property of its gatekeeper, which is the Form-giver, is in one respect greatest in it.

The planet Mercury is the locus of manifestation for the name Just. The property of its follower, the Author [*al-bārī'*], is in one respect most manifest within it.

The planet moon is the locus of manifestation for the name Speaker. The governing property of its follower, which is the Creator, is in one respect strongest within it.

The planet Mars is the locus of manifestation for the name Powerful. The strength of its gatekeeper, who is the Severe, is in one respect strongest within it.

The planet Saturn is the locus of manifestation for the name Generous. The governing property of the name Lord, whose relationship to it is the most perfect, is strongest within it.[39]

The Four Elements

Cosmologists often express the subtlety and ambiguity of qualitative relationships through the idea of the four "pillars" (*ar-*

kān) or "elements" (*ʿanāṣir*). These are the "substances" from which the visible universe is compounded. They possess a certain relationship to the higher realms because of their relative invisibility, which results from their "simplicity" (*basāṭa*), the fact that they are not compound things. In contrast, minerals, plants, and animals are all compounded of the elements. Many texts imply, if not state explicitly, that the four elements themselves pertain to the invisible world, precisely because they have no parts and therefore cannot be present in a world where everything is divisible. In other words, the elements indicate qualities rather than actual manifest things. Thus it is often said that each element exists in pure form only in its own "sphere" (*kura*), while our locus of experience is the place where their four spheres of influence intersect.

Whether or not the pillars coincide precisely with the four things in the cosmos that go by the names earth, water, air, and fire, the cosmologists consistently discuss the pillars in terms of their qualities. In general, earth is dry and cold, water wet and cold, air wet and hot, fire dry and hot. In descriptions of cosmogenesis, the four elements are originally undifferentiated. Then the earth sinks to the center because of its density, fire rises to the top because of its subtlety and heat, water rests above the earth, and air fills up the space between water and fire. In terms of our own discussion, examination of the elements helps explain how heavenly qualities become manifest in different degrees within the earth. The earth as an element (*arḍ* or *turāb*) represents the qualities furthest from heaven, while fire represents those earthly qualities that are closest to the heavenly qualities. Hence the four elements represent four qualitative degrees of earthly existence, degrees that ascend from the lowest to the highest, the densest to the subtlest, the darkest to the brightest, and so on.

This qualitative understanding of the elements is found throughout Islamic texts, whether or not the author is versed in cosmology, just as our own, scientific view of the elements is reflected throughout contemporary literature. Thus, for example, Firdawsī (d. ca. 411/1020), the author of the *Shāhnāma*, the Persian national epic, provides the following description of the creation of the world. Note that he immediately draws moral conclusions from his cosmological considerations:

At the beginning you should correctly grasp
  the substance of the first elements.
God created things from no things
  in order thereby to manifest His power.
He brought the substance of the four elements
  into existence without trouble or time.
A shining fire came forth,
  between water and wind, along with dark earth.
When fire fell into movement,
  its heat brought about dryness.
Then cold appeared from the unmoving,
  and wetness grew up from that coldness.
Once these four elements fell into place
  God used them for the realm of two-or-three-days.
He combined the elements one with the other
  and they put up their heads in every kind.
The quickly circling dome appeared,
  displaying wonders ever new.
The seven [days] became lord over the twelve [months]—
  each assumed an appropriate place.
All these appeared through generosity and gift—
  the Knowing One gave each what it deserved.
The spheres became tied one to another.
  Once the work was completed, they began to turn. . . .
When all this was completed, the human being appeared.
  He was the key to all these locks.
His head went up like a tall cypress,
  he worked his tasks through good speech and intellect.
He received awareness, thought, and intellect.
  He was obeyed by wild animals and tame.
Look at him for a moment through intellect—
  What is man in meaning? One.
Do you think all people are headstrong?
  Do you think they have no other mark?
You were brought out from the two worlds,
  you were nurtured by many intermediaries.
The first in creation, the last to be enumerated,
  is you—take not yourself in play.[40]

Farghānī offers an explanation of how the four elements come into existence within the context of the metaphysics of Ibn al-ʿArabī's school. He is commenting on the Koranic verse quoted above: "Have not the unbelievers beheld that the heavens and the earth were a mass all sewn up, and then We unstitched them, and out of water fashioned every living thing?" (21:30):

> Some people have called that sewn-up material the Greatest Element, others the Element of Elements. This Greatest Element has four pillars, which are fire, air, water, and earth, just as its own origin, the Dust [*habāʾ*], has four pillars, that is, the pillars of Nature [heat, cold, dryness, and wetness]. This Element with its pillars is brought into movement through the original movement of God's love [for creation], which permeates it and which is intrinsic to the All-merciful Breath, of which this material is one of the effects and loci of manifestation. . . .
>
> This movement and power of yearning demands a powerful and power-giving churning of the pillars. This makes manifest within them a hidden trace of heat, and its effects make the subtlest part rise up from that sewn-up material as a vapor or smoke, undifferentiated and unitary in description. This is the sewn-up mass of the heavens.

In discussing the appearance of the individual elements, Farghānī is careful to avoid the absolutizing of terms that is characteristic of the more mythic mode of discourse, as in Firdawsī's discussion of four distinct elements. With most cosmologists Farghānī holds that the elements do not exist in pure form in the manifest cosmos, but only as the domination of a certain tendency within existence. Hence, when we say that the earth is cold and dry, this is not an absolute statement, simply an assertion of a certain dominant tendency. Heat and wetness are also found in earth.

> Then the pillars become differentiated one from another. This is the "unstitching" of the pillars. . . . They become four kinds, each kind of which is dominated by two pillars [of Nature], though it also comprises the other two. The densest kind is dominated by cold and dryness, though the other two are actualized therein. Hence the pillar of earth [*turāb*] comes into existence. This is the unstitching of the earth [*arḍ*]. The second kind is more subtle than the first. It is dominated by cold and wetness, along with the actualization of the other two qualities. Hence the pillar of water comes into existence. The third kind is more subtle than the second. It is dominated by heat and wetness, along with the actualization of the other two qualities. Hence the pillar of air comes into existence. The fourth kind is more subtle than the third. It is dominated by heat and dryness, along with the actualization of the other two qualities. Hence the pillar of fire comes into existence.[41]

This qualitative evaluation of earthly things has many applications. For example, it helps us differentiate among the basic kinds of existent things in the cosmos. There are certain creatures made predominantly of clay (water and earth), such as plants and animals. Some creatures—the angels—are made of light, which is completely outside the elements. Because of their unmixed luminosity, angels are invisible, except in special circumstances when they choose to appear through their power to "imaginalize" (*tamaththul*) themselves, thereby assuming a state of semi-visibility.[42] Then there are jinn, who are made predominantly of fire and, according to some authorities, possess a strong admixture of air. This means that they pertain to the earth but at the same time possess heavenly qualities. Hence they are for the most part invisible, though like certain angels they can choose to make themselves visible. In short, the jinn are "imaginal" beings. Najm al-Dīn Rāzī employs the qualitative distinction between the elements to explain the difference between the bodily life of this world and the mode of existence represented by the bodily resurrection in the next world.

> The this-worldly frame was built from the four elements of earth, wind, water, and fire. But it was dominated by water and earth—"sticky clay" [37:11]. Both of these are sensory and dense. They are perceived by the sense of sight. Wind and fire are subtle and non-sensory and are not perceived by the sense of sight. Hence they are dominated by the bodily frame and latent within it.
>
> In the next world, which is the world of

subtlety, the frame is also built from the four elements. But wind and fire are made dominant, since they are subtle. Earth and water are dominated over and made latent within. Hence the frame will be intensely subtle. The light that is today latent in the heart of the person of faith will be given dominance over his form: "Their light shall run forth in front of them" [57:12]. The verse, "A day on which some faces shall be whitened and others blackened" [3:106], also refers to this meaning.

When the frame is subtle and luminous, it no longer interferes with the spirit. . . . In the same way, a glassmaker removes the earth and opacity from the substance of glass, making it translucent and pure. Thereby its outward and inward dimensions have the same color. Its inside can be seen from its outside, and its outside from its inside. The verse, "Upon the day when secrets are divulged" [86:9], alludes to this meaning. That which is found in the outside dimensions will enter the inside dimensions. . . .

The bodily frame will then be resurrected in this subtlety so that it can enjoy its full share of the bounties of the eight paradises, without any opacity arising from it to interfere with the spirit.[43]

The qualities inherent in the elements tell us something about the kinds of existent things in the cosmos and the difference between this world and the next. In the same way, these qualities allow us to draw conclusions about the nature of human beings. An early and especially interesting use of the qualitative significance of the elements is found in Samʿānī's *Rawḥ al-arwāḥ*. The author is analyzing the qualities that went into the creation of Adam. At the same time, he wants to show that mercy is the predominate divine attribute in the human being, since God's mercy precedes His wrath. Human beings were created as the objects of this mercy. Hence everything in creation directs people toward paradise and felicity. At the outset Samʿānī explains the meaning of the objection that the angels made when God told them that He was going to create a human being and make him His vicegerent. He also pays close attention to the "two hands" and the "feet" of God.

The angels said, "What, wilt Thou place therein one who will do corruption and shed blood?" [2:30]. But God did not reply that He was not doing that. He said, "I know what you do not know" [2:30]. In other words, I know that I will forgive them: You know their disobedience, but I know My forgiveness. . . . In your glorification, you make manifest your own activity, while in My forgiveness I make manifest My own bounty and generosity. . . . "I know what you do not know," which is My love for them. No matter what they are, I love them. . . . Though your felicity lies in your sinlessness, I desire to show mercy to them. You wear the vest of sinlessness, they wear the covering of mercy. . . .

On the day that He created earth for Adam, through His own generosity He made having mercy upon Adam incumbent upon Himself. He said, your Lord "has written mercy against Himself" [6:12]. He wrote Adam's slip through the intermediary of others, but He wrote mercy without intermediary against Himself. For earth is the capital of incapacity and weakness. What can be shown toward the weak except mercy?

Some of the commentators hold that "He created them for mercy."[44] He created you in order to have mercy on you. In its constitution earth is humble and submissive. People trample it underfoot and look down upon it. In contrast, fire seeks through its constitution elevation and eminence. It is always trying to go up. Water has a certain innate purity and natural humility, but earth does not have that purity. However, it does have the humility. When Adam was brought into existence, he came from earth and water. Hence the basis of his work was built upon purity and submissiveness. Then this water and earth, which had become "stinking mud" [15:26] and "sticky clay" [37:11], was honored with the attribute of the hand. For God said, "What prevented you from prostrating yourself to him whom I created with My own two hands?" [38:75]. But fire, which claimed eminence, was made the object of severity through the attribute of the "foot." "The Invincible will place His foot in the Fire, and it will say, 'Enough, enough.'"[45] . . .

God honored earth with the attribute of the hand. Then He fastened His own speech to them: "He fastened to them the word of godfearing" [48:26]. He showed severity to fire through the attribute of the foot.

The attribute of the hand imparts the sense

of lifting up, while the attribute of the foot gives the sense of putting down. Earth was put down through its own attribute. Through His attribute it was lifted up. Fire was lifted up through its own attribute. Through His attribute it was put down.

O earth! O you who are put down through your own attribute and lifted up through My attribute! O fire! O you who are lifted up through your own attribute and put down through My attribute!

Iblis performed many acts of obedience and worship, but all of these were accidental. His innate attribute was disobedience, for he was created of fire, and fire possesses the attribute of claiming eminence. Claiming eminence is the capital of the disobedient.

Adam slipped and we disobeyed. But the attribute of disobedience is accidental, and the attribute of obedience original. For we were created from earth, and the attribute of earth is humility and submissiveness. Humility and submissiveness are the capital of the obedient. God looks at the foundation of affairs and the point around which the compass turns. He does not look at exceptional affairs and accidents.

O dervish! On the day when Adam slipped, they beat the drum of good fortune for all human beings. God set down a foundation with Adam at the beginning of the work. He gave him a capital from His own bounty.

The first example of bounty that He gave Adam was that He placed him in paradise without any worthiness and without his asking. And the first example that Adam displayed of his own capital was his slip.

God made a contract with Adam at the beginning of this business. The condition of the contract was that whenever someone buys something or sells something, he has to give a taste. Adam gave a taste of his capital when he disobeyed the command and ate the wheat. God gave him a taste of the cup of bounty when He pardoned that slip.

No sin is as great as the first sin. This is especially true when the person was nourished on beneficence and nurtured through blessings. The angels had to prostrate themselves before him—the throne of his good fortune was placed upon the shoulder of those brought nigh to God. He was brought into paradise without any worthiness. God gave him a home in the neighborhood of His own gentleness. Since He pardoned the first slip, this is proof that He will pardon all sins.

After all, we have a thousand times more excuses than Adam had. If the darkness of clay is necessary, we have it. If the weakness of earth is necessary, we have it. If the impurity of "stinking mud" is necessary, we have it. If some confused bites of food are necessary, we have them. If the times should have become dark with injustice and corruption, we have that. If the accursed Iblis has to be sitting in wait for us, we have him. If caprice and appetite have to dominate over us, we have that. At the first slip, Adam was excused without any of these meanings. Since we have all these opacities, why should He not forgive us? In truth, He will forgive us.

O dervish! They robbed the human caravan on the day that Adam slipped. "The caravan is secure once it has been waylaid." Once a blind old man was sitting in the hot sun in the Hijaz eating walnuts and dates. Someone asked him, "Why are you eating two foods that are [medicinally] so hot in this terrible heat?" He replied, "Well, they waylaid my caravan and everything that I feared has come to pass. Now I am secure."[46]

The Virtues of the Earth

Which is more excellent, heaven or earth? This question is often implicit in discussions of their respective qualities. Fakhr al-Dīn Rāzī, in the usual dry and systematic fashion of the rational thinkers, offers arguments for both sides without expressing his own opinion. He is commenting on the first Koranic mention of the two terms together (2:22).

The Seventh Question. Is heaven more excellent [*afḍal*], or earth?

Some have said that heaven is more excellent, for several reasons: [1] Heaven is the place where the angels worship, and God is not disobeyed anyplace within it. When Adam committed that act of disobedience in the Garden, it was said to him, "Get down out of the Garden." And God said, "No one who disobeys Me will dwell in My neighborhood."

[2] God said, "We set up the heaven as a well-protected roof" [21:32] and "Blessed is He who has set in heaven constellations" [25:61], but He did not say anything like that concerning earth.

[3] In most cases, heaven is mentioned before the earth in the Koran.

Others say that no, the earth is more excellent, for several reasons: [1] God described a number of regions of the earth as being blessed with His words, [a] "The first house established for the people was that at Mecca, a place blessed" [3:96]; [b] "[A voice called . . .] in the blessed hollow, [coming from the tree: 'Moses . . . ']" [28:30]; [c] "to the Further Mosque, the precincts of which We have blessed" [17:1]. [d] He described the earth of Syria as being blessed, for He said, "all the east and the west of the land that We had blessed" [7:137]. [e] He also described the whole of the earth as being blessed, since He said, "What, do you disbelieve in Him who created the earth. . . . And He set therein firm mountains over it, and He blessed it" [41:9–10]. You might ask what kind of blessing can be found in empty wastelands and dangerous deserts. We would reply that these are the dwelling places and grazing spots of wild animals, and they become the dwelling places of people when they need them. Because of these blessings God says, "In the earth are signs for those having certainty" [51:20]. Although these signs are also seen by those who do not have certainty, only those who have certainty profit from them, so He made them signs for those having certainty, to honor them. In the same way He says, "A guidance for the godfearing" [2:2].

[2] God created the prophets, the noble ones, from the earth, as He said: "Out of the earth We created you, and We shall restore you into it" [20:55]. But He did not create anything out of the heavens, since He said, "And We set up the heaven as a well-protected roof" [21:32].

[3] God ennobled His Prophet through it, since He made all the earth a mosque for him and made its dust pure for him.[47]

Among the four elements, some authorities would certainly rank earth as the most excellent. One reason for this is that on the elemental level it alone is purely itself. In other words, each of the other three elements has an admixture of heavenly qualities, even though it dwells in the lower world. Fire seeks the height of heaven and borrows something of its luminosity. Air is open to luminosity and moves in high domains relative to earth and water. Water, though it seeks lowness, is able through its translucency to become thoroughly illumined by heaven's light. Only earth is fully low and fully dark. This may help explain why Ibn al-ʿArabī holds the earth in great esteem, calling it the subtlest of all elements, in spite of its apparent density. Note that he clearly identifies earth as a single qualitative reality, in spite of its two apparent senses (that is, as element and as counterpart of heaven).

The earth . . . gives all benefits from its own essence and is the locus of every good. Hence it is the mightiest of corporeal bodies. In its movement it vies with no moving thing, since none of these leave the earth's location. Each pillar manifests its authority within the earth, while it is the patient, the receptive, the fixed, the stable. Its shaking was quelled by its mountains, which God placed as its pegs because it was moving from the fear of God.[48] God made it secure through these pegs, so it became quiet with the quiet of those who have certitude. From it the People of Certainty learn their certainty. For it is the Mother from whom we emerged and to whom we return, and from her we will emerge once again.[49] To her we are submitted and entrusted.

Earth is the most subtle of the pillars in meaning. It only accepts density, darkness, and hardness to conceal the treasuries that God has entrusted to it, for God has given it jealousy. . . .

God sent the earth down to the station of the central point of the circumference. Hence through its essence it stands opposite every part of the circumference. Every part of the circumference gazes upon it. Every line from the earth goes out to the circumference equally and in equilibrium, since it gives only in accordance with its own form, while each line from the circumference aims to reach it. If the earth should disappear, the circumference would disappear. But if the circumference should disappear, this would not necessitate the disappearance of the earth. It remains and subsists in this world and the next. It is similar to the Breath of the All-merciful through bringing into existence.[50]

Maybudī provides a beautiful and poetic account of the qualities of earth. Far from being reprehensible because of its lowliness, it allows the highest human qualities to manifest themselves; it is superior in some respects even to the angels.

A dervish overcome with the pain of separation came before Abū Yazīd Basṭāmī. In turmoil and disorder, he had lost his head and feet. He came as a traveler, and in his ecstatic state he said, "O Bāyazīd, what would it matter if this shameless earth did not exist?"

Abū Yazīd became angry and shouted at the dervish, "Were there no earth, the breast would have no burning! Were there no earth, religion would have no sorrow and joy! Were there no earth, love's fire would not flame up! Were there no earth, who would smell the scent of beginningless love? Were there no earth, who would become the familiar of the Eternal Beloved?

"Dervish, Iblis's curse marks the perfection of the majesty of earth. Seraphiel's trumpet was prepared for the sake of the yearning of earth. The questioning [of the dead in the grave] by Nakīr and Munkar acts as deputy for the love in the breast of earth. Riḍwān with all the slaves and serving boys is but earth under the feet of earth.[51] Beginningless grace is a gift and robe for earth. The call from the Unseen World was prepared in the name of earth. The attributes of the Lord adorn the beauty of earth. God's love feeds the mysteries of earth. Eternity's qualities supply provisions for the journey of earth. The pure, incomparable Essence is witnessed by the hearts of earth.

"Before you asked, I asked for you,
  I set up the world all for you.
"A thousand in the city are in love with Me—
  Live in joy: I asked for you."[52]

5

MACROCOSMIC MARRIAGE

The relationship between heaven and earth is that between yang and yin, male and female, husband and wife. We have already quoted the following lines of Rūmī:

> In the view of intellect, heaven is the man
> and earth the woman.
> Whatever the one throws down,
> the other nurtures.[1]

Ibn al-ʿArabī makes the same point in the following passage. He has in mind the Koranic verse, "He revealed its command to each heaven" (41:12).

> God placed between heaven and earth a supra-formal conjunction and an attentiveness toward the children—the minerals, plants, and animals—which He desired to bring into existence in the earth. He made the earth like the wife and the heaven like the husband. The heaven casts something of the command that God revealed to it into the earth, just as the man casts water into the woman through intercourse. When the casting takes place, the earth brings out all the strata of the engendered things that God has concealed within it.[2]

Because of her beauty and virtue, the earth is eminently lovable. Heaven marries her not simply out of duty, but for pleasure and joy. Many Muslim authorities hold that the sexual relationship that marks the consummation of marriage is itself a positive good, whether or not the goal is to have children. Islam's "liberal" evaluation of sexual relationships has often been remarked upon, most notably by nineteenth century missionaries trying to prove the superiority of Christianity's ascetic approach. Nowadays, of course, that criticism has largely been forgotten because of new attitudes, but something of it lingers on, especially in the general Western attitude toward the permissibility for a man to take four wives. The West views monogamy as closer to a "religious" attitude. And of course few Western women have been able to grasp the benefits of polygamy.

However this may be, it is not my purpose here to provide an apologia for the Sharia or Islamic sexual mores. I am merely concerned with bringing out the "deep background" of Islamic attitudes toward relationships, whether or not these pertain to the strictly human realm. Islamic myth and thought often picture relationships in terms of male and female, heaven and earth. Hence it is totally normal that marriage should frequently be employed to explain the nature of the fruitful relationship between the two sides.

The Arabic term most commonly used for marriage, *nikāḥ*, also signifies coitus, but Islamic law makes a clear distinction between legitimate and illegitimate coitus. *Nikāḥ* refers only to the former. The term *nikāḥ* is also used in a figurative sense, such as "The rain married the soil," "The disease married the man," "Drowsiness married his eye."[3] Our authors often use the term in metaphysical or cosmological contexts. In what follows, I translate it sometimes as marriage and sometimes as marriage act, depending on the context.

Fathers and Mothers

We have seen on more than one occasion that the four elements and the three kingdoms born from them are sometimes called the "mothers" and the "children." Ibn al-ʿArabī often employs such terms. For example, the title of chapter 11 of his *al-Futūḥāt al-makkiyya* is "Concerning our fathers, the high things, and our mothers, the low things." High and low, as already noted, are juxtaposed to express the difference between the spiritual and the corporeal. In this particular chapter, Ibn al-ʿArabī is more concerned with the relationship between spirits and souls. Among created things, spirits are the most closely akin to the divine. They are more or less identical with the "divine breath" blown into Adam. For Ibn al-ʿArabī and many others, the qualities of spirits stand at the antipodes of bodily qualities. Between bodies and spirits stand the souls (*nufūs*), which partake of the characteristics of both sides. Hence souls are "imaginal," since they are both luminous and dark, intelligent and ignorant, high and low, and so on.

Through their affinity with bodies, souls are thoroughly permeated by bodily attributes. When our authors consider the contrast between spirits and souls, they set up the same relationships that exist between spirits and bodies. Spirits are pure light while souls are darkness, imbued with the qualities of the elements. We can see the justification for this in everyday experience. For all practical purposes, the body as body can be ignored, since as body it is dead, no different from a corpse. It is the body as living through the soul that is at issue, and that living body cannot be considered apart from the soul. Bodily pain and pleasure are experienced as real by the soul, since life and sensation are attributes of soul, not body. Hence the soul is identical with our embodied self. The distinction between body and soul can be ignored until it becomes relevant to the discussion.

In contrast to both soul and body, the spirit stands beyond normal experience. As the luminous and noumenous reality beyond the soul, the spirit is a father, since all positive qualities descend from it. In contrast, the embodied soul is a mother, since it is the locus wherein the spirit's attributes become manifest. The spirit is rain-giving heaven and the soul fruit-yielding earth.

If soul and body can be considered practically identical in their oppositional relationship to the spirit, from another point of view they are completely different. That is when the similarity and affinity between spirit and soul is taken into account, and the difference between soul and body. As an imaginal reality, the soul reflects the life and luminosity of the spirit, while the body is dead and dark. The soul is, as it were, simply the face of the spirit turned toward the world of lowness and density. If the soul turns back upon itself, it will see its own identity with the spirit. This is the path of spiritual realization and human perfection.

Ibn al-ʿArabī begins the chapter on "fathers and mothers" with a poem summarizing its contents. He speaks for the human individual:

> I am the son of fathers—pure spirits—
> and mothers—elemental souls.

Souls are "elemental" since they are thoroughly imbued with bodily attributes and with the properties of the four elements that make up the body. Hence the qualities of earth, water, air, and fire all manifest themselves within the soul. But spirit is pure light, dwelling beyond the realm of the elements.

> Our locus of manifestation is between spirit and body,
> the result of a union of embracing and pleasure.

We as human beings come into existence as the result of the marriage of spirit and body. The "we" with whom we identify is precisely our soul.

> I come not from one, that I should declare him one,
> but from a group of fathers and mothers.

From a cosmological perspective, human beings come into existence as the result of the marriage between plural properties present within the spiritual and corporeal realities. They are not created directly by God.

> God is to them—when you investigate their task—
> like a carpenter who makes things with tools.
> They are not related to him like his product.
> Thus did the Lord bring us into existence.

In this cosmological scheme, the fathers and mothers—the heavenly and earthly qualities—are the tools through which God creates the human universe. The tools are not the finished product of His work.

> Hence he who declares his Creator one speaks truly,
> and he who affirms causes speaks the truth.
> If you look at the tools, it will take long before
> the attribution goes step by step to the Essence.
> But if you look at Him, while He brings us into existence,
> we will uphold His oneness without any groups.
> The Unique Entity alone gave birth to me;
> all people have the same father, but different mothers.

On the one hand, we have a variety of fathers because of the qualities of the spiritual world. On the other hand, we all have but a single father because of the oneness of God. This is a cosmological application of the principles of incomparability and similarity: From the first point of view, creativity is God's alone. From the second, it is reflected within the creaturely realm. As we will see below, Ibn al-ʿArabī sometimes refers to God as "father" (*ab*) within the cosmological context. This is unusual in Islamic texts, because of the Christian connotations of the term.

Ibn al-ʿArabī begins the prose part of the chapter by affirming a standard theme of Islam, that human beings were God's goal in creation. The microcosm is the crowning glory of the cosmos, since it governs the macrocosm through its knowledge and awareness. As we saw in the last chapter, "God subjected to you" human beings "everything in the heavens and the earth" (45:13). The goal of creating the spiritual and corporeal realities, the fathers and mothers, was nothing but giving birth to the children, the human being specifically.

> The goal of this cosmos was the human being. Human beings are the leader [of all things] [*imām*]. Hence we attributed the fathers and mothers to them. We said, "our fathers, the high things, and our mothers, the low things."

Ibn al-ʿArabī now defines his terms so that we will understand why he refers to high and low realities as fathers and mothers. He has in view the qualitative significance of the terms. What is it that makes a father a father and a mother a mother in the most general sense?

> Everything that exercises an effect [*mu'aththir*] is a father, and everything that receives an effect [*mu'aththar fīh*] is a mother. This is the general rule of this chapter. That which is born between the two from the effect is called a son [*ibn*] or a child [*muwallad*]. . . .
>
> The spirits are all fathers, while Nature is the mother, since Nature is the locus of transmutations. When the spirits turn their attention toward the pillars—the elements—which are receptive toward change and transmutation, the children—the minerals, plants, animals, and jinn—become manifest in Nature. The most perfect of these is the human being.[4]

If the defining characteristics of fathers and mothers are exercising effects and receiving effects, the terms can be employed in a wide variety of contexts.[5] Ibn al-ʿArabī takes speech and architecture as examples:

> The speaker is a father, the listener is a mother, and speech is a marriage. What

comes to exist from this within the understanding of the listener is a son.

Every father is high, since he exercises effects. Every mother is low, since she receives effects. And every determinate relationship between the two is a marriage and a turning of attention. Every result is a son.

From here one understands the words of the speaker when he wants someone to stand up: *Stand*! The object of desire is achieved through the standing. It is the result of the effect of the word *Stand*! If the listener—who is the mother, without doubt—does not stand up, then she is barren. And if she is barren, she is not a mother in this state. . . .

If the architect has knowledge but is not well skilled in workmanship, he casts what he has to the hearing of one who is skilled in the work of carpentry. The speech of the architect is a father, and the reception of the listener is a mother. Then the knowledge of the listener becomes a second father, while his limbs become a mother.

If you like, you can say that the architect is a father, and the craftsman or carpenter is a mother in respect to the fact that he listens to what the architect casts. If the architect exercises an effect upon him, then he has caused what he has in his capacity to descend into the soul of the carpenter. Then a form appears to the carpenter in his inward dimension. It derives from what the architect cast to him and is actualized in the existence of his imagination as subsistent and manifest to him. This form stands in the station of the child of the architect to which the carpenter's understanding gives birth.

Then the carpenter undertakes his work. He is the father in respect to the lumber, which is the mother of the carpentry. He works with his tools, through which the marriage act and the ejaculation of semen take place, that is, every strike with the adz or cutting with the saw. Every cutting, separating, and joining of planks is for the sake of configuring the form. Then the chest becomes manifest, like the child that is born, coming into the world of sense perception.

This is the way you should understand the realities in the hierarchy of fathers, mothers, and children and the way in which results are produced. Any father who does not have the attribute of working [*ʿamal*] is not a father in that respect. He may have knowledge, but the instrument of communication is prevented from speech or allusion in order to make understood, while he himself is not doing the work. Then he is not a father in every respect. He is a mother to the knowledges that are actualized in his soul.[6]

In showing the wide application of the terms father and mother, Ibn al-ʿArabī has in view the spirit of the Koranic revelation, a point that he makes explicit in this chapter on a number of occasions. For example, he points to one of the Koranic verses referring to the creation of Eve from Adam, a verse we have already quoted: "It is He who created you from one soul and made from it its spouse that he might rest in her" (7:189). The verse then says, "Then, when he covered her, she bore a light burden," referring to her pregnancy. "When it became heavy they cried to God their Lord, 'If Thou givest us a righteous son, we indeed shall be of the thankful.'" Ibn al-ʿArabī turns his attention to the verb the Koran employs here, "to cover" (*taghashshā*). He points out that the Koran uses the same verbal root, in the same meaning, to describe the relationship between night and day. He also mentions other verses that employ a similar sexual symbolism. And he points out that both night and day may be considered father or mother, yang or yin, depending upon the point of view. Note in the following the distinction between daytime (*nahār*) and the twenty-four hour "day" (*yawm*), which comprises both nighttime and daytime.

Nighttime and daytime are found in time. God made the two a father and a mother because of what He originates through them. He says, "He makes the nighttime cover the daytime" [7:54]. He says something similar concerning Adam: "When he covered her, she bore." Hence, when the nighttime covers the daytime, the nighttime is a father and the daytime is a mother. Everything that God brings into existence in the daytime is like the children to whom a woman gives birth. . . .

In the same way, God says, "God makes the nighttime enter into the daytime, and makes the daytime enter into the nighttime" [22:61]. Thereby He increased explanation concerning the fact that they perform the marriage act with each other.

Through His words, "And a sign for them is the nighttime: We draw the daytime out from it" [36:37], He explains that the nighttime is daytime's mother and that daytime is born from her. In the same way, the child "is drawn out" from its mother when it comes out of her, and the snake "draws out" from its skin. Hence daytime becomes manifest as a child in another world, different from the world embraced by nighttime. Here daytime is the father. . . .

Hence nighttime and daytime are fathers in one respect and mothers in another respect. All minerals, plants, and animals that God brings into existence in the world of the pillars while nighttime and daytime turn round about are called the children of daytime and nighttime.[7]

Ibn al-ʿArabī makes similar points in another passage:

> God made both daytime and nighttime female and male in order to produce the results, the children, that become manifest among the four pillars. In days in general, the mother of every effect that is born and becomes manifest in the daytime is the daytime, while its father is the nighttime. The mother of that which becomes manifest in the nighttime is the nighttime, while its father is the daytime. Hence "The nighttime enters into the daytime" when the daytime is female, and "The daytime enters into the nighttime" when the nighttime is female.[8]

In discussing the qualities found in cosmic realities, our authors never forget that the root of these qualities is the Divine Reality. Fathers and mothers both manifest divine attributes. Kāshānī reminds us of this fact in commenting on the Koranic verses,

> Thy Lord has decreed that you shall not worship any but Him, and to be good to parents, whether one or both of them attains old age with you. Say not to them "Fie," neither chide them, but speak unto them words respectful, and lower to them the wing of humbleness out of mercy and say, "My Lord, have mercy upon them, as they nurtured me when I was little." (17:23–24)

To worship none but God is the fundamental teaching of Islam, equivalent to *tawḥīd*. Why, in this verse, does the Koran place being good (*iḥsān*) to parents second only to the most basic teaching of Islam? Kāshānī explains:

> God places being good to parents next to *tawḥīd* and considering Him alone as worthy of worship because parents correspond to the Divine Presence in the fact that they are the cause of your existence. And they correspond to the Presence of Lordship in the fact that they nurtured you when you were a helpless and weak infant, without power and motion. They were the first locus of manifestation within which such attributes of God as bringing into existence, lordship, mercy, and kindliness became manifest in relation to you. With all that, their rights need to be observed, while God is independent of that. Hence the most important obligatory duty after *tawḥīd* is being good to them and fulfilling their rights to the extent possible.[9]

Universal Marriage

Ibn al-ʿArabī and his followers devote a good deal of attention to the nature of marriage or sexual intercourse, not as a human phenomenon, but as the universal power of productivity found within every level of existence. One of Ibn al-ʿArabī's lost works is called *Kitāb al-nikāḥ al-sārī fī jamīʿ al-dharārī*, "The book on the marriage act that pervades all atoms."[10] Many passages in the *Futūḥāt* deal with the theme. In general, he looks at marriage as a reality that manifests certain qualities in all things:

> When an act gives rise to something that had no entity before it, that is a property of marriage. There is no act that does not give rise to something in accordance with its own reality and way. Hence marriage is a root of all things. Hence it possesses all-encompassingness, excellence, and priority.[11]

Ibn al-ʿArabī calls chapter 21 of the *Futūḥāt* "Concerning the true knowledge of three sciences of the engendered universe and their entering into each other [*tawāluj*]." He begins the chapter by noting that the topic of the chapter is marriage, and that the root of marriage is found in God Himself.

> This chapter deals with the knowledge of reproduction [*tawālud*] and procreation [*tanā-*

> *sul*]. It is one of the sciences connected to engendered things. Its root is found in the divine science. First we will explain to you its form among the engendered things, and then we will make it manifest to you in the divine science.
>
> The root of every science is found in the divine knowledge, since everything other than God derives from God. God says, "He has subjugated to you what is in the heavens and what is in the earth, all together, from Him" [45:13].
>
> This science of interpenetration [*tadākhul*] permeates all things. It is the science of conjunction [*iltiḥām*] and marriage. It has three kinds: sensory, supra-sensory, and divine.[12]

Sensory conjunction is the sexual act that occurs among animals. Supra-sensory conjunction pertains to the realm of "meanings" or ideas and is illustrated by the syllogism, through which two premises meet and give birth to a conclusion. Divine marriage takes place when God brings a thing into existence. He and the nonexistent thing are male and female, while the existent thing that results from the union is the child.

The discussion of the original divine marriage has to do with the nature of the nonexistent things, also called the immutable entities, or the things of the cosmos as known by God for all eternity. In God's knowledge, they are nonexistent in themselves. Only when God gives them existence do they enter into the cosmos for their determined stay. God in Himself, nondelimited Being, is the father. Thus Ibn al-ᶜArabī writes, "I have alluded to the all-pervading First Father: the all-comprehensive, greatest name that is followed by all the other names."[13] In other words, the First Father is Allah, which embraces all the other names and denotes the Real. The mother is the nonexistent things, while the creatures that enter into existence are the children. Fathers are "high" and mothers "low." The "highness" of the father in this case is the fact that He is Being Itself, the source of all realities. The mother is "low" because she has no existence of her own. She is pure receptivity toward the perfections that the father sends down. Ibn al-ᶜArabī refers to the state of the things in God's knowledge as their "thingness." The term derives from various Koranic verses that refer to the "things" before God creates them, like the verse Ibn al-ᶜArabī quotes in the following.[14]

> The first of the high fathers is manifestly clear. The first of the low mothers is the thingness of the nonexistent possible things. The first marriage is the intention of the command [given to the nonexistent thing, that is, "Be!"]. The first child is the existence of the entity of that thingness.
>
> This father is all-pervasive in fatherness, this mother all-pervasive in motherness, and this marriage all-pervasive in all things. The result is continuous. It is never cut off for anything whose entity is manifest. This is what we call "The Marriage that Pervades all Atoms." As evidence for what we said, God says, "Our only word to a thing, when We desire it, is to say to it 'Be!' and it is" [16:40].[15]

Since this divine marriage is continuous, its celebration is also continuous. The guests at the wedding festivities are the divine names, who rejoice in the fact that their properties become manifest in the cosmos through the marriage. Without this marriage, the Hidden Treasure would remain hidden.

> The divine marriage act is the attentiveness of the Real toward the possible thing in the presence of possibility through the desire of love. . . . The entity of the possible thing is named "wife," the attentiveness through desire and love is called the "marriage act," and producing the result is called the "bestowal of existence upon the entity of the possible thing." . . . The wedding feasts are the rejoicing of the Most Beautiful Names. For the marriage results in a bestowal of manifested existence upon the entities of the possible things, in order that the effects of the names may become manifest. . . . This marriage is constant and continuous in existence. There can be no cessation or divorce in this marriage contract.[16]

It is worth emphasizing that Ibn al-ᶜArabī often discerns the qualities connected with marriage in unexpected places. For example, in the midst of a discussion of dream-visions in the *Futūḥāt*, he cites the Koranic verse, "It is He who forms you in the wombs as He will" (3:6). Then he says,

> Among the "wombs" is imagination. God forms within it imaginal things as He will on the basis of a supra-sensory marriage and a supra-sensory pregnancy. God opens up meanings within that womb. "In any form He will, He composes" them [82:8]. Hence He shows you Islam as a dome, the Koran as butter and honey, and religion as a shirt—long, short, plaited, doubled, clean, dirty—in keeping with the situation of the religion of the dreamer or the one upon whom the clothing is seen.[17] I saw such a thing for a judge of Damascus while he was undertaking judgment in Damascus. He was Shams al-Dīn Aḥmad ibn Muhadhdhib al-Dīn Khalīl al-Jūnī—God give him success, support him with His angels, and protect him in his giving judgments! A speaker was saying to him in the dream, "God has bestowed upon you a clean, long gown. Dirty it not and let it not shrink!" I awoke and mentioned that to him. May God make him one of those who preserve the divine admonition! Hence imagination is one of the wombs within which forms appear.[18]

Ibn al-ʿArabī's teachings on the marriage that pervades all things is systematized by his disciple Qūnawī, who discusses it in some detail in at least three of his works. Qūnawī's style is often much more difficult than that of his master, not because he is more obscure, but because he is careful to use technical terminology of a philosophical rather than mythic type. One of his major concerns was to bridge the gap between Sufism and Islamic philosophy. In what follows, I synthesize his teachings on marriage from three works, translating only occasionally, where the discussion is nontechnical enough to make sense in English.[19] My version is simplified and does not do justice to the subtleties of the original. But it is more useful for our purposes here to provide the flavor of this discussion than to try to provide a thorough analysis that would take many pages.

Qūnawī tells us that there are five fundamental levels of marriage: unseen, spiritual, "natural" or pertaining to the Dominion, elemental or low, and "human" in a peculiar sense.[20]

The first marriage pertains to the level of the Divine Essence inasmuch as It can be understood in terms of certain fundamental names that Qūnawī calls "the keys to the Unseen," after the Koranic verse, "With Him are the keys to the Unseen; none knows them but He" (6:59). A "key" (*miftāḥ*) is an instrument for "opening" (*fatḥ*). The keys to the Unseen open the locked door that is the Divine Essence and allow it to establish certain primary relationships with the cosmos. "The first marriage is the turning of the Divine Essence toward the first, original names—which are the keys to the Unseen of the Divine Essence and to the Presence of Engendered Existence."[21] These keys "open up" engendered existence, the created world, the cosmos. Without the keys there would be nothing other than God. The marriage takes place when the father, Sheer Being, impregnates the mother, who is these Keys to the Unseen. Being in Itself is nondelimited and nonentified; no name can be applied to It. But Being as delimited and defined by the Keys to the Unseen establishes the universal parameters of existence. The child born from this marriage is the Breath of the All-merciful, the divine exhalation within which all created things come into existence as words. Qūnawī also refers to the first child as the "World of Meanings," that is, the world of the divine names and the immutable entities, or the divine knowledge that knows the things before they are given existence.

The second marriage is "spiritual." It is the coming together of active and receptive meanings within the World of Meanings to give birth to the spiritual realities, which dwell in the first created world. Those meanings that reflect the influence and activity of the Keys to the Unseen are known as the "properties of Necessity," since they denote the qualities of the Absolute Being that cannot not be. Other meanings are receptive to these active meanings and are known as the "properties of possibility." In other words, we have here at the level of the meanings what Farghānī calls the "Oneness of Being" and the "Manyness of Knowledge," or the properties of "Necessity" and the properties of "possibility." The meanings give rise to spiritual realities, such as intellects, souls, and angels, which are like mirrors reflecting the qualities of their parents.

The third marriage is known as "natural" or "pertaining to the Dominion." The term *Nature* in Ibn al-ʿArabī's school refers to the whole domain of existence that lies below the purely spiritual realm and thus includes the world of imagination as well as the corporeal world. The term *Dominion* (*malakūt*), as we have seen already, is used in opposition to the *Kingdom* (*mulk*), which is the corporeal world. In this context, Qūnawī is employing the term *Dominion* to refer to an intermediary domain between the spiritual world or "Invincibility" (*jabarūt*) and the corporeal world. The marriage in question takes place when certain high spirits turn toward the level of Nature. The children are those angelic beings who inhabit the heavens, which Qūnawī identifies with the World of Imagination.

The fourth marriage pertains to the low, elemental world. It is the conjunction that takes place between the simple corporeal realities as a result of the influences of the heavenly and spiritual realities. The fruit of the marriage is the production of the compound, corporeal things, that is, minerals, plants, and animals.

Each of the three lower levels of marriage results from the activities of the level or levels that stand beyond it. Each lower level is more restricted and confined than the higher levels. As for the fifth level, Qūnawī tells us that "Marriage has no fifth level, except for the intelligible reality (*maʿqūliyya*) of the coming together of all the levels, and this pertains exclusively to the human being."[22] In other words, human beings, as microcosms, bring together in their reality all the levels of marriage, and this itself is a "marriage" or conjunction of all realities.

Qūnawī discusses these marriages mainly to illustrate the nature of human perfection, which is identical with the perfection of Being's full manifestation. At each level, different children are produced, depending upon how the parents interrelate. Some of the children are more general in scope and property. In other words, they manifest more of the qualities of Being, more of the names embraced by the all-comprehensive name Allah, more of the colors present in pure light.

> For example, there may be a spirit that becomes manifest from a divine turning of attentiveness in respect of one hundred names. It is more perfect and more complete than a spirit that becomes manifest from a divine turning of attentiveness in respect of ten names.[23]

The perfection of each level of marriage is found when complete equilibrium and harmony is established among all the properties of the divine names manifest at that level. The perfection of the final level is found in the perfect equilibrium of everything in existence. This perfect equilibrium is the fully actualized microcosm, the pinnacle of God's creation. Such a microcosm—a prophet or a great friend of God—can come into existence only when all the levels of marriage, including the marriage of his or her physical parents, have taken place in complete harmony. As we saw in chapter 3, Qūnawī describes the state of human perfection in terms of the equilibrium of all the divine names and all the realities of the universe. If any one name or thing dominated over the others, then the person would stand in the "station" of that one name or thing. But perfection is the point at the center of the circle that is unbiased toward any station. It is, in Ibn al-ʿArabī's terms, the "Station of No Station."

> A certain interrelationship is eventually established among the properties of all the levels of equilibrium, that is, the supra-formal level, then the spiritual, then the imaginal or Dominion-related, then the sensory and elemental. This interrelationship does not allow any of the levels to dominate any of the other levels. If a level dominated, then the properties of the dominating level would overcome the properties of the other levels.
>
> The properties of all the levels are combined in the marriage of a pure human being, free of disequilibrium, with a spouse who is a pure locus. This occurs in a place appropriate for that [conjunction] which we have men-

tioned, after the parents have partaken of pure and balanced food. Then the form of a perfect human individual becomes manifest. The properties of the intermediaries and the levels are overcome through the Real's turning His attentiveness toward bringing this form into existence. Or rather, this condition resulting from the combination of intelligible and imaginal realities and the bringing together of the properties and characteristics of all the levels . . . receives an effusion from the Real in perfect equilibrium. The effusion is non-delimited, pure, and manifest according to the properties, forms, and effects of all the levels. Hence this [human] form is a mirror for all. It is imbued with the characteristics of all the levels in such a way that all the properties of the levels are preserved without any change entering in upon the divine effusion and self-disclosure that emanates from this level of human perfection.[24]

Triplicity

More than any other Muslim thinker, Ibn al-ʿArabī sought out the "divine roots" of phenomena by analyzing the nature of the relationships between the absolutely Real and the relatively real. Up until this point we have tried to find the key to the Islamic understanding of marriage in the nature of the yin/yang relationship. Implied by that approach is the existence of a fundamental polarity. But Ibn al-ʿArabī often looks a bit more closely at the relationship between yin and yang and points out that we are not dealing with two terms, but three: the two sides and the relationship itself. When we look at the production of results or offspring (*intāj*), that is, the quality in respect of which marriage is found on every level of existence and in all things, then we see that three things are involved: husband, wife, and the marriage act. This holds true at every level. Hence, all things come into existence because of "triplicity" (*tathlīth*).

At the divine level, the triplicity is found in God Himself. Ibn al-ʿArabī usually cites three divine principles as fundamental for creation: (1) the Essence, or Being, or God in Himself; (2) the desire (*irāda*) on God's part to bring something into existence, or His love for that thing; and (3) the creative word or command. He sees these three principles mentioned in the Koranic verse, "Our only *word* to a thing, when *We desire* it, is to say to it 'Be!' and it is" (16:40). Word and desire are mentioned explicitly, while "We" is the divine Essence.

In the *Futūḥāt*, Ibn al-ʿArabī explains the relationships among these three principles in some detail. The discussions center around the quality of "singularity" or "being odd" as opposed to even. What is the essential quality expressed to us through the divine name, *al-fard*, the Singular? Why is it that this same word is applied to odd numbers? What is the divine quality manifested in the odd numbers that allows them to be called by this term? How does this divine name manifest its qualities in the cosmos? What is the nature of "producing results" (*intāj*)? These are some of the issues that the Shaykh is investigating. Remember that in Islamic mathematics, "one" is not considered a number, so "three" is the first odd number.

> Clearly nothing comes to be from "one." The first of the numbers is two, and nothing whatsoever comes to be from two unless there is a third thing that couples them and relates one of them to the other. It brings the two together [*jāmiʿ*]. At this point what is engendered from them can be engendered in accordance with the situation of the two. The two things may be two divine names, or two supra-sensory or sensory engendered things—whatever they may be. The situation must be like this. This is the property of the name the Singular [*al-fard*], since three is the first singular [i.e., the first odd number].
>
> From this name becomes manifest every possible entity that becomes manifest. No possible thing becomes manifest from the One. It becomes manifest only from a plurality [*jamʿ*], and the smallest plurality is three, which is the singular. Hence every possible thing needs the name the Singular.[25]

In another passage, Ibn al-ʿArabī explains the nature of this triplicity of the Singular on the divine level:

> In the science of the divine things, entering into one another and reproduction are as

follows: Nothing becomes manifest from the Essence of the Real inasmuch as It is an Essence. It must first be ascribed to something else. This "something else" is the fact that the power of bringing into existence is attributed to this Essence. . . .

Once this relationship—the fact that He is powerful—is established, then there has to be a third thing. That third thing is His desire to bring into existence the entity that is intended. God has to turn His attentiveness, through His intention, toward bringing the entity into existence. Rational thought calls this turning "power," while the revealed Book calls it "word." Then the entity is engendered.

Hence creation comes into existence only from singularity, not from unity, since His Unity accepts no second, for this is not the unity of number. Therefore, in the science of the divine things, the cosmos becomes manifest from three intelligible realities. Then all this pervades the engendered universe, since some parts of it are reproduced through other parts, because this is the form of the Root.[26]

The Real brings the cosmos into existence in this manner: The cosmos becomes manifest from an Essence described by power and desire. Desire becomes connected to bringing an existent thing into existence. It is the turning of God's attentiveness. It is like the coming together of the two spouses. Power exercises its influence and brings into existence what He desired.[27]

If reproduction is rooted in a certain triplicity in God, it is reflected in the created triplicity of two things and a relationship, and it is also found on the level of concepts because of the nature of rational thought. Ibn al-ʿArabī frequently refers to the syllogism as a form of "producing results" based on triplicity. For example,

Proofs [*dalīl*] are always triple in configuration—there is no escape from that: two terms [*mufrad*] and that which brings them together [*jāmiʿ*]. This is the third term [*wajh*] in every two premises that cannot be avoided if results are to be produced. "Every *A* is *B*," and "Every *B* is *C*." Hence *B* is repeated, and the proof that *A* is *C* is established. The comprehending term is *B*, since it is repeated in the two premises. Hence every *A* produces the result *C*. This is the goal claimed by the possessor of the claim, since he claimed that every *A* is *C*.[28]

In short, triplicity is found on every level of existence, since marriage is found on every level of existence.

When God wills to make a person manifest from two other people in the realm of sense perception, these two produce that person as their result. But the third cannot become manifest from them as long as a third property does not appear within them. The third property is that one of the two should come to the other through intercourse [*jimāʿ*]. The two of them come together in a specific manner and according to a specific condition. The specific condition is that the locus must be receptive to giving birth, that it must not corrupt the seed that it receives, and that the seed must accept the opening up of the form within it. This is the specific condition. As for the specific manner, it is that the two private parts meet, and that the water or wind is let loose out of passion. Then a third must become manifest, and this third is called a child. The two are called parents. The manifestation of the third is called a birth. The coming together of the two is called marriage [*nikāḥ*] or fornication [*sifāḥ*]. This is a sensory affair, manifest among animate things. . . .

In Nature, [reproduction] takes place as follows: The heaven rains down water, and the earth receives the water. "It swells," that is, becomes pregnant, "and puts forth herbs of every joyous kind" [22:5]. A similar thing happens with the pollination of palms and trees. "Of all things we created a pair" [51:49] for the sake of reproduction.[29]

Ibn al-ʿArabī's best known explanation of the nature of triplicity is found at the beginning of chapter 11 of the *Fuṣūṣ al-ḥikam:*

Know—God give you success—that the whole situation is built in itself upon singularity, to which triplicity belongs. Singularity pertains to three and all the successive singular [i.e., odd] numbers. So three is the first of the singulars. From this Divine Presence, the cosmos comes into existence. For God says, "Our only word to a thing, when We desire it, is to say to it 'Be!' and it is" [16:40]. Here we have an Essence, a desire, and a word. . . .

Then that threefold singularity also becomes manifest within the thing. In respect to it the thing was able to be engendered and become qualified by existence. This singularity is the fact that it is a thing, its hearing, and its obedience to the command of its Engenderer to come into existence. Hence three stand opposite three. The essence of the thing, immutable in the state of its nonexistence, parallels the Essence of Him who brings it into existence. Its giving ear parallels His desire. And its reception, through obeying the command to be engendered, parallels His word, "Be!"[30]

The Pen and the Tablet

Ibn al-ʿArabī finds a salient example of "the marriage that pervades all atoms" in the relationship between the Pen and the Tablet, the two principles of spiritual existence through which the rest of the cosmos was brought into being. He writes,

> A supra-sensory intelligible marriage takes place between the Pen and the Tablet, and a visible, sensory trace. . . . The trace that was deposited in the Tablet was like the sperm that is ejaculated and set within the womb of the female. The meanings deposited within the celestial letters that became manifest from that writing are like the spirits of the children deposited within their bodies.[31]

As noted in the introduction, the Koran mentions both Pen and Tablet in rather ambiguous and seemingly unconnected verses. The hadith literature provides a number of suggestive explanations for these verses and their connection with other verses where neither Pen nor Tablet is mentioned by name. Most of these explanations have to do with the idea of the "measuring out" (*qadar*) of good and evil, that is, the "predestination" that is an article of faith for all Muslims. For example, the Koran says, "Did you not know that God knows all that is in the heaven and earth? Surely that is in a Book; surely that is easy for God" (22:70). Fakhr al-Dīn Rāzī tells us that most authorities consider this "Book" to be identical with the Guarded Tablet. Within it is written everything that comes into existence in the heavens and the earth.[32] Concerning the Koranic mention of the Pen, Rāzī says that it means the "well-known Pen mentioned in the report, 'The first thing God created was the Pen.'" He continues,

> Ibn ʿAbbās said, "The first thing God created was the Pen. Then He said, 'Write what will be until the Day of Resurrection.'" He also said that it is a pen of light whose length is the distance between the heaven and the earth. Mujāhid has related from him that he said, "The first thing God created was the Pen. Then He said, 'Write the measuring out.' So it wrote what would be until the Day of Resurrection. People act out an affair with which He has finished."[33]

Ibn ʿAbbās reports that the Prophet said,

> God created the Tablet from a white pearl. Its two surfaces are of green emerald, and its writing is of light. He looks upon it every day with 360 glances. He gives life and slays, He creates and provides, He exalts and abases, and He does what He will.[34]

The Shiʾite Imams, pillars of learning in early Islam according to Sunnis as well as Shiʾites, often mention Pen and Tablet in senses that make obvious connections with the later explications of Islamic cosmology. Thus some of the Imams say that Pen and Tablet are two angels, thereby connecting them to the luminous world of the spirits.[35] The well known ascetic Sufyān al-Thawrī asked the sixth Imam, Jaʿfar al-Ṣādiq, about the verse "*Nūn*. By the Pen and what they inscribe" (68:1). *Nūn*, written here as a single letter (i.e., *N*), is one of the many isolated letters of the Arabic alphabet that begin various chapters of the Koran. However, this letter is pronounced *nūn*, and the word *nūn* can mean fish (*ḥūt*), ink (*midād*), and inkwell (*dawāt*). The context of the verse suggests that there may be an allusion to one of these latter two meanings. Commentators have suggested this, and some have also proposed that this letter *nūn* refers to the mythical fish upon which the earth is said to rest. The fish in turn swims in the ocean, the ocean is held up by the wind, and the wind is maintained by the divine power.[36] Sufyān relates that Imam Jaʿfar spoke concerning this verse as follows:

"Nūn is a river in the Garden. God said to it, 'Harden!' So it hardened and became ink. Then God said to the Pen, 'Write!' So the Pen wrote in the Guarded Tablet everything that is and will be until the Day of Resurrection. The Ink is an ink of light, the Pen a pen of light, and the Tablet a tablet of light."

Then I said to him, "O son of God's Messenger, explain to me the situation of the Tablet, the Pen, and the Ink with a greater explanation and teach me something of what God has taught you."

He replied, "O Ibn Saʿīd, if you were not one of the people of answers, I would not answer you. Nūn is an angel who conveys to the Pen, who is an angel. The Pen conveys to the Tablet, who is an angel. The Tablet conveys to Seraphiel, Seraphiel conveys to Michael, Michael conveys to Gabriel, and Gabriel conveys to the messengers and the prophets.[37]

The yang/yin implications of Pen and Tablet are plain. The Pen's masculinity needs no explanation, while the Tablet's feminine receptivity is just as obvious. Ibn al-ʿArabī frequently makes use of this symbolism, as we saw above in his description of the marriage of Pen and Tablet. Elsewhere he writes as follows:

Since God created this First Intellect as a Pen, it sought through its own reality a place for its effectivity to write, since it is a Pen. From this search arose the Guarded Tablet, that is, the Soul. Hence the Tablet was the first existent thing to arise from something created, since it arose from the searching that subsisted in the Pen. . . .

The Intellect cast to the Soul everything within itself to the Day of Resurrection, inscribed and arranged. This was a third existent thing, whose level was between the Tablet and the Pen and whose existence came after the Tablet. . . .

The form of the Intellect's acceptance from God was a self-disclosure of the All-merciful out of love between the Self-discloser and that to which He disclosed Himself. From this station God appointed love and mercy between the pair [*zawjayn*], "That he might rest in her" [7:189]. He made the wife to be created from the entity and soul of the husband, as He said: "He created for you, of your own souls, spouses, so that you might rest in them, and He has placed between you love and mercy. Surely in that are signs," that is, marks and indications, "for a people who reflect" [30:21] and come to know that this is the Real.[38]

Just as the human world needed an Adam and an Eve, so also the cosmos as a whole needed a spiritual Adam and a spiritual Eve—Pen and Tablet—to bring the heavens, earth, and everything between the two into existence. Pen and Tablet are the spiritual principles of created duality. In the words of Ibn al-ʿArabī,

In reality the instructor [*al-muʿallim*] is God, while the whole cosmos is a learner, a seeker, poor, and in need. . . . The first teacher [*ustādh*] in the cosmos is the First Intellect, while the first student [*mutaʿallim*] to take from a created teacher is the Guarded Tablet. This is the religious nomenclature, while rational thinkers refer to the Tablet as the "Universal Soul." It is the first existent thing that arises from something created. It is a locus that receives the activity of the Intellect. It is to the Intellect as Eve is to Adam. It was created from the Intellect and was paired [*tazawwuj*] to it, so the Intellect became two [*thany*], just as existence became two through the temporally originated thing, and the divine knowledge became two through the temporally originated Pen.[39]

A father is anything that exercises an effect and a mother is anything that receives an effect. In the same way, a pen is what writes and a tablet is what is written upon. Hence it is not surprising to find discussion of a plurality of tablets in the cosmos. In commenting on the Koranic verse, "God obliterates whatsoever He will, and He establishes; and with Him is the Mother of the Book" (13:39), Kāshānī tells us that the Pen itself is a Tablet in relation to God. Then the Soul is the Tablet upon which the Pen writes. The Soul in turn writes in the heavenly souls, and these write upon matter and produce the corporeal world. Hence the terms *pen* and *tablet*, like so many other correlative terms, have to be understood as designating specific relationships. What is "pen" from one point of view may be "tablet" from another point of view. In the following and in subsequent quotations from Koran commentators, the Koranic verses are italicized.

> *God obliterates whatsoever He will* from the particular tablets, which are the inscriptions fixed within the heavenly souls. Hence what He obliterates ceases to exist in the souls and is annihilated from material substrata. *And He affirms* whatsoever He will within them, so it comes to be. *And with Him is the Mother of the Book*, that is, the Tablet of precedent decree, which is the Universal Intellect, inscribed with everything that has been and will be, from eternity without beginning to eternity without end, in a universal mode, free from obliteration and affirmation.
>
> There are four tablets: The tablet of precedent decree [*qaḍā'*] towers beyond obliteration and affirmation. It is the First Intellect.
>
> The tablet of measure [*qadar*] is the Universal Rational Soul, within which the universal things of the First Tablet become differentiated and attached to their secondary causes. It is named the Guarded Tablet.
>
> The tablet of the particular, heavenly souls is a tablet within which is inscribed everything in this world along with its shape, condition, and measure. This tablet is called the "heaven of this world." It is like the imagination of the cosmos, just as the first [tablet] is like its spirit, and the second [tablet] is like its heart.
>
> Then there is the tablet of matter, which receives the forms of the visible world. And God knows best.[40]

The Intellect and the Soul

That the predominant characteristics of intellect and soul are male and female is not unconnected with the grammatical gender of the words *ʿaql* and *nafs* in Arabic. In any case, the yang/yin relationship between the two is a commonplace in Sufi texts that touch on cosmology. A relatively early example is provided by the Persian poet Sanā'ī (d. 525/1131):

> Know that the father and mother of the subtle world
> are the noble Intellect and the rational Soul.
> Do not single yourself out from this noble pair,
> do not be disloyal to these two roots. . . .
> They give substance to the heaven and the pillars,
> they take care of the world of the spirit.[41]

Just as Intellect takes from God, so the Soul takes from the Intellect. The rest of the universe then falls into line behind these two. At every level there is a parallel relationship established between that which exercises effects by determining the form, and the material or maternal dimension that receives effects and displays the forms. Sanā'ī describes both the Arc of Descent and the Arc of Ascent in terms of these relationships.

> In the kingdom of giving form, the situation consists
> of the Soul and the one that receives the pictures.
> From the first spirit to the last mineral,
> active and receptive are placed in between . . . .
> The Intellect sits waiting for the Command,
> the Soul wounds its heart yearning for the Intellect.
> Form becomes the prisoner of matter,
> the nine spheres are caught by the seven snares.[42]
> Within the Sphere, four substances
> are imprisoned by each other, each an enemy to each.
> The three children come from these four pillars:
> plants, minerals, and animals.
> The plant becomes the food of the animal,
> and the animal becomes the food of the human.
> Then human rationality becomes the food of the angel,
> returning thereby to the Highest Sphere.[43]

As Sanā'ī points out here, the marriage of Pen and Tablet, or Intellect and Soul, gives birth to the cosmos, but in a series of stages. All the cosmologists describe a hierarchy of children. In the view of Ibn al-ʿArabī and others, the first child of the Intellect and Soul is Nature, which in turn becomes the mother of both the imaginal and corporeal worlds. Nature as mother or womb will be discussed in chapter 7. For now it is sufficient to mention it as a feminine principle born from the first father and the first mother. The following passages from Ibn al-ʿArabī describe the relationship between Intellect and Soul in terms of marriage:

> Have you not considered the Universal Soul, the wife [*ahl*] of the First Intellect? When God paired the two in order to manifest the cosmos, the first child who became manifest from the Universal Soul was Nature.[44]

> The Universal Soul . . . is the locus within which the Divine Pen casts, so it is taken in marriage [*mankūḥ*] by an engendered thing that takes in marriage [*nākiḥ*]. Everything below the Soul belongs to the World of Birth [*ʿālam al-tawallud*]—the Intellect is its father and the Soul its mother.[45]

> When God married the Intellect to the Soul in order to manifest the children—not to actualize the pleasure of the consummation[46] —He settled the children in the earth of Nature. Hence Nature exercised an effect upon their constitutions.[47]

One of the first children produced by the marriage of Pen and Tablet was God's Throne, which encompasses the whole cosmos. Cosmologically the Throne is identified with the ninth sphere, which is the starless heaven. As was indicated in chapter 3, the Throne is a locus of pure mercy. Mercy does not become divided into the two feet—mercy and mercy mixed with wrath—until the Footstool, the eighth sphere. Hence, when the All-merciful sits on the Throne, He has but one word. When His feet reach the Footstool, the one word becomes divided into contraries. The fact that the All-merciful sits upon the Throne, thereby encompassing the cosmos, is simply a manifestation of the principle "My mercy precedes My wrath."

> When the All-merciful created the Throne, He sat upon it one in Word, His Word having no contrary. Hence all the Throne is mercy, there being nothing within it contrary to mercy. . . . Intellect is the Throne's father and the Soul is its mother—which is why the "All-merciful" sat upon it: The parents look upon their children only with mercy, and God is the Most Merciful of the merciful, while the Soul and the Intellect are two existent things noble before God and beloved to Him. So He sat upon the Throne only through that which would comfort its parents. . . .
>
> If some of the cosmos falls to choking, that is because there is a mercy that they would not receive if God did not make them drink. The choking is caused by the natural constitution and the conflict with the desire of the soul. . . . This is like a bad-tasting medicine that gives no enjoyment. But within it is mercy for the one who drinks it and uses it, even if the person dislikes it. . . .
>
> God created the Footstool, square in shape, inside the Throne. He let down His two feet. The One Word, which was one in the Throne, became divided. In the Throne this Word was the One Mercy to which all things go back. In the Footstool it became divided into mercy and wrath mixed with mercy. This composition was required by what God desired to manifest in the cosmos, that is, contraction and expansion and all the opposite qualities. For He is Exalter and Abaser, Contractor and Expander, Giver and Withholder.[48]

Though Nature's characteristics are predominantly yin, since it receives the effects of Pen and Tablet, Nature can also manifest yang qualities in relation to other cosmic realities. In the following passage we see Nature not as wife or mother, as is usually the case, but as husband. Here the "Dust" refers to what the philosophers call "Prime Matter" or "Hyle" (*hāyūlā*).[49] The "Universal Body" is a corporeal sphere possessing width, height, and depth that fills the Void. Within it every corporeal thing in the cosmos takes shape.[50]

> Among the things that were cast into the Soul through a most holy, spiritual casting were Nature and the Dust. Hence the Soul was the first mother to give birth to twins. The first thing she cast down was Nature, which was followed by the Dust. Hence Nature and the Dust are brother and sister from a single father and a single mother. Then God married Nature to the Dust. Born from the

> two was the Universal Body, the first body to become manifest. Nature is the father, since it possesses the effectivity. The Dust is the mother, since within it receiving effects becomes manifest. The result is the Body. Then reproduction descended within the cosmos all the way to the earth according to a specific hierarchy.[51]

As mentioned in chapter 2, the Ikhwān al-Ṣafā᾽ provide a number of sets of names that they consider synonymous with the terms Intellect and Soul, or Pen and Tablet. Each name specifies a particular relationship between these two fundamental principles of the created order, a relationship that is repeated throughout the cosmos in other pairs. In explaining the logic of the names, the Ikhwān demonstrate the qualities of the two sides in yin/yang fashion:

> Those who mentioned "matter and form" meant by this that the Intellect is the form of the completion of the Soul and that the Soul is its matter, since the Soul receives the Intellect's effects and the shining of its light. Hence the Intellect deposits the form of completion within the Soul and takes it to the degree of perfection.
>
> Those who spoke of "light and darkness" meant that the light of Intellect is a light with no opacity, while the Soul inclines toward Nature. Hence the Soul's ways become dark when it turns toward Nature, and it forgoes the Intellect. At this point it is dark.
>
> Those who spoke of "Tablet and Pen" meant the Intellect and Soul, since what is written by the Pen appears in the Guarded Tablet.
>
> Those who spoke of "substance and accident" meant that the Intellect is a substance, since it is the father of the substances and the one who substantiates them. It is the element of elements and the one who makes the elements into elements. In the Soul's relationship to the Intellect and in being engendered from it, the Soul is the Intellect's accident, though it is a substance in relation to others. So also others are substance in relation to those below them.
>
> Those who said "spiritual and corporeal" meant by "spiritual" the Intellect, since it is the pure spirit of holiness within which is no opacity and which is not touched by density. They meant by "corporeal" the Soul in relation to the Intellect, since it is united with corporeal things and inclines toward Nature. But the Soul is spiritual, in respect of being turned toward the Intellect, and corporeal, in respect of being turned toward Nature.
>
> Those who spoke of "extension and seizure" meant that the Intellect extends its lights, benefits, and blessings over the Soul, while the Soul seizes what it acquires from the Intellect and passes it on to those below it. Those below the Soul seize and take it from the Soul.
>
> Those who spoke of "love and yearning" meant by "love" that the Intellect turns toward the Soul with love, since the Soul is like the Intellect's instrument. "Yearning" is the Soul's yearning for the Intellect's benefits and receiving its blessings.
>
> Those who spoke of "motion and rest" meant by "motion" that the Intellect comes into motion at the command of its Originator to make manifest the things. By "rest" they meant the rest and peace of the Soul in the Intellect.
>
> Those who spoke of "existence and nonexistence" meant by "existence" the Intellect, which is an existent thing that receives existence by the effusion of generosity from the One Object of worship, other than whom there is no god. Hence the Intellect is the secondary cause of the existence of every existent thing. As for "nonexistence," they may have called the Soul that since it was nonexistent in relation to the Intellect, while the Intellect was prior to the Soul and the root of its existence.
>
> Those who said "time and space" meant by "time" the Intellect, since it is the time of times and the aeon of aeons. From it appeared the movement that is the root of time. They meant by "space" the Soul, since it was a space into which the Intellect cast its benefits. When the Soul accepted that and expanded for the Intellect, the Soul was space and the Intellect was the one situated in space. The Intellect was time, and the Soul was the one situated in time.
>
> Those who said "this world and the next world" meant by "this world" the Soul, since it is the secondary cause of this world's becoming populated and its life. By "the next world" they meant the Intellect, since it is the Abode of Life and the Seat of the All-merciful. The people of this world come from the Intellect and return to it in the next world, while the Soul turns back to the Intellect and returns to it.
>
> Those who said "cause and effect" meant by "cause" the Intellect and by "effect" the

Soul, since the Intellect is the cause of the Soul and the secondary cause of its existence.

Those who said "origin and return" meant by "origin" the Intellect, since it is the root of the origin of the things. By "return" they meant the Soul, since it returns to the Intellect when it acquires from it and receives its own matter.

Those who said "manifest and nonmanifest" meant by "manifest" the Intellect, because of the manifestation of its signs and the clarity of things to which it gives existence. By "nonmanifest" they meant the Soul, since the flow of its faculties are nonmanifest. In the same way, the Soul's spirituality is located within the nonmanifest dimensions of the sensory things, the hidden recesses of the corporeal things, and the subtle centers of the natural things.

The demonstration of this explanation is clear. The sayings of the sages in their goals and intentions have agreed upon it, even if they were diverse in their words, sayings, and expressions.[52]

Ibn al-ʿArabī's followers often illustrate how Intellect and Soul manifest their own divine roots, or those divine qualities to which they correspond on their own level. Primarily, these qualities are activity for the Intellect and receptivity for the Soul, or yang and yin. Thus, for example, Farghānī ties Intellect and Soul back to the two inherent attributes of the Essence, the Oneness of Being and the Manyness of Knowledge. He writes:

The Essence has two inherent attributes: oneness, to which pertains activity, and manyness, to which pertains receptivity. . . . It is through the quality of oneness with its activity that the Greatest Spirit—which is the First Intellect—becomes manifest. . . . The quality of manyness along with its receptivity becomes manifest by means of the Soul.[53]

Natural Children

The Pen and the Tablet give birth to the creatures that make up the "natural world," which embraces all the imaginal and corporeal realities below the spiritual world. In discussing these children, ʿAzīz al-Dīn Nasafī provides a good overview of Sufi cosmological thinking. His primary concern is to bring out relationships between God, the cosmos, and the human being. On each level of existence he describes realities that correspond to what is found on other levels. He begins by setting up the basic duality between spiritual and corporeal, but he soon expands on it in order to bring out the complexities of the actual situation.

Some people say that this First Intellect, which is God's Pen, was addressed by the words, "Write upon this first sphere, which is the Tablet of God!" The Pen replied, "O God, what shall I write?" The command came, "Write everything that was, is, and will be until the Day of Resurrection." The Pen wrote all of this, and the Pen became dry. "God has finished with creation, provision, and fixed terms."[54]. . .

In my opinion, this First Intellect, which is the Pen of God, was addressed as follows: "Write upon yourself and upon the First Sphere."[55] It wrote in the blink of an eye. "His only command, when He desires a thing, is to say to it 'Be!', and it is" [36:82]. Immediately all the intellects, souls, and natures came into existence from the First Intellect. And the spheres, stars, and elements appeared from the First Sphere, were arranged in layers, and became separated from each other. "Have not the unbelievers beheld that the heavens and the earth were a mass all sewn up, and then We unstitched them, and of water We fashioned every living thing? Will they not have faith?" [21:30]. In other words, the First Intellect wrote out all these things that came into existence. And these things that came into existence possess what they possess from themselves and have brought it with themselves. The simples of the universe all came into existence, the "fathers" and the "mothers" were completed, and the Pen became dry.[56]

As Nasafī explains below, "fathers" refer to the unseen, spiritual realities such as intellects and souls. The "mothers" are the heavens, the stars, and the elements that act as receptacles for the effects of the unseen world and give birth to the children: minerals, plants, and animals. In what follows, Nasafī's mention of Adam is particularly interesting and more or less typical for the genre. He looks upon him not as a historical person (though he does not mean to reject that interpretation) but as the mythic first individual. Adam represents a set of qualities that are manifest in every world.

> O dervish! The "Kingdom" is the name of the world of sensory objects, the "Dominion" is the name of the world of intelligible objects, and the "Invincibility" [*jabarūt*] is the name of the world of quiddities [*māhiyyāt*]. Some refer to the quiddities as "immutable entities," some refer to them as "immutable realities," and I refer to them as the "immutable things." Each of these immutable things is as it is. It has never changed from its state and will never change. That is why these things are called "immutable." The Prophet wanted to know and see these things as they are in themselves. [That is why he used to pray,] "O God, show us the things as they are!" . . .
>
> O dervish! The Adam of the Invincibility is one person, the Adam of the Dominion another, the Adam of the Kingdom still another, and the Adam of earth yet another. The Adam of the Invincibility is the first existent thing. He is the Invincibility itself, since all existent things appeared from the Invincibility. The Adam of the Dominion is the first of the world of the Dominion. He is the First Intellect, since the whole world of the Dominion appeared from the First Intellect. The Adam of the Kingdom is the first of the world of the Kingdom. He is the First Sphere, since all the world of the Kingdom appeared from the First Sphere. The Adam of earth is the locus of manifestation for the sciences and the meeting place of the lights. He is the perfect human being, since all sciences appeared from the perfect human being.
>
> O dervish! The Adam of earth is the setting place of lights, since all the lights rose from the rising place of the Invincibility and came down to the Adam of earth. When the light becomes manifest from the Adam of earth, the resurrection will have come and the sun will have risen from its setting place.

One of the signs of the end of time is the "rising of the sun in the west." Here Nasafī provides us with a *ta'wīl* or esoteric interpretation of this idea.[57] The east is the rising place of the sun, the west its setting place. The sun is light, and light is a name of God's Essence. Having created Adam in His own form, God made the sun set in the earth. But at the resurrection, the realities of things will be laid bare. The sun that descended into the darkness of the lower realms and set in Adam's earth rises back up from its setting place. The human being brings the divine form from potentiality to actuality, thereby making the sun manifest once again. Hence various Sufis divide the "resurrection" into a number of kinds. For example, Qūnawī speaks of the lesser resurrection, the greater resurrection, and the greatest resurrection. In the first, the true nature of the human being is bared through death and entrance into the *barzakh*, one of the realms of the World of Imagination. At the greater resurrection, all people are resurrected for the final judgment, and everyone's true nature is laid bare for all to see. At the greatest resurrection, the true nature of the human being as divine form is actualized through the spiritual quest. As Qūnawī puts it, the greatest resurrection is "the Arrival [*wuṣūl*] achieved by the gnostic, the moment when the two created worlds are erased and obliterated by the light of Unity, so that nothing remains but the Alive, the Self-subsistent."[58]

Nasafī continues, providing an implicit commentary on the hadith of the Hidden Treasure:

> To come back to the point: Now that you have known the World of the Invincibility, which is the essence of the cosmos, you should know that the World of the Invincibility desired a mirror in which to see its own beauty and contemplate its own attributes. It disclosed itself, thereby coming from the world of undifferentiation to the world of differentiation. From its self-disclosure two substances came to exist, one made of light and the other of darkness. Darkness is the companion of light since darkness preserves and embraces light and is a niche and guardian of light.

Within the cosmos, light and darkness necessitate each other and are inseparable from each other. Though light is inherently manifest, in itself—in God—it is invisible because of the intensity of its manifestation. Hence darkness is the yin that allows for light's yang to appear. Here Nasafī refers to one of the Koranic allusions to this complementarity by mentioning the word "niche," from the Koran's famous "light verse": "God is the light of the heavens and the earth. The likeness of His light is as a niche wherein is a lamp. . . " (24:35). His light becomes manifest only in a niche, which is darkness.

> One of these two substances was the First Intellect and the other the First Sphere. The first things that reached the shore of existence from the Ocean of the Invincibility were these two substances. That is why the First Intellect is called the "First Substance of the World of the Dominion," while the First Sphere is called the "First Substance of the World of the Kingdom." For the same reason the First Intellect is called the "Throne of the World of the Dominion," while the First Sphere is called the "Throne of the World of the Kingdom."
>
> Both substances descended. They came down into many levels. Hence the intellects, souls, and natures appeared from the First Intellect, while the spheres, stars, and elements became manifest from the First Sphere. The sensory things and the intelligible things appeared. Thereby the simple things [*mufradāt*] of the cosmos were completed, since the simple things of the cosmos are not other than these.
>
> Now that you have understood these introductory remarks, you should know that the spirits, souls, and natures are known as the "World of the Dominion." The spheres, stars, and elements are called the "World of the Kingdom." The spirits, souls, and natures are called the "fathers," while the spheres, stars, and elements are known as the "mothers."

At this point Nasafī turns to a discussion of the "two oceans." These are mentioned in several Koranic verses. For example, "It is He who let forth the two oceans, this one sweet, grateful to taste, and this one salt, bitter to the tongue, and He set between them a *barzakh*, and a ban forbidden" (25:53). "He let forth the two oceans that meet together, between them a *barzakh* they do not overpass" (55:19–20). These two verses provide two of the three Koranic mentions of the term *barzakh*, which plays a major role in Sufi thought. We have seen on several occasions that our authors understand a *barzakh* to be an intermediate reality or world. Thus the World of Imagination is a *barzakh* between the spirits and the bodies, while "the *barzakh*" is the world of the grave between death and resurrection. These two Koranic verses are often understood as an allusion to the three worlds: the spirits, the imaginal things, and the bodies. The spirits are sweet, wholesome, pure, luminous; the bodies are bitter, corrupt, defiled, dark. The imaginal things combine the qualities of both sides.

Nasafī takes the "two oceans" as an allusion to the World of Light and the World of Darkness, and he immediately tells us that these are the spiritual world and the corporeal world. However, both light and darkness have wider implications, since light is a name of God, while darkness is a designation for absolute nothingness. The two terms can allude to a number of possible relationships. Thus Nasafī says that this Ocean of spiritual Light is in fact a created ocean. As soon as we compare it to the Ocean of God's Knowledge and Wisdom, it appears as an ocean of darkness. In contrast, the visible world is the Ocean of Darkness properly speaking. However, the darkness of the visible world also cannot be absolute, since the visible world is called dark in relation to the unseen, just as the invisible world is called dark in relation to God. As soon as we compare the visible world to nonexistence, we see that it is luminous. After all, the term *world* (*ʿālam*) signifies that which is marked (*ʿalam*) and designated (*ʿalāma*), that which is known (*ʿilm*). Things can be known only through manifestation. Hence the world is manifest by definition. The visible world is luminous, even if it is dark in relation to the unseen world. At the same time, "darkness" itself has a certain positive aspect, since light cannot manifest itself without darkness. As Ibn al-ʿArabī puts it, "darkness is a kind of light."[59] It is precisely darkness that allows light to be seen in the lower levels of the cosmos, just as the heavens, stars, and elements allow the spiritual domain to manifest itself.

> O dervish! Now that you have come to know about the World of the Invincibility, the World of the Dominion, and the World of the Kingdom . . . , you should know that the Dominion is the Ocean of Light, while the Kingdom is the Ocean of Darkness. This Ocean of Light is the "water of life" and is found in darkness. In the same way, this Ocean of Light is the Ocean of Darkness in relation to the Ocean of Knowledge and Wisdom, and Knowledge and Wisdom are the water of life found in darkness.

That the "water of life is found in darkness" is a proverbial expression. According to various Koran commentators (explaining Koran 18:83ff.), Dhu'l-Qarnayn set out with Khiḍr searching for the water of life. They left the inhabited world and entered into the "darknesses" that lie beyond it. Khiḍr alone was successful in the quest. Sanā'ī writes, "In this path, good is found in evil—The water of life is found in darkness."[60]

> O dervish! How often have you heard that the water of life is found in the darknesses? But you do not know what the water of life is or what these darknesses are. Some of the travelers say that they have reached this Ocean of Light and seen it. It is an unlimited and infinite light, an endless and shoreless ocean. The life, knowledge, power, and desire of the existent things derive from this light.[61] The sight, hearing, talking, taking, and walking of the existent things derive from this light. The nature, specific characteristics, and activity of the existent things come from this light. Or rather, everything comes from this light. The Ocean of Darkness preserves and embraces this light. It is the niche and guardian of this light and the locus of manifestation for its attributes.
>
> In short, this Ocean of Light is called the "fathers," while this Ocean of Darkness is called the "mothers." These fathers and mothers have wrapped their arms around each other's necks and embraced each other. "He let forth the two oceans that meet together, between them a *barzakh* they do not overpass" [55:19–20]. From these fathers and mothers, children appear. "From the two come forth the pearl and the coral" [55:22]. The "children" are the minerals, plants, and animals.
>
> Minerals, plants, and animals are compound things, and before their existence no compound things are found in the cosmos. The compound things do not come from anywhere, nor do they go anywhere. But the simple things become compound and the compound things become simple once again. "Everything returns to its root."
>
> The wisdom in this composition is that those who have the preparedness may advance, ascend, and turn into the World-displaying Cup and the Universe-reflecting Mirror. Then this Ocean of Light and Knowledge may see its own beauty and contemplate its own attributes, names, and acts.[62]

The World-displaying Cup and the Universe-reflecting Mirror both refer to the station of the perfect human being, the "all-comprehensive engendered thing" who has actualized the divine form and manifests fully the two hands of God. Through the perfect human being, the Hidden Treasure is displayed and God witnesses Himself.

Changing Relationships

Earlier in this chapter we saw an example of how the Ikhwān al-Ṣafā' apply different names to the fundamental cosmic duality depending upon the qualitative relationship in view. In another passage, they explain the principle involved in shifting perspectives. Words are but titles that we give to things to express the relationships that we have in view. If we change our point of view, the words may change. What was matter may become form, and what was form may become matter. And matter is clearly the yin side of the relationship, as indicated already in the fact that the English word is cognate with *mother*.

> Know that all these words are titles and marks. Through them allusion is made to forms, so that distinction can be drawn in ascriptions that are made among them. Thus one form is sometimes called material, sometimes substantial, sometimes accidental, some-

times simple, sometimes compound, sometimes spiritual, sometimes corporeal, sometimes cause, sometimes effect, and so on. In the same way, when some numbers are related to others, one number is sometimes called half, sometimes double, sometimes one-third, sometimes one-fourth, and so on.

An example of this can be a shirt, which is a corporeal, manufactured thing, perceived by sense perception. Its quiddity is a form in cloth, while cloth is its matter. The quiddity of cloth is a form in thread, while thread is its matter. The quiddity of thread is a form in cotton, while cotton is its matter. The quiddity of cotton is a form in a plant, while a plant is its matter. The quiddity of a plant is a form in the natural bodies, which are fire, air, water, and earth. And each of these four is a form in the nondelimited body, which is a form in the Prime Matter. The Prime Matter is a spiritual form effused from the Universal Soul. The Universal Soul is also a spiritual form, effused from the Universal Intellect, which is the first existent thing brought into existence by the Creator.[63]

Ibn al-ʿArabī and his followers were equally concerned to delineate the qualities of things, but characteristically the Sufis looked not to the Greek heritage for their terminology but to the Koran. They were concerned to find the roots of all qualities present in the cosmos in the divine reality, as that reality is described by God's own Word. These qualities depend upon the relationships that exist between God and the creatures. And as we have pointed out more than once, these relationships are precisely God's attributes or names. Some of them are negative in the sense that they declare what He is not. This is the route of incomparability: He is Inaccessible, Pure, Transcendent, Holy. Other relationships are positive, since they tell us what He is, giving news of His similarity: He is Alive, Knowing, Desiring, and so on.

Created things also can be known only through relationships with other things. These relationships are expressed through the qualities that are attributed to things. When the cosmologists look at the Pen and the Tablet, they want to show how the two are connected to God and the visible universe. Pen and Tablet are needed to explain the world as we observe it in terms of what we know about God through revelation. At the same time, Pen and Tablet are known through their qualities, and these appear in all levels of existence. Hence some cosmologists seek to show that the primordial qualities manifested by Pen and Tablet are present everywhere. Ibn al-ʿArabī does this, employing related terminology, when he declares that marriage "pervades all atoms."

If the qualities of Pen and Tablet are found on every level, then Pen is found in Tablet and Tablet is found in Pen. Thus, when the Pen, which is yang in relation to the Tablet, is viewed in relation to God, it becomes yin, a tablet. And when the Tablet, which is yin in relation to the Pen, is viewed in relation to what lies below it, it is yang, a pen.

In the first passage quoted in this chapter from the Ikhwān al-Ṣafāʾ, allusion is made to a series of yang/yin relationships in the pairs being discussed. The Ikhwān say, for example, that the Soul is an accident (yin) in relation to the Intellect, but a substance (yang) in relation to things below itself. In the second passage quoted above they say that what is matter in one respect is form in another. In still another passage they explain that the Intellect and Soul are each in turn a source of light and activity. The Intellect is God's radiance, while the Soul is the Intellect's reflection. The Soul is bright in relation to the corporeal world, but dark in relation to the Intellect.

The relationship of the Soul to the Intellect is like the relationship of the brightness of the moon to the light of the sun, while the relationship of the Intellect to the Creator is like the relationship of the light of the sun to the sun itself. When the moon is filled with the light of the sun, it resembles the sun in light. In the same way, when the Soul receives the effusion of the Intellect so that its excellencies are completed, it resembles the Intellect in its acts.[64]

In a similar passage Ibn al-ʿArabī shows that the Pen is receptive in relation to God, but active in relation to the Tablet.

The First Intellect, which is the first thing to be created from nothing, is the Supreme Pen. No temporally originated thing was found along with it. It was a locus that received effects because of what God caused to occur within it, that is, the arising of the Guarded Tablet from it. In the same way, Eve arose from Adam in the world of corporeal things. Hence this Tablet became an object and a locus for what the Supreme, Divine Pen writes within it. . . . So the Guarded Tablet is the first existent thing to arise from a created thing.[65]

Since the Guarded Tablet or Universal Soul is a spiritual being, born directly from the First Intellect, it is light. But it represents a movement in the direction of Nature, so it embraces the properties of darkness as well. Like any *barzakh*, it brings together the properties of the two sides.

> The Universal Soul arises from the First Intellect. Hence it is the first object of activity to arise from a created thing. It mixes that which acts upon it with that upon which it acts. That which acts upon it is light, while that upon which it acts is darkness, that is, Nature.[66]

Just as the Pen can be considered yin or a "Tablet" in relation to God, so also the Tablet can be considered yang or a "Pen" in relation to what lies below it. In the process of explaining this, Ibn al-ʿArabī tells us why the hadith literature frequently describes the Tablet as an emerald.

> This noble angel, the Guarded Tablet, is also a pen in relation to what lies below it. Every active thing and the locus that receives its activity are pen and tablet. . . . This angel has two relationships: a luminous relationship, which is turned toward the Noble Intellect, and a dark relationship, which is turned toward the Dust, the Ocean of Nature. In itself the Tablet is green because of this delicate and wonderful mixture.[67]

In Ibn al-ʿArabī's cosmology the "Dust" (*habāʾ*) or "Dust Substance" (*al-jawhar al-habāʾī*) is the Universal Hyle or Prime Matter within which everything in the imaginal and corporeal worlds assumes shape. The world of "Nature" appears within the Dust. If the Tablet is the first existent thing to arise from the activity of a created reality, the Dust is the second existent thing to arise in a similar receptive manner, but from the activity of the Tablet, now considered as yang. Looking at the cosmos as a Divine Book, Ibn al-ʿArabī refers to it in the following as the "world of writing and inscription" (*ʿālam al-tadwīn waʾl-tasṭīr*).

> The First Intellect came into existence within the World of Writing and Inscription. It came into existence from nothing. Then "after" that, with no temporal afterness, the Soul arose in the mode of a thing arising from another created thing. It is the Guarded Tablet within which is written everything that will come to be in this abode until the Day of Resurrection. It is God's knowledge concerning His creation. It lies below the Pen—the Intellect—in luminosity and level of brightness. Hence it is like the green emerald, because of the arising of the Dust Substance, which lies within the potentiality of this Soul. Hence the Dust Substance arises from the Soul. It is a dark substance within which there is no light.[68]

Nasafī frequently discusses the way in which realities take on different names according to the point of view. In the following, he is once again discussing the worlds of Invincibility, Dominion, and Kingdom. He shows that each of them can be called by certain key Koranic terms as soon as we envisage their qualities and the corresponding relationships. He is concerned here to bring out the relationship between *nūn*, the Pen, the Guarded Tablet, and God's Book. We saw above that Imam Jaʿfar interpreted *nūn* to be a river in the Garden, ink, light, and an angel. In the present context, Nasafī understands *nūn* to mean "inkwell." Hence we have the Inkwell, the Pen that writes, the Tablet upon which is written, and the Book that is written. What is especially interesting about this passage is the clarity with which Nasafī brings out the directionality of relationships. Each thing needs to be understood in relation to the yang realities above it and the yin realities below it.

> Know—God exalt you in the two worlds—that the World of Invincibility is the Guarded Tablet, the Book of God, and the Inkwell. For the World of Invincibility has two faces, one turned toward God and the other turned toward the Dominion and the Kingdom. The face turned toward God is

called the "Guarded Tablet" and the "Book of God," since everything that has been, is, and will be is written together in the World of Invincibility. "There is not a thing, fresh or withered, but in a Manifest Book" [6:59]. Hence the World of Invincibility is the Guarded Tablet and the Book of God.

The face that is turned toward the Dominion and the Kingdom is called the "Inkwell," since the simple things and the compound things of the cosmos all appeared from the World of Invincibility, becoming manifest and differentiated. As long as they were in the World of Invincibility, they were all concealed and undifferentiated. Hence the World of Invincibility is the Inkwell.

Now that you have come to know about the Guarded Tablet, the Book of God, and the Inkwell, you should know that the First Substance is the Pen of God, since the First Substance was addressed with the words, "Write from this Inkwell!" In the blink of an eye it wrote, and the simple things of the cosmos entered into existence, coming from the world of potentiality to the world of actuality and from the world of undifferentiation to the world of differentiation. The "simple things" of the cosmos are the intellects, the souls, the natures, the spheres, the stars, and the elements. Once the simple things were written, the Pen became dry. "The Lord has finished with creation, character, provision, and fixed terms."

The Pen of the simple things became dry, but the simple things are constantly occupied with inscription, thereby writing out the compound things. "The Inkwell! By the Pen and what they are writing" [68:1]. The "Inkwell" is the World of Invincibility, the "Pen" is the First Substance, and "what they are writing" is the simple things of the cosmos.

O dervish! Each of the simple things of the cosmos has a special task and is constantly occupied with its task in order that the compound things of the cosmos may appear and arrive from them. The "compound things" of the cosmos are the minerals, the plants, and the animals. The existent things of the cosmos are nothing more than this.

O dervish! The World of the Invincibility is the Book of God, and the worlds of the Dominion and the Kingdom are also the Book of God. However, the World of the Invincibility is the undifferentiated book, while the worlds of the Kingdom and the Dominion are the differentiated book. In this differentiated book, the simple things of the cosmos are the letters of the alphabet, while the compound things of the cosmos are the words. That is why the simple things of the cosmos are twenty-eight and the compound things are three: minerals, plants, and animals. For the simple letters of the [Arabic] alphabet are twenty-eight,[69] while the compound things [according to Arabic grammar] are three: nouns, verbs, and particles. . . .

Know that each simple thing of the cosmos is the Guarded Tablet, the Book, the Inkwell, and the Pen, since all the simple things have two faces, a face turned toward the World of the Invincibility and a face turned toward the compound things. The face turned toward the World of Invincibility is called the "Guarded Tablet" and the "Book," since everything that has been, is, and will be in the compound things was written in them by the First Pen from the First Inkwell. The second face, which they have turned toward the compound things, is called the "Inkwell" and the "Pen." It is called the "Inkwell" because all the compound things of the cosmos appeared from the simple things, becoming manifest and differentiated. As long as the compound things were in the simple things, they were concealed and undifferentiated. Hence the simple things are the Inkwell. This second face is called the "Pen" since the simple things are constantly occupied with inscription, writing out the compound things. Once the First Pen wrote the simple things, it became dry. But these pens that write the compound things do not become dry. All are constantly occupied with inscription. "Say: 'If the sea were ink for the Words of my Lord, the sea would be exhausted before the Words of my Lord are exhausted, though We brought replenishment the like of it'" [18:109].

O dervish! The First Pen, which wrote the simple things, and these pens, which write the compound things, did not learn inscription from anyone. Inscription pertains to their essences. The perfection of the simple things goes along with their essences, in contrast to the compound things.[70]

The Faces of the Intellect

Most authorities consider the Pen and Tablet as two levels of spiritual manifestation. But considered independently from the

Tablet, the Pen itself has two faces, since it looks both at God and at the cosmos. The face turned toward God is receptive, while the face turned toward the lower levels of creation is active. On one side stands the Necessary Being, on the other side the world of possible existence. Hence the Pen is a *barzakh* between the two sides, possessing properties of both Necessity and possibility.

The two faces of the Pen help explain why hadiths refer to it both as Pen and Intellect, as in the sayings, "The first thing created by God was the Pen" and "The first thing created by God was the Intellect." When envisaged as a Pen, this reality is considered yang in relation to the worlds below it. When looked upon as an Intellect, it is yin in relation to its divine source. The root meaning of the word *ʿaql* (intellect) is tying, binding, constricting. The intellect delimits, defines, and differentiates that which is undifferentiated. Qūnawī alludes to these points while discussing the process whereby the cosmos comes into existence.

> When God turned the attentiveness of His desire [toward creating the cosmos], this gave rise within the World of Writing and Inscription to a single ontological result that carried the unseen manyness of the relationships. God named it a "pen" and an "intellect."

In other words, the relationships established by the fact that God desired to create a universe appear in the Pen/Intellect. God's "turning the attentiveness of His desire" is Qūnawī's way of expressing the meaning of the hadith of the Hidden Treasure: God created the creatures because of His love or desire to be known.

> This reality is an "intellect" in respect of the face turned toward its Lord, a face that receives from Him bestowal and replenishment. The Intellect is the first entified existent thing that intellectually perceives its own self along with everything that is distinguished from itself. It also perceives everything through which it becomes distinguished from others, in contrast to those who precede it in level, the "enraptured ones."

In Ibn al-ʿArabī's cosmology, the "enraptured angels" (*al-malāʾikat al-muhayyamūn*) are created along with or just before the First Intellect, but their attention is turned exclusively toward God, so they have no awareness of self or others. They stand above the World of Writing and Inscription.[71]

> God called it a "pen" in respect of its face turned toward the engendered world, so it exercises effects upon this world and replenishes it. Moreover, the Pen carries the unseen, undifferentiated manyness that is deposited in its essence so that it may differentiate it in that which becomes manifest from it, whether through a level or in some other way.

Even though the Pen is differentiated in relation to the absolute undifferentiation of God, it manifests God's knowledge of creation in a relatively undifferentiated form. Then, through its activity, this knowledge becomes differentiated within the Tablet.

> Since the Pen is the result of the aforementioned turning of God's attentiveness, it became manifest comprising the characteristics of all-comprehensiveness and unity.

In other words, the Pen is itself the created manifestation of this divine act of turning toward the creation of the cosmos. Inasmuch as it reflects the divine reality directly, the Pen is a single reality that comprehends all attributes, just as Allah comprehends all names. Hence the Pen brings together the real oneness of the Essence and the relative manyness of the names—what Farghānī calls the "Oneness of Being" and the "Manyness of Knowledge."

> The property of the Desire reached its limit through exercising its influence in respect of this face. Thereby the Pen—which was the object of the Desire—became manifest. Then another relationship became entified through a second attentiveness in respect of this entification [of the Pen], not in respect of the Real, since His command is one.

In other words, God's one command—to which the cosmologists find reference in the

Koranic verse, "Our command is but one, like the blink of an eye" (54:50)—gives rise to the Pen. It does not produce the Tablet directly. We saw Ibn al-ʿArabī make this same point by saying that the Pen comes into existence from no created thing, while the Tablet arises from the Pen. As our authors frequently mention, the single command of the One Reality has but a single object, the Intellect. On the basis of this triplicity of Command, Intellect, and relationship, first the Tablet is engendered and then the rest of the cosmos. Qūnawī explains these points in his own typical fashion:

> As a result, a self-disclosure possessing two properties became manifest and entified from the Unseen. One of these properties was the unitary, all-comprehensive property of the Essence. The other has to do with the fact that this very property [of the Essence] became colored by that over which it passed and from which it became distinguished, that is, the Pen. Hence there became entified . . . in the level following the level of the Pen the existence of the Guarded Tablet. . . .
>
> Within the Tablet became manifest the differentiation of the manyness contained in the Cloud [that is, the level of God's knowledge]. Thereby the name Differentiator reached its perfection through having a locus of manifestation. In the same way, the name Governor had reached its perfection of having a locus of manifestation through the Pen.[72]

The yang/yin relationship between the names Governor and Differentiator, discussed in chapter 2, is thus made manifest in the Pen and Tablet.

In the preceding passage, Qūnawī was concerned merely to show why a single reality is called both "Pen" and "Intellect." In the following, his disciple Farghānī wants to show that Pen and Intellect are also identical with the "Muhammadan Spirit" or the "Muhammadan Light," since the Prophet said, "The first thing God created was my spirit" or "my light." Hence he speaks of three faces of the Pen:

> The Supreme Pen has three supra-sensory, universal faces. One is its taking existence and knowledge—in an undifferentiated mode and without any intermediary, perception, or restricting—from the unseen Presence of Him who gives it existence. In respect of this face it is named the First Intellect.
>
> Through the second face it differentiates within the Guarded Tablet that which it had received as undifferentiated. Thus it follows the command, "Write My knowledge in My creation" or "in that which will be." Because of this face it is called the Supreme Pen. This face is the Muhammadan Soul which is alluded to by his saying, "By Him in whose hand is Muhammad's soul."

These two faces represent the yang and yin sides of the Pen, as in Qūnawī's discussion. The third face suggests that the Pen combines the two qualities in a unified whole, just as God combines the names of majesty and beauty.

> Through the third face the Pen carries the property of the First Self-disclosure and acts as its locus of manifestation in itself. In this respect it is the reality of the Greatest Muhammadan Spirit, and in one respect his Light.

If the Pen has three faces, then the Guarded Tablet, which is second in the chain of command, has six faces. Three are receptive toward the faces of the Pen, and three more effuse upon the realities of the cosmos below the Tablet.

> As for the Guarded Tablet, it has six supra-sensory, universal faces.
>
> First is the fact that it is a condition resulting from combining the ray of light effused from and attributed to [the Real] with the properties of the quiddities that are connected to the world of the spirits. This condition comprises the two kinds of words, active and verbal.[73] These words are differentiated such that nothing that enters into existence until the completion of the Day of Resurrection escapes this face. In this respect the Tablet is called "everything" and is referred to in God's words, "We wrote for [Moses] on the tablets something of Everything" [7:145].
>
> The second face is the Tablet's attention toward Him who brought it into existence and its taking of replenishment from Him. This is in fact two faces. The first of the two has no intermediary. In this respect the Tablet is called a spirit attributed to the Divine Pres-

ence and effused from the All-merciful Breath without intermediary. From it the spirits attributed to perfect human beings are blown into them without intermediary, while spirits attributed to others are blown into them with the intermediary of a particular spirit from this face called an "angel."

The second face, which is the third, is an effusion through the intermediary of the Supreme Pen. In accordance with this face the Tablet is called a "Guarded Tablet."

The Tablet's fourth face is its descent and manifestation in respect to some of what its reality and essence comprise. In this descent and manifestation, the Tablet becomes differentiated and assumes imaginal and sensory forms, both simple and compound. These forms are the Throne, the Footstool, the heavens, the earths, and everything in between, that is, the angels, the spheres, the planets, the elements, and the children—minerals, plants, animals, and human beings. . . . In this respect the Tablet is called the "Active, Manifest Book." It is meant by His words, "There is not a thing, fresh or withered, but it is in a Manifest Book" [6:59], and His words, "*Ṭā' Sīn*. Those are the signs of the Koran and a Manifest Book" [27:1].

The fifth face is the attention that the Tablet turns, through the attribute of governing and perfecting, toward that which becomes differentiated from it and manifest in the imaginal and sensory forms. Hence the Tablet governs, guards, and perfects the universal through a universal attribute and the particular through a particular attribute. In this respect it is called the "Universal Soul."

This fifth face turns its attention toward governing in two forms. One of them is the form of universality, and in this respect it is the soul of all the prophets and friends of God except our Prophet. The Prophet's rational soul, which governs his purified form, is a face of the Supreme Pen's differentiation. This same thing was taken in undifferentiated mode by the Guarded Tablet through the command, "Write what will be!" Allusion is made to this in the Prophet's words while swearing an oath: "By Him in whose hand is Muhammad's soul."

The fifth face's second form [i.e., the sixth face] is the particular souls that govern the elemental, particular persons.

In short, the Pen is closer to the Oneness of God, and hence has only three faces. The Tablet is further away, so it is more closely connected to manyness. Here Farghānī comes back to the common theme that oneness dominates over certain realities of the cosmos, while manyness dominates over others. Oneness is closely connected to equilibrium, mercy, and all the names of beauty, while manyness is connected to deviation, wrath, and all the names of majesty. Oneness is the right hand of God, manyness the left hand.

From all of this you have come to know that the relationship of the reality of the Guarded Tablet to the Second Level, known as the Level of Divinity, is stronger. In the same way, the relationship of the Pen to the First Entification is more intense. Just as the First Entification is dominated by the property of undifferentiation and oneness, so also this property dominates over the reality of the Pen. Hence the Pen receives the existence that is effused upon it only in an undifferentiated mode.

In a similar way, since the property of differentiation dominates over the Second, Relational Entification, the reality of the Guarded Tablet received that undifferentiated existence through the intermediary of the Pen as differentiated.[74]

Maḥmūd Shabistarī (d. ca. 720/1320) alludes to two faces of the Intellect in his famous poem, *Gulshan-i rāz* ("The rose-garden of the mystery"). His meaning is made clear by his commentator, Muḥammad Lāhījī (d. 912/1506–7), who also ties in Necessity and possibility, the right and left hands, and Adam and Eve. In the light of the tradition, the parallels he draws should not seem exceptional.

"Just once, look carefully at your own root—
it is your mother's father and her mother."

The poet's meaning is as follows: Look carefully at your own root, which is the Universal Intellect. See that your root, which is the Universal Intellect, became the father of your mother, which is the Universal Soul, while in another respect, it is her mother.

The Universal Intellect is the root and reality of the human being. In respect to the fact that it effuses the Universal Soul and becomes the intermediary for its manifestation, it is the Universal Soul's father. But in respect to the fact that the Universal Soul is born from the Universal Intellect, the Intellect is the Soul's mother.

Since the Universal Intellect is the isthmus between Necessity and possibility and encompasses the two sides, and since Necessity stands on its right side while possibility stands on its left side, the Universal Soul was actualized on the left side, which is the side of possibility. In his reality, Adam is the form of the Universal Intellect, while Eve is the form of the Universal Soul. From here the seeker comes to know why Eve became manifest from Adam's left side.[75]

Finally, I quote a passage from Ibn al-ʿArabī in order to emphasize the importance of the relationship between undifferentiation and differentiation. Ibn al-ʿArabī is commenting on the Koranic passage, "*Nūn*. By the Pen" (68:1). Like Imam Jaʿfar, Ibn al-ʿArabī sees Nūn as the name of an angel. And like Nasafī, he is concerned to bring out the hierarchy of relationships between God and the visible world. He refers to this angel while explaining some of the implications of the fact that God is called King (*al-malik*). He describes a series of levels, moving from God to the Tablet. God as King sets up the kingdom as He desires. He chooses certain close companions, the enraptured angels or cherubim. Then He chooses one of these to be His closest advisor: the veil-keeper or chamberlain (*ḥājib*). He gives His knowledge of creation to this most trusted of friends. The chamberlain then appoints a scribe, the Pen, who writes down the details on the Tablet. Hence the movement is from total undifferentiation in God Himself to relative undifferentiation in the chamberlain. Then the scribe possesses a relatively differentiated knowledge, which is further differentiated through writing in the Tablet. On each created level, from Nūn to the Tablet, there is a receptive face turned toward the higher direction, and an active face turned toward the lower direction.

Since God is named the King, He arranged the cosmos in the hierarchy of a kingdom [*mamlaka*]. Hence He appointed certain of His servants to be His favorites, and these are the enraptured angels, God's sitting companions through remembrance [*dhikr*]. "Those who are with Him wax not too proud to do Him service, neither grow weary, glorifying Him by night and in the daytime and never failing" [21:19–20].

Then God chose one of these cherubim to be the veil-keeper, giving him His knowledge concerning His creation. This is a differentiated knowledge within undifferentiation. Hence God's knowledge is a locus of disclosure to the angel within the angel. He named the angel Nūn. Nūn never ceases living in the seclusion of the Presence of His Knowledge. He is the head of the Divine Chancellery. God—in respect of being the All-knowing—is never veiled from him.

Then God specified another angel from among the angels, below Nūn in rank, whom He named the Pen. He appointed for him a station below Nūn, making him a scribe. God teaches him whatever knowledge of the creatures that He desires through Nūn, but by way of undifferentiated knowledge. One of the things that this undifferentiated knowledge comprises is differentiated knowledge, which is one kind of undifferentiated knowledge. For knowledges have their levels, one of which is the knowledge of differentiation. Hence the Divine Pen possesses none of the levels of undifferentiated knowledge except the knowledge of differentiation in general and some specific differentiated knowledges, but nothing else.

God took this angel, the scribe of His chancellery, and disclosed Himself to him in respect of His name the All-powerful, giving him replenishment through this Divine Self-disclosure. He made this Pen turn its gaze toward the World of Writing and Inscription and created for it a Tablet. He commanded it to write within it everything that He willed to bring about in His creation until the Day of Resurrection specifically. He made the Tablet the pupil and the Pen the teacher.[76]

The Two Wings of Gabriel

Shihāb al-Dīn Suhrawardī al-Maqtūl (d. 587/1191), Ibn al-ʿArabī's older contemporary and the founder of the Illuminationist School of philosophy, demonstrates the reversibility of the yin/yang relationships in cosmic realities in the midst of one of his visionary treatises, "The Song of the Wing of Gabriel." In Suhrawardī's scheme, Gabriel is the lowest of the supreme angels, who are the "greatest words" of God. He stands at the borderline between the unmixed light of the spiritual realm, where all attention is turned toward the Divine, and the mixed light of the lower realms of spiritual existence, where the angelic beings are busy with bringing the visible world into existence. Gabriel's two wings correspond functionally with the First Intellect and the Universal Soul. Hence one is pure light, while the other is light mixed with a small amount of darkness. This mixture prepares the way for the realms that are thoroughly mixed with darkness on lower levels of the cosmos. Suhrawardī refers to Nature as the "world of deception" because it is dark in relation to the spiritual world. Hence Nature gives a relatively free hand to ignorance and misguidance.

> Know that Gabriel has two wings. The first, the right wing, is sheer light. This wing is solely the attribution of his existence to God. He also has a left wing, which has a bit of the mark of darkness upon it, like a spot on the face of the moon. . . . This is the sign of his own existence, one side of which is turned toward nonexistence. When you look at the attribution of his existence to the Real, he has the attribute of the Real. But when you look at the proper claim of his own essence, he can properly claim only nonexistence. This is the concomitant of possible existence. These two meanings are found in the level of the two wings: the attribution to the Real in the right wing, and the respect of his own proper claim in the left wing.

In other words, Gabriel displays the light of the Necessary Being. But he is the manifestation of that Being, not that Being Itself. Hence he is a possible thing. As a result, his light does not belong intrinsically to himself, but to God. He cannot be called pure light, since he himself, in his own specific reality, has no light of his own. Hence his right wing manifests the Oneness and Necessity of Being, while his left wing displays the Manyness and Possibility of Knowledge. His right wing goes back to God, while his left wing displays its effects in the engendered universe.

> The left wing of Gabriel, which has a small amount of darkness, throws down a shadow. From it derives the world of falsehood and deception. Thus the Prophet said, "God created the creatures in darkness, then He sprinkled them with some of His light."[77] "He created them in darkness" alludes to the blackness of the left wing. "Then He sprinkled them with light" alludes to the ray of the right wing. . . .
>
> The world of deception is the song and shadow of Gabriel's wing, that is, his left wing, while enlightened souls derive from his right wing. The realities that God deposits in the minds of human beings all derive from the right wing, as, for example, "He has written faith upon their hearts, and He has confirmed them with a spirit from Himself" [58:22]. But severity, the "Cry" [11:67], and mishaps all derive from the left wing.[78]

In short the two wings of Gabriel reflect the two hands of God: The right wing is related to Oneness, mercy, and beauty, the left wing to manyness, wrath, and majesty.

6

HUMAN MARRIAGE

The macrocosm is identical with the cosmos, or "everything other than God." If the term *macrocosm* is used instead of *cosmos*, this is done to set up a relationship between the whole universe and the human individual, since the two terms are correlative. Frequently our authors draw correspondences between the outward structure of the macrocosm and the inner structure of the microcosm by investigating the relationships among the three basic levels of the human being: spirit, soul, and body. In this case they are studying the microcosm in terms of a "spiritual psychology." In doing so they often speak of "marriage" between the various levels. This is a topic that will be discussed in chapters 8 through 10. Our authors also study relationships between individual microcosms, though here the term *microcosm* is normally not employed, precisely because the term is used to establish relationships between the human being and the macrocosm, not among human beings. Since we have discussed macrocosmic marriage in the previous chapter, it may be appropriate here to investigate the repercussions of macrocosmic marriage on the level of interpersonal relationships. What does marriage within the Divine Reality, between God and the cosmos, and within various levels of the macrocosm other than the human level, tell us about human marriage? And conversely, what do human sexual relationships tell us about God and the macrocosm?

To deal with these sorts of questions, we need to consider those Islamic teachings that have a bearing on the relationship between men and women, and then see how these are placed in the context of God, the macrocosm, and the microcosm. Naturally, Islam in general has a great deal to say about sexual relationships, and it would be impossible in this context to summarize all the relevant legal and social teachings. Instead I will focus on a few key Koranic verses and sayings of the Prophet.

Marriage in Society

There are numerous Koranic verses and prophetic sayings—not to mention the Sunna or prophetic practice—that supply the basis for Islam's generally positive evaluation of human sexual relationships.[1] On one level, Islam sees the sexual relationship as a natural and normal part of God's good creation.[2] Did not God say, "And of everything We created a pair that haply you may remember" (51:49)? "He Himself created the pair, male and female" (53:45). When something was created as one of a pair, it is clearly incomplete without the other. Many traditional sayings emphasize marriage's importance. Among hadiths of the Prophet are the following: "Marriage is my Sunna. He who does not act according to my Sunna does not belong to me."[3] "A person who marries achieves half his religion, so let him fear God in the other half."[4] "Most of the people of the Fire are bachelors."[5] "No building is built in Islam more beloved to God than marriage."[6] "A Muslim man can acquire no benefit after Islam greater than a Muslim wife who makes him happy when he looks upon her, obeys him when he commands her, and protects him when he is away from her in herself and his property."[7]

Given that marriage is the foundation of society and one of the highest goods, it is natural that Islam expects both husband and wife to behave in the best manner toward their spouses. The Prophet said, "The best among you is the one who acts best toward his wife, and I am better than any of you toward my wife."[8] It is true that in these discussions of the relationships between men and women, the tradition typically addresses men. But it is also typical for the tradition to recognize that whatever is applied to men also applies to women, the appropriate adjustments having been made. Thus the Koran usually employs language that grammatically refers to men. But sometimes, clearly in order to prevent the reader from making the mistake of thinking that God is addressing men alone, it brings women into the picture, making the same points that were made elsewhere through grammatically masculine expressions. For example, in the first passage below, only masculine adjectives are employed, in the second both masculine and feminine adjectives:

> And God sees His servants who say, "O Lord, we have faith; forgive us our sins, and guard us against the chastisement of the Fire"—the patient, the truthful, the obedient, the expenders, the askers of forgiveness at daybreak. (3:17)
>
> The submitted ones [masculine] and the submitted ones [feminine], the faithful and the faithful, the obedient and the obedient, the truthful and the truthful, the patient and the patient, . . . for them God has prepared forgiveness and a mighty wage. (33:35)

We can summarize the Muslim view of the benefits of marriage by quoting a few short passages from the great authority Abū Ḥāmid Muḥammad al-Ghazālī (d. 505/1111). It needs to be recognized, however, that in these passages Ghazālī is speaking from the position of a teacher concerned for the good of the general public. Hence he de-emphasizes certain aspects of marriage, such as enjoyment of the sexual act, that are given a positive evaluation by many Sufi authors writing for a more limited audience. From the perspective of the Sharia and the general religious teachings, establishing social responsibility is the primary goal. Hence God's awesome authority and His outward commandments need to be stressed.

> Know that marriage is one part of the way of religion, like eating food. For the way of religion has need of human life and subsistence, and life is impossible without food and drink. In the same way it needs the subsistence of the human species and its procreation, and this is not possible without marriage. Therefore marriage is the cause of the origin of existence, while food is the cause of the subsistence of existence.
>
> Marriage was made permissible for this reason, not for the sake of satisfying one's appetites. On the contrary, God created appetite as a deputy responsible for encouraging people to marry. Then travelers on the path of religion will come into existence and travel on religion's path. Everyone was created for the sake of religion. As God said, "I created jinn and mankind only to be My servants" [51:56].[9]

Ghazālī devotes much of the rest of this chapter to five benefits that marriage provides: having children, protecting one's religion and limiting appetite, being intimate with women, having someone to take care of the affairs of the house, and training oneself in good character traits. Though all these topics deserve amplification, some of Ghazālī's remarks on the benefits of children and intimacy are especially interesting for our purposes.

Ghazālī considers participation in the natural order the first of four merits that a person acquires through having children. In a fashion that typifies Muslim thinking about the created world, he appeals to the signs of the microcosm to show that marriage is the human state desired by God.

The first merit of having children is that a person should have striven for that which is loved by God, that is, human existence and procreation. Whoever understands the wisdom of the created order will have no doubt that God loves this. For God has given His servant an earth worthy of cultivation. He has given him seed. He has turned over to him a pair of oxen and a plow. He has sent a deputy to encourage him to cultivate. If the servant has one iota of intelligence, he knows what God means by all this, even if He should not speak to him with His tongue.

God created the womb. He created the organ of intercourse. He placed the seed of the children in the backs and bodies of men and women. He sent appetite as His deputy to men and women. No intelligent person will miss what God means by all this.

If the person should waste the seed and send away the deputy through some stratagem, without doubt he will remain far from the road of what was meant by his original nature [*fiṭrat*]. This is why the early Muslims and the Companions considered it reprehensible to die while single. So much was this the case that when Muʿādh's two wives died in the plague and he himself caught the plague, he said, "Give me a wife, that I may not die single."[10]

Ghazālī's explanation of the benefits of intimacy (*uns*) reminds us that intimacy is associated with yin names such as Merciful and Loving. Worship and service (*ʿibāda*), in contrast, are associated with yang names such as King and Majestic. Too much dealing with the names of majesty tends to increase awe and constrict the heart. The intimacy and bold expansiveness that one achieves through women remedies this one-sided development of the soul. And of course it should not be thought that the same argument does not apply to women. They also become constricted by too much worship, and they also find ease and expansion through intimacy with men. In this context, men manifest the yin names for them.

The third benefit of marriage is that the heart finds ease through intimacy with women, because of sitting and joking with them. This ease then becomes the cause of an increase in desire for worship. For diligence in worship brings weariness, and the heart contracts. But ease acquired in this way brings back the heart's strength. ʿAlī said, "Do not remove rest and ease completely from the hearts, lest they become blind."

It sometimes happened that the Prophet was overcome by such tremendous unveilings that his bodily frame was not able to tolerate it. He would take ʿĀ'isha's hand and say, "Talk with me, ʿĀ'isha."[11] He wanted to gain strength so that he could carry the burden of revelation. Once he came back to this world and gained full strength, the thirst for that work would overcome him, and he would say, "Give us ease, Bilāl!"[12] Then he would turn back to the ritual prayer.

Sometimes the Prophet would strengthen his mind with a sweet aroma. That is why he said, "Three things of this world of yours were made lovable to me: women, perfume—and the coolness of my eye was placed in the ritual prayer." He put "ritual prayer" last because that is the goal. For he said, "The coolness of my eye is in the ritual prayer," while sweet aromas and women are the ease of the body. Thereby the body gains strength to busy itself with prayer and to gain the coolness of the eye found therein.[13]

Man's Degree over Woman (I)

One of the most famous, and indeed in certain circles, notorious, verses of the Koran is 2:228: "The men have a degree above them [the women]." The passage occurs in a relatively long section having to do with the laws of divorce. The particular verse within which it occurs sets down the woman's waiting period after divorce before she can remarry. The whole verse is as follows:

Divorced women shall wait by themselves for three periods; and it is not lawful for them to hide what God has created in their wombs, if they have faith in God and the Last Day. In such time their husbands have better right to bring them back, if they desire to put things in order. They have [rights over their husbands] similar to those [their husbands have] over them, [all to be maintained] with honor, but the men have a degree above them. God is Inaccessible, Wise.

Certainly the meaning of the clause, "the men have a degree above them" needs to be clarified within its context, though that cannot exhaust its significance, as our authors are the first to note. "The men" are the husbands of these women, and thus Arberry, for example, one of the most careful of Koran translators, practically never adding a word to the text, sees fit to translate the verse, "*Their* men have a degree above them." The verse deals specifically with the context of the marriage relationship established according to the Sharia. It affirms that God gives to men a certain something in which they are one "degree" (*daraja*) "above" or "over" (*ʿalā*) the women. The Koran commentators naturally try to explain what that something is, and interpretations differ.

Maybudī's explanation of this verse provides a good sampling of the usual opinions put forward by the commentators:

> God is saying that the right of the women over the men is just like the right of the men over the women. It is incumbent on both of them to keep the other and the self pure and pleased, to live in happiness, and to provide pleasant company and companionship. Ibn ʿAbbās said, "I love to adorn myself for the woman just as I love that she adorn herself for me, since God said, 'They have [rights] similar to those over them, with honor.'" In the same way God says, "Treat them [women] with honor" [4:19]. The Prophet said, "The best of you is the best of you to his wife."
>
> Saʿīd ibn al-Musayyib reports that the Prophet said, "When a Muslim man intends to come to his wife, God writes for him 20 good deeds and erases from him 20 evil deeds. When he takes her by the hand, God writes for him 40 good deeds and erases from him 40 evil deeds. When he kisses her, God writes for him 60 good deeds and erases from him 60 evil deeds. When he comes into her, God writes for him 120 good deeds. When he stands up to make the ablution, God boasts of him to the angels and says, 'Look at My servant. He stands up in a cold night to wash himself of impurity [*janāba*] seeking the good pleasure of his Lord. I bear witness to you that I have forgiven him.'"
>
> *But the men have a degree above them.* They have more than the women through the dower they contract to give them and the support [*infāq*] they provide for them. In addition they have it through the blood money, since the blood money for a man is twice that for a woman; through inheritance, since men have two shares and women one; through divorce and returning [*rajʿa* (before a full divorce)], since this is in the man's hands, not the woman's; through leading the prayer, leading the people, and the holy war, since these belong to the men, not to the women; through intelligence and religion, since the Prophet said, "I have seen none who fall shorter in intelligence and religion in the eye of the possessor of insight than you [women]." Then a woman said, "O Messenger of God, what is this 'falling short in intelligence and religion'?" He replied, "As for falling short in intelligence, it is that the testimony of two women equals that of one man [according to the Koran], so this is falling short in intelligence. The fact that one of you remains several nights without fasting and breaking the fast in Ramadan pertains to falling short in religion."

It is significant that all the examples provided by the tradition, and the original discussion itself, pertain to social relationships and the rules and regulations set down by the Sharia. We are dealing here with men and women as social beings having strictly defined gender roles. And these roles, in the Islamic view, are established by God. We have not yet entered into the domain of the interpretation of these rules and regulations for any level other than the social. Even the hadith, "Women fall short in intelligence and religion," is explained in a strictly Shariite sense. Maybudī continues his commentary in the same vein, looking at the most outward and socially relevant aspects of the verse:

> *They have [rights] similar to those over them, with honor. But the men have a degree above them.* Concerning this verse, Saʿīd ibn al-Musayyib relates the following from Ibn ʿAbbās:
>
> When the Day of Resurrection comes, God will gather together the jurists and ulama, and they will stand in a row. Then a man will come with a woman. He will say, "My Lord, Thou art the Judge, the Just. Be-

fore marriage, she and I were forbidden to each other. Then, through marriage, we became permitted to each other, and she had enjoyment the like of my enjoyment. Why then didst Thou make incumbent upon me the giving of a dower to her?"

God will say, "Did you take a dower from him?" She will say, "Yes." He will say, "Who commanded you to do so?" She will point to the jurists.

Then God will say to the jurists, "Did you command her to take a dower from him?" They will say that they did, and He will ask them on what basis they did so. They will say, "O Lord, Thou hast said in Thy book, 'Give the women their dowers as a free gift'" [4:4]. God will say, "You have spoken the truth."

Then the husband will say, "But why didst Thou make incumbent upon me a dower for her, when we were the same in enjoyment?"

God will say, "Because I made it permissible for you to take enjoyment from others while she was with you, but I forbade her to take enjoyment from others while you were with her. Since I permitted you and forbade her, I wanted to give her that which would make you equal, so I appointed for her the dower."

The account continues in the same vein. The man asks why he must support her and why he alone must support their children, and he is given answers. Then he says,

"Thou hast said in Thy book, 'The men have a degree over them.' Yet we are equal. What then is this degree?"

God replies, "Your degree above her is that I have given you permission to divorce her if you like and keep her if you like, but she does not possess that."[14]

In turning to a more inward sense of the verse, Maybudī points to the importance of the rights that God has over human beings as their Creator and Sustainer. He quotes a number of hadiths, such as God's words reported by the Prophet, "I will not observe the right of My servant until My servant observes My right." Nevertheless, God usually forgives and forgoes His rights.

But as for the rights of human beings, there is no indulgence, so most of God's vengeance takes place here. It has even been said that if a person should have the merit of seventy prophets but has a single claimant against whom he has transgressed in the measure of half a grain, he will not go to paradise until that claimant is satisfied.

Hence the rights of the creatures must be maintained and one must strive mightily to observe them—especially the rights of women and wives. In this verse the Lord of the worlds represents them and asks the husbands to take care of them. The Prophet said, "The best of you is the best to his wife, and I am the best to my wife." He said, "I counsel you to be good to your wives, for they are your helpers. They own nothing of their own, and you have taken them only as a trust from God, making their vulvas lawful through a word." In other words, these women are in your hands and are God's trust with you. Be good to them and desire the best for them, especially that they be pious and worthy, since a pious and worthy woman is the cause of a man's ease and his help in religion.

One day ʿUmar ibn al-Khaṭṭāb said to the Prophet, "O Messenger of God, what should I take from this world?" He replied, "Let each of you take a tongue that remembers God, a heart that thanks Him, and a wife who has faith," a pious and worthy woman. Look at the high rank he has given a worthy wife, for he has placed her next to remembrance and gratitude! It is well known that the remembrance of the tongue and the gratitude of the heart are not of this world. On the contrary, they are the reality of religion. Hence the pious woman that the Prophet placed next to them is the same. That is why Abū Sulaymān Dārānī said, "A worthy spouse is not of this world, but of the next." In other words, the worthy spouse allows you to be free to engage in the work of the next world. When you keep to your worship, if a boredom should appear such that the heart is wearied and you fall behind in worship, looking at her and witnessing her gives intimacy and ease to the heart. That power of worship will return and your desire to obey God will be renewed.[15]

In commenting on the same Koranic verse, Ṭabrisī demonstrates a less "liberal" approach than that found in Maybudī. He speaks for the more legalistically minded ulama, and he does not temper his position with any appeal to the more inward dimensions of understanding:

The verse *They have [rights] like those over them, with honor* is one of the marvelous statements, embracing many important points. By it God means everything that goes back to good companionship, freedom from harm, and equality in portions, provision, and clothing. In the same way, the husband has rights over the wife, like the obedience toward him that God has made incumbent upon her, that no one should enter her bed but he, that she should preserve his water and not try to make it come out.

It is related that the wife of Muʿādh said, "O Messenger of God, what is the right of the wife over the husband?" He replied, "That he not hit her in the face and not abuse her, that he feed her with what he eats, that he clothe her in what he wears, and that he not keep himself apart from her." It has also been related that he said, "Fear God in the affair of women, for you have taken them in trust from God, you have made their vulvas lawful with the word of God. Among your rights over them is that they not spread your bed for someone whom you dislike. If they do that, strike them with a striking not severe. They have the right over you that you provide for them and clothe them with honor."[16]

Ṭabrisī's commentary on the verse "The men have a degree above them" quotes the views of many of the early Muslims and does not differ substantially from Maybudī's review of the same material. Toward the end of the passage, however, he takes a rather extreme view of men's degree over women. In support of his position, he quotes the following prophetic saying on the authority of the fifth Shiʿite Imam, Muḥammad al-Bāqir:

A woman came to the Messenger of God and said, "O Messenger of God, what is the right of the husband over the woman?"

He replied, "That she obey him and not disobey him; that she not give alms from her house without his permission; that she not fast of her own accord without his permission and she not hold herself back from him, even mounted on a camel; that she not leave her house without his permission, for if she leaves without his permission, she will be cursed by the angels of heaven, the angels of earth, the angels of wrath, and the angels of mercy until she returns to her house."

The woman said, "O Messenger of God, which person has the greatest right over a woman?"

He replied, "Her husband."

She said, "Do I have rights over him similar to the rights he has over me?"

He replied, "No, not one in a hundred."

She said, "By Him who sent you with the Truth, no man will ever own my neck!"

The Prophet also said, "Were I to command someone to prostrate himself before another, I would command the woman to prostrate herself before her spouse."[17]

Of course there is more than one way to interpret these sayings. Some might read them as clear proof that Islam aims to subjugate women in society. But those who read between the lines may see them as clear proof of the dominating power of women in Islamic society. On one level, such sayings clearly mean to stress the importance of the marriage bond as the foundation of the community. They also set up a certain irreversibility in the husband/wife relationship. The husband has his functions and the wife has hers, and the two should not be mixed.

However, the firmness with which the superiority of men is stressed in this last saying points to a certain power within women that needs to be faced. If men are so superior, why does the point have to emphasized so much? They should be able to take care of themselves. But in fact, men in many ways are weaker than women, so they need the backing of God and the prophets to set up the right relationship. In one passage Ibn al-ʿArabī takes this position, and he supports it by referring to the implications of a certain Koranic verse that was revealed in reference to two of the Prophet's wives, ʿĀʾisha and Ḥafṣa. He is discussing the divine name the Strong (*al-qawī*) and the various realities in the cosmos that manifest it. He begins by reminding us that the cosmos comes into existence through a marriage between the Necessary Being and the possible things. God as Creator and giver of existence stands in need of the immutable entities which become His "wife." He can do nothing without them. On the level of the relationship between man and woman, man is impotent without woman. And since woman is a microcosm, she focuses within herself the strength of every receptive reality in existence. She brings together in herself the power of the whole cosmos. As a result, nothing in the universe is stronger.

> There is nothing in the created world greater in strength than woman, because of a mystery known only by those who know that within which the cosmos came into existence, by what movement the Real brought it into existence, and the fact that it comes from two premises. For the cosmos is a result. The one who takes in marriage [*nākiḥ*] is a seeker, and a seeker is poor and needy. The one who is taken in marriage [*mankūḥ*] is the sought, and the sought has the mightiness of being the object of need. And appetite predominates. Thus has been made clear to you the place of woman among the existent things, what it is in the Divine Presence that looks upon her, and why it is that she manifests strength.

Note that "appetite" (*shahwa*) in the human realm reflects the love (*maḥabba*) and desire (*irāda*) of God for creation. God "loved" to be known. This was a desire for the cosmos. It dominates over the reality of the Lord. Hence the vassal rules the Lord.

> God has indicated the strength singled out for the woman in His words concerning ʿĀʾisha and Ḥafṣa: "If you two support one another against him, God is his Protector, and Gabriel, and the righteous among the faithful; and, after that, the angels are his supporters" [66:4]. All of this in order to vie in strength with two women! And here God mentions only the strong, those who possess power and strength![18]

Man's Degree over Woman (II)

When we leave the social level, which is the concern of the Sharia, other interpretations of the verse of man's "degree above women" become possible. It is worth noting that ʿAbd al-Razzāq Kāshānī passes over most of the verses in this section of the Koran in silence, not wishing, it seems, to find in them any inward significance, although he accepts in principle that every Koranic verse has a number of inward senses. Qushayrī's *Laṭāʾif al-ishārāt* offers extremely brief interpretations for the two sections of the verse we have been considering. Recall here that the title of his work means "Subtle allusions."

> *They have [rights] similar to those over them, with honor.* In other words, he has the obligation to expend property for her, and she has the obligation to serve him because of this. *But the men have a degree above them* in excellence, while the women have the advantage [*maziyya*] of weakness [*ḍaʿf*] and the incapacity of mortal nature [*ʿajz al-bashariyya*].[19]

Note first that Qushayrī, in keeping with the more esoteric approach of his commentary, pays no attention to the actual rules and regulations of the Sharia, but rather to the inner spirit of the verse. By calling woman's weakness an advantage, he is alluding to a positive view of the yin reality typical of an approach to the Koran that seeks out meanings related to inwardness. We just saw how Ibn al-ʿArabī draws a surprising conclusion on the basis of this quality of woman.

Awareness of one's weakness, incapacity, and yin position in relationship to the Real is the state of servanthood (*ʿubūdiyya*). As was noted earlier, being a servant is the proper human relationship with God, a necessary prerequisite for actualizing the yang qualities that pertain to vicegerency. Hence, Qushayrī's "subtle allusion" here suggests that men can be deluded by their natural state of projecting and displaying yang attributes. They tend innately toward claiming authority and vicegerency, but this is a great danger, since they have no valid claim to it without first attaining servanthood. In contrast, women have the advantage of relative weakness and incapacity in the outward domain. Hence they will be less inclined to make unjustified claims. They have the advantage of a kind of natural servanthood.

Attributing yang qualities to oneself is perilous because all yang qualities belong by right to God. As Rūmī puts it, alluding, through "king" and "dust," to yang and yin qualities,

> If I be a king but without Thee, then how false are this "I" and "we"! But if I am dust and with Thee, how comely is my I-hood![20]

Recognizing one's own yin qualities in face of God is an aid to *tawḥīd*, since it makes a person ascribe all power, strength, glory, creativity, and so on to the Real. As the Prophet put it, in a saying that traditional Muslims frequently recite: "There is no strength and no power except in God, the High, the Tremendous." In any case, this discussion pertains more to the psychological or microcosmic dimension of reality, so we will return to it in chapter 9.

Ibn al-ʿArabī demonstrates a concern to explain the nature of the "degree" that men possess above women in several passages. Typically, he does not pay a great deal of attention to the social applications of the degree, but rather to the cosmological and metaphysical significance. In other words, he is especially concerned to show what it is in the nature of reality that establishes this degree and determines its qualities. As he puts it, "That degree is ontological [*wujūdī*], so it does not disappear."[21]

In one passage, Ibn al-ʿArabī sees the fundamental root of the relationship between husband and wife in the yang/yin relationship between God and the cosmos. To support this position, he cites two Koranic verses that show an interesting parallel. God "stands over" (*qāʾim*) or takes care of every soul just as men "stand over" (*qawwām*) women. Here his argument is simply an appeal to the Word of God.

> God made Himself descend among His creatures by standing over their best interests and what they earn. He says, "What, is He who stands over every soul through what it earns . . . ?" [13:33], just as He says, "Men stand over the women for that God has preferred one of them over the other in bounty" [4:34], since the women are men's family [*ʿāʾila*]. It has been related that the Messenger of God said, "The creatures are God's family,"[22] so He stands over them, since the creatures incline toward Him. That is why they are His family.[23]

In several passages, Ibn al-ʿArabī sees man's superiority over woman to lie in the relationship established through Eve's creation from Adam. Note in the following that he brings out a masculine side to Eve's reality not often encountered. He also finds a kinship between Eve and Jesus, both of whom were created by the intermediary of a single human being.[24]

> The first existent human body to become manifest was Adam. He is the first father of this kind. . . . Then God separated out from him a second father for us, whom He called a mother. Hence it is correct to say that this first father has a degree above her, since he is her root. . . .
>
> God brought Jesus into existence from Mary. Hence Mary settled in the station of Adam, while Jesus settled in the station of Eve. For just as a female came into existence from a male, so a male came into existence from a female. Hence God finished with the like of that through which He began, by bringing into existence a son without a father, just as Eve came to be without a mother. Hence Jesus and Eve are two siblings, while Adam and Mary are their two parents.
>
> "The likeness of Jesus, in God's sight, is as the likeness of Adam" [3:59]. God compared the two in terms of the lack of male parentage. He set this down as a proof to show that Jesus' mother was free of blame. He did not compare him to Eve—even though the situation would warrant that—since the woman is a place of suspicion, because of pregnancy. She is the locus within which birth takes place, while the man is not a locus for that. And here the aim of the proofs is to remove all doubts. . . .
>
> The meaning of the likeness is that Jesus is like Eve. However, the denier might be beset by doubts about that, since the female is, as we said, the place for that which issues from her, and hence suspicions might occur. Hence the comparison was made with Adam so that Mary would be shown to be free of that which commonly occurs. Hence the manifestation of Jesus from Mary without a father is like the manifestation of Eve from Adam without a mother. And he is the second father.
>
> When Eve was separated from Adam,

> God filled her place in him with appetite for the marriage act with her. Through that took place the "covering" [7:189] for the sake of the manifestation of procreation and reproduction.[25]

Ibn al-ʿArabī sometimes connects the verse of the degree to the superiority of heaven over earth. Here he provides a cosmological justification for male superiority, not simply one based on the text of the Koran—though the Koran is also brought to bear. The following is found in a chapter called "Concerning the true knowledge of how men and women come together in certain divine abodes."

> "Humanity" [*insāniyya*] is a reality that comprehends both male and female, so men do not possess a degree over women in respect of humanity. In the same way the human being shares with the macrocosm in the quality of being a world. Hence the cosmos does not possess a degree over the human being in this respect.
>
> Yet it has been established that "The men have a degree above" the women, just as it has been established that "The creation of the heavens and the earth is greater than the creation of mankind" [40:57]. . . . God also said, "Are you stronger in creation or the heaven He built?" [79:27], and He mentions what pertains to heaven. Then He mentions the earth, and that He spread it and what pertains to it. All this serves to demonstrate the superiority of these two over the human being.
>
> We have found that the degree by which heaven and earth are more excellent than the human being is exactly the same as that by which the man is more excellent than the woman. It is that human beings receive the activity of the heaven and the earth and are between the two and derive from them. That which receives activity does not possess the strength of the one that acts upon it.
>
> In the same way, we find that Eve received the activity of Adam and was taken out and engendered from his shortest rib. By that she fell short of reaching the degree of him who acted upon her. Hence, she knows the level of the man only to the extent of that from which she was created, that is, the rib. Hence her perception falls short of the reality of the man.
>
> In the same way the human being knows the cosmos only to the measure in which his existence is taken from it, no more. Hence the human being will never reach the degree of the cosmos in its totality, even if he is an epitome [*mukhtaṣar*] of it. Likewise the woman will never reach the degree of the man, even though she is the choicest part [*naqāwa*] of this epitome.
>
> The woman is similar to Nature in respect of being a locus that receives activity [*maḥall infiʿāl*]. But the man is not like that, for the man simply casts the water into the womb, nothing more. The womb is the locus of engendering and creation. Hence the entities of this species appear from the female, since she receives engendering and activity in the stages of creation, creation after creation, until the person emerges as a faultless human being.[26] In this measure men are distinct from women.
>
> That is why women fall short of the intelligence of men: They understand only to the measure that the woman takes of the creation of the man at the root of configuration. As for the fact that they fall short in religion, that is because recompense follows the measure of works, and works come into existence only from knowledge. Knowledge follows the measure of receiving the cosmos, and the degree of receiving the cosmos follows the measure of the preparedness at the root of configuration. Woman's preparedness falls short of the preparedness of man, since she is a part of him. Hence woman must be described as falling short of man in religion.
>
> But this chapter demands the attribute in which men and women come together. That lies in what we mentioned: the fact that they stand in the station of receiving activity. All of this is in respect to the realities.

The "realities" for Ibn al-ʿArabī are the divine roots of things, or the inherent characteristics of things determined by their mode of being. The realities lie at the deepest level of existence and become manifest in the cosmos as the actual situations. At this point in the discussion, Ibn al-ʿArabī turns to the concrete situations of men and women in the world. He points out that the Koran makes them share in qualities:

> As for that which occurs for men and women, that is like God's words, "The submitted [masculine] and the submitted [feminine], the faithful and the faithful, the obedient and the obedient, the truthful and the truthful, the patient and the patient, the hum-

ble and the humble, those who fast and those who fast, those who guard their private parts and those who guard, those who give in charity and those who give in charity, those who remember God much and those who remember, [for them God has prepared forgiveness and a mighty wage]" [33:35]. Or it is like God's words, "The repenters [masculine], the worshipers, the praisers, the fasters" [9:112] and His words, "The repenters [feminine], the worshipers, the fasters" [66:5]. The Messenger of God said, "Many have reached perfection among men, but among women only Mary the daughter of ʿImrān and Āṣiya the wife of Pharoah."[27] Hence men and women come together in the degree of perfection. But men are more excellent in the degree of most-perfectness [*al-akmaliyya*], not that of perfection. For though men and women are both perfect through prophethood [*nubuwwa*], men are more excellent through messengerhood [*risāla*] and "being sent" [*baʿtha*], since no woman has had these two degrees.[28] . . .

God has made men and women share in the prescription of the Sharia [*taklīf*]. Though women are singled out for rulings that do not pertain to men, men are singled out for rulings that do not pertain to women, even if "Women are the likes of men."[29]

In still another passage, Ibn al-ʿArabī rejects the idea that man's degree stems from the fact that Eve was created from Adam. Though he seems to be contradicting what he says in the above passage, in fact he is merely adding some precision by pointing out that the myth of Eve's creation from Adam's left rib teaches us that woman is dominated by yin qualities to a degree that is not true for man. This passage is found in a short subchapter called "Concerning dependence upon that which falls short [*nāqiṣ*] and inclination toward it." He explains that this title refers to dependence upon any created thing other than the perfect human being, since full perfection is found in him or her alone. Someone who depends upon the perfect human being—for example, upon a prophet or a great saint—is not depending upon that which falls short, since the perfect human being becomes manifest in the form of God. Ibn al-ʿArabī continues:

But everything else in the phenomenal world falls short of this level, just as the woman falls short of the man by the degree that stands between them. Even if the woman becomes perfect, this degree means that her perfection will not be that of the man. Some people claim that the degree is the fact that Eve came into existence from Adam, so she became manifest only through him. Hence he has the degree of being a secondary cause, and she can never reach him in that. But this is a situation in a particular entity [that is, Eve], and we would counter it with [another particular entity, that is,] Mary in relation to the existence of Jesus. Hence the "degree" is not that he is the secondary cause of her becoming manifest.

The fact is that the woman is the locus that receives activity, while the man is not like that. The locus that receives activity does not possess the level of activity, so it falls short. But in spite of the falling short, there is dependence upon it and inclination toward it, since it receives activity in itself and with itself.[30]

In other words, man has no superiority over woman simply because Eve was created from Adam, since Jesus—the spirit and word of God and one of the greatest of perfect human beings—was created from Mary, without any human intermediary. Rather, man's degree has to do with the dominance of yang in his case and yin in hers. Perhaps it is necessary to add that Muslims have never questioned the virgin birth of Jesus, since the Koran supports it explicitly.

In still another passage, Ibn al-ʿArabī attributes man's degree over woman to the fact that the cosmos can never reach the station of God because of the peculiar relationship that is established between them: cosmic receptivity and divine activity. He is commenting on the Koranic verse, "He has no equal" (112:4).

Here He means by "equal" consort [*ṣāḥiba*], because of those who said that the Messiah was the son of God and Ezra was the son of God.[31] The equal is a likeness. But the woman can never be like the man, since God says, "The men have a degree above them." Hence she is not his equal. For the locus that receives activity is not the equal of that which acts upon it. The cosmos is the locus that receives God's activity, so it is not God's equal. Eve is the locus that receives Adam's activity, so he has the degree of activity over her. Hence she is not his equal in this respect.

Since He said, "The men have a degree above them," He did not allow Jesus to be the locus that receives the activity of Mary, lest the man should be the locus that receives the activity of the woman, as Eve had received that of Adam. Hence Gabriel or the angel "became imaginalized to her as a mortal man without fault" [19:17]. He said to her, "I am but a messenger come from your Lord, to give you a boy most pure" [19:19]. Hence he gave her Jesus. Thus Jesus received the activity of the angel who was imaginalized in the form of a man. That is why he came out in the form of his father—a male, a mortal man, a spirit. Hence he brought together the two forms possessed by his father, who was the angel, since his father was a spirit in respect of his entity and a mortal man in respect of his becoming imaginalized in the form of a mortal man.[32]

Mutual Love

For Ibn al-ʿArabī as for other Muslim thinkers, the myth of Adam and Eve has many applications. For example, it provides a rationale for the love that appears between a man and a woman. But it also makes clear that the two loves are not identical, precisely because of the "degree" that separates the sexes. The hierarchical relationship set up by that degree defines the yang and yin qualities on each side.

When the body of Adam became manifest, as we mentioned, he had no appetite for the marriage act. But the Real knew that reproduction, procreation, and marriage would be brought into existence in this abode. And marriage, in this abode, is for the sake of the subsistence of the species.[33] Hence He brought Eve out from Adam's short rib. Thereby she fell short of the degree of the man, as God says, "The men have a degree above them." Hence the women will never reach the men.

Eve came from the rib because ribs are bent. Thereby she may bend toward her children and her spouse. The bending of the man toward the woman is his bending toward his own self, since she is a part of him. The bending of the woman toward the man is because she is created from the rib, and within the rib are bending and inclination.

When Eve was taken from Adam, God filled the empty space with appetite for her, since existence does not allow a vacuum to remain. When He filled the vacuum with "air" [*hawā*ʾ],[34] Adam bent toward her just as he bends toward his own self, since she is a part of him. And Eve bent toward him, since he is the homeland from which she was configured. Hence Eve's love is the love of homeland,[35] while Adam's love is the love for himself. That is why the man's love for the woman is manifest, for she is himself. But in love for men the woman is given the power called "shame" [*ḥayā*ʾ], so she is strong in concealment, for the homeland is not united with her in the same way that she is united with Adam.

God formed within that rib everything that He had formed and created in the body of Adam. Hence the configuration of the body of Adam in His form was like the potter's configuration of what he configures from clay and baking. But the configuration of the body of Eve was like the carpenter's configuration of the forms that he carves in wood. When He had carved her in the rib, set up her form, proportioned her, and balanced her, He blew into her of His own spirit. Then she stood up alive, speaking, a female. Hence He made her a locus for tilling and cultivation, because of the existence of sowing, which is procreation. Hence Adam rested in her, and she rested in him. She was "a garment" for him, and he was a "garment" for her. God says, "[Permitted to you, upon the night of the Fast, is to go in to your wives.] They are a garment for you, and you are a garment for them" [2:187]. Appetite permeated all his parts, so he sought her.[36]

Ibn al-ʿArabī provides a similar explanation for the love between men and women when explaining why the gnostics, those men who have reached perfection, incline toward women:

The longing [*ḥanīn*] of the gnostics toward women is the longing of the whole toward its part, like the loneliness of dwellings for the inhabitants that give them life. Moreover, God filled up the place in the men from which woman was taken with inclination [*mayl*] toward her. His longing toward her is the longing and bending of the large toward the small.[37]

According to a sound hadith that will be discussed in detail in the next chapter, "The womb is a branch (*shajana*) of the All-merciful." The Arabic word for womb (*raḥim*) derives from the same root as the words mercy (*raḥma*) and All-merciful (*raḥmān*). The mother's womb is the locus of God's life-giving mercy. Ibn al-ʿArabī sees one of the meanings of the hadith in the relationship between man and woman, since, just as the womb is a branch of the All-merciful, so Eve is a branch of Adam:

> The station of the woman in relation to the man at the root of coming into existence is the same as the station of the womb in relation to the All-merciful, since she is a branch of him, for she emerged in his form. Certain hadiths have reported that "God created Adam in the form of the All-merciful,"[38] and it has been established that the womb among us is a branch of the All-merciful. Hence in our relationship with the All-merciful God placed us in the station of Eve in relation to Adam, and this is the locus of procreation and the manifestation of the entities of the children. In the same way, we are the locus for the manifestation of the acts of God, since the act, though it belongs to God, becomes manifest only through our hands. It does not become attributed to Him in the sensory realm except through us.
>
> Were we not a branch of the All-merciful, it would not be correct for us to be ascribed to God. That is the fact that we are His servants, and "The client of a people is one of them." Our poverty and need toward God is the poverty of the part toward the whole. Were there not this much relationship, the Divine Inaccessibility and the Absolute Independence would not incline toward us, nor would He look upon us. Through this ascription we have become the locus of disclosure for that Inaccessibility. Hence His Essence is witnessed only in us, because of the divine form in which He created us. So our kingdom is all the divine names. There is no divine name of which we do not possess a portion. No affair occurs in us whose property does not permeate the Root. . . .
>
> Since Eve is a branch of Adam, God placed love and mercy between the two, thereby calling our attention to the fact that there is love and mercy between the womb and the All-merciful. . . . The love placed between the two spouses is permanency in marriage, which leads to reproduction. The mercy placed between them is the longing found by each of the spouses toward the other. Each longs for the other and finds rest therein.[39]
>
> In the case of the woman, this longing is that of the part for its whole, the branch for its root, the stranger for her homeland. The man's longing for his spouse is the longing of the whole for the part, since through the part he can rightly be called the whole, but with the part's disappearance, this name does not belong to him. It is the longing of the root for its branch, since the root replenishes the branch. Were it not for the branch, the lordly power of giving replenishment would not become manifest from the root.
>
> In the same way, if there were no engendered universe, it would not be correct to say that God is "Lord" over Himself. But He is a Lord, so there must be a cosmos. And He is always a Lord, so the immutable entities will never cease gazing upon Him through their poverty, [asking Him] to clothe them with the name of existence. He never ceases gazing upon them with the eye of mercy, because of their calling to Him. Hence He never ceases as a Lord in the state of our nonexistence and the state of our existence. Possibility belongs to us and Necessity to Him. . . .
>
> Hence love and mercy are the seeking of the whole for its part and the part for its whole. The two join together, and from this conjunction become manifest the entities of the children. Then the name parenthood can correctly refer to the two. Hence the existence of the children gives a property to the parents that they did not possess, that is, parenthood. But the Lord is not like that, since He is a Lord from eternity without beginning. For the possible thing is always described by possibility, whether or not it exists, since God looks upon it in its state of nonexistence from eternity without beginning. The priority of nonexistence is the possible thing's beginningless attribute. Hence it remains forever a vassal, even if it does not exist. This is the difference between that which is necessary for God and that which is necessary for the servant in respect of the naming and the level that appears for it through the existence of the child.[40]

Later in the same chapter, Ibn al-ʿArabī wants to correct those who think that women are inferior to men in their possibilities of spiritual attainment. They can even, he says, become the Pole (*quṭb*), the supreme spiritual ruler of the age upon whom the existence of the cosmos depends. Moreover, women have certain attainments that men cannot reach, a point to which allusion is made in the very word "woman" (*mar'a*) that is applied to them. Apparently some Sufis had cited the hadith Ibn al-ʿArabī mentions in the following as proof that women could not become the Pole.

> Women share with men in all levels, even in being Pole. You should not let yourself be veiled by the words of the Messenger of God, "A people who give the rule of their affairs to a woman will never prosper."[41] We are speaking about the rulership given by God, not the rulership given by people, while the hadith speaks of someone who is given rulership by the people. If the only thing that had reached us concerning this matter were the words of the Prophet, "Women are the likes of men," that would be enough, since it means that everything to which a man can attain—stations, levels, or attributes—can also belong to any woman whom God wills, just as it can belong to any man whom God wills.
>
> Do you not notice God's wisdom in the extra which He has given to the woman over the man in the name? Concerning the male human being, He says *mar'*, and concerning the female He says, *mar'a*; so He added an *a*—or an *at* in construct form—to the name *mar'* given to the man. Hence she has a degree over the man in this station, a degree not possessed by him, in contradistinction to the degree given to men in the verse, "Men have a degree above them" [2:228]. Hence God blocked that gap [alluded to in the verse] with this extra in *mar'a*.[42]

What then is Ibn al-ʿArabī's position on the degree? It would not be possible to state it on the basis of the above passages without inconsistency. My own reading is that whenever Ibn al-ʿArabī takes the point of view of a specific quality in men or women, he reaches a conclusion appropriate for the quality. In the last analysis, however, we enter into the imponderables of the divine form, which opens up to infinity. Here God does what He wants, and in that respect no distinction can be drawn between men and women.

Women Made Lovable

If men and women fall short of each other by a certain degree, yet they find fulfillment in each other precisely for that reason. What separates them gives rise to the desire that brings them back together. In the same way, God's love for the cosmos brings it into existence, "so that the Hidden Treasure might be known." Thereby "other than God," difference, diversity, separation, make their appearance. But just as this love brought the world into existence, so also it brings creatures to the perfections for which they were created. Thereby it reunites them with God. God "loved to be known." Without the original separation demanded by the cosmos, a separation that begins on the human level in ignorance of God, the subsequent knowledge of God by the "other" would not have been possible.

The Sufis see one of the most striking expressions of the inherent presence of love in the cosmos in the prophetic saying, "Three things of this world of yours were made lovable to me: women, perfume—and the coolness of my eye was placed in the ritual prayer."[43] The Prophet is by definition the most perfect human being and the most perfect male. His love for women shows that the perfection of the human state is connected with love for other human beings, not simply with love for God. More specifically, it shows that male perfection lies in women and, by implication, female perfection in men. Ibn al-ʿArabī provides several insightful explanations of this hadith, situating it in various contexts.

In the chapter of the *Futūḥāt* on supererogatory acts (*nāfila*) like extra prayers and fasting, Ibn al-ʿArabī points out that such acts of worship are ranked in degrees according to the excellence of the required worship whose form they take. Thus, for example, if the mandatory ritual prayer is more excellent than the mandatory alms, so also supererogatory ritual prayer is better than supererogatory alms. If Abū Ḥanīfa, the founder of the Hanafite school of law, called marriage the best of all supererogatory acts, this is because marriage is the best of all obligatory acts. And the reason for this must be sought in God's love to make the Hidden Treasure manifest.

Marriage is the best of the supererogatory good deeds. It has a root, and that is the obligatory marriage. Anything in addition to that is supererogatory. The obligatory marriage is of two kinds, that is, its occurrence: It may occur because of the relationship of unqualified love. And it may occur because of the relationship established by a person's love for reproduction and procreation.

When marriage occurs because of the love for reproduction and procreation, then it joins the divine love when there was no cosmos. He "loved to be known." Hence He turned His desire toward this love for the things while they were in the state of their nonexistence. They were the root [of creation] through the preparedness of their possibility. He said to them, "Be!" and they came to be, that He might be known by every sort of knowledge. Temporally originated knowledge as yet had no object, since the one who knows by means of it was not yet qualified by existence.

This was a love that sought the perfection of knowledge and the perfection of existence, for neither existence nor knowledge gains perfection without the cosmos. And the cosmos becomes manifest only through God's turning His attentiveness toward the entities of the possible things by way of love, in order that the entities may achieve the perfection of existence and knowledge. This is a state that resembles marriage for the sake of reproduction.

Obligatory marriage is the best of obligatory acts, so its supererogatory form is the best supererogatory good deed. . . . Abū Ḥanīfa said that marriage is the best of the supererogatory good deeds. What he said is true—he truly struck the mark. The Messenger of God was made to love women, and he married more than any other prophet. The reason for this is that in marriage is found something of the realization of the form in which the human being was created. However, only a small number of people know this, and that by way of unveiling. Or rather, only a small number of gnostics among the Folk of God know this.[44]

God created the human being in His own form, and hence the human is the most perfect form in the cosmos, the goal of creation, the pinnacle of the cosmos. This is one reason that God made the Prophet love women—through women the perfect form enters into existence. But it is not the only reason, since the joy given by the marriage act is itself inherently beautiful and lovable. This is proved by the fact that the inhabitants of paradise have sexual relationships simply for pleasure, not for producing children.

God made the Prophet love women and gave him the strength for marriage. He praised the state of being a husband and blamed abstaining from sexual intercourse. The Prophet was made to love women because they are the locus that receives the activity of engendering the most perfect form, that is, the human form, more perfect than which there is no form. Not every locus of receiving activity has this specific perfection. Hence love for women is one of the things through which God favored His Messenger, for He made him love them in spite of the fact that he had few children. Hence the desired goal was nothing but the marriage act itself, like the marriage act of the people of the Garden, which is strictly for pleasure, not for producing offspring.[45] . . . And this [pleasure in the marriage act] is an affair outside the requirement of the love for the locus that receives the activity of engendering [children].

Do you not see—if you understand the meanings of the Koran—how the Real "assigned to you earth for a bedding" [2:22] and how He created Adam from the earth, making him a locus that receives activity? The Messenger of God said, "The child belongs to the bedding."[46] In other words, the child belongs to the master of the bedding, while the bedding is the woman. In the same way, God made Adam a vicegerent in the earth from which he was created. Thereby Adam was made a "master of the bedding," since he has the form of Him who brought him into existence. Hence God gave him the power of activity [through the divine form and being the master of the bedding] just as He gave him the power of receiving activity [through being a product of the bedding].[47]

Here Ibn al-ʿArabī alludes to the fact that Adam contains both yin and yang characteristics within himself. In the same way, Eve has both yin and yang qualities, as was pointed out earlier. All created realities are ambiguous, capable of being considered yin or yang depending on the point of view. This helps explain why the Prophet said, "Women are the likes of men." As Ibn al-ʿArabī remarks,

"Women are the likes of men." Do you not see that Eve was created from Adam? Hence she has two properties: the property of the male at the root and the property of the female as accident. Hence she is ambiguous [*mutashābih*].[48]

Eve's ambiguity can be seen in the fact that she acts upon Adam just he acts upon her. Adam's "acting upon her" is inconceivable without her acting upon him, since the ability of the yang force to act is given to it by the yin force. As Ibn al-ʿArabī points out in continuing the above passage, yin is present in yang, giving it the ability to be yang:

Humanity is the locus that brings together male and female. But how can the reality of the active be compared with that which receives activity from something active within it? However, the active one acts only upon that which resembles it. For the active one is the first thing within which receiving activity appears. There becomes manifest within it the form of that which receives its activity. Through this strength that which receives activity receives the activity. This is like the divine names Originator, Deviser, and Real.

These divine names refer to the fact that God creates out of "nothing." But in Ibn al-ʿArabī's understanding, the "nothing" out of which the cosmos is created corresponds to the nonexistent immutable entities. They are nothing because they do not exist in themselves. However, they are known by God. The point of all this is that the active (God, Adam) is able to act upon the receptive (the immutable entities, Eve) because the receptive acts upon the active. Adam gave birth to Eve because Eve acted upon Adam by being present within him. The Lord brings the vassal into existence because the Lord is defined by the vassal and has no meaning apart from it. Yin has yang within it, and yang has yin. Ibn al-ʿArabī makes clear that he has this inseparability of the two terms of the relationship in mind in the continuation of this discussion. Having mentioned the divine names that demand creation out of nothing, he explains that this divine creativity cannot mean that there is yang without yin. As Rūmī would put it, how can one hand clap?[49] Rather, yin is already present within yang: The entities are present within the knowledge of the Creator before they are given existence.

We have already demonstrated concerning God's knowledge of the cosmos that this knowledge follows its object. Knowledge is an attribute of the Knower. That which gives the knowledge is the actual situation of the object of knowledge. Then the Knower gives rise to the coming into existence of the object of knowledge. In the same way, the Deviser gives rise to the coming into existence of that which is devised; He makes it manifest within existence.

Hence yin is found within yang. If yang loves yin, it is because yin is yang itself. If the Prophet (the perfect image of God) was made to love women, it is because women reflect God. In Rūmī's words again, "She is the radiance of God, she is not your beloved. She is the Creator—you could say that she is not created."[50]

From this you will understand why God made Muhammad love women. He who loves women as the Prophet loved them has loved God, who brings together all reception of activity. For He has been given knowledge by the objects of knowledge. Thus it can be said concerning Him that He is the Knower. Hence He is the first to receive activity from an object of knowledge.

Jesus's reception of activity from Mary became manifest opposite Eve's reception from Adam. "Surely in that is a reminder for him who has a heart" [50:37]. Thereby such a person can understand God's words, "O people, We created you from a male," as in the case of Eve, "and a female" [49:13], as in the case of Jesus, and from both together, as in the case of the rest of the offspring, the children of Adam. This encompasses the creation of all people.

Ibn al-ʿArabī now turns to an autobiographical remark that is worth quoting, at least to make clear that these speculations on the nature of male and female were not without practical results in the lives of our authors.

> I used to dislike women and sexual intercourse as much as anyone when I first entered this Path. I stayed that way for about eighteen years until I witnessed this station.[51] Before that, I had feared the divine displeasure because of this, since I had come across the prophetic report that God had made women lovable to His Prophet. For he did not love them because of nature. He loved them because God had made them lovable to him. When I was sincere toward God in turning my attentiveness toward Him in that, because of my fear of His displeasure—since I disliked what God had made lovable to His Prophet—that dislike disappeared from me. Praise belongs to God! He made them lovable to me. I am the greatest of creatures in care for them and the most observant of their rights. For in this I am "upon insight" [12:108]. This derives from my being made to love. This is not a love deriving from Nature.[52]

The love that the Prophet had for women is obligatory on all men, since he is the model of perfection who must be emulated. Ibn al-ʿArabī explains this while discussing how the gnostic takes help from women:

> He takes help from them for their sake, as the Messenger of God took it when he commanded them to give alms. For he was striving in their deliverance, since he saw them as the majority of the people of the Fire.[53] Hence he felt pity for them, since they came to be from him. This is a human being's pity for himself. Moreover, women are the locus within which the form of perfection is engendered. Hence love for them is obligatory [*farīḍa*] and a way of following the Prophet. The Messenger of God said, "Three things of this world of yours were made lovable to me: women, perfume—while the coolness of my eye was placed in the ritual prayer." Thereby he mentioned women. Do you think that which would take him far from his Lord was made lovable to him? Of course not. That which would bring him near to his Lord was made lovable to him.
>
> ʿĀ'isha, the Mother of the Faithful, understood what women were taking from the heart of the Messenger of God when he chose them and they chose him. God wanted to console these women [that is, the Prophet's wives], to show affection for them in that time, and to take care of them, even if that was against the desire of the Messenger of God. Hence He said, "Thereafter women are not lawful to thee, neither for thee to take other wives in exchange for them, though their beauty please thee, except what thy right hand owns" [33:52]. Out of mercy for him because of the love of women that He placed in his heart, God left for him the property of the right hand.[54] This was one of the most difficult [*ashaqq*] verses to come down upon the Messenger of God. Hence ʿĀ'isha said, "God would not chastise the heart of His Prophet! By God, the Messenger of God did not die before He made women lawful to him."[55]
>
> He who knows the measure of women and their mystery will not renounce love for them. On the contrary, one of the perfections of the gnostic is love for them, for this is a prophetic heritage and a divine love. For the Prophet said, "were made lovable to me." Hence he ascribed his love for them only to God. Ponder this chapter—you will see wonders![56]

The "mystery" of women lies in the fact that the sexual act provides the occasion for experiencing what Ibn al-ʿArabī calls God's "greatest self-disclosure." From the perspective of incomparability, God is unknown and cannot be experienced. But from the perspective of similarity, God shows Himself in all things and can be experienced through all things. The whole cosmos and everything within it is God's self-disclosure. But the greatest locus of experiencing God's self-disclosure is the sexual act.

The fact that Islam considers sexual relationships one of the greatest pleasures of paradise is well-known.[57] There is no suggestion that this is for the sake of producing children. The prophets and great friends of God experience already in this life that paradisial state. Their marriages replicate the marriages of the blessed in the Garden. If children happen to be born as a result, that is fine, but the goal was the pleasure. Ibn al-ʿArabī expands on this theme in a chapter on the Pole (*quṭb*), who is the greatest friend of God in any given era and acts as the primary means whereby the worlds are interconnected. He is the perfect human being par excellence, the true servant of the name that embraces all divine names. "Servanthood"—a yin relationship, let it be recalled—is the highest human situation, the station of perfection itself, especially servanthood to the name Allah, to God as He is in Himself.

> Through God's self-disclosure in marriage, the Pole knows what encourages him to seek marriage and to become completely enamored of it. For neither he nor any other gnostic realizes his servanthood more thoroughly than in what he realizes in the marriage act—not in eating, or drinking, or putting on clothes to ward off harm. But he does not desire marriage for offspring, but strictly for the sake of appetite. He makes procreation present in himself because of a command of the Sharia, while procreation in this is an affair of nature, for the sake of the preservation of the species in this abode.

The word *shahwa*, translated here as "appetite" in order to maintain consistency throughout this book, can also be rendered as passion or desire or concupiscence. The Koran says of the people of the Garden that "They shall dwell forever with the objects of their souls' appetite" (21:102). Or again, "Therein you shall have all the objects of your souls' appetite, all that you call for" (41:31). Arberry renders these two verses as follows: "They shall dwell forever in that their souls desire." "Therein you shall have all that your souls desire, all that you call for." In Ibn al-ʿArabī's view, this "appetite" or passion that is given free rein in the Garden is the same as the appetite that people experience in this world. For, as pointed out above, human appetite reflects God's attribute of desire and love. Within human beings, it incarnates God's desire for creation and His joy in bringing the world into existence. In order for human beings to develop their appetite in a healthy and wholesome manner, fully in accord with the nature of the Real Itself, they must keep it within the bounds set down by the Sharia. Then appetite will follow the course of what God desires for mankind. Once human beings reach the Garden, their appetite is freed from all outside constraint, since at this stage of human perfection appetite coincides with God's desire by its very nature. Like the activity of angels and beasts, the activity of the felicitous in the Garden flows with the Tao. Ibn al-ʿArabī continues:

> The marriage act of the possessor of this station is like the marriage act of the people of the Garden, strictly for appetite, since it is the greatest self-disclosure of God. However, it is hidden from mankind and jinn except in the case of those of God's servants whom He singles out. In the same way, the marriage act of the beasts is strictly for appetite.
>
> Many of the gnostics have remained oblivious of this reality, since it is one of the mysteries grasped only by a few of the People of God's Solicitude. Within marriage is found complete nobility denoting the weakness [*ḍaʿf*] that is worthy of servanthood. There is something of the severity of enjoyment [*qahr al-ladhdha*] that annihilates the person from his strength and his claims. It is a delicious severity. For severity precludes taking enjoyment in it for the one who is overcome by it, since enjoyment of severity is one of the specific characteristics of the one who is severe. Its enjoyment is not a characteristic of the one who is overcome by it, with the single exception of this act.

Here again Ibn al-ʿArabī stresses the Islamic view that human perfection is found in submission to God. Every positive good begins in servanthood. In the sexual act, the human being is overwhelmed by the power of pleasure, thereby gaining a foretaste of the bliss of the paradisial relationship with God. The pleasure manifests God's severity (*qahr*), which is normally juxtaposed with His gentleness (*luṭf*). The relationship between the two is that between majesty and beauty, wrath and mercy. But here the utter submission to severity leads not to separation and wrath but to unparalleled joy.

> People have remained oblivious of this nobility, making the marriage act an "animal appetite." Thereby they declare themselves beyond it, even though they name it with the noblest of names, that is, "animal" [*ḥayawānī*]. In other words, it is one of the characteristics of the living being [*ḥayawān*]. What is more noble than life? What they believe to be an ugliness in their eyes is identical with words of praise in the view of the perfected gnostic.[58]

The Fuṣūṣ al-ḥikam

Ibn al-ʿArabī devotes much of the last chapter of his most celebrated book, the *Fuṣūṣ al-ḥikam*, to explaining why the Prophet's character is summed up in the hadith that tells us that women, perfume, and the ritual prayer were made lovable to him. What he has to say in the *Fuṣūṣ* about love for women parallels the above passages from the *Futūḥāt*, but provides a good deal of elaboration. Small sections of this *Fuṣūṣ* passage have sometimes been quoted in studies of women in Islam, but no one has put the passage into its context within Ibn al-ʿArabī's overall teachings, nor have scholars looked in detail at the commentary tradition.[59]

As usual, Ibn al-ʿArabī is looking at the "divine roots" of things, their situation in relation to God that determines their mode of appearance in this world. The key to his discussion lies in the title of the chapter, which is "A ringstone of wisdom of singularity [as embodied] in a Muhammadan Word." Each of the twenty-seven chapters of the *Fuṣūṣ al-ḥikam* (The ringstones of wisdom) deals with the incarnation of wisdom in a specific prophet. Muhammad, as the last and greatest of the prophets, is given the last chapter of the work. "Singularity," as explained in the previous chapter, means not only uniqueness but also the quality of being odd as opposed to even. The first of the odd numbers is three, and three is connected to the quality of "producing results" (*intāj*). Nothing can be produced from one or two. Until the two interrelate through a third element, there can be no production, no results, no creation, no cosmos. Hence God does not create the cosmos with respect to His Unity, only with respect to the interrelationship of three of His attributes. This three that produces the cosmos is the first of the odd numbers, hence the first of the "singulars." Singularity, then, implies not only uniqueness, but also principiality, productivity, bringing into existence. The quality of being "singular" relates directly to the idea, well known long before Ibn al-ʿArabī, that the Prophet in his innermost reality is the principle of creation. He is the "Reality of Realities" from which all other realities derive.

In what follows, I will quote important passages from this discussion in the *Fuṣūṣ* and refer also to some of the more significant explanations provided by the commentators. The text of the *Fuṣūṣ* is given in italics. Ibn al-ʿArabī begins the chapter as follows:

> *His is the wisdom of singularity because he is the most perfect existent in the human species. That is why the whole affair began with him and is sealed with him. For he was a prophet while Adam was between water and clay. Then, in his elemental configuration, he was the Seal of the Prophets. And three is the first of the singulars. Every singular beyond one derives from it.*

Here Ibn al-ʿArabī alludes to Muhammad as the most perfect human being. As such, he manifests the divine name Allah, since he brings together all the divine names in a comprehensive unity. At the same time, his innermost reality, called by such names as the "Muhammadan Reality" and the "Reality of Realities," is the principle that gives rise to the cosmos and is manifest in the Breath of the All-merciful—the Supreme Barzakh—as well as in the Supreme Pen. Hence the Prophet's innermost reality is identical with the marriage act that gives rise to the cosmos. The very fact that he is the most perfect existent in human form—

created in God's form—shows that he is the fruit of the original creative movement in the divine reality. He is the first creation and as such the locus of manifestation for singularity, which is identical with triplicity.

Jandī explains that at the level of his reality or immutable entity, the Prophet possesses true singularity in the World of Meanings, since his immutable entity is the greatest and most all-embracing immutable entity, that is, the Reality of Realities. Then, at the level of his spirit, he was a prophet sent out to the spirits of all the prophets. Finally, at the level of his corporeal form, he was the seal of the prophets. Hence he was unique in entity, spirit, and body, and these make up his triplicity.[60] Qayṣarī remarks that he is the first triplicity since, as the Muhammadan Spirit or First Intellect, he manifests both the Essence and the level of Divinity that embraces all the names, so these three levels—Essence, Divinity, and First Intellect—make up his reality.[61]

> *Hence he is the most perfect proof of his Lord, since he was given the "all-comprehensive words." They are the things named by the names taught to Adam. . . .*

"I was sent with the all-comprehensive words" is a sound hadith.[62] According to Jandī, "the things named by the names taught to Adam" are infinite, but they can be summarized in three categories, and these correspond to yang, yin, and the full manifestation of the Tao: (1) the active and effect-producing realities and entities pertaining to the Necessary Divine Being; (2) the engendered and activity-receiving realities pertaining to the possible vassal; (3) the all-comprehensive realities pertaining to human perfection.[63]

> *So his reality yields singularity, since he is triple in configuration. Hence he said concerning the love that is the root of the existent things, "Three things of this world of yours were made lovable to me," because of the triplicity in himself. Then he mentioned women and perfume, while the coolness of his eye was placed in the ritual prayer. Hence he began with woman and he ended with the ritual prayer.*
>
> *The reason for this is that woman is a part of the man in the root of the manifestation of her entity. A human being's knowledge of his soul is prior to the knowledge of his Lord, since his knowledge of his Lord is the result of his knowledge of his soul. That is why the Prophet said, "He who knows his soul knows his Lord." . . .*

ʿAbd al-Razzāq Kāshānī makes explicit that this whole discussion is based on the correspondence that is found between two pairs: man and woman, and spirit and soul.

> The woman is the outward form of the soul, while the man is the outward form of the spirit. The soul is a part of the spirit, since the soul is one of the entifications that is included under the entification of the first spirit, which is known as the "True Adam." The soul is one of the descents of this spirit. Hence the woman is in reality a part of the man, and every part is a proof of its root. So the woman is a proof of the man and the man of the woman, for the Prophet said, "He who knows his own soul knows his Lord." The proof is prior to that which is proven. Hence he placed the woman first.[64]

> *So Muhammad was the clearest proof of his Lord, since each part of the cosmos is a proof of its root, which is its Lord.*

In explaining this passage, Kāshānī points out that everything in the cosmos is a proof of the Lord, since everything is His sign. But Muhammad, as the most perfect human being, proves his Lord perfectly on all levels of existence, since he is the most perfect of microcosms and thereby fully conforms to the metacosm. His human level corresponds exactly to the Divine Presence, the reality of God inasmuch as it embraces everything that exists.

> Knowledge of the most perfect of human beings, the one who was defined and entified through the First Entification, is the most complete of knowledges. And that individual is Muhammad.
>
> First, his immutable entity: The entity of Muhammad, in respect of being entified through the greatest, all-comprehensive *bar-*

zakh-reality, is identical with the One Essence in respect of Its being entified through the First Entification.

Second, his form: The Muhammadan form brings together the presences of the exclusive unity of the Essence and the inclusive unity of the divine names on all the levels of possibility, that is, spirit, heart, soul, imagination, and body. In a similar way, the "Divine Presence" is the Essence with all Its names and forms. These comprise the entities of the cosmos, its active realities, and its receptive realities. These are: the Mother of the Book, which is the Universal Spirit that comprises all spirits; the Guarded Tablet, which is the universal heart that comprises all hearts; the World of Imagination; and the Nondelimited Body, which comprises all the corporeal bodies of the cosmos.[65]

Mutual Longing

The woman is a part of the man, as Ibn al-ʿArabī explains in passages already quoted. All the more so are women part of the Prophet, the most perfect of men. Hence,

> *Women were made lovable to him—so he longed for them—only because the whole longs for its parts.*

Next Ibn al-ʿArabī explains that man's longing for woman is a mirror image of God's longing for the human being, and the root of God's longing for the human being is found in His statement, "I blew into him of My own spirit" (15:29). In fact, God is longing for Himself in the human being.

> *He has explained that He blew into him of His own spirit, so He yearns only for Himself. Do you not see that He has created him upon His own form, since he derives from His spirit? . . .*

Qayṣarī's explanation of this passage is especially interesting, since he brings out the mutuality of the relationships between God and the human being on the one hand, and between man and woman on the other.

> In respect of the reality, the woman is identical with the man, but in respect of the entification, each is distinct from the other. At root the woman becomes manifest from the man, so she is like a part of him. She becomes separate and manifest in feminine form. Hence the Prophet's yearning for them was of the type of the yearning of the whole for its part. The Prophet explained this through his words.
>
> On the divine side, the situation is the same, since His words, "I blew into him of My spirit," proves that the relationship of Adam to his Lord is exactly the relationship of the part to its whole and the branch to its root. Every whole yearns for its part and every root yearns for its branch. Thereby interrelationship is established between the two sides. Hence each one became lover in one respect and beloved in another respect.[66]

> *That God should refer to the spirit through "blowing" alludes to the fact that it derives from the Breath of the All-merciful. For through this Breath, which is the blowing, the entity of the human being became manifest. . . .*
>
> *Then God split off from him a person in his form whom He named "woman." She became manifest in his form. Hence he longs for her as a thing longs for its own self, and she longs for him as a thing longs for its homeland. Hence women were made lovable to him, for God loves the one whom He created in His own form and before whom He made the angels—the beings made out of light—prostrate themselves. This was in spite of the greatness of their measure and station and the elevation of their natural configuration. From here arises the correspondence* [munāsaba].

Kāshānī explains that there is a correspondence in form between the man and the woman, just as there is one between God and the human being.[67]

> *The form is the greatest, grandest, and most perfect correspondence. For it is "one of a pair"* [zawj]. *In other words, it made the Being of the Real into two. In the same way, the woman makes the man two through her existence. She turns him into one of a pair.*

In other words, says Qayṣarī, the human form makes the form of the All-merciful into one of a pair, just as the form of the woman makes the form of the man one of a pair.[68] Here we have Ibn al-ʿArabī's teachings about the Lord's need for a vassal and God's need for a divine thrall. Interrelationship lies at the root of existence. Without cosmos, "God" is not a god, since divinity is defined precisely in terms of cosmos. Without woman, man is not a man, since man is defined by woman. This is part of the mystery of the "strength" of the woman to which Ibn al-ʿArabī alluded in the passage quoted above: The cosmos turns the Real into a God and woman turns man into man. Without cosmos, there is no god. Without woman, there is no man.

> *Thereby triplicity becomes manifest: the Real, man, and woman. The man longs for his Lord, who is his root, just as the woman longs for him.*

Kāshānī points out that spirit and body have a corresponding love for each other:

> The body is in the form of the spirit, which is one and unique. Hence the bodily form makes the spirit two and turns it into one of a pair. Such also is the relationship between the He-ness and existence. Hence love brings about interrelationships on every level.[69]

Qayṣarī points to the corresponding appearance of triplicity in the microcosm through spirit, heart, and soul. Hence there is mutual love between spirit and heart and between heart and soul.[70]

> *Hence his Lord made women lovable to him, just as God loves him who is upon His own form. Hence love occurs only toward the one who is engendered from him. Or it may take place toward the one from whom a person is engendered, that is, the Real. This is why the Prophet said, "were made lovable to me." He did not say "I loved" on his own behalf. His love was for his Lord, in whose form he existed, even his love for his woman. He loved her through God's love for him, as an assumption of a divine character trait.*[71]
>
> *When the man loves the woman, he seeks union, or the ultimate union that takes place in love. And there is no union in the form of the elemental configuration greater than the marriage act. That is why appetite pervades all his parts. And that is why he is commanded [by the Sharia] to make a major ablution.*

The major ablution (*ghusl*) is necessary after the sexual act, while a minor ablution (*wuḍū*ʾ) is required after becoming impure through such activities as going to the toilet.

> *The purification is general, just as the annihilation within her in actualizing the appetite is general. For God is jealous lest His servant should believe that he takes enjoyment in someone other than He.*

As pointed out already, God's jealousy (*ghayra*) is connected to the existence—or apparent existence—of the other (*ghayr*). The "other" is everything that has the qualities of engendered existence and possibility. But in reality, there is no "other," if by that is meant something that has true and inherent existence, independent of the Real. The gnostic knows the actual situation, as Qayṣarī points out:

> The gnostic, in his state of taking enjoyment, believes that he is taking enjoyment in the Real, who becomes manifest within that form. Hence he is busy with the Real, not with the other. So in this case there is no jealousy. However, that form is entified and distinct from the station of the perfect Divine All-comprehensiveness. Hence it is stained with the stain of having been originated in time. It is sullied by imperfections and impurities. Hence God made the major ablution incumbent upon him, that he may become pure of the imperfections he gained by turning his attention toward the form and busying himself with it. The Shaykh alludes to this with his next words:
>
> *Hence He purifies him through the major ablution, so that he will return to looking upon Him in the one within whom he is annihilated, since there is none other than He.*

Witnessing God in Women

We now come to the heart of the discussion, which is that the witnessing or contemplation of God in woman is the most perfect kind of witnessing given to a human being. It is useful to recall here that representatives of the Muslim sapiential tradition do not allow that God can be seen *in Himself*, that is, in His own Essence. God's Essence stands beyond every sort of delimitation, entification, and relationship. There is "no thing" that could be witnessed by a something. However, God can be witnessed as He discloses Himself (*tajallī*). And He discloses Himself in every existent thing.

Given the earlier discussions in the chapter, it is clear that Ibn al-ʿArabī's primary concern is to bring out the nature of the perfect witnessing of God that is given to the most perfect of human beings and those who follow in his footsteps. The tradition holds that God reveals Himself most completely and perfectly in the human being, made in the image of the name Allah, the name that comprehends every name, every reality, every ontological possibility. Hence witnessing God in the human being must be the most perfect form of witnessing. However, one can then ask if witnessing God is more perfect in the form of men or the form of women. Ibn al-ʿArabī answers with the latter, especially since women "were made lovable" to the Prophet. He could not have been made to love something other than God, since nothing other than the Real is truly worthy of love. "There is no beloved but God" is a theme found throughout Sufi literature, though rarely expressed in these particular words. Rūmī provides the most detailed and accessible explanation of the fact that all love is in fact directed only toward God.[72] But it takes a prophet or a gnostic to experience this.

In short, Ibn al-ʿArabī holds that witnessing God in the female human form is the most perfect mode of witnessing. He also provides us with a rational explanation for this fact. But it should be remembered that Ibn al-ʿArabī is speaking not primarily as a rational thinker, but as a gnostic who himself has tasted the realities. He himself knows through his own experience that this is the most perfect form of witnessing.

The gist of his explanation is that by witnessing God in woman, a man sees Him as both yang and yin, as embracing both majesty and beauty, distance and nearness, activity and receptivity, left hand and right hand.

> *When the man witnesses the Real in the woman, this is a witnessing within a locus that receives activity. When he witnesses Him in himself in respect to the fact that the woman becomes manifest from himself, then he has witnessed Him in an agent. When he witnesses Him in himself without calling to mind the form of that which was engendered from himself, then his witnessing takes place in a locus that receives the Real's activity without intermediary.*
>
> *Hence his witnessing of the Real in the woman is the most complete and the most perfect, since he witnesses the Real in respect to the fact that He is both agent and locus of receiving activity.*

Jandī explains why woman is the most complete locus of witnessing as follows:

> The man witnesses the Real within a locus of receiving activity in the state where the locus both receives and acts. He witnesses God in a locus that brings together [1] receiving activity while it is active while being receptive, [2] acting while it is receiving activity, and [3] receiving activity while it is active. But here there are hidden mysteries, forbidden to those who are not worthy.[73]

The mystery of Jandī's own explanation can perhaps be clarified by looking at other commentaries on this key passage. According to Kāshānī, this witnessing of the Real during sexual intercourse is most perfect,

> because it takes place in a locus of receiving activity, while that locus receives activity from an agent. At the same time, both are one in the unitary reality, since the marriage act of the witnessing gnostic brings together the witnessing of the Real receiving activity while He is performing an act. So He is active while receiving activity and receives activity while being active.[74]

Qayṣarī was clearly not satisfied with the explanation of his teacher or his teacher's teacher, since his explanation bears little outward resemblance to theirs:

> The witnessing of God's activity is that the Real, manifest in the form of the woman,

takes control of and acts upon the soul of the man through a universal taking of control. He makes him obey and love his own soul.

The witnessing of His receiving of effects is that this form is the place man controls. It is under his hand and his command and prohibition.

It may also be that the way in which He is active through the woman is that the reality of the woman is identical with the reality of the man, since masculinity and femininity are the reality's accidents. Hence that human reality acts within her, and it itself is acted upon. Its activity and receiving activity are the same.[75]

ʿAbd al-Raḥmān Jāmī provides a more straightforward explanation:

The man witnesses the Real in respect to the fact that He is both agent and locus of receiving activity at the same time, without any separation between the two. He witnesses the Real within her in respect of His being the agent, since she has an effect within the soul of the man by exciting him. He witnesses Him in respect of His receiving activity, since she becomes affected by him during intercourse.[76]

However, [he witnesses Him] in himself in respect only of the fact that he is a locus of receiving activity.

Qayṣarī explains:

When he witnesses Him in his own soul without calling to mind the form of the woman, he witnesses Him as a locus of receiving activity, since he is one of those things that are the objects of God's activity and His creations.[77]

This is why the Prophet loved women—because of the perfection of witnessing the Real within them. For the Real can never be witnessed disengaged from some material, since God in His Essence is independent of the worlds. Since the situation is impossible in this respect, and witnessing takes place only in some material, then the witnessing of the Real in women is the greatest and most perfect witnessing.

Marriage and Creation

Having explained why the gnostic experiences the sexual act as the supreme instance of witnessing God in the full splendor of His self-disclosure, Ibn al-ʿArabī turns to the metaphysical and cosmological dimensions of marriage. The marriage act gains its nobility from the fact that its archetype is God's creative act itself.

The greatest of unions is the marriage act. It is equivalent to God's turning His attentiveness toward creating him whom He creates in His own form. Hence He sees Himself in him. He proportions and balances him and blows into him of His own spirit, which is His Breath.

[Qayṣarī:] The marriage act is equivalent to God's turning His attentiveness toward creating the human being in order that He may witness within him His own form and entity. That is why He proportions and balances him and blows into him of His own spirit. In the same way, the active partner of the marriage act turns his attention toward bringing a child into existence in his own form. He blows into the child something of his own spirit as contained in the sperm drop. He wants to witness his own soul and entity within the mirror of the child and make him his vicegerent after him. Hence the well-known marriage act is equivalent to the original marriage act in eternity without beginning.[78]

Hence his manifest dimension is a creature while his nonmanifest dimension is the Real.

[Qayṣarī:] The manifest dimension of the human form that He proportions and balances is a creature described by servanthood. The nonmanifest dimension is the Real, since his nonmanifest dimension derives from the spirit of God, which governs and acts as Lord over the manifest dimension. Or rather, it is God's Entity and Essence that has become manifest through the spiritual form.[79]

That is why He describes himself as governing this outward frame. For He said, "He governs the affair from the heaven," which is the high, "to the earth" [32:5], which is the lowest of the low, for it is the lowest of the four elements.

Jandī tells us that here Ibn al-ʿArabī is alluding to the five universal divine marriages that give rise to the production of the five worlds: the World of Meanings, the

World of Spirits, the World of Souls, the World of Images, and the World of Sensory Objects.[80] Kāshānī takes inspiration from Jandī's allusions and writes a detailed explanation of the passage. It is worth quoting, since it provides another explanation of Universal Marriage and illustrates that this whole discussion cannot be separated without distortion from the metaphysics and cosmology within which it is embedded. Notice how clearly Kāshānī explains that the universe depends upon the interplay of yang and yin forces for its existence.

> The Shaykh said *his manifest dimension is creation while his nonmanifest dimension is the Real* only because the He-ness that is entified within the World of the Unseen in the form of the inward spirit governs the outward form, gives shape to it, and becomes manifest through it. This spirit is identical with the form that governs this outward frame called the "cosmos."
>
> The One Essence has five descents down to the World of the Visible, or the World of Sense Perception—which is the last world—in the form of acting and receiving activity. That is why they have been compared to marriage acts and have been called the "Five Marriages." But this is a single reality in acting and receiving activity. Its manifest dimension is the cosmos, and its nonmanifest dimension is the Real. And the nonmanifest dimension governs the manifest dimension. In reality, He is the Manifest and the Nonmanifest, for these descents are nothing but the entifications and modalities of the One Essence. They take the forms of name-derived, effect-producing forms and their effect-receiving forms.
>
> The first descent is the self-disclosure of the Essence in the forms of the unmade immutable entities. This is the World of Meanings.
>
> The second is the descent from the World of Meanings to the spiritual entifications. This is the World of Disengaged Spirits.
>
> The third is the descent to the entifications of soul. This is the World of Rational Souls.
>
> The fourth is the imaginal descents. These become embodied and take shape without matter. This is the World of Imagination. The philosophers call it the World of the Conforming Souls. In reality, this is the imagination of the cosmos.
>
> The fifth is the world of material bodies. It is the World of Sense Perception and the World of the Visible.
>
> The four preceding descents are the levels of the Unseen. Whatever is lower is like the result of what is higher. It is actualized through activity and the reception of activity. That is why this has been compared to the marriage act. All this is identical with the Real's governing of the cosmos.[81]
>
> *The Prophet loved women only because of their level and the fact that they are a locus that receives activity. In relation to him they are like Nature in relation to the Real. For within Nature He opened up the forms of the cosmos through the attentiveness of desire and the divine command. This, in the world of elemental forms, is the marriage act. In the world of the luminous spirits it is resolve* [himma], *and in the world of meanings it is the ordering of premises to produce conclusions. All this is the marriage of the Prime Singularity in each of these respects.*

These allusions to different kinds of marriage acts prompt Qayṣarī to provide his version of the "marriage that courses through all things":

> The first marriage is the coming together of the divine names in order to bring into existence the World of Spirits and their forms within the Breath of the All-merciful, which is called "Universal Nature." Then the luminous spirits come together to bring into existence the world of natural and elemental bodies. Then there are other marriages that produce the three children and what pertains to them.
>
> Since these instances of coming together—of the names, the luminous spirits, and the meanings that produce conceptual results in demonstrations—lie outside the property of time, the Shaykh makes all of them the marriage act of the Prime Singularity. In other words, it is the marriage act through which the Prime Singularity is actualized. In ontological level this Singularity is the One Essence, the divine names, and Universal Nature.

In other words, the primary Singularity/Triplicity that brings about the cosmos is God as Essence or Nondelimited Being, God as named by the names, and God as manifesting Himself through the Breath of the All-merciful.

The other instances of coming together that produce the three children are the second and third marriages. They end with the fourth marriage, which is the last of the universal marriages.

Here Qayṣarī most likely has a view toward the teachings of Qūnawī, who maintains that there are four universal marriages, as we saw in the last chapter.

Since the effectivity of the luminous spirits takes place through resolve and turning attentiveness, while the effectivity of premises takes place through a specific order, the Shaykh mentioned "resolve" for the World of Spirits and the "ordering of premises" for the meanings. All these things are branches of the first marriage and are contained within it in one of the three modes: the marriage act in elemental forms, resolve in the World of Spirits, and the ordering of premises in the World of Meanings.[82]

Perfect Sexual Union

It should not be imagined that Ibn al-ᶜArabī is prescribing sexual activity as a means of achieving spiritual realization. At least, he is not doing so any more than the Prophet did when he said, "Marriage is one-half of religion." Rather, he is describing the modalities of human perfection, achieved only by the prophets and the great friends of God. No doubt in order to preclude any misunderstanding, Ibn al-ᶜArabī now turns to the fact that this type of witnessing of God is not possible for the vast majority of people. For, as he frequently points out in the *Futūḥāt*, most people are "animal human beings" (*al-insān al-ḥayawān*). They have not attained to the perfection of the divine form latent within themselves. Hence they are governed by the characteristics that they share with other animals.

When a person loves women within these bounds, that is a divine love. But when someone loves them only out of natural appetite, then he falls short of the knowledge of this appetite. For him the marriage act becomes a form without a spirit. Though in actual fact that form possesses a spirit, it is not witnessed by the one who comes to his wife, or to whatever female it may be, strictly for taking pleasure, but not knowing in whom. He remains ignorant of his own soul just as someone else remains ignorant of him as long as he does not name himself with his tongue so that he might be known. . . . Such a person loves the taking of pleasure, so he loves the locus within which it is found, that is, the woman. However, the spirit of the question has remained hidden from him. Were he to know it, he would know in whom he takes pleasure and who it is that takes pleasure. Then he would be perfect.

[Jandī:] The Shaykh is talking about the witnessing of the Real within the locus in which the man takes pleasure. The man must witness the Real through a single witnessing that brings together the agent and the recipient of the act. At the same time he must witness Him as not confined or delimited through His entification within either of the two, or both together, or the combination of the two, or being free from the combination. On the contrary, he must witness Him as not delimited by any of these modalities and as incomparable with all of them, together or apart. Then he is the perfect man, the one who takes enjoyment in the Real in every single entity and every single entification. He is unique in his time, unparalleled among his peers and his companions. He is one of the perfect human beings, or one of the rare Singulars.[83]

Though Ibn al-ᶜArabī has not mentioned the Singular or Solitary (*fard*) in his discussion, he clearly has him in mind, since this chapter is devoted to the Wisdom of Singularity. According to his teachings, the Singulars are friends of God who have the same spiritual rank as the Pole. They are not given the Pole's specific cosmic function, nor are they under his command. It is even possible that their knowledge of God may be superior to his.[84]

The woman stands below the degree of the man according to God's words, "The men have a degree above them." In the same way, the one who is created in the divine form stands below the degree of Him who configured him in His form, though he has His form. Through the degree whereby the Real is distinguished from him, the Real is independent of the worlds and a First Agent. The form is a second agent. Hence the human being does not have the firstness that belongs to the Real. Thereby the entities become distinguished through the levels. Hence every gnostic "gives to each that has a right its right."

Here Ibn al-ᶜArabī alludes to the ontological and cosmic hierarchy that lies at the root of all things. He refers to the sound hadith, "Give to each that has a right its right."[85] Each thing has a right to existence and attributes according to its own essence. The gnostic acts according to justice, which is defined as putting each thing in its proper place. Hence the gnostic acts in a manner that is exactly appropriate to every situation. He observes the rights of God, men, and women.

Hence Muhammad's love of women derived from God's making him love them and the fact that God "gives each thing its creation" [20:50]. Its creation is identical with its right. Hence he only gave the right to the thing inasmuch as the thing deserved it in its very essence.

[Kāshānī:] The Real becomes entified within each spirit that is entified, whether for the gnostic or other than the gnostic. Or rather, in all things He gives every thing that has a right and a level what is worthy for it according to its reality and essence. Hence He gives the locus of receiving activity its creation in its receiving activity and its posteriority in degree. That is its right. Likewise He gives the agent its creation in its activity and its priority. That is its right. He gives the gnostic who knows all this the witnessing of the Real within all things and the enjoyment of it. That is his creation and his right. And He gives to other than the gnostic his creation, which is the enjoyment without his having the spirit. That is his right. Similar words can be said for everything.[86]

[Qayṣarī:] The verifying gnostic gives each possessor of a right its right. Hence the love for women found in Muhammad's heart derived from God's giving him love. In other words, He made the Prophet's heart love women because of the requirement of the very essences of women that they be men's objects of love and the requirement of men's essences that they be loved by women. This giving by God is identical with the right of the thing to which the right is given. Hence Muhammad's love of women was identical with Muhammad's right, since the essences of men require the love of women. Nevertheless, from another point of view, the man is loved and desired by the woman, and the woman is his lover and desirer. Through the fact that each of them brings together the attribute of being the lover and the beloved, interrelationship is established between them. Love pervades all loci of manifestation. Each of them is lover from one point of view and beloved from another point of view. Hence love sets up the interrelationship between the Real and the creature.[87]

He put women first because they are the locus that receives activity. In the same way Nature precedes those who come into existence from it as forms. And in reality, Nature is nothing other than the Breath of the All-merciful. Within it the forms of the cosmos, both the high and the low of the cosmos, were opened up through the fact that the "blowing" pervades the hylic substance specifically within the World of Bodies. . . .

The Symbolism of Grammatical Gender

Ibn al-ᶜArabī now turns to a "Taoist" perception of reality. In truth, the ultimate reality is feminine, since the Essence of God "receives" all forms in the same way that God as Knower (as we saw above) receives all knowledge from the objects of His knowledge. But this divine receptivity cannot be made too explicit, if only because of the social dangers inherent in such a perspective, as we saw in chapter 2. Hence the Prophet only alludes to this perspective through the grammatical gender of the words that he employed in his saying.

Then the Prophet made the feminine gender dominate over the masculine, since he wanted to give great importance to women. For he said "three things" in the feminine form, not in the masculine form. But he mentioned "perfume," which is masculine, and it is the habit of the Arabs to make the masculine gender dominate over the feminine.

You say, "The Fatimas and Zayd came," using a masculine plural verb. You do not use the feminine plural. So the Arabs make the masculine gender dominate over the feminine, even if the masculine is one and the feminines are many. And the Prophet was an Arab. Hence he observed here the meaning that he wanted to convey. For that which had not been exercising an effect upon his love was made lovable to him. Thereby God taught him something that he did not know, and God's bounty upon him was great. Hence he made the feminine dominate over the masculine with his words, "three things." What a great knowledge he had of the realities! How great was his observance of rights!

Then he made the end [of his words] *correspond to the beginning in feminine gender, while he placed the masculine between the two. For he began with "women" and he ended with "prayer," and both words are feminine. Perfume stands between the two, just as the masculine stands between two feminines in existence. For the man is placed between an Essence from which he becomes manifest and a woman who becomes manifest from him. Hence he is between two feminines: the feminine gender of the Essence and the real femininity of the woman. In a similar way, "women" is a real feminine, while "prayer" is an unreal feminine. Between the two, "perfume" is like Adam between the Essence, from which he comes into existence, and Eve, who comes into existence from him.*

If you want to say [that he does not come into being from the Essence, but] *from a divine attribute, "attribute"* [ṣifa] *is also feminine. If you want to say* [that he comes into being] *from the divine power, "power"* [qudra] *is also feminine. Take whatever position you like. You will not find anything but the feminine having priority, even in the case of those who claim that God is the "cause" of the cosmos, for "cause"* [ʿilla] *is feminine.*

Jandī sums up the significance of this discussion in a long passage that is rewritten with a bit more clarity by Kāshānī. Both authors see the root of all yang and yin in the Nondelimited Reality, or the Essence of God, which is both active and receptive to activity.

This passage is one of the more abstruse discussions to be found in the *Fuṣūṣ* commentaries, which are not known for their clarity and simplicity. For the most part the translation of the passage follows Kāshānī. However, the sections in brackets { } follow Jandī's original version when I found it clearer than Kāshānī. In this section I observe the gender of the feminine pronouns in English, translating consistently as "she" where I would normally translate "it." I leave the masculine pronouns as "it" or "he," depending on the context.

The Shaykh says that the Prophet made the feminine gender dominate over the masculine gender, even though he was the most eloquent of the pure Arabs. . . . He did this because he paid perfect attention to observing the rights of things, after having reached the furthest limit of the verification of the realities.

The reason for this is that the origin of anything is called the "mother" [*umm*], since the branches branch off from the mother. Do you not see how God says, "[Fear your Lord, who created you from a single soul,] and from her He created her spouse, and from the two of them scattered forth many men and women" [4:1]? "Women" are feminine, while the "soul" from which creation took place is also feminine. In the same way, the root of the roots, beyond which there is no beyond, is called the "Reality" [which is feminine]. . . . The same is true of "Entity" and "Essence"—all these words are feminine.

By making the feminine dominate over the masculine the Prophet wanted to point to the state of women: They embrace the meaning of being the root from which things branch off. The same is true of Nature, or rather, of the Reality. Although the Reality is the father of all things because She is the Absolute Agent, She is also a mother. She brings together activity and the reception of activity. Hence She is identical with the locus of receiving activity in the form of that locus, and She is identical with the agent in the form of the agent. Her own reality demands that She bring together entification and nonentification. Hence She becomes entified through every male or female entification, just as She is incomparable with every entification.

In respect of Her entification through the First Entification, She is the One Entity that requires equality and equilibrium between activity and reception of activity, manifestation and nonmanifestation. In respect of being nonmanifest within every form, She is an agent, while in respect of being manifest, She receives activity. This is like what was explained concerning the spirit's governing the body.

The First Entification may be witnessed inasmuch as It is manifest in Its own Essence through that Essence's nonentification and nondelimitation. For entification, in its very essence, must be preceded by nonentification. The Reality, in the respect that She is She, is actualized within every entified thing. Hence this entification demands that it be preceded by nonentification. Or rather, every entification, in respect of the Reality and disregarding the delimitation, is nondelimited. Hence the entified thing is supported and sustained by the Nondelimited. In respect of that Nondelimited Root, it receives activity and makes the Root manifest. And that Root is active within it and hidden. Hence it is a locus of receiving activity in respect of being entified within itself after having been nondelimited, even though the Entity is one.

{As for nonentification, if we consider It in the sense of the negation of entification, then knowledge of that depends on entification. Without entification, nonentification could not be actualized in knowledge. Hence in knowledge nonentification receives the activity of entification and actualization from that which is entified through the First Entification.}

If we consider the Reality nondelimited either by entification or by nonentification, then She possesses priority over the two. Then the two—entification and nonentification in the sense of negation—are preceded by the Reality and receive Her activity, since the two are relationships possessed by Her equally.

{Hence both activity and reception of activity are established for the First Entification and That which becomes entified within It.}

Through the First Entification the Reality leaves the nonmanifestation of Her Essence to become manifest within Her first and greatest visibility. Each of the Five Descents is a manifestation after a nonmanifestation, or a visible after an unseen. In respect of entifying and delimiting the Nondelimited, each locus of manifestation and self-disclosure acts upon the Nondelimited. Hence, in this respect, it is correct to say that the entified thing and the entification exercise activity and effectivity within the Reality.

Hence wherever the Reality travels and in whatever face She becomes manifest, She possesses activity and the reception of activity, fatherhood and motherhood. Hence it is correct to give the feminine gender to the Reality, the Entity, and the Essence. But the all-comprehensive *barzakh*, who is the true Adam, stands between two feminines.[88]

Kāshānī ends this discussion after providing brief explanations of the other feminine words mentioned in Ibn al-ʿArabī's text. But Jandī continues expanding upon the complementarity of yin and yang that are found in the Reality, which Herself is the inward dimension of that all-comprehensive *barzakh* known as the reality of the human being. For human beings, made in the form of God, bring together in their innermost nature every quality found in the Reality in a completely harmonious fashion. They manifest the two hands of God. Hence in their outward existence, to the extent that they reach the perfection of the human state, they are the face of the Tao. Jandī continues:

> You should realize that the Root Reality, which is the origin of the human reality, receives through Her own reality both activity and reception of activity, both manifestation and nonmanifestation. For indeed, these relationships are the modalities of Her own Essence. Hence they do not change or disappear. This one, all-comprehensive Reality demands the *barzakh*-reality that brings together nondelimitation and delimitation, entification and nonentification, manifestation and nonmanifestation, activity and reception of activity. The human *barzakh*-reality receives the activity of the Entity between the First Entification and the Nonentification of the Essence. She [the *barzakh*-reality] brings together these two while keeping them separate. She becomes manifest through the triplicity of the First Singularity, which is the origin of the Prophet's configuration and the root of his existence.
>
> Femininity is the description of that which receives activity in its essence. In the same way, masculinity is the quality of that which is active. The actual situation stands between the Real, nonmanifest or manifest, and a creature, also nonmanifest or manifest, within the two stations of firstness and lastness and with the two relationships of manifestation and nonmanifestation, or unseenness and visibility. But the Reality is one in all. And ac-

tivity and the reception of activity belong to Her truly and by Her very essence in all these relationships—manifestation and nonmanifestation, unseenness and visibility, creatureliness and realness, Lord and servant—in respect of the Unity of the Entity.

Hence the all-comprehensive *barzakh* is active between two things that receive activity, like the masculine gender between two feminines. The Prophet made these mysteries and realities manifest in respect of his having been given the "all-comprehensive words" in all his words and acts. Likewise he took into account singularity in all things. Hence he gave priority to the true femininity that belongs to the Essence, the Reality, the Entity, the Divinity, the Lordship, the Attribute, and the Cause—depending on the diversity of viewpoints and considerations. He also put the feminine gender last through "ritual prayer," in respect of the word. And he placed "perfume," which is masculine, between two feminines. So what a great knowledge he had of the realities, as the Shaykh said! Know this, for these discussions, even though they have been mentioned repeatedly in this book, are extremely difficult for people to understand when the Reality has not been unveiled to them.[89]

Spiritual Counsel

The foregoing passages should make clear that Ibn al-ʿArabī and many of his followers perceived absolute Reality as predominantly yin in a manner analogous to the Taoist conception of the Tao. Hence, even though the Essence transcends all distinctions, they conceived of It as a personal "She," not the impersonal "It" that English grammar would demand. Ibn al-ʿArabī brings out a practical consequence of this divine femininity while explaining the significance of addressing God by the second person singular pronoun while reciting the *Fātiḥa* (the Koran's opening chapter that is included as part of every cycle of the mandatory ritual prayer). He says that people have no choice but to address God through prayer, whether they employ the masculine or feminine pronoun in doing so. "For," he says, "I sometimes employ the feminine pronoun in addressing God, keeping in view the Essence."[90] Again, this does not mean that Ibn al-ʿArabī is advising people to address God as feminine; he is simply remarking that to do so is a possibility, provided one understands the profound reasons that allow one to do so. But he would certainly not recommend this form of address, since it pertains to the same touchy domain that is dealt with in the *Fuṣūṣ* passages just quoted.

I bring this chapter to a close by reminding the reader of the context of Ibn al-ʿArabī's teachings on woman as image of God. Ibn al-ʿArabī did not write the *Futūḥāt* or the *Fuṣūṣ al-ḥikam* for everyone. He directed both books toward people who consider spiritual perfection as the goal of human life. His teachings are not primarily theoretical or philosophical, no matter how abstract or irrelevant they may appear to some people. He is trying to map out the cosmos and the soul so that serious practitioners of spiritual discipline may achieve the goal of union with God.

In short, Ibn al-ʿArabī's teachings on the spiritual significance of sexuality are a guide for those few members of the human race who have the intellectual and spiritual gifts to put them to practical use. For people in general, he has no prescriptions outside the Shariite teachings on human relationships; in other words, he accepts the "patriarchal" orientation of those Islamic teachings that stress God's incomparability and difference. But he has further advice for those who are making a serious attempt to integrate all dimensions of their own existence into the Real. Such people should recognize that God's similarity and sameness with the cosmos allow for a totally positive evaluation of the feminine dimensions of reality.

Ibn al-ʿArabī devotes the last chapter of the *Futūḥāt*, one of the longer chapters of the book, to counselling the spiritual traveler. There he makes clear how all the "abstract" discussions of his works have direct applications to life. In one section he talks about the trials that people face in their everyday existence. He has in mind several Koranic verses, such as 64:14–15: "O believers, you have an enemy in your wives and children, so beware of them . . . ; your wealth and your children are only a trial." To undergo a trial is be tested, and the author of the test is God. Ibn al-ʿArabī mentions four divine blessings through which men are tried: women, children, wealth or possessions, and position. He devotes several pages to explaining how a person can pass the test of having been given one or more of these blessings. The first test he deals with is women. Here we see an explicit statement of the practical application of what he says elsewhere in his works concerning human sexual relationships.

> You should return to God through trials, for "God loves everyone who undergoes trials and who turns toward Him." So said the Messenger of God.[91] And God says, "He created death and life to test you, which of you is best in works" [67:2]. Trial and testing have the same meaning, which is none other than the examination of human beings in their claims. "It is only Thy trial," that is, Thy examination, "whereby Thou misleadest whom Thou wilt," that is, Thou bewilderest him, "and Thou guidest whom Thou wilt" [7:155], that is, Thou makest clear for him the way of deliverance in the midst of the trial.
>
> The greatest of trials are women, possessions, children, and position—these four. God tests His servant with all of them or with one of them. If the servant acts correctly while the trial is directed toward him, returns to God during it, does not stop with it in respect of its entity, and takes it as a blessing through which God has blessed him, then God will bless him through it. Thus the servant refers the trial back to God and stands in the station of true gratitude, to which God commanded His prophet Moses. For God said to Moses, "O Moses, thank me with true gratitude." Moses replied, "My Lord, what is true gratitude?" God said to him, "Moses, when you see that every blessing comes from Me, that is true gratitude."[92] . . .
>
> As for being tried by women, the form of the return to God in loving them is to see that the whole loves its part and longs for it. Hence the whole loves only itself. For the woman, at root, was created from the man—from his short rib. Hence in relation to the man's self, the woman was put in the place of the form upon which God created the perfect human being, that is, the form of the Real. Hence the Real made her a locus of disclosure for the man. When something is the locus of disclosure for something else, the viewer sees only himself in that form. When the man sees his own form in this woman, his love for her and inclination toward her intensifies, since she is his form. At the same time, it has become clear to you that his form is the form of the Real upon which he was brought into existence. Hence he sees only the Real, but with an appetite of love and a joy in union. He becomes annihilated within her with a real annihilation and a true love. He coincides with her through likeness. Hence he becomes annihilated within her, for there is no part of him that is not in her. Love may permeate all his parts such that he devotes his whole self to her. That is why he becomes annihilated in his like with a complete annihilation, in contrast to his love for something that is not his like.

In other words, a human being can become totally absorbed in love for another human being (or in love for God), but not in love for any other created thing. Ibn al-ʿArabī makes this point explicitly in another context:

> Love cannot absorb the whole of the lover unless his beloved is God or one of his own kind, a woman or a man. No other love can absorb a human being totally. We say this because in his essence a human being coincides with nothing but the one who is upon his own form. When he loves that person, there is nothing in himself that does not find its corresponding part in his beloved. There remains nothing left over in him that would allow him to remain sober. His outward dimension is enraptured by his beloved's outward dimension, and his inward dimension by his beloved's inward dimension. Have you not noticed that God is named "the Outward and the Inward" [57:3]? So the human being's love for God and for his fellow human beings absorbs him totally, whereas no love for anything else in the cosmos can do that. When a person loves one of the forms found in the cosmos, he turns to it with the corresponding part of himself, while the rest of himself remains sober in its occupation.
>
> As for the reason that the human being is totally absorbed by his love for God, this is because he is made in God's form. Hence he coincides with the Divine Presence with his total self, for all the divine names have be-

come manifest within him. . . . When God is his Beloved, he is annihilated in this love much more thoroughly than in his love for his fellow human beings, since, in loving a human being he loses the outward dimension of his beloved when his beloved is not with him; but when God is his Beloved, he witnesses Him constantly. Witnessing his Beloved is like a food for his body through which he grows and flourishes. The more he witnesses Him, the more he loves. . . . This is what the lovers find when they come together with their Beloved. They are never sated by witnessing Him. Their burning desire is never taken away from them. As much as they look upon Him, they increase in their ecstasy and yearning for Him, though they are present with Him.[93]

To return to the passage already begun, we see that Ibn al-ʿArabī is telling us that a man can overcome the trial of being stricken by love for a woman by recognizing that his absorption in her is in fact his absorption in the divine image, which is, at root, nothing but God. Hence by loving her he is loving God. He continues,

He becomes one with his beloved to the extent that he says [in the words of al-Ḥallāj],

I am the one I love,
and the one I love is I.

In this station, someone else said, "I am God."

Hence, if you love a person who is like you with such a love, your witnessing within this person will turn you back to God with such a turning. Then you will be one of those loved by God.

Another path in love for women is as follows: They are loci of receiving activity and engendering in order that every kind may become manifest. There is no doubt that God loves the entities of the cosmos in the state of the nonexistence of the cosmos only because those entities are loci of receiving activity. When He turns toward them in respect of the fact that He is Desiring, He says to them "Be!" and they come to be. Hence His kingdom becomes manifest within existence through these entities. These entities give to God His right in His Divinity; hence He is a god. They worship Him in all His names through their states, whether or not they know these names. Hence God has no name left over in the form and state of which the servant does not stand up, even if he does not know the fruit of that name. This is what the Messenger of God said in His supplication concerning the names of God: "[O God, I ask Thee by every name by which Thou hast named Thyself] or kept to Thyself in the knowledge of Thy Unseen or taught to any one of Thy creatures."[94] In other words, he prays concerning each of His names that he come to know its entity so that he may differentiate it from other names through knowledge. For there are many things in a human being's form and state that he does not know, while God knows these from him.

When the person loves a woman because of what I mentioned, his love for her takes him back to God. She becomes the blessing of trial for his sake, and God loves him for his returning to Him through loving her.

As for the fact that in this love the man is attached to a specific woman and no other, even though the realities that we mentioned permeate every woman, this is because of a spiritual affinity between these two individuals at the root of their configuration, natural constitution, and the gazing of their spirits. Sometimes this affinity goes on until a fixed date, and sometimes there is no fixed date, or rather, the final date is death, and the devotion does not disappear. Take, for example, the Prophet's love for ʿĀʾisha, for he used to love her more than he loved any of his other wives. So also was his love for Abū Bakr, who was her father. These secondary affinities determine the individuals. But the first cause is what we mentioned.

The fact of a specific affinity toward certain people seems to contradict the idea that a person of spiritual attainment should love God in all His creatures without any discrimination. The tradition speaks of the "nondelimited" (*muṭlaq*) love of the friends of God, the fact they they love God in all things, hear His speech in all things, and see His face in all appearances. Ibn al-ʿArabī now explains that there is no contradiction between loving God in all things and loving specific things more than others.

The nondelimited love, nondelimited hearing, and nondelimited vision that belong to some of the worshipers of God is not singled out for one individual rather than another in the cosmos. Everyone present for such a person is his beloved and keeps him occupied. Nevertheless, there has to be a specific inclination toward certain individuals because of a specific affinity, despite this nondelimitation. There is no escape from this, since the configuration of the cosmos yields this in its members—there has to be delimitation. The perfect human being is the one who brings together nondelimitation and delimitation. An example of the nondelimitation is the words of the Prophet, "Three things of this world of yours were made lovable to me—women." Here he did not single out one woman rather than another. An example of delimitation is what has been related concerning his loving ʿĀ'isha more than his other wives, because of a divine, spiritual affinity that delimited him toward her rather than toward anyone else, even though he loved women.[95]

7

THE WOMB

In the Chinese view, everything comes under the sway of the Tao. Heaven and earth follow the Tao, as do the Ten Thousand Things. In ancient times, the sage-emperors were in perfect harmony with the Tao, and hence their kingdoms dwelt in peace and equilibrium. If the world is now in turmoil, that is because human beings do not follow the Tao as they should. If on the one hand the Tao governs all things, on the other hand human beings have the peculiar ability to upset the balance.

Universal Worship

Muslim thinkers would have little trouble grasping these basic ideas of the Chinese tradition. They can be rewritten in Islamic terms as follows: The heavens and the earth and everything between the two obey the laws of God since they are His creatures. Their obedience can be called "submission to the Real," or "Islam." Nothing refuses to obey the Real, since everything is submitted to Him by the very fact that He brings all things into existence. "To Him is submitted (*islām*) everyone in the heavens and the earth" (3:83). Hence everything in the universe constantly worships Him—"Everything in the heavens and the earth glorifies God" (57:1, 59:1, 61:1).

Human beings are no different from other creatures. Hence, in one sense of the word *islām*, they are submitted to God by definition. But the term *islām* has several senses. In another sense, it refers to voluntary submission to God by following one of the religions brought by the prophets. In this sense, humans can choose not to submit themselves. To reject this kind of submission is to go against the will of God and to corrupt the harmonious interaction of heaven and earth. Corruption takes place first on the microcosmic scale when spirit and soul fail to interact fruitfully. Corruption then spreads to the macrocosm, since human beings are God's vicegerents in the earth. If they refuse to perform their duties, they ruin the earth.

In still another sense, *islām* refers to the historical religion that goes by the name. But even people who are "Muslim" in this sense may choose not to submit to God's will. Merely to be a member of the religion is no guarantee that one understands its teachings or puts them into practice in the proper way. One can be a "Muslim" in this historical sense without having submitted oneself to God.

In short, the term *islām* refers both to the way things are and to the way things should be, and hence it is a worthy candidate for an Arabic word to translate Tao. In the first broad sense of the word *islām*, all things are Muslims. In the second sense, few human beings are truly Muslim. In the first sense the Tao is the principle of heaven and earth from which nothing can escape, while in the second sense the Tao represents a right way that human beings alone have the power to transgress. Other Koranic concepts illustrate the same ideas.

To say that "Everything in the heavens and the earth" praises and glorifies God is to say that things "worship" or "serve" Him, two words that translate the Arabic word *ʿibāda*. The term *ʿabd* (slave or servant) comes from the same root. We have already met this as one of the highest human qualities, without which human vicegerency—the goal of creation—is impossible. In the broadest sense, to be an *ʿabd* is the inescapable ontological condition of all creatures. It derives from the fact that "He created you and what you do" (37:96). Human existence as well as human activity are God's creations, like all other things in the universe. Hence the Koran refers to all things as servants: "None is there in the heavens and the earth that comes not to the All-merciful as a servant" (19:93). All creatures serve God, whether they want to or not. But like *islām*, the term *ʿabd* is also used in a more specific sense. Then it refers to the observance of the laws of religion, or doing the work of God by voluntarily following His commandments.

All things worship God in their own way, but human beings can also reject worship and upset the balance between heaven and earth. Hence the Koran sometimes qualifies itself in statements concerning universal worship and submission: "Have you not seen how before God prostrate themselves all who are in the heavens and all who are in the earth, the sun and the moon, the stars and the mountains, the trees and the beasts, and many of mankind?" (22:18). The whole Koranic message is, of course, directed at those "many" of mankind who do not submit. Inasmuch as human beings do not submit themselves to God's will, they become the "lowest of the low" (95:5), as the Ikhwān al-Ṣafāʾ point out:

> Know, my brother, that the human being who is heedless of worship and engrossed in disobedience is less than an animal, less than a plant, and less than the minerals, restored to the "lowest of the low." For mineral substances receive form, but he does not receive it. The plant prostrates and bows itself to its Lord, but he does not prostrate himself. The animal obeys man, but he does not obey his Lord, nor recognize him, nor find Him.[1]

In discussing the worship of all things, the Ikhwān usually keep in view the analogy between God and the human vicegerent. Hence they see the worship of animals as identical with the service they render to people. This obscures the central Koranic teaching, brought out by many Sufis, that all worship is directed toward God.[2] In the following passage, the Ikhwān elaborate upon this idea of universal worship. What is especially noteworthy is the way in which their argument is centered upon the idea of worship as a quality that is manifest in different modes throughout the cosmos. Note that they describe the worship in question in terms that recall the complete receptivity of the servants to the divine command and their submission to it. Worship is the yin dimension of the cosmos.

> The movement of the mineral substances to worship and admitting the Originator is the fact that they receive imprint [*naqsh*] and form. This is their worship, obedience, subjection, and humbleness. Among them are those that enjoy and yearn for obedience. Among them are those that are quicker in reception, more beautiful in form, greater in measure, more than this, and less than this. Among them are those that are heedless of this. They do not receive the form and do not melt in fire. They have no radiance or purity, and no one profits from them, such as hard and solid stones and rocks and salty earth.
>
> The worship of plants is the movements that appear from them and their turning right and left with the wind. Thereby they bow and prostrate themselves. They glorify and call God holy through the rustling of their leaves, the movements of their branches, the splendor and blossoms that appear from them, and the submission of their fruits to animals. Among them are those that give no profit and are fit only for the fire.
>
> The worship of animals is their service [*khidma*] to mankind, their going with him when he goes, their patience in the work they do for him. Among them are the disobedient, the deniers, the rejecters of obedience to human beings, and their enemies, like savage beasts and varieties of wild animals.
>
> The worship of human beings is that which God has made incumbent upon them

and to which He has guided them. This is the greatest of the earthly worships and the most tremendous animal science. The human being possesses the excellence of rational speech, the nobility of power over what stands below him, the perfection of creation, and the uprightness of his stature. He brings together the two worlds. He is like the boundary that lies on the two boundaries and the intermediary between the two sides.[3]

In short, when human beings worship God through total submission, they become perfect vicegerents, thereby bringing together the two hands of God and manifesting the full range of divine attributes. No other creature can compare to them.

The Sufis of Ibn al-ʿArabī's school frequently discuss worship as a quality of all things. Their approach is much less anthropocentric than that of the Ikhwān, since they consider this worship to be directed toward God without intermediary. All things manifest the divine names, so all things render service to Allah, the name that encompasses all names. ʿAbd al-Razzāq Kāshānī illustrates the typical approach of this school in commenting on Koran 16:48. His *taʾwīl* departs only slightly from the literal sense. In fact, his reading is much more "literal" than that of those who would see the verse as referring simply to everyday reality and nothing more. The verse says, "Have they not seen all things that God has created casting their shadows?" It does not qualify "all things" by making them those corporeal realities that would cast shadows by nature. If we say that the Koran means only things like mountains, trees, animals, and humans that have "shadows" in the most literal sense of the term, then we would be rejecting the verse's explicit statement. Hence Kāshānī suggests that we need to understand both *thing* and *shadow* in the widest senses of the terms. "Thing" can be taken to refer to the entities, whether or not they exist. The entities, as we have noted before, are also called the essences, the realities, the quiddities, and the objects of God's knowledge. The "shadows" cast by the entities are the creatures that enter into the various worlds of existence—spiritual, imaginal, and corporeal. They are shadows since they dim the infinite light of God by making it finite and perceptible. Light is invisible, but a shadow can be seen. The Light of God is incomparable, but the luminous being of an angel can be perceived in appropriate circumstances. A shadow, on whatever level it is witnessed, alerts us to the infinite light of God.

Have they not seen all things that God has created, that is, every created essence and reality, whatever it may be among the created things, *casting their shadows*? In other words, their frames and forms assume bodily form and imaginalized form. For everything has a reality, which is the "Dominion" of that thing and its root through which it is it, as God says, "In His hand is the dominion of each thing" [36:83]. And each thing has a shadow, which is its attribute and locus of manifestation, or its body, through which that thing becomes manifest. *To the right and to the left*, that is, in the direction of good and evil, *prostrating themselves before God*, submitting themselves to His command and being obedient, not refusing what He desires in them. In other words, their frames move in the directions of good and evil works by His command, *while they are abased*, submissive, making themselves lowly before His command, overpowered.

To God prostrates or submits *itself everything in the heavens*, the world of the spirit. This refers to the Inhabitants of the Invincibility and the Dominion and the disengaged, holy spirits. *And every creature on the earth*, the world of bodies. This refers to the crawling creatures, the human beings, and the trees. *And the angels*, all the souls and the earthly and heavenly faculties. *They do not claim eminence*: They do not refuse to submit themselves. *They fear their Lord*: they are broken and they receive effects. They are receptive toward His activity with the receptivity of one who fears. *Above them*, because of His overpowering sway, His exercising effects, and His elevation beyond them. *And they do what they are commanded*, willingly and submissively, such that the activity of no one else embraces them.[4]

Kāshānī makes similar points in commenting on Koran 13:15:

To God prostrate themselves all who are in the heavens and the earth. These are the spiritual realities, such as the entities of the substances and the Dominion of the things.

> *As do their shadows*. These are their frames and bodies, which are the "idols" of those spiritual things and their shadows. That is why, when the Prophet prostrated himself at this verse, he would recite, "Prostrated before Thee is my face, my blackness, and my imagination."[5] He meant the reality of his essence, the blackness of his person, and the imagination of his soul; or, his existence, his entity, and his person. *Willingly or unwillingly*: whether they want to or refuse to do so. The meaning demands that this be said, since some of them are willing and some of them unwilling. *In the mornings and the evenings*: constantly.[6]

By serving and worshiping God and singing His praise, everything tells us something about its specific relationship to His Essence. All things are signs of their Lord, giving news of how He relates to His creatures. We saw in chapter 1 the importance of the Koranic term *sign* (*āya*), which is employed to refer to any phenomenon that gives news of God, whether it be a prophet, a prophetic message, a prophetic miracle, or simply the things of the natural world. In the writings of the Sufis, few ideas are as basic as that everything in the cosmos is a sign of God because it manifests God's names and attributes. Rūmī summarizes this idea clearly:

> Consider the creatures as pure and limpid water, within which shine the Attributes of the Almighty.
>
> Their knowledge, their justice, their kindness—all are stars of heaven reflected in flowing water.[7]

It is this quality of being a sign that most clearly expresses the yin relationship of all created things to God.

The Mercy of Existence

The signs of God give news of the divine reality. The names of God provide in summary form the knowledge given by the signs. On the basis of a well-known saying of the Prophet, Muslim thinkers generally speak of the divine names as numbering ninety-nine, though many more are found in the sources. The name Allah is the supreme and all-comprehensive name, since all other names refer back to it. It is Allah who is Knowing, Powerful, Desiring, and so on. But the Koran says, "Call upon Allah, or call upon the All-merciful—whichever you call upon, to Him belong the names most beautiful" (17:110). While alluding to the all-comprehensiveness of the name Allah, the verse also suggests that the name All-merciful (*al-raḥmān*) somehow shares in this quality.

The All-merciful is God inasmuch as He shows mercy to everything. God says in the Koran, "My mercy embraces all things" (7:156). Following various allusions in Ibn al-ʿArabī's works, Qūnawī identifies mercy (*raḥma*) with *wujūd*, which in this sense of the term denotes both Being, or the absolute Reality of God, and existence, or that Reality inasmuch as it is reflected in the universe and therefore brings it to be. Of all conceivable divine attributes, only *wujūd* and knowledge "embrace all things." But the creatures do not profit simply by the fact that they are the objects of God's knowledge. As long as they are objects of knowledge and nothing else, they have no existence of their own. They reap benefit only when God shows mercy to them by bringing them to be. Hence *wujūd* is the root of every blessing. In this sense God's bestowal of *wujūd* on the things is identical with His mercy toward them. This is the "mercy of the All-merciful" that we have already met. Qūnawī writes,

> God is called "All-merciful" inasmuch as He spreads His nondelimited *wujūd* over the things that become manifest through His manifestation.[8] For mercy is *wujūd* itself, and the "All-merciful" is the Real inasmuch as He is a *wujūd* spread over everything that becomes manifest through Him and inasmuch as He possesses through His *wujūd* the perfection of receptivity toward every property in every time and in accordance with every level—properties that rule over every state.[9]

Note that the All-merciful—*wujūd* or Being—is receptive to all properties: It is yin. This is the point that Ibn al-ʿArabī alluded to through his assertion that the cosmos derives from the feminine. We will return to this point shortly.

If in one respect the names Allah and All-merciful seem to be identical, since both are to be "called upon" (as we saw in the above Koranic verse) and both "embrace all things," in another respect the name Allah is more inclusive, since it embraces nonexistence as well as existence. If "mercy" is existence (*wujūd*), and existence is an attribute that applies to that which is "found" (*mawjūd*), then mercy has been bestowed upon all those things that may be found in the cosmos, that is, everything other than God. Hence mercy is the attribute of God inasmuch as He turns His attention toward bringing the cosmos into existence, or inasmuch as He is Manifest through His own Being. But God is also Nonmanifest, refusing to show Himself to any "others." According to Qūnawī, the name All-merciful does not refer to God from this point of view:

> The All-merciful is a name of the pure and eternal Essence in respect of the fact that the lights of existence shine out from the presence of His majesty upon the [nonexistent] entities of the possible things [thus bringing them into existence]. This name has no relationship with the Unseen He-ness in respect of the fact that It is the Unseen He-ness. Rather, this name pertains exclusively to the presence of the manifest. In contrast, the name Allah embraces both the unseen and the visible, the manifest and the nonmanifest.[10]

The name All-merciful never becomes exhausted by bestowing existence upon the entities and bringing them out from the level of nonmanifestation to manifestation. The Prophet said, "On the day God created mercy, He created it as one hundred mercies and kept ninety-nine mercies with Himself. To all His creatures He sent out but a single mercy."[11] The Prophet also said,

> God created a hundred mercies on the day He created the heavens and the earth, each mercy of which would fill what is between the heaven and the earth. Of these He placed one mercy in the earth. Through it the mother inclines toward her child, and the birds and animals incline toward each other. When the Day of Resurrection comes, He will complete those mercies with this mercy.[12]

Ibn al-ʿArabī expanded on the Koranic and prophetic references to God's mercy and its relationship with creation by developing the image of the "Breath of the All-merciful," a term which is found in the hadith literature and which we have already discussed. He explains the qualities implied by the term "Breath of the All-merciful" something like this:

Before the creatures enter into existence, God embraces them within His own Reality as so many latent possibilities of manifestation. It is as if God, prior to creating the universe, has drawn a deep breath. He then feels distressed by holding all the creatures in a nonmanifest state, just as a person holding his breath feels constricted. So God exhales, thereby showing mercy to all things, giving birth to the cosmos, and relieving His own constriction. And this exhalation takes the form of articulated speech, since God is the Speaker—He never remains silent. This mythic description of God's "distress" (*kurb*) pertains to the same level of reality as the love for creation expressed in the hadith of the Hidden Treasure: "I loved to be known." This love or distress is also described as the demand of the divine names to experience the manifestation of their own properties.

For Ibn al-ʿArabī and his followers, the Breath of the All-merciful is the substance of creation, pure mercy or pure existence. The individual things or creatures are so many articulated words within the Breath, or specific shapes and forms assumed by existence. As Qūnawī explains in the passage quoted above, the All-merciful is God inasmuch as "He possesses through His Being the perfection of receptivity toward every property in every time and in accordance with every level." In other words, the All-merciful is God considered as a yin reality, inasmuch as She is the matrix within which the things take shape. In the same way, the term "Breath of the All-merciful" makes explicit the implications of the name All-merciful by providing an analogy to explain how God shows mercy to all things. His Breath, which is not other than Himself from the point of view of similarity, receives the articulations known as "words" or "creatures." If there were no words in the Breath, God would be silent. But the All-merciful speaks. Thereby we perceive God in the mode of similarity. When we hear His words by perceiving His creation, we are alerted to the fact that these are certain words and not others. And we know that an infinite Breath can say anything and talk forever. The Breath can be articulated by any word. Just as God is considered yang when He is looked upon as the distant Creator, so also God is considered yin when She is looked upon as the receptive substance underlying all things and giving shape to all things.

Inasmuch as each creature articulates the All-merciful Breath through its own reality, it possesses a yang nature in respect to God as yin. In one respect the Breath precedes the word in existence and reality, so the Breath is yang and the word yin. But the word acts upon the Breath by defining it and differentiating it from pure Breath and from other words, so the word is yang and the Breath yin. Moreover, Breath without word is inconceivable—since this is the Breath of the All-merciful, whose goodness does not allow Him to remain silent. In the same way, it is impossible to conceive of God without a divine thrall, Lord without a vassal, Creator without a creature. This is a constantly recurring theme in Ibn al-ʿArabī's writings: that the realities of the things make God receptive. For example, he writes,

> Though God in His Essence is Independent of the worlds, it is known that He is described by generosity, munificence, and mercy. Hence there must be objects of mercy and objects of generosity. That is why God says, "When My servants question thee about Me—surely I am near. I respond to the call of the caller when he calls to Me" [2:186]. God answers the caller through munificence and generosity.[13]

In other words, the gentle and beautiful qualities connected to God's similarity and nearness make God receptive toward the creatures. Moreover, this receptivity and response on God's part is the root of every receptivity and response in the cosmos. No Muslim thinker can doubt that God is active in relation to the cosmos. Hence all activity reflects His activity. But to speak of God's receptivity is further from the mind. The "patriarchal" view of God is normal for the Sharia that pertains to all Muslims, but the "matriarchal" view pertains to the spiritual path, the Ṭarīqa, so not everyone can appreciate it. Ibn al-ʿArabī alludes to this point in the midst of a discussion of the characteristics of water. He points out that water has effects upon the other elements, for example, by purifying the air. But it also can be affected by the other elements. Then he generalizes the discussion to include all the elements:

> God has made each of the four pillars both producer of effects and receptive toward effects. The root of this in the divine knowledge is His words, "When My servants question thee about Me—surely I am near. I respond to the call of the caller when he calls to Me." When anything in the cosmos is receptive toward effects, this derives from the divine response. As for the divine root of the active, that is obvious to everyone. We call attention to something only when most people may remain heedless of it.[14]

And most people are heedless of the fact that receptivity or yin is as much a divine attribute as activity or yang.

One way of explaining God's receptivity is, of course, to speak of God's two hands, the giving hand and the receiving hand. In other terms, the divine reality brings together all qualities, both the qualities of the Real and those of the creatures. The creaturely qualities, after all, stem from His qualities. Hence, on every level, the Real and the creature are intertwined: On the divine level, God has such "creaturely" qualities as receptivity and response. On the creaturely level, the things have such "divine" qualities as activity and control. All of this is rooted in the "marriage that permeates every atom," thereby displaying yin and yang in all things. Ibn al-ʿArabī makes some of these points while discussing the properties of the divine name the Strong (*al-qawī*).

> The reason for all this is the interpenetration of creation and the Real and of the Real and creation through the self-disclosure in the divine and engendered names. The actual situation manifests the Real in one respect and creation in another respect in each and every engendered thing. The Divine Presence Itself brings together the property of the Real in creation and creation in the Real. Were this not the case, God could not be described in such terms as the following: The servant makes Him wrathful and angry, so the Real becomes wrathful and angry. The servant makes Him pleased, so He becomes pleased. As for the fact that the Real makes the servant angry, wrathful, and pleased, everyone knows about that. This all belongs to the science of entering into one another [*tawāluj*] and interpenetration [*tadākhul*].
>
> Were it not for the existence of the property of strength, none of this would take place. For weakness is a strong hindrance. Look at the property of strength and see how it permeates weakness! Thus, you say concerning a weak person: The weakness has become so strong that he is unable to move. Hence you ascribe strength to weakness. You describe it by its opposite. From here you will understand the words of Abū Saʿīd al-Kharrāz [d. 286/899]. He was asked, "Through what do you know God?" He replied, "Through the fact that He brings opposites together." . . .[15]
>
> Through strength, weakness becomes strong. And through the stronger, strength becomes weak. This is the difference between the stronger and the strong, like the nearer and the near. Everything nearer is near, but everything near is not nearer. Everything stronger is strong, but everything strong is not stronger.[16]

In short, qualities interpenetrate on every level. Yin and yang are both present in all things. What is yin may become yang simply by a change in the point of view. All this goes back to the Real, which is both yin and yang. At the same time, there is a yin/yang relationship between the Real and each thing. From the perspective of the specific qualities of the things, including existence, each quality is received from the Real, so the thing is yin. But from a slightly different perspective, the Breath of the All-merciful receives the qualities of the things, just as our breath is delineated and articulated by our words. Hence the Real is yin and the creature yang.

Nature as Wife and Mother

The intellectual tradition, and more particularly the philosophers and Sufi sages, employed a great array of rational demonstrations and analogies to develop the idea that the cosmos manifests the signs of God. For example, they adopted the idea of "nature" (*ṭabīʿa* or *ṭabʿ*) from the Greek philosophers and, especially among the Sufis, explained it in ways harmonious with the Koranic teachings on signs. The basic meaning of the Arabic root *ṭ.b.ʿ.* is to seal, stamp, or impress with a signet or stamp. Nature is that which receives impressions or imprints from a higher level of existence. It is the cosmos viewed as the place wherein the signs of God are made manifest.

In the view of the Ikhwān al-Ṣafā', Nature is the "faculty" or "power" or "strength" (*quwwa*) of the Universal Soul, which is the "spirit of the cosmos." Nature is the activity (*fiʿl*) performed by this spirit, while the four elements are the matter within which Nature displays its activity. Nature permeates the elements and the three children, governing them and giving them motion and rest. It completes each of them, taking each to its ultimate goal.[17] Though Nature is the "activity" of the Universal Soul, it is clearly subordinate and governed by the Soul and receives effusion by means of the celestial bodies, which are the instruments (*adawāt*) of the Soul. Hence, say the Ikhwān,

> The engendered things below the sphere of the moon begin from the least complete and lowest states, advancing to the most complete and most excellent. This takes place during the passage of time and hours, since

> Nature does not receive the effusion of the celestial bodies all at once. Rather it receives it gradually, little by little, just as a bright student receives from a skilled teacher.[18]

The dual aspect of Nature, as both receptive and active, is also discussed in the teachings of Ibn al-ᶜArabī, though he develops Nature's feminine symbolism in some detail. According to his view, Nature in the widest sense refers to the Breath of the All-merciful, within which are imprinted the words or creatures, whether these be spiritual or corporeal. We saw in the previous chapter that in the *Fuṣūṣ* he identifies the qualities of Nature with those of women. Then he says, "In reality, Nature is nothing other than the Breath of the All-merciful."[19]

But Ibn al-ᶜArabī employs the word *Nature* in two basic meanings. If in one sense it is the divine receptivity or the All-merciful Breath, in a narrower sense it refers to the corporeal world inasmuch as it is governed by the spiritual world, receiving its imprint. In this second case also Nature is clearly yin. It is described as "wife" or "woman" (*marʾa*) in relation to the spirit, which is "husband" or "man" (*rajul*). Nature is the mother (*umm*) who gives birth to the creatures, the children (*awlād, mawālīd*).

Nature is the domain wherein appear the "four natures"—heat, cold, wetness, and dryness. These four manifest the qualities of the spiritual world and ultimately go back to certain fundamental names of God. For example, Ibn al-ᶜArabī refers to the analogical connections between the four natures, various cosmological realities, and the Four Pillars of Divinity—the divine attributes life, knowledge, desire, and power. Each of these divine attributes has an "imprint" (*ṭabᶜ*), that is, a "nature" within the corporeal things.

> The cosmos demands four relationships from the divine realities: life, knowledge, desire, and power. . . . Life and knowledge are the two roots in these relationships, while desire and power stand below them. The root is life, since it is a precondition for the existence of knowledge. Then knowledge is connected to all things, since it is connected to the Necessary Being, the possible thing, and the impossible thing.
>
> Desire stands below knowledge, since it becomes connected only to the possible thing. This happens when God gives preponderance to one of the possible thing's two sides: existence and nonexistence. It is as if life seeks desire, since desire, as it were, receives its activity, for desire is more inclusive in connection than power. Power is the most limited in connection, since it becomes connected to bringing the possible thing into existence, but not to making it nonexistent. Hence it is as if power receives the activity of knowledge. For power in relation to desire is like knowledge in relation to life.
>
> Once the levels of these divine relationships have been distinguished, the active is distinguished from that which receives activity. Then the cosmos emerges in this form: active and receptive to activity.
>
> In relation to God, the whole cosmos is receptive and originated. But in respect to itself, some of it is active and some receptive.

This, in a nutshell, is a conclusion that was reached in chapter 2: The cosmos is yin in relation to God as yang. Then within the cosmos itself, some parts are yang and some yin, depending on the relationships envisaged. Ibn al-ᶜArabī continues by illustrating how the divine names that reflect yang and yin are the roots of various cosmological realities. Note that the issue is always qualitative correspondence, and this is established at least partly by the reports that come through revelation. "Natural" phenomena—for example, cold—can never be separated from human phenomena—for example, knowledge and certainty—since the qualities that the natural and human worlds manifest derive from the same roots.

> God brought the First Intellect into existence from the relationship life. He brought the Soul into existence from the relationship knowledge. The Intellect was the precondition for the existence of the Soul, just as life was the precondition for the existence of knowledge. The two things that receive the activity of the Intellect and the Soul are the Dust and the Universal Body. These four are the root of the manifestation of the forms in the cosmos.
>
> However, between the Soul and the Dust stands the level of Nature. It has four realities. Two of them are active, and two are

loci that receive activity. But all of them stand at the level of receiving activity in relation to that from which they have come forth.

These four realities are heat, cold, wetness, and dryness. Dryness receives activity from heat, and wetness receives activity from cold.

Heat derives from the Intellect, and the Intellect derives from life. That is why the "nature" [*ṭab*ᶜ (literally, imprint)] of life within the elemental bodies is heat.

Cold derives from the Soul, and the Soul derives from knowledge. That is why, when knowledge becomes established it is described as the "coldness of certainty" or "snow." For example, the Prophet said that when he felt the coolness of God's fingers between his breasts, he came to know the knowledge of the ancients and the later folk.[20]

Since dryness and wetness receive activity from heat and coldness, desire seeks dryness, which is on its level, and power seeks wetness, which is on its level.

Since power is connected only to bringing into existence, it is more worthy of having life as its nature. For "life," in corporeal bodies, is heat and wetness.[21]

Ibn al-ᶜArabī frequently discusses Nature itself as a receptive reality. He often juxtaposes it with spirit, which is active. He does this in the following passage while reminding us that yin and yang are inseparable. Just as creation has an effect upon the Creator by making it a Creator, so also Nature has an effect upon the World of the Command, which is the world of activity proper to spiritual beings.

> A woman in relation to a man is like Nature in relation to the Divine Command, since the woman is the locus for the existence of the entities of the children, just as Nature in relation to the Divine Command is the locus of manifestation for the entities of the corporeal bodies. Through Nature they are engendered and from it they become manifest. There can be no Command without Nature and no Nature without Command.[22]

The World of the Command, as we saw in chapter 4, is invariably contrasted with the World of Creation. So also the natural level is usually contrasted with the spiritual level, since Nature receives the spirits' imprints and reflects their light. The spirit governs while Nature is governed, the spirit is the husband, Nature the wife. In the following, Ibn al-ᶜArabī employs the terms soul and spirit synonymously.

> When a natural form that has the receptivity to be governed becomes manifest and when a particular soul becomes manifest governing it, the form is like the female, while the governing spirit is like the male. Hence the form is the wife, while the spirit is the husband.[23]

Nature's outstanding characteristic is the ability to receive and manifest the activity of the spiritual realities that dwell above and beyond it. Ibn al-ᶜArabī insists on Nature's receptivity in a curious anecdote about one of the spirits, who wanted to give the property of activity, which belongs to spiritual beings—or, as Ibn al-ᶜArabī says here, to the forms that place their stamp upon Nature—to Nature itself.

> One of the spirits desired to make the property of the form that it governed join with the property of Nature, within which that form had come into existence. It wanted to make the form descend so that its properties would be those of the level of Nature. But the form can never descend to Nature's level. The Teacher [the First Intellect?] said to it, "What you desire is impossible. The form cannot perform the activity of Nature, since Nature is receptive toward the form. What does the level of that which is active have in common with the level of that which receives activity?" . . .
>
> When this ignorant spirit was unable to join the form to Nature, its own mother, it said, "Perhaps that is because of my inability and incapacity to perceive knowledge in this." . . . So it asked from God that the form have the same reception toward activity as Nature. But it found that the receptacles within which form exercises effects could not receive what was received by those forms that had the receptivity for the effect of Nature. The Real gives to things, as mentioned, only in accordance with the preparedness of the recipient of the gift. The recipient cannot receive that which is not allowed by its preparedness.[24]

Love for Parents

Human beings are the children of Nature, and hence her qualities permeate them. But they also take after their father, the Spirit. This Spirit is the "Attributed Spirit" (*al-rūḥ al-iḍāfī*) mentioned in the Koranic verses that attribute it to God, such as "I blew into him of My spirit" (15:29). In Ibn al-ʿArabī's view, the rational soul—also called the human spirit—is born from the Attributed Spirit and Nature. Nature is the mother of spiritual as well as corporeal possibilities. Body and soul are two faces of the same human reality.

> The human being is the son of his mother in reality, without doubt. Hence the spirit [i.e., the rational soul] is the son of the nature that is the human being's body. Nature is the mother who nurses it. It is configured in her belly and nourished by her blood. It must have food for its frame to subsist.[25]

But Nature is passive and weak compared to the Spirit. As long as human beings are dominated by the natural and bodily side of their realities, they will have no resistance toward things that draw them away from the Divine Light. When their mother pulls them away from their father, they will not be able to stand up to her unless they are confirmed by God Himself.

> In this human configuration, Nature's property demands a great lassitude, since there is no intermediary or veil between her and the spirits, which possess strength and authority over her. Hence fear clings to her as a shadow clings to the person that throws it. Those who are companions of Nature cannot be strong unless they are confirmed by the Spirit. Then the lassitude of Nature will not exercise its effects over them. Otherwise, what is greatest in them is the flow of Nature.
>
> However, the spiritual reality of such a person, which is the governing soul, also comes to exist from Nature, since she is its mother. Even if the soul's father is a spirit, the mother has an effect upon the son, since he was engendered in her womb and nourished by what was with her. Hence the soul does not gain strength through its father unless God confirms it with a holy spirit that gazes upon it. Then it will gain strength over the property of Nature and she will no longer exercise total effectivity upon it, even though her effect will remain, since it cannot disappear completely.[26]

Maybudī makes a similar point while discussing the importance of intelligence or intellect (*ʿaql*) in the human being. He is commenting on a Koranic verse that speaks of "signs for those who have intellect" (2:164). He explains what this intellect is, and he traces it back to its cosmological source in the First Intellect. Then he provides us with a Persian translation of the famous hadith of the Intellect, adding at the end a section I have not seen in the Arabic versions. Clearly he wants to remind us that however exalted Intellect may be, it depends utterly upon God. All of its power and authority is derivative and depends upon His aid. The spirit within us needs the divine confirmation to overcome the hold of Nature.

> Intellect [*ʿaql*] is the fetter [*ʿiqāl*] of the heart. In other words, it holds the heart back from everything except the Beloved and prevents it from unworthy desires. In the view of the Sunnis, intellect is light and its place is the heart, not the brain. It is the precondition for being addressed by God, but its existence does not mean that God will necessarily address a person. Intellect is identical with the instrument of knowledge, not with the root of knowledge. Intellect gives benefit and profit because the heart can come to life through it. The Koran says, "[It is only a Remembrance and a Clear Koran], that he may warn whosoever is alive" [36:69–70], that is, whosoever has intellect. Hence, those who have no intellect are not considered to be alive. Do you not see that God does not address the mad man? Nor does He address a corpse. The reason is that they have no intellect. . . .
>
> The intellect of the servant is a divine gift and a lordly bestowal. The servant's obedience is earned, but obedience cannot be put in order without that gift, and that gift cannot function without God's bestowal of success [*tawfīq*]. Thus it has been reported that the Inaccessible Lord created the Intellect. He said to it, "Stand up." It stood up. He said, "Sit." It sat. He said, "Come." It came. He said, "Go." It went. He said, "See." It saw.

Then He said, "By My inaccessibility and majesty, I have created nothing more noble and honored than you. Through you I shall be worshiped and through you I shall be obeyed."

Because of these caresses, the Intellect felt pleased with itself. The Lord of the worlds did not let that pass. He said, "O Intellect, look behind yourself. What do you see?" The Intellect looked behind itself and saw a form lovelier and more beautiful than itself. It said, "Who are you?" The form said, "I am that without which you are useless. I am the success that God gives."

Intellect, though you be noble, become low!
Heart, be no longer heart, but blood, blood!
Come under the veil of that waxing Beauty!
Come without eyes, go without tongue![27]

In certain respects, the spirit, who is the father of the soul, has a greater claim upon it than Nature, the mother. But in another respect, the good behavior and loving kindness that are due toward parents demands that human beings turn more attention to their mother. This is a point of fundamental importance in the Islamic perspective and helps explain where it parts company with much of Christianity. This world is good and full of God's bounty. The body is good. It is a divine gift, to be cherished as such. Marriage is good, not only for the sake of procreation but also in itself inasmuch as it is a mode of enjoying the divine bliss that creates us. The mother, who is Nature, deserves as much love and respect as the father, the spirit.

The Prophet was asked, "Among people, who is most deserving of loving kindness [*birr*]?" He answered, "Your mother." The questioner asked, "After her, who?" He replied, "Your mother." He asked, "After her, who?" He said, "Your mother. Then your father."[28]

The word *birr* is itself significant. In his *Lexicon* Lane defines it as benevolent and solicitous regard or treatment or conduct to parents and others; piety towards parents and towards God; and goodness or beneficence; kindness, good and affectionate and gentle behavior, and regard for the circumstances of another. The adjectival form is *barr*, and this is also a name of God (52:28): *Al-Barr* is the Lovingly Kind, the Beneficent, the Benevolent. One says in Arabic, *al-umm barra bi waladihā*, "The mother is lovingly kind toward her child," or, as Lane renders it, "The mother is maternally affectionate toward her child." Moreover, the same word *barr* means the land as opposed to the sea (*baḥr*) and is so employed in several Koranic verses. A prophetic saying concerning *tayammum*, or ritual purification with earth when water is not present, says, "Wipe yourselves with the earth, for it is lovingly kind to you."[29] So *birr* or "loving kindness" is a divine attribute that permeates existence and is manifest especially in mothers and in the earth. And just as the earth is loving and kind to us, we must be loving and kind to it. Moreover, all the good qualities of the earth are epitomized in one's mother. She deserves the highest love, kindness, and goodness in return. The Prophet's great-grandson, ʿAlī ibn al-Ḥusayn, reflects the Muslim attitude toward mothers in his "Treatise on Rights":

> The right of your mother is that you know that she carried you where no one carries anyone, she gave to you of the fruit of her heart that which no one gives to anyone, and she protected you with all her organs. She did not care if she went hungry as long as you ate, if she was thirsty as long as you drank, if she was naked as long as you were clothed, if she was in the sun as long as you were in the shade. She gave up sleep for your sake, she protected you from heat and cold, in order that you might belong to her. You will not be able to show her gratitude, unless through God's help and giving success.[30]

Such hadiths and sayings have many social repercussions, but clearly the "mother" in question has more meanings than one. Ibn al-ʿArabī writes,

> The human being brings together Nature and Light. Nature makes demands upon him and Light makes demands upon him. Light is charged to stay hidden and to refrain from much of what it merits and what its own reality demands because of Nature's best interests. Light is commanded to fulfill the right of Nature. This is illustrated by the Prophet's words when he was asked to whom loving

kindness should be shown. He replied "Your mother" three times. Then the fourth time he said, "Your father." So he preferred loving kindness toward the mother over that toward the father, and Nature is the mother. This point was also made in the Prophet's words, "Surely your soul," that is, your animal soul, "has a right upon you, and your eye has a right upon you."[31] These are all the rights of the mother, who is the human being's nature. The father is the Divine Spirit, that is, Light.[32]

In the last analysis, the rights of the spirit outweigh those of Nature, since the receptivity inherited from Nature needs to be turned in the right direction. Nature is receptive to all things, darkness as well as light, ignorance as well as knowledge, evil as well as good. Hence the spirit, which is identical with light, knowledge, and good, makes demands upon her. The human being, caught between father and mother—spirit and Nature—must choose the father if the two pull in different directions.

> Nature . . . courts her spouse, seeking childbirth, for she loves sons. She has a tremendous affection for her children. Because of this affection, she seeks to attract them to herself. If she trains them, they will recognize no other. That is why you will see that most sons are servants only of the natural level. They do not leave aside sensory things and natural objects of pleasure. Only a few do that—the ones who gaze upon their father. They are those who have become spiritualized [*al-mutarawḥinūn*]. Their mark is not that they cease to undergo variation in forms, since undergoing variation in forms belongs to them just as it belongs to the people of Nature. What marks the spiritualized ones as sons of their father is that they rid themselves of natural appetites, taking only what allows their configuration to subsist. Thus the Prophet said, "A few mouthfuls to firm up his backbone are enough for the son of Adam."[33] Their aspiration should lie in joining with their father, who is the Divine Spirit, . . . the word of God blown into Nature.[34]

Qūnawī makes a similar point while explaining the meaning of a well-known hadith that sets up a series of images, each of which is yang in one respect and yin in another. In the process, he suggests another significance for the "two hands of God" that created the human being.

> When God created the earth, she began to sway. So He created the mountains and said to them, "Overwhelm her!" Then she became steady.
>
> The angels wondered at the strength of the mountains. They said, "O Lord, is there any of Thy creatures stronger than the mountains?"
>
> He said, "Yes, iron."
>
> They said, "O Lord, is there any of Thy creatures stronger than iron?"
>
> He said, "Yes, fire."
>
> They said, "O Lord, is there any of Thy creatures stronger than fire?"
>
> He said, "Yes, water."
>
> They said, "O Lord, is there any of Thy creatures stronger than water?"
>
> He said, "Yes, wind."
>
> They said, "O Lord, is there any of Thy creatures stronger than wind?"
>
> He said, "Yes, the son of Adam. He gives charity with his right hand and conceals it from his left."[35]

In discussing this hadith, Qūnawī suggests that the meaning is plain down to wind, but few people are aware of why the human being should be superior to wind or why God should have inspired the angels with this knowledge.

> The human being has a right hand and a left hand that are manifest. These are the two hands of his form. He also has a right and a left hand that are nonmanifest: his spirituality and his nature. The religion has taken this into account. It alludes to it in God's words, "The earth altogether shall be His handful on the Day of Resurrection, and the heavens shall be rolled up in His right hand" [39:67]. Since the heavens are the place of the spirits and have become manifest from the Real by means of them, they are more strongly related to the World of Spirits [than the earth]. Hence God attributed them to His right hand, while He attributed the earth and the natural forms within it to the other hand, to which He alluded with the term *handful*. . . .
>
> You should know that the mystery of the words that the Prophet relates from his Lord, "He gives charity with his right hand, concealing it from his left," is as follows: What incites the human being to charity is a spirit-

ual, lordly inciter, completely empty of the properties of Nature. But this is exceedingly difficult. What makes it so difficult is that the human being is a combination of spiritual and natural attributes, and they are thoroughly mixed together. A person's spirituality may be strengthened to the extent that his natural faculties and attributes are absorbed into his spirituality and he is able to exercise free disposal with his spirit without any influence from his nature. Then he will possess the ultimate limit of power and strength. What is more, through that he will be superior to many of the angels, since the angel's innate disposition is that its acts are empty of natural attributes. In the angel this is not considered surprising, nor is it counted as something great, since nothing contends against it.

But in this world, natural faculties and attributes contend with the spiritual, and the ruling power of Nature is exceedingly strong. How should it not be? For the spirit of the human being becomes entified only after and in accordance with the natural constitution. Hence the ruling power of the spirit and its attributes, which are attributed to the suprasensory right hand of the human being, do not overcome the ruling authority of his natural constitution, which possesses the left hand direction. If they did, all his spiritual acts would be delivered from the stain and properties of his nature. This does not occur as long as the interrelationship and mixture between the spiritual and natural attributes remain, unless there should be a lordly confirmation and a tremendous strength and power, as we indicated.[36]

The Womb as Microcosm

The elevated station of the mother in the Islamic tradition is reflected in the stress that is placed on observing the rights of "womb relatives." As noted in the previous chapter, the Arabic word *womb* (*raḥim*) is derived from the same root as the word *mercy* (*raḥma*). The dictionaries define the womb as the receptacle for the young in the belly or the place where the young originate. The word also signifies a blood tie, kinship, or a close family relationship. *Raḥma* is defined as mercy, pity, compassion, tenderness; the inclination to favor someone. It is the natural attribute of a mother toward the fruit of her womb. Various hadiths make this point. For example,

> We were with the Messenger of God in one of his battles. He passed a tribe and asked, "Who is this tribe?" They replied, "We are Muslims."
>
> A woman was tending her oven. She had her son with her. When the flames of the oven shot up, she pulled back her son. Then she came to the Prophet. She said, "Are you the Messenger of God?" He said, "Yes." She said, "I ask you by my father and my mother: Is God not the Most merciful of the merciful?" He replied, "Indeed He is." She said, "Is God not more merciful to His servants than the mother to her child?" He replied, "Indeed He is." She said, "A mother would not throw her child into the fire."
>
> The Messenger of God looked down and began weeping. Then he raised his head to her and said, "Among His servants, God will only chastise the one who is defiant and rebellious, the one who rebels against God and refuses to say, 'There is no god but God.'"[37]

The connection between mercy and womb is clear in both the form and meaning of the words. In addition four different sayings of the Prophet connect the womb to the the All-merciful and to His Throne. The sayings speak of "cutting off the womb," which is an expression that signifies breaking the ties of blood relationship, or acting unkindly toward one's relatives. In contrast, "joining the womb" means to act with kindness and tenderness toward one's relatives. The hadiths are as follows:

1. God said, "I am God and I am the All-merciful. I created the womb and I gave it a name derived from My own name. Hence if someone cuts off the womb, I will cut him off, but if someone joins the womb, I will join him to Me."[38]

2. God created the creatures. When He finished with them, the womb stood up and seized the All-merciful by the belt. The All-merciful said, "What is this?" It replied, "This is the station of whoever seeks refuge from being cut off." God said, "Indeed it is. Will you not be satisfied that I join him who joins you and cut him off who cuts you off?" The womb

replied, "Yes, I will." God said, "Then that is yours."[39]

3. The womb is attached to the Throne and says, "If someone joins me, let God join him, but if someone cuts me off, let God cut him off."[40]
4. The womb is a branch of the All-merciful. God said to it, "When a person joins you, I will join him, but when he cuts you off, I will cut him off."[41]

These sayings are enough to establish the sanctity of the womb and family relationships in Islam. Our concern, however, is to look at the cosmological significance of the qualities implied in the term *womb*. We will return to these sayings shortly.

Many cosmologists see the growth of the embryo into a complete human being as an analogical repetition of what takes place in the cosmos through the creative act of God's mercy. The basic movement of the embryo in the womb is from undifferentiation to differentiation. In each earlier stage, everything is present potentially, like a tree in a seed. Each stage is yin or earth in relation to the previous stage, since it actualizes what was potential. At the same time, it is yang in relation to what follows, heaven in relation to the next earth.

The Ikhwān al-Ṣafā' are especially fond of the analogy between the embryo and the cosmos, developing it most fully in their treatise, *Fī masqaṭ al-nuṭfa* (Concerning the place where the sperm drop falls).[42] On one level, this treatise deals with astrology, since it discusses the influence of the stars and planets upon the growth of the child in the womb. But what is interesting for our purposes is the way in which the Ikhwān develop the analogies and correspondences between the macrocosm and the microcosm.

The first sections of the treatise describe the development of the embryo through eight full months. After the eighth month it is complete and ready for birth, though many factors will influence the exact date of birth. Each monthly stage is marked by the "governance" (*tadbīr*) of one of the planets (or one of the heavens). I quote from the section concerning the fourth month of pregnancy, which is governed by the middlemost planet, the sun. The sun, as we have seen, manifests the spirit more clearly than any other planet, since it is most intense in light. According to the Prophet, it is at the end of the fourth month that the spirit is breathed into the embryo.[43] The stages to which the Ikhwān refer are mentioned in Koran 22:5: "We created you of dust, then of a sperm drop, then of a lump of flesh, formed and unformed. . . . And We establish in the wombs what We will, till a stated term, then We deliver you as infants."

> When the fourth month from the entrance of the sperm arrives, the governance is given over to the sun. The faculties of the spiritual things assume mastery over the lump of flesh. The spirit of life is breathed into it, and the animal soul permeates it. This is because the sun is the leader of the planets in the celestial sphere. The sun's soul is the spirit of the whole cosmos. It has mastery over all the engendered things below the sphere of the moon, especially over the animal children that have wombs. It has its greatest specific properties in human beings, since its corporeal body in the cosmos is like the corporeal heart within the human frame. The rest of the planetary and celestial bodies are like the organs and articulations of the body. . . .
>
> When the sperm drop falls into the womb, the sun must dwell in some degree of one of the constellations. It travels its course for four months from the entrance of the sperm to the end of the fourth constellation. During this time it passes through one third of the celestial sphere. . . . Then it will have completed the natures of the constellations: the fiery, earthy, airy, and watery. Thus the natures of the four elements will have mixed in compounding the structure of the embryo. The constitution will have reached equilibrium [*iʿtidāl*], the form will have been impressed, and the disposition will have been configured. At this point the shapes of the bones have appeared, the joints have been mounted, the composition put in order, the muscles connected to the bones, the veins extended through the flesh. Thus the bodily structure appears "formed and unformed."[44]

Nasafī provides an account of the process of the growth of the embryo that is worth quoting in some detail, since it provides a clear and basic account of the "evolutionary" development of a human being in the typical fashion. For Nasafī, as for the Ikhwān al-Ṣafā' and others, the development of the human body replicates the development of the outer world, beginning from the four elements, then the appearance of minerals, plants, and animals, then the appearance of the various levels of spirit. In truth the embryo is a Hidden Treasure within the womb, and it makes manifest its own attributes, motivated by a love to be known. At the same time, this is a "return" to God whereby the human being becomes the second vicegerent, ultimately identical in a certain respect with the first vicegerent—the First Intellect—from which the cosmos had entered into existence. Like the Ikhwān al-Ṣafā', Nasafī has various Koranic verses in view.

> The human being is a single substance, and everything that gradually comes into existence in the human being was already existent in that single substance. Everything becomes manifest in its own time. That single substance was the sperm drop. In other words, all the parts of the human being, whether substances or accidents, existed in the sperm drop. Everything that is useful for reaching human perfection is already found there. This is to say that the sperm drop is writer, pen, paper, ink, book, and reader.
>
> O dervish! The sperm drop of the human being is the first substance of the microcosm, the essence of the microcosm, the seed of the microcosm. The world of love is the microcosm: The sperm drop is in love with itself. It wants to see its own beauty and witness its own attributes and names. It will disclose itself, become clothed in the attribute of actuality, come from the world of undifferentiation into the world of differentiation, and become manifest in many forms, shapes, meanings, and lights. Thus its beauty will become manifest and its attributes, names, and acts will appear.
>
> When the sperm drop falls into the womb, for a time it is a sperm drop, for a time a blood clot, and for a time a lump of flesh. In the midst of the lump of flesh appear bones, veins, and nerves until three months pass. Then, at the beginning of the fourth month, which is the turn of the sun, it comes to life. Sensation and volitional movement gradually appear within it, until the fourth month passes.
>
> When the fourth month passes, the body and spirit are actualized and the creation of parts and organs is completed. The blood that gathers in the mother's womb becomes the food of the child and reaches it through the navel. The body, spirit, and parts of the child gradually reach perfection, until eight months pass. In the ninth month, when Jupiter's turn arrives,[45] the child is born from the mother's womb into this world. . . .
>
> When the sperm drop falls into the womb, it becomes round, since water by its nature is round. Then by means of the heat that it has in itself and the heat of the womb, the sperm drop gradually begins to grow. Its subtle parts become separate from its solid parts. When it completes its growth, the solid parts from the whole sperm drop turn toward the center of the drop, while the subtle parts from the whole drop turn toward the encompassing surface. In this way the sperm drop becomes four layers, each of which encompasses what is below itself. In other words, that which is solid goes to the center and becomes established in the middle of the drop. That which is subtle goes to the encompassing surface and becomes established in the highest level of the drop. That which is beneath the highest level but connected to it has a lesser subtlety, while that which is above the center but connected to it has a lesser solidity than the center. In this way the sperm drop comes to have four strata.
>
> The center, which is in the middle of the drop, is called black bile. Black bile is cold and dry and has the nature of earth, so it had to fall into the place of earth. The stratum that is above the center, connected to it, and encompasses it is called phlegm. Phlegm is cold and wet and has the nature of water, so it had to fall into the place of water. The stratum that is above phlegm, connected to it, and encompasses it is called blood. Blood is warm and wet and has the nature of air, so it had to fall into the place of air. The stratum that is above blood, connected to it, and encompasses it is called yellow bile. Yellow bile is hot and dry and has the nature of fire, so it had to fall into the place of fire.
>
> The one substance that was called "sperm drop" became four elements and four natures, and all this took place in one month.
>
> When the elements and natures were completed, the three children appeared from the four elements and natures: First the mineral, second the plant, third the animal. In other words, the Apportioner apportioned these

four elements and natures and brought all the organs of the human being into manifestation, both the inward and the outward organs. These organs are the minerals. He sent to each organ a certain measure of black bile, phlegm, blood, and yellow bile. To some He sent the four in equal measures, to some in disparate measures, as wisdom demanded. All the inward and outward organs appeared. He joined them all to each other and brought into existence the channels of food, life, sensation, and volitional movement until the minerals were completed. This all took place in the second month.

When the organs were completed, the minerals were completed. Then faculties appeared in each outward and inward organ: the faculty of attraction, retention, digestion, repulsion, transformation, nourishment, and growth. These faculties are called "angels."

Nasafī continues by describing how the vegetal spirit comes into existence in the liver, the animal spirit in the heart, and the psychic spirit in the brain. Each of these spirits has its own specific functions. Finally the human spirit arrives, but here a major difference can be discerned.

> The human being shares with other animals in these three spirits—the vegetal, animal, and psychic. A human being is distinguished from other animals through the human spirit. The human spirit is not of the same kind as the other three, since the human spirit belongs to the high world, while the vegetal, animal, and psychic spirits belong to the low world.[46]

However, Nasafī then explains that these different kinds of spirit are in fact but a single spirit. This one spirit is put into relationship with the bodily world in different modes according to specific limitations pertaining to various levels of the cosmos. In the last analysis, the spirit pertains to the higher world and the body to the lower. If in all cases we speak of spirit and body, this is because the spirit governs the body, while the body is receptive to the spirit's activity.

> The body belongs to the World of the Kingdom and the spirit to the World of the Dominion. The body belongs to the World of Creation and the spirit to the World of Command. Since it has become clear that the spirit is not more than one, we can know the spirit as the following: The spirit is a substance that perfects and moves the body, on the level of plants through nature, on the level of animals through choice, and on the level of human beings through choice and intellect.[47]

The Womb as Nature

Human beings develop in the womb in a manner that parallels the order followed by God in creating the macrocosm. In the womb the infant grows to completion and reaches deliverance by dying to the womb in order to be born into the world. In the world the human being grows to spiritual perfection and reaches deliverance through death to this world and birth into the next. The analogy between these two processes was never lost on our authors. At the beginning of the treatise, "On how the particular souls become configured in the human, natural bodies," the Ikhwān al-Ṣafā' develop it in some detail:

> The body is related to the soul just as the womb is related to the embryo. When the embryo's structure is completed within the womb and its form is perfected there, it comes out into this abode complete in creation, flawless in its sense faculties. It takes benefit from life here and enjoys its bliss until a fixed time. So also is the situation of the souls in the next abode: The particular souls complete their essences by coming out of potentiality into the confines of actuality by means of the knowledges and sciences that they acquire through the senses. Then forms reach perfection through the virtues they gain by way of intelligibles, experiences, and acts of ascetic discipline as well as through governing those things that need to be managed. These things are putting the affairs of the soul's livelihood in good order through the path of the mean, smoothing the way to the Return according to the norms of guidance, and polishing the soul through beautiful character traits, correct opinions, and righteous works—all of this by means of the body, put together from blood and flesh.

If the soul parts from the body having true insight about itself and its affairs, having known its own substance, conceived of its own essence, and seen with clear vision the affair of its own world and its own beginning and Return, and having disliked existence along with the body, then it will stay separate from matter, become independent in its essence, and have no need in its substance for attachment to corporeal things. It will then advance to the Higher Plenum and enter into the ranks of the angels. It will witness those spiritual affairs and see face to face those luminous forms that it did not perceive through the five senses and that were not conceived of by human intuitions. This is mentioned in prophetic symbols, since the Prophet said that in the Garden there is "What no eye has seen, what no ear has heard, and what has never passed into the heart of any mortal,"[48] that is, bliss, joy, happiness, pleasure, repose, and ease. Thus God says, "Therein shall be all the objects of the souls' appetite and whatever the eyes delight in, and therein you shall dwell forever" [43:71]. He also says, "No soul knows what comfort is laid up for them secretly, as a recompense for what they were doing" [32:17].

However, if the creation of the embryo does not reach completion in the womb and its form is not perfected therein, or there occurs to it an accident in the soul or a crookedness in one of the organs, then it will not benefit completely from life in this abode and its bliss will not be perfect, like the blind, the dumb, the deaf, the chronically ill, the crippled, and so forth. Such will be the state of the particular souls when they part from human bodies.[49]

Rūmī sometimes compares the birth of the child to the perfection of the soul achieved through "dying before you die," or the voluntary death that is the goal of the spiritual path.

Although the mother suffers the pain of childbirth, the embryo breaks out of its prison.

The woman weeps at the birth: "Where is the refuge?" The child laughs: "Deliverance has come!"[50]

Until mothers feel the pain of childbirth, the child finds no way to be born.

The Trust is within the heart and the heart is pregnant; all the exhortations of the saints act as a midwife.

The midwife says, "The woman has no pain. Pain is necessary, for it will open a way for the child."[51]

Ṣadr al-Dīn Qūnawī develops the analogy between the womb and the macrocosm in some detail while commenting upon the four hadiths of the womb cited above. He considers them far more than simple rhetorical devices used to emphasize the importance of family ties. Why was it necessary, after all, to mention the Throne, God's belt, and other details of the unseen world? The Prophet certainly had the social situation in mind, but the social implications can not exhaust the meaning, especially since three of the four hadiths are *ḥadīth qudsī*, that is, sayings of the Prophet in which God's own words are quoted.

Hence Qūnawī sets out to explain the significance of these sayings on a deeper level that is not accessible without confirmation from God. Before beginning his explanation he refers to this deeper level of knowledge by thanking God for "His blessing me, giving me knowledge, and clarifying [the meaning of these texts] for me; He has allowed me to share with the most perfect of His creatures [that is, Muhammad] in coming to know these secrets and disclosing these sciences hidden from 'others.'"

Qūnawī's explanation is based on the identification of the womb with Nature. The womb clings to the Throne because, according to Ibn al-ʿArabī and his followers, the Throne is the sphere that encompasses the corporeal universe. If, according to the Koran, "The All-merciful sat upon the Throne" (20:5), this is because God, who is Being, envelops the universe. The radiance of His Being is the very existence of the universe, the All-merciful Breath whereby the cosmos subsists.

The Throne marks the demarcation line between the unseen and the visible worlds, or the World of Command and the World of Creation. Both worlds exist through the radiance of Being, but in two different modes. The "belt" of the All-merciful alludes to the line that distinguishes the two worlds. The All-merciful is present in both worlds through His radiance, but the world above the belt is manifest to the angels and spiritual beings, while the world below the belt is the locus of the "pudendum" or "shame" (*ʿawrāt*). This is the domain of corporeal things, which are concealed from the spiritual beings by God's loincloth. Hence the angels were ignorant of Adam's rank, blaming him and praising themselves. For when God told them He was setting a vicegerent in the earth, they replied, "What, wilt Thou set therein one who will do corruption therein and shed blood, while we proclaim Thy praise and call Thee Holy?" (2:30).

Qūnawī concludes by explaining why Nature should be held in high esteem—why "cutting off" Nature from oneself is to cut oneself off from God. Here he is being critical of a certain current in the philosophical tradition, especially among the heirs of Neoplatonism and Hermeticism, including the Ikhwān al-Ṣafāʾ. Such philosophers sometimes blamed Nature for the darkness that holds the soul back from seeing its ultimate good.

> Though these hadiths deal specifically with the womb, each of them has mysteries not found in the others. Altogether they include great mysteries, many inaccessible branches of knowledge, and general questions whose knowledge is important. The first of these is the knowledge of the reality of the womb; then the knowledge of its being a branch of the All-merciful; the knowledge of the name All-merciful; the knowledge of why the womb is attached to the Throne; the knowledge of its joining; the knowledge of its being cut off; the knowledge of the belt of the All-merciful; the knowledge of the womb's seizing the All-merciful's belt; the knowledge of its standing; the knowledge of its seeking refuge; the knowledge of God's answering it with exactly what it asked for; the knowledge of its prayer in respect to being attached to the Throne; and the knowledge of its properties. All of these are mysteries about which nothing has been written in any book. I do not know, or it has not reached me, that anyone has undertaken to explain the images of these hadiths. . . .
>
> "Womb" is a name for the reality of Nature. Nature is the reality that brings together heat, cold, wetness, and dryness. This means that Nature is identical with each of these four without opposition, but none of the four is identical with it in every respect, only in some respects.
>
> The womb is "attached to the Throne" in the respect that in the view of those who verify the truth, all existent corporeal bodies are natural, while the Throne is the first of these corporeal bodies. Reports of the Sharia have come concerning this fact, and the unveilings of the perfect human beings all give witness to its correctness.
>
> The womb is a "branch of the All-merciful" because mercy is identical with existence, since it is mercy that "embraces all things." Nothing embraces all things except existence, since it embraces everything, even that which is called "nonexistence." . . .
>
> Since mercy, as we have established, is a name of existence, the "All-merciful" is the name of the Real inasmuch as He is identical with Being. As for the fact that Nature is a branch of the All-merciful, that is because the existent things are divided into the manifest and the nonmanifest. The corporeal bodies are the forms of the manifest dimension of existence, while the spirits and meanings are the entifications of the nonmanifest dimension of existence. The Throne is the place where the division takes place. So understand!
>
> The "womb seized the All-merciful by the belt" because the All-merciful is a lordly self-disclosure through existence, comprising the world of spirits and meanings as well as the world of corporeal bodies. The world of spirits precedes the world of corporeal bodies in existence and level. Moreover, in one respect it possesses the degree of causation toward the womb. Hence it possesses height and corresponds to the first half of the form of the Divine Presence. That is why the womb is attached to the Throne, for the Throne is the first of the world of corporeal bodies and it encompasses all manifest forms. Through it what is manifest becomes distinguished from what is nonmanifest.
>
> The "belt," which holds up the loincloth, is the beginning of the second, lower half, which is concealed by the loincloth. The loincloth is the world of Nature and the locus of the concealment of the Real within the self-disclosures that lie in the depths of Nature, and these are the pudendum. That is why the angels, who were commanded to

prostrate themselves to Adam, were ignorant of these self-disclosures. They shied away from Adam's natural configuration and blamed him, while they praised themselves.

The womb "sought refuge from being cut off" because it sensed the distinction that was made between it and the world of spirits and the Presence of the All-merciful Breath, which is the station of complete nearness to the Lord. It pondered the state of distance after nearness and feared the cutting off of the Lordly replenishment because of the separation that it sensed. While answering its prayer God announced to it that He would continue the replenishment and make permanent the joining in respect of the divine and essential withness [*maʿiyya*] and compass. The womb became happy at that, gained peace, and rejoiced in God's answer to it concerning exactly what it had asked. So its prayer for him who joins it and against him who cuts it off continues.

The term *withness* derives from the Koranic verse, "He [God] is with you wherever you are" (57:4)—whether in the spiritual world or the natural world. Qūnawī now turns to a basic point that helps explain Islam's great respect for this world, marriage, and reproduction. Before its entrance into this world, the human spirit is not actually separate from its One Source. The body alone allows for separation, distinction, differentiation, individualization. Thereby the spirit, which knows by its very essence, comes to know others—and having known others, it knows itself. Self-knowledge is impossible without other-knowledge, since "Things become known through their opposites." If there were no opposition between body and spirit, earth and heaven, there could be no differentiation between the two or awareness of their specificities. Without the body, the microcosmic Hidden Treasure remains hidden. Rūmī frequently refers to these points, as in the verse, "The body did not exist and I was a spirit with Thee in heaven; between us was none of my speaking and listening."[52] Without "speaking and listening," there is no interaction and no awareness of self. Through earthly existence, the spirits gain self-awareness and realize the worth of their original abode. As Rūmī says, "The birds of consciousness . . . were sent from the spheres . . . to realize the worth of union with God and to see the pain of separation from Him."[53] Qūnawī continues:

> To "join the womb" is to recognize its position and to honor its measure. Were it not for what becomes constituted through Nature's four pillars, the human spirit would not become outwardly entified and the human being would not have been given the ability to combine knowledge of universals and particulars. Or rather, the human spirit's knowledge of universals would also have remained absorbed, just as God reported about this with His words, "And God brought you out from the bellies of your mothers when you knew nothing" [16:78].[54] Through the natural configuration and the characteristics, faculties, and instruments that God placed within it, the human being brings together both spiritual and natural characteristics, properties, and perfections. Through this bringing together, he is able to seek access to the realization of the *barzakh*-reality that encompasses the properties of Necessity and possibility. Thereby his conformity [with the Real] is perfected and his parallelism [with Him] is established. He becomes manifest in the form of the Divine Presence and the form of the whole cosmos, both outwardly and inwardly. So understand! These are some of the properties of its joining that can be mentioned.

The human being is created with the two hands of God and made in His form, so he comprehends all the worlds. This is the very definition of what it means to be human. It is impossible to be human without being at the same time a *barzakh*, an isthmus that separates and joins all dualities, all oceans found in reality: God and Cosmos, Being and Nothingness, Right Hand and Left Hand, Spirits and Bodies, Light and Darkness, Beauty and Majesty, Mercy and Wrath. As the locus of manifestation for God's left hand, the body is the absolutely essential yin reality without which yang is barren or, rather, without which yang does not exist. Spirit and body are equally necessary and deserve equal respect. Criticism of the body reflects ignorance of reality.

> The cutting off, concerning which God says that "He will cut off him who cuts it off," takes place through belittling the womb, ignoring its position, and disregarding its

rights. The person who disregards its rights and belittles it has disregarded God and ignored the specific characteristics of the names that God has deposited within it, names in respect to which it is supported by and related to God. Were its position with God not high, God would not have reported His answer to it with His words, "When a person joins you, I will join him, but when he cuts you off, I will cut him off."

Among the ways in which Nature is belittled and cut off is the blame ascribed to it by the recent philosophers. They have described it as dark and opaque and sought deliverance from its properties and the shedding of its attributes. Suppose that they had known that this is impossible; that every perfection acquired by a human being after parting from the natural configuration is one of the results and fruits of the spirit's companionship with the natural constitution; that after parting, the human being passes from the forms of Nature to worlds that are the loci of manifestation for Nature's subtle realities; and that in those worlds, all the felicitous reach the vision of God promised by religion, a vision that is reported to be the greatest of God's blessings given to the People of the Garden. So Nature is a reality upon which the witnessing of God depends. How then could they have allowed Nature to be belittled?

As for the state of the elect among the Folk of God, such as the perfect human beings and those who approach them, they achieve the witnessing of God and verified knowledge of Him in this world. But that is made possible for them only with the help of this natural configuration. This is true even of the everlasting, essential self-disclosure [of God], after which there is no veil and below which there is no resting place for the perfect human beings. For the perfect ones agree that if they do not achieve this self-disclosure within this natural configuration, they will not achieve it after parting from this configuration. There is an allusion to this in the Prophet's words, "When the child of Adam dies, his works are cut off,"[55] and his words, "There is a group of the People of the Garden from whom the Lord is not hidden or veiled."[56]

The fact that the womb "stands" and prays means that through the attribute of poverty it has turned the attention of its own essence toward God.[57] God refers to the attention He turns toward creation through replenishing it as "standing," for He says, "What, is He who stands over every soul through what it earns . . . ?" [13:33].

Know this and ponder what has been placed for you in the commentary on this hadith, which contains sublime sciences and hidden mysteries. You will prosper and reach salvation, God willing.[58]

4

Spiritual Psychology

8

STATIC HIERARCHY

The microcosm is the human individual. Everything in the macrocosm is reflected in the microcosm. And both microcosm and macrocosm manifest the Metacosm. This is the law of correspondence. The goal of the seeker is to integrate the three realities, to "make them one" (*tawḥīd*).

If the macrocosm is the world "out there," the microcosm is the world "in here." The Muslim cosmologists see reference to the three realities and their integration in the Koranic verse, "We shall show them Our signs upon the horizons and in themselves, until it is clear to them that He is the Real" (41:53). The relative reality of the signs in the macrocosm and microcosm points to the absolute reality of the Real, the Metacosm. When the seeker truly realizes that "There is none real but the Real," he achieves *tawḥīd*.

Principles of Ta'wīl

We have seen repeatedly the importance our authors give to the Koran. As the word of God in the form of a book, the Koran manifests the Metacosm within the macrocosm in a mode especially adapted to the needs of the microcosm. God creates both cosmos and the human being through the word *Be*, so language lies at the heart of existence. It is latent in every individual thing. Both the cosmos and the human individual manifest the divine Word. Our authors view both macrocosm and microcosm as books because of their totality or all-comprehensive nature.

By revealing the nature of God in a linguistic mode that appeals to the intelligence—a quality that sets human beings apart from most other creatures—the Koran makes possible the establishment of correspondences between the divine and human worlds. It is true that God is unknowable and incomparable. But this unknowable God is God as He is in Himself without taking His relationship with the cosmos into account. As soon as we see God and cosmos, Lord and vassal, King and servant, we can describe the relationship in terms of divine attributes. This is the perspective of similarity. The Koran, as God's word, reveals these relationships as they are. It manifests guidance to a world which, left to its own devices, sinks ever deeper into error and misguidance.

In short, our authors see the Koran as the one certainty in a world of ambiguity. But though it be truth in itself, there remains the problem of how to understand the Koran. At this point ambiguity and uncertainty reenter the picture. Interpretation of the Koran lies at the heart of Islamic intellectuality, and different interpretations explain most of the diversity that is found in Islamic law and thought.

One particular mode of interpretation is of particular interest in the present context. This is *ta'wīl*, sometimes called "esoteric hermeneutics." Henry Corbin has devoted a great deal of attention to bringing out its centrality for the sapiential tradition, especially the branch of it that he calls "Shiʿite gnosis." Here I want to look at some of the characteristics that are found in one of the important modes of *taʾwīl*.

Taʾwīl derives from the same root as the word *awwal*, "first," which is a name of God. The word *taʾwīl* means to return, to cause to return, to reduce to, to find that to which a thing can be reduced. Since God is the First in relation to all things, many authorities understand the term to signify taking a thing back to the First, demonstrating a thing's relationship with the First, tying things back to God. At the same time, many Muslim thinkers draw no real distinction between *taʾwīl* and *tafsīr* or "commentary." Both terms are taken to mean explanation or exegesis of the Koran. But when distinctions are drawn between the two, *taʾwīl* is often said to refer to the reading of Koranic verses with a view toward implications hidden below or behind the surface meaning. Or, it may simply be that *tafsīr* is commentary based upon what has been handed down to us by tradition, while *taʾwīl* adds a dimension of personal meditation.[1]

For many Sufis, *taʾwīl* is based on a knowledge of the esoteric meaning of the Koran that is given by God Himself. This knowledge cannot be brought to hand by ordinary learning. It can be acquired only through submitting oneself to God's will as manifested in the Koran. Once a person yields to the Koran, the Koran gives of itself. The seeker must be yin to the Koran's yang. When Rūmī compares the Koran to a bride (*ʿarūs*), one might suppose that he has in mind her submission to the husband. Quite the opposite: He means that the husband must submit to the will of the wife. Only by giving oneself to the other do we gain worthiness for the other's gift of self. Did not the caliph ʿUmar, renowned for his severity and military prowess, say that a husband must be a child before his wife, in other words, yin before yang?[2] As Rūmī himself puts it,

> Since God created Eve so that Adam "might rest in her" [7:189], how can Adam cut himself off from her?
>
> Even if a man is [a hero like] Rustam and greater than [the great warrior] Ḥamza, still he is captive to his old woman's command.
>
> The Prophet, to whose speech the whole world was enslaved, used to say, "Talk with me, O ʿĀʾisha!" . . .
>
> The Prophet said that women totally dominate men of intellect and Possessors of Hearts.[3]

It is in this context that one must understand Rūmī's comparison of the Koran to a bride. Remember also that traditionally a Muslim man never saw his wife's face until she unveiled herself after the wedding.

> The Koran is like a bride. Although you pull the veil away from her face, she will not show herself to you. When you investigate the Koran, but receive no joy or unveiling, it is because your pulling at the veil has caused you to be rejected. The Koran has deceived you and shown itself as ugly. It says, "I am not that beautiful bride." It is able to show itself in any form it desires. But if you stop pulling at its veil and seek its good pleasure; if you water its field, serve it from afar, and strive in that which pleases it, then it will show you its face without any need for you to draw aside its veil.[4]

One of the foremost practitioners of the science and art of *taʾwīl* in the Sufi sense is ʿAbd al-Razzāq Kāshānī, author of *Taʾwīl al-Qurʾān*, a work that has often been mistakenly attributed to Ibn al-ʿArabī. We have had occasion to quote from it in earlier chapters, and we will hear from it more now that we have turned to the microcosm, to which Kāshānī pays most of his attention. At the very beginning of his work, Kāshānī explains why he wrote the book and how he came to have mastery over the science of *taʾwīl*. The passage demonstrates the spirit that infuses most Sufi works dealing with Koran commentary.

> I used to dedicate myself to recitation of the Koran and I used to ponder its meanings with the strength of faith, all the time persevering in my litanies. But my breast was constricted and my heart upset. Even though the Koran's meanings did not bring about the opening of my heart, my Lord did not turn my attention away from them. Finally I be-

came intimate and familiar with them. I tasted the sweetness of their cup and their drink. Now I was joyful in soul, opened in breast, ample in mind, expanded in heart, spacious in inmost mystery, glad in moment and state, happy in spirit, all through that opening [*futūḥ*].[5] Opening seemed to come constantly, as both an evening draught and a morning draught. At each verse meanings were unveiled to me that my tongue fell short of explaining. My power was not equal to recording and listing them. My strength had not the endurance to spread and expose them.

Then I remembered . . . the words of the Prophet: "There is no verse of the Koran that does not have an outward sense, an inward sense, a limit, and a place to which one may ascend."[6] From it I understood that the outward sense is *tafsīr*, the inward sense is *ta'wīl*, the limit is the meaning of the Word beyond which understandings go no further, and the place to which one may ascend is that to which one may rise up from the meaning, in order to witness the all-knowing King.

It has been related that the foremost truth-telling Imam, Ja'far ibn Muḥammad al-Ṣādiq, said, "God has disclosed Himself to His servants in His Word, but they do not see." It has also been related that he fell down in a swoon while performing the ritual prayer. When asked about that, he said, "I kept on repeating the verse until I heard it from Him who spoke it."[7]

Hence I decided to make notes on some of what has come to me in my momentary states. These are the mysteries of the realities of the inward senses and the lights of the illuminating truths of the places to which ascent is made. But I made no note on that which pertains to the outward senses and the limits. For God has determined for them a defined limit. It has been said, "He who makes *tafsīr* according to his own opinion has become an unbeliever."[8] But as for *ta'wīl*, that should not be left alone and ignored. For it differs according to the states and moments of the listener in the levels of his wayfaring and the disparity of his degrees. Whenever he rises beyond his present station, the door to a new understanding is opened to him. Through it he becomes aware of a subtle meaning already there. . . .

I do not maintain that I have reached the limit in what I have set down—by no means! For the modalities of understanding are not exhausted by what I have understood. God's knowledge is not delimited by what I have come to know. At the same time, my understanding does not stop with what I have mentioned. On the contrary, often so many senses have occurred to me in the written word that I have been perplexed at all the things they embrace.[9]

The specific kind of *ta'wīl* that I want to consider here takes as its starting point the self-evident—at least for our authors—correspondence that exists between the cosmos and the human being. Hence it is based on relationships among the three realities. Practitioners of *ta'wīl* in this sense read the Koran with a view to showing that the verses that ostensibly refer to the world "out there" have another, deeper meaning, that refers to the world "in here." The verses of the Koran, after all, are God's "signs," just as the phenomena of nature and the soul are God's signs. Every verse that mentions a phenomenon gives to it a linguistic valuation that ties it to God. The thing is a sign, the revealed word that refers to it is a sign, and our understanding of the revealed word is a sign made possible by the presence of that very sign within us. "We shall show them Our signs upon the horizons and in themselves." "He who knows himself knows his Lord."

Shaykh Maḥmūd Shabistarī sums up this perspective in lines of poetry that correlate various chapters and verses of the Koran with the structure of the cosmos. His words quoted below introduce a long section on meditation, first on the signs of the macrocosm, then on the signs of the microcosm. Since all this depends upon the Koran, he first shows how the Koran itself is connected to the major "signs" or "verses" (*āya*) of the cosmos. The actual details of the correspondences are not as important as the fact that correspondences do in fact exist. Anyone who witnesses God's self-disclosure (*tajallī*) in the cosmos will necessarily see these correspondences. The perspective of similarity demands interrelationships among all things. Remember that in the following the word *verse* translates *āya* and also means "sign."

When a person's soul receives God's
self-disclosure,

he sees the whole cosmos as the Book of the Real.
Accidents are the vowel marks, substances the letters,
the ontological levels like verses and stops.
Each of the worlds is like a specific chapter,
one like al-Fātiḥa, another like al-Ikhlāṣ.
The first verse is the Universal Intellect,
like the first word of "In the name of God."
Second is the Universal Soul, the Light verse [24:35],
since it is like a lamp in extreme brilliance.
The third verse is the Throne of the All-merciful.
Read the fourth verse as the Footstool.
Then come the bodies of heaven,
within which are the "seven verses" [15:87].
Now look at the body of the elements,
each of which is a radiant verse.
After the elements come the bodies of the three children,
and these are verses that cannot be counted.
The last thing to come down was the human soul,
for the Koran concludes with "People" [sura 114].[10]

The correspondence between macrocosm and microcosm allows us to read Koranic verses describing macrocosmic phenomena as referring also to the human person. Heaven and earth, for example, may refer to spirit and soul, or soul and body. At first reading, the correspondences may seem arbitrary, but the more one becomes familiar with the world view that underlies this way of thinking, the more one sees a principled science of qualitative evaluation, taking all qualities back to God as He reveals Himself in the Koran.

If the work of Kāshānī, for example, is studied in isolation, the logic of the correspondences he draws is seldom clear. But as soon as he is placed in the tradition that we have been discussing, his interpretations are seen to fit in harmoniously. One of the best preparations for understanding Kāshānī's work is to study the treatises of the Ikhwān al-Ṣafā', who constantly investigate the qualitative correspondences among the worlds. Unlike Kāshānī, however, the Ikhwān are concerned not only with the text of the Koran but also with other texts, especially the hadith literature. And they derive a good deal of their terminology and modes of explication from the Greek philosophical heritage.

Like later authors, the Ikhwān al-Ṣafā' often refer to their *ta'wīl*s as "allusions." Ibn al-ʿArabī suggests that the Sufis employed this word to defend themselves against the attacks of the jurists, the exoteric and literal-minded legalists who could see nothing beyond the surface meaning.[11] This may also be the case for the Ikhwān. In the following they provide a typical example of *ta'wīl*, investigating the significance of the prophetic custom of eating food with three fingers, not with the full hand. They point out that "food" is the nourishment of the body, and that a corresponding custom pertains to partaking of knowledge, the nourishment of the soul.

One of the practices of the prophetic norm and the beautiful acts of right conduct is to use three fingers to partake of food, which is the nourishment of the body. In this custom the one who established the norm for souls seems to have made an allusion, admonishing and inciting them to seek knowledge from three routes. For knowledge is the nourishment of the soul, just as food is the nourishment of the body. And the states of the soul are similar to the states of the body, because the connection between the two is so strong.

One of the routes by which the soul partakes of knowledge is the faculty of reflection [*fikr*], through which the soul perceives the intelligible existents. By this route the prophets take revelation from the angels.

The second route is hearing [*samʿ*], by which the soul receives the meanings of words and the tidings of absent things denoted by the sounds.

The last is the route of sight [*naẓar*], by which souls witness existent things that are present.

Sciences must be acquired by these three routes, as God has admonished us. For He said, "It is He who made for you hearing and eyes and hearts—little thanks you show" [23:78]. Thereby He blames those who do not make use of these blessings. He also says, "They have hearts, but understand not with them. They have eyes, but see not with them. They have ears, but hear not with them. They are like cattle—no, they are even more misguided" [7:179]. He also says, "Deaf, dumb, blind—they do not understand" [2:171]. They are deaf to the realities, dumb to the subtleties, blind to the supra-sensory, intelligible objects that are seen with the eye of the heart. God does not mean to blame them for not hearing sounds, not seeing colors, and not knowing the affairs of livelihood. No, He blames them only for not understanding the affair of the return to God [*maʿād*], as He said, "They know an outward dimension of the life of this world, but of the next world they are heedless" [30:7].[12]

Names of the Unseen

The human microcosm can be divided into two fundamental dimensions corresponding to heaven and earth: the unseen and the visible, or spirit and body, or the Dominion and the Kingdom. Complications arise immediately because of the variety of words that are employed to refer to the inner, invisible dimension of the human being. The Koran employs three primary words, *rūḥ* (spirit), *qalb* (heart), and *nafs* (soul, self), while using other words, such as *ʿaql* (intellect), to refer to certain qualities of the same dimension. The semantic fields of the Koranic terms overlap, and our authors use the terms in ways that reflect the fluidity of their meanings.

Most texts that deal in any detail with the unseen realities of the macrocosm and/or the microcosm distinguish between various levels or degrees of the unseen dimension. Even those who draw no distinction between the terms *spirit* and *soul* will differentiate among a number of levels within the spirit or the soul. Some speak of the vegetal, animal, and human spirits, while others refer to the same realities as the vegetal, animal, and human souls. In order to distinguish among these levels, the Muslim cosmologists and psychologists speak of relationship between the various levels, or of differing intensities in which the levels manifest certain qualities. Invariably they envisage a hierarchy. Terms such as *lower* and *higher* refer to a trajectory leading from the simplest signs of life and activity, as found, for example, in plants, to the perfection of these same qualities as found in human beings and beyond.

What is of particular interest here is the relationship envisaged between any two levels, since this is frequently discussed in terms of activity and receptivity, with the upper level usually being active and the lower level receptive. In Sufi texts in particular, the higher and dominant dimension of the inward human reality is called *rūḥ* (spirit), while the lower and receptive dimension is called *nafs* (soul). The demarcation lines are never very clear, since we are dealing with an invisible realm where exact boundaries cannot be drawn. Moreover, boundaries shift as relationships change. Something that has the qualities of *rūḥ* from one point of view may have the qualities of *nafs* from another point of view.

Considered as an invisible dimension of the cosmos, spirit and soul are marked by a number of conspicuous attributes, most salient among them being life, since the unseen dimension of existence animates the visible realm. As Rūmī puts it,

> Have not the earthen clods—the bodies—come to life through the radiance of the spirit? Marvelous shining light! Wonderful life-increasing sun![13]

As in Latin, Hebrew, and other languages, the words for soul and spirit allude to this animating power. *Rūḥ* (spirit) derives from the same root as *rīḥ* (wind), while *nafs* or soul is written the same as *nafas* (breath). We perceive the presence of the spirit for reasons analogous to our knowledge of the existence of wind: The rustling of the leaves. In the same way, the breathing of a breather signifies the presence of life and the soul. The moment the breath is gone, the soul also disappears. In Rūmī's words, "The poor body will not move until the spirit moves. Until the horse goes forward, the saddlebag stands still."[14]

Signs of the Microcosm

For most authors of the intellectual tradition, the various names applied to the inward dimension of the human being do not refer to distinct and autonomous entities, but to different qualities or degrees of a single reality. Ghazālī makes this point clearly in his magnum opus, *Iḥyāʾ ʿulūm al-dīn*. I take the following passages from *Kīmiyā-yi saʿādat*, which summarizes in simple and elegant Persian many of the *Iḥyā*ʾ's important discussions. At the very beginning of the work, he explains this view of the human self, and he clearly identifies this view—as do the other authors with whom we are dealing—with the essence of the Islamic teachings.

Note the basic correspondences that Ghazālī draws. These are normative for the whole tradition. The human being is compounded of a large number of qualities, and the nature of these qualities can be understood by finding in the macrocosm the realities that make them manifest. These qualities display the three "directions" of existence: ascending (angelic), descending (demonic), and dispersive (animal). The dispersive tendency is in turn divided into two kinds, represented in the macrocosm by two basic kinds of animals: Beasts (*bahīma, sutūr*) and predators (*sibāʿ, dadagān*). The predominant quality of the first is appetite (*shahwa*) and of the second anger (*ghaḍab*). These are the two fundamental tendencies of the animal soul. The term *shahwa* has usually been rendered into English in philosophical works as "concupiscence," while *ghaḍab* has been translated as "irascibility." Since both terms are Koranic and used in a wide variety of contexts, from everyday speech to philosophy, I prefer to employ common English words that provide something of the broad sense of the terms.

Both appetite and anger, in their own places, are positive. "Appetite" is the faculty or power that attracts the soul toward anything that is agreeable to it, such as food and the sexual act. "Anger" is the faculty that turns the soul against anything disagreeable and defends the organism from threats. It can manifest itself in violence or flight. Both faculties are absolutely essential to the survival of all animals, including human beings. But in human beings, appetite and anger must be made subservient to the angelic faculty known as "intellect," which is by nature obedient to the will of God. The angels, as the Koran puts it, "disobey God not in what He commands them and do what they are commanded" (66:6). Here is Ghazālī's explanation of these points:

> Know that the key to knowledge of God is knowledge of one's own soul. That is why it has been said, "He who knows his own soul knows his Lord." That is also why God said, "We shall show them Our signs upon the horizons and within their souls, until it is clear to them that He is the Real" [41:53].
>
> In short, nothing is closer to you than you. If you do not know yourself, how will you know the other? Moreover, you may think that you know yourself and be mistaken, for this kind of knowing is not the key to the knowledge of the Real. The beasts know this much of themselves—since of yourself you know no more than the outward head, face, hands, feet, flesh, and skin. Of the inward dimension you know that when you are hungry, you eat bread, and when you are angry, you fall on the other person, and when appetite dominates, you make for the marriage act. All the beasts know that much.
>
> Hence you must seek your own reality. What thing are you? From whence have you come? Where will you go? For what work have you come to this dwelling place? Why were you created? What and where is your felicity? What and where is your wretchedness?

The terms *felicity* (*saʿāda*) and *wretchedness* (*shaqāʾ* or *shaqāwa*) are employed by the Muslim authorities to refer to the ultimate state of the soul in paradise or hell. The locus classicus for the terms is Koran 11:105–8, in reference to the Day of Resurrection: "On the day it comes, no soul shall speak save by His leave. Some of them shall be wretched and some felicitous. As for the wretched, they shall be in the Fire. . . . And as for the felicitous, they shall be in the Garden." By extension, "felicity" is employed to refer to the proper final end of anything, not just human beings, while "wretchedness" refers to failure to achieve this end.

> Some of the attributes that have been gathered together within you belong to the beasts, some to the predators, some to the devils, and some to the angels. Of all these, which are you? Which one is found in the reality of

your substance? Which ones are alien to you and borrowed? If you do not know this, you can not seek your own felicity. For each of these has a different food and a different felicity:

The food and felicity of the beasts lie in eating, sleeping, and mating. If you are a beast, strive day and night to keep the business of your stomach and private parts in order.

The food and felicity of the predators lie in tearing, killing, and being angry. The food of the devils lies in stirring up evil, deceiving, and duping. If you are one of them, busy yourself with your work so that you may reach your ease and felicity.

The food of angels and their felicity lie in witnessing the beauty of the Divine Presence. Envy, anger, and the attributes of beasts and predators have no access to them. If you have an angelic substance at your root, strive to know the Divine Presence. Find a way to witness that Beauty and deliver yourself from the hand of appetite and anger. Seek to know why these attributes of beasts and predators that are found in you were created. Were they created to make you their prisoner, to make you serve them, and to take forced labor from you? Or so that you may make them prisoner in the journey you have ahead of you and take forced labor from them? So that you could make one of them into your mount and the other into your weapon? So that, in these few days when you live in this dwelling place, you may employ them to hunt, with their help, the seed of your felicity? Then, when you bring the seed of your felicity to hand, you can place them under your feet and turn your face to the resting place of your own felicity: The elect call it the "Divine Presence," and the common people call it "paradise." . . .

If you want to know yourself, you should know that when you were created, two things were created: One is this outward frame, which is called the body. It can be seen with the outward eye. The second is the inward meaning, which is called the soul, the spirit, and the heart. It can be recognized through inward insight but cannot be seen with the outward eye. Your reality is that inward meaning. Everything else follows upon it. Everything else is its soldier and servant.

We will refer to this reality as the "heart." When we speak of the heart, you should know that we mean the human reality, which is sometimes called spirit and sometimes soul. By "heart" we do not mean the piece of flesh placed in the left side of the chest, since that has no importance. Beasts and corpses also have that, and it can be seen with the outward eye. Everything that can be seen with the eye belongs to this world, which is called the "visible world."

The heart's reality does not belong to this world. It has come into this world as a stranger and a passerby. The outward piece of flesh is the heart's mount and instrument. All the parts of the body are its soldiers. The heart is the king of the whole body, and its attribute is knowing God and witnessing the beauty of His presence. Religious prescriptions are made for it, and it is addressed by God. Rebuke and punishment apply to it, and fundamental felicity or wretchedness belong to it. In all of this, the body follows the spirit.

The knowledge of the reality of the heart and its attributes is the key to the knowledge of God. Strive to know it, since it is a precious substance, of the same substance as the angels. Its fundamental quarry is the Divine Presence. It came from there and will return there. It has come here as a stranger in order to trade and till.[15]

In *Iḥyāʾ ʿulūm al-dīn* Ghazālī makes similar points but in much more detail, explaining how the terms *soul, heart, spirit,* and *intellect* can all refer to the same reality but from different points of view.[16] Sufis such as ʿAzīz al-Dīn Nasafī present the same sort of ideas but with less of a view toward the abstract mode of logical discussion employed by theologians and philosophers and more attention to the qualitative symbolism of the terms. In the following, Nasafī divides the spirit into five levels, according to the qualities that are manifest at each level. In the lower levels, the attributes of plants and animals are displayed, while in the higher levels, the all-inclusive divine attributes become more and more apparent.

Know that human beings have a natural spirit located in the liver, on the right side. They have an animal spirit located in the heart, on the left side. They have a psychic spirit located in the brain. They have a human spirit located in the psychic spirit. And they have a holy spirit located in the human spirit.

The holy spirit is like fire, the human

spirit like oil, the psychic spirit like a wick, the animal spirit like a glass, and the natural spirit like a niche. This is the meaning of God's words, "God is the light of the heavens and the earth. The likeness of His light is as a niche wherein is a lamp (the lamp in a glass, the glass as it were a glittering star) kindled from a Blessed Tree, an olive that is neither of the East nor the West, whose oil would almost shine, even if no fire touched it" [24:35].[17]

The reality of these words in the view of the People of the Sharia is that when a child is in the womb of its mother for three forty-day retreats—which is four months—God sends an angel to blow this human spirit into the child. The spirit belongs to the World of Command and was created many thousands of years before the child's body, but it had remained in God's neighborhood. After three forty-day retreats the child comes to life.[18]

The human spirit has been called by several names according to various relationships and viewpoints:

In respect of the fact that it can increase or decrease and change from state to state it is called the "heart" [*qalb*].[19]

In respect of the fact that it is alive and bestows life on the body it is called the "spirit."

In respect of the fact that it knows itself and gives the quality of knowing to the other, it is called the "intellect."

In respect of the fact that it is truly simple and cannot be divided into parts, it is called the "spirit of the Command."

In respect of the fact that it comes from the higher world and is the same kind as the angels it is called the "angelic spirit."

In respect of the fact that it is disengaged, detached, pure, and purified, it is called the "holy spirit."

This is what is meant by the words of him who says that the prophets and friends of God have five spirits, the people of faith have four spirits, and the unbelievers and children have three spirits. This also explains what some people mean when they say that the prophets and friends of God have ten spirits.

Dervish, if someone says that the human being has one hundred spirits and one hundred intellects, that also would be correct, since a single thing can be called by a hundred names in keeping with a hundred viewpoints. No plurality and multiplicity become necessary for that thing. This means that it may be said that for every praiseworthy or blameworthy attribute a human being possesses, he has a spirit, such as the angelic spirit or the satanic spirit. The reason for this is that the spirit is a single reality, but this single reality has the receptivity for imperfection or perfection. In other words, it is receptive toward low and base works, and it has the preparedness for high and noble works. This is the meaning of the verse, "The unbelievers of the People of the Book and the idolaters shall be in the fire of Gehenna, therein dwelling forever. They are the worst creatures. But those who have faith and do righteous works—they are the best creatures" [98:6–7].

Hence the human being is called by any attribute by which he is qualified. In respect of any attribute, he can be said to possess a spirit or an intellect. Hence, everyone who has more character traits and attributes has more spirit and intellect. Though the substance of intellect and the substance of spirit is not capable of increase and decrease in respect of substance, it is receptive to imperfection and perfection in respect of the fact that it receives accidents and attributes. Hence it is referred to in terms of manyness and fewness.[20]

Note here that Nasafī sees receptivity as the fundamental attribute of the human reality. It is this yin quality, almost infinite in scope, that allows human beings to change and develop in every conceivable direction. Receptivity is the key to human nature, as the Muslim philosophers, among others, point out clearly. We will return to this point in the next chapter.

Spirit

Characteristically, Sufi authors based their explanations of the human situation on the verses of the Koran and the hadiths of the Prophet. When discussing the human spirit, they paid particularly close attention to the verses that allude to some sort of identity between the human and divine spirits. It needs to be remembered here that the Koran never mentions the term *divine spirit* (*al-rūḥ al-ilāhī*) as such. In several verses it mentions "the spirit" (*al-rūḥ*), and the commentators generally consider this to be identical with the greatest of the angels. Thus the cosmographer Qazwīnī (d. 682/1283) tells us that the spirit is the greatest angel and occupies one row by itself, while the rest of the angels occupy a second row. He cites in proof the Koranic verse, "On the day the Spirit and the angels stand in ranks" (78:38).[21]

The ambiguous nature of the spirit comes to the fore in several Koranic verses where the human spirit is mentioned, since these make clear that this spirit is not different from God's own spirit, whatever may be the relationship between "God's spirit" and God. The Koran speaks of God's spirit in three verses connected to the creation of human beings. In each case, God is said to proportion Adam's clay, then to blow something of His own spirit into it:

> And when thy Lord said to the angels, "See, I am creating a mortal from a clay of molded mud. When I have proportioned him, and blown into him of My spirit, fall you down, prostrating yourselves before him!" (15:28–29 and 38:72)
>
> And He originated the creation of man out of clay, then He fashioned his progeny of an extraction of mean water, then He proportioned him, and He blew into him of His spirit. (32:7–9)

In the Islamic view, God is not a "spiritual" being, as Christian authors often maintain, but the Creator of all spirits. Hence in creating the macrocosm, God created two basic worlds, the spiritual and the corporeal, or the unseen and the visible. The spiritual domain is inhabited by spirits, intellects, and angels, all of whom are basically identical in substance, though diverse in function and certain qualities—hence the diversity of the names. The "substance" of the angels, according to a well-known hadith, is light, and light is associated with manifestation, knowledge, and awareness.

Although the spirit is created, it retains an ambiguity that does not allow us to disentangle it completely from the divine domain. Hence it is commonly said that the reality of the spirit is difficult for human beings to grasp, and the following Koranic verse is cited in support of this view: "They will ask you about the spirit. Say, 'The spirit is from the command of my Lord, and of knowledge you are given but little'" (17:85). Rūmī says,

> It is understood from "Say: 'The spirit is from the command of my Lord'" that the spirit's explanation cannot be uttered by the tongue.[22]

Though many authorities read this verse to imply that the spirit cannot be understood, they do not mean to say that no knowledge of it can be acquired. What is being said is that the spirit cannot be defined as it is in itself, in contrast to, for example, the body, which can be known, described, measured, dissected, and so on. However, if discursive knowledge of the spirit in itself is unavailable, a great deal of discursive knowledge about the *attributes* of the spirit is in fact provided both by human experience and revealed texts. These attributes, in turn, delineate the relationships that are established between the spirit and the body. Typically, for example, the spirit is said to "govern" (*tadbīr*) the body, and here the relationship is clear. But even when the intrinsic attributes of spirit, such as life, are mentioned, the relationship with the body is understood, since the body—in and of itself—is dead. It can live only through the spirit's presence within it. Rūmī makes this point in the following verse, though he seems to have the Arabic term *soul* in mind rather than *spirit*, since he uses a feminine image:

> When the soul (*jān*) goes, place me beneath the earth—When the lady leaves, the house gathers dust.[23]

Ghazālī provides one of the earliest and most detailed descriptions of the spirit and its relationships with other realities in *Iḥyāʾ ʿulūm al-dīn*.[24] The following is from his *Kīmiyā-yi saʿādat*:

> As for the reality of the heart—what thing it is and what its specific attributes are—the revealed Law has not given permission [to

discuss this]. That is why the Messenger of God did not explain it, as God said, "They will ask you about the spirit. Say, 'The spirit is from the command of my Lord.'" He received permission to say no more than that the spirit is a divine business and it pertains to the "World of the Command."

Concerning the World of Command, the Koran says, "Verily, His are the creation and the command" [7:54]. The World of Creation is on one side and the World of Command on the other. When area, measurement, and quantity have access to something, that is called the "World of Creation." At root, *khalq* means to arrange in measure [*taqdīr*], but the human heart has no measure or quantity. That is why it cannot be divided into parts. If it could be divided into parts, then one side of it could be ignorant of something and the other side have knowledge of the same thing. It would be knowing and ignorant in the same state. But this is absurd.

Though the spirit cannot be divided into parts or touched by measure, it is "created." The word *khalq* also means creation, just as it means to arrange in measure. In this meaning, the spirit is part of creation, but in the other meaning it pertains to the World of Command, not the World of Creation, since the World of Command consists of those things to which area and measure have no access.

Hence those who suppose that the spirit is eternal [*qadīm*] are mistaken, and those who say that it is an accident are also mistaken. For an accident cannot subsist in itself, only through subordination. But the spirit is the root of the human being, while the whole frame is subordinate to the spirit. How could the spirit be an accident?

Those who say that the spirit is a body are also mistaken, since the body can be divided into parts, but the spirit cannot. However, there is something else which is also called "spirit" and which can be divided into parts, but that spirit is also possessed by animals. As for the spirit which I refer to as "heart," that is the locus for the knowledge of God. Animals have no such thing. It is neither body nor accident. On the contrary, it is a substance of the same kind as the substance of the angels.

To know the reality of the heart is difficult, and permission to explain it has not been given. At the beginning of walking on the path of religion, there is no need for knowledge of it. On the contrary, the beginning of the path of religion is spiritual struggle [*mujāhada*]. When a person performs the spiritual struggle as he should, then he will himself actualize this knowledge, without hearing it from anyone. This knowledge is part of the "guidance" to which God refers in His words, "Those who struggle in Us—surely We shall guide them on Our paths" [29:69]. If a person has not yet finished his struggle, it is not permissible to tell him of the reality of the spirit. However, before struggle one must know the army of the heart, since he who does not know this army cannot undertake the holy war [*jihād*].[25]

This "struggle" on the path of God is the true "holy war," incumbent on all Muslims. Note that grammatically the two terms, *mujāhada* and *jihād*, are two different forms of the same word. The first, however, is used almost exclusively to refer to the inward struggle, while the second is used for both inward and outward struggles. The Prophet established the superiority of the inward struggle in his famous saying upon returning from a battle with the unbelievers, "I have returned from the lesser *jihād* to the greater *jihād*."[26]

Najm al-Dīn Rāzī looks at the Koranic ascription of the human spirit to God and concludes that its special relationship with the divine reality puts it at the top of the hierarchy of created things. Hence it is intimately connected with the creative word of God, "Be!" (*kun*), which is written with the two Arabic letters *kāf* and *nūn*.

Know that the human spirit belongs to the World of Command and is singled out for a nearness to the Presence possessed by no other existent thing. . . .

The World of Command consists of a world that does not accept measure, quantity, or extent. In contrast, the World of Creation accepts measure, quantity, and extent. The name "Command" was given to the World of the Spirits because it became manifest as a result of the indication "Be!" without temporal delay or material intermediary. Although the World of Creation also appeared through the indication "Be!", it did so through the intermediary of material things and the extension of days. "He created the heavens and the earth in six days" [7:54].

In God's saying, "Say, 'The spirit is of my Lord's command,'" there is an indication that the spirit, in all its wondrous nature, arose from the *kāf* and the *nūn* of the address *kun* with neither matter nor hyle. It found life from the attribute of "He, the Alive" [2:255]. It subsisted through the divine attribute of self-subsistence [2:255]. The spirit is itself the matter from which the World of Spirits is derived. The World of Spirits in turn is the origin of the World of the Dominion. And the World of the Dominion is the source of the World of the Kingdom. The whole World of the Kingdom subsists through the World of the Dominion. The World of the Dominion subsists through the World of Spirits. The World of Spirits subsists through the human spirit. And the human spirit subsists through God's attribute of self-subsisting. . . .

Whatever comes into being in the Worlds of the Kingdom and the Dominion does so by means of an intermediary, with the exception of the existence of the human being, for his spirit first appeared at the indication "Be!" without any intermediary. The form of his bodily frame was also kneaded without intermediary: "I kneaded the clay of Adam with My two hands for forty days." And when it was time for the pairing [*izdiwāj*] of the spirit with the bodily frame, the human being was honored with "I blew into him" without intermediary. Thereby he was singularly ennobled with the attribution "of My spirit," as if God wished to say, "a spirit that is alive with My life." Just as the spirit was brought into existence by God's command, so too did God attribute the existence of the spirit to His command—"of my Lord's command." And because the life of the spirit was brought into existence by the divine attribute of life-giving, this too He attributed to Himself, saying, "of My spirit."[27]

In an approach closer to the school of Ibn al-ʿArabī, Nasafī analyzes the spirit in terms of the divine attributes present within it. God is absolute and nondelimited Light, while the substance of the angelic or spiritual world is created light. The attributes of this created light can be known from the point of view of either incomparability or similarity. If we take the first point of view, we see that created, angelic light is utterly different from uncreated Light, possessing no common measure accessible to our understanding. It remains a mystery why God and His Prophet chose to employ the same word for two completely different realities. But from the point of view of similarity, if the Prophet chose to call the angels "light," they must reflect in a rather direct way that which can properly be called "light," God Himself. Hence the attributes of God predominate in their nature. They possess unity, life, knowledge, and so on, in contrast to creatures made of clay, which are multiple and in themselves dead, ignorant, and so on. Nasafī makes many of these points in the following passage:

The human being has a manifest dimension and a nonmanifest dimension. In other words, he has a body and a spirit. The spirit is truly simple and cannot be divided into parts. It belongs to the World of Command. The body is compound and can be divided into parts. It belongs to the World of Creation.

Having learned this much, you should know that every compound thing has within itself manyness and parts. When a thing has manyness and parts, each of its attributes and acts is singled out for one of its parts and organs. For example, if that thing sees, hears, takes, and speaks, it hears through one part, speaks through another part, and sees through another part.

When a thing is simple, it has no manyness and parts. None of its attributes and acts is singled out for a part or an organ, since there are no parts or organs. It has no front and back, no head and foot, no right and left. Hence its attributes subsist through its own self. If such a thing should see, hear, speak, and have knowledge, it does each through the same thing through which it does the rest.

Now that you have come to know this much, you should know that the human spirit, which is truly simple, is living, knowing, hearing, seeing, and speaking. Its attributes do not resemble the attributes of the bodily frame, since the frame hears from one place, sees from another place, and speaks from another place. But if the human spirit is alive, you have to say that it is all life. If it knows, you have to say that it is all knowledge. If it hears, you have to say that it is all hearing. If it sees, you have to say that it is all sight. If it speaks, you have to say that it is all speech. For its attributes and acts have no instruments and organs. This is the meaning of the saying, "God created Adam in His own form." This is also the meaning of "He who knows himself knows his Lord."[28]

The business of the spirit is governing the body. In other words, from the point of view of the inherent structure of the cosmos, the spirit is heaven and the body is earth, the spirit yang and the body yin, the spirit lord and the body servant, the spirit high and the body low. Nasafī refers repeatedly to this relationship in explaining how the one spirit can come into contact with a multiplicity of bodily parts.

> The human frame is a world. Or rather, it is many worlds. The human spirit is the lord of this world. In this world, no organ is empty of the spirit, while the spirit belongs to none of the organs.
>
> Dervish, if it is said that cream is neither in the milk nor outside the milk, and milk is neither in the cream nor outside the cream, this is correct. For no part of the cream is empty of milk and no part of the milk is empty of cream. That is why, in this world, the spirit is not near to some parts and far from others, or present with some and absent from others. The crown of the head of this world, which is the Throne, and the bottom of its foot, which is under the earth of this world, are identical. Both are governed without any distinction of place. Moreover, the spirit's control of this world does not take place through reflection, thought, instrument, or limb. That is why it is said that no business ever distracts the spirit from any other business. "No task distracts it from any other task." In other words, when it governs the head, this does not distract it from governing the foot, and when it governs the foot, this does not distract it from governing the hand.[29]

The difference between spirit and body lies in the qualities possessed by each. Although God is present in all things in respect of the Breath of the All-merciful, since His Breath is their very substance, in another respect He is more intensely present in some things than in others, since the divine attributes manifest themselves in different degrees, thus giving rise to qualitative diversity. Some things are more luminous and some less. The distinction between the most luminous and the least luminous things in a cosmos that manifests every possible degree of luminosity allows us to speak of light and darkness as relatively absolute differences. A candle next to the sun is, in effect, dark. This sort of ranking in degrees applies to every attribute. Thus, for example, the spirit is near to God, the body far from Him. The spirit is knowing, the body ignorant. The spirit is alive, the body dead. The spirit is desiring, the body without desires. The Ikhwān al-Ṣafāʾ allude to these points in the following:

> The substances of the souls possess a station and nobility with God not possessed by the substances of the bodies, since souls have a close relationship with Him, while the relationship of the bodies is far. This is because the substances of the souls are alive in themselves, knowing, and active, while the substances of the bodies are dead and receive the activity of their likes.[30]

Soul

The term *nafs* may be translated as "soul" or "self." As remarked earlier, many authors make no distinction between *nafs* and *rūḥ*, dealing rather with different degrees of a single reality that may be called by either name. When authors distinguish between the two, the purpose is the same as in dividing either into degrees: To show how a single, invisible reality, the inward dimension of the human being, possesses a variety of qualities and how these qualities manifest themselves in different modes. In other words, the inward/outward or unseen/visible dichotomy drawn by Muslim authors is never a simple, dualistic, mind/body split. On the contrary, the inward and invisible dimension is itself complex. In order to bring out its complexity, one investigates how it manifests a great variety of divergent qualities whether at the same time or in different circumstances. These qualities can then be classified into hierarchical groups. There is nothing artificial about the hierarchies, since they pertain to the very nature of the qualities.

The typical philosophical mode of dealing with the structure of the microcosm is to divide it into levels of soul or spirit, the inherent and salient attribute of which is life. Then the vegetal soul possesses qualities such as growth, nutrition, attraction, expulsion, digestion, and retention. The animal soul possesses in addition the five senses, imagination, appetite, and anger. The human soul adds to these intelligence and reflective thought.

Hierarchy is inherent to the discussion, since to speak of a plant is to speak of something that to a certain degree rules over the inanimate world precisely because of its basic qualities. In the same way, to speak of an animal is to speak of something that possesses the vegetal qualities plus an added something that gives it power over plants. Likewise, the human being possesses "three spirits," since it has vegetal, animal, and human qualities. It is superior to the animals through the intelligence that sets it apart from the whole macrocosm.

This "great chain of being" found within qualities ties directly into the divine attributes. All the qualities found in inanimate objects, plants, animals, and humans have their roots in the divine names. In truth, there is "no life but God's life, no knowledge but God's knowledge, no power but God's power, no desire but God's desire." To the extent that these qualities are found in the cosmos, they show that all things are signs of God.

The tripartite division "body, soul, and spirit" plays the same role. Through it we come to understand that the movement from outward to inward involves an increasing intensity of ontological qualities. The trajectory of increase leads ultimately to infinite and absolute Being.

When spirit and soul are differentiated, soul commonly acts as a kind of *barzakh* (isthmus) between spirit and body. The spirit is made of light and, like the angels, totally disengaged from the bodily world. It is a single, simple reality. In contrast, the body is made from clay, which is dark and has many parts. There can be no direct connection between the luminous and disengaged reality that is the spirit and the dark conglomeration of parts that is the body. The soul possesses the qualities of both sides and acts as the intermediary between the two.

If the spirit is light and the body clay, the soul is fire. It is a mixture of light and clay, both one and multiple at the same time. It is subtle and luminous enough to establish a link with the spirit, but dense and dark enough to maintain contact with the body.

Koranic support for the spirit's higher rank can be found in several verses that ascribe to it qualities never given to the soul. Thus, as we saw above, the Koran attributes the spirit directly to God, in verses such as "I blew into him of My spirit." The word *nafs*, which also functions as a reflexive pronoun and in many Koranic usages can be translated "self" just as well or better than "soul," is usually envisaged at a lower level than *rūḥ*. In the sense of self the Koran sometimes uses the term *nafs* to refer to God. For example, Jesus is quoted as saying to God, "Thou knowest what is in my self but I know not what is in Thy self" (5:116). But the Koran makes no suggestion that the *nafs* of human beings and God are somehow intimately connected, as it does with the *rūḥ* of human beings and God. Commonly the Koran refers to the soul or self of human beings as that which is held responsible for activity and which will be rewarded or punished in the next world.

The Sufi authors were particularly concerned to ground their terminology in the Koran, in contrast to the Muslim philosophers, for example, who were deeply influenced by the translated works of the Greek philosophers. Hence the Sufis usually looked upon the spirit as intimately connected to God, while the soul or self represents the human being in an aspect of greater separation. In the Sufi cosmological texts, the spirit normally precedes the soul because of the natural hierarchy of the universe and the order of creation. The spirit pertains to the highest level of the cosmos, and everything else is ranked below it, step by step.

The hierarchical priority of the spirit is connected to an existential priority, in the sense that the soul comes into existence after the spirit and is in some respect less real than the spirit. In this connection the soul is often referred to as the spirit's child. More commonly, however, the relationship is envisaged as one that has already been established. The spirit dominates, since from it the divine qualities flow into the soul, qualities such as life, knowledge, desire, power, speech, hearing, and sight. The soul is receptive to these attributes and then makes them manifest through the body. The soul's natural relationship with the spirit is one of acceptance and receptivity.

The spirit fecundates the soul, and the soul gives birth to bodily activities in the visible world. In respect of this relationship, the spirit is frequently called the "husband," the soul the "wife." When the two of them marry in harmony, like Adam and Eve, they make the earth of the body fruitful and bring about the possibility of the return to the primordial unity from which they arose. Rūmī is not atypical in envisaging the relationship between intellect (the spirit inasmuch as it possesses the power of discernment and the luminosity of awareness) and soul in terms of the original couple. Nor is he atypical in thinking that the original relationship has been lost and must be restored through the establishment of unity (*tawḥīd*): "If duality were to leave our heart and spirit for a moment, our intellect would be Adam, our soul Eve."[31]

Once spirit and soul live in conjugal harmony, each performing the function proper to the relationship, the inward human dimension lives peacefully with the innermost reality (God) and with the outermost reality (the body). If their marriage fails and complementarity is not achieved, they cannot fulfill their proper functions.

In the spiritual psychology developed by the Sufis, the relationship between the male and female dimensions of the invisible human reality was frequently employed to describe the ideal and less than ideal psyches. But one has to read the texts carefully in order not to be misled by negative or positive evaluations of the feminine or masculine characteristics. The male/female relationship needs to be viewed in the whole context. In one respect the male side will be praised and the female side blamed, and in another respect the opposite is the case. Each attribute, male and female, may contribute to the ideal equilibrium or detract from it, depending on the situation envisaged. We will return to this point in the coming chapters.

Intellect

Intellect or intelligence (*ʿaql*) is a quality that is highly praised in the Koran and the hadith literature. Though the Koran does not use the noun itself, it employs its verbal form about fifty times. Translators usually render the verb with such words as "understand." Intelligence allows a person to grasp the significance of the signs of God. Note that in one verse the Koran locates it in the heart.

> Surely in the creation of the heavens and the earth and the alternation of night and day . . . there are signs for a people having intelligence. (2:164)
>
> And when it is said to them, "Follow what God has sent down," they say, "No; but we will follow such things as we found our fathers doing." What? And if their fathers had no intelligence whatsoever and were not guided? (2:170)
>
> And when you call to prayer, they take it in mockery and sport. That is because they are a people who have no intelligence. (5:58)
>
> Surely in that there are signs for a people who have intelligence. (13:4, 30:24)
>
> What, have they not journeyed in the land, so that they have hearts to intellect with or ears to hear with? It is not the eyes that are blind, but blind are the hearts within the breast. (22:46)

As we saw in previous chapters, macrocosmically the First Intellect is considered the first reality to emerge from the One, or God's initial step in bringing the manyness of the cosmos into existence. It plays an intermediary role and shares in both the oneness of the Real and the manyness of the things. As in the macrocosm, so in the microcosm: Intellect is the spirit considered as the most luminous dimension of the human being, the nearest to God, and thus the first dimension of the microcosm to enter into existence. The microcosmic applications of the hadith in which the Prophet says that intellect was the first thing created by God were obvious from earliest times. This is especially so in Shiʿite sources, which have a special fondness for intellect.

Intellect is that which discerns the hidden and unveils the unknown. Luminosity is inseparable from it, since light is that which removes darkness and obscurity. Also associated with intellect are the other positive qualities connected to the divine name Light, such as life, knowledge, desire, and power.[32] In fact, Light is one of the names of God's Essence, so it denotes the very nature of the Divinity. Like the sun that shines because it is the sun, God is luminous because He is God. His Light in itself is His Being, while in its manifestation it is existence, the cosmos, "everything other than God." Hence that which is luminous with a pure and unsullied light reflects all the divine names.

Early expressions of these ideas applied to the microcosm are found in a number of hadiths from Shiʿite collections. For example, the following is related from the Prophet:

> The intellect [*ʿaql*] is a fetter [*ʿiqāl*] against ignorance. The soul is like the worst of beasts. If it does not have intellect, it wanders bewildered, since the intellect is a fetter against ignorance.
>
> God created the intellect and said to it, "Turn away from Me" so it looked away. Then He said, "Turn toward Me," so it turned toward Him. Then He said, "By My might and majesty, I have created no creature greater than you nor more obedient than you. Through you I shall begin and through you I shall bring back. What is for you shall be rewarded, and what is against you shall be punished."
>
> Then from intellect branched off deliberation [*ḥilm*], from deliberation knowledge, from knowledge right guidance [*rushd*], from right guidance abstention, from abstention guarding, from guarding shame, from shame gravity, from gravity continuity in the good, from continuity in the good aversion to evil, and from aversion to evil obedience to the good counselor.[33]

The hadith goes on to mention ten good qualities that branch out from each of the ten qualities mentioned here. Thus we have an early version of the lists that in Sufi texts came to be called the "stations" (*maqāmāt*) of the spiritual path.

The sixth Shiʿite Imam, Jaʿfar al-Ṣādiq, provides a similar list of attributes or positive character traits connected to intellect, but he contrasts them with the negative qualities connected to intellect's opposite, ignorance (*jahl*). Implicit to this discussion is the fact that the attributes of intellect pertain to the prophets, while those of ignorance pertain to Iblis and his followers. The Koran repeatedly identifies the function of the prophets with guidance (*hudā* or *hidāya*), which is a divine attribute, since God is the Guide (*al-hādī*). And it identifies Iblis with misguidance (*iḍlāl*), as in the verse "This is of Satan's doing; he is surely a blatant misguiding enemy" (28:15). Of course, misguidance is also a divine attribute, since God is made the subject of the verb in about thirty Koranic verses, though few authorities would add the name Misguider (*al-muḍill*) to the lists of the Most Beautiful Names. The Koran places too much stress on the underlying unity of reality (*tawḥīd*) to allow Iblis to escape from God's control. But guidance leads to human felicity, while misguidance leads to wretchedness. If, from the divine point of view, the two attributes participate in the same task of making the Hidden Treasure manifest, from the human point of view they lead to profoundly different ends. In other words, guidance pertains to God's right hand, and misguidance to His left hand.

In the Koran God says, "We have appointed for every prophet an enemy" (6:112, 25:31). So also, every prophetic quality—every quality that aids in guidance—has an enemy. Both in the outside world and the inside world, the friends and enemies of God are defined by their attributes. In the microcosm, guidance is innate to the intellect, so intellect is the prophet's microcosmic analogue. As the Safavid philosopher Mullā Muḥsin Fayḍ Kāshānī (d. 1090/1679) puts it, "Intellect is a revealed law [Sharia] within the human being, just as the revealed law is an intellect outside of the human being. . . . In short, the source of all good qualities and the origin of all perfections is the intellect."[34] The enemies of intellect are the enemies of human perfection and the Prophet. They are the friends of Satan and misguidance.

Imam Jaʿfar's description of the contrasting attributes of intellect and ignorance illustrates that from early times Muslim thinkers were concerned to establish qualitative differences among the realities of both the outside world and the soul. How could they not be? For the Koran itself constantly attributes certain qualities to the faithful and the opposite qualities to the unbelievers. Notice, at the beginning of the hadith, the correlation between intellect and the right hand and the implication that ignorance stands on the left. Note also that the Imam uses the imagery of the king and his soldiers, as Ghazālī did after him.

> God created the Intellect—the first creature among the spiritual beings [*rūḥāniyyūn*]—from His light on the right side of His Throne. He said to it, "Turn away from Me" so it turned away. Then He said, "Turn toward Me," so it turned toward Him. Then He said, "I have created a great creature and ennobled him above all My creation."
>
> Then He created ignorance from the briny, dark ocean. He said to it, "Turn away from Me" so it turned away. Then He said, "Turn toward Me," but it did not turn. Then He said, "Have you waxed proud?"[35] So He cursed it.
>
> Then God appointed for the Intellect fifty-seven soldiers.[36] When ignorance saw how God had ennobled the Intellect and what He had given it, it conceived a hidden enmity toward it. Ignorance said, "O Lord, this is a creature like me. Thou hast created him, ennobled him, and given him strength, while I am his opposite and I have no strength against him. Give me soldiers the like as Thou hast given him."
>
> So God said, "Yes, and if you disobey Me after this, I will send you and your army away from My neighborhood and mercy." Ignorance said, "I am satisfied." So God gave it fifty-seven soldiers.

The rest of the hadith lists the opposing soldiers of the two camps, as summarized in Table 11.[37]

Table 11 Soldiers of Intellect and Ignorance According to Imam Jaʿfar al-Ṣādiq

SOLDIERS OF INTELLECT	SOLDIERS OF IGNORANCE
good (intellect's vizier)	evil (ignorance's vizier)
faith	disbelief
acknowledgement	denial
hope	despair
justice	injustice
satisfaction	anger
gratitude	ingratitude
desire	disheartenment
trust	greed
clemency	cruelty
mercy	wrath
knowledge	ignorance
understanding	stupidity
modesty	shamelessness
renunciation	craving
gentleness	encroachment
reverence	impudence
humility	pride
deliberation	haste
intelligence	foolishness
silence	idle talk
resignation	waxing proud
surrender	doubt

Table 11 Continued

SOLDIERS OF INTELLECT	SOLDIERS OF IGNORANCE
patience	uneasiness
forgiveness	vengeance
wealth	poverty
remembrance	distraction
remembering	forgetting
fond attachment	cutting off
contentment	greed
sharing	withholding
amity	enmity
faithfulness	treachery
obedience	disobedience
meekness	aggression
safety	affliction
love	hate
truthfulness	lying
truth	vanity
trustworthiness	betrayal
purity	adulteration
sagacity	dull-wittedness
kind masking	unveiling
guilelessness	deceptiveness
concealing	disclosing
ritual prayer	neglect
fasting	fast breaking
struggle	shirking
hajj	breaking the covenant
safeguarding one's words	backbiting
loving kindness to parents	undutifulness
reality	lip service
the approved	the disapproved
covering	displaying
guarding	proclamation
fairness	fervor
accommodation	infringement
cleanliness	filth
shame	boorishness
going straight to the goal	overstepping boundaries
ease	hardship
easiness	difficulty
blessing	obliteration
rightness	excessiveness
wisdom	caprice
gravity	frivolity
felicity	wretchedness
repentance	persistence
asking forgiveness	self-deception
mindfulness	carelessness
supplication	disdainfulness
liveliness	indolence
joy	sorrow
familiarity	separatedness
generosity	stinginess

The Spirit's Kingdom

We have seen two references in this chapter to the analogy between the spirit and the king. In chapter 1 a short passage from the Ikhwān al-Ṣafā᾽ was quoted comparing the soul to a king and the body to his city. Ghazālī provided an influential and far more detailed version of this analogy in *Iḥyā᾽ ʿulūm al-dīn*. Just as the king's fundamental function is to govern the kingdom, so also the spirit's fundamental function is to govern the body. A king has ministers and servants, and so also does the spirit. I quote from the briefer version of the analogy found in *Kīmiyā-yi saʿādat*. Remember that Ghazālī uses the term *heart* to refer to the inward dimension of the human being, whereas others may refer to the same reality as "spirit" or "soul." In Ghazālī's view, intellect is the heart's vizier, providing it with right guidance. In other words, as mentioned above, intellect is the microcosmic equivalent of a prophet.

> Know that the body is the kingdom of the heart, and the heart has many armies in the body. "And none knows the armies of thy Lord save He" [74:31]. The heart was created for the next world. Its business is the seeking of felicity. Its felicity lies in the knowledge of God. It acquires knowledge of God by coming to know the handiwork of God, which is the whole cosmos. It acquires knowledge of the wonders of the cosmos by way of the senses. The senses subsist through the bodily frame.
>
> Hence knowledge is the heart's prey, senses its snare, and the frame its horse and the carrier of its snare. That is why it needs the frame.
>
> The frame is compounded of water, earth, heat, and dampness. That is why it is weak. It stands in danger of destruction from within, because of hunger and thirst, and from without, because of fire and water, and because of the intentions of enemies, wild animals, and so on.
>
> Because of hunger and thirst, the frame needs food and drink. Hence it needs two armies, one outward, like hand, foot, mouth, and teeth; and one inward, like appetite for food and water.
>
> For the sake of fending off outward enemies, it needs two armies: one outward, like hand, foot, and arms; and one inward, like anger and wrath.
>
> Since it cannot seek a food which it does not see and cannot fend off an enemy which it does not see, it has need of perceptual faculties. Some of these are outward, that is, the five senses—eye, nose, ear, taste, and touch. Some are inward, and they also are five: the faculties of imagination, reflection, memory, recall, and intuition. Each of these faculties has a special business. If one of these should be defective, the human business in religion and this world will also be defective.
>
> All these armies, outward and inward, are under the command of the heart. It is the commander and king of them all. When the heart commands the tongue, at once the tongue begins to speak. When it commands the hand, it takes. When it commands the foot, it goes. When it commands the eye, it looks. When it commands the faculty of reflection, it thinks. By nature and obedience all of these are made to follow the heart's command. Thereby the heart will protect the body so that it may take its provisions, accomplish its hunt, finish trading for the next world, and scatter the seeds of its felicity.
>
> The obedience of this army to the heart is like the obedience of the angels to God. They cannot disobey God in any command. On the contrary, by nature and obedience they follow His command.
>
> Knowing the details of the heart's army is a long process. What has to be said here can be made known to you through an analogy:
>
> Know that the analogy of the body is a city. Hand, foot, and organs are like the craftsmen of the city. Appetite is like the tax-collector. Anger is like the police chief. The heart is the city's king, while intellect is the king's vizier. The king needs all these to keep the kingdom in order.
>
> The problem is that appetite is a liar, a meddler, and a troublemaker. Whenever intellect—the vizier—tells appetite to do something, it acts opposite his command. It always uses some pretext to take all the property in the storehouses of the kingdom as tax.
>
> Anger, which is the police chief, is evil tempered and exceedingly fierce and harsh. It likes nothing better than killing, breaking, and spilling.
>
> The king of the city should always consult with the vizier. The king must keep the lying tax collector chastened and he must not listen to anything he says in opposition to the

vizier. He must give the police chief control over the tax collector in order to prevent him from meddling. But he must always keep the police chief beaten and broken, so that he will not place his foot outside its boundaries. When the king does this, the business of the kingdom will be kept in order.

In a similar way the heart/king should work according to the instructions of the intellect. It must keep appetite and anger under the control and command of the intellect and it must not place the intellect in their power. Then the business of the kingdom of the body will be correct and it will not be cut off from the path of felicity and the way of reaching the Presence of Divinity. But if the heart makes intellect the prisoner of appetite and anger, the kingdom will be destroyed and the king will be wretched and ruined.[38]

The relationship between spirit and its various faculties is that between a king and his servants. But here the yang/yin polarity becomes more subtle, since everything that dwells between spirit as such and body as such has two faces, one turned toward the spirit and the other toward the body. In respect of the first face, the spirit is high and bright, while the thing itself is low and dark. In respect of the face that looks down toward the body, the middle reality takes on the attributes of spirit.

If we begin at the top of the created hierarchy, we see spirit as God's servant and vicegerent. It is yin in relation to God and yang in relation to everything below it. Each of the spirit's underlings is also a yin reality in relation to the spirit and a yang reality in relation to what it controls. But in some cases, there are several intermediaries before we reach the lowest realm, so the yin/yang relationship keeps on switching back and forth. Ghazālī brings this out while expanding upon his analogy. Each level is the servant or assistant (*khādim*) of the level that lies above it, being assisted in its turn by the level that lies below it.

From everything that has been said you have come to know that appetite and anger were created for the sake of food, drink, and preserving the body. Hence both are assistants of the body. The body was created to carry the senses. Hence the body is the assistant of the senses. The senses were created to spy for the intellect. They were to be its snare through which it might know the wonders of God's handiwork. Hence the senses are the assistant of the intellect. The intellect was created to be the heart's candle and lamp, so that through its light the heart might see the Presence of Divinity, which is the heart's paradise. Hence intellect is the assistant of the heart. The heart was created to gaze upon the beauty of the Presence of Divinity. When it busies itself with this, it is the servant and assistant of the threshold of the Divine Presence. That is the meaning of God's words, "I created jinn and mankind only to serve Me" [51:56].[39]

We have here a hierarchical set of relationships stretching from the inanimate objects, which are yin in relation to appetite and anger, to God Himself, who is yang in relation to all. But all this pertains to the natural and normative state of the human being. It does not mean that relationships necessarily observe this order. In fact, relationships are usually upset, which is why human beings are addressed by revelation. We will return to this point in detail.

Heaven and Earth

The structure of the human being is typically described in terms of worlds, levels, or activities. These terms are in no way exclusive, since worlds are defined in terms of levels—which indicate relationships with other worlds—and the activities that pertain to specific levels. What is peculiar about the microcosm is that it brings together and harmonizes all the worlds, levels, and activities found in the macrocosm.

Since the basic worlds are two, spiritual and corporeal, the description of how the microcosm functions centers upon how these two worlds interrelate. In the simplest analysis, as we have just seen in Ghazālī's description of the kingdom of the heart, the higher world is yang and the lower yin. In other words, the stress is laid upon the proper relationship between heaven and earth as reflected in the human being.

Hence those authors who apply *ta'wīl* to the Koranic text often read verses mentioning heaven and earth as applicable to spirit and body. For example, the first verse juxtaposing heaven and earth in the Koran is the following: "O people, serve your Lord . . . , who assigned to you earth for a bedding, and heaven for a building, and sent down out of heaven water, wherewith He brought forth fruits for your provision. So set not up compeers to God willingly" (2:22). After explaining certain allusions found in the macrocosmic sense of the verse, Maybudī adds:

> The Masters of the Realities have commented [*tafsīr*] on this verse in a different way and have seen a different intimation. They say that these are likenesses [*mathal*] that God has placed in this verse. The earth is the likeness of the body, the heaven the likeness of the intellect, and the water that comes down out of heaven is the likeness of the knowledge that is actualized through intellect. The fruits are the likeness of the servant's praiseworthy behavior on the basis of knowledge.
>
> Thus the allusion of the verse is as follows: God is that lord who has created you as a person, a form, and a body. Then He adorned the body with the beauty of intellect. Then by means of intellect He gave knowledge, cleverness, and science. From that knowledge great fruits were produced. Those fruits are praiseworthy behavior, within which are found your soul's food and its good life. Since that Lord shows such kindness and mercy to you, why do you worship others along with Him and associate partners with Him?[40]

Kāshānī frequently makes heaven and earth correspond to spirit and soul or body in applying *ta'wīl* to Koranic verses, as in his summary of the meaning of the above verse:

> God spread out for them the earths, their souls. He built over them the heavens, their spirits. He sent down out of heaven water, which is the knowledge to profess the unity of His acts. Therewith He brought forth from that earth the plant of surrender, good works, acts of obedience, and beautiful character traits, to provide their hearts through them with fruits, which are certainty, states, and stations, such as patience, thanksgiving, and trust.[41]

Here Kāshānī follows Sufi technical terminology that we have met: The character traits actualized by the soul as it gradually achieves its perfection are the "stations" (*maqāmāt*) of the spiritual path. The ongoing and ever-changing transformations and transmutations that the soul experiences are "states" (*aḥwāl*).[42] In this perspective, "spirit" is the divine light within the human being, while "soul" is the inward reality that experiences the actualization of the divine light through becoming more and more illuminated.

In another typical passage, Kāshānī comments on one of the many Koranic verses (2:164) that urge people to use their intelligence to understand the signs of the macrocosm:

> *Surely in the creation of the heavens and the earth*: Surely in the bringing into existence of the heavens, which are the spirits, hearts, and intellects, and the earth, which is the souls. *And the diversity of night and day*, the light and darkness that differentiate the two. *And the ship*, the body, *that runs in the sea*, the Nondelimited Body *with profit to men* in gaining their perfections. *And the water*, knowledge, *that God sends down from heaven*, the spirit, *therewith reviving the earth*, the soul, *after it was dead* through ignorance. *And His scattering abroad in it all manner of crawling thing*, the animal faculties that live through the life of the heart. *And the turning about of the winds*, the forceful winds that increase God-given acts, *and the clouds*, the self-disclosure of lordly attributes, *subjected*, or arranged, *between heaven*, the spirit, *and earth*, the soul. *Surely there are signs*, indications, *for a people who have intelligence* illumined with the light of the Sharia and disengaged from the stain of sensory intuition.[43]

According to implications of the hadith of the Hidden Treasure, God creates heaven and earth in order to manifest His own perfections through "everything between the two," the Ten Thousand Things. Heaven and earth are the two principles upon which creation is built. So also, God creates spirit and body to manifest His own perfections within His own "form," which is the human being. As divine images, human beings are the loci wherein the divine names and attributes reach full actuality. In commenting on Koran 13:3, Kāshānī correlates earth with the body. When heaven's rain falls on the earth, the earth gives birth to the Ten Thousand Things: When the spirit effuses its light upon the body, the body gives birth to the soul. The soul, as conjunction of spirit and body, is the locus within which all the perfections of heaven and earth become outwardly manifest. In other words, the body is the womb wherein the child—the heart—is born.

It is He who stretched out the earth, the body, *and set therein firm mountains*, the bones, *and rivers*, the veins. *And of every fruit*, character traits and perceptions, *He placed there pairs*, that is, two contrasting kinds, such as generosity and stinginess, shame and shamelessness, licentiousness and continence, timidity and courage, wrongdoing and justice; and such as black and white, sweetness and sourness, freshness and rottenness, heat and cold, smoothness and roughness.

He makes the night, the darkness of corporeal things, *cover the day*, the spiritual things. In the same way the spiritual faculties are covered by organs and the spirit is covered by the body.

Surely in that there are signs for a people who reflect on God's handiwork and the correspondence between its two worlds, the microcosm and the macrocosm.

And in the earth, the body, *are tracts neighboring each to each*, like bones, flesh, fat, and nerves. *And gardens* of trees, which are natural, animal, and human faculties; *of grapes*, which are appetitive faculties, from which is squeezed the wine of the soul's caprice, and intellective faculties, from which is squeezed the wine of loving kindness with the squeezing of love. *And fields sown*, the vegetal faculties. *And palms*, the other outward and inward faculties. *In pairs*, like the two eyes, two ears, and two nostrils, *and not in pairs*, such as the tongue, the instrument of reflection, intuition, and recall. *Watered with one water*, the water of life. *And some of them We prefer above others in fruit*, that is, in perceptions and acquired habits. Thus the objects of intellect's perception are preferred over those of the senses, and sight is preferred over touch. So also the acquired habit of wisdom is preferred over temperance, and so on. *Surely in that are signs for a people who have intelligence* to perceive the marvels of His making.[44]

In commenting on Koran 14:32–34, Kāshānī illustrates the proper relationship between spirit and body:

It is God who created the heavens, the spirits, *and the earth*, the body. He *sent down out of heaven*, the world of holiness, the *water* of knowledge, *wherewith He brought forth* from the earth of the body the *fruits* of wisdoms and virtues, *to be your provision* so that your heart might be strengthened through them. *And He subjected to you the ship*[45] *to run at His command; and He subjected to you the rivers* of knowledge through deduction, discovery, induction, and classification. *And He subjected to you the sun*, the spirit, *and the moon*, the heart, *untiring* in their courses through unveiling and contemplation. *He subjected to you the night*, the darkness of the attributes of the soul, *and the daytime*, the light of the spirit, for seeking livelihood, the next life, ease, and illumination. *And He gave you of all you asked Him* with the tongue of your preparednesses [*istiʿdād*], for everything asks Him with the tongue of its preparedness for a perfection that is effused upon it along with the question, without lag or delay. Thus God says, "All those in the heavens ask from Him; each day He is upon some task" [55:29].[46]

In commenting on Koran 6:99, Kāshānī again shows how a description of God's creativity in the macrocosm can easily be applied to the microcosm by observing qualitative correspondences.

It is He who sent down out of heaven, the spirit, *water*, knowledge. *And thereby We have brought forth every plant*, every kind of character trait and virtue. *And then We have brought forth* from the plant a *green* condition, which is the soul. It is a lovely, beautiful ornament and a joy through knowledge and character. *We bring forth from* that condition, which is the fresh, tender soul, *close-*

> *compounded grain*, that is, ordered, noble, and pleasing works and truthful intentions, from which the heart gains strength. *And out of the palm tree*, the intellect, *from its spathe*, its intellection, *thick-clustered dates*, gnostic sciences and realities. *Ready to the hand*, easy to partake of, since they are manifest through the light of the spirit, as if they were self-evident. *And gardens of grapes*, which are states and tastings. More particularly, they are various kinds of love in the heart, whose extract and choicest wine intoxicates. *Olives*, reflection, *and pomegranates*, truthful imaginings, which are noble aspirations and worthwhile intentions. *Like each to each*, as, for example, intellections, reflections, gnostic sciences, realities, works, and intentions; or love for the Essence, and love for the divine attributes. *And each unlike to each*, as for example, the kinds of love compared to the kinds of works. Or "like each to each" in level, in strength and weakness, in being disclosed and hidden, "and each unlike to each" in the same things. . . . *Surely, in all this are signs for a people who have faith* through knowledge. They are those who have attained certainty in these signs and states that we have enumerated.[47]

The earth is good, as the Koran often reminds us. But there is a real danger that the equilibrium between heaven and earth may be upset. We cannot partake of the earth in any way we see fit. If people deal with the earth while ignoring its relationship with heaven, they will bring about its corruption. To be a true vicegerent, ruling over the earth and its creatures with justice, the human being must be a true servant, submitting his or her will to the Real. The Tao establishes guidelines for activities, and these must be observed to keep the microcosm and macrocosm in order. Satan, who incarnates the tendency in the soul to turn away from the spirit, must be avoided. Kāshānī explains some of these points in commenting on Koran 2:168:

> *O people, eat of what is in the earth*: Partake of the pleasures and enjoyments that are in the low direction, the world of the soul and the body, in a manner that is *lawful and good*. In other words, partake of them according to the law of justice, with the permission of the Sharia and the approval of the intellect, in the measure of need and necessity. Do not overstep the limits of equilibrium, through which things are good and give profit, entering into the limits of immoderation, for these are *the steps of Satan*. That is why God says, "Verily the squanderers are brothers of Satan" [17:27]. *He is a clear enemy to you*. He wants to destroy you and make you hateful to your Lord by the performance of blameworthy acts of immoderation, for God "does not love the immoderate" [6:141].
>
> You should know that balance [*ʿadāla*] in the world of the soul is the shadow of familiarity [*ulfa*] in the world of the heart. Equilibrium [*iʿtidāl*] is familiarity's shadow in the world of the body. Familiarity is the shadow of love in the world of the Spirit, and love is the shadow of true Oneness. Hence equilibrium is the fourth shadow of Oneness. Satan flees from the shadow of God and is unable to bear it. Hence he always steps outside the domains of these shadows to the sides of immoderate acts. When he cannot do that, then he goes to the side of extremes, as in love and familiarity. That is why ʿAlī said, "You will never see the ignorant person except falling short or going too far, since the ignorant person is Satan's plaything."[48]

If heaven can be divided into seven heavens, as the Koran tells us, this also has its parallels in the microcosm. Kāshānī explains this in commenting on Koran 2:29:

> *It is He who created for you what is in the earth*. The earth is the low direction, which is the elemental world. *Altogether*, since all these things are the origins of your creation and the material for your existence and subsistence. *Then He lifted Himself straight*, that is, He turned His intention straight *to heaven*, the high direction. "Then" indicates the disparity between the two directions and the two kinds of bringing into existence: origination [*ibdāʿ*] and engendering [*takwīn*].[49] This does not indicate a delay between the times [of coming into existence], which would necessitate that the earth was created before the heaven. He put them in order as "seven" heavens in accordance with what the common people see, since the eighth and the ninth heavens are the manifest Footstool and Throne.
>
> The reality is that the low direction is the corporeal world, like the body and its limbs, because its level is lowly in relation to the spiritual world, which is the high direction

called the "heaven," and also because of the disparity between Creation and Command.

He *proportioned them as seven heavens.* This alludes to the levels of the world of spiritual things. The first is the World of the Dominion over the earth, the faculties of the soul, and the jinn. The second is the World of the Soul. The third is the World of the Heart. The fourth is the World of the Intellect. The fifth is the World of the Inmost Mystery [*sirr*]. The sixth is the World of the Spirit. The seventh is the World of the Hidden [*khafā*ʾ], which is the spiritual mystery, not the heart mystery. ʿAlī referred to all this when he said, "Ask me about the paths of heaven, since I know them better than the paths of the earth." The paths of heaven are the states [*aḥwāl*] and the stations [*maqāmāt*], such as renunciation, trust, satisfaction, and so forth.[50]

9

DYNAMICS OF THE SOUL

One of the primary concerns of the Sufis was to map out the various stages or "stations" (*maqāmāt*) of spiritual development undergone on the path to God. At the beginning the individual self or soul has little similarity with the spirit that is God's Breath. It stands at a level of imperfection deriving from the natural human tendency to "forgetfulness" (*ghafla*), represented mythically by the negative side of Adam's fall. Revelation appears as a message from God that "reminds" (*tadhkīr*) the soul that its own luminosity stands witness to a covenant made with God before the entrance into this world (cf. 7:172). Once a person accepts the message, he or she enters onto a long path of struggle (*mujāhada* or *jihād*) against the soul's negative tendencies.

Struggle on the Path to God

A human being possesses a variety of inward tendencies or dimensions represented by such words as *soul*, *spirit*, and *intellect*. Without these dimensions there could be no question of "struggling against oneself." One way to picture the relationship among these dimensions is to see human consciousness as situated on a vertical axis connecting the lowest dimension of reality—the visible world—with the highest dimension, the incomparable God. This is the "static" picture of the microcosm drawn in the previous chapter, where heaven and earth interrelate in harmony at every level. God is heaven, the spirit earth. The spirit is heaven, the soul earth. The soul is heaven, the body earth.

But this picture of the human individual as microcosmic harmony is normative. It describes the ideal relationship between human beings and God, taking into account all the intermediary levels of consciousness and experience, or all the different qualities that must be actualized in certain modes. In any given human individual, the relationships may not correspond to the ideal. The purpose of life will then be to rectify the relationships.

This static and normative picture of the microcosm gives us a model that allows us to distinguish between what we are and what we should be. Based as it is on the structure of the macrocosm, it is seen to pertain to the objective nature of things. A human being whose inward nature corresponds to the macrocosmic order is seen to be in equilibrium with the Real. If the inner relationships do not follow this order, the person is out of kilter with God and the cosmos.

Of course, from a certain point of view, everything is in perfect order, even if it is out of kilter. God has issued the command "Be!" and all things have come into existence in their proper places. The tradition calls this particular command the "engendering command" (*al-amr al-takwīnī*). Through saying "Be!" God engenders all things. This is the Breath of the All-merciful through which God speaks every possible word. It corresponds to the two hands of God, through which He makes all things. But God also issues the "prescriptive command" (*al-amr al-taklīfī*). This second command takes the normative picture of the cosmos into account. It draws a qualitative distinction between God's right and left hands. Through this command God tells us that all paths do not lead to felicity and that every situation does not necessarily present us with optimum conditions from our point of view. The heaven and earth of the microcosm are not necessarily in balance, even if the macrocosmic heaven and earth follow the Tao. In order to put our own heavens and earths back into equilibrium, we as human beings—God's servants and vicegerents—must change our outlooks and habits. This is the perspective that religion commonly takes, and it is the perspective that makes the "spiritual quest" a human imperative.

Here arises a perennial question, to which we have already alluded in chapter 7: If God is the principle of heaven, earth, and everything between the two, then all things must conform to Him by their very natures. Yet we see that human beings bring about a rupture of equilibrium. In the midst of the Real's cosmic equilibrium is found a disequilibrium caused by human beings. How can certain things work against their own ontological root?

One way to explain this discrepancy between the two commands of God—the engendering and prescriptive—is to tie things back to the divine names, or to appeal to the different requirements of the two hands of God. The argument can be summarized as follows: On one level, the all-comprehensive name Allah demands the cosmos as it is. On another level, certain less comprehensive names, such as the Guide, have in view felicity, or ultimate human happiness. Felicity is connected to mercy, kindness, love, nearness. It is the human actualization of the attributes of beauty and gentleness that are allied with God's similarity. But felicity can be achieved only if human beings establish a relationship with the Guide, which manifests itself in the teachings brought by the prophets.

The very possibility of the existence of felicity on God's right hand depends upon the existence of its opposite, wretchedness, on His left hand. If there were no wretchedness and all things were equally felicitous, we could not speak of felicity. We might as well say that all things are equally wretched. The experience of felicity depends upon the existence of misery. "Things become distinguished through their opposites." As Rūmī remarks, "If you write upon a black page, your script will be hidden, since both are the color of tar."[1]

Like other qualities, felicity has degrees, and these decrease steadily until they merge imperceptibly into their opposite, wretchedness. A Sufi saying catches the point nicely: "The felicity of the pious is the wretchedness of the saints." Something that is felicity in the eyes of the common people may be constraint and misery for the enlightened. That is why Sufis commonly speak of having no interest in paradise. By definition, paradise is different from God, and therefore limited and defined. The infinite aspirations of the true seekers can be satisfied only by the Infinite. There are many variations on this theme in Sufi literature. One of the most famous is the prayer of the great woman saint Rābiʿa (fl. second/eighth c.), who was one of the first to make the language of love central to Islam's spiritual vocabulary:

> O God, whatsoever Thou hast apportioned to me of worldly things, do Thou give that to Thy enemies; and whatsoever Thou hast apportioned to me in the world to come, give that to Thy friends; for Thou sufficest me.[2]

The quality of wretchedness, localized eschatologically in hell, sets human beings into relationship mainly with the names that declare God's distance and incomparability: Mighty, Invincible, Magnificent, Majestic, King, Inaccessible, Avenger, Intensely Severe. God remains far from His servants, and they are deprived of all that follows upon His nearness: mercy, love, paradise, felicity. The Koran makes the point explicitly: "No indeed, but on that Day they shall be veiled from their Lord, then they shall roast in Hell" (83:15). Being distant from God is equivalent to torment.

In short, the engendering command brings all things into existence, including paradise and hell. It follows upon the very nature of God as the reality that comprehends all ontological qualities. God as "Allah" assumes every possible relationship with His creatures: incomparability and similarity, wrath and mercy, severity and gentleness, vengeance and forgiveness, left hand and right. These qualities must exist because they belong to the nature of existence itself. They are rooted in Being, which is the Real. And everything, as the Arabic proverb tells us, returns to the root from which it arises. The Koran frequently reminds us that all things "return to Allah." But all things do not return to Allah inasmuch as He is Forgiving, Merciful, Gentle. Some return to Him inasmuch as He is Avenger, Wrathful, Severe.[3] Ibn al-ʿArabī frequently makes this point, as does his student Qūnawī. For example, the latter writes as follows:

> Though every path takes us to God in respect to one of the divine names—since, in one respect, every name is identical with the Named—this yields no profit or felicity. For the names, in respect of their realities and effects, are diverse. What does Harm-giver have in common with Benefit-giver, or Bestower with Withholder? What does Avenger have in common with Forgiver, or Kind and Beneficent with Severe?[4]

On the one hand, human souls are situated on a vertical axis that sets them into relationship with the Real at any given moment. On the other hand, they experience changing relationships on a second, horizontal axis, which is temporal extension. If we look at any microcosm in its day to day existence, we find nothing static about the relationships among its invisible qualities. They change from moment to moment. The enormous extent of these changes in the long term can be judged by tracing human trajectories from birth to death.

The Koran often recalls the "stages" (*aṭwār*) of human life that begin within the womb. We had occasion to refer to these in chapter 7. All the early stages relate directly to God's engendering command. When human development reaches the stage where it makes sense to speak of responsibility, the prescriptive command comes into play. This command has a bearing upon everything that makes human beings truly human. Only in respect of the prescriptive command do right and wrong, beautiful and ugly, moral and immoral, perfection and imperfection, good and evil, felicity and wretchedness, take on direct relevance to the human state. At this point, we have to distinguish between the vertical axis that actually exists in a human being and the vertical axis that should exist. What actually exists was brought into existence by the engendering command. What should exist is described by the prescriptive command, which provides norms for the human state. The horizontal axis is the scene wherein relationships can be put into the right order.

The prescriptive command sets down a desired relationship between heaven and earth, spirit and soul, soul and body. Its goal is to reestablish harmony among the qualities present within the self and, as a result, between the microcosm and the macrocosm. Through it God warns about the undesirable relationships that corrupt the Tao of human and cosmic life. He sets down various means whereby relationships can be brought back into their proper and normative standing.

The possibility of upsetting the balance of heaven and earth goes back to human freedom. Since people are made in God's image, they share to a certain degree in His free choice. To that extent they can reject the prescriptive command and will be held responsible for their choice. When they do reject their role as servants of the Real, they upset the proper cosmic relationships by arrogating the rights of the vicegerent to themselves. Instead of submitting to God's will (*islām*), they refuse the divine guidance and try to take control of their own destinies. Here they are being misled, since they can never wrest control from the Real. The power that misleads them is known as "Iblis" or "Satan." As mentioned earlier, he manifests the divine name Misguider. His task is to bring about separation and dispersion in order that all the possibilities latent in existence may become manifest. Without distance there can be no nearness, without misguidance no guidance, without wretchedness no felicity, without hell no paradise. This is why the Sufi philosopher ʿAyn al-Quḍāt Hamadānī (d. 525/1131) can talk of Muhammad and Iblis as two lights of God:

> "By the sun and her brightness! By the moon who follows her!" [91:1–2]. . . . Do you know what this sun is? It is the Muhammadan light that comes out of the beginningless East. And do you know what this moon is? It is the black light of Iblis that comes out of the endless West.[5]

ʿAyn al-Quḍāt brings out some of the implications of the existence of these two lights in the following:

> Dear friend, wisdom is this: Everything that is, was, and will be, may not and must not be any different. There can never be whiteness without blackness. Heaven is not proper without the earth. Substance cannot be imagined without accident. Muhammad could not exist without Iblis. There can be no obedience without disobedience or unbelief without faith. Such is the case with all the opposites. This is the meaning of the saying, "Things become distinguished through their opposites." Muhammad could have no faith without Iblis's unbelief.
>
> If it were possible that God not be "the Creator, the Author, the Form-giver" [59:24], then it would be possible for Muhammad and the faith of Muhammad not to be. If it were conceivable that He not be "the Invincible, the Magnificent" [59:23], "the Intensely Severe" [12:39], then it would be conceivable that Iblis and his unbelief not exist. Thus it is clear that Muhammad has no felicity without the wretchedness of Iblis. Abū Bakr and ʿUmar would not exist without Abū Jahl and Abū Lahab.[6] This is the meaning of the saying, "There is no prophet who does not have a counterpart in his community." There is no friend of God whose days are not accompanied by an ungodly person. There is no prophet without a forgetful person, no truth-teller without someone ungodly.[7]

Harmony between heaven and earth, spirit and soul, God and cosmos, is established when people bring into balance within themselves the two hands of God, or the two dimensions of their own nature. Like God Himself, of whom they are the image, their two basic dimensions are yang and yin, activity and receptivity, majesty and beauty. To reestablish the normative hierarchy, their receptivity must be open toward the divine guidance. And their activity must be directed against their own limited awarenesses. The first attribute is known as "submission" and "servanthood." The second attribute is known as "struggle" (*jihād, mujāhada*). This is the "greater holy war." According to the famous hadith mentioned in the previous chapter, the Prophet spoke of leaving the lesser holy war and returning to the greater holy war (*al-jihād al-akbar*). When asked what struggle could be greater than the struggle against the unbelievers, he replied that it was the struggle against one's own soul. The macrocosmic battle against the forces of the enemy, Iblis, has an important role to play in human existence. However, given the murkiness of human affairs, it is often extremely difficult to discern just who the enemy really is. This is why Muslim authorities, after the initial century or two of Islam, have rarely agreed on the legitimacy of any given war. And this is why "holy war" is not incumbent upon everyone, even though some authorities have made it one of the pillars of Islam. However, the greater holy war—the struggle against the enemy within—is indeed incumbent upon everyone, because it is the active face of submission to the will of God. Like everything else, the soul has two faces. The face turned toward God must submit to Him, and the face turned toward everything other than God must struggle against the forces of misguidance. And the first and foremost of these "others" is the soul itself. If it turns away from the divine command, it must be contended with.

To the extent that people refuse to submit to God and to contend with their own negative tendencies, they remain imperfect and forgetful. Like those human beings who have actualized true servanthood and vicegerency, they contain within themselves a vertical axis reaching from body to God, but it does not conform to the Tao of human affairs. If they do not rectify their inward states, they will meet God after death as Wrathful, Avenger, Intensely Severe.

Commonly the struggle to establish right relationships is pictured as a path. This path has an explicit or implied ascent, since it leads to greater and greater actualization of goodness and virtue, or emergence from the various kinds of darknesses into the one light. The Koran employs this last image repeatedly:

> God is the Friend of those who have faith: He brings them forth from the darknesses into the light. (2:257)
>
> [This is] a Book We have sent down to thee, that thou mayest bring forth mankind from the darknesses to the light by the leave of their Lord. (14:1)
>
> It is He who blesses you, and His angels, to bring you forth from the darknesses into the light. (33:43)
>
> It is He who sends down upon His servant signs, clear signs, that He may bring you forth from the darknesses into the light. (57:9)
>
> Why, is he who was dead, and We gave him life, and appointed for him a light to walk by among the people, as one who is in the darknesses, and comes not forth from them? (6:122)

The goal of the ascent into light is to reestablish harmony on all the inner levels of the human being. Harmony with other harmonious human beings is then seen as the natural result of the individual's own inner harmony. As Rūmī puts it,

> The spirits of wolves and dogs are separate, every one, but the spirits of God's lions are united.
>
> I refer to their spirits by a plural noun because that one spirit is a hundred in relation to bodies.
>
> In the same way the light of the heaven's sun is a hundred in relation to the courtyards of houses.
>
> But all the lights are one when you remove the walls from between.[8]

At each level of the microcosm, the lower dimension must submit to the higher dimension, the darkness must allow the light to shine. Finally the innermost dimension of the human reality, called by such names as "inmost mystery" (*sirr*) and "most hidden" (*akhfā*), submits itself to God. But here the language of submission and dominance disappears, since *tawḥīd*, or the true profession of God's unity, has been achieved. Hence the tradition employs words such as *union* or *unification*. At this stage a person comes to know what he or she is in truth, in reality. The identity of the innermost dimension of the self with the divine is perceived as having always been the situation. The true, normative hierarchy of the cosmos is actualized and firmly fixed within the individual. Ibn al-ʿArabī makes the point in typical fashion. He is commenting on the well-known sound hadith in which God says,

> I love nothing that draws My servant near to Me more than [I love] what I have made obligatory for him. My servant never ceases drawing near to Me through supererogatory works until I love him. Then when I love him, I am his hearing through which he hears, his sight through which he sees, his hand through which he grasps, and his foot through which he walks.[9]

Ibn al-ʿArabī writes,

> In reality, it is the Real who governs the cosmos [just as the spirit governs the body]. . . . So He is the spirit of the cosmos, its hearing, its sight, and its hand. . . . This is known only by those who draw near to God through supererogatory good works. . . . When the servant draws near to Him . . . , He loves him, and when He loves him He says, "I am his hearing, his sight, and his hand." . . . God's words "I am" show that this was already the situation, but the servant was not aware.[10]

The great Persian poet Ḥāfiẓ (d. 792/1389) makes the point in allusive verses that summarize the whole tradition. He refers to the goal of the path as the mythical, "world-displaying cup" of King Jamshid:

> For years my heart sought Jamshid's cup from me —
> What it had in itself it tried to find in others.
> It asked for the pearl that is outside existence and place
> from those lost on the shore of the Ocean.[11]

Union with God is perfect accord with the divine will. At the inmost center of the being, the person lives in perfect harmony with the Tao. As a result, all other levels of the being are brought into harmony with the inmost center. Each lower level "serves" the higher levels and is in turn served by the lower levels.

When Sufi texts envisage the soul as something that must be transformed, they typically describe a development through three stages, basing themselves on Koranic terminology. The lowest stage, the "soul commanding to evil" (*al-nafs al-ammāra bi'l-sū'*), belongs to ordinary mortals overcome by forgetfulness. The next stage, the "blaming soul" (*al-nafs al-lawwāma*), pertains to those who have begun to struggle on the path to God. They recognize their own weaknesses and blame themselves for their failures to adhere to the normative guidelines set down by the prescriptive command. The final stage, the "soul at peace" with God (*al-nafs al-muṭma'inna*), is achieved by those who reach the fullness of human perfection.[12]

According to the normative ideal, human beings should turn their attention toward the upper reaches of the vertical axis and "ascend" to the World of the Command and to God Himself. This is achieved while people live upon the horizontal, temporal axis. Those who cling to life in the visible world and neglect their human possibilities as God's designated servants and vicegerents are dominated by the "soul that commands to evil." Those who remember their true nature and undertake the task of turning their attention toward perfection and nearness to God reach the stage of the "blaming soul." Those who persevere in their struggle against their own forgetful tendencies and succeed in attaining perfection achieve the soul "at peace."

If the transformation of the soul can be described in terms of a journey or ascent from imperfection to perfection, or from forgetfulness to remembrance and mindfulness, it can also be understood as a passage from dispersion to unity. The human reality, though single, has multiple faculties and dimensions. Its oneness lies in the direction of the divine/human spirit, while its multiplicity pertains to the side of the body with its many parts and functions. Here the geometrical image is that of a circle. The center of the circle is the spirit, while its circumference is the body. The more the soul turns toward its own center or source, the more it becomes integrated and whole. The more it turns toward the circumference, the more it becomes dispersed and partial. "Perfection" or full "remembrance" then corresponds to awareness situated at the center of the circle. The circumference no longer attracts the soul, thereby drawing it into dispersion, but instead represents the soul's active and conscious self-manifestation within the bounds of its own perfected nature.

No matter how the ascent to human wholeness and integration is described, relationships among different dimensions or qualities of the human being are constantly at issue. Terms such as *soul*, *spirit*, *heart*, *inmost mystery*, and *most hidden* designate the subtle dimensions of the human reality in terms of certain qualities. This is clearly and explicitly the case in the three levels of soul: commanding to evil, blaming, and at peace. In the discussions of spiritual psychology, such concepts serve to describe certain groups of qualities that need to be juxtaposed with other qualities, whether within the microcosm, the macrocosm, or God Himself. The purpose of the explanations is to allow people to come to grips with the forces inside themselves within the context of the prescriptive command.

The Soul's Evil

The three levels of the soul—in some texts expanded to four or five—are derived from Koranic passages that refer to the soul in connection with diverse qualities: evil, blaming, and peace with God. Were one to study all the references to the soul in the Koran and Hadith, one would surely come to the conclusion that the soul itself has no specific qualities. Rather, the souls of different people have diverse qualities, and these souls are no different from the realities of their own selves.

Sufi texts frequently build on this picture

of the soul as the inner dimension of the human reality possessing a great number of possibilities, many of them negative. Abū Ṭālib al-Makkī (d. 386/996) provides an early example of this approach:

> The soul is afflicted with four diverse qualities. The first are the meanings of the attributes of Lordship [*rubūbiyya*], like pride, invincibility, love of praise, mightiness, and independence. It is also afflicted with the character traits of the satans, such as guile, cunning, envy, and suspicion. And it is afflicted with the natures of the beasts, that is, the love of food, drink, and the marriage act. And with all this, it is also held responsible for the qualities of servanthood, such as fear, humility, and lowliness. The servant is not a pure servant until he is purified of the first three meanings. When he realizes the attributes of servanthood, then he is pure of those attributes of lordship that afflict him.[13]

Here we see the constantly recurring theme that all perfection is found in servanthood or pure submissiveness toward God. But this is a servanthood toward God alone, as Makkī stresses in continuing the discussion. For, he asks,

> How can the person be a servant of the Lord if he is a servant of a servant? When he is led by something, that is his god. When he falls in line behind something, that is his lord. In the view of those who have realized their deiformity [*al-muta'allihūn*], this is to associate other gods with God; and in the view of those who have assumed lordly attributes [*al-rabbāniyyūn*], this is to be confused about Lordship. Such a person has fallen on his face and is inverted, according to the supplication of the Messenger: "Let the servant of the dinar fall on his face, the servant of the dirham fall on his face, the servant of his wife fall on his face, and the servant of the cooking pot fall on his face!"[14] . . . These are the possessors of souls that command to evil. Their souls have been seduced, follow caprice, and are opposed to the Master.[15]

Given the fact that most people—as Ghazālī and others frequently tell us—follow the negative tendencies of the soul, it is not surprising that the Sufis often employ the term *soul* without qualification to refer to the soul that commands to evil. Thus from earliest times we find definitions of the soul that focus exclusively on the blameworthy character traits that it can assume and stress its opposition to the qualities of the spirit. If the spirit is intelligent and good, the soul is ignorant and evil.

In the chapter on terminology in *Kitāb al-Luma'*, Abū Naṣr al-Sarrāj (d. 378/988) explains the expression "So and so has no soul" (or, "So and so has no self") as follows:

> This means that the character traits of the soul do not appear within him. For the soul's character traits are anger, severity, seeking greatness, covetousness, eager desire, and envy. If a servant is free of these and similar plagues, they say that he has no soul. They mean that it is as if he has no soul. Thus Abū Sa'īd al-Kharrāz said, "There is a man who returns to God and attaches himself to God. He stands motionless in nearness to God having forgotten his own soul and everything other than God. If you were to say to him, 'Who are you and where are you going,' he would have no other answer than to say, 'God,' since he knows none other than God. This is because of the recognition of God's tremendousness that he finds in his heart."[16]

The famous Sufi Abū 'Abd al-Raḥmān al-Sulamī (d. 412/1021) devotes a short treatise to "The defects (*'uyūb*) of the soul and their cure." Although he begins with a brief explanation of the three basic levels of the soul—commanding to evil, blaming, and at peace—he limits himself to a discussion of the soul that commands to evil. He describes seventy negative character traits innate to the soul and explains how they can be overcome. His concluding remarks convey the tone of the work:

> I have explained in these chapters some of the defects of the soul so that the intelligent person may deduce from them what is beyond them; and so that the person who is confirmed by God with His giving success and showing the right way may come out of these defects. I admit that it is impossible to enumerate fully the soul's defects. How could that be possible? For the soul is defective in all its attributes and is never empty of defects. How can one count the defects of something when the whole of it is defective and God has described it as "commanding to

evil"? However, it may be that the servant can gain well-being from some of its defects through some of these cures. He may be able to free the soul from one of its defects through that cure. May God give us the success to follow right conduct! May He eliminate from us sources of forgetfulness and appetite! May He place us in His shelter, compass, safekeeping, and care! For He is powerful over that and bestower of that, through His mercy and bounty.[17]

In his classic *Risāla*, Qushayrī (d. 465/1072) defines the soul as follows:

> Literally, the *nafs* of something is its existence. The Sufis do not apply the term *soul* to mean existence, nor the bodily frame. They only mean by "soul" those qualities of the servant that are defective and those character traits and acts that are blameworthy.[18]

ʿAyn al-Quḍāt brings out the qualities of the soul by contrasting them with those of the heart and spirit:

> Dear friend, human beings do not have a single attribute. On the contrary, they have many attributes. In every child of Adam there are two instigators: one from the All-merciful, one from Satan. The frame and the soul are satanic, while the spirit and heart pertain to the All-merciful. The first thing that came into the frame was the soul. If the heart had come first, it would never have let the soul into the world. Relative to the heart the frame is dense. The soul has the attribute of darkness. The frame is from earth and also has darkness. These two have become each other's intimate and familiar. The homeland of the soul is the left side, while the heart's homeland is the "breast." At every moment, the soul is increased in caprice and misguidance, while the heart is adorned with the light of knowledge. "Is he whose breast God has opened up to submission, so he follows a light from his Lord . . . ?" [39:22].[19]

Many Sufis were concerned to show that even the negative characteristics of the soul have a positive side to them, since they are created by God. As soon as we take the divine names into account, we see that certain names demand the soul's reality. As we have pointed out before, God's incomparability and all the attributes of severity and majesty that go along with it demand that creatures be nothing more than servants, with all the abasement and lowliness that this implies. Moreover, such divine names as Avenger, Harsh in Punishment, and the Best of Deceivers demand that there be servants who deserve to face these names. And God shows vengeance and deception only to the wrongdoers. On the macrocosmic scale, these facts demand the existence of Iblis and unbelievers. On the microcosmic scale, they demand the existence of the soul that commands to evil. This perspective is commonly met with in the works of Ibn al-ʿArabī and his followers. But it is also found in authors who had no connection to his school, like ʿAyn al-Quḍāt—as we saw in passages quoted above—or like Ibn al-ʿArabī's contemporary, Rūzbihān Baqlī. In *Mashrab al-arwāḥ*, Rūzbihān discusses the "true knowledge of the soul" as follows:

> The soul is an instrument of God's severity. From it branch out all evil and corruption. God says, "Verily the soul commands to evil" [12:53]. In its very essence the soul comprises the attributes of severities and is prepared to receive the inspiration of wickedness. God says, "By the soul and Him who proportioned it and inspired in it its wickedness and its godfearing" [91:7–8]. The one who examines the clothing of the Eternal's severity worn by the soul will know the Real in the quality of invincibility, inaccessibility, magnificence, and tremendousness. The Prophet said, "He who knows his own soul knows his Lord." One of the shaykhs says, "The soul does not speak the truth and the heart does not lie." The gnostic says, "The soul is the hidden inspirations and thoughts of severity that come upon the person from the horizon of Eternity's deception."[20]

In another passage of the same work, Rūzbihān devotes a section to the visionary experiences of the travelers on the path to God. They see all things in appropriate forms, including the soul. It appears as a wife who "rests" in her husband, her husband being the activity of God. But if she should turn away from the heart, spirit, and intellect—the luminous dimension of the human reality—then she will fall prey to satanic insinuations:

> When the lights of the divine attributes are unveiled to the spirit and the heart, the soul is seen in imaginal forms as the bride of the acts of the Creator. She rests in those acts and enjoys the neighborhood of the heart and the spirit. She gains peace with the affair of the heart, intellect, and spirit.
>
> But if she should become opaque and turn presumptuous before the intellect, then she becomes infatuated. God shows her the callings of the appetites and the mysteries of misleading forces from the direction of the severities. These take the form of satanic imaginings. God has affirmed the truth of this in the texts of His Book where He says, "and inspired in it its wickedness and its godfearing" [91:8]. The gnostic says, "The vision of the soul is the witnessing of the severities of eternity without beginning."[21]

Conflicting Character Traits

The qualitative nature of the terms employed to refer to the human reality can be illustrated with all sorts of texts. One particularly interesting area that brings it out clearly is the discussion of ethics. The Arabic term used for the science of ethics, *akhlāq*, is the plural of *khuluq* and means literally "character traits." These may be good or bad, praiseworthy or blameworthy. The good and the bad are commonly cited as opposites, as we saw in Imam Jaʿfar al-Ṣādiq's comments on the opposing soldiers of intellect and ignorance.

When spirit is seen as luminous and soul as dark, praiseworthy character traits belong to the luminous side of the self and blameworthy traits to the dark side. A slightly deeper analysis shows that the dark side is not really dark, or at least not absolutely so. It is dark in relation to the luminous side. It becomes firmly fixed in darkness only if it refuses to submit to the luminosity from which it derives and clings to its own constricting and privative nature. Spirit, for example, is inherently generous, while the soul should follow the spirit and adopt the same quality. But the "soul that commands to evil"—a crony of Satan—urges people to stinginess. It follows the darkness instead of the light. It points out with its inherent guile that generosity leads to poverty and should be avoided. "O possessors of faith, expend of the good things you have earned, and of that We have produced for you from the earth. . . . Satan promises you poverty and commands you unto indecency. But God promises you His pardon and bounty" (2:267–68).

The science of ethics was developed extensively by representatives of the philosophical tradition on Greek models. But the Koran and Hadith are full of references to character traits, both human and divine, and those authorities who wanted to show the Koranic roots of ethics had no difficulty doing so. One of the most prominent representatives of this latter tradition was Ghazālī, who discusses ethics in detail in many of his works. At the beginning of the twenty-first book of the *Iḥyāʾ ʿulūm al-dīn*, he devotes a section to "explaining the wonders of the heart."[22] He acknowledges the importance of this section in his own eyes by summarizing it in Persian at the beginning of *Kīmiyā-yi saʿādat*. We have already had occasion to quote parts of this summary.[23] After discussing the various meanings given by different authorities to the terms heart, soul, spirit, and intellect, Ghazālī explains his own reasons for choosing the term *heart* as the fundamental designation for that dimension of the human reality that must be transformed by the spiritual life. In brief, he defines "heart" as the essence of the human being, "spirit" as the source of perception and awareness, "soul" as the human self inasmuch as it undergoes transformation, and "intellect" as the heart to the extent that it perceives the realities of things.[24] The four terms all refer to the subtle reality of the human being, but from different points of view.

Ghazālī's discussion of the nature of the human self is complex and cannot be dealt with here. He provides a much more detailed and scholarly description of the structure of the self than in the passages quoted from him earlier. In the present context, we can look at one part of his analysis in order to bring out an approach to spiritual psychology that is typical for the tradition.

Ghazālī sees the human self as made up of different tendencies or attributes that must be brought into equilibrium (*iʿtidāl*) before human beings can reach the perfection for which they were created. Note that the Arabic word for equilibrium, *iʿtidāl*, derives from the same root as the word for justice, *ʿadl*, which is normally defined as putting everything in its proper place. The establishment of equilibrium within the self corresponds to the establishment of justice in human society. Both terms, equilibrium and justice, play central roles in philosophical discussions of ethics.

Ghazālī refers to the two primary tendencies of human beings as "lordly" (*rabbānī*) and "satanic" (*shayṭānī*). The first is ascending and the second descending. The first is intellect, which attracts toward God. This is the inner light that recognizes the teachings of the prophets as one in substance with itself. The satanic tendency pulls away from God and tries to keep the soul occupied with the outer world. It incarnates the divine attribute of misguidance and draws toward wretchedness. As long as the satanic tendency dominates, the individual will remain at the stage of the soul that commands to evil. This is the state of most people, who are overcome by forgetfulness. If the ascending tendency gains the upper hand, the soul will eventually achieve the stage of peace with God.

As pointed out already, the soul has two other tendencies that are basically dispersive. They pull the soul this way and that, but in themselves they are neither ascending nor descending. One is appetite, the power of the soul that seeks to obtain everything necessary for survival. The other is anger, the soul's power to fend off everything detrimental to survival. These two faculties are inherent to the animal soul and necessary for life. Though they work on the horizontal plane, they can be employed to help in ascending or descending. The manner in which they are employed will depend on whether the satanic or the lordly tendency predominates in the soul.

In explaining these points with an analogy, Ghazālī personifies the four tendencies as a wise man (intellect), a satan (satanity), a pig (appetite), and a dog (anger). At the beginning, he describes the pig and the dog in completely negative terms. As he develops the analogy in some detail, it becomes clear that their negativity is not inherent, but depends upon their being put to use in the wrong way. Throughout he employs a typical qualitative evaluation that is quickly tied back to divine attributes.

> The pig is appetite, for a pig is not blameworthy because of its color, shape, and form, but because of its greed, burning thirst, and eager desire. The dog is anger, for the rapacious predator and the vicious dog are not "dog" and "predator" because of their form, color and shape. The true meaning of "predatoriness" is rapacity, animosity, and viciousness.
>
> Within the human being are found the rapacity and anger of the predatory beast and the eager desire and lust of the pig. Through covetousness the pig invites to indecency and abomination. Through anger the predator invites to wrongdoing and harm. The devil never ceases stirring up the appetite of the pig and the anger of the predator. He goads on the one with the other and makes their natural instincts appear beautiful to them.
>
> The wise man—who is the likeness of the intellect—is commanded to repel the cunning and deception of the satan by employing his penetrating insight and his illuminating and clarifying light to unveil the satan's dissimulations. The wise man has to break the covetousness of the pig by making the dog its master, since anger can break the force of appetite. He must also repel the rapacity of the dog by making the pig dominate and rule over it. If the wise man is able to achieve this, equilibrium will be established and justice will appear in the kingdom of the body. All will walk upon the Straight Path.

Once equilibrium has been established through the rule of the intellect, every attribute of the soul plays a positive role. Appetite and anger are wholly good as long as they are kept in proper harmony and correct balance through the intellect's governance. Ghazālī continues by pointing out that if the wise man does not succeed in governing the other dimensions of the self, the others will overcome him and place him at their service. Then he will spend his time devising stratagems and sharpening his wits so that the pig can eat its fill and the dog can be content. He will remain forever a servant of the dog and the pig. And this is the situation of most people, since most of their aspiration is centered in the stomach and private parts and in vying with their enemies.

Next Ghazālī turns to a dimension of experience that soon after him became central to the sapiential tradition—the World of Imagination. He alludes to the visions of the "unveilers" (*mukāshif*), those adepts of the spiritual path who perceive the realities of things through imagination in appropriate images. As he remarks in several places, images perceived through imagination reveal the spirit and reality of things more clearly than the corporeal forms of the things.[25]

What is really strange about people is that they criticize idol worshipers for worshiping stones. But suppose the covering were lifted from them and the reality of their own situation were unveiled. Suppose they were shown the reality of their situation in images, as the unveilers are shown images in sleep or wakefulness. Then they would sometime see their own soul bending before a pig, prostrating itself before it. Or they would see themselves bowing before it, awaiting its indication and command. Whenever the pig needed to seek some object of its appetite, they would rise up immediately in its service and bring the object. Or they would see themselves bending before a rapacious dog, worshiping it, obeying it, giving ear to what it requires and requests. They would sharpen their wits to come up with stratagems to obey it. Through all this, they are striving to make their satan happy, for it is he who stirs up the pig and urges on the dog, sending the two out in his service. Hence they are worshiping their satans by worshiping the pig and the dog.

Every servant of God should watch carefully over his movement and his rest, his speech and his silence, his standing and his sitting. He should look with the eye of insight. Then, if he is just with himself, he will see that he is striving all day to serve these three. This is the utmost limit of wrongdoing, since he has made the master a slave, the lord a vassal, the commander a servant, and the ruler the ruled. The intellect is worthy of leadership, domination, and authority, but this person has put it under the sway of the dog, the pig, and the satan.[26]

At this point it hardly needs mentioning that the proper hierarchy of the human microcosm is envisaged here with imagery reduplicating the proper relationship between God and the world, heaven and earth, spirit and soul, Lord and servant, yang and yin. The luminosity of the intellect should be dominant, since it is heaven's nature to rule the earth.

When the proper relationship between heaven and earth is upset, the result can only be the corruption of everything between the two. Within the human microcosm, this means that all the character traits proper to the heart will be distorted and perverted. Continuing the above passage in a discussion reminiscent of Imam Jaʿfar al-Ṣādiq's description of the soldiers of ignorance, Ghazālī details the character flaws and ugly moral traits found in those who are not ruled by intellect.

Then Ghazālī describes what will happen if the right relationship can be established. If lord dominates over vassal—heaven rules over earth—equilibrium and justice will be established and all the negative tendencies found in the soul will be transformed into positive ones. Appetite and the qualities that go along with it are negative only if ruled by the satan. They are positive when governed by the intellect. Among the virtues that grow out of appetite and its allies are chastity, contentment, tranquility, ascesis, piety, godfearing, joyful expansion, modesty, and gracefulness. Anger and its accompanying vices are transformed into traits such as courage, generosity, forbearance, patience, clemency, forgiveness, steadfastness, and gravity.

Ghazālī summarizes his points by comparing the heart to a mirror that reflects everything around it. Through its receptivity, it is able to acquire every attribute in existence. If the heart lives in a situation where the order of creation is inverted so that the intellect is subjugated and obscured, it becomes cloudy and dark. If the proper equilibrium is established, the mirror of the heart reflects the luminosity of the spiritual realm and, in effect, gains the attributes of heaven. Through remembering (*dhikr*) God and becoming adorned by His attributes, the heart attains to the stage of the "soul at peace."

> The heart is like a mirror, and all these things surround it and have an effect upon it. Their traces constantly reach it. The praiseworthy effects that we have mentioned increase the polish, luminosity, and brilliance of the heart's mirror. Finally the plain evidence of the Truth sparkles within it and the desired goal of religion is unveiled. The Prophet alludes to this kind of heart with his words, "When God desires good for a servant, he appoints for him an admonisher from within his heart," and his words, "When a person has an admonisher within his heart, God has given him a protector."[27] This is the heart within which the remembrance of God becomes firmly established. "In God's remembrance are hearts at peace" [13:28].
>
> Blameworthy effects are like a dark smoke mounting up on the heart's mirror. The smoke keeps on piling up on it until the heart becomes dark and black, totally veiled from God. God calls this "sealing" and "rust." He says, "No indeed, but what they were earning has rusted upon the hearts" [83:14]. Likewise He says, "Did We will, We would smite them because of their sins, sealing their hearts so that they do not listen" [7:100].

Note here that the word the Koran employs for "sealing," *ṭabʿ*, is one of the two words from a single root that come to be used in the intellectual tradition for nature (the other being *ṭabīʿa*). "Nature," conceived of as a yin reality, carries the imprint or "seal" of the spirit. It has nothing of its own other than receptivity. At the same time, the spirit tends to be covered and concealed through being impressed in matter. This becomes a seal over the heart, preventing it from perceiving the spirit's light. Ghazālī has this dual sense of the word *ṭabʿ* in mind in the next sentence.

> Thus He connects "not listening" because of sealing/nature to sins, just as He connects "listening" to godfearing [*taqwā*]. For He says, "Fear God and listen" [5:108]. "Fear God and God will teach you" [2:282].
>
> When sins pile up, hearts are sealed. Then the heart is blind to the perception of the Real and to the well-being of religion. It considers the business of the next world insignificant and gives great importance to the affair of this world, turning its attention exclusively toward it. When the affair of the next world, along with the warning it contains, knocks on its hearing, it goes in one ear and out the other. This affair does not take rest in the heart, nor does it move the person to repentance and preparing himself. Such people are the ones "who have despaired of the world to come, even as the unbelievers have despaired of the inhabitants of the tomb" [60:13].
>
> This then is the meaning of the "blackening" of hearts through sins, as mentioned in the Koran and the Hadith. Maymūn ibn Mahrān says, [quoting the Prophet,] "If the servant commits a sin, a black spot appears in his heart. If he repents, refrains, and asks forgiveness, it becomes polished. If he returns, the black spot increases until it overcomes his heart. That is its 'rust.'"[28]
>
> The Prophet said that the heart of the person of faith is bare, a lamp shining within it, while the heart of the unbeliever is black and upside down. Obeying God by opposing the appetites polishes the heart, while performing acts of disobedience blackens it. When a person turns toward acts of disobedience, his heart turns black. When someone follows an evil deed with a good one and erases its effect, his heart does not become dark, but its light is decreased. It is like a mirror upon which someone breathes. Then he wipes it off and breathes on it again. Then he wipes it off again. It will not be completely clear of dullness.[29]

The Soul's Receptivity

When earth is fecundated by heaven, it yields every sort of fruit and flower. When the mirror of the soul is receptive to the light effused by the spirit, it acquires every sort of virtue and praiseworthy character trait. To upset the harmony between heaven and earth is to corrupt the world. To upset the harmony between spirit and soul is to pervert the individual. The normal and normative condition of the soul is to be receptive to the lights that come down from the spirit. Through this receptivity, the soul becomes luminous and is transmuted into a spiritual substance. The alchemical elixir turns the soul's lead into gold. The soul ascends from the world of darkness into the world of light. The descending tendency that is all too often present results from the soul's inability to see the light, its lack of receptivity toward that which lies beyond itself, its satisfaction with its own limitations, or the deceptions of Satan. All these expressions refer to the limitations inherent in the lower realms of existence.

The Muslim philosophers see the possibility of the soul's transformation as deriving from its quality of receptivity, even though they do not contrast the term *soul* with *spirit* as clearly as do many Sufi authors. In their treatise entitled "How the particular souls develop within the human, natural bodies," the Ikhwān al-Ṣafā' expand on the analogy of knowledge as food for the soul, referred to in the previous chapter. The goal of acquiring knowledge is not to gain information but to develop the praiseworthy character traits, the virtues (*faḍā'il*). These in turn depend upon the soul's being open to what lies above it and its ascending into the luminous world of the spirit. The plethora of adjectives in the following passage is not simply a rhetorical device. On the contrary, the Ikhwān are listing the qualities that are acquired by the soul in its ascension into the world of light. The point of the discussion is not that "the soul is transformed"—that is easy enough to say. At issue are questions such as, what are the attributes that are acquired by the soul? What are the ontological qualities that the soul comes to manifest? Ultimately, how does the soul become similar (*tashabbuh*) to God?

> You should know, my noble, pious, and compassionate brother—God confirm you and us with a spirit from Him—that the soul's knowledge and wisdom is like the body's consumption of food and drink. First, bodies are given milk. Then they partake of food and drink, which are their nourishment. Thereby their small parts grow, their incomplete parts develop, their thin parts fatten up, and their weak parts strengthen. Their splendor and perfection are uncovered. They reach their furthest limits and their ultimate goals and beauties through milk, then through food and drink, which are their nourishment and matter.
>
> In the same way, the states of the souls are similar to the states of the bodies. . . . For the substances of the particular souls become substantialized through various kinds of knowledge. Their essences grow through wisdom. Their forms become illumined through sciences. Their reflective faculties become strengthened through mathematical exercises. Their thoughts take on light through the rules of the disciplines. Their intellects become expanded to receive the disengaged, spiritual forms. Their aspirations rise up and yearn for everlasting affairs. They gain a strong determination to reach the furthest limits and to ascend to the highest levels by gazing upon the sciences of the Divine. They travel in the spiritual, lordly ways and devote themselves to the noble affairs of wisdom, following the way of Socrates. They follow Sufi practices [*taṣawwuf*], asceticism, and monastic discipline in the manner of Christ. They attach themselves to the unswerving religion, which is for the souls to become similar to their universal substance and to attain to their high world and their union with their First Cause.

"Unswerving religion" (*al-dīn al-ḥanīfī*) is identified both with Islam and with the way of Abraham. It has sometimes been translated as "primordial religion." The Koran uses the term *ḥanīf* in the singular or plural in twelve instances, all suggesting a person who follows the best form of religion. For example, "Abraham in truth was neither a Jew nor a Christian. He was submitted [*muslim*], unswerving" (3:67). "Say: 'As for me, my Lord has guided me to a straight path of right religion, the creed of Abraham, unswerving'" (6:161). By employing this term, the Ikhwān have in mind Islam on its most universal level. Though they use philosophical terminology in talking of the unswerving religion, they do not mean philosophy, since that was the first path they cited, and the three paths form an ascending hierarchy. Like most members of the sapiential tradition, they see no contradictions among the ways of Socrates, Christ, and Muhammad. But the philosophical way is dominated by certain intellectual qualities such as concern for the divine wisdom. The way of Christ and the Sufis is dominated by a certain concern for actualizing the purely spiritual domain of reality. And the way of Muhammad is seen as balancing all positive tendencies. The passage continues:

> Such souls hold fast to His handle that protects from error, desire His good pleasure, and seek nearness to Him through becoming united with the sons of their own kind in their spiritual world, their luminous locus, and their abode of life—as God says, "Surely the abode of the next world—that is life, did they but know" [29:64]. If the abode itself is life, then what do you think, my brother, about the inhabitants of the abode? How could their attribute and their bliss be anything other than that said by God? "[Surely the godfearing shall dwell amid gardens and a river], in a sitting place of truthfulness, in the presence of a King Omnipotent" [54:55]. So understand these allusions, pointers, and symbols!
>
> The soul is awakened from the sleep of forgetfulness and aroused from the drowsiness of ignorance. It struggles and throws off from itself the corporeal shells, the bodily coverings, the natural habits, the character traits of predatory beasts, and ignorant opinions. It becomes purified of the grime of material appetites. Then it is delivered, springs up, and stands. Its essence is illuminated and its substance irradiated. Its lights shine and its sight is made piercing. Then it sees that spiritual form, it observes those luminous substances, and it witnesses those hidden affairs and concealed mysteries whose perception is impossible through the corporeal senses and the bodily faculties. No one witnesses them but the person whose soul has been delivered by the rectification of his character [*tahdhīb khuluq*]. For these things are not connected to a natural desire or tied to corporeal appetites that they could appear to these and be examined.
>
> When the soul examines those affairs, it becomes attached to them and clings to them as a lover becomes attached and clings to his beloved. It becomes united with them as light becomes united with light. It subsists along with them through their subsistence and remains through their remaining. It takes delight in their repose and ease. It smells their fragrance and enjoys their joys—joys that human tongues are unable to express, for the minds of great thinkers fall short of imagining the depths of their attributes. Thus God says, "No soul knows what comfort is laid up for them secretly, as a recompense for what they were doing" [32:17]. He also says, "Therein are the objects of the souls' appetites and what delights the eyes, and therein you shall dwell forever" [43:71].[30]

After developing the analogy of food for the body and the soul in some detail, the Ikhwān draw conclusions that illustrate clearly many of the points that we have been making concerning normative guidelines for establishing wholeness in the soul:

> There is no honor in eating a great deal. Food and drink are necessary only to the extent that they appease hunger and thirst. When these are appeased, it makes no difference whether they were appeased through many kinds of food or through a piece of barley bread and some pure water. Thus Jesus said to the apostles, "Eating barley bread and drinking pure water today in this world is plenty for him who wishes to enter paradise tomorrow."
>
> Honor and praise must lie in gaining the virtues of wisdom, becoming illumined by the light of knowledge, and coming to see the signs and proofs of the knowledge of the realities of things. It lies in wisdom, deiformity [*taʾalluh*], asceticism, Sufi practices, clinging to the ways of those who have assumed lordly attributes [*rabbāniyyūn*]. It is thinking little of the affair of the body and attaching great importance to the affair of the soul. It is a strong desire to deliver the soul from the darkness of ignorance, save it from the sea of Matter, and free it from the prison of Nature. It is coming out of the depths of bodies, ascending to the World of the Spirits, and entering into the ranks of the angels, as God says: "To Him good words go up, and the righteous deed—He uplifts it" [35:10]. By "righteous deed" He means the spirit of those who have faith. He says, "Surely the lovingly kind shall be in bliss" [83:22], and He says, "The book of the lovingly kind is in the high ones, and what shall teach you what the high ones are?" [83:18]. By the "high ones" He means the souls of the lovingly kind. He says, "Till, when they have come thither, and its gates are opened, and its keepers will say to them, 'Peace be upon you! Well you have fared; enter in, to dwell forever'" [39:73].

> And He says, "And the angels shall enter unto them from every gate: 'Peace be upon you, for that you were patient. Fair is the Ultimate Abode!'" [13:23–24].[31]

The Islamic philosophical tradition follows the Ikhwān al-Ṣafā᾽ in considering the soul's transmutation through its receptivity to higher realities as the goal of human existence. The Leading Master (*al-shaykh al-ra᾽īs*) of the philosophers, Avicenna (d. 428/1037) speaks for the whole tradition when he explains the perfection of the rational soul, that is, the normative ideal that it must achieve. The key idea is the soul's transformation through receiving what lies beyond it. It begins as a "material intellect" (*al-ᶜaql al-hayūlānī*). Here, as in all of his philosophy, Avicenna wants to describe "the path which the intellect has to traverse in order to progress from the stage of pure potentiality to total actuality."[32] At the beginning of its becoming, the specific quality of the soul that can be illumined by the light of the spirit has not yet received its luminous form. When the soul reaches the pinnacle of its perfection, it has actualized all the qualities of the spiritual realm.

"Material" in "material intellect" does not mean "made out of matter" in a modern sense, but "not having received form" in an Aristotelian sense. At the beginning of the soul's becoming, its rational and intellectual qualities—and these are precisely the qualities that give it a specifically human identity—have not yet been developed, though the animal and vegetal faculties are present. Hence the material quality of the intellect refers to the soul's potential to become fully human. As Avicenna himself remarks, it is customary to refer to the rational soul as the "'material intellect,' that is, potential intellect, by analogy to matter."[33] But the soul will not necessarily become fully human, quite the contrary. For at this stage its human potentiality is like clay waiting to receive imprinted shapes. If the wise man dominates, the true human being will emerge. But the pig, the dog, and the satan are also vying for control. If the light of the intellect finally gains total control over the soul, the soul will itself be transmuted into the Active Intellect (*al-ᶜaql al-faᶜᶜāl*).

This whole process represents the inherent movement of existence toward its full manifestation. As the Sufis put it, this is the Hidden Treasure making Itself known. The Treasure can be truly known only by that "other" which is not other. The light of the Real must be fully and wholly reflected in a human being, made in the Real's image. This is the culminating point of the return of the cosmos to God. Just as existence manifested itself through the Arc of Descent and reached its lowest point in matter, so once again it rises up through the three children and human beings until it reaches its full splendor in the perfect human being, who is a prophet or a great friend of God. Avicenna encapsulates the cosmological teachings of the philosophical tradition in the following words:

> It is necessary that you know that when existence begins from the One, each thing that follows upon it is lower in level than the One. And existence keeps on descending in degrees. The first of these degrees is the degree of the spiritual, disengaged angels who are called "intellects." Then come the levels of the spiritual angels who are called "souls." These are the angels that perform works. Then are the levels of the heavenly bodies, some of which are nobler than others. Finally existence reaches the last of these bodies.
>
> After that begins the existence of matter receptive to the forms of corruptible, engendered things. The first thing in which existence clothes itself is the form of the elements. Then the elements ascend in degree little by little. The first thing found among them is lower and baser than that which follows. The lowest thing in existence is matter, then the elements, then the compound inanimate things, then the plants, then the animals. The most excellent of animals is the human being. The most excellent of human beings is he whose soul reaches perfection by becoming an active intellect and acquiring the character traits that are the practical virtues. The most excellent of these is he who has the preparedness for the level of prophecy.[34]

Avicenna's terminology in this discussion strays too far from the Koran and the hadith literature for the taste of most Sufis, but the Sufi view of the nature of the cosmos and the human role within it is not substantially different. Sufis stress the role of the First Intellect at the beginning of the Arc of Descent. But most of them would agree that the Active Intellect stands at the end of the Arc of Ascent and that the perfection of existence is achieved only by the prophets—and the friends of God. The Active Intellect is precisely the fully actualized perfection of the divine form. In contrast, the First Intellect, standing at the beginning, possesses all perfections only potentially. Ibn al-ʿArabī writes, "Perfection in the perfect human being is actualized [*biʾl-fiʿl*], while in the First Intellect it is potential [*biʾl-quwwa*]."[35]

In the following passage, Avicenna describes the perfected soul in relation to the various levels of the cosmos and God. He refers to the cosmos as the "whole" (*al-kull*) and to God as the "Origin of the whole" and as "Absolute Comeliness, Absolute Good, and Absolute Beauty." As in the above passage, he avoids—in a manner typical for much of the writings of the earlier philosophers—terminology with a specifically religious color.

> The perfection peculiar to the rational soul is for it to become an intellective world within which is imprinted the form of the whole, the intelligible order of the whole, and the good that is effused upon the whole. [Its intellective world] begins with the Origin of the whole and moves on to the noble substances: First the nondelimited spiritual substances, then the spiritual substances connected in a certain way to bodies,[36] then the higher corporeal bodies with their dispositions and faculties. The soul continues in this manner until it realizes fully within itself the disposition of all existence. It becomes an intelligible world, parallel to the entire existent cosmos, and witnesses That which is Absolute Comeliness, Absolute Good, and Absolute Beauty while being united with It. The soul's intelligible world becomes impressed with Its likeness and disposition, strung upon Its thread, and joined to It in substance.[37]

What Avicenna calls "becoming impressed with Its likeness and disposition," the specifically religious terminology calls submission (*islām*) to God. The Sufis are completely explicit in stating that the soul attains perfection in servanthood (*ʿubūdiyya*), the quality of being an *ʿabd*, which is precisely the quality of submission to the Lord. As Ibn al-ʿArabī puts it, "At root the servant was created only to belong to God and to be a servant perpetually. He was not created to be a lord."[38] That is why Ibn al-ʿArabī, who was more careful than any other representative of the Islamic tradition to ascribe attributes to their rightful owners, speaks of servanthood as the highest human station, attained only by the perfect human being. In order to attain to perfection, he says, "The servant returns to his own specific characteristic, which is the servitude that does not compete with Lordship. . . . In all of this he secludes himself from governing his own affair."[39] Or again: "The perfect human being is separated from him who is not perfect by a single intangible reality, which is that his servanthood is uncontaminated by any lordship whatsoever."[40]

Like Avicenna, the philosopher Bābā Afḍal Kāshānī (fl. seventh/thirteenth c.) sees the soul's ascent to perfection as a movement from pure receptivity to pure activity. Typically, Bābā Afḍal describes this movement in terms of the ascending levels of existence. He makes use of the Persian language to distinguish between two fundamental senses of the word *wujūd* in Arabic: being (*būdan*) and finding (*yāftan*). The cosmos, which is *wujūd* or existence, can be divided into four ascending levels. Each higher level embraces the perfections of the lower levels. The lower two levels are merely "being." The higher two are also "finding":

> The difference between being and finding is that being may exist without finding, like the being of elemental and mineral bodies, which has no finding. But finding cannot exist without being.
>
> Each of these two kinds is then divided into two more kinds: potential being and actual being, potential finding and actual finding.
>
> Potential being is the lowest level of existence. It is the existence of material things in a matter, similar to the existence of a tree in a seed and the existence of an animal in the embryo.

> Actual being, without finding, is like the existence of elemental and other bodies.
>
> Potential finding belongs to the soul. The meaning of the word soul [*nafs*] and the word self [*khwud*] is the same.
>
> Actual finding belongs to the intellect. That which is potential in the soul is actual in the intellect.[41]

In another treatise, Bābā Afḍal employs terminology that shows without question that he has in mind the active/receptive, yang/yin dichotomy. He is explaining that knowledge is indispensable to the spiritual journey whereby the soul is transformed.

> The purpose of listing the various sciences and explaining the kinds of knowledge is to awaken the human soul from forgetfulness and lack of awareness of its own substance. To awaken the soul is to take it to the limit and perfection of existence [*wujūd*]. For existence has four levels: acted upon [*karda*], agent [*kunanda*], known [*dānasta*], and knower [*dānanda*].
>
> That which is acted upon is the lowest level. It is the whole corporeal world.
>
> That which knows is the highest level. It is the source and end of existence.
>
> The agent and the known lie between these two levels.
>
> The bodily things are acted upon, the souls and spirits are agents, and the realities of disengaged things are known. By these realities I mean the reality of agents, the reality of things that are acted upon, and the reality of knowledges. Intellect is the knower.
>
> The perfect human being brings together the acted upon, the known, the agent, and the knower. Within such a person the acted upon is joined to the known and the agent with the knower. . . . He joins his own Origin through all four, with God's guidance and bounty.[42]

In still another passage, Bābā Afḍal summarizes the stages of human perfection, culminating in the full actuality of the intellect through knowledge of God. He is in the midst of discussing why, among the four causes delineated by Aristotle, the final cause is precisely "final" and the most fundamental. Notice that each actuality, which is the actualization of full activity (*fiʿl*), is in turn a receptivity toward what lies beyond. The ultimate final cause and absolute agent is Real Being.

> It is possible that for every final cause there be another final cause. For example, the simple, elemental body exists for the sake of the compound body. Hence the compound body is the final cause of the simple, elemental body.
>
> Composition exists for the sake of the equilibrium of the opposite and disharmonious natures. The equilibrium of the natures exists so that there will be worthiness for receiving the power of the spiritual soul. The worthiness for receiving the soul exists for the sake of knowledge and intellect. Knowledge and intellect exist for the sake of Nondelimited Being. And Nondelimited Being belongs to the He-ness and Essence. . . . The noblest cause is the final cause and perfection.[43]

The great philosopher of the Safavid period, Mullā Ṣadrā (d. 1050/1641), reflects both the philosophical and Sufi traditions when he describes the movement of the soul to the station of the Active Intellect:

> If you look at the soul's substance in this world, you will find that it is the principle of all bodily faculties. It employs all the animal and vegetal forms. But if you look at its substance in the World of the Intellect, you will find that, at the beginning of its original disposition, it is pure potentiality without any form in that world. However, it can emerge from potentiality into actuality in respect of the intellect and the intelligible.
>
> The soul's original relationship to the form of the World of Intellect is the relationship of a seed to the fruit and an embryo to the animal. Just as the embryo is actually an embryo and potentially an animal, so also the soul is actually a mortal and potentially an intellect. To this point God alludes with His words, "Say: 'I am only a mortal like you. To me it has been revealed that your God is one God'" [18:110]. The soul of the Prophet resembles other mortal souls in this [mortal] configuration. But when his soul, through divine revelation, emerged from potentiality to actuality, it became the most excellent of creatures and nearer to God than every prophet and angel. For the Prophet said, "I have a time with God when no angel brought nigh or prophet sent out embraces me."[44]

The Prophet in the perfection of his soul is the example par excellence of what the specifically religious teachings refer to as the "vicegerent of God," the person who rules the cosmos and determines its shape in keeping with God's prescriptive command. The Sufis would remind us that this Active Intellect, like the First Intellect, has two faces, one turned toward God and the other turned toward the cosmos. Through the first face it receives the divine effusion, through the second it actively rules the cosmos. It is both servant and vicegerent.

In short, the perfection of the yang side of human nature pertains specifically to intelligence, to what Avicenna calls the "Active Intellect." But implicit within this perfection is the submission to the Origin, or rather, identity with It. The perfection of the yin side of human nature pertains to this submission and receptivity of the soul.

Ibn al-ʿArabī devotes much of his attention in his voluminous works to outlining the possible modalities of the soul's perfection. In referring to the femininity of the soul that must be actualized, he brings the issue down to the concrete level of the discipline that is imposed by a Sufi master. The question is whether or not a male disciple on the path to God may have friends (*rafīq*) among women. In other words, is it possible for him to have a legitimate "Platonic" relationship with members of the opposite sex, or must he limit his relationships to the female members of his own family? Ibn al-ʿArabī provides an interesting answer, pointing to a dimension of the soul that every man on the spiritual path—and every woman, of course—must realize. He concludes that such friendship is not legitimate, except in the case of the gnostics, those who have attained to spiritual perfection.

> The disciple should not have friends among women until he becomes a woman in his own soul. When he becomes feminine, becomes joined with the lower world, and sees how the higher world is enamored of him, then he will constantly witness his own soul in every state, moment, and influx as a woman taken in the marriage act [*mankūḥ*]. He should not see his soul in his formal unveiling and his state as a male or that he is a man in any sense. On the contrary, he must see himself as an utter woman. From that marriage act he must become pregnant and bear children. Then it is permissible for him to take friends among women. Inclining toward them and loving them will do him no harm.
>
> As for the gnostics, they are free, since they witness the holy hand of God, which is free in taking and giving.[45]

This idea is not limited to Ibn al-ʿArabī, though he is more explicit than most in his language. In Islamic India the image of the soul as a longing female becomes a mainstay of devotional poetry. It is true that this image is also present in various forms of Hinduism, but the Muslims would not have adopted it so readily if it had not already been implicit in their own tradition.[46]

Manliness and Chivalry

One of the great pre-Islamic virtues taken over by the Muslims is *murūʾa* (manliness), which is derived from the word *marʾ* (man). Lane quotes the classical Arab dictionaries in defining it. It consists

> in abstinence from things unlawful, or in chastity of manners, and the having some art or trade; or in abstaining from doing secretly what one would be ashamed to do openly; or in the habit of doing what is approved, and shunning what is held base; or in preserving the soul from filthy actions, and what disgraces in the estimation of men; or in good manners, and guarding the tongue, and shunning impudence; or in a quality of the mind by preserving which a man is made to persevere in good manners and habits. . . . In a word, [it is] virtue; or rather manly virtue or moral goodness.[47]

The Sufis looked upon manliness as one of the virtues that become established in the soul when it manifests the active qualities of the spirit. In his Persian *Ṣad maydān* ("One hundred fields of battle"), which describes the waystations of the path to God, Khwāja ʿAbdallāh Anṣārī has this to say about manliness:

Manliness is to lose oneself and to live in oneself. God says, "Be those who stand firmly in justice" [4:135].

The pillars of manliness are three things: to live with oneself by intellect, with the creatures in patience, and with God through need.

The mark of living with oneself by intellect is three things: knowing the measure of oneself, seeing the dimensions of one's own work, and striving for one's own good.

The mark of living with the creatures in patience is three things: being satisfied with them when they are strong, seeking out excuses for them, and deciding in their favor when you are strong.

The mark of living with God through need is three things: necessarily giving thanks for whatever comes from Him, necessarily excusing oneself for whatever one does for Him, and seeing that His choice is correct.[48]

As a character trait, manliness is closely connected with *futuwwa*, which signifies generosity, liberality, and nobleheartedness. We will follow the normal custom and translate the term as "chivalry." It derives from *fatā*, meaning "young man." Chivalry has formed the background of the moral order in the guild organizations throughout Islamic history.[49] The Sufis adopted it early on as one of the leitmotifs of their spiritual and social teachings.[50] The perfect exemplar of chivalry is ʿAlī, the cousin and son-in-law of the Prophet, fourth caliph, first Imam of the Shiʿites, greatest warrior of Islamic history, and patron saint of the guilds. According to some sources, after the battle of Uhud, when ʿAlī demonstrated his unparalleled valor, an angel was heard calling out, "There is no sword but Dhu'l-Fiqār, there is no *fatā* but ʿAlī."[51] This saying has gained the status of a proverb throughout the Islamic world.

Qushayrī provides a number of sayings concerning chivalry by Sufi masters in his famous *Risāla*:

The root of chivalry is that the servant strive constantly for the sake of others.

Chivalry is that you do not see yourself superior to others.

The one who has chivalry is the one who has no enemies.

Chivalry is that you be an enemy of your own soul for the sake of your Lord.

Chivalry is that you act justly without demanding justice for yourself.

Chivalry is a beautiful character.[52]

Anṣārī provides us with two descriptions of chivalry in the context of the spiritual path. The first is from his Persian *Ṣad maydān*:

God says, "They were chivalrous youths who had faith in their Lord" [18:13].

What is chivalry? To live in young-manliness and freedom. Chivalry is of three kinds: a kind with God, a kind with the creatures, and a kind with oneself

To be chivalrous with God is to strive in servanthood with all one's strength. To be chivalrous with creatures is not to blame them for a defect that you know comes from yourself. To be chivalrous with oneself is not to accept the temptations, embellishments, and adornments of your own soul.

Chivalry with God has three marks: You never tire of seeking knowledge, you never cease remembering Him, and you stick to companionship with good people.

Chivalry with the creatures has three marks: You never have suspicions concerning what you do not know from them, you cover over what you do know, and thereby you become an intercessor for the faithful.

Chivalry with oneself has three marks: You busy yourself with seeking out your own defects, you show gratitude for the blessing of having your defects covered over, and you never cease in your fear [of God].[53]

Anṣārī's second description of chivalry comes from his Arabic classic, *Manāzil al-sāʾirīn* (The waystations of the travelers):

God says, "They were chivalrous youths who had faith in their Lord, and We increased them in guidance" [18:13]. The subtle point in chivalry is that you witness nothing extra for yourself and you see yourself as not having any rights. It has three degrees:

The first degree is to abandon quarreling, to overlook slips, and to forget wrongs.

The second degree is that you seek nearness to the one who goes far from you, honor the one who wrongs you, and find excuses for the one who offends you. You do this by being generous, not by holding yourself back, by letting go, not by enduring patiently.

> The third degree is that in traveling the path you do not depend upon any proofs, you do not stain your response [to God] with [any thought of] recompense, and you do not stop at any designation in your witnessing.
>
> You should know that he who compels his enemy to intercession and has no compunction about not pardoning him has never smelt the scent of chivalry. According to the science of the elect, he who seeks the light of Reality by means of rational arguments will never be able to claim chivalry.[54]

Authors such as Qushayrī and Anṣārī consider manliness and chivalry as two stations or two virtues among many. But some Sufis put these virtues at the height of human qualities, just short of perfection itself. ʿAbd al-Razzāq Kāshānī voices this opinion at the beginning of his Persian *Tuḥfat al-ikhwān fī khaṣā'iṣ al-fityān* (The gift to the brethren on the characteristics of the chivalrous young men). He makes chivalry the final stage before reaching *walāya*, "sanctity," or being a friend of God.

> Chivalry consists in the manifestation of the light of the original nature [*fiṭra*] and its gaining mastery over the darkness of the bodily configuration. All the virtues become manifest within the soul and all ugly qualities disappear.
>
> The human original nature comes to be delivered from the blights and accidents of the soul's attributes and motives. It is freed from the veils of natural wrappings and the ties of corporeal attachments. Then it becomes pure and luminous. It gains preparation and yearns for its own perfection. It recoils from base goals and lowly aims. It deems it necessary to turn away from ugly qualities and blameworthy character traits. It pulls aside from the belt of this-worldly chaff and the clothing of the faculties of anger and appetite. Through high aspiration it passes beyond transitory affairs and turns toward high and noble things. It becomes eagerly desirous and passionately fond of manifesting virtues and perfections within its own nature. This state is called "manliness."
>
> The human being perseveres in these affairs until the force of the soul is broken, its strength and evil are overcome, and subdual and firmness become the person's second nature. The person remains firm in purity, radiance, luminosity, and subtlety. Then all the kinds of moral integrity [*ʿiffa*] and courage become firmly rooted within him. All the varieties of wisdom and justice become manifest from him in actuality. This is called "chivalry."
>
> Hence manliness is to gain the deliverance and purity of the original nature, while chivalry is this nature's luminosity and radiance. Just as manliness is the foundation and basis of chivalry, so also chivalry is the foundation and basis of being the friend of God [*walāya*]. A person without manliness cannot possibly gain chivalry. A person without chivalry cannot possibly become God's friend. For manliness is the sign of the connection of the servant to God through the wholesomeness of the original nature. That is why ʿAlī said, "Overlook the slips of the possessors of the attributes of manliness, for none of them slips without his hand being taken by the hand of God." In the state of his falling away, God takes his hand. The pivot of manliness is moral integrity. When moral integrity is completed, manliness is complete.[55]

Sufis frequently employ the term *rajul*, another word meaning man as opposed to woman, to refer to the great friends of God, those who have attained to the station of human perfection. Ibn al-ʿArabī constantly uses the term, but he is careful to point out that it is not gender specific. For example, he describes the process whereby "the human being becomes purified through the light of intellect and guidance after having emerged from the darkness of nature and caprice." The person then reaches a state wherein he is called a "man." "The perfection of manliness [*rujūliyya*] lies in what we have mentioned, whether the person be male or female."[56] Towards the beginning of a long section of the *Futūḥāt* classifying the different types of God's friends, he cites the example of those friends called the "Substitutes":

> Everything we mention about these men by the term *men* may include women, though most often men are mentioned. One of God's friends was asked, "How many are the Substitutes [*abdāl*]?" He answered, "Forty souls." He was asked, "Why do you not say forty men?" He answered, "Because there may be women among them."[57]

About a woman Sufi Ibn al-ʿArabī remarks, "I have never seen one more chivalrous than her in our time."[58] In short, a host of good qualities is associated with being a "man" or a "young man," though these qualities may be possessed by women as well as men. These in turn are connected with the struggle (*jihād*) of the soul against itself and the victory of the spiritual warrior in the battle against his or her lower nature. The achievement of manliness and chivalry verges on the achievement of human perfection, which is connected to the full activity of the intellect and the full receptivity of the soul toward God.

Negative Masculinity

The qualities of the lord, such as knowing, ruling, control, kingship, and domination, belong by right to God alone. Within the microcosm, they pertain by nature and right to the spirit, while the opposite qualities, those of the vassal and the servant, define the soul's correct relationship with the spirit. Hence yang qualities such as highness, brightness, and control are virtues when found in the spirit, because they are light's inherent qualities in relation to darkness. These same yang qualities also belong to the soul by right when the soul's relationship with the body is taken into account. The soul must dominate over the body for the same reason that the spirit must control the soul. Though these yang qualities are only dimly present in the soul, they may be intensified through the soul's receptivity to the spirit's light. As long as the soul remains fully receptive to the spirit, it can gradually change from the soul that commands to evil into the soul at peace with God.

When the soul is contrasted with the spirit, it corresponds to the earth. Hence it possesses all earthly qualities, which are summed up as the characteristics of the four elements: earth, water, fire, and air. Like the qualities of the earth as contrasted with those of heaven, the qualities of the elements may be positive or negative, depending on the relationship envisaged. The soul that commands to evil is associated most commonly with fire, since it has a close kinship with Satan and the other jinn, who were created from fire. We have noted already certain negative qualities of fire, such as pride and seeking greatness. These qualities lie on the yang side of things, since they manifest a masculine assertiveness that allows fire to consume everything that it dominates. But when the soul manifests the qualities of fire, they work to its detriment, since they prevent it from seeing light and becoming light. In other words, the soul that commands to evil asserts control in realms in which by right it should be yin, while it yields in realms in which by right it should be yang.

The normative situation of the soul demands that it should be the servant of the spirit and the master of the faculties through which it aids the body. These faculties include appetite and anger—the pig and the dog. But if the soul submits to the pig and the dog, it puts the wise man into the satan's service and follows a path that leads to wretchedness. Iblis dominates over Adam and leads him into loss. The soul assumes attributes proper to Satan. These are by and large domineering, since they control, but for the wrong ends.

Muʾayyid al-Dīn Jandī makes use of the qualitative distinction between the elements to explain the relationship between Adam and Iblis. Why did Iblis refuse to bow himself before Adam? When God asked him this question, Iblis replied, "I am better than he. Thou createdst me of fire, and him Thou createdst of clay" (7:12). The qualities of fire demand self-assertion and rising up in fury. The qualities of clay demand submission and acquiescence.

> The realities [of the human being and Iblis] are different, so opposition, counteractivity, and enmity occur in the world of form. This follows upon the real opposition in the realities and the fact that the configuration of each of the two is opposed to the configuration of the other in the greatest part. The greatest part in the configuration of the human being is water, then earth. These two—through their realities, forms, powers, and spiritual essences

—give softness, yielding, obedience, reception, submission, faith, fixity, gravity, affection, tranquility, reverent fear, abasement, servanthood, lowliness, knowledge, forbearance, patient waiting, and similar attributes. But the greatest part in the configuration of Iblis and the satans is fire, and it—through its reality, form, and spiritual essence—yields seeking exaltation, claiming eminence, fickleness, inconstancy, triviality, pride, haughtiness, ruling power, self-magnification, unbelief, denial, spite, and envy.[59]

When the soul is dominated by the qualities of fire, it sees its own substance as "better" than clay and refuses to acknowledge that its light derives from something beyond itself. It sees its own fiery nature as unmixed light and acts as if the light were its own. Iblis is unable to see beyond his own limitations. As Rūmī puts it,

> Of Adam, who was peerless and unequaled, the eye of Iblis saw naught but clay.[60]

> Iblis saw things separately: He thought that we are apart from God.[61]

> Do not gaze upon Adam's water and clay, like Iblis: Behold a hundred thousand rose-gardens behind that clay![62]

Rūmī's spiritual psychology is based largely on the dichotomy between soul and spirit considered as possessing the attributes of light and fire, though he prefers the term *intellect* to *spirit*.[63] Intellect has a luminous substance like the angels or the prophets, while soul has a dark, fiery, and rebellious substance like Iblis.

> The angels and the intellect are of one nature, but for the sake of God's wisdom they assumed two forms:
>
> The angel acquired wings and feathers like a bird, while the intellect put aside wings and acquired splendor. . . .
>
> Both angel and intellect are finders of God; both aided Adam and prostrated themselves to him.
>
> The soul and Satan were also one from the beginning and were enemies and enviers of Adam.[64]

> When Solomon leaves the palace, the jinni takes over as king: When self-restraint and intellect go, your soul commands to evil.[65]

Rūmī commonly compares the soul to the dog, the pig, the cow, and especially the donkey. He may have in view the docility of the soul in face of the world, but more commonly he sees in these animal traits the soul's active anger and stubbornness. Intellect—the distinguishing feature of the rational, human soul—is able to control the animal qualities and either transmute them or put them to work for the soul's good.

> The intellect is luminous and seeks the good. How then can the dark soul vanquish it?
>
> The soul is in its own bodily home, and your intellect is a stranger: At its own doorstep, a dog is an awesome lion.[66]

> You have abandoned Jesus and nurtured his ass. That is why, like an ass, you must remain outside the curtain. . . .
>
> Have mercy on Jesus, not the ass! Let not your animal nature rule your intellect.[67]

Of course in Rūmī's view, love is even higher than intellect, for love erases all duality between lover and beloved. If on the one hand the soul must submit to the intellect, on the other hand the intellect is but a fly in face of all-conquering Love. Rūmī often makes this point when explaining the Prophet's *miʿrāj* (ascent to God). Gabriel, who guided the Prophet to the "Lote Tree of the Far Boundary," could ascend no further, for his wings would burn. Gabriel is the angel of revelation and prophecy. Like the prophets, he has a microcosmic equivalent in the intellect.

> Intellect is a shadow, God the sun: How can a shadow stand up to the sun?[68]

> The intellect of the saints is like Gabriel's wing—it takes you mile by mile to the shade of the Lote Tree.[69]

> I had wings like Gabriel—six hundred wings were mine. When I arrived at *His* side, what use were wings?[70]

> I am with the King, I am both slave and King—how can Gabriel find room where there are only God and I?[71]

In short, the soul may be considered as a positive and good reality, in which case its attributes are of the yin type connected with servanthood, submission, and obedience. The soul perfectly submitted to God's will is then called "the soul at peace." In Rūmī's terms, it has reached the stage of union where the slave is no different from the king. This same yin soul also has yang attributes, but these are established in relation to the soul's faculties, such as appetite and anger, and the body. The soul at peace with God is in perfect control of its own attributes and the body that it governs.

When the soul is considered as a negative and bad force, its attributes are again of both a yin and a yang type. The yin negativity of the soul is that it should surrender to the dictates of the dog, the pig, and the satan. Its yang negativity is that it should acquire attributes proper to Iblis. In either case, this is the soul that commands to evil.

Finally a soul may be neither fully yin nor fully yang in either sense of the two terms. Such a soul is the "blaming soul."

In all these cases, the judgment as to whether the soul's qualities are positive or negative has to do with the soul's relationship with the spirit on the one hand and with the body on the other.

As pointed out above, many Sufi authors employ the term *soul* almost exclusively to refer to the soul that commands to evil. But most of these authors are also aware of the soul's ambiguity, so its positive sense sometimes comes out. For example, Shihāb al-Dīn ʿUmar Suhrawardī (d. 632/1234) provides a clear picture of the two sides of the soul in his *ʿAwārif al-maʿārif* (Gifts of mystic knowledge), even though on the whole he pays little attention to theoretical concerns. This work has probably been the single most influential handbook of practical Sufism in the Islamic world. In most of what Suhrawardī says concerning the soul he has in view the sayings of earlier Sufi masters. Thus, for example, at the beginning where he refers to the definition of the soul as a purely negative reality, having in view the nature of the soul that commands to evil, he takes most of the discussion from the Sufi classic *Qūt al-qulūb* by Abū Ṭālib al-Makkī.[72] When he provides his own view, however, he explains the situation with greater attention to changing relationships and takes into account the soul at peace with God.

> It has been said that the soul is a subtle reality [*laṭīfa*] placed within the bodily frame and that from it arise blameworthy character traits and attributes. In the same way the spirit is a subtle reality placed within the heart, and from it arise praiseworthy character traits and attributes. Just as the eye is the locus of vision, the ear the locus of hearing, the nose the locus of smell, and the mouth the locus of taste, so also the soul is the locus of blameworthy qualities and the spirit the locus of praiseworthy qualities.
>
> All the character traits and attributes of the soul derive from two roots: inconstancy [*ṭaysh*] and covetousness [*sharah*]. Its inconstancy derives from its ignorance, and its covetousness from its eager desire [*ḥirṣ*].
>
> In its inconstancy the soul is like a ball on a smooth, descending surface. Because of both its innate disposition and its situation, it never ceases moving.
>
> In its eager desire the soul is like a moth that throws itself on the flame of a lamp. It is not satisfied with a small amount of light without pouncing upon the source of the light that holds its destruction.
>
> Because of its inconstancy the soul is hurried and lacks self-restraint [*ṣabr*]. Self-restraint is the substance of the intellect, while inconstancy is the attribute, the caprice, and the spirit of the soul. Nothing can overcome inconstancy except self-restraint, for intellect uproots caprice.[73]
>
> Because of its covetousness the soul is greedy and eagerly desirous. It is these two qualities that became manifest in Adam when he was greedy for everlasting life and eagerly desirous of eating from the tree.
>
> The attributes of the soul have roots in its coming into existence. For it was created from earth, and hence it has qualities in keeping with earth. It has been said that the quality of weakness in the human being derives from earth, the quality of stinginess from clay, the quality of appetite from "stinking mud" [15:26], and the quality of ignorance

from "dry clay" [15:26].[74] It has been said that God's words, "[He created man of a dry clay] like baked clay" [55:14] display a quality in which there is something of satanity, since there is fire in baked clay. From this derive guile, cunning, and envy.

When someone knows the roots of the soul and its innate dispositions, he will know that he has no power over it without seeking the help of its Creator and Originator. The servant will not realize his humanity until he governs the animal motivations within himself through knowledge and justice. Justice is to make sure neither to fall short nor to go too far. Thereby the person's humanity and supra-sensory reality gain in strength and he perceives the attributes of satanity and the blameworthy character traits within himself. The perfection of humanity demands of him that he not be pleased with his soul in that. Then there will be unveiled for him those attributes through which he contends with Lordship, that is, pride, mightiness, seeing the self, being pleased with oneself, and so on. He sees that pure servanthood is to abandon contending with Lordship.[75]

"Contending with Lordship" (*tanāzuʿ maʿ al-rubūbiyya*) is a direct and explicit reference to the negatively yang qualities of the soul. This is the quality of Iblis, who argued with God concerning the affair of Adam. The qualities of the Lord are always juxtaposed with those of the servant, and servanthood is precisely *islām*, submission to the divine will. From this perspective, any claim to the qualities of the Lord appears as the soul's wrongful usurpation of the rights of the spirit or God, as we saw in the previous section.

Though the qualities of earth are frequently portrayed as positive in relation to the qualities of fire, they may also be considered negative, as we just saw. For the soul's earth-like submission to the dictates of appetite and anger upsets the right relationship between heaven and earth. Thus, for example, Najm al-Dīn Rāzī describes the earth's negative qualities while describing the ascent of the soul on its way to perfection. Since earth is the lowest level of creation, its negative qualities are the first that must be overcome on the "return" (*maʿād*) to God. Rāzī does not have in mind the compulsory return to God, which everyone experiences through death, but the voluntary return that takes place on the spiritual journey when a person dies to his own limitations.

First, one must step outside the waystation of earth, which is the last waystation of this world. The spirit reached it after becoming attached to this world. It is also the first waystation of the next world in the soul's return to God. That is why, when someone is put into the earth [after death], they say, "This is the last of the waystations of this world, and the first of the waystations of the next world."

But the dead are taken without their own free choice. The living person on the spiritual journey passes beyond the attributes of earth, not the form of earth. The attributes of earth are darkness, opacity, density, and heaviness. From the characteristic of darkness arise ignorance and blindness. From the characteristic of opacity are born attachment, clinging, and mixing with all things, and this produces dispersion. From the characteristic of density appear lack of mercy, lack of kindness, and hardness of heart. From the characteristic of heaviness appear meanness of nature, vileness, lowliness, baseness, lack of aspiration, contemptibleness, laziness, and disagreeableness.

The traveler has borrowed all these blameworthy attributes from earth. He has left there as a pledge generosity, manliness, chivalry, high aspiration, pity, mercy, kindness, knowledge, certainty, purity, truthfulness, concentration, delicacy, luminosity, and buoyancy. He cannot pass beyond the station of clay without giving its qualities back. And he cannot find the way to his own world without retrieving and taking back those attributes that he had brought from there and left with the earth as a pledge.

In the same way, he has borrowed blameworthy attributes from the other three elements: water, fire, and air. In place of each he has left praiseworthy qualities as security. So also is the case with the heavenly spheres, the stars, and the other worlds.

When the traveler returns all the loans, takes back his pledges, and goes back to his original resting place, he is appointed to the kingship of vicegerency. . . . Once he becomes king of the kingdoms, whatever he had previously borrowed that he had to return becomes his property. He controls them through ownership. As deputy and vicegerent of God,

> he employs all the worlds of the Unseen and the Visible as his own servants.[76]

In short, by giving up the negative attributes acquired by immersion in the lower world, the human being ascends to the degree of vicegerency, where he controls the cosmos on behalf of God. As the Active Intellect, he brings all things in the universe under his sway.

Adam, Eve, and Iblis

We have seen that the soul, when contrasted with the spirit, is that dimension of the human reality furthest from the light of God, while the spirit is close enough to be considered inherently luminous. Inasmuch as the soul is receptive to the spirit's light, it is completely positive. But inasmuch as it remains far from the luminous center of the cosmos, it is dark and ignorant. To the extent that it is unaware of its own darkness and makes no attempt to overcome it, it is a negative dimension of the person. In this respect the soul is a hindrance to human perfection and may lead to wretchedness. It is evaluated negatively: It is the "soul that commands to evil."

In his esoteric commentary on the Koran, Kāshānī frequently contrasts spirit and soul. Sometimes he views the soul as a good and positive reality, sometimes as a negative reality, depending on the verse. His interpretation of the myth of Adam and Eve is especially interesting. He discusses the microcosmic meaning of Satan—Iblis—and his relationship to the soul. He identifies Iblis with the faculty of the soul known as *wahm*, which I have been translating as "sensory intuition."[77] Human beings share this faculty with animals. According to the usual explanation given in texts on psychology, sensory intuition provides an immediate, but sometimes mistaken, awareness of the non-sensory state of a sensory thing. Neither the senses nor imagination can grasp this state, whether the thing is present or absent. For example, sensory intuition alerts us to the fact that qualities such as enmity, truthfulness, rapaciousness, and kindness may be present in a person or an animal. As Avicenna puts it, this faculty "perceives the non-sensible intentions that exist in the individual sensible objects, like the faculty which judges that the wolf is to be avoided and the child is to be loved."[78] Kāshānī remarks that sensory intuition is able to perceive particular meanings, but not universal meanings. Perhaps he means that it can grasp certain states of a person's soul, such as love or hate, but it cannot perceive the universal mercy and vengeance that pertain to the divine realm. In any case, sensory intuition is clearly an intermediary faculty situated somewhere between intellect and sense perception. The soul dominated by sensory intuition possesses a certain luminosity in relation to corporeal things, but it is a mixed and ambiguous luminosity, like that of fire. Since the faculty is also possessed by animals, it clearly ranks below reflection or thought (*fikr*), not to mention intellect.

Note that Kāshānī does not ascribe moralistic evil to the microcosmic Iblis. Sensory intuition has its limitations and cannot go beyond them. It has always had these limitations, and they are what they are. Sensory intuition plays a positive and necessary role on its own level. But like appetite and anger, it has to be kept in place. If a person follows sensory intuition instead of intellect, Iblis instead of the prophets, he is displaying the depths of ignorance and misguidance and will end up in wretchedness. Prophetic wisdom alone, which is grasped only through intellect, can lead a person outside the limitations of the animal soul.

Like Ghazālī, Kāshānī employs the term *heart* to refer to the essence of what makes a human being human, or what the philosophers call the "rational soul."[79] Thus in his *ta'wīl*, Adam corresponds to the heart, Eve to the soul, and Iblis to sensory intuition. We begin with God's teaching Adam the names (2:31).

> *He taught Adam the names, all of them.* In other words, He cast into the human heart the characteristics of the things through which they are known to be themselves as well as

their benefits and harms. . . . *When We said to the angels, "Prostrate yourselves to Adam."* Their prostration to him is their submission to him, their becoming lowly before him, their obedience to him, and their being subjected to him. *So they prostrated themselves, except Iblis.* Iblis is the faculty of sensory intuition. Sensory intuition does not belong to those angels who are purely earthly and veiled from the perception of meanings by the perception of forms, or it would necessarily obey the command of God willingly.[80] Nor is it one of the heavenly, intellective angels, or it would perceive the nobility of Adam. It would conform with Adam's intellect and willingly yield to him out of love and out of seeking the good pleasure of God. Sensory intuition is a jinn. In other words, it pertains to the lower Kingdom and the earthly faculties. It grew and was nurtured among the heavenly angels because of its perception of particular meanings and its ascent to the horizon of the intellect. Hence in dumb beasts sensory intuition stands in the place of intellect in human beings.

Sensory intuition *refused* because it did not submit to the intellect and refrained from accepting its ruling power. It *claimed eminence* because of its counting itself superior to things created from clay and to the heavenly and earthly angels, for it failed to grasp its own limits, that is, the fact that it perceives particular meanings connected to sensory objects. It transgressed its own stage by delving into intelligible meanings and universal rulings. *He was one of the unbelievers,* those who were veiled in eternity without beginning from intelligible and spiritual lights, not to speak of the light of Oneness.[81]

We said, "Adam, dwell with your wife in the Garden." The heart's wife is the soul. The soul is called *ḥawwāʾ* [Eve, literally "red inclining to blackness"] because it is inseparable from the dark body, and *ḥuwwa* is a color dominated by blackness. In the same way the heart is called *ādam* [Adam, literally "tinged with blackness"] because it is connected to the body through imprinting [*inṭibāʿ* (i.e., through becoming immersed in nature, *ṭabʿ*)], though the heart is not inseparable from the body. *Udma* [from the same root as *ādam*] is brownness, or the color that tends toward blackness. Were it not for its attachment to the body, the heart would not be called "tinged with blackness."[82]

The Garden within which the two of them were commanded to remain is the heaven of the World of the Spirit, which is the Meadow of Holiness. In other words, God said, "Stay within the heaven of the spirit."

And eat thereof easefully where you desire. In other words: Spread out and make yourselves comfortable in receiving heaven's meanings, sciences, and wisdoms. These are the foods of the heart and the fruits eaten by the spirit. Spread out to any extent whatsoever, in any level, state, and station that you desire, since it is everlasting, not cut off, not forbidden. *But draw not nigh this tree, lest you be wrongdoers* [*ẓālimūn*], those who put light in the place of darkness [*ẓulma*].[83] For "wrongdoing" [*ẓulm*] in common usage means putting something in the wrong place, while literally it means failing in what is right and in the obligatory portion.

Then Satan caused them to slip therefrom. He made them slip from their station in the Garden into the abyss of Nature by enticing them with corporeal pleasures and having them forever. *He brought them out of what they were in,* bliss and constant repose.[84]

Kāshānī clarifies Satan's role in his commentary on a second, more detailed Koranic account of these events. Iblis tells God that he refused to bow himself because his qualities were better than those of Adam. The section begins with the verse,

> He said, "What prevented you from prostrating yourself when I commanded you?" Said he, "I am better than he. Thou createdst me of fire, and him Thou createdst of clay." Said He, "Get down out of it. It is not for you to claim eminence here, so go forth. Surely you are among the humbled." (7:12)

Note that the analysis of Iblis's nature depends upon the qualities associated with fire. As pointed out in Chapter 4 and elsewhere, fire correlates with the imaginal realm. Kāshānī mentions sensory intuition as belonging to the World of Dominion (*malakūt*), which is the unseen world as opposed to the World of the Kingdom. Imagination is unseen inasmuch as it shares in certain spiritual characteristics, though it belongs to an unseen realm much closer to the visible world than disengaged spirits.

"Thou createdst me of fire." The faculty of sensory intuition was created from the

most subtle parts of the animal spirit. . . . It is the hottest thing in the body, so He called it a fire. Heat demands ascent and self-elevation. We have already explained that every faculty of the World of Dominion oversees the characteristics of what is below it, but not what is above it. It oversees both the perfections and characteristics of the body and those of the animal spirit. Since sensory intuition is veiled from the characteristics of the human spirit and heart, this veiling takes the form of its denial and causes its refusal and claiming eminence. It transgresses its own proper domain by making judgments about intelligible meanings and disengaged things. It refuses to accept the judgment of the intellect. This takes the form of its refusal to prostrate itself.

"*It is not for you to claim eminence here*," since claiming eminence is to pretend to possess excellent attributes of the self that one does not possess. The spiritual presence to which you claim to belong would not elevate itself above the intellect. "*So go forth.*" You are not one of the people of this presence. They are the mighty. "*Surely you are among the humbled*," one of the faculties of the soul that are inseparable from the low direction and remain constantly in lowliness by being tied to bodily things.[85]

The Koranic account continues by telling how God banished Satan and gave him respite until the Day of Resurrection. Then God addresses Adam, telling him to live in the Garden but to avoid the tree. "Then Satan whispered to them, to reveal to them that which was hidden from them of their shameful parts. He said, 'Your Lord has prohibited you from this tree lest you become two angels, or lest you become immortals'" (7:20).

To reveal to them that which was hidden from them of their shameful parts. In other words, Satan wanted to make manifest to them through their inclining toward Nature what had been veiled from them while they were disengaged from natural things, bodily enjoyments, base character traits, animal acts, and predatory and beastly attributes. Human beings are ashamed to manifest any of these and disapprove of spreading them about. Manliness prompts them to conceal them, since these are shameful things in the view of the intellect, so they scorn and despise them.

He said, "Your Lord has prohibited you from this tree lest you become two angels, or lest you become immortals." In other words, Iblis made them have the sensory intuition that joining with corporeal nature and hylic matter would give them the pleasures, perceptions, and acts of angels as well as immortality. . . .

And he swore to them, "Truly, I am for you two a sincere adviser." So he caused the two of them to come down. He made them come down to attachment to Nature and repose within it. *By delusion*, for he deluded them by dressing himself in the dress of sincere advisers and making them have the sensory intuition that bodily pleasures and the chieftainship of human beings would last forever. He enticed them with the benefits of the body and the appetites of the soul.

And when they tasted the tree, their shameful parts were revealed to them, so they took to stitching upon themselves leaves of the Garden. In other words, they began to conceal the blights of Nature through good manners and beautiful customs. These branch out from intellectual opinions and are deductions of the practical intellect. The two of them were hiding those blights with practical stratagems.

And their Lord called to them, "Did I not prohibit you from this tree?" The form of the prohibition is that which is firmly fixed within the intellect: inclination toward disengagement [from Nature], perception of intelligible things, and the avoidance of material and sensory things. *"And say to you, 'Verily, Satan is for you a manifest enemy'?"* This is what God inspires to the intellect: It must contradict the rulings of sensory intuition, oppose its perceptions, and stand firm in acting contrary to it and resisting it. God's "call to them" in this is that they are apprised of this meaning through an inspired thought. They are reminded of it after becoming attached to and immersed in the pleasures of Nature, when they reach maturity and when the lights of intellect and understanding become manifest to them.

They said, "Lord we have wronged ourselves." This is because within Nature the rational soul becomes aware of its imperfections, the snuffing out of its light, and the breaking of its strength. It has now been incited to seek perfection through becoming disengaged. "*And if Thou dost not forgive us*," by effusing upon us true knowledges, "*we shall surely be among the lost*," those who waste their original preparedness, which

> is the substance of felicity and subsistence, by employing it in the abode of annihilation. Thereby they would be deprived of reaching perfection through becoming disengaged because they kept on clinging to the imperfections of Nature.[86]

God then sends Adam and Eve down to this world, in a passage parallel to that discussed above. Next the Koran addresses the children of Adam, telling them what conclusions they should draw from the story. God has sent down a "garment" to cover those "shameful parts" that were exposed when Adam and Eve ate of the fruit. The shameful parts are the ugly character traits that grow up in the rational soul when it becomes attached to this world. The garment is the revealed law, the Sharia, which rectifies character traits and brings the soul into harmony with intellect. Through the guidance of the Sharia the intellect is able to disengage itself from immersion in the darkness of Nature, and the soul can then follow suit. Intellect, we should recall once again, is that dimension of the microcosm that corresponds to the prophets in the macrocosm. Hence its inherent characteristic is the light of guidance. However, it can be brought from potentiality into full actuality only when a person follows the prophets, accepts the revealed law, and possesses the receptivity of servanthood. The soul, considered here in its negativity, conceals the light.

> *Children of Adam! We have sent down on you a garment to cover your shameful parts.* In other words, [We have sent down] a Sharia that will conceal your ugly attributes and indecent acts. *And plumage*, that is, a beauty that will keep you far from resembling slovenly cattle and adorn you with good character traits and beautiful works. *And the garment of godfearing*, which is the attribute of piety and being on guard against the attribute of the soul, *that is better* than all the pillars of the revealed laws, since that is the root and foundation of religion. . . .
>
> *That is one of God's signs*, one of the lights of His attributes, since avoiding the attributes of the soul will not be achieved or made possible unless the self-disclosures of God's attributes become manifest. The Sufis allude to this with their words, "God will not take control of anything of the servant without replacing it with something better of its own kind." *Perhaps*, when the self-disclosures become manifest, *you will remember* your luminous, original garment, or the neighborhood of God, within which you were dwelling through the guidance of the lights of the divine attributes.
>
> *Let not Satan tempt you* away from entering the Garden and being inseparable from it. For he would strip you of the garment of the Sharia and godfearing, *as he brought your parents out of the Garden, stripping them of their* original, luminous *garments*.[87]

In another part of his commentary, Kāshānī ties sensory intuition into the negative masculinity of the soul while commenting on the Koranic verse, "When We let the people taste mercy after hardship has touched them, lo, they have a deception against Our signs. Say: 'God is swifter at deception'" (10:21). He begins by explaining why hardship and suffering are good for the soul. They make it aware of the limitations and narrowness of the lower direction and cause it to turn its aspiration upward. In contrast, well-being leads to self-satisfaction and arrogance.

> *When We let the people taste mercy after hardship has touched them.* It was mentioned that the different kinds of affliction, such as hardship, distress, and different types of misery, break the covetousness of the soul, subtilize the heart through removal of the veils that are the soul's attributes, refine the densities of nature, and remove the wrappings of caprice. Hence in the state of hardship people's hearts incline by nature toward their Origin, because here they return to the requirements of their original nature, go back to their fundamental luminosity and innate capacity, and incline toward the ascension that is in their root because of the removal of the hindrance. Or rather, inclination toward the high direction and the luminous origins is the innate disposition of the natures of all faculties relating to the Dominion. This is true even of the animal soul, if it is purified from the dark, bodily conditions, since remaining low is one of the bodily accidents. This is even so for the beasts and wild creatures: When their situation becomes difficult in times of barrenness and days of drought, they gather together, lifting their heads to heaven,[88]

as if their Dominion understands that effusion comes down from the high direction. So they seek replenishment from it.

In the same way, when outward blessings become abundant for people and natural supplies and corporeal desires are complete, the soul is strengthened by replenishment from the low direction. Then its faculties become presumptuous through elevating themselves over the heart. The veils become dense and coarse. Caprice gains mastery and becomes dominant. Ruling authority comes to belong to corporeal nature. Dark, bodily conditions accumulate. The heart takes on the condition of the soul and becomes hard and coarse. It becomes insolent and blessings make it reckless. Hence it disbelieves and becomes blind, deviating toward the low direction, since now it is far from the luminous condition.

To the extent that the soul gains mastery over the heart, sensory intuition gains mastery over intellect. Hence satanity gains mastery, since the intellective faculty is a prisoner in the shackles of sensory intuition, commanded by it, employed for its goals and put to work for its hopes. These hopes are acquiring the pleasures of the soul, replenishing it by means of the world of filth, and strengthening its attributes by means of the world of Nature. Satanity prepares the material of gratifications by means of reflective thought. Hence the heart becomes veiled through rust and is unable to receive all the attributes of God. That is the meaning of His words, *Lo, they have a deception against Our signs. Say: "God is swifter at deception."* For God conceals true severity in outward gentleness. All the while He prepares the chastisement of the "fires," which are deprivation, the "serpents," which are the conditions of vile qualities, the "black scorpions," and the "garment of tar" within this apparent mercy.[89]

The Soul's Animals

Kāshānī's allusion to the nature of the torments of the grave leads into a question closely related to the perfection and completion of the soul, that is, the afterlife, belief in which is one of the principles of Islam. Most authors of the intellectual tradition read the detailed descriptions of the afterlife given in the Koran and the Hadith as delineating the possible qualities that the soul may assume. At the beginning of its becoming, the soul is pure receptivity. If the qualities and character traits which it gradually adopts as its own conform with the luminosity of the spirit, then it ends up in felicity. If, on the contrary, the soul clings to the limitations and darkness of the lower realms of reality, it will fail to be uplifted by the qualities of the spirit. Instead it will ignorantly arrogate to itself the rights of spirit and intellect, and eventually it will find itself in wretchedness. Kāshānī refers to these two basic routes that the soul can take in explaining Koran 7:8, one of the several Koranic references to the scales that will be set up on the Day of Resurrection.

> *He whose scales are heavy.* In other words, the things weighed for him excel because they are "subsisting works, deeds of righteousness" [18:46]. *They are the prosperers*, the ones who achieve the attributes of their original nature and the bliss of the Garden of the Attributes in the station of the heart.
>
> *And he whose scales are light.* In this case the things weighed are the passing, sensory things. *They have lost their souls* by selling them for immediate and quickly disappearing pleasures and annihilating them within the Abode of Annihilation, even though souls are the wares of subsistence.
>
> You should know that the "tongue" of the scales of God is the attribute of justice. One of the pans is the world of sense perception, while the other is the world of intellect. When a person's earnings are of the abiding intelligible things, virtuous character traits, and good works joined with right intentions, then the scales are "heavy." In other words, they possess worth and weight, since nothing is worth more than continuous subsistence. But when a person's acquisitions are of the passing sensory things, transitory pleasures, corrupt appetites, base character traits, and ruinous evils, then the scales are "light." In other words, they have no worth and are not counted. There is no lightness lighter than annihilation. The "loss" of such people is that they wasted their original preparedness by seeking the chaff of this world and acquiring the hopes of the soul, since they became manifest in the attributes of their souls. They "wronged" the attributes of God by crying

lies to them, that is, by concealing them with the attributes of their own souls.[90]

If the soul fails to actualize the attributes of God that are latent within itself as a divine image, it will not become human. In other words, a person who at first had the potentiality to actualize the fullness of human nature instead will remain dominated by the qualities of the animal soul, which are the qualities that we see manifest around us in the animal kingdom. In the next world, when the veils are lifted and the true nature of things is exposed for everyone to see, such a soul will become manifest in its own proper attributes. Hence it will appear as an animal. This, in the view of our authors, is the true meaning of transmigration (*tanāsukh*).

Both the Koran and the hadith literature provide many examples of the close correspondence between works and the reward or punishment of the next world. The qualities present within a person in this world become manifest outwardly and concretely within the next world. For example, the Prophet said,

> If any owner of camels does not pay the alms tax that is due on them . . . , when the Day of Resurrection comes, a soft sandy plain will be spread out for him, as extensive as possible. He will find that not a single young camel is missing, and they will trample him with their hoofs and bite him with their mouths. Just as often as the last of them passes over him, the first of them will be brought back to him, during a day whose length will be fifty thousand years. Then judgment will be pronounced among mankind, and he will see whether his path takes him to paradise or to hell.[91]

The intellectual tradition explains such events by having recourse to the World of Imagination, which is neither purely spiritual nor purely corporeal. There disengaged spiritual realities become manifest as appropriate corporeal forms, and material things are transmuted into images that display their true nature.

Human beings, as microcosms, possess the qualities of all things within themselves, though not necessarily in an actualized mode. Since they are made in the form of God, they can actualize all the attributes of God. By the same token, they have the ability to actualize some divine attributes and not others. They can develop on the basis of all sorts of combinations and permutations of qualities. Inasmuch as these qualities manifest divine attributes, they are positive. But as soon as the prescriptive command and human felicity are taken into account, some combinations of qualities are positive and some negative. The right and left hands of God are not equal.

Animals are the closest children of the elements to human beings, so human attributes have strong affinities with animal attributes. What separates an animal from a human is the partiality of the animal's constitution, as opposed to the potential totality of the human form. An animal manifests one divine attribute, or two, or ten. But human beings have the potentiality to manifest every attribute, since they are created in the form of the all-comprehensive name of God. This, in the view of the sapiential tradition, helps explain the relevance to human life of myths and fables about animals, the most famous example in Islamic literature being *Kalīla wa Dimna*, also known as *The Fables of Bidpai*.

Almost all our authors compare certain attributes in the human being to the traits of well-known animals. They have good precedents for this in the Koran and the Hadith. For example, the Prophet was asked about the Koranic verse, "On the day the Trumpet is blown, and you shall come in troops" (78:18). He replied,

> Ten groups of my community will be gathered separately. God will have distinguished them from those who have faith and changed their forms. Some will be in the form of monkeys. Some will be in the form of pigs. Some will be upside down, their legs on top and their faces on bottom, and they will be sliding on their faces. Some will be blind and wavering. Some will be deaf, not understanding. Some will be chewing their own tongues . . . .
>
> As for those who are in the form of monkeys, they are the slanderers. Those in the form of pigs acquired property through unlawful means. Those upside down took usu-

ry. The blind are those who transgressed in passing judgment. The deaf and dumb are those pleased with their own works. Those chewing their own tongues are the ulama and judges whose acts conflicted with their words.[92]

Shiʿite sources provide many examples of such sayings. The following is a particularly good illustration, though I have not been able to trace it to any of the authoritative collections. The addition of a star and a planet at the end is perhaps meant to keep us from taking the saying too literally. ʿAlī is reported to have quoted the Prophet as saying,

> People who are metamorphosized [*mamsūkh*] [in the next world] become one of thirteen: elephant, bear, pig, monkey, eel, lizard, bat, scorpion, worm, spider, rabbit, Canopus, and Venus. . . . The elephant was a tyrannical pederast who left neither wet nor dry alone. The bear was an effeminate man who let other men come to him. The pig was a Christian man. The monkey was one of those who transgressed the sabbath. The eel was a cuckold. The lizard was a thief. The bat used to steal fruit. The scorpion was a stinging man from whose tongue no one was safe. The worm was a backbiter who caused separation among his friends. The rabbit was a woman who did not purify herself after menstruation or anything else. Canopus was a man who took the tithe. Venus was a Christian woman.[93]

The Ikhwān al-Ṣafā' provide lists of the analogical correspondences between animals and human character traits in their discussions of the microcosm. I quote a long passage which again is a good illustration of the type of thinking involved.

> The animals are many kinds, and each of them has a characteristic different from the others. Human beings share with them in all the characteristics. But animals have two characteristics that embrace all the others: seeking benefits and fleeing from harmful things.
>
> However, some animals seek benefits through severity and domination, such as predators. Some seek them through blandishments, like dogs and cats. Some seek them through artifice, like spiders. And all this is found in human beings. Kings and sultans seek benefits through domination, beggars through asking and humility, artisans and merchants through artifice and friendliness.
>
> All animals flee from harmful things and enemies, but some repel the enemy from themselves by killing, severity, and domination, like predators, and some through fleeing, like rabbits and deer. Some animals repel through weapons and armor, like hedgehogs and turtles, and some through fortifying themselves in the earth, like mice, vermin, and serpents. And all of this is found in human beings: They repel enemies through severity and domination. If they fear for themselves, they wear weapons. If they cannot master the enemy, they flee from him. If they cannot flee, they defend themselves through fortifications. Sometimes people repel their enemies with artifice, just as the crow overcame the owl in the book *Kalīla wa Dimna*.
>
> As for the fact that human beings share with the engendered things in their characteristics, you should know, my brother—God confirm you, and us, with a spirit from Him—that every kind of animal has a special characteristic imprinted within its nature, and all of these are found in human beings. Human beings are brave like the lion, timid like the rabbit, generous like the rooster, stingy like the dog, chaste like the fish, proud like the crow, wild like the tiger, sociable like the dove, clever like the fox, gentle like the cow, swift like the gazelle, slow like the bear, mighty like the elephant, servile like the camel, thieving like the magpie, haughty like the peacock, guiding like the sand grouse, astray like the ostrich, skillful like the bee, strong like the dragon, dreadful like the spider, mild like the lamb, spiteful like the donkey, hard working like the bull, headstrong like the mule, dumb like the whale, great talkers like the nightingale and the parrot, usurping like the wolf, auspicious like the sandpiper, harmful like the rat, ignorant like the pig, sinister like the owl, and full of benefit like the bee.
>
> In short, there is no animal, mineral, plant, pillar, celestial sphere, planet, constellation, or existent thing possessing a characteristic without that characteristic or its likenesses being found in the human being. . . .
>
> This explains why the sages have said that the human being alone stands after all multiplicity, just as God alone stands before all multiplicity.[94]

Ghazālī frequently employs the imagery of animals, as in the passage quoted at the beginning of this chapter. A work usually attributed to him describes the structure of the soul, showing how the characteristics of all creatures are found within it:

> Human beings were created at a level between beast and angel, and within them are found a totality of faculties and attributes. In respect of being nourished and growing, they are plants. In respect of sensation and movement, they are animals. In respect of their forms and statures, they are like pictures painted on a wall. But the characteristic for which they were created is only the faculty of intellect and the perception of the realities of things.
>
> Those who employ all their faculties in order to reach knowledge and good works through them are similar to the angels and worthy of joining with them and being called lordly angels. . . .
>
> Those who turn their aspiration toward following bodily pleasures and eating as the beasts eat have come down to the horizon of the beasts. Such people become dull like a bull, covetous like a pig, mad like a dog, spiteful like a camel, proud like a leopard, or evasive like a scorpion.[95]

Sufi texts frequently describe the negative tendencies of the soul in terms of animal characteristics. Samʿānī is typical:

> O dervish, the human being was given a place of peril: In one instant, he attains to the degree of Gabriel and Michael—rather, he passes beyond them. And through a single thought he becomes a dog or a pig. If he goes forward in accordance with knowledge and intellect, then we have a noble angel: "This is no mortal man, this is but a noble angel!" [12:31]. If he follows his appetites and makes his heart the threshold of Satan, then we have a worthless beast. He may be greedy like a pig, fawning like a cat, spiteful like a camel, proud like a panther, sly like a fox, mean like a dog. "The likeness of him is as the likeness of a dog" [7:176].
>
> The human being is an all-comprehensive city. His essence is a container for all the meanings of the cosmos. The wisdom in this is as follows: The Lord of Inaccessibility wanted to apprise him of the treasuries of knowledges and make him witness all the meanings of the cosmos. But the cosmos is exceedingly vast and the face of the earth is very wide. There was no way that mortal human beings could travel all around the cosmos in its entirety, given their short life and their incapacity in their affairs. Hence the divine wisdom required and requested from the divine power that an abridged transcription be made of the root of the macrocosm. This was then recorded in the microcosm. Then He placed this abridged tablet before the child, the intellect, and He made him bear witness to it: "He made them bear witness to their own souls: 'Am I not your Lord?' They replied, 'Yes, we bear witness'" [7:172].[96]

As a microcosm, the soul contains all the animal characteristics, and any one of them may dominate over it. The only way to overcome these characteristics is to strive in the way of religion (*dīn*). As Samʿānī puts it,

> These Men who entered into this path fought a war against their selves, a war that had no way to peace. For they found the soul to be the opponent of religion. How can the man who has religion make peace with the opponent of religion? Sometimes they described the soul as a beast, sometimes as a serpent, sometimes as a dog, sometimes as a pig. Every picture they described it with was correct, except the picture of religion.[97]

Rūmī constantly uses animal imagery in his poetry to bring out the qualities and character traits of different types of people or simply to express the general human situation. Like Ghazālī and others, he divides creatures into three basic kinds—angels, human beings, and animals—citing also a prophetic saying to this effect. His position is no different from that of others, but his way of expressing himself shows something of the laughing warmth of his personality:

> The situation of the human being is like an angel's wing being attached to a donkey's tail. Hopefully that ass, through the radiance and companionship of the angel, will itself become an angel.[98]

One of the clearest explanations of the principle of qualitative correspondence at work here is provided by Nasafī. The following is taken from a chapter entitled, "Explaining Adam and Eve."

You should know that just as Adam, Eve, and Iblis are found in the macrocosm, so also they are found in the microcosm. And just as predators, beasts, satans, and angels are found in the macrocosm, so also they are found in the microcosm.

O dervish! The human being is the microcosm. Intellect is this world's Adam. The body is Eve. Sensory intuition is Iblis. Appetite is the peacock.[99] Anger is the serpent. Good character traits are paradise. Bad character traits are hell. The faculties of intellect, the faculties of the spirit, and the faculties of the body are the angels. O dervish! Satan is one thing and Iblis is another. Satan is Nature, while Iblis is sensory intuition.

O dervish! Form is of no account—meaning must be considered. Names are of no account—attributes must be considered. Lineage is of no account—excellence must be considered.

A dog is not low and vile through its form as a dog. It is low and vile because of the attribute of predatoriness and viciousness. When this attribute is found in a human being, that human being is a dog through the attribute.

A pig is not low and vile because of its form as a pig. It is low and vile because of the attribute of eager desire and covetousness. When this attribute is found in a human being, that human being is a pig through the attribute.

Satan is not low and vile because of his form as a satan. He is vile and bad because of disobedience and teaching evil. When this attribute is found in a human being, that human being is a satan through the attribute.

Iblis is not driven away and distant because of his form as Iblis. He is driven away because of the attribute of pride, self-satisfaction, envy, and disobedience. When this attribute is found in a human being, that human being is an Iblis through the attribute.

The angel is not noble and good through its form as an angel. It is noble and good through its obedience and heeding commands. When this attribute is found in a human being, that human being is an angel through the attribute.

You should think of all things in these terms.

The business of God's vicegerent is to make all these attributes subjected and obedient to himself. He puts each of them to work in its own place. Without his command, none of them will do anything. God's vicegerent is Solomon. All these work for Solomon.[100]

O dervish! The angel and Iblis are a single power. As long as this power is not obedient to Solomon, it is called "Iblis." Solomon puts one of them in chains. When it obeys Solomon, it is called an "angel." Then Solomon puts it to work. Some build, some dive.[101]

Hence the work of Solomon is to change attributes, not to eliminate attributes, since this is impossible. He makes the disobedient obedient. He teaches the one who behaves badly right conduct. He makes the blind seeing and the deaf hearing. He brings the dead to life. Hence the intellect, which is God's vicegerent, is Adam, Solomon, and Jesus.

If the situation is different from this, then all these things subjugate Solomon and make him obey them. Hence Solomon becomes the prisoner of the dog and the pig, the slave of the devil and the satan. He must serve them every day, searching out their wants. . . .

O dervish! Though a person like this has the form of a human being, in meaning he is a devil and satan, or a dog and a pig.[102]

In reading the descriptions of the afterlife provided by the Koran and the Hadith, many authorities came to the conclusion that at death the soul is transferred to the World of Imagination, where essences and meanings are experienced directly, without the intermediary of the corporeal body. Through the growth of the soul in this world, all its sensory faculties pertaining to the animal level of existence come to be developed. After death, these faculties continue to function without the body. The imaginal realities are perceived by the senses, like corporeal things, but they are far more intense in existence, like spiritual things. Moreover, it is here that "qualitative correspondence" plays a dominating ontological role. The body has disappeared, so its darkness can no longer fend off the realities of things. Character traits are seen for what they are, hypocrisy is unmasked, moral ugliness—or beauty—assumes concrete form. "Today We have lifted thy covering," says God to the soul that has just died, "so thy sight today is piercing" (50:22). These ideas are expressed in perhaps the most appropriate form by poets of the spiritual tradition, especially Rūmī. The philosophical and cosmological underpinnings of eschatology are dealt with most thoroughly by Ibn al-ʿArabī and Mullā Ṣadrā, though from Suhrawardī al-Maqtūl onward, the appeal to the World of Imagination is standard procedure.[103]

Already Ghazālī refers to the appropriate nature of the images perceived after death. In a passage from the *Iḥyā*ʾ quoted from him earlier, he remarks that if people were to perceive their own situation in appropriate imaginal forms, they would see themselves bowing before pigs and dogs. In the parallel passage in *Kīmiyā-yi saʿādat*, he extends the discussion to the afterlife:

> If people were to be honest and remove the veil of forgetfulness, most of them would see that, day and night, they have tightened the belt of service before the desires and caprice of their own souls. And this in reality is their state, even though in form they are human. But tomorrow, at the resurrection, meanings will be laid bare. Form will appear in the color of meaning. If a person is dominated here by appetite and greed, tomorrow he will be seen in the form of a pig. If he is dominated by anger, he will be seen as a dog.[104]

In the next world, the soul experiences its own character traits as the "snakes and scorpions" promised to the wrongdoers by various prophetic sayings. Rūmī makes the point clearly:

> Man's existence is a jungle: Beware of his existence if you breathe the breath of the spirit!
>
> There are thousands of wolves and pigs in our existence: good and evil, fair and foul.
>
> Man's properties are determined by the trait that predominates: If gold is more than copper, then he is gold.
>
> Of necessity you will be given form at the resurrection in accordance with the character trait that predominates in your existence.[105]

Mullā Ṣadrā provides detailed philosophical explanations of the nature of the afterlife in many of his works. In brief, he explains that the soul moves from potentiality to actuality. But each soul's ultimate actuality is different, and it will appear in the next world according to its own specific nature.

> There is no human soul that does not acquire a certain kind of actuality in this engendered universe, an actualization of existence. Then it acquires an independent existence after the dissolution of the elemental body. Each soul acquires through its acts and works certain conditions of character and traits of second nature. These give to it a correspondence within itself with one of the four genera of substances, that is, the angel, the satan, the beast, and the predator. Then the soul is resurrected according to that which has become firmly rooted within it. He who is dominated by knowledge and wisdom becomes an angel in actuality. He who is dominated by cunning and trickery becomes a satan in actuality. He who is dominated by appetite and greed becomes a beast in actuality. And he who is dominated by anger and love of leadership becomes a predator in actuality.[106]

Mullā Ṣadrā then says that the reports that have come down from Plato and earlier philosophers concerning their belief in the transferal of wretched souls into the bodies of animals must be understood in this light. Here he is following an interpretation going back at least to Avicenna, who writes,

> It has been related that one of the sages said that if the soul has done evil, then, after it is separated from the bodily frame, it will return to another body similar to it in that evil trait. Thus, if the evildoing was based on the pull of appetite, the soul will come into the body of a pig. If the evildoing grew up out of becoming angry, causing harm, and making people suffer, then the soul will come in the body of a lion. . . .
>
> This and similar things related from the sages are all allusions [*ishārāt*]. They said such things so that the common people would avoid evildoing. . . . What they meant by these allusions was to [exhort their readers to] empty the soul of evil attributes, since, if these attributes remain, it would be as if they had remained in the body. . . . Then the soul would receive effects from the bodily faculties. . . . This would prevent the soul from seeking for its own perfection and would hold it back from knowledge and intellection, which are the act of the soul in its own substance. Then it would have no awareness of the pleasure that is singled out for it alone.
>
> Although the soul's connection with the body will be terminated after it leaves the

body, nevertheless, if the body's effect remains, the soul will be as if it were still in the body. And the evil condition that the soul gains through connection with the body is an effect either from the side of the bestial appetite or from the side of the anger and wrath that is an attribute of predatory animals. After separation, it is as if those effects upon the soul are the body of a beast or a predatory animal.[107]

Ibn al-ᶜArabī makes the same point, but he states explicitly that all this actually occurs within the World of Imagination:

> It was here that the people who believe in transmigration slipped. They saw or heard that the prophets sometimes gave news about the passage of spirits into these forms in the World of Imagination, forms that accord with the character traits of the spirits. They saw these same character traits in animals. So they imagined that the words of the prophets, messengers, and men of knowledge refer to the animals that exist in this lower world. . . . They were mistaken in their view and in their interpretation of the words of the messengers.[108]

Purifying the Soul

The goal of human life is to purify the soul and allow it to rejoin the world of luminosity from which it descended. This theme permeates the intellectual tradition. We can take Avicenna as the spokesman of the philosophers. He sums up his conclusions in one of his important works:

> We have established the situation of the true Return. We have proven that felicity in the next world is earned by making the soul incomparable. "To make the soul incomparable" is to keep it far from those bodily conditions that conflict with the causes of felicity. This making the soul incomparable is acquired by character traits and second natures. Character traits and second natures are earned through specific acts. Their characteristic is that the soul turns away from the body and sense perception and constantly remembers its own Source. When it keeps on going back to its own Essence, it no longer receives the activity of bodily states.[109]

Najm al-Dīn Rāzī can speak for the Sufis. In *Mirṣād al-ᶜibād*, he describes the human soul in terms that sum up many of the points that have been made in the present chapter. He names this section of his book "Concerning the Purification of the Soul and the True Knowledge Thereof." As usual, he begins by quoting the Koran and the Hadith to set down the theme that will be discussed.

> God says, "By the soul and Him who proportioned it and inspired in it its wickedness and its godfearing—truly he prospers who purifies it, and he is lost who obscures it" [91:7–10]. The Prophet said, "Your worst enemy is your soul that is between your two sides."[110]
>
> Know that the soul is an enemy with the face of a friend. Its cunning and deception have no end. To repel its evil and subjugate it is the most important of tasks. For the soul is the worst of all enemies, worse than the satans, this world, and the unbelievers. . . .
>
> To train the soul and bring it back to a state of well-being and to make it advance from the attribute of commanding to evil to the level of being at peace with God is a great task. The perfection of human felicity lies in purifying the soul, while the perfection of human wretchedness lies in letting the soul flow in accordance with Nature. That is why God says, after several oaths, "Truly he prospers who purifies it, and he is lost who obscures it."
>
> The reason for this is that the purification and training of the soul result in knowing the soul, and knowing the soul entails knowledge of God. For "He who knows his own soul knows his Lord." Knowledge stands at the head of all felicity. . . .
>
> In the technical terms of the People of the Path, the soul is a subtle vapor whose source is the form of the heart. The physicians call it the animal spirit. It is the source of all blameworthy attributes, just as God said: "Truly the soul commands to evil" [12:53]. . . . The souls of other animals have the same relationship with their bodies in terms of form. However, the human soul has certain attributes that are not found in the souls of animals. One of these attributes is subsistence. A taste

of the World of Subsistence has been placed in the human soul. After separation from the frame it will subsist, whether in paradise or hell. . . .

Subsistence is of two kinds: One kind always was and always will be. This is the subsistence of God. The second kind was not, then came to be, and after this will subsist by means of the Real's subsistence. This is the subsistence of spirits, the Dominion, and the next world. . . . The human soul was given a taste of both kinds of subsistence.

The soul gained a taste of the subsistence of the Real when Adam's clay was kneaded. One of the precious pearls that God concealed in that base earth through His own Divinity was everlasting subsistence.

As for the taste of the subsistence of the spirits, that was placed within him at the time when the spirit and frame were paired through the controlling power of "I blew into him of My spirit" [15:29]. The likeness of this is that a man and woman should couple. From them two children are engendered in a single belly. One is male and resembles the father, the other is female and resembles the mother.

In the same way, from the pairing of spirit and frame two children appeared: the heart and the soul. The heart is a boy who is similar to the father. The soul is a girl who is similar to the mother, the earthy frame. In the heart are found all the praiseworthy, high, spiritual attributes, and in the soul all the blameworthy, low attributes. However, since the soul was born of spirit and frame, some of the attributes of subsistence and a few of the praiseworthy attributes that pertain to spirituality are found within it. . . .

[In the mother's womb] the sperm drop becomes a blood clot and the blood clot becomes a lump of flesh. . . . When three forty-day periods pass, the lump of flesh becomes worthy of becoming connected to the spirit. . . . When the child enters existence and reaches puberty, the soul reaches the perfection of soulness. After this it is worthy of carrying the prescriptions imposed on it by the Sharia. If the Sharia had been addressed to the person earlier, he would not have been able to carry the prescriptions, since his nurturing was still incomplete. . . .

Now that you have learned the true knowledge of the soul as appropriate for this summary, listen to an intimation that will tell you where its training and purification are to be found.

Know that the soul has two inherent attributes that it inherits from its mother. All other blameworthy attributes are born from these two roots and represent their activity. These two inherent attributes are caprice and anger.

We have not yet met caprice paired with anger, though this is commonly seen in Sufi texts. The word *caprice* (*hawā*) is employed synonymously here with *appetite* (*shahwa*). Like other authors who prefer the word *caprice* to *appetite*, Rāzī probably does so because *appetite* has too many connections with the philosophical tradition (which most Sufis do not defend), while *caprice* is a key Koranic term. The Koran employs it to sum up all the negative tendencies of the soul. In short, to follow caprice is to turn away from the Real. We have already met the term in such Koranic verses as 23:71: "Had the Real followed their caprices, the heavens and the earth and everything within them would have been corrupted." The literal meaning of the word is to drop, fall, tumble. By extension it means to fall for, to fall in love, love, passion. Rāzī has this extended meaning of the term in mind, as we will see shortly. For now, he turns to explaining the connection between these two attributes and the four elements, from which the soul's mother—the body—is compounded. Note that Rāzī connects caprice and anger rather explicitly with the negative yin and yang tendencies of the soul. Caprice or appetite is passive and falls for anything that pulls it away from God. In contrast, anger stands up arrogantly against the truth and the Real.

Both caprice and anger are specific characteristics of the four elements, which are the mother of the soul. Caprice is to incline and to go straight to the low. Thus God says, "By the star when it falls [*hawā*]" [53:1], that is, when it comes down. It is said that this verse refers to the return of the Prophet from his *miʿrāj*. He came from the high world to the low world. This inclination and going straight to the low is the characteristic of water and earth.

Anger is self-exaltation, seeking eminence, and seeking domination. These are the attributes of wind and fire.

These two intrinsic attributes of the soul are inherited from the mother. They are the leaven of hell. All the descending degrees of hell are born from them. At the same time, these two attributes—caprice and anger—must be present in the soul. Through the attribute of caprice the soul attracts benefits, and through the attribute of anger it repels harm. Through the two its existence subsists and is nurtured in the world of generation and corruption.

However, these two attributes must be kept in equilibrium. A deficiency of either results in the deficiency of soul and body, and an excess of either results in a deficiency of intellect and faith.

Here Rāzī almost certainly has in view the prophetic saying, "Women fall short in intellect and religion." For these "women" mentioned by the Prophet manifest the characteristics of the soul that commands to evil. And the soul that commands to evil is precisely the soul dominated by caprice and anger.

The purification and training of the soul consists in bringing these two attributes, caprice and anger, back to equilibrium. The scales in which they are to be weighed in every situation is the code of the Sharia. Thus, both soul and body will remain without fault, and both intellect and faith will advance. Each of these will be used in its proper place according to the command of the Sharia.

People should observe the rights of godfearing and not try to find excuses for neglecting the Sharia's commands. The Sharia and godfearing are the scales through which all attributes are kept in equilibrium. They prevent some attributes from dominating over others. Such are the attributes of beasts and predators. In beasts the attribute of caprice dominates over the attribute of anger, while in predators the attribute of anger dominates over the attribute of caprice. Beasts necessarily fall into eager desire and covetousness, while predators enter into gaining mastery, severity, domination, killing, and hunting. Hence the two attributes must be kept in equilibrium so that the person will not fall into the station of beasts or predators and other blameworthy attributes will not be born.

If caprice oversteps the bounds of equilibrium, then covetousness, eager desire, expectations, meanness, vileness, appetite, miserliness, and treachery appear. The equilibrium of caprice is that it should attract benefits—which is its specific characteristic—in the measure of imperative need and at the time of need. If it inclines toward more than it needs, covetousness appears. If it inclines before the time of need, eager desire is born. If it inclines in order to provide for the future, then expectations become manifest. . . . If the attribute of caprice is dominated over and deficient at the root of the disposition, then femininity, hermaphroditism, and lowliness will appear.

At this point it probably does not need to be remarked that this "femininity" (*unūtha*) is the negative femininity of the soul, the opposite of "manliness." It is the state of the soul that commands to evil because of its passivity toward everything below it. In a similar way, the hermaphrodite (*khunthā*) is lukewarm, neither man nor woman in the path of God, always wavering.

If the attribute of anger passes the bounds of equilibrium, then evilness of temper, seeking eminence, enmity, violence, fury, headstrongness, thirst for self-rule, instability, untruthfulness, self-satisfaction, boastfulness, self-exaltation, and pride will be born. If the person cannot express his anger, rancor will appear on the inside. If the attribute of anger is deficient or dominated over at the root, this will result in want of zeal, lack of jealousy, cuckoldry, sloth, lowliness, and incapacity.

One is a cuckold (*dayyūth*) when one's wife sleeps with another man. "Lack of jealousy" (*bī ghayratī*) is not to care when she does. The wife is the soul, and the "other man" is anything other than her husband, the spirit. Note once again that "jealousy" (*ghayra*) and "other" (*ghayr*) are intimately connected in both form and meaning. To be jealous is to turn away from all "others" and aim for God with single-minded attentiveness. For God is a jealous God, who wants no "others" to be worshiped in place of Himself. Perseverance in "jealousy" or the negation of "others" is to avoid *shirk* (associating other gods with God) and to establish *tawḥīd*.

If both attributes—caprice and anger—should dominate, then envy will appear. For, through the domination of caprice, people incline toward something that they see with someone and they like. Because of the domination of anger, they do not want that person to have it. So this is envy: You want something possessed by another and you do not want that person to have it.

Each of these blameworthy qualities is the source of one of the descending degrees of hell. When these attributes gain mastery over the soul and dominate over it, the soul inclines toward godlessness, wickedness, killing, plundering, inflicting injury, and all sorts of corruption.

When the angels looked with angelic glance on the Dominion of Adam's frame, they witnessed all these attributes. They said, "Wilt Thou place therein one who will work corruption there and shed blood?" [2:30]. They did not know that when the elixir of the Sharia was placed upon these blameworthy, bestial, predatory, satanic attributes, they would all turn into praiseworthy, angelic, spiritual, All-merciful attributes. Hence the Real replied to the angels, "I know what you know not" [2:30].

The basic function of the Sharia is to turn all the forces of the soul in directions that will help the soul reach felicity. As Ibn al-ʿArabī frequently remarks, all the soul's faculties and character traits are innate and cannot be uprooted. Hence they must be redirected, and this is the function of "guidance" or prophecy. Even negative character traits become positive when they submit to God's will.[111] Hence Ibn al-ʿArabī, like other Sufis, disagrees with a certain philosophical approach that speaks of eliminating negative character traits. Rāzī reflects that concern in what follows. His criticism of the philosophers is reminiscent of that of his contemporary Qūnawī in his discussion of the positive nature of the "womb" (above, pp. 221-22).

The alchemy of the Sharia does not efface these attributes totally, or that would also be a deficiency. It is here that the philosophers fell into error. They imagined that caprice, anger, appetite, and other blameworthy attributes must be totally effaced. They toiled for years, but those attributes were not totally effaced. However, they did become deficient. From that deficiency, other blameworthy attributes appeared. For example, when caprice is negated, femininity, hermaphroditism, vileness, and low aspiration appear. When anger is deficient, want of zeal, weakness in religion, lack of jealousy, cuckoldry, and cowardice appear.

The characteristic of the Sharia and the alchemy of religion is to bring each of these attributes back to equilibrium and employ each in its proper place. The Sharia acts to dominate over each of these attributes. They become like a tame horse for the Sharia, so it rides them wherever it wants. These attributes do not dominate over the Sharia such that it would become a prisoner to the soul wherever the soul inclines. Then the attributes would be like a rebellious horse that refuses to be tamed. Without wanting to, the horse throws itself and its rider into a pit or against a wall, and both are destroyed.

Once the attributes of caprice and anger are brought into equilibrium in the soul through the elixir of the Sharia and godfearing, such that the soul employs these attributes only according to the Sharia, then praiseworthy attributes appear within the soul, like shame, generosity, liberality, courage, forbearance, humility, manliness, contentment, self-restraint, gratitude, and other praiseworthy character traits. The soul leaves the station of commanding to evil and enters the station of peace with God. It becomes a mount for the pure spirit. Like Burāq, the soul will cross over the low and the high waystations and stages and take the spirit to the ascending levels of the Highest of the High and the advanced degrees of Two Bows' Length.

Here Rāzī describes the ascent of the soul in terms of the Prophet's *miʿrāj*. Through becoming the worthy servant, submitted to the Sharia, the soul is transformed into a celestial Burāq—the angelic steed that took the Prophet to the heavens. Then only can the soul reach the "Highest of the High," a term we have already met. "Two Bows' Length" is derived from an allusive Koranic description of the Prophet's ascent: "He drew near and suspended hung, two bows' length away or nearer" (53:8-9). According to some interpreters, the pronoun "he" refers to the Prophet, and the verse is describing his nearness to God. For many of Ibn al-ʿArabī's followers, the two stations—"Two Bows' Length" and "Or Nearer"—are the highest degrees of human perfection.

The first is achieved by the prophets and great friends of God, while the second is reached only by Muhammad.[112]

> Then the soul is worthy to be addressed by the words, "O soul at peace, return to thy Lord, well pleased, well pleasing" [89:27–28]. . . .
> When the spirit returns to its own world, it must have the Burāq of the soul, since it cannot go on foot. When it came into this world, it was mounted on the Burāq of the Blowing: "I blew into him of My own spirit" [15:29]. . . .
> The soul needs the two attributes caprice and anger. Whether it goes to the high or the low, it cannot go without them. That is why the shaikhs have said, "If not for caprice, no one would travel the path to God.". . .
> When the soul reaches peace with God, having dominated over the attributes of both caprice and anger and having heard the address "Return!", then it turns the face of caprice and anger away from the lowest and directs it toward the highest. The desired goal of the two becomes nearness to the Presence of Inaccessibility, not the enjoyments of the bestial and predatory worlds. When caprice aims for the high, it turns completely into love and passionate affection. When anger turns its face to the high, it turns into jealousy and aspiration.

"Jealousy," as pointed out above, can be understood only in terms of the "others." The jealous spirit will never be a cuckold, since it does not allow its wife, the soul, to look at anything but God.

> Through love and passionate affection, the soul turns its face toward the Presence, and through jealousy and aspiration, it refuses to stop at any station or to look at anything other than the Presence of Inaccessibility. So these two instruments, caprice and anger, are the spirit's most perfect means for reaching the Presence.
> Earlier, in the World of the Spirits, the spirit did not have these two instruments. Like the angels, it was satisfied with its own station. It was content to witness a single light and brightness from the candle of Unity's Majesty. For [the angels say] "None of us there is but has a known station" [37:164]. The spirit was not brave enough to take a single step beyond that station. Like Gabriel it used to say, "If I advance a fingertip, I will be consumed by fire."

Having told us about the spirit's original situation, Rāzī turns to the advantages that the spirit gained by being connected with earth.

> When the spirit became acquainted with the earth, the soul was born as the child of its pairing with the elements. From the soul, two children—caprice and anger—arose. Caprice was "very ignorant," anger "a great wrongdoer."

Here Rāzī ties the negative femininity and masculinity of the soul to two Koranic terms attributed to human beings in the verse of the Trust, which alludes to the unique role that humans play in creation. God says, "We offered the Trust to the heavens and the earth and the mountains, but they refused to carry it and were afraid of it. And the human being carried it—surely he is very ignorant, a great wrongdoer" (33:72). As Rūmī remarks, "Human beings are able to perform that task which neither the heavens nor the earth nor the mountains can perform. When they perform that task, they will no longer be 'very ignorant, great wrongdoers.'"[113]

> When the soul turns its face toward the low, these two—the very ignorant and the great wrongdoer—keep on throwing it into pits of destruction. The spirit is also their prisoner, so all of them are being destroyed.
> Then God's giving success becomes the soul's friend. The lasso of the attraction of "Return to thy Lord!" calls the soul—which has the attribute of a wild horse—to the high world and the Presence of Inaccessibility. Once the spirit, an intelligent rider, reaches its own "known station," it wants to draw in its reins like Gabriel.

With his words, "an intelligent rider," Rāzī wants to remind us that intellect is the attribute of the prophets and the angel of revelation, Gabriel. As we saw above, intellect can go only so far in its approach to God. At a certain point love must take over. Intellect is too cool and collected to risk the dangers of the unknown. But, as Rūmī puts it, "Love is that flame which, when it blazes up, burns away everything except the

Everlasting Beloved."[114] That is why the soul must possess the attributes of caprice and anger to reach its goal.

> The soul, which has the attribute of a wild horse, like a mad moth throws itself upon the candle of Unity's majesty with the two wings of being "very ignorant" and a "great wrongdoer"—caprice and anger. It says good-by to its own metaphorical existence and seizes the neck of union with the candle. Then the candle transforms its metaphorical moth existence into the true existence of the candle. As I put it,
>
> O you who sit around the candle,
> content with a single ear from its harvest,
> Place your souls on your palms, like moths—
> perhaps then will you embrace the candle.
>
> Until the soul reaches perfection through its work of being a great wrongdoer and very ignorant, one cannot know the soul perfectly in this station: What is it? Why was it created? For which task and to which station has it come?
>
> Once this work has become completely manifest from the soul, it passes beyond the madness of the moth and gives light by being a candle. For God says, "I am for him hearing, sight, and tongue. Through Me he hears, through Me he sees, and through Me he speaks."[115] Then the reality of "He who knows himself knows his Lord" will be realized. In other words, whoever knows his own soul as a moth will know the Presence as a candle.
>
> Were it not for Thee,
> we would not know caprice.
> Were there no caprice,
> we would not know of Thee.[116]

10

THE HEART

For many Muslim authorities, knowledge of the human heart is the key to knowledge of God, the macrocosm, and the microcosm. As the rational soul in its full perfection, the heart is the goal of creation. Made in God's image, it embraces all of reality. Only through the human heart can true equilibrium between God and the cosmos be established.

In the Koran and the Hadith

The Koran employs the term *qalb* (heart) 132 times, while employing near synonyms on several occasions. The root meaning of the word is to overturn, return, go back and forth, change, fluctuate, undergo transformation. The Koran uses a number of verbal forms from the same root in this meaning. It uses the term *heart* itself in a variety of senses, all of which point to the heart's centrality in the human being. Taken together, the various Koranic uses of the term suggest that the word's etymological sense—turning, overturning, changing—is not far in the background, since the heart is the locus of good and evil, right and wrong. Both the people of faith and the unbelievers have hearts. But to provide a thorough survey of the Koranic use of the term would take up far too much space. Instead I will attempt to classify the major senses of the term, providing a small number of examples. In almost every case, hadiths confirm what is found in the Koran.

Broadly speaking, the Koran pictures the heart as the locus of that which makes a human being human, the center of the human personality. And since human beings are intimately tied to God, this center of the person is the place where they meet God. This meeting has both a cognitive and a moral dimension.

Since the heart is the true center of the person, God pays special attention to it and less attention to the actual deeds that people do. "There is no fault in you if you make mistakes, but only in what your hearts premeditate" (33:5). "God will not take you to task for a slip in your oaths; but He will take you to task for what your hearts have earned; and God is Forgiving, Clement" (2:225; cf. 2:118, 8:70). A hadith tells us that, "God looks not at your bodies or your forms, but He looks at your hearts."[1]

Since the heart is the place where God looks, it is the key to hypocrisy, certainly the worst character trait in Muslim eyes. "God knows what is in your hearts" (33:51). "The hypocrites are afraid, lest a sura should be sent down against them, telling thee what is in their hearts" (9:64; cf. 3:154, 3:167, 9:64, 48:11).

The heart is the place where God reveals Himself to human beings. His presence is felt in the heart, and revelation comes down into the hearts of the prophets. "Know that God comes in [*yaḥūl*] between a man and his heart, and that to Him you shall be mustered" (8:24). "[Gabriel] it was who brought [the Koran] down upon thy heart by the leave of God, confirming what was before it, and for a guidance and a good tidings to those who have faith" (2:97). "It is a sending down by the Lord of the worlds, brought down by the Faithful Spirit upon thy heart" (26:192–94). "His heart [*fu'ād*] lies not of what he saw; what, will you dispute with him what he sees? And he saw him another time" (53:11–13). According to the hadith authority Muslim, these verses refer to the Prophet's seeing Gabriel with the heart on two occasions.[2] According to Ibn ʿAbbās, they mean that the Prophet saw God.[3] Sufi authors frequently cite the *ḥadīth qudsī*, "My heavens and My earth embrace Me not, but the heart of My gentle and meek servant with faith does encompass Me."

The heart is a place of vision, understanding, and remembrance (*dhikr*). "Upon the Day when the first blast shivers, . . . hearts upon that day shall be athrob, and their eyes [i.e., the eyes of the hearts] shall be humbled" (79:8). "What, have they not journeyed in the land? Have they no hearts to use intelligence or ears to hear with? It is not the eyes that are blind, but blind are the hearts within the breasts" (22:46). "Surely We have laid coverings upon their hearts lest they understand it, and in their ears heaviness" (18:57). "What, do they not ponder the Koran? Or is it that there are locks upon their hearts?" (47:24). "Surely in that there is a reminder to him who has a heart, or will give ear while he is a witness" (50:37). "Obey not him whose heart We have made forgetful of Our remembrance so that he follows his own caprice, and his affair has become all excess" (18:28). "Whenever a new Remembrance comes to them from their Lord, they listen to it in sport, their hearts neglectful" (21:2). "We have created for Gehenna many jinn and men; they have hearts, but understand [*fiqh*] not with them; they have eyes, but perceive not with them; they have ears, but hear not with them. They are like cattle; no, they are even more misguided. Those—they are the forgetful" (7:179). "Their valor is great, among themselves; you think of them as a host, but their hearts are scattered. That is because they are people who have no intelligence" (59:14). The Prophet said, "Verily God brings hearts to life through the light of wisdom."[4] In Bukhārī, Īmān 13 is called "The chapter on the words of the Prophet, 'I am the most knowledgeable of God among you' and that knowledge [*maʿrifa*] is the act of the heart, because of God's words, 'But He will take you to task for what your hearts have earned' [2:225]."

Faith grows up in the heart, while guidance turns the heart in the right direction. By the same token, the heart is the place of doubt, denial, unbelief, and swerving from the right path. It is where Satan directs his attention, trying to instill misguidance. "You do not have faith; rather say, 'We submit,' for faith has not yet entered your hearts" (49:14). "No affliction befalls, except it be by the leave of God. Whosoever has faith in God, He will guide his heart. And God has knowledge of everything" (64:11). "Those—He has written faith upon their hearts, and He has confirmed them with a Spirit from Himself" (58:22). "And We increased them in guidance, and We strengthened their hearts" (18:13–14). "It is He who sent down tranquility into the hearts of the believers, that they might add faith to their faith" (48:4). "And those who do not believe in the world to come, their hearts deny, and they have waxed proud" (16:22). "Our Lord, make not our hearts to swerve after that Thou hast guided us; and give us mercy from Thee" (3:8). "Those whose hearts are filled with doubt, so that in their doubt they go this way and that" (9:45). The Prophet said, "Surely Satan flows in people like blood, so I fear that he will throw evil into your hearts."[5] He also said, "When the call to prayer is made, Satan turns away while breaking wind. When it is finished, he comes forward, and when the second call is made, he turns away. When the call is finished, he comes forward in order to pass between a man and his heart. He says to him, 'Remember such and such' until he does not know if he has prayed three cycles or four."[6]

Through the heart the Koran can be grasped and unity achieved. The Prophet said, "When it [the Koran] falls into the heart and becomes firmly rooted there, it gives benefit."[7] He said, "This Koran is God's banquet, so take from it what you can, for I know of nothing smaller than a house within which is naught of the Book of God. The heart that has naught of the Book of God within it is a ruin, just as a house that has no occupants is a ruin."[8] Another hadith tells us that "A branch of the heart of the son of Adam lies in every stream bed. If someone allows his heart to follow all the stream beds, God will not care in which stream bed He destroys him. But if someone trusts in God, He will save him from branching."[9]

Koranic verses locate such virtues as purity, piety, confirmation, softness, expansion, peace, love, and repentance in the heart. However, these virtues are not inherent to the heart. They must be put there by God. If God does not purify the heart, it will be sick, sinful, evil, hard, harsh, full of hate, anxious, and so on. "Those are they whose hearts God desired not to purify; for them is degradation in this world . . . " (5:41). In the Koran, Abraham prays, "Degrade me not upon the day when they are raised up, the day when neither wealth nor sons shall profit except for him who comes to God with a faultless heart" (26:87–89). One of the Prophet's supplications reads, "O God, wash away from me my offenses with the water of snow and hail, purify offenses from my heart as Thou purifiest dirt from white cloth, and remove me far from offenses as Thou hast removed the east from the west."[10] The Prophet was asked, "Who is the most excellent of people?" He replied, "Every one whose heart is swept and whose tongue is truthful." They said, "We recognize the one whose tongue is truthful, but whose heart is swept?" He said, "He is the godfearing and pure, who has no sin, no wrongdoing, no rancor, and no envy."[11] "Whosoever venerates the offerings made to God—that is of the godfearing of the hearts" (22:32). "Those are they whose hearts God has tested for godfearing; they shall have forgiveness and a mighty wage" (49:3). "Remember God's blessing upon you when you were enemies, and He brought your hearts together, so that by His blessing you became brothers" (3:103). "But God has made you love faith, decking it out fair in your hearts, and He has made detestable to you unbelief and ungodliness and disobedience" (49:7). "It was by some mercy of God that thou wast gentle to them; hadst thou been harsh and hard of heart, they would have scattered from about thee" (3:159). "And We set in the hearts of those who followed him tenderness and mercy" (57:27). "Whosoever fears the All-merciful in the Unseen, and comes with a penitent heart . . ." (50:33). "Those who have faith, their hearts being at peace in God's remembrance—in God's remembrance are at peace the hearts of those who have faith and do righteous deeds" (13:28).

Sickness (*maraḍ*) is the most common negative attribute that the Koran attributes to the heart (e.g., 2:10, 8:49, 9:125, 47:20, 47:29, 74:31). "What, is their sickness in their hearts, or are they in doubt, or do they fear that God may be unjust toward them?" (24:50). "When the hypocrites, and those in whose hearts is sickness, . . . " (33:12; cf. 33:60). "And conceal not the testimony; whoso conceals it, his heart is sinful" (2:283). Other negative qualities include rage and fierceness. "And He will remove the rage within their hearts; and God turns toward whomsoever He will" (9:15). "When the unbelievers set in their hearts fierceness, the fierceness of pagandom . . . " (48:26).

The heart should be soft and receptive to the divine guidance, light, and love. But the hearts of the wrongdoers are hard and harsh. "God has sent down the fairest discourse as a Book, . . . whereat shiver the skins of those who fear their Lord; then their skins and their hearts soften to the remembrance of God" (39:23). "Then your hearts became hardened thereafter and are like stones, or even yet harder" (2:74). "So for their breaking the covenant We cursed them and made their hearts hard" (5:13). "Is he whose breast God has opened unto submission (*al-islām*), so that he follows a light from his Lord . . . ? But woe to those whose hearts are hardened against the remembrance of God! They are in manifest error" (39:22). "Is it not time that the hearts of those who have faith should be humbled to the Remembrance of God and the Truth which He has sent down, and that they should not be as those to whom the Book was given aforetime, and the term seemed over long to them, so that their hearts have become hard, and many of them are ungodly?" (57:16).

These passages from the Koran and the Hadith and many more like them show that the heart has no fixed nature. However, there are normative qualities that the heart should have, and any heart that does not have them is faced with the danger of deviation, misguidance, and wretchedness. Several hadiths point to the instability of the heart, its ability to accept any quality whatsoever. The heart, in keeping with its root meaning, never stands still. In many supplications recorded by Bukhārī (Qadar 14 etc.) the Prophet calls to God with the words, "O He who makes hearts fluctuate [*yā muqallib al-qulūb*]!" He also said the following: "The heart of the child of Adam is between two fingers of the Invincible. When He wants to make it fluctuate [*taqlīb*], He makes it fluctuate." So he often used to say, "O He who makes hearts turn about [*muṣarrif al-qulūb*]!"[12] "The heart is like a feather in a desert of the earth. The wind blows it to one side and the other."[13] One of the Prophet's wives reported that he used to pray with the words, "O He who makes hearts fluctuate, fix my heart in Thy religion!" She asked him about that, and he replied, "O Umm Salama, there is no child of Adam whose heart does not lie between two of God's fingers. Whomsoever He wants, He makes to go straight, and whomsoever He wants, He makes to swerve."[14]

Between Spirit and Soul

It would be possible to cite numerous references, especially from poetry, showing how the later tradition reflects the picture of the heart provided by the Koran and the Hadith.[15] Instead I will turn back to our authors to illustrate how they bring out the pivotal importance of the heart for the human being. They illustrate clearly that they followed the Koranic description of the heart as an indefinable reality that assumes a wide variety of qualities. But they were concerned primarily with bringing out the normative qualities that the heart should possess and showing how human perfection depends upon actualizing these qualities. For our authors, the heart is the divine form within us that must be brought from potentiality to actuality. Through perfection, it comes to manifest both hands of God. And its growth from imperfection to perfection can easily be understood as the play of relationships set up by a series of yin/yang qualities.

From the perspective of the engendering command, God has created the heart as it is, perhaps dominated by guidance, perhaps by misguidance. But from the perspective of the prescriptive command, the heart is called upon to assume a whole series of positive qualities, such as guidance, faith, intelligence, understanding, light, certainty, and so on. In actual fact, the heart is caught between the two sides—light and darkness, spirit and body. It may be dominated by the "soul that commands to evil," in which case it is predominantly dark. It may stand in the middle between spirit and soul, in which case light and darkness are contending. When light gains the upper hand, the soul "blames" itself for not conforming wholly to the spirit. Only in the greatest of human beings, the prophets and the friends of God, has the soul attained to "peace" with God, such that light is in total ascendence. Only in them can we speak truly of the heart. Other people, though human from a certain point of view, have not attained to the fullness of human nature. They are not, to use the common expression, "Possessors of Hearts" (*aṣḥāb al-qulūb*).

One of the most detailed early discussions of the nature of the heart is given by Abū Ṭālib al-Makkī in *Qūt al-qulūb* (Food of the hearts), a work that has been extremely influential in the Sufi intellectual tradition. Ghazālī, for example, made thorough use of it in writing his great *Iḥyā'*. As the title suggests, this long work is concerned with the perfection of the heart throughout. Especially interesting for our purposes is chapter 30, a thirty-two page section that deals with "Mention of the different kinds of incoming thoughts experienced by the People of the Hearts; the attribute of heart; and comparing the heart to lights and substances." "Incoming thoughts" (*khawāṭir*) are all the thoughts that occur to the mind (or rather, to the heart). They are "incoming" because they come from someplace. The Sufi psychologists employ this term precisely to set up a relationship between the thought in the heart and its source. In general, they discern four sources for all thoughts: God, the angels, the soul, and the satans. To know where one's thoughts come from in any given instance is a fundamental prerequisite for putting them into action or avoiding what they suggest. In keeping with the usual format of such works, most of what Makkī has to say is quoted from earlier authorities. I quote a few short passages to give his evaluation of certain important qualities of the heart.

The heart is the locus for the remembrance of God (*dhikr*), just as it is the place where caprice (*hawā*) appears and turns the individual this way and that.

> God says, "The godfearing, when a visitation of Satan touches them, remember, and then they see" [7:201]. Hence He reports that the clarity of hearts is remembrance, through which the heart sees. He also reports that the door to remembrance is godfearing, through which the servant remembers. Thus godfearing is the door to the next world, just as caprice is the door to this world. God commanded remembrance and reported that it is the key to godfearing, since it is the cause of protecting oneself, which is avoidance and renunciation. For He says, "Remember what is in it; haply you will be godfearing" [2:63]. He reports that He made the Explication manifest for the sake of godfearing through His words, "So God explicates His signs to people; haply they will be godfearing" [2:187].
>
> God says, "O human being! What has deceived you as to your generous Lord, who created you, and proportioned you, and balanced you?" [82:6]. He says, "We created the human being in the most beautiful stature" [95:4]. He says, "And of everything We created a pair" [51:49]. Included in this proportioning, balancing, pairing, and stature are the outward instruments [*adāh*] and the inward motives [*gharaḍ*]. These are the bodily senses and the heart. The instruments of the body are the outward attributes, while the motives of the heart are the inward meanings. God has balanced them through His wisdom, proportioned them according to His will, and given them a proper and firm stature with His making and handiwork.
>
> The first inward meanings are the soul and the spirit. These are two places for the encounter of the enemy and the angel, who are two persons who inspire with wickedness and godfearing.
>
> Among these meanings are two motives firmly placed in two places—intellect and caprice—deriving from two decrees in the will of the Decreer. These two decrees are giving success and misleading.
>
> Among them are two lights that shine in the heart by the specification of the mercy of Him who gives mercy. These are knowledge and faith.
>
> These are the instruments, the unseen senses and meanings, and the tools of the heart.
>
> In the midst of all these instruments, the heart is like the king, while these are his soldiers that discharge their duty to him. Or the heart is like a polished mirror, while these tools become manifest around it and are seen within it. . . .
>
> In short, the incoming thoughts are six. They limit and detract from the heart. Beyond them are the treasuries of the Unseen and the Dominion of Power. They are God's ready soldiers possessing manifest authority from Him.
>
> The heart is one of the treasuries of the Dominion. God, who makes it fluctuate, has in accordance with His will placed within it some of the subtle realities of the realms of desire and fear and irradiated it with some of the lights of tremendousness and invincibility. . . .
>
> The first two incoming thoughts are those of the soul and the enemy. The common people among the faithful are not able to eradicate them. These incoming thoughts are blameworthy and judged to be evil. They come only as a result of caprice and the opposite of knowledge.
>
> The next two are the incoming thoughts of the spirit and the angel. The elect of the faith-

ful are not able to eradicate them. They are praiseworthy, and they come only as a result of the Real and that which is denoted by knowledge.

The next incoming thought comes from intellect. It stands among the previous four. . . . The incoming thought of the intellect is sometimes with the soul and the enemy and sometimes with the spirit and the angel, because of a wisdom from God in His making and the ordering of His handiwork. Thus the servant enters into good and evil in accordance with a clear rationality and a sound witnessing and discernment. Then the reward or punishment that results from it returns to him. . . . The intellect's innate nature is discernment and judging between good and evil. The soul's innate nature is appetite and commanding to caprice.

The sixth incoming thought is that of certainty. It is the spirit of faith and the increase of knowledge. . . . This incoming thought is singled out for the elect; only those who have certitude find it. They are the Witnesses and the Sincere Devotees. This thought comes only through the Real. . . . They are the ones whom God has described by the Reminder and to whom the Prophet has ascribed making pronouncements. God says, "Surely in that there is a reminder for him who has a heart" [50:37], that is, him whose heart God has undertaken to protect. The messenger of God says, "When something scratches your heart, leave it. Sin cuts into the heart."[16] In other words, sin has an effect upon the heart and cuts into it, because of the heart's fineness, purity, softness, and subtlety. When a man asked the Prophet about loving kindness and sin, which are two roots of good and evil, he answered: "Ask for a pronouncement from your heart, even if the pronouncers give you a pronouncement."[17] . . . Another hadith tells us that "Loving kindness is that through which the heart gains peace, even if I keep on giving you pronouncements."[18] This is the description of the heart that undergoes unveiling through remembrance and the quality of the soul that comes to rest through increased tranquility and loving kindness.[19]

A more systematic early analysis of the Koranic verses dealing with the heart and related terms is provided by al-Ḥakīm al-Tirmidhī, who died toward the end of the fourth/tenth century. He is the author of a treatise called "An explanation of the difference between the breast, the heart, the inner heart, and the kernel." He discerns four levels of the heart, corresponding to an ever-deepening certainty and rootedness in God. He correlates the four levels with four levels of the soul, adding the "inspired soul" (*al-nafs al-mulhama*) to the three levels with which we are already familiar. Some of the correspondences that he sets up are shown in Table 12.

In the concluding chapter of the treatise, called "The Lights of the Heart," Tirmidhī associates many qualities with each of the four levels.

Even though their names differ, the lights that I described at the beginning of the book—such as the light of submission, the light of faith, the light of gnosis, and the light of asserting God's unity [*tawḥīd*]—are all similar and not opposite. From each of these lights, in keeping with its level, are born benefits that differ from the benefits born from the others. . . .

Each of these lights is like a mountain. Submission is a mountain whose earth is the breast, faith is a mountain whose place is the heart, gnosis is a mountain whose mine is the inner heart, and the assertion of unity is a mountain whose resting place is the kernel.

On top of each mountain is found a bird. The bird of the breast's mountain is the soul that commands to evil, the bird of the heart's

Table 12 Corresponding Qualities According to al-Tirmidhī

BREAST	HEART	INNER HEART	KERNEL
soul that commands to evil	inspired soul	blaming soul	soul at peace
a person submitted to the Sharia (*muslim*)	a person of faith (*muʾmin*)	a gnostic (*ʿārif*)	one who asserts God's Unity (*muwaḥḥid*)

mountain is the inspired soul, the bird of the inner heart's mountain is the blaming soul, and the bird of the kernel's mountain is the soul at peace.

The soul that commands to evil flies in the valleys of associating others with God, doubt, hypocrisy, and similar things. God says, "The soul commands to evil, except inasmuch as my Lord has mercy" [12:53].

The inspired soul flies sometimes in the valleys of godfearing and sometimes in the valleys of wickedness. "By the soul and Him who proportioned it and inspired in it its wickedness and its godfearing" [91:7–8].

The bird of the mountain of gnosis is the blaming soul. Sometimes it flies in the valleys of self-exaltation, mightiness, looking upon God's gifts [to itself], pride, and joy in God's blessings. Sometimes it flies in the valleys of poverty, humility, disparaging itself, and seeing its own lowliness, misery, and destitution. Along with all this it blames its possessor for its states. "Nay, I swear by the blaming soul!" [75:2].

The bird of the mountain of the kernel is the soul at peace. It flies in the valleys of contentment, modesty, firmness in *tawḥīd*, and the sweetness of remembering [*dhikr*] God. It corresponds to the spirit. God has cleansed from it the defilement of contention. God says, "O soul at peace, return unto thy Lord, well pleased, well pleasing" [89:27–28]. And He says, "Then repose, and ease, and a garden of delight" [56:89]. . . .

The substance of the soul is a hot wind like smoke. It is dark, evil in conduct. But at root its spirit is luminous. It increases in well-being [*ṣalāḥ*] through God's giving success. It must also have beautiful conduct and correct humility. But it does not increase in well-being until the servant opposes its caprice, turns away from it, and subjugates it through hunger and austerities.

The blaming soul is nearer to the Real, but it is full of guile and fawning dissimulation. Only shrewd gnostics recognize it.

The soul at peace has been purified by God of the defilement of darknesses. It has become luminous and resembles the spirit. It walks in obedience to God, being led without refusal. It becomes obedient through obeying God. This is the soul of the sincere devotee [*ṣiddīq*] whose secret and public sides have been filled [with light] by God.

I have compared these lights to mountains only because the light of submission in the breast of the submitted one is too firm and too well established for anyone to remove it as long as God preserves it.[20]

Another early Sufi, Abū Ibrāhīm Mustamlī Bukhārī, summarizes the qualities associated with the heart that were to dominate the tradition down to modern times.[21]

We know that the spirit is luminous, heavenly, Throne-like, high, and lordly. We know that the soul is earthly, low, dark, and satanic. And we know that the heart fluctuates between these two. The attribute of the spirit is all pleasantness and conformity, while the attribute of the soul is all loathsomeness and opposition. The heart stands between the two and turns about. Because of its fluctuating it is called the "heart" . . . . Sometimes it goes toward the high and becomes one with the spirit, sometimes it comes toward the low and becomes one with the soul. When it becomes one with the spirit, it dominates over the soul. Then nothing but conformity and obedience appear. When it becomes one with the soul, it dominates over the spirit. Then nothing but opposition and disobedience appear.

The turning about of the heart is like the turning about of the celestial sphere. Sometimes it brings the sun under the world and makes the world dark, and sometimes it brings the world under the sun and makes it luminous. The spirit is like the sun, and the soul is like the earth. The heart is like the celestial sphere. Sometimes the heart brings the spirit under the soul, though the spirit itself remains in place, just as the disk of the sun remains in place. However, the spirit becomes veiled by the soul, just as the sun becomes veiled by the earth. It does not become incapable of giving light. In one case, the darkness of night appears, in the other the darkness of wrongdoing.

Sometimes the sphere brings the sun. The veil of the earth disappears and the world becomes luminous. In one case the brightness of daytime comes, in the other the brightness of conforming [to the revealed law].[22]

In a similar way, ʿAyn al-Quḍāt Hamadānī identifies God's two fingers that make the heart fluctuate with heaven and earth.[23] He tells us that the heart's exalted place has to do with the fact that it is worthy of God's gaze.

What a shame that you have no heart! If you had one, it would tell you what the heart is. The heart is in charge. Seek for the heart and bring it to hand! Do you know where the heart is? Seek for it "between two fingers of the All-merciful." Would that the beauty of "two fingers of the All-merciful" would lift up the veil of magnificence. Then all hearts would find healing. The heart knows what the heart is and who the heart is. The heart is the place where God looks, and the heart alone is worthy of that, for "God looks not at your forms or your works, but He looks at your hearts."[24] O friend, the heart is God's looking-place. When the frame takes on the color of the heart and becomes the same color as the heart, He also looks at the frame.[25]

Aḥmad Samʿānī provides us with a typical expression of the heart's exalted stature in *Rawḥ al-arwāḥ*:

O chivalrous young man! You must wait many long years for trees to give fruit so that you may take some produce. If you want a tree to give fruit earlier and give better fruit, you must take a graft from another tree. Glory be to God! So many blessings are found in cutting!

Many thousands of years before Adam walked forward, the angels were walking around and performing acts of obedience. But they did not reach the station, level, and degree that Adam reached at the first instance. Yes, they were trees full of fruit. But they were not grafted from another branch.

Once the circle of engendering reached the point of the people made of clay and once it was determined that they would remain in this world for only a short time, the Presence of the Unseen prepared a subtle reality in the spirit. Then the tree of human existence was grafted on to that. Thus human beings were able to reach in a short period of time what others could not reach in a long period. For they took no help from their own constitution, but from the solicitude of the Teacher. May the evil eye stay far away—for He made them very beautiful!

Once the body became the companion of the spirit, a heart appeared between the two. It was called the "point of loving purity" [*nuqṭa-yi ṣafā*]. No other creature has a heart. The heart is not that lump of flesh that if you threw ten of them to a dog would not satisfy it. That is simply an outward marking place so that opinions and understanding may gain some good manners. But the inner meaning of the heart is pure of that.

From the spirit the heart took subtlety and from the earth gravity. It came to be praised by both sides and was well pleasing to both. It became the locus for the vision of the unseen.

The heart is neither spirit nor bodily frame. It is both spirit and bodily frame. If it is spirit, where does this embodiment come from? And if it is a bodily frame, why does it have subtlety? It is neither that nor this. But it is both that and this.

Since the heart came into existence from these two meanings, the disparity of states and diversity of steps appeared. The spirit does one work, the soul does another. The heart is a prisoner in between, having read its sentence of poverty. If it inclines toward the spiritual substance, the work of the spirit becomes manifest. If it leans toward the corporeal substance, the work of the body appears. That is why the Master of the Two Worlds, the Messenger to the Two Weighty Ones, said in this station, "The heart is like a feather in a desert. The winds make it fluctuate from side to side."

The chameleon of creation and the wonder of the mystery of original disposition is [the human being,] a point in the earth. Sometimes God praises him with a praise whose foot rises above the head of the angels. Sometimes He blames him with a blame of which Iblis would be ashamed. "The repenters, the worshipers" [9:112] are human beings. And so also are the "ungrateful" [100:6], the "fretful" [70:19], the "impatient" [70:20], the "grudging" [70:21], the "great wrongdoers" [33:72], the "very ignorant" [33:72], and the "unthankful" [42:48].[26]

In his Koran commentary, Rashīd al-Dīn Maybudī pays special attention to the near synonyms that are applied to the heart in the Koran. Taking advantage of the fact that he is writing in Persian, he calls the heart itself *dil*, and then refers to each of four other terms, including *qalb*, as a "curtain" (*parda*) over the heart. He sees the curtains as an ascending scale of spiritual perfections, similar to the four degrees discussed by Ḥakīm Tirmidhī: submission, faith, witnessing, and love.

The human heart has four curtains: The first is the breast [*ṣadr*], the resting place of the covenant of submission [*islām*], according to God's word, "Is he whose breast God has opened up to submission . . . ?" [39:22]. The second curtain is the heart [*qalb*], the place of the light of faith, according to His words, "He has written faith upon their hearts" [58:22]. The third curtain is the inner heart [*fu'ād*], the pavilion of the witnessing of the Real, in accordance with His words, "His inner heart lies not of what he saw" [53:11]. The fourth curtain is the innermost heart [*shaghāf*], the place where one puts down the carpet of love, in accordance with His words, "Love for him has rent her innermost heart" [12:30].

Each of these four curtains has a characteristic, and God looks upon each in a special way. When the Lord of the worlds desires to pull someone who has shied away from Him into the path of His religion with the lasso of gentleness, He first gazes upon his breast, so that it may become pure of caprices and innovations. Then the person's feet will become steadfast on the road of the Sunna.

Then God turns His gaze to his heart, so that it may become pure of the stains of this world and blameworthy moral traits, such as self-satisfaction, envy, pride, lip service, greed, enmity, and frivolity. The person sets out on the path of abstinence [*wara*ʿ].

Then He gazes upon his inner heart and keeps him back from attachments and created things. He opens the fountainhead of knowledge and wisdom in his heart. He makes the light of guidance a gift for its core, as He said, "So that he follows a light from his Lord" [39:22].

Then He gazes upon his innermost heart, a gaze—what a gaze! A gaze that is a picture upon the soul, that brings the tree of joy to fruit, that opens the eye of revelry. A gaze that is a tree, while the companionship of the Beloved is its shadow. A gaze that is wine, while the heart of the gnostic is its cup. When this gaze reaches the innermost heart, it removes it from water and clay. Then the person steps into the lane of annihilation [*fanā*']: Three things are negated by three things: Seeking is negated by the Sought, knowing is negated by the Known, and love is negated by the Beloved.

The Shaykh of the Way [ʿAbdallāh Anṣārī] said, "I threw away the two worlds for the sake of love, and I threw away love for the sake of the Beloved. Now I dare not say "I am I,' nor dare I say 'He.'"

I have an eye filled with the form of the Friend—
Happy am I with my eye when my Friend is there.
To set eye and Friend apart is not good —
He sits in the eye's place, or the eye is He.[27]

Few Sufis paid as much attention to the qualitative side of existence as Rūzbihān Baqlī of Shiraz. Even his theoretical works read like poetry. They present not so much a theory of spiritual perfection as a verbal textile woven of qualities tasted by the gnostic through unveiling. In his *ʿAbhar al-ʿāshiqīn* (The jasmine of lovers), Rūzbihān explains how the human lover, having traversed various stages of love, reaches a state where he or she is ready to love the Divine Beloved:

> The soul is nurtured through human love until love becomes firmly rooted in the inmost mystery. The heart is cleansed of the soul's passing thoughts through the fire of love. Then the soul that commands to evil attains peace under the heel of love's dominating power. The intellect is taught the waystations of love. The sensory soul and the animal soul take on the color of meaning. The journey through the waystations of human love reaches completion in the spirit. The spirit acquires the rules of right conduct and the science of the path of love.[28]

In another work, Rūzbihān devotes a chapter to describing the qualities that come to be acquired by the perfected heart. The following represents less than half the chapter, which goes on in the same vein:

> The form of the children of Adam is the likeness of engendered existence. The heart is like the Throne. It is the place where the spirit sits.[29] Just as heaven is the staircase of the ascent [*mi*ʿ*rāj*], so the frames of form are the ladder into the heart's world. Just as the World of the Kingdom is veiled, so also between you and the heart, which is the throne of the spirit, are found one hundred thousand veils. These include the five senses, the four natures, accidents, character traits, soul, caprice, satans, and so on. Until you pass beyond them, you will not reach the spirit's resting place.
>
> Within the heart the lights of God are directed to the site of the spirit. God manifests Himself there without veils. Between this heart, which in form is a lump of flesh, and that heart, which is the site of the spirit, are

found seven hundred thousand veils, from outside to inside.

Indeed, since God Himself has built the heart, He calls it His own house, just as He calls the Kaaba His own house. He opened the door of the outward Kaaba and shut the door of the inward Kaaba. For the outward Kaaba is the place that creatures visit. The door has to be open, since it belongs to the common people. But the door of the inward Kaaba must be kept shut, since it is the place that God visits. It belongs to the elect. . . .

God formed the heart like an oyster and threw it into the ocean of form. He concealed the spirit in the pearl. Unless you enter into the ocean of forms, you will not reach the oyster of the holy spirit. . . .

Between the corporeal heart and the spiritual heart lie great distances. Within the spiritual heart the spirit has one hundred thousand windows turned toward the chambers of the Dominion. Through those windows it sees the marvels of the Unseen and the wonders of the King. The spirit sends effusion from that place to the human attributes. From the window of contraction it sees the lights of *tawḥīd*. From the window of expansion it grasps pure singularity. From the window of fear it falls into tremendousness itself. From the window of love the effects of beauty enter in upon it. From the window of yearning it witnesses with every eye. From the window of love it takes the wine of familiarity. From the window of eternity it is struck with the blow of annihilation. From the window of endlessness it is taken into the bridal chamber of subsistence.

That house is God's domain. There He plays the backgammon of verification with the stone of disengagement against the one who witnesses Him. It is the place of revelation, the house of knowledge, God's treasury, the home of joy, the corner of grief, the treasure chest of comeliness, the mountain of Moses, the locus of God's self-disclosure, the brightness of lordship, and the everlasting garden. Its seeds are faith, its trees gnosis, its fruit love. It is the cage of wisdom for the bird of gnosis. It is the house of descent and the ocean of lordship's wonders. At every moment the pearls of gnosis rain down on it from the heaven of *tawḥīd*.[30]

In his Arabic *Mashrab al-arwāḥ*, Rūzbihān has this to say about the "true knowledge of the heart":

The heart has an outward dimension and an inward dimension. Its outward dimension is the pine-cone shaped lump of flesh. That is the locus of the spirit, the intellect, the inmost mystery, the subtle reality, the army of the angel, and the soldiers that are incoming thoughts.

The original heart is the blessed, holy, subtle reality. Its locus is the natural, receptive, original disposition. This subtle reality is the place in which is seen the light of the Unseen and the source of the Lord's decree. Sometimes this heart is unveiled for the people of unveiling. This heart is called "heart" because of its fluctuation in the witnessing of attributes. God says, "Surely in that there is a reminder for him who has a heart" [50:37]. The Prophet said, "There is in the body a lump of flesh: when it is sound, the whole body is sound, and when it is corrupt, the whole body is corrupt. Indeed, it is the heart."[31]

The form of the heart is corporeal, but the reality of the heart is heavenly, spiritual, Dominion-related, luminous, and lordly. It rests only in the remembrance of God: "In God's remembrance are the hearts at peace" [13:28]. One of the Sufis said, "The person of faith has a heart, but the gnostic has no heart." He also said, "The heart of the person of faith rests in God's remembrance, but the heart of the gnostic rests in God." The gnostic says, "The heart is that which fluctuates in the breast according to the quality of intentions and determinations. In the Unseen it examines the coming of the lights of the divine attributes."[32]

Najm al-Dīn Kubrā differentiates among soul, heart, and spirit as follows:

Soul, heart, and spirit give expression to a single thing. However, soul is used when that thing is defiled and hardened, heart when it becomes purified, and spirit when it gains nearness to God. Sometimes the Sufis differentiate among the realities and say that the heart is inside the soul, the spirit inside the heart, and the inmost mystery inside the spirit.[33]

Kubrā often discusses the changing qualities of the heart during the spiritual journey in his Arabic classic, *Fawā'iḥ al-jamāl*. I quote a single passage:

> Know that the subtle reality which is the heart . . . fluctuates from state to state, like water that takes on the color of its container. . . . That is why it is called a "heart," because of its fluctuation. In the same way, it is called a heart because it is the heart of existence and the meanings. The heart is subtle and accepts the reflection of things and meanings that circle around it. Hence the color of the thing that faces the subtle reality takes form within it, just as forms are reflected in a mirror or in pure water.[34]

The Heart in the School of Ibn al-ᶜArabī

Ibn al-ᶜArabī provides the most detailed discussions of the heart found in any Ṣufi writings. His primary concern is to show how this subtle human reality, once it attains to the fullness of manifestation in the perfect human being, displays God in His infinite self-disclosure. As in all of his discussions, Ibn al-ᶜArabī is especially concerned to bring out the roots of the heart's nature in the divine reality. In brief, he tells us that the heart alone is adequate to receive the self-disclosure of God. As both incomparable and similar, God is at once inaccessible and present. That dimension of the human subtle reality known as "intellect" perceives God as incomparable. It can comprehend God only in terms of His name Nonmanifest. In keeping with the root meaning of the term *ᶜaql*, intellect "constricts" and "confines" God to transcendence and incomparability. In contrast, that dimension of the human reality known as "imagination" perceives disengaged realities in sensory form. It alone is able to grasp God in His self-disclosure through the name Manifest. But intellect and imagination each perceives one-half of reality. Only the heart, through its "fluctuation" from one state to another, is able to perceive God as both Manifest and Nonmanifest, both similar and incomparable, both present and absent, both near and far.[35]

In ᶜAbd al-Razzāq Kāshānī's explanations of the Koranic verses dealing with Adam and Eve, we saw that the qualities of Adam and Eve correspond to those of the heart and the animal soul. Kāshānī reads these verses as alluding to the original and normative state of human beings and as pointing to the way of overcoming the rupture of equilibrium that took place when the qualities pertaining to the lower dimension gained the upper hand. In *Iṣṭilāḥāt al-ṣūfiyya* (The technical terms of the Sufis), Kāshānī defines the heart as follows:

> The heart is a luminous, disengaged substance halfway between the spirit and the soul. It is that through which true humanity [*al-insāniyya*] is realized [*taḥaqquq*]. The philosophers refer to it as the "rational soul." The spirit is its inward dimension [*bāṭin*], and the animal soul is its mount and its outward dimension, halfway between it and the body. Thus the Koran compares the heart to a glass and a shining star, while it compares the spirit to a lamp. This is in His words, "The likeness of His light is a niche, within which is a lamp, the lamp within a glass, the glass as it were a shining star, kindled from a blessed tree, an olive tree neither of the east nor the west" [24:35]. The tree is the soul, the niche is the body. The heart is the intermediate reality in existence and in levels of descents, like the Guarded Tablet in the cosmos.[36]

Kāshānī provides a more detailed explanation of this famous "light verse" of the Koran in his *Taʾwīlāt*, where he also explains the rest of the verse: "Its oil would almost shine, even if no fire touched it. Light upon light. God guides to His Light whom He will." Note how the soul, which Kāshānī often portrays in a negative light, has now been utterly transmuted into the soul at peace. Through its receptivity to the light of the spirit, it has attained its perfection. Hence it is nothing but good. Kāshānī also employs here the philosophical term *Active Intellect* to refer to the source of the light and guidance to which the soul must be receptive.

> *The likeness of His light*, that is, the attribute of His Being and Its manifestation within the worlds through making them manifest, *is a niche, within which is a lamp*. The niche is an allusion to the body, because it is

dark in itself and becomes illuminated by the light of the spirit, to which He alludes by "lamp." The body becomes a grillwork window because of the crossbars, the senses. The light sparkles from behind the crossbars, like a lamp in a niche. *The glass* is an allusion to the heart that is illumined by the spirit and illuminates everything around it by shining its light upon them. In the same way a flame illuminates a whole lamp and throws light upon others. God compares the glass to *a shining star* because of its spaciousness, its exceeding luminosity, the elevation of its place, and the multiplicity of its rays, since this is the state of the heart.

The tree from which the glass is *kindled* is the holy soul, purified and pure. It is compared to a tree because of the branching out of its branches and its many kinds of faculties that grow up out of the earth of the body. Its branches reach up within the space of the heart to the heaven of the spirit. He described it as *blessed* because of the great abundance of its benefits and uses, that is, the fruits that are character traits, works, and perceptions. Also, it has a strong growth through advance in perfections. Through it the felicity of the two abodes and the perfection of the two worlds are actualized. Upon it depend the manifestation of lights, mysteries, gnostic sciences, realities, stations, earnings, states, and mystic gifts. The soul is singled out for the *olive tree* because its perceptions are particular and oppressed by the weight of material appendages. In a similar way, the whole olive is not equally good. Also, the peak of the soul is fully prepared to be inflamed and illumined by the light and fire of the Active Intellect, which is connected to it by means of the spirit and heart. This is like the oil that makes the olive receptive to catching fire.

The meaning of the soul's being *neither of the east nor the west* is that it is halfway between the west and the east. The west is the world of bodies, the place where the divine light has set and has become concealed by dark veils. The east is the world of spirits, which is the place of the rising of the light and its appearance from luminous veils. For the soul is more subtle and luminous than the body, but denser than the spirit.

Its oil. This is the soul's preparedness for the holy light pertaining to its original nature hidden within itself. *Would almost shine*. In other words, it would almost come forth into actuality and reach perfection through itself, sending forth radiance. *Even if no fire*, that is, the Active Intellect, *touched it*, and if no light from the spirit of holiness reached it. For it has a strong preparedness and exceeding purity. *Light upon light*. In other words, this light that shines upon it from actualized perfection is a light added to the light of the fixed preparedness, which shines in the root. It is as if it is a doubled light. *God guides to His Light*, which is manifest in itself and makes other things manifest through His giving success and guidance, *whom He will*. These are the people to whom He shows solicitude so that they may achieve felicity.[37]

Kāshānī contrasts spirit and soul in dozens of passages in his *Taʾwīlāt*, since the whole drama of human existence to which the Koran addresses itself is played out in the relationship between the two. The heart is caught between them, sometimes pulled toward light and felicity, sometimes toward darkness and wretchedness. If it ascends toward spirit, it will attain to its perfection as rational soul. If it descends into the soul dominated by bodily limitations, it will be cut off from light. The following commentary on Koran 8:63 is typical:

He has made their hearts familiar through agreement in purpose and deliverance from the bounds of the attributes of soul. For the soul's attributes demand conflict and stubborn opposition, since the soul relies upon the world of opposition and is diverse through the four natures. As long as the heart stays with the soul and its desires, and the soul's attributes gain mastery over the heart, then the soul will drag the heart to the low direction. The heart's goals will be particularized in accordance with the soul's interests. The heart will seek that which someone else withholds from it, and enmity and hatred will occur. The faculty of anger will gain mastery, and anger seeks position, honor, subordination, domination, leadership, and sovereignty. Then pride, refusal, disdain, and scorn will appear. This will lead to mutual cutting off, breaking up, antagonism, and quarreling.

The more the heart moves away from the low direction by turning its attention to the high direction and becoming illuminated by the lights of the Oneness of the attributes or of the Essence, it rises above the station of the soul and joins with the spirit. Its goals cease to be mutually exclusive. There is no rivalry in them, since they can be achieved by one person without someone else being deprived of them. The heart inclines toward those who are of the same kind as itself in purity through essential love, because of the strength of the affinity.

The closer the heart is to Oneness, the stronger is the power of love within it, because of the intensity of nearness to Him whose religion it follows. This is similar to the lines that move from the circumference of a circle toward its center. In keeping with the strength of faith, the familiarity among them becomes more intense.

Hadst thou expended all that is in the earth, thou couldst not have made their hearts familiar, since everything in the low direction increases their enmity and their competition, because of the strength of their greed and their falling upon each other because of it. *But God made their hearts familiar*, through the light of Oneness that yields spiritual love and familiarity in the heart. For love is the shadow of Oneness, familiarity the shadow of love, and balance the shadow of familiarity.[38]

In another passage, Kāshānī clarifies his understanding of four different terms that are applied to the self from various points of view: spirit, soul, intellect, and breast. As in the above passage, the development of human perfection is tied to the spiritual world, while loss and misguidance derive from the limitations of the soul. He is commenting on the following verse: "You might have seen the sun, when it rose, inclining from their Cave towards the right, and, when it set, passing them by on the left, while they were in a broad fissure of the Cave" (18:17). This verse is found in the story of the Seven Sleepers of Ephesus, whom the Koran calls the "Companions of the Cave." Kāshānī has already suggested that the Seven Sleepers refer to seven spiritual realities found in the human being: spirit (*rūḥ*), heart (*qalb*), theoretical intellect (*al-ʿaql al-naẓarī*), practical intellect (*al-ʿaql al-ʿamalī*), reflection (*fikr*), inmost mystery (*sirr*), and most hidden (*akhfā*). The "cave" in which they sleep is the body.

You might have seen the sun, that is, the spirit, *when it rose*, that is, ascended through becoming disengaged from the wrappings of corporeality. Then it became manifest from its own horizon, *inclining* and turning through its love *from their Cave*, the body, *towards the right*, the direction of the World of Holiness. This is the direction of works of loving kindness: good deeds, virtues, beautiful works, acts of obedience. It is the way of the lovingly kind, since they are the "Companions of the Right." *And, when it set*, that is, when the spirit sank into the body and became veiled by it, it became concealed by the body's darknesses and blights. The disconnectedness and dispersion of the Companions of the Cave make the spirit's light die down, since they are *on the left*, the direction of the soul. This is the path of evil works, so the Companions become absorbed in acts of disobedience, evil deeds, evils, ugly moral qualities, and the way of the ungodly, who are the "Companions of the Left." *While they were in a broad fissure of the Cave*. In other words, they were in the wide playing field of their body, which is the station of the soul and Nature. For within the body there is a spacious area in which the light of the spirit does not reach them.

You should know that the face of the heart that is turned toward the spirit takes illumination from the spirit's light and is called "intellect." It incites to the good and is the place to which the angel's inspiration has access. The heart's face turned toward the soul is dark through the darkness of its attributes. It is called the "breast." It is the place where Satan whispers, as God says: "He who whispers in people's breasts" [114:5].

When the spirit moves and the heart turns toward it through the face in the spirit's direction, the heart becomes illumined and strengthened through the intellectual faculty, which incites and causes yearning toward perfection. Hence it inclines toward good and obedience. But when the soul is set in motion and the heart turns toward it through the face in the soul's direction, it becomes darkened and veiled from the light of the spirit. The intellect is darkened and inclines toward evil and disobedience. In these states the angel seeks access through inspiration and the satan through whispering.[39]

Since the intellect manifests the light of guidance in the microcosm, it corresponds not only to the prophets but also to their books. Hence the Koran frequently refers to the Torah, the Gospel, and itself as guidance. The Koran has two primary names, *al-qurʾān* and *al-furqān*. Ibn al-ʿArabī and his followers frequently juxtapose the two terms, pointing out that one of the literal meanings of the first term is "that which brings everything together and combines them into a harmonious whole." In contrast, the second term means "that which discerns and differentiates." In a parallel way intellect has two basic functions, which one might call "synthesis" and "analysis." In the following passage Kāshānī shows once again how intellect, heart, spirit, and soul are interrelated, emphasizing the character traits that belong respectively to spirit and soul as contrasting tendencies. He is commenting on Koran 17:82–84:

> *And We send down from the Koran*. In other words, from the intellect that harmonizes all [*qurʾānī*], We send down, gradually, the stars that are the differentiations of the intellect that discerns [*furqānī*]. One by one these stars reach the existence that manifests the Real in accordance with the manifestation of the divine attributes. In other words: We differentiate that which is undifferentiated and hidden within your essence in a plain differentiation, manifest to you. This will then be *a healing for* the illnesses of the hearts of those who have preparedness, *those* in your community *who have faith* in the Unseen—illnesses like ignorance, doubt, hypocrisy, blindness of heart, rancor, envy, etc. Thus We shall purify them. *And a mercy*, giving them perfections and virtues and adorning them with wisdoms and knowledges. *But it increases the unbelievers*, those who have little portion of perfection because of their bodily conditions and attributes of soul, *only in loss*. For their souls increase in manifesting their own attributes, such as denial, obstinacy, haughtiness, stubbornness, dissimulation, and hypocrisy. All these are added to what they had of doubt, ignorance, blindness, and straying.
>
> *And when We bless the human being*, through outward blessings, *he turns away*, since he stands with the soul and the body. The bodily faculties are finite. They do not have the circumspection to deal with the infinite affairs that may possibly occur and are connected to the causes of blessing. . . . Hence people see nothing but the immediate. They claim eminence because their soul is master of their heart and becomes manifest in their ego [*anāʾiyya*]. Such a person flees from the heart *and withdraws aside*. In other words, he goes far from the Real and into the side of the soul. He is enwrapped by the side of the soul and turns away from the Real. So also he goes in the direction of evil. *When evil visits him, he is in despair*, since he is veiled from the Powerful and His power. Were he to look with the eye of insight, he would see God's power in both states. He would gain certainty that in the first state gratitude is the tie of blessings, while in the second state patience wards off adversity. Hence he would show gratitude and have patience. He would know that the Giver of blessings is powerful. He would not turn away from Him in arrogance and insolence after the blessing. He would fear its disappearance without forgetting the Giver of blessings. He would not despair in adversity because of anxiety and grief. Rather, he would hope for its removal while showing deference to the side of Him who gives affliction.
>
> *Say: "Everyone works according to his own manner,"* that is, according to his own character traits and the disposition that dominates over him in keeping with his station. When a person's station is the soul and his manner accords with its nature, then he will work as we said, turning away and despairing. When his station is the heart and his manner is a virtuous character, he will work in accordance with gratitude and patience. *"So your Lord knows very well who is best guided"* among those who perform works *"as to the way"*: He knows that there is a worker of good according to the character of the heart and a worker of evil according to the nature of the soul. He gives them recompense in keeping with their works.[40]

Kāshānī's microcosmic interpretation of the archetypal spiritual journey of Islam, the ascent (*miʿrāj*) of the Prophet to the Divine Presence, clearly places the spirit at the summit of the microcosm and contrasts it with all the negative character traits associated with the soul. The Koranic verse is 17:1: "Glory be to Him who carried His servant by night from the Holy Mosque to the Further Mosque, the precincts of which We have blessed, that We might show him some of Our signs. He is the Hearing, the Seeing." Note that God carried His *servant*. For only in servanthood, which is utter submission and total abandonment of any self-control (*taṣarruf*), is the human being a proper receptacle for the divine self-disclosures. The "Holy Mosque" in the outside world is the Kaaba, while the "Further Mosque" is al-Aqṣā in Jerusalem. It perhaps needs to be stressed that Kāshānī is in no way denying the bodily nature of the Prophet's *miʿrāj*, which is accepted by practically all Muslims. Rather, he wants to suggest what takes place in the microcosm when the servants of God make their non-bodily ascents in imitation of the Prophet.

> *Glory be to Him who made His servant travel.* In other words, the Prophet declared God incomparable with material appendages and the imperfections of similarity through the tongue of his state, which was disengagement and perfection in the station of servanthood, within which there is no exercise of self-control whatsoever. *By night,* that is, within the darkness of the bodily blights and the natural attachments, since ascent and advance take place only by means of the body. *From the Holy Mosque,* from the station of the heart. The heart is too holy for the circumambulation of the idolaters—the bodily faculties—and the commission of their indecencies and mistakes. And it is too holy for the pilgrimage of the animal faculties, whether the beastly or the predatory. The twin evils of their going to one extreme and the other extreme are exposed, since they are naked of the clothing of virtue. *To the Further Mosque,* which is the station of the spirit, the furthest from the corporeal world. This takes place through the witnessing of the self-disclosures of the Essence and the "glories of the Face."[41]
>
> Remember here what we said earlier, that each station can be put in order only after the traveler advances to what lies beyond it. Then you will understand that His words, *that We might show him some of Our signs,* refers to the witnessing of the divine attributes. Although viewing the self-disclosures of the attributes takes place in the station of the heart, the Essence described by those attributes is not witnessed to perfection in majesty and beauty until advance to the station of the spirit. God is saying, "that We might show him the signs" of Our attributes inasmuch as they are ascribed to Us and We are witnessed through them and appear in their forms. *He is the Hearing*: He hears his invocations in the station of the inmost mystery, seeking annihilation. *The Seeing*: He sees the strength of his preparedness, his turning his attentiveness toward the locus of witnessing, his being attracted toward Him through the strength of love and the perfection of yearning.[42]

Kāshānī continues his analysis of the relationship between spirit, soul, and heart in commenting on the next several verses of the Koran (17:2–7), which outwardly deal with a topic completely different from the previous verse.

> *And We gave Moses,* the heart, *the Book,* knowledge. *And We made it a guidance for the Children of Israel,* in other words, for the faculties that are the tribe of "Israel," the spirit. *"Take not unto yourselves any guardian apart from Me"*: Thirst not for self-rule in your acts and seek not independence through seeking your perfections and shares. Earn not in accordance with your own motivations. Entrust not your affairs to the satan of sensory intuition, or he will entice you with bodily enjoyments, nor to the intellect of everyday livelihood, or it will employ you for arranging its own affairs and putting them in order. On the contrary, entrust your affair to Me, that I may govern you with the provisions of knowledges and gnostic sciences, the conditions of character traits and virtues. I will perfect you with the replenishment of lights from the world of the heart and the spirit and with the confirmation of holiness. I will send down upon you something of the worlds of the Dominion and the Invincibility. That will deliver you from need for the earnings of the human world. These earnings are *the offspring of those we bore with Noah,* who is the intellect, in the ship of the Sharia and practical wisdom. *He was a thankful servant* because of his knowledge of God's blessings and his employing them in the mode that was proper.
>
> *And We decreed for the Children of Israel,* the faculties, *in the Book,* the Guarded Tablet: *"You shall work corruption in the earth twice."* The first time you shall work corruption in the station of the soul when it is "commanding to evil" by seeking your appetites and your enjoyments. *"You shall ascend exceedingly high"* through your seeking mastery over the heart and your dominating and gaining exaltation over it. Thereby you will prevent it from its perfection and you will employ its faculty of reflection to gain your objects of desire and hope.
>
> The second time refers to the station of the heart: Once you become clothed in virtues,

illumined by the light of the intellect, and manifested in the splendor of your perfections, then you will work corruption by making manifest your own perfections and veiling the heart by means of your virtues from witnessing the self-disclosure of *tawḥīd*. And luminous veils are stronger than dark veils, since they are fine and subtle and give form to perfections at which one must stop. Then *you shall ascend* in the station of your original nature through the ruling authority of intellectual conditions and human perfections.

So when the promise of the evil consequence *of the first of these came to pass, We sent against you servants of Ours*. These were attributes of the heart, lights of the Dominion, and views of the intellect. They were *possessors of great might*, authority, and severity. *And they went through the habitations*, that is, your places and loci. They slew some of you by subdual and severity. They cursed the offspring of bodily conditions and the vile qualities of the soul. They plundered the possessions of the sensory organs and the bestial and predatory pleasures. *And it was a promise* made by God *performed* by His bringing into existence the faculty of perfection. He sought in your preparedness and in purifying it the proofs of intellect in its original nature.

Then We gave back to you the turn to prevail over them. We gave you good fortune by illuminating you with the light of the heart, your turning toward the breast, and your devotion to what is demanded by the vision and view of the intellect. *And We succored you with possessions*, that is, beneficial knowledges, intellectual and Shariite wisdom, and sciences of the heart, *and children*, virtues of character and luminous conditions. *And We made you a greater host* through the greatness of virtues, virtuous habits, and beautiful character traits. *If you do good* by acquiring perfections of character and views of the intellect, *it is your own souls that you do good to, and if you do evil* by acquiring vile qualities and bodily conditions, *it is to them likewise*.

The final stage of the heart's perfection is achieved through the annihilation (*fanā'*) of the human attributes and the subsistence of the divine qualities within the human being. Annihilation takes place through the manifestation of God's left hand: the attributes of majesty and severity. Subsistence occurs when the right hand shows itself. Annihilation is one of the demands of *tawḥīd*, since everything unreal is effaced by the Real. Hence Kāshānī refers to it as "annihilation in *tawḥīd*." But here submission through annihilation turns into the oneness of the qualities of the servant and the Lord. By achieving the station of subsistence, the individual follows God by following the desires of his or her own heart.

Then, when the promise of the second time *came to pass* through annihilation in *tawḥīd*, *We sent against you servants*, that is, holy lights, the self-disclosures of majesty, the glories of the severe divine attributes, the armies of the sultan of tremendousness and magnificence, *so that they would make your faces worse*. In other words, they would annihilate your existences through *tawḥīd*, and you would be overcome by the grief of the loss of perfections through severity and negation. *And* they would *enter the Temple* of the heart, *as they entered it the first time*. Then their effect, which is knowledges and virtues, reached you. *And* they would *destroy utterly* and annihilate by means of the attributes of God *that which they had ascended to* by becoming manifest in the perfection and virtue of the heart and being pleased with its vision, adornment, and joy. *Perhaps your Lord will have mercy upon you* after the severity that annihilates and effaces you in the self-disclosure of His attributes. He will have mercy by bringing you to life and stirring you up through subsistence after annihilation. Then He will fix you in "what no eye has seen, what no ear has heard, and what has never passed into the heart of any mortal."[43] *But if you return* by undergoing variegation in the station of annihilation by manifesting your ego, then *We shall return* through severity and annihilating. *And We have made Gehenna*, which is Nature, *a confinement*, that is, a place of imprisonment within which people are confined by the chastisement of being veiled and deprived of reward. *For the unbelievers*, that is, for the ones who are veiled from the lights. They are the ones who remained in corruption the first time.[44]

The Birth of the Heart

Soul as a negative force pulls the individual away from the light of guidance and intellect, while spirit draws him or her toward God. From this point of view, the relationship between spirit and soul is one of tension and conflict. But if the soul submits to the light of the spirit, the relationship is one of harmony and equilibrium. Hence the smooth and peaceful relationship between spirit and soul is frequently compared to a marriage similar to that between the First Intellect and the Universal Soul. This happy and fruitful marriage gives birth to the heart, which is a child in the image of God.

In this analogy, the true and perfect child is the full and perfected rational soul. For although "rational soul" is the characteristic of human beings, few people actualize it. Hence, as we saw in chapter 1, Ibn al-ʿArabī contrasts the "perfect human beings" (*al-insān al-kāmil*), who are the prophets and the great friends of God, with "animal human beings" (*al-insān al-ḥayawān*), who are the rest of the human race.[45] Most people, in short, are ruled by the soul's animals, if not by its satan. Rūmī, along with many other authors, calls the perfect human beings who have truly actualized the rational soul "possessors of hearts."

> Experience shows that the spirit is nothing but awareness. Whoever has greater awareness has a greater spirit.
>
> Our spirit is greater than the animal spirit. Why? Because it has more awareness.
>
> Then the angel's spirit is greater than ours, for he transcends the rational senses.
>
> Then the spirit of God's friends, the Possessors of Hearts, is even greater. Leave aside your astonishment!
>
> That is why the angels prostrated themselves before Adam: His spirit was greater than their existence.[46]

If the perfected rational soul is to be actualized, its parents—spirit and soul—must marry, give birth to it, and nurture it. Only through perfect activity and perfect receptivity can husband and wife bring the child to its perfected nature. The child will then embrace all the qualities of the parents within itself, and through the child the parents will live in perfect harmony.

One of the earliest authors to develop this imagery was Shihāb al-Dīn Suhrawardī in *ʿAwārif al-maʿārif*:

> The human, high, heavenly spirit pertains to the World of Command, while the mortal [*basharī*], animal spirit pertains to the World of Creation. The mortal, animal spirit is the locus where the high spirit comes down and alights. The animal spirit is a subtle corporeal thing and carries the faculties of sensation and movement. The animal spirit arises from the heart. Here by the heart I mean the well-known lump of flesh deposited on the left side of the body. The animal spirit spreads out within the hollows of the veins and arteries. This spirit belongs to all animals. From it are effused the faculties of the senses. It is this spirit whose support depends for the most part on food in order to put God's norm into effect. The science of medicine acts upon it by putting the mixture of the humors into equilibrium.
>
> When the high, human spirit arrives at the animal spirit, the animal spirit gains a certain kinship with it and becomes distinct from the spirits of the other animals, since it acquires another attribute. It becomes a "soul," a place for rational speech and inspiration. God says, "By the soul and Him who proportioned it and inspired in it its wickedness and its godfearing" [91:7–8]. It becomes "proportioned" when the human spirit arrives at it and cuts it off from the genus of the spirits of the animals. Hence the soul is engendered when God engenders it through the high spirit.
>
> When the soul, which is the animal spirit in the human being, is engendered from the high spirit within the World of Command, this is like Eve's being engendered from Adam within the World of Creation. Between the high spirit and the animal spirit appeared a mutual familiarity and love like that found between Adam and Eve. Each of them tastes death by being separated from its companion. God says, "He made from [the one original soul] its spouse that he might rest in her" [7:189]. So Adam rested in Eve, and the high, human spirit rested in the animal spirit and made it into a soul.
>
> From the resting of the spirit in the soul the heart was engendered. By this heart I mean the subtle heart whose place is the lump of flesh. But the lump of flesh belongs to the World of Creation, while this subtle reality belongs to the World of Command.
>
> When the heart is engendered from the spirit and soul in the World of Command, this is like the offspring of Adam and Eve being engendered in the World of Creation. Were there no mutual rest between the

spouses, one of whom is the soul, the heart would not have been engendered.

Among hearts, some are apprised of the father, who is the high spirit, and incline toward him. That is the confirmed heart, which is mentioned by the Messenger of God as related by Ḥudhayfa. He said, "There are four kinds of hearts: There is a bare heart within which is a shining lamp, and this is the heart of the person of faith. There is a black and inverted heart, and this is the heart of the unbeliever. There is a heart bound by attachments, and this is the heart of the hypocrite. And there is a layered heart, within which are both faith and hypocrisy. The faith within it is like a plant nourished by sweet water, while the hypocrisy within it is like a boil nourished by pus and filth. The heart will be judged by whichever nourishment dominates over it."[47]

The inverted heart inclines toward the mother, which is the soul that commands to evil. There is also a heart that wavers in its inclination toward her. Its property will belong to felicity or wretchedness in accordance with the dominant inclination of the heart.

The intellect is the substance of the high spirit, its tongue, and that which points to it. It governs the confirmed heart and the purified soul at peace just as the father governs a loving child and the husband a virtuous wife. The servant governs the inverted heart and the soul that commands to evil as a father governs a recalcitrant child and a bad wife. Hence the intellect is turned away in one respect and attracted toward them in another respect, since it cannot do without them.

Various people have offered differing opinions on the place of the intellect. Some hold that its place is the brain, some that its place is the heart, and both fall short of perceiving the reality of the situation. The reason they differ is that the intellect does not stay still in a single manner. Sometimes it is attracted to the loving child, sometimes to the recalcitrant child. The heart has a relationship with the loving child, and the brain with the recalcitrant child. When people look at the governing of the recalcitrant child, they say that intellect's place of rest is the brain. When they look at the governing of the loving child, they say that its place of rest is the heart.

The high spirit aims to rise up to its Master out of yearning, bending, and freeing itself from engendered things. Both heart and soul are among the engendered things. When the spirit ascends, the heart bends toward it as the longing, loving child bends toward his father. The soul longs for the heart, her child, as the longing mother longs for her child. When the soul longs, it rises up from the earth. Its roots driven into the low world are withdrawn. Its caprice vanishes and its matter is cut off. It renounces this world and withdraws from this abode of delusion, turning toward the abode of everlastingness.

The soul, who is the mother, had made herself endure the earth through her innate disposition. For she was engendered from the animal spirit that is similar in kind to the earth, and she supported herself by resting in the natures, which are the pillars of the low world. God says, "And had We willed, we would have raised him up through them [Our signs]. But he inclined toward the earth and followed his own caprice" [7:176]. When the soul, who is the mother, rests in the earth, the inverted heart is attracted to her. This is the child that inclines toward its crooked and imperfect mother rather than to its upright and perfect father. At the same time, the spirit is attracted to the child, who is the heart, because of the father's innate attraction to its child. At this point it fails in the reality of standing up for the right of its Master.

In these two attractions become manifest the property of felicity and wretchedness. "That is the ordaining of the Inaccessible, the Knowing" [6:96].[48]

The Heart's Birth According to ʿIzz al-Dīn Kāshānī

Suhrawardī's brief explication of the heart and its relationship with its parents was expanded upon considerably by ʿIzz al-Dīn Maḥmūd Kāshānī (d. 735/1334–35) in his Persian *Miṣbāḥ al-hidāya* (The lamp of guidance), a work that was inspired by the *ʿAwārif* and has enjoyed a wide popularity wherever Persian has been read, especially in the Indian subcontinent.

Like other authorities, ʿIzz al-Dīn insists on the impossibility of providing an exact definition of the soul, since the term is applied to the whole inward dimension of the human reality, which is unlimited in the direction of God. Each human soul is made up of a wide range of tendencies and faculties. These belong not to the visible world that is accessible to observation but to the unseen world that can be grasped only through the revelations given to the prophets, or through individual spiritual experience on the basis of those revelations. But each human being's grasp of the soul will be different, since each individual represents a unique image of God. No one can have access to the whole range of possibilities encompassed by the soul.

> Our purpose is to provide knowledge of the soul, even though knowledge of all its attributes is impossible, for it possesses the characteristics of a chameleon. Moment by moment it displays a new color, hour by hour it assumes another shape. It is the Hārūt of the Babylon of existence:[49] At each moment it presents another painting, at each breath it begins another trick. In the fact that the knowledge of the divine is connected to and made conditional upon the knowledge of the soul [in the hadith, "He who knows his own soul knows his Lord"], we should see an allusion to the fact that it cannot be known in all its attributes. No creature can reach the innermost depth of the soul's knowledge, any more than one can reach the innermost depth of the knowledge of God. And just as it is impossible to know the soul as it is in itself, so also it is difficult to tie down its states in a worthy manner. Hence ʿAlī said, "I and my soul are like a shepherd and his sheep. Whenever I gather them from one side, they run off in another direction."[50]

ʿIzz al-Dīn then proceeds to describe the three stages of the soul: the soul that commands to evil, the blaming soul, and the soul at peace. He points out that corrupt and blameworthy character traits derive from the soul that commands to evil, while the praiseworthy character traits that begin to manifest themselves in the blaming soul and become firmly established in the soul at peace derive from the spirit. But as to the exact nature of the spirit, that is even more mysterious than the nature of the soul. Nevertheless, it is possible to grasp the relationship between spirit and soul by examining the structure of the cosmos. Hence he turns his attention to the creation of the universe and God's blowing the spirit into the human being. He calls the attributed spirit that God blew into the human being when creating him the "Greatest Spirit." This Spirit has two "visions" (*naẓar*), one for looking at majesty and the other for looking at beauty. Through one of these visions "it contemplates the majesty of God's beginningless Power, and through the other it gazes upon the beauty of His endless Wisdom." Both of these visions are referred to as "Intellect," but the one that contemplates majesty and power is directed toward God, while the one that contemplates beauty and wisdom is directed toward creation. According to ʿIzz al-Dīn, these two faces of the Intellect are mentioned in the versions of the hadith of the First Intellect that refer to the two directions in which the Intellect "turned": "The first thing God created was the Intellect. He said to it, 'Turn this way,' so it turned toward God. Then He said to it, 'Turn that way,' so it turned away from God."

Majesty and power are clearly the yang side of the Divine Reality, while beauty and wisdom are the yin side. If the former are seen in God, this is because of His incomparability and distance. In contrast, creation manifests beauty and wisdom inasmuch as it reflects God and displays His nearness and similarity. Wisdom is demonstrated by putting everything into its proper place with a view toward ultimate truth and felicity. As Ibn al-ʿArabī says, wisdom is the divine attribute that rules over arrangement, order, and hierarchy, that is, "cosmos" in the original Greek sense.[51]

> The noblest existent thing and the nearest object of contemplation to the Presence of Inaccessibility is the Greatest Spirit, which God attributed to Himself with His words, "[I blew into him] of My spirit" or "of Our spirit." Terms such as the Great Adam, the First Vicegerent, the Divine Interpreter, the Key to Existence, the Pen of Existentiation, and the Garden of the Spirits all express its attributes.
>
> The first prey caught in the snare of existence was the essence of this Spirit. The Eternal Will appointed it to His vicegerency in the World of Creation. He turned over to it the keys to the treasuries of the mysteries and gave it permission to exercise control over the cosmos. He let a tremendous river flow down

upon it from the Ocean of Life, so that it constantly takes replenishment from the effusion of life and conveys it to the various parts of the engendered universe.

From the resting place of all-comprehensiveness, that is, the Holy Essence, the Greatest Spirit takes the forms of the divine words to the locus of dispersion, which is the World of Creation. It takes them from the Undifferentiated Reality and displays them in the entities of the differentiated things.

The divine generosity gave this Spirit two visions, one for the contemplation of the majesty of the beginningless power and the other for gazing upon the beauty of the endless wisdom. The primordial intellect that is turned toward God is the outward expression of the first vision. Its result is love for God. The creaturely intellect that is turned away from God is the outward expression of the second vision, as mentioned in the report, "He said to it, 'Turn that way,' so it turned away from Him." Its result is the Universal Soul.

Whenever the Attributed Spirit is replenished by an effusion from the All-comprehensive Reality, the Universal Soul becomes its receptacle and the locus of its differentiation.

This activity and receiving activity, or strength and weakness, bring about between the Attributed Spirit and the Universal Soul the relationship of masculinity and femininity and the customs of mutual love and intimate embracing. Because of this mixture and pairing between the two, the children—the things of the engendered universe—are brought into existence. They enter into the world of manifestation at the hand of the midwife—God's ordainment—from the placenta of the Unseen. Hence all creatures are the offspring of the Soul and the Spirit, while the Soul is the offspring of the Spirit, and the Spirit is the offspring of the Command. For God created the Spirit by Himself without any intermediate cause, and this is alluded to by the word "Command." In the same way, He created all creatures by means of the Spirit, and these are called "Creation." "Verily, His are the Creation and the Command. Blessed is God, the Lord of the worlds" [7:54].[52]

As God's one creature through which all other creatures come into existence, the Spirit comprehends all the divine names and attributes, of which the cosmos in its full amplitude and deployment is the outward manifestation. The Spirit is the first point on the Arc of Descent, while those human beings who achieve the station of perfection or vicegerency complete the Arc of Ascent. The Spirit is God's first vicegerent, through which the effusion of existence reaches all things, and human beings are His last vicegerent, taking existence back to its Source.

Since every vicegerent must bring together all the attributes of the one who appoints him, the divine bounty and infinite generosity clothed the Spirit in the vicegerency of existentiation through all His beautiful and majestic names and attributes. He made the Spirit honored and venerated in the royal seat of creation. Then, when the Circle of Engendering reached its final point, which coincided with the beginning point, the form of the spirit came to be reflected in the mirror of the existence of the Adam made of earth. All the divine names and attributes disclosed themselves in him. Then God called out, "Verily I am placing in the earth a vicegerent" [2:30].[53]

The news of Adam's vicegerency spread among the Higher Plenum. On the firman of his vicegerency these words were inscribed: "Verily God created Adam in His own form." On the banner of his nobility this verse appeared: "He taught Adam the names, all of them" [2:31]. The reins of subjugation and the halters of ordainment were placed in the hand of his control. The angels were commanded to prostrate themselves to him. They did not have the perfection of all-comprehensiveness that he had. Some of them are the locus of manifestation for the attribute of beauty, and nothing else. These are the angels of gentleness and mercy. Others are the locus of manifestation for the attribute of majesty, and nothing else. These are the angels of severity and chastisement. But God made Adam bring together the attributes of beauty and majesty. He made him a locus for gentleness and severity, mercy and wrath. He expressed this through His words, "What I created with My own two hands" [38:75]. Hence Adam knew God by means of all the names. But the angels knew God only through that name for which they were the locus of manifestation. They allude to this with their words, "We know nothing but what Thou hast taught us" [2:32].

Hence human beings were made God's vicegerent upon earth because they were created in the divine form and manifest the properties of both hands of God. The properties of the two hands are reflected in the dual nature of the spiritual world, as represented by the Greatest Spirit (the First Intellect) and the Universal Soul. Through its distance from creation, the spirit reflects majesty and severity. In contrast, the Soul reflects the caring qualities of gentleness and kindness through its relative nearness to creation, multiplicity, and differentiation. Spirit and Soul are then reflected in the human pair, Adam and Eve, and in the spirit and soul of each human individual. Kāshānī continues:

> Just as Adam's existence in the visible world is the locus of manifestation for the Spirit's form in the unseen world, so also Eve's existence in the visible world is the locus of manifestation for the Soul's form in the unseen world. Her birth from Adam—for God says, "He created from [the one soul] its spouse" [4:1]—is a likeness of the birth of the Soul from the Spirit. Thus the effect of the pairing of Soul and Spirit and the relationship established there between masculinity and femininity were transferred to Adam and Eve.
>
> Just as the created things emerged from the Spirit and Soul, so also the seed of the offspring—which was entrusted to Adam's reins [7:172]—was brought into existence through the pairing of Adam and Eve. Hence the existence of Adam and Eve is a transcription of the existence of the Spirit and Soul. Moreover, in each human individual, another transcription was made from the transcription that is the existence of Adam and Eve. This takes place through the pairing of the particular spirit and the particular soul and the birth of the heart from between the two.[54]

Both men and women manifest Spirit and Soul, but the Spirit predominates in men while the Soul predominates in women. This may be the reason, Kāshānī suggests, that God sent prophets only in male form. He indicates through his last sentence that he is not sure of his own interpretation.

> The birth of the form of the male derives from the form of the Universal Spirit, but mixed with the attributes of the Soul. The birth of the form of the female derives from the form of the Universal Soul, but mixed with the attribute of the Spirit. Hence no prophet was sent in the form of a woman, for prophecy is related to masculinity because it controls human souls and exercises effects within the World of Creation.[55] Moreover, the means of manifestation of the prophets is the Spirit, and the Spirit gives rise to the masculine form. But God knows best.[56]

The heart that is born between spirit and soul is not born once and for all, since it continues to come into existence instant by instant through the ever-changing relationship between its parents. In the same way, the cosmos is reborn instant by instant—as the Ashʿarite theologians suggested and as Ibn al-ʿArabī maintains with great vigor—since it is constantly being reborn as the result of the marriage of Universal Spirit and Universal Soul. Since "Everything is perishing except the Face of God" (28:88), only the Face or Essence of God is fixed and stable. Kāshānī, like earlier authorities, identifies the experience of the constant flux of creation with the heart's fluctuation.

Though the heart constantly fluctuates in its states, it is always conditioned by its mother, the soul. As the soul moves away from the stage of commanding to evil and advances toward the stage of peace with God, the heart undergoes a concordant transformation. But like its father and mother, the heart cannot truly be known.

> Knowledge of the attributes of the heart as they are in themselves is impossible. It is even difficult to speak about the heart, since it undergoes constant fluctuation in the stages of the states and constant advancement in the ascending degrees of perfection. Because of this fluctuation it is known as the heart.

The "states" (*aḥwāl*), as pointed out earlier, are the ever-changing experiences undergone by the travelers on the path of God. As ephemeral gifts from God, they are contrasted with the "stations" (*maqāmāt*), which are permanent earnings.

> Since the states are divine gifts, and since these gifts never end, the fluctuation and ad-

vance of the heart in the ascending degrees of perfection and the rising stages of beginningless beauty and majesty are infinite. Hence the heart's attributes and states cannot be contained within the limits of reckoning and the reckoning of limits. If a person speaks in an attempt to limit and reckon them, he will know for certain—if he looks carefully—that in reality he is defining only the limits of his own perception and clarifying only the share of his own preparedness. Several thousand divers into the oceans of gnostic sciences have plumbed the depths of the ocean of the heart's knowledge, and no one has reached the bottom or fully explained the inmost depth of its wonders and marvels. Moreover, not everyone who found a trace of it has brought back news, nor has everyone who has grasped one of its precious pearls held it out to be seen. ʿAlī ibn Sahl Ṣūfī says, "From the time of Adam till the coming of the Hour, people will be saying, 'My heart, my heart.' I would like to see one person who can describe to me what thing the heart is and what its qualities are. But I have not found that one."[57]

Though any human being has a heart, father and mother do not always marry in harmony to produce a perfect child. The true heart represents the coming together of the qualities of yang and yin in perfect balance. It is the locus where heaven and earth work in harmony, where the unseen and the visible meld and become inseparable. It is the possession only of the prophets, the great sages, and the friends of God, those who have reached the goal of human life.

Let me tell of the meaning of the heart in the tongue of allusion: It is the point from which the Circle of Existence comes into movement and through which it reaches perfection. Within it the mystery of eternity without beginning meets the mystery of eternity without end. The first glance at it reaches the furthest range of sight. The beauty and majesty of the Abiding Face are disclosed to it. Terms such as the Throne of the All-merciful, the Descending Place of al-Qur'ān and al-Furqān, the Isthmus between the Unseen and the Visible and between the Spirit and the Soul, the Meeting Place of the Two Seas of the Dominion and the Kingdom, the Viewer of the King and the one whom He views, the Lover of God and His Beloved, and the one who carries and is carried by the Secret of the Trust and the Divine Bounty, all express its qualities.

What was desired from the pairing of spirit and soul was the offspring that is the existence of the heart. A relationship was established between the Kingdom and the Dominion in order for the heart to have an object of vision and a place for witnessing. Its form took shape through love itself, while its insight is illuminated with the light of contemplation.

When the soul was separated from the spirit, love and quarrel appeared on both sides. When the two loves were paired, the form of the heart was born. Like an isthmus [*barzakh*], it became the intermediary between the sea of the spirit and the sea of the soul. It stood at their meeting place. Thereby if in their flowing either should infringe upon or transgress against the other, it could prevent that: "[He let flow the two seas that meet together,] between them an isthmus they do not overpass" [55:19–20].

The reason that the form of the heart appeared from love itself is that wherever the heart sees beauty, it clings to it, and wherever it finds loveliness, it embraces it. It is never without an object of gaze, a beloved, a heart's ease. Its existence subsists through love, and love's existence through it.

In human existence, the heart is like the Throne of the All-merciful. The Throne is the great heart in the macrocosm, and the heart is the small throne in the microcosm. All hearts are encompassed by the Throne, just as the particular spirits are embraced by the Greatest Spirit, and the particular souls are under the Universal Soul.

Like the Throne, the heart has a form and a reality. Its form is the pine cone shaped lump of flesh deposited in the left side of the body. Its reality is the lordly subtle reality [*laṭīfa-yi rabbānī*] mentioned earlier. The rational soul and the animal spirit are intermediaries between the reality and form of the heart, for the reality of the heart is sheer subtlety, while its form is density itself. Between the absolutely dense and the absolutely subtle, there can be no relationship of any sort whatsoever. Hence the rational soul and the animal spirit, both of which have a face turned toward the World of Subtlety and a face turned toward the World of Density, became the intermediaries between the form and the reality of the heart.

Every effect that emerges from the heart first reaches the soul, which receives it in respect of its subtle face. Then in respect of its dense face it conveys it to the animal spirit. In the same way, the animal spirit takes it in respect of its subtle face and entrusts it to the outward form of the heart in respect of its dense face. From there, it is spread out to the regions of the body.

In the same way, the effusion of mercy from the Presence of Divinity first reaches the reality of the Throne. From there it reaches the Bearers of the Throne, and they convey it to the form of the Throne, from which it reaches the regions of the visible world.[58]

The Heart's Birth According to Ibn al-ʿArabī's School

When we turn to the school of Ibn al-ʿArabī, we find several authors discussing the birth of the heart. Qūnawī devotes a section to it in one of his short unpublished works, *Taḥrīr al-bayān fī taqrīr shuʿab al-īmān*. His major ideas are brought out well by his disciple, Saʿīd al-Dīn Farghānī, who frequently discusses the heart. Farghānī makes the same associations as the other authors that we have looked at, but the key idea in his teaching, following his master, is that of equilibrium (*iʿtidāl*). The perfect heart is only realized when all the qualities present in the microcosm are fully actualized in proper balance and harmony. Farghānī refers to the birth of the heart from its placenta, the soul, in the following commentary on Ibn al-Fāriḍ's verse, "Be empty of gratifications, rise up from your own nadir. Then be firm and grow."[59] First he paraphrases the verse in Persian:

> Become empty of everything desired by your own soul. Rise up from the nadir of your own existence. Be firm in that emptiness. Have patience in the abandonment of gratifications so that you may grow up through the growth of the heart. Then the doors of increase will be opened to you.
>
> His meaning is as follows: The world of sensation and sensory things has fallen to a nadir and a lowness in relation to the world of the spirit and spiritual things. The more a person inclines toward sensory gratifications and enjoyments, the more he descends into the lowness and nadir of his own existence. Hence, if he abandons gratifications and enjoyments and becomes empty of them, he will become more complete in relation to the World of the Spirits. His spirituality will dominate over his corporeality. Then he will advance from his own lowness to a high level.
>
> The poet says that since you are seeking guidance, you should abstain from your corporeal gratifications so that you may advance from the nadir to the zenith. When you become firm in abandoning the gratifications and desires of the soul—which are the soul's modes of disequilibrium—then the child/heart, who is concealed and overcome within your placenta/soul, will lift up its head. The heart is the form and the central point of the soul's equilibrium. It will be like a plant that grows up out of the earth of your constitution and soul. It is nurtured through the aid of a spiritual gaze by means of the water of repentance, abstinence, and sincerity.[60]

In the introduction to the Arabic version of his commentary, Farghānī discusses five levels of the heart pertaining to five major stages in the path to human perfection. In four out of five cases he describes the appearance of the heart as a birth. The first and lowest level, "the particular, relative heart," pertains to the soul that has passed through a number of the important preliminary stations of the Sufi path. The second level, called the "true heart," is born of the mutual love between its father and mother, who are spirit and soul. It displays the properties of the divine name "the Manifest." The father of the second heart now becomes the mother of the third heart, while its father is the inmost mystery (*sirr*). This heart displays the properties of the divine name "Nonmanifest." The fourth heart is that of the perfect human being and brings together the properties of both the Manifest and the Nonmanifest. Finally, the fifth heart belongs exclusively to Muhammad and is the source of all the other hearts. Farghānī's long discussion is full of technical terms pertaining to the teachings of Qūnawī. In what follows I quote only a few especially relevant sections:

> Once the soul has realized these stations, while remaining constantly in remembrance

> [*dhikr*] of God through concentration and through repelling incoming thoughts, then the properties of being veiled and the properties and effects of the soul's manyness disappear from it. When the properties of manyness become weak in the soul, the effect of its own all-comprehensive oneness becomes manifest. This oneness had been concealed within the properties of manyness. This is the particular, relative heart that pertains specifically to the soul. It is not the true heart.[61]

In contrasting spirit and soul, Farghānī refers to the activity that pertains to the Oneness and Necessity of Being and the receptivity that pertains to the manyness and possibility of the existent things, an idea with which we are already familiar. He refers to the spirit as the "spiritual spirit" (*al-rūḥ al-rūḥāniyya*) in order to distinguish it from the "animal spirit" or animal soul. Note that he does not make the activity of the spirit absolute. On the contrary, he simply means to say that, all things taken into consideration, activity belongs to it more than it does to the soul.

> The relationship of activity to the spiritual spirit is stronger because of its intense tie with the Presence of Necessity, since that Presence's oneness is manifest within it. And the relationship of receiving activity is more intense in the human, animal soul, because of its strong tie with the Presence of Possibility, since that presence's characteristic—which is manyness—becomes manifest within it.
>
> The inmost mystery, the spirit, and the soul each witnessed the manifestation of its own specific perfection as being bound to the others. Inclination to perfection belongs to their very essences and is manifest in each of them. The reason for this is that they are permeated by the original love of the Divine Essence [mentioned in the hadith, "I was a Hidden Treasure so I loved to be known"]. . . .
>
> That property of love made each of them move toward its companion. Hence through its properties the spiritual spirit longed for the human soul as the contented husband longs for his willing wife. The soul also, through its properties and original faculties, longed for the spirit as the contented and pleasing wife yearns for the husband who is devoted to her. Each of the two inclines toward the other. They come together and mix with all the unitary and equilibrium-related effects contained in each. . . . Through the property of their coming together is born from the placenta of the soul's all-comprehensiveness the child, who is the true heart. The child brings together all the properties of the parents along with those of the inmost mystery. He becomes manifest as a mature child, devoted to his parents. This unitary and all-comprehensive heart, which is godfearing and purified of all the properties of every mode of disequilibrium, becomes a mirror and a locus of self-disclosure for Him who discloses Himself in the oneness of His attributes.[62]

Farghānī tells us that this true heart reflects God inasmuch as He is the Manifest, and he devotes several pages to describing the various stations of perfection that this heart achieves. But God is also the Nonmanifest, and the heart should also achieve the perfections of nonmanifestation. This can occur only when the spirit becomes the wife of the inmost mystery. "Then there is born from the placenta of the spirit the child/heart, receptive to the self-disclosure of Nonmanifest Being." Through this receptivity the heart comes to know its own reality within the knowledge of God.[63]

The fourth stage of the heart is actualized when the spiritual traveler is freed from being dominated by the self-disclosure of God in the manifest or the nonmanifest domains. This takes place when both names, the Manifest and the Nonmanifest, disclose themselves to the person in their perfections that pertain to the "universal categories of their entifications."

> Then between the two names is born the reality of the ocean-like heart that brings together the two Presences. . . . From the east of this perfect, all-embracing and all-comprehensive heart rises the sun of the perfect, all-comprehensive self-disclosure of the Essence. . . . Now the traveler is able to put on any garment he wishes and become manifest in any locus of manifestation that he desires.[64]

ʿAbd al-Razzāq Kāshānī makes use of the image of the marriage of spirit and soul and the birth of the heart in a number of places in *Taw'īl al-Qur'ān*. For example, the following is his *ta'wīl* of Koran 4:36:

Serve God. Pay exclusive attention to Him and to annihilation within Him, for that is the extreme of self-abnegation. *And associate naught with Him* in affirming His existence. *And be good to parents.* Be good to the spirit and the soul, from which the heart was born. The heart is your reality. You belong only to it. Fulfill your parents' rights and respect them as they should be respected, by taking effusion from the spirit and turning your attention toward it through assent and reverence. Purify and preserve the soul from the defilements of love for this world and becoming abased before greed, covetousness, and the like. Protect her from the evil of Satan and his enmity toward her. Help her through clemency and zeal by giving her fully her rights and keeping gratifications away from her.[65]

Kāshānī employs similar imagery in providing a *taʾwīl* of the Koranic story of Zachariah, who prayed that God would give him a child. He is the spirit and his wife is the soul. She is barren because she has not yet given birth to the heart. And John is their child, the heart. He is called "John," *yaḥyā*, which in Arabic can be read to mean "he lives," because the heart has everlasting life.[66]

In commenting on Koran 30:21, Kāshānī illustrates the nature of the love that should exist between spirit and soul. Notice that the relationship is not one-sided. Both spirit and soul give and receive, act and are acted upon. But the situation here corresponds to the relationship between God and the divine thrall, or the Lord and the vassal: The soul acts by receiving the activity of the spirit and thereby making the spirit spirit. Without a vassal, the Lord cannot be a Lord. Without a soul, the spirit cannot be spirit.

And among His signs, that is, among His acts and attributes through which one obtains access to His Essence through knowledge and wayfaring, *is that He created for you, of your souls, spouses*. In other words, He created for you spouses for the spirits from the souls, *that you might rest in them*, and support yourselves through them and incline toward them through love, exercising effects, and accepting effects. *And He has set between you* from both sides *love and mercy*. Hence through receptivity and receiving effects the soul loves the light of the spirit and its exercising effects. Thereby it finds rest from inconstancy and is purified. God blesses the soul through the child, the heart, within the placenta of preparedness, as a loving kindness toward her. The soul is guided through the child's blessing. She assumes its character traits and is delivered.

The spirit loves the soul by exercising effects within her and effusing light upon her. God has mercy upon the spirit through the blessed child by means of loving kindness and sympathy. Through the child's blessing the spirit climbs up. Through the child its perfection becomes manifest.

Surely in that are signs, or attributes and perfections, *for a people who reflect* upon their souls and their essences, their innate dispositions, and what has been deposited within them.[67]

The Soul as Virgin Mother

The ideal soul receives the infusion of the spirit and gives birth to the heart. This is the soul at peace. Sometimes our authors compare this soul to the Virgin Mary, while Jesus is the heart to whom she gives birth. Rūmī, in a slight variation on this theme, depicts the human body as Mary. He is explaining why the pain of love and longing are necessary on the path to God.

As long as Mary did not feel the pain of childbirth, she did not go toward the tree of good fortune. "And the pangs of childbirth drove her to the trunk of the palm tree" [19:23]. That pain took her to the tree, and the barren tree bore fruit.

The body is like Mary, and each of us has a Jesus within. If the pain appears, our Jesus will be born. But if no pain comes, Jesus will return to his Origin on that same hidden road by which he came. We will be deprived of him and reap no benefit.[68]

Kāshānī interprets Mary in a similar microcosmic sense in commenting on Koran 3:42–45:

And when the angels, the spiritual faculties, *said to Mary*, the purified and pure soul,

"God has chosen you," because you have freed yourself of appetites, *"and"* He has *"purified you"* of ugly character traits and blameworthy attributes. *"He has chosen you above all women."* Women are the appetitive souls that are colored with blameworthy acts and despicable habits. *"Mary, be obedient to your Lord"* through your duties, which are acts of obedience and worship. *"And prostrate"* yourself in the station of brokenness, lowliness, poverty, incapacity, and asking forgiveness. *"And bow yourself"* in the station of humility and fear *"with those who bow,"* those who are humble. . . .

The angels said to *Mary*, the soul, *"God gives you good tidings of a Word,"* the heart, which is a gift *"from Him."* His *"name is 'Messiah,'"* since he will "anoint" [*masḥ*] you with light.

"High honored shall he be in this world" because of his perception of particular things and his governing of the best interests of livelihood. He shall be the best, the purest, and the most correct that can be. Both the "human beings," that is, the outward faculties, and the "jinn," the inward faculties, shall obey him, follow him, attend to him, and glorify him. *"And in the next world,"* since he perceives universals and holy sciences and he undertakes to govern the return to God and guidance to the Real. Hence We give to him the Kingdom of the Heaven of the spirit and We honor him. He is one of those *"near stationed to God,"* receptive to His self-disclosures and unveilings.[69]

The Perfected Heart

If we suppose that intellect and soul have been perfected and live together in utter harmony, then the heart will have been born. But the soul, this virtuous "woman," is none other than her husband, since her union with the intellect is complete and total. Heaven and earth have achieved such perfect harmony that their properties cannot be distinguished. Their oneness is precisely the heart itself, which is identical with the Tao. And indeed, the essence of the true human being is the heart.

In the midst of the *tawḥīd* that has been established, relationships can be discerned in any given situation. Is the perfect soul yin? Yes, since it has submitted itself to the will of heaven. Is it yang? Yes, since it incarnates the will of heaven that rules over the Ten Thousand Things. Is the perfect intellect yin? Yes, since it is receptive to the light of God. Is it yang? Yes, since it irradiates the soul.

One can also express this state of union by saying that the heart has two faces. One looks at God, the other at the cosmos. Inasmuch as the heart looks at God and receives from Him, it is His servant. Inasmuch as it looks toward the cosmos and governs it, it is God's vicegerent. Thus Qūnawī writes that a human being considered as an integrated whole—as having actualized the perfections of all the divine attributes—is yin only in respect to the Presence of All-comprehensiveness (*ḥaḍrat al-jamʿ*), which is designated by the all-comprehensive name Allah. And this occurs only after the person achieves total and utter annihilation (*fanāʾ*) of the limiting attributes of the soul:

> When receiving activity [*infiʿāl*] embraces both the outward and inward dimensions of the human being and complete annihilation has been achieved, then the situation pertains to the Presence of All-comprehensiveness. For the human being as a whole does not act as a locus for the reception of activity except in relation to this Presence.[70]

Human beings who attain to this station of perfection function as the heart of the macrocosm, since only within them are all the qualities of heaven and earth, or all the properties of the two hands of God, fully realized. Hence Qūnawī and his followers sometimes refer to the perfect human being as the "heart of all-comprehensiveness and existence." Such a person comprehends the attributes of heaven, earth, and the Ten Thousand Things and has become a totally integrated whole that embraces all reality. As servant and vicegerent, he or she stands at the center of existence, tying all things together. This individual human being is "the point at the center of the ontological circle," a circle which is all of existence, or everything other than God. Qūnawī refers to some of these ideas in examining the notion of heart and showing how it can be understood to exist on the five levels of the microcosm.[71]

> Know that every heart has five faces: [1] a face turned toward the Presence of the Real with no intermediary between it and the Real; [2] a face through which it stands opposite the World of the Spirits and in respect to which it takes from its Lord what its preparedness requires by means of the spirits; [3] a face specific to the World of Imagination, from which it enjoys favors to the extent of its relationship with the station of all-comprehensiveness and according to the equilibrium of its constitution and character traits and the right order of its states in its activities, presence, and knowledge; [4] a face turned toward the World of the Visible and specific to the names Manifest and Last; and [5] an all-comprehensive face that pertains to the Unity of All-comprehensiveness. This face is turned toward the level of the He-ness that is described by Firstness, Lastness, Manifestation, and Nonmanifestation and the bringing together of these four descriptions. Each of these faces has a locus of manifestation among human beings. . . .
>
> When a person is the form of the "heart of all-comprehensiveness and existence," he is like our Prophet, for his station is the point at the center of the ontological circle. The five faces of his heart are turned toward each world, presence, and level. He comprises the properties of all things and becomes manifest through all their qualities through his all-comprehensive face.
>
> Know that the greatest things that God described by all-embracingness are mercy, the human heart, and knowledge. Concerning the capacity of mercy He said, "My mercy embraces everything" [7:156]. Concerning mercy and knowledge together He said through the tongue of the angels, "Our Lord, Thou embracest all things in mercy and knowledge" [40:7]. And concerning the all-embracingness of the human heart he said, "My heavens and My earth embrace Me not, but the heart of My servant with faith does embrace Me." . . .
>
> As for the all-embracingness of the heart that embraces God, that consists of the *barzakh*-reality that pertains exclusively to the true human being, who is the heart of all-comprehensiveness and existence.[72]

The perfect human being is a *barzakh* or "isthmus" in respect of embracing all the qualities of both God and the macrocosm and bringing them together within a single reality that is both yin and yang, servant and vicegerent.

In another work, Qūnawī discusses the gradual perfection of the soul through its ascent in the "stations," a word that signifies literally a place of standing or halting. Any attribute of created things that can become manifest in the human being may be a person's station. In effect, human beings may stand anywhere, depending upon the qualities that dominate over their characters. If luminosity and beautiful character traits dominate, they stand with the angels. If ugly and limiting animal traits dominate, they stand with the beasts. Throughout a person's life, each stage of becoming can be called a "station." The ideal and ultimate station is that of all-comprehensiveness, which is the mirror image of the divine name Allah, in the form of which human beings were created. Allah possesses all qualities while not being limited and defined by any one of them. Correspondingly, the perfect human being possesses all qualities but is free of any constriction. Hence the highest human station is to be free of every station, what Ibn al-ʿArabī calls "the station of No Station."

Qūnawī commonly refers to the station of No Station as "equilibrium" (*iʿtidāl*), since it stands equidistant from every station and is free from the dominating influence of each. Hence the perfect human being stands at the "point at the center of the circle of existence," the point from which all qualities are generated and which is dominated by no quality. To be dominated by any station whatsoever is to leave the center and to be less than total. It is to be less than fully human. It is to dwell in disequilibrium or deviation (*inḥirāf*). Having attained equilibrium, the perfect human being turns his or her attention only toward the Essence or He-ness, the absolutely nondelimited Reality.

> The true human being gains freedom from the bondage of the stations and climbs up. Through the equilibrium of perfection and the middle, he is delivered from the properties

that attract to the sides and to the states of disequilibrium. Then he turns his attention toward the Presence of the He-ness, which possesses the unity of the comprehension of all-comprehensiveness.[73] It is described by manifestation and nonmanifestation, firstness and lastness, comprehensiveness and differentiation. . . .

But the human being may incline away from the middle toward one of the sides through an attracting and overwhelming affinity. He may be overpowered by the property of some of the names and levels and leave equilibrium. Then he will take up residence within the circle of that overpowering name and become related and ascribed to it. He will worship God in respect to that name's level and depend upon that name. The name will become his ultimate goal and the limit of his desires. The name will turn him this way and that in respect of its state and station until he passes beyond it.[74]

True Men and True Women

We can summarize Islamic spiritual psychology as follows: The human soul is situated on a vertical axis. It can ascend by moving toward the spirit or descend by moving away. God's attribute of guidance, which shows itself most directly in the macrocosm through the prophets and in the microcosm through the intellect, calls upon the soul to return to its origin. But the attribute of misguidance, incarnate in the satans and the soul that commands to evil, calls upon the soul to follow the animal qualities and to move away from God.

In the "normal," forgetful state, the soul is passive or "feminine" toward appetite and anger, while it is active or "masculine" toward God and the intellect. Here both yin and yang are inappropriate and therefore blameworthy. In both cases the normative order of heaven and earth has been upset by the qualities that dominate over the microcosm. This is the state of the soul that commands to evil.

In contrast, if the soul ascends through the various stages of the blaming soul and attains to the soul at peace, which is none other than the yin side of the intellect, then it manifests praiseworthy yin and yang. Its receptivity and yielding are its complete surrender to the light of God. Its activity and domination are its mastery of appetite, anger, and all forces that call upon it to become engrossed in the lower world.

Islamic sources are full of accounts of women that can be read as criticisms. In the view of the intellectual tradition, critical references to women have in view those qualities that are typically manifested by people who incarnate the negative receptivity of the soul. In contrast, when women are praised—far less often, since praiseworthy souls are much rarer than blameworthy souls—the object of praise is those qualities that are incarnate in the receptivity of the soul at peace with God. If "women" are sometimes put into the same category as hermaphrodites, this is because they both lack manliness, the active qualities of the intellect.

Samʿānī refers to both women and hermaphrodites in negative terms while providing a *taʾwīl* of a Koranic verse that commands the Prophet's wives not to display themselves to strangers. He is in the midst of explaining why self-satisfaction and pride is the worst affliction that can overcome the traveler on the path to God. After all, Iblis reached great proximity to God through his good works. According to some accounts, he was even made the teacher of the angels. But then he refused to bow before Adam and said, "I am better than he" (38:76). His vision of his own self was his downfall. He was a woman because he surrendered to his lower self. He was hermaphrodite because he possessed certain male qualities by achieving a high spiritual station, but then negated them by claiming them for himself.

> O dervish! If you dwell in a station of distance from God and regret not having arrived, that is better than having a station of nearness and being self-satisfied because of your arrival. Self-satisfaction is the beginning of the end, and regret is the precursor of blessing. In short, you must clear your own self out of the way, you must tear off the clothing of your mortal nature, you must pour earth on your earthly eyes. In this path, those who show themselves have the property of hermaphrodites.

In the rulings of the Sharia, women have been commanded to conceal and cover themselves. "Display not your beauty as did the pagans of old" [33:33]. But when we look at the mysteries of the Ṭarīqa and the allusions of the masters of Reality, then we see the following: To manifest one's own soul in the Path is more blameworthy and corrupting than to remove curtained ladies from behind their veils and auction them off naked before strangers.

There was someone in the time of Adam who spoke of himself. Though he was the teacher of the angels and their leader, when he made his own self appear, he became a hermaphrodite and a woman on the Path. God said to him, "Go far from My Presence. Go, for I have given you the lower world. Go down into the cave of delusion. Adorn that dustbin for the eyes of those who have no aspiration."[75]

Rūmī typically reads all mention of women that suggests negative qualities as referring to the soul that commands to evil. For example,

When the Prophet said, "Put the females behind," he meant your soul. For it must be put last, and your intellect first.[76]

Having told a story about a man and a woman, Rūmī then clarifies the meaning, lest we take the story literally and miss the point:

A tale about man and woman has been related. Consider it as a likeness of your soul and your intellect.

This "woman" and "man," which are soul and intellect, are very necessary for the existence of good and evil.

Day and night in this abode of dust these two necessary beings are in war and altercation.

The woman always desires the necessities of the household—reputation, bread, food, and position.

Like a woman, the soul sometimes displays humility and sometimes seeks leadership in order to remedy its plight.

The intellect indeed knows nothing of these thoughts. Its mind contains only longing for God.[77]

In this qualitative view of things, a "man" is someone whose intellect or spirit dominates over his or her soul, whatever the person's physical gender. A man incarnates the qualities of the First Intellect in relation to the Universal Soul, or heaven in relation to earth. In the same way, a "woman" is someone whose intellect and spirit are subjugated by the soul's negative tendencies: Heaven has been wrongly dominated by earth. At the same time, a "woman" also has masculine qualities, but these are the negative masculine tendencies of the soul as incarnate in Iblis. And a "man" has feminine qualities, the positive feminine attributes of the soul at peace with God. This is how Rūmī explains male and female in the following:

Alas for those whose intellects are feminine and whose ugly souls are masculine and prepared.

Without question their intellects are vanquished and they will be taken only to loss.

Happy are those whose intellects are masculine and whose ugly souls are feminine and helpless.

Their partial intellects are masculine and dominant, intelligence has negated the feminine soul. . . .

Animal qualities prevail in "women," because they tend toward color and scent.

When the ass perceived the color and scent of the pasture, all arguments fled from its nature.[78]

In short, a "man" is someone who possesses the qualities of manliness and chivalry, and these include all the positive qualities of the soul. Many more passages could be cited showing how the term man is used in this normative sense. For example, ʿAṭṭār tells the following anecdote about Abu'l-Ḥasan Kharraqānī:

It has been related that a man came to Shaykh Abu'l-Ḥasan and said, "I want to put on the *khirqa* [i.e., the cloak of the Sufis]." The Shaykh replied, "I have a question. If you can answer it, you are worthy of the *khirqa*. If a man puts on the chador of a woman, does he become a woman?"

The man replied, "No."

The Shaykh said, "If a woman puts on a

> man's clothing, will she ever become a man?"
>
> He replied, "No."
>
> The Shaykh said, "You also—if you are not a man in this Path, you will not become a man by putting on the *khirqa*."[79]

An Arabic saying, traceable at least to the seventh/thirteenth century, contrasts ideal manliness with negative femininity: "The seeker of the Lord is male, the seeker of the next world is hermaphrodite, and the seeker of this world is female."[80] As already pointed out, "hermaphrodites" are lukewarm on the path to God, wavering between the ascending and descending tendencies of soul. Such a person may have overcome the desires of the soul that commands to evil to a certain degree, but not enough to aspire to perfection. For perfection entails actualizing all the names of God through union with the Real. In this saying the suggestion seems to be that a person who seeks after paradise—at least in the limiting sense of the term—is still looking for the sensory delights and enjoyments promised in the Koran. Hence the soul has not completely overcome its lower nature, attached to the sensory and outward level.

Many sayings are found in the early accounts of the Sufis that ascribe masculinity to women. For example, the famous Sufi Abū Yazīd (d. ca. 260/874) said about the wife of Aḥmad ibn Khaḍrūya (d. 240/854), "If someone wants to see a man hidden in women's clothing, let him look at Fāṭima."[81] Someone ignorant of the context might think that Abū Yazīd is disparaging Fāṭima's femininity. But this is hardly the case. On the contrary, by calling a woman a "man" the Sufis meant to show that she had attained to the fullness of the human state in which the soul serves the intellect. One can hardly be a perfect woman without first being perfectly human. In other words, a female human being can be fully female only when she is a "man" in the normative sense. A woman's specific gender characteristics reach the fullness of their actuality only in the wake of her human perfection. She also is made in God's image—though generally speaking in her outward form she manifests God's love, beauty, mercy, kindness, and gentleness more directly than a man. Only when she is fully herself by being fully one with God can she be fully human and fully female. That is why Mary, whom Muslims look upon as perfectly feminine, can be considered perfectly masculine without in any way compromising her femininity. ʿAṭṭār quotes the following saying with approval: "When tomorrow on the Day of Resurrection the call goes up, 'O men!', the first person to step into the ranks of men will be the Virgin Mary."[82] Rūmī makes a similar point, though he calls attention to the fact that such a man in woman's clothing is truly rare. And he also points out that such a man in *man's* clothing is almost as rare. Most men are "women" in men's bodies.

> Since women never go out to fight the holy war, how should they engage in the Greater Holy War [against the soul that commands to evil]?
>
> Except rarely, when a hero like Rustam is hidden in a woman's body, as in the case of Mary.
>
> In the same way, women are hidden in the bodies of those men who are feminine [in the path of God] from faintness of heart.[83]

In short, if we look at the dominant qualities in most people from the point of view of the Islamic sapiential tradition, we see that they are "women," since they are passive toward the pig, the dog, and the satan. In the qualitative perspective, the fact that "women fall short in intelligence and religion," as the Prophet said, is self-evident. Intelligence and religion are the hallmarks of guidance. "Woman" in the negative sense of the term refers to someone dominated by the soul that commands to evil. By definition such a soul has turned away from guidance by following ignorance and satan. Everyone who follows satan is a "woman."

We reach the conclusion that very few people deserve to be called "men" in the positive and normative sense of the word. But many people—according to Ghazālī and Ibn al-ʿArabī almost everybody—should be called "men" in the negative sense. For a "man" in this negative meaning is someone whose soul is dominated by the fiery qualities proper to Iblis, or someone whose soul is masculine through commanding to evil and whose intellect is feminine through submitting to the soul.

What then is the Muslim view of women? It depends on whom you ask, and it depends on what you mean by the term. As in any tradition, there are many views. Until you define your terms, you will not be able to grasp the subtleties of the discussion.

POSTSCRIPT

Several years ago I gave a talk to some of my colleagues at Stony Brook on "Feminine-Masculine Complementarity in Islamic Spiritual Psychology." I drew certain conclusions concerning the loss of true femininity and true masculinity. One of the sharpest minds in the room belonged to a philosopher, who happened to be a woman. She participated vigorously in the discussion and defended what I had to say against the criticisms of some of the males present. Afterward she told me that the reasoning was valid. However, there was no basis for the fundamental premise: that intellect is masculine and soul feminine. One of my goals in writing this book has been to answer her objection. I am grateful to her for her remarks on that occasion.

I hope that I have demonstrated that Islamic views of the gender qualities of intellect, soul, and other realities are not motivated simply by the will to power or some individual or social ill. Our authors were sincere Muslims. As such, they put God first. Once God is first and the ego is second, certain conclusions follow. The two chapters on theology should have suggested that Islam's metaphysical basis is hardly flimsy. It is based squarely on an analysis of the nature of reality. If such analyses do not satisfy modern sensibilities, this does not prove that they are intellectually bankrupt or wrong. It merely shows that the modern West perceives reality in a profoundly different way.

The section on cosmology should suggest that Muslim evaluations of the nature of the universe have nothing to do with proto-science, or with science in the modern sense. The Islamic view of the cosmos grows up out of an ontology that differentiates clearly between the Real and the unreal, the Absolute and the relative. However, this distinction does not yield a universe of white and black. Quite the contrary, it gives us a practically infinite scale of grays, from the darkest possible to the lightest possible. Pure white light—the Absolute—stands beyond the scale but determines its nature.

Islamic cosmology offers a sophisticated appraisal of ontological qualities that ties everything back to the One, thereby expressing *tawḥīd*. It is not especially "systematic," since our authors are constantly changing their standpoints depending on the qualities they have in view. Hence it is open ended, capable of infinite variation.

Within *tawḥīd*, relationships are fundamental, since the relationships set up the scale of grays. Any two things that are related to each other—and all things are related to each other—can be looked at as white and black. But the more closely we examine a given relationship, the more we see that there is only gray. Nevertheless, the degree of intensity has immense importance. Muslims did not find themselves in a relativistic universe, since differing degrees of relativity were established by the Real, which stands beyond all the degrees. Outside of every scale stands a divine name.

But here we are not talking simply about

gray. What is at issue is an indefinite variety of colors. Each hue varies from the darkest to the brightest. And outside each scale stands the absolute color from which the relative shades derive.

As soon as we look at relationships between any two things, it becomes clear that in the perspective of a given color, one of the things is more intense and one less intense. One is yang and one yin. God created the universe in pairs because existence (not Being) is inconceivable without distinction. God is Being, the universe is existence. God is the sun, the universe its rays. And this is said, of course, from within the perspective of similarity. In no way does it compromise the divine transcendence, the perspective of incomparability.

In short, differing qualities or intensities in qualities can always be described in terms of yin and yang, female and male. The Islamic tradition attributes qualities to God and the cosmos, heaven and earth, male and female. These things can then rightly be analyzed in terms of qualitative correspondence, and such analysis tells us something of the nature of reality. Moreover, in the Islamic intellectual tradition, knowledge of reality is the goal of human life. Through knowing Absolute Reality and acting accordingly, we establish a relationship that is able to step beyond all relativism. That relationship is called "felicity," or "paradise," or "union with God," or "*tawḥīd*."

Nowadays some people might assume that a woman's duty in writing a study of Islam is to help undermine Islam's patriarchal structure. In a sense, I am doing that, since I have brought out the "matriarchal" elements in Islamic thought clearly enough. But to bring out the feminine stress of Islamic spirituality does not necessarily mean criticizing the masculine stress of the Sharia and Kalām.

In many circles today hierarchy is bad by definition. I look at the problem in a slightly different light. Hierarchy is not bad, since it is built into reality. To deny that is to be blind. Those who do deny it invariably do so in order to set up other hierarchies that they prefer. They are not blind, but they do have agendas.

Rather than try to overthrow the hierarchy, I prefer to acknowledge it for what it is, but to clarify the relationships in imitation of Confucius, trying to "rectify the names." Hierarchy cannot be avoided in Islamic thought because Islam's premise is the Shahāda: "There is no reality but the Real." God is the Real and the cosmos is unreal. That in turn sets up the infinite scale from white to black. To break with the hierarchy means to overthrow the most fundamental of Islamic principles.

If we simply accept that Islam acknowledges hierarchy and work within that framework, a great deal can be done toward addressing those fundamental human concerns that do in fact inform criticisms of hierarchy. We have to understand how the tradition defines male and female and use the terms with all their proper nuances. Too often the issues are confused because the terms have not been understood. If we define "male" simplistically and consider it good and only good, we will include in that good all the negative sides to masculinity, thereby giving a free hand to every negative masculine force. If we consider "female" bad and only bad, every positive feminine quality gets trampled underfoot. But analogous things will happen if we decide that male means bad and female good.

If certain Muslims evaluate "women" negatively, the problem may be that they are unable to see beyond surface appearances and elementary Islamic teachings. In recent times most Muslims, especially those involved with public affairs, have lost sight of the sapiential current of their religion. They understand something about the Sharia, and perhaps Kalām, both of which stress God's incomparability and the yang divine names. Hence such Muslims perceive Islam's positive evaluation of "men" and negative evaluation of "women," but they are rarely able to escape the reification of qualities that characterizes so much of modern thought. In other words, they cannot distinguish between the symbol and what is symbolized, or the object and the quality incarnate within it. They cannot grasp that the primary thrust of the discussion concerns male and female qualities, not men and women.

Those Muslims who place almost exclusive stress upon the incomparability of God, emphasizing the yang qualities of the divine reality, naturally evaluate "men" in a positive light, while seeing "women" largely in terms of the negative femininity of the soul that commands to evil. This point of view devalues, if it does not deny, God's similarity. As a result, we have but a single set of parameters for male and female. The male is good, because the male incarnates intellect and struggle against the forces of deviation. The female is bad, because the female incarnates the soul that commands to evil and acquiescence to every satanic whisper.

But in fact, if we look at Islamic thought in the broader terms that I have investigated in this book, we see that both feminine and masculine are double edged swords. Each has a negative and a positive evaluation. If the rigidly "patriarchal" stress of some contemporary Muslims is to be softened, this can happen only when they place renewed stress on femininity as a positive quality and masculinity as a negative quality. And Muslims will be able to do this as Muslims—not as imitation Westerners—only if they look once again at the spiritual and intellectual dimensions of their own tradition.

Many Islamic movements in the modern world seem unwilling or unable to grasp the nuanced appreciation of masculine and feminine provided by the intellectual tradition. In some cases we see that Muslims have adopted the worst and most negative tendencies of the modern world as their own. Thus, for example, few Muslim activists today have any sensitivity toward beauty or nature. All the problems of the ecological crisis—which are the clear results of a negative masculinity run amuck—are being adopted with glee. There is no question of "returning to the Middle Ages," as many Westerners read the scene. On the contrary, we see a headlong rush into a position of power and domination through any means, technology in particular. It is precisely the element of control and domination found in technology that make political activism so attractive and so dangerous. Yet, from the perspective of the sapiential tradition, this urge to establish control over society and the environment is a submission to the descending and dispersive tendencies of the soul and a revolt against the ascending and unifying tendencies. It is the worst of both worlds, masculine and feminine.

One might object that Islam tells us that human beings are God's vicegerents. Hence they have the right to control the environment. But this is to ignore the fact that "vicegerency" is the goal, not the actual situation. True vicegerency—not the counterfeit form found in modern technology—depends utterly upon submission to God. It is achieved in spite of the servant's personal desires, not because of them. *You* cannot desire to be God's vicegerent, since "you" are the ego that must be erased in order for full submission to be established. Servanthood is the sine qua non. Without servanthood, the urge to vicegerency becomes what we see before our eyes: the rape of the environment and the destruction of all those values and institutions that help human beings achieve servanthood and peace.

Moreover, there is another side to false vicegerency or negative masculinity. That is false servanthood or negative femininity. These are two sides of the same coin. We cannot criticize "masculine" impulses without criticizing "feminine" tendencies, any more than we can praise either in isolation. The one who claims greatness and vicegerency without right is Iblis: "I am better than he—You created me of fire, and You created him of clay" (38:76). This "I am better than he" is the slogan of negative masculinity. It is the motivating force behind much of modern civilization and contemporary culture (need I speak of competition, sports, achievement . . . ?). Iblis's point of view goes hand in hand with shortsightedness and failing to recognize the signs of God.

But Iblis's "masculine" quest for domination coincides with a "feminine" receptivity to everything that pulls toward dispersion and distance from God. The negative femininity—or negative "servanthood"—that goes along with the masculine urge to control is surrender to all the impulses in the self and the world that turn human beings away from the guidance of God and the prophets.

My "feminist agenda" is to help those Muslims who are so inclined to reestablish the vision of the Divine Feminine, which is the Essence of God. The sapiential perspective allows people to see feminine qualities situated at the peak of reality. The Real in Itself is receptive to every entification, every thing. It gives birth to the bipolar God who is both merciful and wrathful, yin and yang, mother and father. The mercy of this bipolar God precedes Her wrath, which is to say that Her femininity is more real and fundamental than Her masculinity.

Nevertheless, I have no hesitations about referring to this God whose mercy predominates as "He," as is normal within the Islamic tradition. If Muslims call God "He," it is because the first and most necessary relationship of human beings to God is submission (*islām*). We are receptive and He is active. Although ultimate Reality is in a certain sense more deeply "feminine" than "masculine," It is not so in relation to us considered as individual egos and collectivities. In human society, negative femininity and negative masculinity dominate the scene. And this is nothing new, since these negative gender traits mark the fundamental tendency of human beings since the time of Adam. That, at least, is the Islamic view. It explains why God has had to send "124,000 prophets" to human beings. People constantly surrender to their lower appetites and passively fall back into forgetfulness (*ghafla*) and ignorance. Then they make use of their controlling power as vicegerents to shape the world in terms of their own egos. History is the story of the descent into negative masculinity and negative femininity.

If the right order is to be reestablished in the cosmos, human beings have first to be women in the positive sense. The flip side of this statement is that they also have to be men in the positive sense. In other words, the Muslim psychologists maintain that human spirits and intellects must be submitted to God and in turn must rule the souls. Then only is it possible to make headway against the corruption of the cosmos and society.

Islam did not keep the mystery of the divine feminine in the background for no good reason. If too much emphasis is placed upon the sacrality of the receptive, earth dimension of reality, the negative tendencies of the soul can easily take advantage of the situation. I am reminded of a button I saw at a New Age fair: "You are perfect just the way you are." To accept the soul just the way it is, with all the natural tendencies pulling toward darkness and deviation, is in the Islamic view the height of folly. By emphasizing the sacrality of the near, the soul, the earth, we run the danger of accepting things just the way they are. Things *are* perfect just the way they are, but that is God's point of view, not our point of view. That is the perspective of the engendering command, which brings guidance and misguidance into existence. It is not the perspective of the prescriptive command, which sets down the means for achieving felicity and avoiding wretchedness and which discerns between God's right and left hands.

As was suggested at the end of chapter 2, the knowledge that God's mercy precedes His wrath can easily lead to the corruption of the soul. To depend upon mercy and ignore wrath is to allow the soul to become "boldly expansive." The soul rises up and asserts itself. But this is the soul that is a friend of Iblis.

The soul that is a friend of the prophets and God must sink down and annihilate itself. It must will to erase its own caprice, appetite, and anger through submission to the divine will. Thereby the primacy of intellect is stressed, and human beings may eventually achieve the perfection of intellect's full actualization. The divine form is brought from potentiality to actuality and the Active Intellect becomes vicegerent in the cosmos.

If God's feminine face is stressed too much, right relationships will be upset, just as they are upset when His masculine face is stressed too much. To see God as loving, merciful, close, and intimate without having first realized God as dominating, wrathful, distant, and awe-inspiring results in the magnification of the soul that commands to evil. To claim exemption from domination by this soul is to claim superiority to Adam.

"I am better than he." This soul that wants intimacy before awe is the negatively feminine soul, the soul that is at ease with appetite, anger, and this world. And it quickly makes peace with such negatively masculine qualities as drive, conquest, domination, control, and exploitation.

There seems to be some deep wisdom in the fact that traditionally all Chinese, even Taoists, are Confucianists and accept the Confucian yang depiction of the Tao, at least on one level. The Confucian perspective sets up a hierarchy of relationships based upon the primacy of heaven over earth. These relationships determine the social hierarchy and make for a stable society. In contrast, the Taoists depict the Tao in yin colors. Receptivity becomes the principle, and the hierarchies of society appear as hindrances to perfection. In theory, social order is overthrown. Fortunately, the Taoists never assumed power. And in fact, in practice, most Taoists observed the social code, because they knew it was a necessary framework for stability. If they overthrew the received order, they did so in their inward lives. There they could pass beyond Tao as yang and preach that "everything is perfect just the way it is."

So also in Islam: The Sharia deals with hierarchies based on distance from God, on God as King and Commander. The divine attributes that are stressed pertain to majesty and severity. In contrast, the Ṭarīqa or spiritual path deals with the elimination of these hierarchies of distance in the inward realm through nearness to God. The divine attributes that are stressed pertain to beauty and gentleness.

If one still asks why it was not the other way around—why the Goddess was not put first—Muslim cosmologists might answer that this has to do with human propensities and capacities. One establishes a relationship with the Merciful, the Kind, and the Loving through that which is near to God, the spirit. And the spirit is from the outset concealed from our awareness. The vast majority of people, in fact, have no interest in reaching God either by one route or the other. They have more immediate and more "real" things to worry about. As Rūmī says, "Women are attracted by colors and scents." Only "men" can love God. But to be true men, their intellects must be actualized. Intellect is the divine light that corresponds to prophecy. Most people reject the prophets when they come—a constant theme of the Koran—and most people have no truck with the intellect in this sense. "Reason" and rationality are another matter, especially in the domineering form they take through the scientific method and technology. Intellect is a positive masculine power only when submitted to God. When it sets itself up as independent, it serves Iblis. Its controlling power is placed at the disposal of the pig, the dog, and the devil. How else could Ghazālī read the history of scientific and technological progress?

When the First Intellect descends in the form of a prophet, it has to set up a framework within which the door to the inward realm can be opened. In the case of Islam, the prophetic message was addressed to everyone so that the right social order could be established. God's masculine face was preached to all because it can be grasped by anyone. When the King says do it, you do it. But when the Beauty says come here, all too many people say, "Who, me?" Or, before she makes the invitation, they try to take her. Love is not the domain for the shortsighted, the fainthearted, the weak willed, the slaves of appetite, the "women." Yet society must be built on these very "women," since there are few men. Once the structure is established, there is always room for a woman to become a man. And in fact, without the structure, no human being ever becomes a man. Submission precedes vicegerency.[1]

There are a number of interesting hadiths that speak about the relationship between men and women at the end of time. Like accounts of the Last Days in other religions, the Islamic accounts tend to be mysterious, referring to the such things as the "Beast of the Earth," Gog and Magog, the descent of the Messiah from heaven, and so on. In most instances, these accounts are far from explicit and have given rise to all sorts of interpretations. The particular accounts that I have in mind seem straightforward, but the fact that they speak of a highly abnormal situation suggests that we are supposed to give some thought to them. They are not necessarily meant to be taken literally. For example, Bukhārī and Muslim both give us the following hadith:

> Among the signs of the last hour will be that knowledge disappears, ignorance is established, fornication prevails, wine is drunk, men become few, and women become many, so that fifty women will have but one man to stand over them.[2]

The first few signs listed here are clear enough and widespread enough for everyone to recognize them. But, you say, we don't have to worry yet, because women outnumber men only by a small fraction. However, by now the reader knows that Muslims often mention men and women as designations for certain collections of qualities and characteristics. A "man" takes care of a "woman" because of the correct ontological relationship between yang and yin. Here we are being told that only a few men will be left, and many women. In other words, most human beings will be dominated by negative yin qualities.

I suspect that our authors would maintain that the problem today is not that men and women are "unequal," but that there are hardly any true men or true women left in the world. No longer are there any female souls to be found—at peace with God. Most peoples' souls are negatively male, commanding to evil. Lalla, the famous eighth/fourteenth century yogini and poetess of Kashmir, used to walk around naked, because there were no men before whom she could feel embarrassed. One day she saw the patron saint of the Kashmiri Muslims, Sayyid ʿAlī Hamadānī (d. 786/1385). Then she put on clothes.[3] She had never before met a man, only people in masculine form who were in fact women.

Writing in the seventh/thirteenth century, Najm al-Dīn Rāzī looks back and sees Islamic society already far from perfect at the time of the famous Sufi saint Ḥusayn b. Manṣūr al-Hallāj (d. 309/922). For he has this to say about al-Ḥallāj's sister:

> Ḥusayn ibn Manṣūr had a sister who laid claim to manliness on this path. She was also beautiful. She would come into Baghdad with half of her face covered by a veil and the other half exposed. A great one came to her and said, "Why do you not cover your face entirely?"
>
> She replied, "You show me a man, and I will cover my face. In the whole of Baghdad there is only half a man, and that is [my brother] Ḥusayn. Were it not for him, I would leave this half uncovered also."[4]

APPENDIX I
CHRONOLOGICAL LIST OF AUTHORS CITED

ʿAlī (ibn Abī Ṭālib). d. 40/661
ʿAlī ibn al-Ḥusayn. d. ca. 95/713
Muḥammad al-Bāqir. d. ca. 117/735
Jaʿfar al-Ṣādiq. d. 148/765
Ikhwān al-Ṣafāʾ. fl. fourth/tenth c.
Sarrāj, Abū Naṣr al-. d. 378/988
Kalābādhī, Abū Bakr al-. d. 380/990
Makkī, Abū Ṭālib al-. d. 386/996
Tirmidhī, al-Ḥakīm al-. d. late fourth/tenth
Firdawsī. d. ca. 411/1020
Sulamī, Abū ʿAbd al-Raḥmān al-. d. 412/1021
Kharraqānī, Abuʾl-Ḥasan. d. 425/1033
Avicenna (Ibn Sīnā). d. 428/1037
Bukhārī, Abū Ibrāhīm. d. 434/1042–43
Qushayrī, Abuʾl-Qāsim al-. d. 465/1072
Hujwīrī, ʿAlī ibn ʿUthmān. d. ca. 465/1072
Anṣārī, Khwāja ʿAbdallāh. d. 481/1088
Ghazālī, Muḥammad al-. d. 505/1111
Maybudī, Rashīd al-Dīn. d. after 520/1126
Hamadānī, ʿAyn al-Quḍāt d. 525/1131
Sanāʾī d. 525/1131
Samʿānī, Aḥmad. d. 534/1140
Ṭabrisī, Faḍl. d. 548/1153–54
Suhrawardī al-Maqtūl. d. 587/1191
Kāshānī, Bābā Afḍal. fl. seventh/thirteenth c.
Rāzī, Fakhr al-Dīn. d. 606/1209
Rūzbihān Baqlī. d. 606/1209
ʿAṭṭār, Farīd al-Dīn. d. 618/1221
Kubrā, Najm al-Dīn. d. 618/1221
Suhrawardī, Shihāb al-Dīn. d. 632/1234
Ibn al-Fāriḍ. d. 632/1235
Ibn al-ʿArabī. d. 638/1240
Rāzī, Najm al-Dīn. d. 654/1256
Rūmī, Jalāl al-Dīn. d. 672/1273
Qūnawī, Ṣadr al-Dīn. d. 673/1274
Farghānī, Saʿīd al-Dīn. d. 695/1296
Nasafī, ʿAzīz al-Dīn. d. ca. 695/1295
Jandī, Muʾayyid al-Dīn. d. ca. 700/1300
Bayḍāwī, Qāḍī ʿAbd Allāh. d. ca. 700/1300
Shabistarī, Maḥmūd. d. ca. 720/1320
Kāshānī, ʿIzz al-Dīn. d. 735/1334–35
Kāshānī, ʿAbd al-Razzāq. d. 736/1335
Qayṣarī, Sharaf al-Dīn. d. 751/1350
Ḥāfiẓ. d. 792/1389
Jāmī, ʿAbd al-Raḥmān. d. 898/1492
Lāhījī, Muḥammad. d. 912/1506
Mullā Ṣadrā. d. 1050/1641
Kāshānī, Mullā Muḥsin d. 1090/1679

APPENDIX II
NOTES ON AUTHORS CITED

ʿAlī (ibn Abī Ṭālib) (d. 40/661)
The cousin of the Prophet and husband of the Prophet's daughter Fāṭima. He was the fourth caliph of the Sunnis and the first Imam of the Shiʿites.

ʿAlī ibn al-Ḥusayn ibn ʿAlī, Zayn al-ʿĀbidīn (d. ca. 95/713)
The son of ʿAlī's son Ḥusayn and the fourth Imam of the Shiʿites. He is known especially for his collected prayers, *al-Ṣaḥīfat al-sajjādiyya*.

Anṣārī, Khwāja ʿAbdallāh (d. 481/1088)
His most famous work is his *munājāt* (Intimate prayers), written in rhymed Persian prose. He is also the author of one the most influential descriptions of the spiritual stations, in Arabic, *Manāzil al-sāʾirīn*, and a Persian life of the saints.

ʿAṭṭār, Farīd al-Dīn (d. 618/1221)
One of the most famous of the Persian poets. Among his translated works are *The Conference of the Birds* (*Manṭiq al-tayr*), *The Ilāhināma*, and, in prose, *Muslim Saints and Mystics* (*Tadhkirat al-awliyāʾ*).

Avicenna (Ibn Sīnā) (d. 428/1037)
The foremost of the Muslim Peripatetic philosophers and one of the greatest of the medieval physicians. He wrote scores of books, mostly in Arabic but some in Persian.

Bayḍāwī, Qāḍī ʿAbdallāh ibn Imām al-Dīn (d. ca. 700/1300)
Author of one of the most influential commentaries on the Koran, *Asrār al-tanzīl*, as well as several works on jurisprudence, logic, Kalām, and history.

Bukhārī, Abū Ibrāhīm Mustamlī (d. 434/1042–43)
Author of a long commentary in Persian on Kalābādhī's *al-Taʿarruf*. Not to be confused with the famous Bukhārī, author of one of the most authoritative collections of Hadith.

Farghānī, Saʿīd al-Dīn (d. 695/1296)
A disciple of Ṣadr al-Dīn Qūnawī, he wrote a long commentary in two versions, first in Persian and then in Arabic, on Ibn al-Fāriḍ's "Poem of the Way." The first was written as a summary of lectures delivered by Qūnawī. Farghānī systematized the teachings of Ibn al-ʿArabī and Qūnawī.

Firdawsī (d. ca. 411/1020)
Author of the Persian national epic, the *Shāhnāma* (Book of kings).

Ghazālī, Abū Ḥāmid Muḥammad al- (d. 505/1111)
One of the most famous of the Muslim authorities of the early period. His autobiography detailing how he became a well-known scholar and then left his post in search for certainty has often been studied and translated. His most famous work is *Iḥyāʾ ʿulūm al-dīn* (The revivification of the sciences of the religion), in which he brings out the inner meaning of Islamic practices and ethical ideals. He summarizes this work in his Persian *Kīmiyā-yi saʿādat* (The alchemy of felicity).

Ḥāfiẓ, Shams al-Dīn Muḥammad (d. 792/1389)
According to most specialists, the greatest of the Persian poets.

Hamadānī, ʿAyn al-Quḍāt (d. 525/1131)
A Sufi and philosopher who was executed at the age of 33 on trumped-up charges of heresy. His *apologia* has been translated into English. He is the author of works in both Arabic and Persian, including more than a hundred Persian letters to disciples.

Hujwīrī, ʿAlī ibn ʿUthmān (d. ca. 465/1072)
Author of one of the earliest Persian manuals of Sufi teaching and practice, the *Kashf al-maḥjūb* (translated by Nicholson). His tomb in Lahore is one of the favorite places of Muslim pilgrimage in the subcontinent.

Ibn al-ʿArabī, Muḥyī al-Dīn (d. 638/1240)
Known as the "Greatest Master," he brought together all the Islamic sciences in a grand synthesis that has been influential throughout the Islamic world, both on the intellectual and popular levels, down to modern times. His most famous work is the *Fuṣūṣ al-ḥikam* (Ringstones of wisdom).

Ibn al-Fāriḍ, ʿUmar (d. 632/1235)
Perhaps the greatest of Arabic poets, his most famous work is the "Poem of the Way" (*Naẓm al-sulūk*), a 750 verse compendium of Sufi teachings.

Ikhwān al-Ṣafāʾ (fl. 4th/10th c.)
Little is known about the personal identity of these "Brethren of Purity." They rewrote Neoplatonic and Pythagorean natural philosophy and metaphysics in Islamic terms in a series of about fifty treatises.

Jaʿfar al-Ṣādiq (d. 148/765)
The sixth Shiʿite Imam, an authority on the Islamic sciences for both Shiʿites and Sunnis.

Jāmī, ʿAbd al-Raḥmān (d. 898/1492)
Sometimes called the "seal of the [Persian] poets," he is the author of fifty works on hadith, biography, Arabic grammar, music, and Sufism. He was a great devotee of Ibn al-ʿArabī and played an important role in popularizing his teachings.

Jandī, Muʾayyid al-Dīn (d. ca. 700/1300)
A spiritual disciple of Ṣadr al-Dīn Qūnawī, he is the author of the most influential of the more than 100 commentaries written on Ibn al-ʿArabī's *Fuṣūṣ al-ḥikam*. He also wrote a number of works in Persian, including *Nafkhat al-rūḥ* (The blowing of the spirit), which has been published.

Kalābādhī, Abū Bakr al- (d. 380/990)
Author of a famous early compendium of Sufi teachings, *al-Taʿarruf* (translated by Arberry as *The Doctrine of the Sufis*). Kalābādhī takes great care to show that Sufi beliefs do not conflict with those of the followers of Kalām.

Kāshānī, ʿAbd al-Razzāq (d. 736/1335)
One of the best known commentators on Ibn al-ʿArabī's *Fuṣūṣ al-ḥikam*, he is the author of several other doctrinal works in Arabic, including an important esoteric commentary on the Koran, as well as some Persian works. He is famed for his correspondence with the Sufi ʿAlāʾ al-Dawla Simnānī (d. 736/1336) in which he defends the teachings of Ibn al-ʿArabī.

Kāshānī, Bābā Afḍal (fl. seventh/thirteenth c.)
An important philosopher who wrote almost exclusively in Persian. He is the author of a large number of quatrains, and his prose is masterly. He has works on logic in the style of Avicenna, but devotes most of his attention to the nature of the human soul, with special regard to the more mystical currents in Neoplatonism.

Kāshānī, ʿIzz al-Dīn (d. 735/1334-35)
He wrote works in both Arabic and Persian, but his most famous and influential book is *Miṣbāḥ al-hidāya* (The lamp of guidance), a compendium of mainly practical teachings on Sufism in beautiful Persian prose.

Kāshānī, Mullā Muḥsin Fayḍ (d. 1090/1679)
One of the foremost scholars of Safavid Iran, a poet and author of works in philosophy, theology, jurisprudence, Hadith, and Sufism.

Kharraqānī, Abuʾl-Ḥasan (d. 425/1033)
His sayings are often quoted in the compendiums of Sufi teachings.

Kubrā, Najm al-Dīn (d. 618/1221)
A great Sufi teacher who was given the title *walī-tarāsh* (sculptor of saints) because of his many well-known disciples. Author of an important work in Arabic and a few Persian treatises, he is looked back upon as the founder of the Kubrawī Order.

Lāhījī, Muḥammad ibn Yaḥyā (d. 912/1506)
The great commentator on Shabistarī's *Gulshan-i rāz* and a poet who used the pen name Asīrī. His *dīwān* has been published.

Makkī, Abū Ṭālib al- (d. 386/996)
Author of the first comprehensive manual of Sufi practical and psychological teachings, *Qūt al-qulūb* (Food of the hearts).

Maybudī, Rashīd al-Dīn (d. after 520/1126)
Author of one of the most important Koran commentaries in Persian, *Kashf al-asrār wa ʿuddat al-abrār* (The unveiling of the mysteries and the preparation of the pious). Printed in ten volumes, it explains each Koranic verse in three sections: literal meaning, historical and doctrinal background, and spiritual significance. Taken separately, the third sections make up a major compendium of Sufi teachings, drawing heavily on the sayings of Maybudī's teacher, Anṣārī.

Muḥammad al-Bāqir (d. ca. 117/735)
The fifth Shiʿite Imam.

Mullā Ṣadrā (d. 1050/1641)
The greatest philosopher of the Safavid period. He taught in Shiraz and wrote about fifty books, mainly in Arabic.

Nasafī, ʿAzīz al-Dīn (d. ca. 695/1295)
A Sufi of Kubrawī lineage whose works, all in Persian, helped popularize the teachings of Ibn al-ʿArabī.

Qayṣarī, Sharaf al-Dīn Dāwūd (d. 751/1350)
One of the most famous commentators on Ibn al-ʿArabī's *Fuṣūṣ al-ḥikam*. A student of ʿAbd al-Razzāq Kāshānī, he is the author of several Arabic works on philosophical Sufism.

Qūnawī, Ṣadr al-Dīn (d. 673/1274)
Ibn al-ʿArabī's step-son, he is the author of about a dozen important Arabic treatises that were extremely influential in determining the way Ibn al-ʿArabī would be interpreted by later Sufis. He also wrote a few short Persian works.

Qushayrī, Abuʾl-Qāsim al- (d. 465/1072)
Author of *al-Risāla* (The treatise), one of the most important early works on Sufi biography and teachings. He also wrote a Koran commentary and other works, some having to do with Kalām.

Rāzī, Fakhr al-Dīn (d. 606/1209)
A well-known theologian, especially famous for his attack on the philosophy of Avicenna. His "Great Commentary" is a mainstay of Koran interpretation, though its dry and pedantic approach puts it off to the side of the sapiential tradition.

Rāzī, Najm al-Dīn (d. 654/1256)
A well-known Sufi of Kubrawī lineage, he is the author of a great handbook of Sufi teachings, *Mirṣād al-ʿibād* (translated into English by Algar).

Rūmī, Jalāl al-Dīn (d. 672/1273)
The most famous of the Persian Sufi poets, translated and studied in the West by several scholars.

Rūzbihān Baqlī (d. 606/1209)
Known as a great lover of God, he usually writes in an ecstatic style that make his works both a pleasure to read and difficult to fathom. Among his Arabic works is an important commentary on the Koran that has not yet been published.

Samʿānī, Aḥmad (d. 534/1140)
Author of the first and one of the longest commentaries on the divine names in Persian, *Rawḥ al-arwāḥ fī sharh asmāʾ al-malik al-fattāḥ* (The ease of spirits in explaining the names of the All-conquering King). Only recently published, this work of astonishing beauty has remained unknown to all but a few specialists. It is a precious source for Sufi teachings written in the most attractive manner possible, and always with a sense of humor.

Sanāʾī Ghaznawī (d. 525/1131)
One of the greatest of the Persian Sufi poets.

Sarrāj, Abū Naṣr al- (d. 378/988)
Author of *al-Lumaʿ* (The flashes), an early exposition of Sufi teachings.

Shabistarī, Maḥmūd (d. ca. 720/1320)
Author of a number of short works, including his masterpiece, the one thousand verse poem, *Gulshan-i rāz* (The rosegarden of the mystery), which explains elliptically many of the basic teachings of Ibn al-ʿArabī's school.

Suhrawardī, Shihāb al-Dīn Abū Hafṣ ʿUmar (d. 632/1234)
He was the nephew of the founder of the Suhrawardī Sufi Order and held an important political position under the caliph in Baghdad. His *ʿAwārif al-maʿārif* (Gifts of mystic knowledge) is considered a classic of Sufi practical and ethical teachings.

Suhrawardī al-Maqtūl, Shihāb al-Dīn Yaḥyā (d. 587/1191)
The founder of the Illuminationist School of philosophy, he took inspiration from both Zoroastrianism and Sufism to modify the dominant Peripatetic school. He is the author of several Arabic doctrinal works and a number of visionary treatises in exquisite Persian prose. He was put in prison on political grounds and died there, perhaps executed, at the age of 38.

Sulamī, Abū ʿAbd al-Raḥmān al- (d. 412/1021)
Author of several important works on Sufism, including a Koran commentary and *Ṭabaqāt al-ṣūfiyya*, one of the most famous Arabic works on the lives of the Sufis.

Ṭabrisī, Faḍl ibn al-Ḥasan, al- (d. 548/1153–54)
A Shiʿite from Tafrish near Qum in Iran, he is the author of an important commentary on the Koran and works in jurisprudence, Hadith, history, and other fields.

Tirmidhī, Muḥammad ibn ʿAlī al-Ḥakīm (d. late fourth/tenth c.)
He was one of the few Sufis of the early period who presented Sufi teachings in a relatively theoretical manner, and thus is called al-Ḥakīm, the "sage" or "philosopher." He is especially famous for his work, *Khatm al-awliyāʾ* (The seal of sanctity). He should not be confused with Tirmidhī, the author of one of the standard collections of Hadith.

NOTES

Introduction

1. Published as *Isuramu Hooriron Josetsu* (Tokyo: Iwanami Shoten, 1985).

2. I published an English translation as *Temporary Marriage in Islamic Law* (London: Muhammadi Trust, 1987).

3. I put "before" in quotation marks, since most authorities see this as a logical and ontological relationship, not a temporal one.

4. Bad' al-khalq 1. Al-Bukhārī also gives us the variant, "God was, and nothing was before Him" (Tawḥīd 22). As Ibn al-ʿArabī sometimes points out, in the case of God, the verb *kān* (was) has no temporal significance, so it is equivalent to "is."

5. *Ta Chuan* 11.5. The translation is my own. Cf. Wilhelm, *I Ching* 318.

6. *Ta Chuan* 11.7. Cf. Wilhelm, *I Ching* 319.

7. "By God, were it not for the Shariʿa brought by the divine report-giving, no one would know God! If we had remained with our rational proofs—which, in the opinion of the rational thinkers, establish knowledge of God's Essence, showing that 'He is not like this' and 'not like that'—no created thing would ever have loved God." (*al-Futūḥāt al-makkiyya* II 326.12; quoted in Chittick, *The Sufi Path of Knowledge* [hereafter SPK] 180).

8. "Putting the *Te* Back into Taoism," in J. Baird Callicott and Roger T. Ames (eds.), *Nature in Asian Traditions of Thought* (Albany: SUNY Press, 1989) 120.

9. The saying is considered suspect by the specialists in the science of hadith, while the yang authorities condemn it outright. For the representatives of the yin perspective, however, it is true, since it epitomizes the metaphysical underpinnings of their position. They are not overly concerned with whether or not the Prophet actually said it. As Ibn al-ʿArabī remarks, it is "sound on the basis of unveiling [i.e., mystical vision], but not established by way of transmission" (quoted in SPK 391).

10. *Mathnawī* II 2680 (quoted in Chittick, *The Sufi Path of Love* 101). Hereafter this book will be referred to as SPL.

11. *Chuang Tsu* 17.6.

12. The wrath that demands the destruction of "others" is frequently connected to the attributes of Oneness and Severity mentioned in a Koranic verse alluding to the Last Day: "Whose is the Kingdom today? God's, the One, the Intensely Severe" (40:16). Thus the sixth/twelfth century Sufi author Aḥmad Samʿānī talks of three divine attributes—power, oneness, and wisdom—that demand respectively creation, destruction, and resurrection: "Bringing into existence [*ījād*] at the beginning is required by power, destroying [*iʿdām*] in the middle is required by oneness, and the return [*iʿāda*] is required by wisdom. Through power He scattered the seed of creation in the ground of wisdom. Many kinds of vegetation sprang up—some were sweet-smelling flowers, others liver-scraping thorns. Then from the World of Oneness the wind of jealousy sprang up and the storm of severity blew. He clothed the cosmos in the garment of nonexistence. With the hand of severity He removed the collar of existence from the neck of the existent things and the creatures." Samʿānī, *Rawḥ al-arwāḥ* 4–5.

13. For a relatively detailed explanation of how the names of gentleness and the names of severity interact in order to produce an ever-renewed creation, cf. Jāmī, *Lawāʾiḥ: A Treatise on Sufism* 32–33. Jāmī's views are based firmly on those of Ibn al-ʿArabī (cf. SPK, especially chapter 6).

14. Rūmī, *Mathnawī* V 3423 (cf. SPL 29).

15. Ibid. III 4404 (cf. SPL 163).

16. *Ta Chuan* 1.1,5. Cf. Wilhelm, *I Ching* 280, 281.

17. *Chuang Tsu* 2.6.

18. Ibn al-ʿArabī, *Inshāʾ al-dawāʾir* 21.

19. *Ta Chuan* 5.1–2.

Chapter 1. The Three Realities

1. On occasion, the human being is seen as the greater reality because of a certain qualitative superiority having to do with human vicegerency. Then the human being is the macrocosm and the cosmos is the microcosm. For example, Samʿānī (*Rawḥ al-arwāḥ* 180) writes, "Though the human structure is small from the point of view of your sense of sight, in terms of the meanings, elevations, treasures, and mysteries that are deposited within it, it is the greater cosmos [*ʿālam-i akbar*]."

2. Lane, *Arabic-English Lexicon* 135.

3. Maybudī, *Kashf al-asrār* VIII 545–46.

4. Ibn al-ʿArabī, *Futūḥāt* II 214.16 (SPK 150).

5. Maybudī completes the text of the hadith to which he has been alluding: "God created the creatures in darkness, then He poured His light down upon them." In the standard sources we have a similar version: "God created His creatures in darkness, then cast to them something of His light" (Tirmidhī, Īmān 18; Aḥmad II 176).

6. Maybudī, *Kashf al-asrār* VII 455.

7. It is remarkable that Western scholars have paid such little attention to the importance of the divine names in Islamic thought. D. Gimaret points to this truly astonishing gap in Western studies of Islam in the introduction to his groundbreaking work, *Les noms divins en Islam*. He cites twenty-one commentaries on the divine names written before al-Ghazālī. However, he limits his own investigation mainly to works written by philologists and specialists in Kalām.

8. Ikhwān al-Ṣafāʾ, *Rasāʾil* II 456–59.

9. Ibid. 466–68.

10. Nasafī, *Insān-i kāmil* 147–48.

11. For further elaborations on this theme, cf. SPK, chapter 1.

12. The term ranking in degrees (*al-tarāfuʿ fiʾl-darajāt*) derives from the Koranic name of God, *rafīʿ al-darajāt* (40:15), the "Uplifter of degrees." I translate it with a view toward Ibn al-ʿArabī's later elaboration of the same doctrine, where the key term is *tafāḍul*, or "ranking in degrees of excellence" (cf. SPK 51–52).

13. Ikhwān al-Ṣafāʾ, *Rasāʾil* IV 207–9.

14. Jāmī, *Naqd al-nuṣūṣ* 71–72; Jāmī, *Sharḥ-i rubāʿiyyāt* 53–54.

15. Cf. the first sentence of chapter 1 of the *Fuṣūṣ al-ḥikam*, a chapter that is dedicated to "the Wisdom of the divine name Allah as embodied in the word Adam." Austin translates *al-kawn al-jāmiʿ* as "all-inclusive object" (Ibn al-ʿArabī, *Ibn al'Arabi* 50).

16. The hadith is found in a number of different versions in Muslim and other standard sources. One of the texts reads, "If you did not sin, God would take you away and bring a people who sin, so that they would ask His forgiveness, and He would forgive them" (Muslim, Tawba 11).

17. Samʿānī, *Rawḥ al-arwāḥ* 312.

18. Ibn al-ʿArabī, *Futūḥāt* II 530.25.

19. Jāmī, *Silsilat al-dhahab* 66–69.

20. Ikhwān al-Ṣafāʾ, *Rasāʾil* II 473.

21. Nasafī, *Zubdat al-ḥaqāʾiq* 324–25, 327.

22. I have tried to avoid inappropriate gender-specific language throughout this book, but sometimes the demands of literal accuracy outweigh the concern for contemporary sensitivities. The Arabic sentence here quoted has two masculine pronouns and two masculine verbs. However, there is no implication that this saying, or similar instances of usages of the masculine gender, excludes women. According to the ancient rules of Arabic grammar, the masculine gender always takes precedence over the feminine. In chapter 6 we will see Ibn al-ʿArabī come to some interesting conclusions because of this rule.

23. This is one of a handful of texts relevant to our discussion available in good English translation, and the reader will find in it a great deal of background material for the present work (Cf. Rāzī, *The Path of God's Bondsmen*, trans. H. Algar). If I depart from Algar's translation in the passages I quote, it is in order to maintain terminological and stylistic consistency.

24. This hadith is often cited in Sufi sources, but it is not found in the standard hadith collections.

25. Rūmī, *Mathnawī* IV 1709 (SPL 83).

26. Ibid. III 2300 (SPL 83).

27. Rāzī, *Mirṣād al-ʿibād* 65–82 (cf. *Path of God's Bondsmen* 94–109). This last poem is by Firdawsī, the author of the *Shāhnāma*, the Iranian national epic. We will quote it again in its own context in chapter 4.

28. For his views, cf. M. Chodkiewicz, *Le Sceau des saints*.

29. Ibn al-ʿArabī, *Futūḥāt* III 154.18 (SPK 276).

30. Rūmī, *Mathnawī* III 3901–3, 3905 (SPL 79). Rūmī's ideas have nothing to do with evolutionism in a Darwinian sense, nor are they anything exceptional in the intellectual climate of Islam. R.A. Nicholson pointed out long ago that Rūmī's evolutionary description of the growth of the soul is deeply rooted in the Islamic philosophical tradition and paralleled by Neoplatonic and Aristotelian teachings (Rūmī, *Mathnawī* VIII 214–16). But this has not prevented many people from seeing in his teachings a kind of proto-Darwinism, as pointed out by Schimmel (*Triumphal Sun* 329–32). Chittick has brought out rather clearly some of the profound differences between "evolution" in the traditional Islamic sense and the Darwinian sense in SPL 72–82.

31. Ibn al-ʿArabī, *Futūḥāt* II 390.35.

32. Ibid. 383.33. Cf. Ḥakīm, *al-Muʿjam al-ṣūfī* 1057–58.

33. Ibid. IV 398.15.

34. Ibid. I 136.30 (Y 2,300.5).

35. Ibn al-ʿArabī, *Inshāʾ al-dawāʾir* 45.

36. The identification of Iblis with *wahm* or "sensory intuition" will be discussed in some detail in chapter 9.

37. Nasafī, *Insān-i kāmil* 142–43. Ibn al-ʿArabī and his followers develop this symbolism of letters and words in order to illustrate the complexity of relationships that must be considered when God and the cosmos are taken into account. However, they are not concerned with establishing an exact system of correspondences or with being consistent. Attention is paid not so much to the correspondences between, for example, certain creatures and certain words, but to the relationships established between the various levels of linguistic expression, whether spoken or written. Cf. D. Gril, "Les science des lettres," in Chodkiewicz, *Les Illuminations de la Mecque* 385–487. For varying schemes by one of Ibn al-ʿArabī's direct disciples, cf. Ṣadr al-Dīn al-Qūnawī, *al-Nafaḥāt al-ilāhiyya* 80–81; *Iʿjāz al-bayān* 85–86; *Miftāḥ al-ghayb* 271–74.

Chapter 2. Divine Duality

1. Anṣārī, *Manāzil al-sāʾirīn* 113.

2. Cf. SPK, chapter 19.

3. Rūmī, *Mathnawī* I 20 (cf. SPL 9).

4. Ibn al-ʿArabī, *Futūḥāt* III 289.4 (SPK 34).

5. Ibid. 441.31 (SPK 35).

6. Rūmī, *Dīwān* 21880–84.

7. For details on Ibn al-ʿArabī's position, cf. SPK, especially chapter 4.

8. Samʿānī, *Rawḥ al-arwāh* 17.

9. Cf. W. Chittick's introduction to the eighth-century book of supplications by ʿAlī ibn al-Ḥusayn, the great-grandson of the Prophet (*The Psalms of Islam: al-Ṣaḥīfat al-sajjādiyya*).

10. SPK 38.

11. Ibid. 64.

12. Chittick has given a rough outline of how this might be done in his introduction to the *Psalms of Islam*.

13. Rūmī, *Dīwān* 12409 (cf. Schimmel, *Triumphal Sun* 128).

14. Ibn al-ʿArabī, *Fuṣūṣ al-ḥikam* 183 (cf. *Ibn Al'Arabi* 231).

15. Idem, *Futūḥāt* II 486.7.

16. Idem, *Fuṣūṣ al-ḥikam* 81 (cf. *Ibn Al'Arabi* 92).

17. Idem, *Futūḥāt* III 363 (quoted in SPK 61).

18. Ibid. IV 40.35.

19. Ibid. I 118.4 (Y 2,221.11).

20. Idem, *Fuṣūṣ al-ḥikam* 83 (cf. *Ibn Al'Arabi* 95).

21. Idem, *Futūḥāt* III 465.3 (cf. SPK 337–38).

22. Ibid. IV 276.33.

23. Ikhwān al-Ṣafā', *Jāmiʿat al-jāmiʿa* 79.

24. Idem, *Rasā'il* III 179.

25. Many of these dualities are explained below in chapter 5 (pp. 412–15).

26. Ikhwān al-Ṣafā', *Rasā'il* III 201–2.

27. Ibid. II 461–62.

28. Rāzī, *Mirṣād* 211 (cf. *Path of God's Bondsmen* 304).

28. Ibn al-ʿArabī, *Futūḥāt* II 459.25 (SPK 84).

30. Samʿānī, *Rawḥ al-arwāḥ* 17.

31. Rūmī, *Fīhi mā fīhi* 176 (cf. SPL 48).

32. Idem, *Majālis-i sabʿa* 29 (cf. SPL 71).

33. Jāmī, *Silsilat al-dhahab* 69–70.

34. Ibn al-ʿArabī, *Futūḥāt* III 163.19.

35. Ibid. 296.11.

36. Ibid. 171.8.

37. Ibid. I 100.30 (Y 2,128.10), 100.25 (Y 2,127.15).

38. Ibid. 100.15 (Y 2,126.11).

39. Farghānī's scheme follows Ibn al-ʿArabī's teachings rather closely. For a set of diagrams taken from Ibn al-ʿArabī's works that help clarify the nature of the relationships Farghānī is discussing, cf. Chittick, "Ibn ʿArabī and His School" 75–79.

40. Farghānī, *Muntahā al-madārik* I 82–83.

41. Ibn al-ʿArabī, *Futūḥāt* I 232.3 (Y 3,405.5).

42. Samʿānī, *Rawḥ al-arwāḥ* 90.

43. Ibid. 151; cf. 206. This marvelous work repeatedly comes back to the myth of Adam, providing many fascinating perspectives on the Islamic view of human nature.

44. Farghānī, *Muntahā al-madārik* I 83.

45. Ibid. II 3.

46. Farghānī's use of the term *waḥdat al-wujūd* does not coincide with the definition given to it by all members of Ibn al-ʿArabī's school. Cf. Chittick, "Rūmī and Waḥdat al-Wujūd."

47. The opponents of the philosophers frequently accuse them of denying God's knowledge of the particulars, thus contradicting the explicit text of the Koran. Many supporters of the philosophers say that the opponents are misreading and misinterpreting the philosophical position.

48. Farghānī, *Mashāriq al-darārī* 345.

49. Farghānī's formulation is by no means original. He is simply building on the teachings of Qūnawī and Ibn al-ʿArabī. Cf. Chittick, "Rūmī and Waḥdat al-Wujūd," where Farghānī's teachings on the Oneness of Being and the Manyness of Knowledge are situated within the development of Ibn al-ʿArabī's school. I cite Farghānī here in preference to other figures because he is particularly explicit in bringing out the active and receptive qualities found in the two sides.

50. Farghānī, *Mashāriq al-darārī* 344.

51. Idem, *Muntahā al-madārik* I 47.

52. Idem, *Mashāriq al-darārī* 349 (cf. Arberry, *The Poem of the Way* 44, lines 1282–85).

53. Ibn al-ʿArabī, *Futūḥāt* I 90.23 (Y 2,78.5; cf. SPK 84).

54. Idem, *Futūḥāt* II 107.26.

55. See, for example, the passage from the *Futūḥāt* translated into English in Chodkiewicz et al., *Les Illuminations de la Mecque* 97–98. Cf. the passage from Ibn al-ʿArabī's *Kitāb al-jalāl wa'l-jamāl* translated in ibid. 506–7, and in Ibn al-ʿArabī, "On Majesty and Beauty" 7–8.

56. Cf. SPK 312ff.

57. Ibn al-ʿArabī, *Futūḥāt* III 136.8 (SPK 323).

58. Cf. SPK 364–66.

59. Cf. SPL 195ff.

60. Schimmel, *Triumphal Sun* 231. Cf. ibid. 231–34.

61. Rūmī, *Mathnawī* VI 4303–4 (cf. SPL 206–12).

62. Ghazālī ascribes this saying to Kaʿb al-Aḥbār (d. 32/652), to whom the early Muslims were indebted for much of their knowledge of Judaism. The full text is as follows: "Moses said, 'O Lord, art Thou near that I should whisper to Thee? Or art Thou far that I should call out to Thee?' He replied, 'I sit with him who remembers Me.' Moses said, 'What if we should be in a situation such that we consider Thee too great to be remembered, such as impurity or the privy?' He said, 'Remember Me in every situation.'" Ghazālī, *Iḥyāʾ ʿulūm al-dīn* II.5.3 (141–42).

63. This is a sound *ḥadīth qudsī*. Cf. Graham, *Divine Word and Prophetic Word* 127, 130.

64. The term *madhhab* commonly designates the school of the Sharia that one follows, while *mashrab* commonly designates a person's intellectual persuasion. The Sufis find the locus classicus for the latter term in Koran 2:60, which tells how Moses struck the rock with his staff and twelve springs gushed forth: "Now the people knew their drinking places." People have a great variety of "drinking places," because of the great variety of capacities or preparedness. In Sufi technical terminology, *shurb* (drinking) stands between *dhawq* (tasting), which is the beginning of a waystation of spiritual growth, and *rī* (quenching), which is the full actualization of that waystation (cf. SPK 220). The subject of Rūzbihān Baqlī's work *Mashrab al-arwāḥ*, "The drinking place of the spirits," from which I quote below, is the different stages and modes of spiritual realization.

65. Samʿānī, *Rawḥ al-arwāḥ* 154–55.

66. Rūzbihān, *Mashrab al-arwāḥ* 262.

67. Rūmī, among others, also refers to the self-disclosures of God's beauty and gentleness to the soul as beautiful women and brides. Cf. SPL 288ff.

68. Kubrā, *Die Fawāʾiḥ al-Ǧamāl* 44–45.

69. For a wide selection of early texts on many of these contrasting pairs, cf. J. Nurbakhsh, *Sufism* II–IV.

70. There is an allusion here to a sound hadith in which the Prophet describes the Day of Resurrection when God gives him the power of intercession. He speaks for many, and those in whose hearts is found a barleycorn of faith are delivered from hell. But he keeps on exclaiming, "My community, my community," and removes more and more from the Fire (cf. Robson, *Mishkat al-masabih* 1181–83). According to the Sufi Abū ʿAlī al-Daqqāq (d. ca. 405/1015), no one possesses the character trait of chivalry (*futuwwa*) to perfection except the Prophet. "For on the Day of Resurrection, everyone will say, 'My soul, my soul!' But he will say, 'My community, my community!'" (al-Qushayrī, *al-Risāla* 471).

71. Bukhārī translates this into Persian as *gustākhī*, and Arberry renders it as "boldness." I choose "bold expansiveness" to call attention to the connection with *basṭ* or "expansion," which is one of the technical terms (contrasted with contraction, *qabḍ*) employed to indicate the servant's proper relationship with the names of gentleness and beauty.

72. Allusion to Koran 2:55: "And when you said, 'Moses, we will not have faith in you till we see God openly'; and the thunderbolt took you while you were beholding."

73. Kalābādhī, *al-Taʿarruf* 106–7; Bukhārī, *Sharḥ-i taʿarruf* III 162–64. Cf. Arberry, *The Doctrine of the Sufis* 108–9.

74. SPK 227. Cf. SPL 288–93.

75. Hujwīrī, *Kashf al-maḥjūb* 490–92. Cf. R. A. Nicholson, *The Kashf al-Mahjūb* 376–77.

76. Cf. Nurbakhsh, *Sufism* III 61–90, for many examples of definitions and descriptions from important Sufi texts.

77. Kubrā, *Die Fawāʾiḥ al-Ǧamāl 46.*

78. Though Muslims commonly understand this to mean that everyone should follow the historical religion of Islam, Koranic usage identifies *islām* as the attribute of a number of pre-Islamic prophets and the apostles of Jesus.

79. Cf. Ibn al-ʿArabī, *Futūḥāt* II 326.12 (SPK 180).

80. Cf. Ernst, *Words of Ecstasy in Sufism.*

81. See especially the fine summary of Sufi teachings and the role of women in Sufism by Annemarie Schimmel, "The Feminine Element in Sufism," in her *Mystical Dimensions of Islam*

426–35. Cf. Elias, "Female and Feminine in Islamic Mysticism."

82. Bukhārī, ʿIlm 49 (cf. Robson, *Mishkat* 10–11).

83. Muslim, Īmān 52 (cf. Robson, *Mishkat* 13–14).

84. ʿAṭṭār, *Tadhkirat al-awliyā*ʾ 672.

Chapter 3. The Two Hands of God

1. Cf. SPK, chapter 2, the section on "The Two Denotations of the Names" (pp. 36–37).

2. The hadith is found, without the expression "it is no concern of Mine" (*lā ubālī*) in Tirmidhī, Mālik's *al-Muwaṭṭa*ʾ, and Abū Dāwūd (cf. Graham, *Divine Word* 161–62). The expression "It is no concern of Mine" is mentioned here by Maybudī and often cited by Ibn al-ʿArabī. This longer version of the hadith is found in Ḥakīm Tirmidhī's collection, *Nawādir al-uṣūl* (cf. Farghānī, *Mashāriq al-darārī* 632).

3. Maybudī, *Kashf al-asrār* IX 442.

4. Rāzī, *al-Tafsīr al-kabīr* VIII 65. Rāzī also tells us that there are medical reasons for the distinction made between right and left having to do with the makeup of the human body.

5. Maybudī, *Kashf al-asrār* VIII 435.

6. Tirmidhī, Tafsīr sūra 113,3.

7. Ibn al-ʿArabī, *Futūḥāt* III 430.22.

8. Muslim, Musāfirīn 201; Nasāʾī, Iftitāḥ 17.

9. Qūnawī, *Sharḥ al-ḥadīth*, no. 21.

10. Maybudī, *Kashf al-asrār* IX 284.

11. Ṣadūq, *al-Tawḥīd* 154.

12. Ibid. 153.

13. Qushayrī, *Laṭāʾif al-ishārāt* V 263.

14. Ṭabrisī, *Majmaʿ al-bayān* VIII 485–86.

15. Maybudī, *Kashf al-asrār* VIII 369.

16. Rāzī, *al-Tafsīr al-kabīr* VII 221–22.

17. Bayḍāwī, *Anwār al-tanzīl* 606.

18. Muslim, Qadar 17.

19. Samʿānī, *Rawḥ al-arwāḥ* 180–81.

20. Ibn al-ʿArabī, *Futūḥāt*, II 129.7 (Y 13,167.8).

21. Ibid. III 76.31.

22. Bukhārī, Tawḥīd 7. Other versions are found in Bukhārī, Muslim, Tirmidhī, and Aḥmad (cf. SPK 412n4).

23. Ibn al-ʿArabī, *Futūḥāt* II 281.23.

24. Ibid. III 76.33.

25. Ibid. 432.15.

26. Ibid. 463.13 (cf. SPK 361).

27. Ibid. II 439.21 (cf. SPK 360).

28. SPK 172.

29. Farghānī, *Muntahā al-madārik* I 58–59.

30. Ibn al-ʿArabī, *Futūḥāt* I 122.11 (Y 2,237.14).

31. Ibid. III 295.

32. Ibid. 294.

33. Ibn al-ʿArabī frequently adds this phrase to passages which speak of God's "similarity" in order to remind his readers that even in His similarity God remains incomparable. They should not imagine that an ordinary, literal reading can do justice to the text.

34. Ibn al-ʿArabī, *Futūḥāt* II 70. Cf. ibid. 3, where the same point is made (quoted in SPK 278).

35. Ibid. I 263.

36. Ibid. II 67.17.

37. Ibid. 468.10.

38. Ibid. II 3–4 (cf. SPK 277–78).

39. Ibid. III 75.14.

40. Ibid. I 37.30 (Y 1,169.12).

41. Ibid. 120.13 (Y 2,229.9).

42. I read "we fear"—rather than "it fears" as in the ʿAfīfī edition—following the alternative reading given in this edition and more particularly in the texts of the commentators Jandī, Kāshānī, and Qayṣarī.

43. As pointed out in the previous chapter, intimacy is the human response to God's beauty, while awe responds to His majesty. The major commentators on the *Fuṣūṣ* such as Jandī, Kāshānī, and Qayṣarī read the present passage as making this connection. But in doing so they ignore the reversed word order here and the fact that in some of his works, Ibn al-ʿArabī provides a different analysis of the nature of these attributes by reversing the usual relationships. Cf. the sources mentioned in chapter 2, note 55.

44. Ibn al-ʿArabī, *Fuṣūṣ al-ḥikam* 54–55 (cf. *Ibn al'Arabi* 55–56).

45. Jandī, *Sharḥ fuṣūṣ al-ḥikam* 9.

46. Ibn al-ʿArabī, *Fuṣūṣ al-ḥikam* 68 (cf. *Ibn al-'Arabi* 73).

47. Ibid. 69 (cf. *Ibn al'Arabi* 74). For a detailed discussion of nondelimitation and its place in Ibn al-ʿArabī's teachings, cf. SPK 109–12.

48. The term *nonentification* is not part of Ibn al-ʿArabī's usual vocabulary. For a discussion of its meaning according to Qūnawī, cf. Chittick and Wilson, *Fakhruddin ʿIraqi* 6ff.

49. Rūmī employs the images and symbols of love and was totally uninterested in the metaphysical speculations of Ibn al-ʿArabī and his followers. Yet his poetical descriptions of the two complementary qualities of jealousy provide an interesting and down to earth application of what Jandī is talking about. Chittick calls these two complementary qualities "smashing idols" and "maintaining veils." On the one hand God eliminates all others, so that He alone will be worshiped. On the other He sets up the veils that prevent the others from reaching His inviolable Presence. Cf. SPL 304–10.

50. Cf. SPK, chapter 20.

51. Ibn al-ʿArabī often employs the term *kufr*, "concealing" or "unbelief," in such a context. Thereby he points to the ontological root of not having faith in God: the fact that the reality of things is concealed. Cf. *Futūḥāt* II 214.12, 567.30, 592.20; III 92.11.

52. Jandī, *Sharḥ fuṣūṣ al-ḥikam* 181–85.

53. The term *proportioning* (*taswiya*) is taken from the Koran, where it is employed in seven verses in the sense of God's preparing the body for the reception of the spirit. For example, "And when thy Lord said to the angels, 'I am creating a mortal of clay. . . . When I have proportioned him, and blown My spirit into him, fall down, prostrating yourselves" (15:28). This explains the meaning of the often mistranslated passage at the beginning of the first chapter of the *Fuṣūṣ*: "The Real brought the whole cosmos into existence as a proportioned shape, without a spirit. Hence it was like an unpolished mirror. But one of the characteristics of the divine decree is that He never proportions a locus without its acting as a receptacle for a divine spirit, which is called 'a blowing into it.'" (Ibn al-ʿArabī, *Fuṣūṣ* 49; cf. *Ibn Al'Arabi* 50).

54. Cf. Chittick and Wilson, *Fakhruddin ʿIraqi* 11.

55. Kāshānī, *Sharḥ fuṣūṣ al-ḥikam* 26–28. Kāshānī provides a similar interpretation of the two hands in his *Ta'wīlāt* or esoteric commentary on the Koran (*Ta'wīlāt* II 366).

56. I translate *man* as "nothing" rather than "no one" following Ibn al-ʿArabī (cf. SPK 412n7).

57. Qayṣarī, *Sharḥ fuṣūṣ al-ḥikam* 86–87, 89–90.

58. As noted above, Qūnawī's *al-Fukūk* deals only with the chapter headings of the *Fuṣūṣ*. Othman Yahia attributes a commentary to the second author, Saʿīd al-Dīn Farghānī, but this is probably an error; Farghānī is too important an author for such a commentary to have remained otherwise unknown.

59. A hadith to this effect is found in Muslim, Janna 44.

60. The prayer is found in Muslim, Dhikr 73, and other standard sources.

61. Qūnawī, *Sharḥ al-ḥadīth*, no. 21.

62. As was pointed out at the beginning of this chapter, Ibn al-ʿArabī frequently makes this point.

63. "Unmade" (*ghayr majʿūl*), since God did not make it the way it is. Rather, it manifests the nature of Reality Itself, and God has known it as long as He has known Reality, which is to say forever. The concept of "making" (*jaʿl*) plays a role in Ibn al-ʿArabī's teachings on the nature of predestination (*qadar*) and is much elaborated upon in later Islamic philosophy. Cf. SPK 297.

64. For a brief survey of Ibn al-ʿArabī's teachings on these points, cf. SPK 369–73. Many of

Kāshānī's discussions are reflected in Bayrak, *The Most Beautiful Names*.

65. The Solitaries (*afrād*) are a group of the highest ranking friends of God who are independent of the Pole (*quṭb*). Cf. SPK 413n23.

66. Cf. Ibn al-ʿArabī's explanation of three basic approaches to knowledge of God, SPK 347.

67. Qūnawī, *al-Tafsīr al-ṣūfī* 385–88/*Iʿjāz al-bayān* 269–72.

68. For Ibn al-ʿArabī's views on the Breath of the All-merciful, cf. SPK 127–32.

69. Qūnawī, *al-Nafaḥāt al-ilāhiyya* 225–26; also quoted in Jāmī, *Naqd al-nuṣūṣ* 117.

70. For Ibn al-ʿArabī's views on preparedness and the relationship between the divine effusion or self-disclosure and the receptivity of the things, cf. SPK 91–94.

71. On the Cloud in Ibn al-ʿArabī's teaching, cf. SPK 125–27.

72. Farghānī describes the two mercies in *Mashāriq al-darārī* 551.

73. On the question of the perfection of the whole cosmos, in spite of the evils found within it, cf. "The Perfection of Imperfection," in SPK 294–97.

74. Farghānī, *Muntahā al-madārik* I 63–64.

75. Cf. Arberry, *The Poem of the Way* 73, lines 2308–20.

76. Ibn al-ʿArabī frequently discusses these two points of view in terms of the "engendering command" that brings both the Garden and the Fire into existence and the "prescriptive command" that brings the Sharia into existence and leads to human felicity. Cf. below, chapter 9, pp. 249–52.

77. Ibn al-ʿArabī, *Futūḥāt* II 163.26 (cf. SPK 174).

78. "Attraction" (*jadhba*) is God's attracting power, normally balanced with "wayfaring" (*sulūk*), the spiritual traveler's own efforts. If attraction completely overcomes wayfaring, the result is the loss of conscious control of self (cf. SPK 266–67). Such "attracted ones" have the outward appearance of madmen, but are respected and even venerated by the pious.

79. Cf. chapter 320 of the *Futūḥāt*, which is dedicated to "The true knowledge of the waystation of the glorification by the two handfuls" (Ibn al-ʿArabī, *Futūḥāt* III 75.5)

80. Farghānī, *Muntahā al-madārik* II 214–19.

Chapter 4. Heaven and Earth

1. Maybudī, *Kashf al-asrār* IX 322.

2. Ibid. 325–26.

3. Kāshānī, *Taʾwīlāt* I 381. On dominion and kingdom, cf. I 382.

4. Always in the singular, though there is some Koranic basis for speaking of several "earths," as many cosmologists do. Koran 65:12 reads, "God is He who created seven heavens, and of the earth their like."

5. See also 15:85, 21:16, 26:24, 30:8, 38:27, 44:38, 46:3, etc., some of which are quoted below.

6. Ibn al-ʿArabī, *Futūḥāt* II 350.4.

7. Ibid. 285.10.

8. Nasafī, *Kashf al-ḥaqāʾiq* 224–25.

9. Cf. Ibn al-ʿArabī's diagram of God's Footstool in *Futūḥāt* III 423, where the seven Gardens embrace the sphere of the fixed stars and the other heavens (the diagram is put in the context of Ibn al-ʿArabī's cosmology in Chittick, "Ibn ʿArabī and his School" 78).

10. See also 4:1, 6:98. The grammatical gender of the words in some of these passages sets up an interesting relationship: "Soul" is grammatically feminine, while "spouse" is masculine. In verse 7:189, "It is He who created you from one soul and made from it its spouse (*zawj*) that he might rest in her," the context shows clearly and the commentators agree that Adam is referred to as the "single soul." But the pronoun referring to this soul is feminine. Then the pronouns quickly switch, so that Adam becomes masculine and the "spouse" feminine. If we were to observe the grammatical gender, we could translate the verse as follows: "It is He who created you from one soul [i.e., Adam] and made from her [the soul] her spouse [Eve] that he [Adam] might rest in her [Eve]." The verse in any case refers to the manner in which yin arises from Adam, the primordial androgyne containing both male and female. The play of the pronouns might be read, in Sufi style, as a divine "allusion" (*ishāra*) to the presence of yin in yang and yang in yin.

11. Ibn al-ʿArabī, *Futūḥāt* II 285.12.

12. Ikhwān al-Ṣafāʾ, *Jāmiʿat al-jāmiʿa* 96.

13. Kāshānī, *Taʾwīlāt* I 80–81.

14. Ibid. 356.

15. Rūmī, *Mathnawī* VI 1847–60.

16. Kāshānī, *Taʾwīlāt* I 717.

17. Muslim, Istiqṣāʾ 13: Abū Dāwūd, Adab 105. Cf. SPK 249.

18. Maybudī, *Kashf al-asrār* I 90. Fakhr al-Dīn Rāzī provides a systematic analysis of the passage in his usual style, finding seven points where the verse provides a good analogy for the situation of the hypocrites, and providing a detailed explanation for the similes on the basis of the science of rhetoric (Rāzī, *al-Tafsīr al-kabīr* I 297–301).

19. Suyūṭī provides a similar saying in *al-Jāmiʿ al-ṣaghīr* (*Fayḍ al-qadīr* II 496, no. 2375).

20. Qushayrī, *Laṭāʾif al-ishārāt* III 224–25.

21. Many hadiths are cited to this effect in the standard sources (cf. Wensinck, *Concordance* VII 108, lines 24–30).

22. Maybudī, *Kashf al-asrār* V 191–93.

23. Kāshānī, *Taʾwīlāt* I 638–39.

24. Ibid. 380.

25. Ibid. 318–19.

26. Rūmī, *Dīwān-i Shams* 3761 (SPL 50).

27. Idem, *Mathnawī* V 599 (SPL 50).

28. Idem, *Dīwān-i Shams* 26832 (SPL 50).

29. Idem, *Mathnawī* I 1134 (SPL 49).

30. Idem, *Dīwān-i Shams* 25634–35 (SPL 50).

31. Cf. Jāmī, *Naqd al-nuṣūṣ* 29–30.

32. SPK 14.

33. Cf. Robson, *Mishkat al-masabih* 1264.

34. SPK 366.

35. *Al-Malaʾ al-aʿlā*, i.e., the angels, the inhabitants of the spiritual world. The term is Koranic.

36. Qūnawī, *Fakk al-khutūm* 275. Cf. idem, *Sharḥ al-ḥadīth*, no. 22.

36. Allusion to various Koranic verses mentioning Abraham, e.g., "Our messengers came to Abraham. . . , and he made no delay in bringing a roasted calf" (11:69; cf. 51:25–26).

38. The Alive is said to comprehend the other names in respect to the fact that each of them depends upon life. God could not be merciful or knowledgeable or vengeful if He were not alive. Hence the name Alive is sometimes called the Leader of the Leaders, that is, the first of the primary names of God, which are usually said to correspond to the seven listed here. Cf. above, p. 63.

39. Farghānī, *Muntahā al-madārik* I 61–62.

40. Firdawsī, *Shāhnāma* I 14–16.

41. Farghānī, *Muntahā al-madārik* I 59–60.

42. For some of Ibn al-ʿArabī's views on imaginalization by angels and human beings, cf. Chodkiewicz, *Illuminations* 290ff.

43. Rāzī, *Mirṣād al-ʿibād* 404–6 (cf. *Path of God's Bondsmen* 391–92).

44. Apparently an allusion to Koran 11:118–19: People "cease not to differ, except those on whom thy Lord has mercy, and for that He created them."

45. On this hadith, cf. chapter 3, note 22.

46. Samʿānī, *Rawḥ al-arwāḥ* 224–26.

47. Rāzī, *al-Tafsīr al-kabīr* I 324–25. The reference at the end is to a hadith in which the Prophet says that he has been given five things never given to any prophet before him, including the fact that "the earth was made for me pleasant, pure, and a mosque [literally: a place of prostration]" (Muslim, Masājid 3). The Prophet also calls the earth a mosque in other hadiths. For example, "Whenever the time of prayer arrives, pray, for the earth is a mosque for you" (Bukhārī, Anbiyāʾ 40).

48. Cf. Koran 59:21 etc.

49. Allusion to such Koranic verses as 20:55: "Out of the earth We created you, and to it We shall make you return, and from it We shall cause you to emerge a second time."

50. Ibn al-ʿArabī, *Futūḥāt* II 455.2.

51. Riḍwān is the angel in charge of the Garden.

52. Maybudī, *Kashf al-asrār* VIII 374–75.

Chapter 5. Macrocosmic Marriage

1. Rūmī, *Mathnawī* III 4404 (cf. SPL 163).

2. Ibn al-ʿArabī, *Futūḥāt* I 131.23 (Y 2,277.15).

3. Cf. Lane, *Lexicon*, under *nakaḥa*.

4. Ibn al-ʿArabī, *Futūḥāt* I 138.17 (Y 2,309.2).

5. If Ibn al-ʿArabī can demonstrate this philosophically, the poets for their part constantly make use of the principle of analogical correspondence in devising imagery. Thus, for example, in Rūmī's view, "Every act in the world can be conceived as a birth; every cause is the mother of a result" (Schimmel, *Triumphal Sun* 125). On Rūmī's use of the image of the "mother," cf. ibid. 124–28.

6. Ibn al-ʿArabī, *Futūḥāt* I 139.10 (Y 2,311.6), 140.3 (Y 2,315.4).

7. Ibid. 141.5 (Y 2,319.10).

8. Ibid. II 445.18. For an expanded discussion, with a few conclusions showing some of the relevance to qualitative thinking, cf. Ibn al-ʿArabī, *Ayyām al-sha'n* 7–8.

9. Kāshānī, *Ta'wīlāt* I 717.

10. Yahya, *Histoire et classification*, no. 544.

12. Ibn al-ʿArabī, *Futūḥāt* II 167.18.

12. Ibid. I 170.7 (Y 3,101.2).

13. Ibid. 139.20 (Y 2,312.10).

14. Cf. SPK 88–89.

15. Ibn al-ʿArabī, *Futūḥāt* I 139.14 (Y 2,311.14).

16. Ibid. III 516.4 (cf. SPK 86).

17. These are standard examples of imaginal experience, mostly derived from various hadiths. Cf. SPK 122, 397n14.

18. Ibn al-ʿArabī, *Futūḥāt* III 508.17.

19. Most of this material, plus a great deal more, is found in al-Fanārī's commentary on Qūnawī's *Miftāḥ al-ghayb* (*Miṣbāḥ al-ins* 159–64). Al-Fanārī takes much of his explanation from Qūnawī's *Sharḥ al-ḥadīth* (no. 22), and his commentary on the opening chapter of the Koran (Qūnawī, *al-Tafsīr al-ṣūfī* 180–92/*Iʿjāz al-bayān* 73–85).

20. Clear correspondences can be drawn between these five levels and the well-known "Five Divine Presences," a term apparently coined by Qūnawī. It is interesting to note that Ibn al-ʿArabī often talks of three fundamental "presences," as he talks of three fundamental "marriages" in the passage quoted above. In both cases it may have been Qūnawī who expanded them to five in a systematic manner.

21. Qūnawī, *Miftāḥ al-ghayb* 161.

22. Ibid. 163.

23. Ibid.

24. Ibid.

25. Ibn al-ʿArabī, *Futūḥāt* III 126.1.

26. Ibid. I 171.15 (Y 3,107.11).

27. Ibid. II 413.3.

28. Ibid. 440.25.

29. Ibid. I 170.11 (Y 3,171.10).

30. Idem, *Fuṣūṣ al-ḥikam* 115 (cf. *Ibn al'Arabi* 141).

31. Idem, *Futūḥāt* I 139.29 (Y 2,314.2).

32. Rāzī, *al-Tafsīr al-kabīr* VI 259.

33. Ibid. VIII 260.

34. Majlisī, *Biḥār al-anwār* LIV 376. Majlisī records several similar reports from Ibn ʿAbbās himself (without reference to the Prophet), often with significant differences in detail. Cf. ibid. 372–75.

35. Ibid. 369, 370.

36. For the various interpretations of *nūn*, cf. Maybudī, *Kashf al-asrār* X 186–87; Rāzī, *al-Tafsīr al-kabīr* VIII 259–60.

37. Majlisī, *Biḥār al-anwār* LIV 368.

38. Ibn al-ʿArabī, *Futūḥāt* II 428.8. In the continuation of this passage, Ibn al-ʿArabī draws a conclusion that may seem surprising to the Christian sensibility, which would make marriage an inseparable bond. Muslims, in contrast, consider marriage as a contract that may be brought to an end through divorce. Though divorce is not encouraged, neither is it forbidden. "The profit of reflecting upon this is that when a man marries a woman and he finds rest in her, and when God places between them love and mercy, he knows that God desires their union. But rest in the companion may be removed from one of them or both of them, and love may disappear. For love is the fixity of this rest, which is why it is called "love" [*wadd* (literally "stake")], while God is named *al-wadūd*, since His love for those servants He loves is firmly fixed. Mercy may disappear from between them, or from one of them toward the companion, so that the one turns away from the other. Then he will know that God desires their divorce, so he may undertake that." *Futūḥāt* II 428.17.

39. Ibn al-ʿArabī, *Futūḥāt* III 399.12,28.

40. Kāshānī, *Ta'wīlāt* I 645.

41. Sanā'ī, *Ḥadīqa* 305.

42. In other words, the seven planets differentiate and define the nine heavens. Without the seven planets, there could only be the first and second heavens, the starless sphere and the sphere of the fixed stars.

43. Sanā'ī, *Ḥadīqa* 311.

44. Ibn al-ʿArabī, *Futūḥāt* III 99.19.

45. Ibid. II 429.29.

46. By adding this condition, Ibn al-ʿArabī acknowledges that intercourse has two legitimate aims: children and pleasure. I will have more to say about these aims in the next chapter.

47. Ibn al-ʿArabī, *Futūḥāt* III 231.13.

48. Ibid. 431.9, 432.18.

49. Cf. Ḥakīm, *al-Muʿjam al-ṣūfī* 1095–96.

50. Cf. Ibn al-ʿArabī, *Futūḥāt* I 122 (Y 2,237), II 675, III 119, 433; idem, *ʿUqla* 56–57.

51. Ibn al-ʿArabī, *Futūḥāt* I 140.13 (Y 2,316.7).

52. Ikhwān al-Ṣafā', *Jāmiʿat al-jāmiʿa* 67–69.

53. Farghānī, *Muntahā al-madārik* II 3–4.

54. This is a hadith, found in some of the standard later sources (cf. SPK 409n17).

55. The first sphere, beginning from the top, is the starless heaven or the Throne of the All-Merciful.

56. Nasafī, *Insān-i kāmil* 189.

57. Again, this does not imply that Nasafī is denying a more literal interpretation, since that pertains to a different realm of existence. One of the principles of *ta'wīl* in the view of our authors is that the more inward interpretations do not contradict the more outward interpretations. On each level of existence a sacred "fact" has one or more significances different from what it means on another level.

58. Quoted in Chittick, "Eschatology" 400.

59. Ibn al-ʿArabī, *Futūḥāt* II 648.4 (SPK 140).

60. Gawharīn, *Farhang* I 9–12.

61. Remember that these four attributes are the "pillars" of divinity, the fundamental attributes of the Divine Reality that are reflected in all creatures.

62. Nasafī, *Insān-i kāmil* 161–64.

63. Ikhwān al-Ṣafā', *Rasā'il* III 234–35.

64. Ibid. II 462.

65. Ibn al-ʿArabī, *Futūḥāt* I 139.14 (Y 2,313.6).

66. Ibid. II 304.19.

67. Ibn al-ʿArabī, *ʿUqla* 56.

68. Idem, *Futūḥāt* II 675.7.

69. Nasafī divides the twenty-eight simple things into fourteen from the World of the Dominion and fourteen from the World of the Kingdom. In the World of the Dominion, they include ten degrees of spirits plus the four natures. The first spirit is Adam, the second the spirit of Muhammad, and so on through the different types of prophets and friends of God down to the tenth, the spirits of the faithful. The fourteen simple things of the World of the Kingdom are Eve, the Throne, the Footstool, the seven heavens, and the four elements. Here "Adam and Eve" refer to the primordial cosmic pair produced from the First Substance. One of them was differentiated to become the World of Spirits, and the other to become the World of Bodies. Cf. Nasafī, *Insān-i kāmil* 55–57.

70. Nasafī, *Insān-i kāmil*, 390–93.

71. Ḥakīm, *al-Muʿjam al-ṣūfī*, 1124. Cf. SPK 413.

72. Qūnawī, *Iʿjāz al-bayān*, 134–35/*al-Tafsīr al-ṣūfī*, 241–42.

73. The "active words" are the words of God that are the spirits of all creatures, while the "verbal words" are the divine revelations delivered by the prophets (Farghānī, *Muntahā al-madārik* I 49).

74. Farghānī, *Muntahā al-madārik*, I 49–50.

75. Lāhījī, *Sharḥ-i Gulshan-i rāz* 195.

76. Ibn al-ʿArabī, *Futūḥāt* I 294.32 (Y 4,353.2).

77. For the hadith, see chapter 1, note 5.

78. Suhrawardī, *Majmūʿa-yi āthār-i fārsī* 220–22. Cf. idem, *The Mystical and Visionary Treatises* 32–33.

Chapter 6. Human Marriage

1. Some of the ascetical Sufis of the early period seem to oppose this attitude, as pointed out by Tor Andrae (*In the Garden of Myrtles* 41ff.). But he concludes that "their practical attitude was quite different. Their critics maintained that the Sufis possessed three outstanding qualities: they enjoyed food, sweet things and women. . . . Most of the mystics were married, and several of them had more than one wife." (Ibid. 49–50).

2. As Abdelwahab Bouhdiba remarks, "Sexual pleasures are conceived by Islam as constitutive of the earthly conditions of life and, as such, they must be welcomed by Muslims" (*Sexuality in Islam* 88). This work is often insightful, but the author pays no attention to the sapiential tradition that might have allowed him to offer Islam's own explanation of the psychological roots of the questions he deals with.

3. Ibn Māja, Nikāḥ 1.

4. Ghazālī, *Iḥyā'* II.2.1 (II 15). A slightly different version is found in Ṣuyūtī, *al-Jāmiʿ al-ṣaghīr* (*Fayḍ al-qadīr* VI 103). The hadith is also found in Shiʿite sources (cf. ʿĀmilī, *Wasāʾil al-shīʿa* XIV 5).

5. ʿĀmilī, *Wasāʾil al-shīʿa* XIV 8.

6. Ibid. 3.

7. Ibid. 23.

8. Ibn Māja, Nikāḥ 50.

9. Ghazālī, *Kīmiyā-yi saʿādat* 301/238. "To be My servants" is usually translated as "to worship Me" or "to serve Me." In any case, the point is that servanthood is the foundation of proper human existence.

10. Ibid. 302–3/239.

11. The hadith is frequently cited, especially in Sufi sources, but scholars do not seem to have found a source for it before Ghazālī (cf. Furūzānfar, *Aḥādīth-i Mathnawī* 20–21).

12. Bilāl was the Prophet's muezzin. He used to say to him, "Stand, O Bilāl, and give us ease through the prayer!" (Abū Dāwūd, Adab 78; Aḥmad ibn Ḥanbal V 364, 371).

13. Ghazālī, *Kīmiyā-yi saʿādat* 305/241.

14. Maybudī, *Kashf al-asrār* I 610–12.

15. Ibid. 613–14. The rest of Maybudī's discussion is derived from *Kīmiyā-yi saʿādat* and follows it rather closely.

16. Ṭabrisī, *Majmaʿ al-bayān* I 327.

17. Ibid. This second hadith is also found in Sunni sources (Abū Dāwūd, Nikāḥ 40; Ibn Māja, Nikāḥ 4; Aḥmad ibn Ḥanbal IV 381, V 228, VI 76).

18. Ibn al-ʿArabī, *Futūḥāt* II 466.10. For a related commentary on the same passage, cf. ibid. IV 84.34.

19. Qushayrī, *Laṭāʾif al-ishārāt* I 193.

20. Rūmī, *Dīwān* 33594 (SPL 193)

21. Ibn al-ʿArabī, *Futūḥāt* II 171.4.

22. The hadith is not found in the standard sources.

23. Ibn al-ʿArabī, *Futūḥāt* IV 228.3.

24. Henry Corbin offers interesting speculations on the significance of this correlation, but he does not pay close attention to the texts. See his *Creative Imagination in the Ṣūfism of Ibn ʿArabī*, especially pp. 162ff.

25. Ibn al-ʿArabī, *Futūḥāt* I 136.13 (Y 2,298.5).

26. Allusion to various Koranic verses concerning the stages which the embryo passes through before birth. For example, "He creates you in your mothers' wombs, creation after creation, in threefold shadows" (39:6).

27. The hadith is found in several of the standard sources, including Bukhārī (Anbiyā' 32, 46, etc.) and Muslim (Faḍā'il al-Ṣaḥāba 70).

28. Apparently Ibn al-ʿArabī is attributing prophethood to Mary and perhaps Āsiya as well. Here his position would differ from most authorities, though the idea that Mary was a prophet was supported by his fellow Andalusians Ibn Ḥazm (d. 456/1064) and al-Qurṭubī (d. 671/1273). Cf. Smith and Haddad, "The Virgin Mary in Islamic Tradition and Commentary."

29. The saying is a hadith found in Tirmidhī (Ṭahāra 82) and other standard sources. Ibn al-ʿArabī, *Futūḥāt* III 87.18.

30. Ibn al-ʿArabī, *Futūḥāt* II 471.21.

31. Allusion to Koran 9:30: "The Jews say, 'Ezra is the son of God.' The Christians say, 'The Messiah is the son of God.'"

32. Ibn al-ʿArabī, *Futūḥāt* III 181.35.

33. Ibn al-ʿArabī adds the proviso "in this abode" because marriage in paradise is strictly for enjoyment.

34. *Hawā'* is from the same root and almost identical in pronunciation with *hawā*, "caprice" or "desire." The empty space was filled with air, which in this context implies desire and love.

35. Ibn al-ʿArabī has in mind here the saying, often cited as a hadith, "The love of the homeland is part of faith" (*ḥubb al-waṭan min al-īmān*).

36. Ibn al-ʿArabī, *Futūḥāt* I 124.27 (Y 2,248.6).

37. Ibid. II 190.9.

38. According to Jāmī, this hadith is found in *Rawāya maʿānī al-akhbār* of Muḥammad ibn Isḥāq ibn Yasār (fl. second/eighth c.). Cf. Jāmī, *Naqd al-nuṣūṣ* 94.

39. Allusion to Koran 7:189: "It is He who created you from one soul and made from it its spouse that he might rest in her."

40. Ibn al-ʿArabī, *Futūḥāt* III 88.28.

41. The hadith is found in several slightly differing versions. Bukhārī (Maghāzī 82, Fitan 18), Tirmidhī (Fitan 75), Nasā'ī (Quḍāt 8), Aḥmad ibn Ḥanbal (V 43, 51, 38, 47).

42. Ibn al-ʿArabī, *Futūḥāt* III 89.22.

43. The hadith is found in Nasā'ī (ʿIshrat al-Nisā' 1) and Aḥmad ibn Ḥanbal (III 128, 199, 285), without, however, the word "three things" (*thalāth*), which plays an important part in Ibn al-ʿArabī's interpretation, as we will see below. Ghazālī provides the text as Ibn al-ʿArabī reads it in *Iḥyā'* II.2.1 (II 21). Shiʿite sources give several sayings of the Prophet and the Imams of similar import. For example Jaʿfar al-Ṣādiq said, "The more the servant's love for women increases, the more his faith increases in excellence." Cf. ʿĀmilī, *Wasā'il al-shīʿa* XIV 9–11.

44. Ibn al-ʿArabī, *Futūḥāt* II 167.10.

45. On the pleasure of the Garden as contrasted to that of this world, cf. Ibn al-ʿArabī, *Futūḥāt* II 193.8.

46. This hadith, as well as its variants, "The child belongs to the master of the bedding" and "to the lord of the bedding" occurs numerous times in all the standard sources (Wensinck, *Concordance* V 109, lines 51–58).

47. Ibn al-ʿArabī, *Futūḥāt* IV 243.8.

48. Ibid. 84.21.

49. Cf. SPL 209.

50. Rūmī, *Mathnawī* I 2437 (SPL 189).

51. If Claude Addas is right that Ibn al-ʿArabī means by "entering the path" the beginning of his training at the hand of a shaykh and that this took place when he was 20 (cf. Addas, *Ibn ʿArabī* 68), he would have been 38 when he reached this station. This corresponds nicely with the fact that he saw himself consecrated as the "Seal of Muhammadan Sanctity" at the age of 38 in 598/1202. In his terminology, a "Muhammadan" friend of God is one who inherits directly from Muhammad, without the intermediary of other prophets, such as Jesus or Moses. Upon fully realizing his own "Muhammadan" nature, he would naturally be made to love women.

52. Ibn al-ʿArabī, *Futūḥāt* IV 84.22.

53. Allusion to the hadith, "The majority of the people of the Fire are women," which comes in several versions (Bukhārī, Ḥayḍ 6, Kusūf 9, Bad' al-Khalq 8; Muslim, Kusūf 17, etc.).

54. The "property of the right hand" here is the slave girl, with whom Islamic law allows sexual relationships.

55. The second sentence of this saying, with the exception of "By God," is found attributed to ʿĀʾisha in Tirmidhī, Tafsīr sūra 33, 19.

56. Ibn al-ʿArabī, *Futūḥāt* II 190.11.

57. Bouhdiba goes a bit overboard when he calls the chapter of his *Sexuality in Islam* that deals with paradise "The Infinite Orgasm." It is worth noting that the analysis by Bouhdiba and others has in turn led to criticisms that give a new twist to the old missionary approach to Islam. M.E. Combs-Schilling remarks, "Christianity's imagination of paradise is asexual, while Islam's is one of infinite male orgasm. For those who would ennoble the sexual act, Islam's imagination has some advantages; it speaks of sexuality in highly poetic and lyrical terms. Yet this imagination is profoundly limited, for it does not apply sacrality to sex between partners on earth. It does not allow the man to have sacred sex with a real woman, only with the imagined huris in heaven. . . . In Islam's imagination, sacred sex is biased towards the man and towards heaven, so that it profoundly interferes with the depth of intimacy that males and females can experience on earth. It does not allow the man to spiritually, emotionally, and sexually invest where he plausibly could" (*Sacred Performances* 96). Even if the Islamic concept of the sacred had not been misrepresented here, one would wonder where the author gained her prophetic ability to see into the souls of Muslim men and women over history and tell us what they have and have not experienced and then to mandate a norm in their sexual relationships. How does she know what is and is not spiritually plausible? At least traditional Muslim authors are frank in their anthropology. One wishes that this author could have told us what a human being is and how she can be sure of her definition.

58. Ibn al-ʿArabī, *Futūḥāt* II 574.1.

59. Henry Corbin provides a fascinating and highly original meditation on the significance of Ibn al-ʿArabī's teachings on woman as divine image based upon this and other passages (cf. *Creative Imagination* 157–75). Most of the passages upon which he bases his arguments are translated in the previous and present chapters, along with a great deal of other material that helps clarify the context.

60. Jandī, *Sharḥ fuṣūṣ al-ḥikam* 671.

61. Qayṣarī, *Sharḥ fuṣūṣ al-ḥikam* 470.

62. Cf. SPK 395n17.

63. Jandī 672.

64. Kāshānī, *Sharḥ fuṣūṣ al-ḥikam* 327.

65. Kāshānī 328.

66. Qayṣarī 472.

67. Kāshānī 332.

68. Qayṣarī 475.

69. Kāshānī 332.

70. Qayṣarī 475–76.

71. On the concept of "assuming the character traits" of God as the basis for all positive human traits, cf. SPK 283–86.

72. Cf. SPL 200–6.

73. Jandī 679.

74. Kāshānī 333.

75. Qayṣarī 477.

76. Jāmī, *Sharḥ fuṣūṣ al-ḥikam* II 329.

77. Qayṣarī 477.

78. Qayṣarī 477–78.

79. Qayṣarī 478.

80. Jandī 679.

81. Kāshānī 333–34.

82. Qayṣarī 479.

83. Jandī 680.

84. Cf. SPK 413n23.

85. Cf. SPK 400n12.

86. Kāshānī 335.

87. Qayṣarī 480.

88. Kāshānī 336; Jandī 682–83.

89. Jandī 683–84.

90. Ibn al-ʿArabī, *Futūḥāt* I 424.34.

91. Aḥmad I 103.

92. According to Ibn al-ʿArabī Ibn Māja quotes this in his *Sunan* from the Prophet, but the hadith is not indexed in Wensinck.

93. Ibn al-ʿArabī, *Futūḥāt* II 325.25. Cf. SPK 285–86.

94. Aḥmad I 391, 452.

95. *Futūḥāt* IV 453.34.

Chapter 7. The Womb

1. Ikhwān al-Ṣafāʾ, *Rasāʾil* IV 212.

2. Ibn al-ʿArabī frequently discusses this point. Cf. SPK 294, 311–12, 349, 404n18.

3. Ikhwān al-Ṣafāʾ, *Rasāʾil* IV 210–11.

4. Kāshānī, *Taʾwīlāt* I 679–80.

5. I was not able to trace this hadith.

6. Kāshānī, *Taʾwīlāt* I 638.

7. Rūmī, *Mathnawī* VI 3172–73 (SPL 43).

8. "Things" here renders *shuʾūn* (tasks), a term derived from Koran 55:29. In Ibn al-ʿArabī's teachings, *shuʾūn* refers to everything God undertakes in the cosmos, or everything toward which He turns His creative power. More specifically, it alludes to the fact that each thing undergoes constant transformation and change. Cf. SPK 98–104.

9. Qūnawī, *Iʿjāz al-bayān* 382/*al-Tafsīr al-ṣūfī* 513.

10. Idem, *Tabṣirat al-mubtadī* 86.

11. Bukhārī, Riqāq 119.

12. Muslim, Tawba 21.

13. Ibn al-ʿArabī, *Futūḥāt* III 289.23 (cf. SPK 65).

14. Ibid. II 453.16.

15. Ibn al-ʿArabī frequently quotes this saying. Cf. SPK 67, 115, 116, 375.

16. Ibn al-ʿArabī, *Futūḥāt* IV 282.25.

17. Ikhwān al-Ṣafāʾ, *Rasāʾil* II 132–33.

18. Ibid. 427.

19. Ibn al-ʿArabī, *Fuṣūṣ* 219.

20. A hadith that has come in several versions in standard sources. Cf. SPK 68.

21. Ibn al-ʿArabī, *Futūḥāt* I 293.8 (Y 4,344.11).

22. Ibid. III 90.18 (cf. SPK 141).

23. Ibid. 99.7.

24. Ibid. 99.16.

25. Ibid. I 276.18 (Y 4,247.12).

26. Ibid. III 125.3.

27. Maybudī, *Kashf al-asrār* I 442.

28. Muslim, Birr 1; Bukhārī, Adab 2; Tirmidhī, Birr 1; Abū Dāwūd, Adab 120; Ibn Māja, Adab 1; Aḥmad V 3, 5.

29. Cited in Lane, *Arabic-English Lexicon*, under *barr*.

30. ʿAlī ibn al-Ḥusayn, *The Psalms of Islam* 287.

31. The hadith is found in several versions in all the standard sources. Cf. Wensinck, *Concordance* I 486.

32. Ibn al-ʿArabī, *Futūḥāt* II 354.22.

33. In Tirmidhī (Zuhd 47) and Aḥmad (IV 132), the hadith reads as follows: "A human being fills no container worse than his belly. A few bites to firm up his backbone are enough for the son of Adam. If he must, then a third [of his belly] for his food, a third for his drink, and a third for himself."

34. Ibn al-ʿArabī, *Futūḥāt* III 125.8. In the same passage Ibn al-ʿArabī makes clear that he means the spirit that the Koran attributes to God Himself ("I blew into him of My spirit").

35. Tirmidhī, Tafsīr 96. I follow Qūnawī's text in *Sharḥ al-ḥadīth*, which has a few slight differences from Tirmidhī's text.

36. Qūnawī, *Sharḥ al-ḥadīth*, no. 15.

37. Ibn Māja, Zuhd 35.

38. Aḥmad ibn Ḥanbal I 191, 194.

39. Muslim, Birr 16; Bukhārī, Tafsīr sūra 47, Tawḥīd 35; Aḥmad II 330, 383, 406.

40. Muslim, Birr 17; Aḥmad II 163, 190, 193, 209.

41. Bukhārī, Adab 13; Tirmidhī, Birr 16; Aḥmad I 190, 321; II 295, 382, 406, 455, 498.

42. Ikhwān al-Ṣafāʾ, *Rasāʾil* II 417–55.

43. In a sound hadith found in the standard sources, the Prophet says, "The creation of each of you is brought together in his mother's belly for forty days. Then he is a blood clot for an equal period. Then he is a lump of flesh for an equal period. Then God sends forth an angel that is commanded by four words. It is said to the angel, 'Write his words, his provision, his time of death, and whether he is felicitous or wretched.' Then the spirit is blown into him." Bukhārī, Badʾ al-Khalq 6, etc. It is for this reason that "All Muslim jurists believed that the foetus became a human being after the fourth month of pregnancy" (B. Musallam, *Sex and Society in Islam* 57).

44. Ikhwān al-Ṣafāʾ, *Rasāʾil* II 423–24.

45. The nine months are governed by the seven planets beginning from the outermost planet and moving to the innermost, then beginning again from the outermost. Hence the order is: Saturn, Jupiter, Mars, Sun, Venus, Mercury, Moon, Saturn, Jupiter (cf. Ikhwān al-Ṣafāʾ, *Rasāʾil* II 434–42).

46. Nasafī, *Insān-i kāmil* 16–23.

47. Ibid. 34.

48. On this sound *ḥadith qudsī*, cf. Graham, *Divine Word* 117–19.

49. Ikhwān al-Ṣafāʾ, *Rasāʾil* III 5–6.

50. Rūmī, *Mathnawī* III 3560–61 (SPL 184).

51. Ibid. II 2518–20 (SPL 241).

52. Rūmī, *Dīwān* 19132 (SPL 70).

53. Ibid. 7192–94 (SPL 70).

54. Cf. the remarks by the Ikhwān al-Ṣafāʾ: "The human being is a whole made of two substances. One is the corporeal body and the other is the spiritual soul. The most incomplete and lowest state of his soul is that it should be simple, without knowing anything, as God said, 'God brought you out of the bellies of your mothers not knowing anything' [16:78]. The most complete state of the soul is that every virtue within the soul's potentiality should be brought out into actuality. This is that the human being should become a person of true faith, a knower of the Lord, a philosopher, a sage, a Verifier, as God said, 'And you were taught what you did not know, neither you nor your fathers' [6:91]. And He said, 'He taught the human being what he did not know' [96:5]. And He said, 'Be you lordly' [3:79]." *Rasāʾil* III 31.

55. The hadith is found in a number of versions in Muslim (Waṣiyya 14), Abū Dāwūd (Waṣiyya 14), Tirmidhī (Aḥkām 36), Nasāʾī (Waṣāyā 8), and Aḥmad II 316, 350, 372.

56. The hadith is not indexed in Wensinck.

57. "Poverty" (*iftiqār*), called "possibility" (*imkān*) by the philosophers, indicates that created things are utterly dependent upon God for everything they are. Cf. SPK 44–46 and passim.

58. Qūnawī, *Sharḥ al-ḥadīth*, no. 20.

Chapter 8. Static Hierarchy

1. Cf. Maybudī's discussion in *Kashf al-asrār* II 20–21.

2. Ghazālī quotes ʿUmar as follows: "ʿUmar, with all his severity [*khushūna*], used to say: 'A man must be like a child with his family [*ahl*], but when they want him to be the lord of the house, then he should be like men." (*Iḥyāʾ* II.2.3 [II 29]; in his Persian translation of this saying [*Kīmiyā-yi saʿādat* 315/249], Ghazālī clearly understands *ahl* to mean "wife," since he uses a singular verb).

3. Rūmī, *Mathnawī* I 2426–28, 33 (cf. SPL 168–69).

4. Idem, *Fīhi mā fīhi* 229 (cf. SPL 273).

5. The "opening" of the door to unseen knowledge is a familiar theme in Sufi writings and is referred to in the title of Ibn al-ʿArabī's magnum opus, the "Meccan Openings," *al-Futūḥāt al-makkiyya*. Note that all the qualities Kāshānī correlates with opening have to do with the expansiveness and intimacy that result from establishing a relationship with the yin divine names.

6. The hadith is often quoted by our authors, but it is not found in the standard sources. Cf. SPK 412n5.

7. Jaʿfar al-Ṣādiq, the sixth Shiʿite Imam from whom I have already had occasion to quote, is the author of an important *taʾwīl* of the Koran that has not been critically edited.

8. This is a saying of the Prophet. Kāshānī follows the text provided by Ibn al-ʿArabī, who says it is found in Tirmidhī. However, the version there is slightly different (cf. SPK 405n16).

9. Kāshānī, *Ta'wīlāt* I 4–5.

10. Lāhījī, *Sharḥ-i Gulshan-i rāz* 733.

11. Cf. SPK 246–47.

12. Ikhwān al-Ṣafā', *Rasā'il* III 13.

13. Rūmī, *Dīwān* 35280 (SPL 28).

14. Ibid. 14355 (SPL 28).

15. Ghazālī, *Kīmiyā-yi sa'ādat* 13–16/9–11.

16. Cf. the translation of this section in McCarthy, *Freedom and Fulfillment* 365–68.

17. Cf. Kāshānī's detailed explanation of this verse in chapter 10 (pp. 299–300).

18. The mention of "forty-day retreats" (*chilla*) no doubt has to do with the Sufi practice by the same name. It also refers to the hadith, quoted above in chapter 7, note 43, where the Prophet mentions three forty-day periods.

19. The root meaning of the term *qalb*, as will be explained in chapter 10, is that which fluctuates.

20. Nasafī, *Kashf al-ḥaqā'iq* 72–73.

21. Murata, "Angels" 327.

22. Rūmī, *Dīwān* 21284 (SPL 27)

23. Ibid. 8676.

24. Much of this section is translated in McCarthy, *Freedom and Fulfillment* 363ff.

25. Ghazālī, *Kīmiyā-yi sa'ādat* 16–18/12–13.

26. Though not found in the standard hadith sources, this saying is frequently cited. Cf. Bayḍāwī, *Anwār al-tanzīl*, on Koran 22:78; Maybudī, *Kashf al-asrār* III 213, VI 405. Cf. the fine study by J. Renard, "Al-Jihād al-Akbar: Notes on a Theme in Islamic Spirituality."

27. Rāzī, *Mirṣād al-'ibād* 210–11 (cf. *Path of God's Bondsmen* 220–21).

28. Nasafī, *Kashf al-ḥaqā'iq* 74–75.

29. Ibid. 75–76.

30. Ikhwān al-Ṣafā', *Rasā'il* II 461.

31. Rūmī, *Dīwān* 25842 (cf. SPL 164).

32. The same term *intellect* is also used in negative senses, especially in Sufi texts. Then it is identified with the clever reasoning of those philosophers, jurists, and theologians who obscure the truth. Hence Rūmī, for example, discerns between the "partial intellect" that is the domain of the mind veiled from the divine light, and the "universal intellect" that is possessed by the prophets and friends of God. Cf. SPL 35–37. Ibn al-'Arabī frequently criticizes the limitations of intellect or "reason," as Chittick usually translates *'aql* (cf. SPK, index).

33. Majlisī, *Biḥār al-anwār* I 117.

34. Kāshānī, *Ā'īna-yi shāhī* 8 (cf. "Two Seventeenth-Century Tracts" 277).

35. These are the words of God to Iblis when he refused to prostrate himself before Adam (38:75).

36. Various versions of the hadith enumerate from seventy-one to eighty-one qualities, with the version cited below giving seventy-five.

37. Al-Kulaynī, *al-Uṣūl min al-kāfī* I 30–34. For other versions, cf. Majlisī, *Biḥār al-anwār* I 109–11, 158–59.

38. Ghazālī, *Kīmiyā-yi sa'ādat* 18–20/13–15.

39. Ibid. 20–21/15–16.

40. Maybudī, *Kashf al-asrār* I 114.

41. Kāshānī, *Ta'wīlāt* I 28.

42. For detailed explanations of the meanings of these two terms, cf. SPK 263–69, 278–83, and passim.

43. Kāshānī, *Ta'wīlāt* I 103.

44. Ibid. 631.

45. Kāshānī does not provide an explanation for ship here, but he probably reads it as referring to the body, as in the passage quoted above.

46. Kāshānī, *Ta'wīlāt* I 656.

47. Ibid. 392.

48. Ibid. 106–7.

49. "Origination" is creation from nothing, while "engendering," as Kāshānī uses the term here, means creation from a pre-existent matter.

50. Kāshānī, *Ta'wīlāt* I 34–35.

Chapter 9. Dynamics of the Soul

1. Rūmī, *Dīwān* 3762 (SPL 50).

2. Arberry, *Muslim Saints and Mystics* 51.

3. For a much more detailed discussion of the two commands, cf. SPK 291ff.

4. Qūnawī, *Iʿjāz al-bayān* 292/*al-Tafsīr al-ṣūfī* 409. Cf. *Futūḥāt* II 93.19 (SPK 55)

5. Hamadānī, *Tamhīdāt* 126.

6. Abū Bakr and ʿUmar were of course two of the Prophet's closest companions and became the first and second caliphs after him, while Abū Jahl and Abū Lahab were the Prophet's archenemies.

7. Hamadānī, *Tamhīdāt* 187.

8. Rūmī, *Mathnawī* IV 414–17 (SPL 71).

9. Bukhārī, Riqāq 38. Cf. Graham, *Divine Word* 173–74.

10. Ibn al-ʿArabī, *Futūḥāt* II 563.29 (cf. SPK 326).

11. Ḥāfiẓ, *Dīwān* 96. Cf. *The Dīvān-i-Hāfiz* I 258.

12. This classification is frequently discussed in Sufi texts. Cf. Schimmel, *Mystical Dimensions* 112.

13. Makkī, *Qūt al-qulūb* 177 (chapter 25).

14. Bukhārī gives the text of the hadith as follows: "Let the servant of dinars, dirhams, velvet, and fine clothes fall on his face. If these are given, he is pleased, and if these are not given, he is not pleased" (Jihād 70, Riqāq 10; cf. Ibn Māja, Zuhd 8).

15. Makkī, *Qūt al-qulūb* 177 (chapter 25).

16. Sarrāj, *Kitāb al-lumaʿ* 360.

17. Sulamī, *ʿUyūb al-nafs* 107.

18. Qushayrī, *Risāla* 305.

19. Hamadānī, *Tamhīdāt* 195.

20. Rūzbihān Baqlī, *Mashrab al-arwāḥ* 151–52.

21. Ibid. 126.

22. See the partial translation by R.J. McCarthy in *Freedom and Fulfillment* 363–82.

23. Cf. above, pp. 230–31.

24. McCarthy, *Freedom and Fulfillment* 365–67.

25. Cf. Chittick, "Eschatology" 396.

26. Ghazālī, *Iḥyāʾ* III.1.5 (III 9); cf. McCarthy, *Freedom* 376–78.

27. Neither of these two hadiths is cited in Wensinck, but the first is given by Suyūṭī in a slightly different form in *al-Jāmiʿ al-ṣaghīr (al-Fayḍ al-qadīr* I 256, no. 378).

28. Maymūn ibn Mahrān is a respected authority in the science of Hadith who died in 117/735. Ibn Māja (Zuhd 29) cites a different version of this hadith on the authority of Abū Hurayra.

29. Ghazālī, *Iḥyāʾ* III.1.5 (III 9–10).

30. Ikhwān al-Ṣafāʾ, *Rasāʾil* III 8–9.

31. Ibid. 15.

32. Gutas, *Avicenna* 86.

33. Quoted in Gutas, *Avicenna* 17.

34. Ibn Sīnā, *Kitāb al-najāh* 299.

35. Ibn al-ʿArabī, *Futūḥāt* III 430.18.

36. Avicenna probably has in mind the appearance of angels in bodily form. As has already been pointed out, the later tradition refers to this realm of spiritualized corporeality, or corporealized spirituality, as imagination.

37. Ibn Sīnā, *Kitāb al-najāh* 293.

38. Ibn al-ʿArabī, *Futūḥāt* III 136.8 (SPK 324).

39. Ibid. II 153.26 (cf. SPK 322). For a detailed discussion of the nature of servanthood in Ibn al-ʿArabī's view, cf. SPK 321–24 and passim.

40. Ibn al-ʿArabī, *Futūḥāt* II 603.16 (cf. SPK 372).

41. *Rahanjām-nāma*, in Kāshānī, *Muṣannafāt* 58.

42. *ʿArḍ-nāma*, in Kāshānī, *Muṣannafāt* 153.

43. *Rahanjām-nāma*, in Kāshānī, *Muṣannafāt* 74–75.

44. Mullā Ṣadrā, *ʿArshiyya* 242–43 (cf. Mullā Ṣadrā, *Wisdom* 148–49).

45. Ibn al-ʿArabī, *Futūḥāt* II 192.5.

46. Cf. Schimmel, *Mystical Dimensions* 434; idem, *As Through a Veil* 152–54. The Ismailis were particularly fond of this analogy. Cf. A. S. Asani, "Bridal Symbolism in Ismāʿīlī Mystical Literature of Indo-Pakistan," in R.A. Herrera (ed.), *Typologies of Mysticism*, forthcoming.

47. Lane, *Lexicon*, under *m.r.*ʾ, form 1. I have modified the text slightly to avoid the references to sources.

48. Anṣārī, *Ṣad maydān* 253–54.

49. Cf. Cl. Cahen and Fr. Taeschner, "Futuwwa," *Encyclopedia of Islam*, new ed., III 961–69. For some of the spiritual significance of the term, cf. S.H. Nasr, "Spiritual Chivalry."

50. Cf. Sulamī (d. 412/1021), *The Book of Sufi Chivalry*.

51. Mufīd, *Kitāb al-Irshād* (translated by Howard) 56, 58.

52. Qushayrī, *Risāla* 472–73.

53. Anṣārī, *Ṣad maydān* 362–63.

54. Idem, *Manāzil al-sāʾirīn* 47–48.

55. Kāshānī, *Tuḥfat al-ikhwān* 4–5.

56. Ibn al-ʿArabī, *Futūḥāt* II 588.6.

57. Ibid. 7.7.

58. Austin, *Sufis of Andalusia* 154.

59. Jandī, *Sharh fuṣūṣ al-ḥikam* 185. For a parallel passage in Ibn al-ʿArabī's *Futūḥāt*, cf. I 131–32 (Y 2,278–79).

60. Rūmī, *Mathnawī* III 2759 (SPL 83).

61. Idem, *Dīwān* 16532 (SPL 83).

62. Ibid. 18226 (SPL 83).

63. Cf. Schimmel, *Triumphal Sun* 269–72 and passim.

64. Rūmī, *Mathnawī* III 3193–94, 96–97 (cf. SPL 89).

65. Idem, *Dīwān* 5798 (cf. SPL 33).

66. Idem, *Mathnawī* III 2557–58 (cf. SPL 35).

67. Ibid. II 1850, 1853 (cf. SPL 34). For many more examples, cf. Schimmel, *Triumphal Sun* 93–124; SPL, index, under animals, ass, beasts, cow, dog, etc.

68. Rūmī, *Mathnawī* IV 2111 (SPL 222).

69. Ibid. VI 4139.

70. Rūmī, *Dīwān* 5791 (SPL 223).

71. Ibid. 34953 (SPL 223).

72. Cf. Makkī, *Qūt al-qulūb* 175 (chapter 25).

73. That intellect combats caprice (*hawā*) is a standard theme of Sufi texts. Cf. below, pp. 284ff.

74. The ideas in this sentence are also taken from Makkī, *Qūt al-qulūb* 176–77.

75. Suhrawardī, *ʿAwārif al-maʿārif* 452–53 (chapter 56).

76. Rāzī, *Mirṣād al-ʿibād* 373–75 (cf. *Path of God's Bondsmen* 363–64).

77. Modern scholars have not been able to agree on how to translate *wahm*, a term that plays a role in philosophical psychology. According to Avicenna, it is one of the five internal senses. Most commonly it has been rendered as estimation, following the early Latin translations from Arabic. P. Morewedge suggests that "prehension" is more accurate. He criticizes various attempts at translation made by historians of Islamic philosophy including not only estimation, but also nervous response, instinct, apprehension, conception, and imagination ("The Internal Sense of Prehension (*Wahm*) in Islamic Philosophy"). I choose "sensory intuition" because it seems to correspond to what Kāshānī is talking about better than any other term I can think of. In addition, the word *wahm* is frequently used in the texts to mean fantasy and misguided thinking without any technical implications. Like the English word *intuition*, it is a part of everyday vocabulary. However, *wahm* usually has a negative connotation, and in the present context, "sensory" helps bring this out.

78. F. Rahman, *Avicenna's Psychology* 31.

79. Kāshānī, *Taʾwīlāt* I 35.

80. The angels are ranked in many degrees, and the types of angels that Kāshānī mentions here clearly belong to the lowest reaches of the hierarchy, since they only perceive forms and not the meanings behind the forms. In other words, they function on the level of imagination, but they do not go into the world of disengaged spirits. But since they are "angels," they submit to the will of God, for obedience pertains to the very substance of the angels.

81. The root meaning of *kufr*, commonly translated as "unbelief," is covering and concealing. Hence our authors look for the significance of the term in the root sense. The "unbelievers" are those who cover and veil the blessings of God, and by the same token, it is they who are covered and veiled from His blessings.

82. These etymologies are not necessarily meant to be taken seriously on the linguistic level, since Kāshānī's interest is *ta'wīl*. He wants to bring out the "allusions" (*ishāra*) and hidden meanings found in the words.

83. Wrongdoers could be translated "darkdoers" to make Kāshānī's point, since the word has a common root with *ẓulma* (darkness).

84. Kāshānī, *Ta'wīlāt* I 39–41.

85. Ibid. 425.

86. Ibid. 427–28.

87. Ibid. 429.

88. Cf. Ikhwān al-Ṣafā', *Rasā'il* III 233, where the same example is given to prove that all things "find" (*wujūd*) God.

89. Kāshānī, *Ta'wīlāt* I 527–28.

90. Ibid. 423–24.

91. Tabrīzī, *Mishkāt* 155; cf. Robson, *Mishkat* 371.

92. Ṭabrisī, *Majma' al-bayān* X 423–24.

93. Ibn Abī Jumhūr, *al-Mujlī* 507.

94. Ikhwān al-Ṣafā', *Rasā'il* II 474–75.

95. Ghazālī, *Mīzān al-'amal* 209–10.

96. Sam'ānī, *Rawḥ al-arwāḥ* 177.

97. Ibid. 89.

98. Rūmī, *Fīhi mā fīhi* 107. For other passages, cf. SPL 85–87.

99. According to Muslim accounts of the events in the Garden of Eden, the peacock acted as the intermediary between Satan and the serpent. The serpent then allowed Satan to hide in its mouth in order to gain entry into the Garden. Cf. Kisā'ī, *Tales* 36–39.

100. Solomon stands for the vicegerent because he was given an unparalleled kingdom in answer to his prayer, "My Lord, forgive me, and give me a kingdom such as may not come to anyone after me" (38:35).

101. Allusion to Solomon's power over the satans mentioned in Koran 38:37: "And the satans, every builder and diver, and others also, coupled in fetters."

102. Nasafī, *Insān-i kāmil* 149–51.

103. For a survey of the tradition, cf. Chittick, "Eschatology." For Ibn al-'Arabī's contribution to the theory of imagination, cf. SPK, especially chapter 7. For Ibn al-'Arabī's eschatological views, cf. J. Morris in Chodkiewicz, *Illuminations*, pp. 119–90; also Chittick, "Death and the World of Imagination." For the eschatological tradition at its height, cf. Mullā Ṣadrā, *Wisdom of the Throne*.

104. Ghazālī, *Kīmiyā-yi sa'ādat* 23/18.

105. Rūmī, *Mathnawī* II 1416–19 (cf. SPL 103–4).

106. Mullā Ṣadrā, *al-Ta'līqāt* 476–77. Cf. Mullā Ṣadrā's discussion of these points in *Wisdom of the Throne* 144–49.

107. Ibn Sīnā, *Tarjama-yi risāla-yi aḍḥawiyya* 13–14, 50–51.

108. Ibn al-'Arabī, *Futūḥāt* III 66.23.

109. Ibn Sīnā, *al-Najāh* 307.

110. The hadith is not indexed in Wensinck.

111. Cf. SPK, chapter 16.

112. Cf. Chittick and Wilson, *Fakhruddin 'Iraqi* 147–48.

113. Rūmī, *Fīhi mā fīhi* 14 (cf. SPL 63).

114. Idem, *Mathnawī* V 588.

115. On this sound *ḥadīth qudsī*, cf. above, note 9.

116. Rāzī, *Mirṣād al-'ibād* 173–86 (cf. *Path of God's Bondsmen* 190–200).

Chapter 10. The Heart

1. Muslim, Birr 32.

2. Muslim, Īmān 284.

3. Aḥmad I 223.

4. Mālik, *al-Muwaṭṭa*ʾ, ʿIlm 1.

5. Bukhārī, Badʾ al-Khalq 11, etc.

6. Bukhārī, Badʾ al-Khalq 11.

7. Muslim, Musāfirīn 175.

8. Dārimī, Faḍāʾil al-Qurʾān, 1.

9. Ibn Māja, Zuhd 14.

10. Bukhārī, Daʿawāt 39, 44, 46, etc.

11. Ibn Māja, Zuhd 24.

12. Aḥmad II 173.

13. Aḥmad IV 419.

14. Tirmidhī, Daʿawāt 89.

15. For a large number of citations from two authors who epitomize the Persian and Arabic Sufi traditions, Rūmī and Ibn al-ʿArabī, cf. the indexes to SPL and SPK.

16. Cf. Aḥmad ibn Ḥanbal V 252, 256.

17. Dārimī, Bayʿ 2.

18. A version near to this is found in Dārimī, Bayʿ 2. Cf. Aḥmad IV 228.

19. Makkī, *Qūt al-qulūb* I 233–35 (chapter 30).

20. Tirmidhī, *Bayān al-farq* 79–83. Cf. Tirmidhī, "Psychological Treatise" 244–46.

21. For a rather typical example of a contemporary discussion of the heart completely rooted in this tradition, by a professor of theology at Tehran University, cf. Mīrzā Aḥmad Āshtiyānī, *Maqālāt-i Aḥmadiyya dar ʿilm-i akhlāq* 13–15.

22. Bukhārī, *Sharḥ-i taʿarruf* II 167–68. Part of the text is found in the abridged version, *Khulāṣa-yi sharḥ-i taʿarruf* 174.

23. Hamadānī, *Tamhīdāt* 259.

24. ʿAyn al-Quḍāt may have distorted this hadith. The nearest saying to it in the standard sources is the following: "God looks not at your forms or your possessions, but He looks only at your works and your hearts." Ibn Māja, Zuhd 9; Aḥmad ibn Ḥanbal II 285, 539.

25. Hamadānī, *Tamhīdāt* 146.

26. Samʿānī, *Rawḥ al-arwāḥ* 298–99.

27. Maybudī, *Kashf al-asrār* VIII 411–12.

28. Rūzbihān Baqlī, *ʿAbhar al-ʿāshiqīn* 99.

29. Allusion to Koran 20:5: "The All-merciful sat upon the Throne."

30. Rūzbihān Baqlī, *Risālat al-quds* 67–68.

31. Bukhārī, Īmān 39; Muslim, Masāfāt 107, etc.

32. Rūzbihān Baqlī, *Mashrab al-arwāḥ* 152–53.

33. Persian text from an untitled ms. provided by F. Meier in Kubrā, *Die Fawāʾiḥ al-Ǧamāl* 170.

34. Kubrā, *Die Fawāʾiḥ al-Ǧamāl* (Arabic text) 7.

35. On the heart in Ibn al-ʿArabī's teachings, see SPK 106–9 and passim.

36. Kāshānī, *Iṣṭilāḥāt al-ṣūfiyya* 167–68.

37. Idem, *Taʾwīlāt* II 140–41.

38. Ibid. I 483–84.

39. Ibid. 751.

40. Ibid. 729–30.

41. Allusion to the hadith, "God's veil is light [or fire]. Were He to remove it, the glories of His face would burn away everything perceived by the sight of His creatures" (Muslim, Īmān 293; Ibn Māja, Muqaddima 13). Ibn al-ʿArabī cites it in a slightly different form (cf. SPK 401n19; Chodkiewicz, *Illuminations* 95–96).

42. Kāshānī, *Taʾwīlāt* I 705–6.

43. Cf. chapter 7, note 48.

44. Kāshānī, *Taʾwīlāt* I 706–9.

45. Cf. SPK 275–77.

46. Rūmī, *Mathnawī* II 3326–30 (cf. SPL 31–32; 37, 39–40, 62, etc.).

47. Ghazālī quotes the same hadith in discussing the heart (*Iḥyāʾ* III.1.5 [III 10]). A similar text is found in Aḥmad III 7.

48. Suhrawardī, *ʿAwārif al-maʿārif* 449–51 (chapter 56).

49. Hārūt is an angel, mentioned in Koran 2:102, who came down to Babylon along with his fellow angel Mārūt and taught the inhabitants sorcery. Cf. Kisā'ī, *Tales* 47–48.

50. Kāshānī, *Miṣbāḥ al-hidāya* 83–84. The saying of ʿAlī is also cited in Sarrāj, *Kitāb al-lumaʿ* 132.

51. Cf. SPK 174.

52. Kāshānī, *Miṣbāḥ al-hidāya* 94–95.

53. Ibid.

54. Ibid. 96.

55. Note that on this point Kāshānī differs with Ibn al-ʿArabī (see above, page 180).

56. Kāshānī, *Miṣbāḥ al-hidāya* 96.

57. Ibid. 97. ʿAlī ibn Sahl ibn Azhar Iṣfahānī (d. 280/893) is one of the eminent Sufis mentioned by Hujwīrī, who also gives a longer version of this saying (Hujwīrī, *The Kashf al-Mahjúb* 143–44).

58. Kāshānī, *Miṣbāḥ al-hidāya* 98–99.

59. Cf. Ibn al-Fāriḍ, *Poem* 25 (lines 575–77).

60. Farghānī, *Mashāriq al-darārī* 210–11.

61. Idem, *Muntahā al-madārik* I 95.

62. Ibid. 98–99.

63. Ibid. 102.

64. Ibid. 103. Farghānī is alluding here to the power of the gnostic to enter into any world of the cosmos in an appropriate form. Cf. Ibn al-ʿArabī's discussion of this point in Chodkiewicz, *Illuminations* 287–300.

65. Kāshānī, *Ta'wīlāt* I 256.

66. Ibid. II 10.

67. Ibid. 259–60.

68. Rūmī, *Fīhi mā fīhi* 20–21 (cf. SPL 241).

69. Kāshānī, *Ta'wīlāt* I 185–86.

70. Qūnawī, *Miftāḥ al-ghayb* 324.

71. These correspond to the well-known "Five Divine Presences." Cf. Chittick, "The Five Divine Presences."

72. Qūnawī, *Fakk al-khutūm* 246–50; cf. Jāmī, *Naqd al-nuṣūṣ* 200–1.

73. *Aḥadiyya jamʿ al-jamʿ*, one of the terms Qūnawī and his followers employ to refer to the station of the most perfect of the perfect human beings.

74. Qūnawī, *Iʿjāz al-bayān* 270–71/*al-Tafsīr al-ṣūfī* 386–87.

75. Samʿānī, *Rawḥ al-arwāḥ* 286–87.

76. Rūmī, *Mathnawī* II 1856. The hadith reads, "Put them [feminine] behind, since God has put them behind." The text is given by Munāwī in *Kanz al-ḥaqā'iq* (Furūzānfar, *Aḥādīth-i Mathnawī* 60). The sense in the original context is that the women should stand behind the men during the communal prayer. As for God's "putting them behind," that probably refers to Eve's creation after Adam.

77. Rūmī, *Mathnawī* I 2617–22.

78. Ibid. V 2459–64, 66–67. For several more examples of such verses, cf. SPL 163ff.

79. ʿAṭṭār, *Tadhkirat al-awliyā* 668.

80. Cited from Jamāl al-Dīn Hanswī (d. 1260) by A. Schimmel, "Women in Mystical Islam" 147.

81. ʿAṭṭār, *Tadhkirat al-awliyā'* 349. Cf. Arberry's translation, *Muslim Saints* 175; Nurbakhsh, *Sufi Women* 85.

82. ʿAṭṭār, *Tadhkirat al-awliyā'* 72. Cf. Arberry's translation, *Muslim Saints* 40; Nurbakhsh, *Sufi Women* 22; Smith, *Rabia* 2.

83. Rūmī, *Mathnawī* VI 1883–85.

Postscript

1. Combs-Schilling reflects a good deal of current scholarship when she remarks that the Mediterranean monotheisms, Islam in particular, "pull the female out of the cosmic dramas, push her away from the momentous settings, and relegate the female instead to the role of the nature-bound individual" (*Sacred Performances* 267). The reason for this was, in short, that "God stepped out of nature, and women fell from the holiest places" (ibid. 257). From the point of view of the tradition I have discussed in this book, such evaluations have in view the fact that the monotheisms place a "feminine" value on the qualities found in the soul that commands to evil. In Islam's general view of history, if "God steps out of nature," this means that human beings, men as well as women, lose the ability to see God in nature. The mythic reason for this is that Adam's fall repeats itself in history. In other words, human beings in general have a tendency to forget (*ghafla*) the Real, and this general forgetfulness increases over time, only to be slowed by the coming of prophets. The more "God steps out of nature," or the Real becomes further removed from human awareness, the more the universe becomes opaque. People no longer see things as signs of God, but rather as discrete entities. The prophets come in order to "remind" (*tadhkīr*) them of the Reality that has now largely been lost to sight. But the Reality is now in fact an unseen God, a God far away from perception, a God of incomparability, a King who issues commands. The sacrality of the earth—which is another way of expressing the idea of God's nearness and "similarity"—now has to be reestablished. But this cannot take place without the prior recognition of God's absolute and incomparable Reality and the relegation of the "female"—the yin qualities of the divine—to the background.

2. The hadith is found with minor differences in many sources, including Bukhārī, ʿIlm 21, Nikāḥ 110, Ḥudūd 20, Ashraba 1; Muslim, ʿIlm 9; Tirmidhī, Fitan 34. The word translated as *"man to stand over them"* (*qayyim*) alludes to the Koranic verse, "The men stand over the women" (4:34).

3. R.C. Temple, *Lalla the Prophetess* (Cambridge, 1924) 8, as quoted in Schimmel, *Islam in the Indian Subcontinent* 44.

4. Rāzī, *Mirṣād al-ʿibād* 119 (cf. *Path of God's Bondsmen* 141).

BIBLIOGRAPHY

Abū Dāwūd. *al-Sunan*. Edited by A.S. ʿAlī. Cairo: Muṣṭafā al-Bābī al-Ḥalabī, 1952.

Addas, Claude. *Ibn ʿArabī ou La quête du Soufre Rouge*. Paris: Gallimard, 1989.

Aḥmad (ibn Ḥanbal). *al-Musnad*. Beirut: Dār Ṣādir, n.d.

ʿAlī ibn al-Ḥusayn. *The Psalms of Islam: al-Ṣaḥīfat al-sajjādiyya*. Translated by W.C. Chittick. Oxford: Oxford University Press, 1988.

ʿAmilī, Muḥammad ibn al-Ḥusayn al-Ḥurr al-. *Wasāʾil al-shīʿa*. Edited by ʿA. al-Rabbānī al-Shīrāzī. Tehran: al-Maktabat al-Islāmiyya, 1383–89/1963–69.

Andrae, Tor. *In the Garden of Myrtles: Studies in Early Islamic Mysticism*. Albany, N.Y.: SUNY Press, 1987.

Anṣārī, Khwāja ʿAbdallāh. *Manāzil al-sāʾirīn*. Edited by S. de Laugier de Beaurecueil. Cairo: L'Institut Français d'Archéologie Orientale, 1962.

———. *Ṣad maydān*. Edited by R. Farhādī. In *Manāzil al-sāʾirīn*. Kabul: Bayhaqī, 1976.

Arberry, A.J. *The Doctrine of the Sufis*. See Kalābādhī.

———. *The Poem of the Way: Translated into English Verse from the Arabic of Ibn al-Fāriḍ*. London: Emery Walker, 1952.

Āshtiyānī, Mīrzā Aḥmad. *Maqālāt-i Aḥmadiyya dar ʿilm-i akhlāq*. Tehran: Dār al-Kutub al-Islāmiyya, 1336/1957.

ʿAṭṭār, Farīd al-Dīn. *Tadhkirat al-awliyāʾ*. Edited by M. Istiʿlāmī. Tehran: Zuwwār, 1346/1967. Partly translated by A.J. Arberry as *Muslim Saints and Mystics*. Chicago: University of Chicago Press, 1966.

Austin, R.W.J. "The Feminine Dimensions in Ibn al-ʿArabi's Thought." *Journal of the Muhyiddin Ibn ʿArabi Society* 2 (1984) 5–14.

———. *Sufis of Andalusia*. London: George Allen & Unwin, 1971.

Avicenna. See Ibn Sīnā.

Awn, P. *Satan's Tragedy and Redemption: Iblīs in Sufi Psychology*. Leiden: Brill, 1983.

Bayḍāwī, al-. *Anwār al-tanzīl wa asrār al-taʾwīl*. N.p.: al-Maṭbaʿat al-ʿUthmāniyya, 1329/1911.

Bayrak, Sheikh Tosun. *The Most Beautiful Names*. Putney, Vt.: Threshold Books, 1985.

Bouhdiba, Abdelwahab. *Sexuality in Islam*. Translated from the French by Alan Sheridan. Boston: Routledge & Kegan Paul, 1985.

Bukhārī. *al-Ṣaḥīḥ*. N.p.: Maṭābiʿ al-Shuʿab, 1378/1958–59.

Bukhārī, Abū Ibrāhīm Mustamlī. *Sharḥ-i taʿarruf*. Lucknow, India: 1328/1910. Abridged version as *Khulāṣa-yi sharḥ-i taʿarruf*. Edited by Aḥmad ʿAlī Rajāʾī. Tehran: Bunyād-i Farhang, 1349/1970.

Chittick, W.C. "Death and the World of Imagination: Ibn al-ʿArabī's Eschatology." *The Muslim World* 78 (1988) 51–82.

———. "Eschatology." In Nasr, *Islamic Spirituality: Foundations* 378–409.

———. "The Five Divine Presences: From al-Qūnawī to al-Qayṣarī." *The Muslim World* 72 (1982) 107–28.

———. "Ibn ʿArabī and his School." In Nasr, *Islamic Spirituality: Manifestations* 49–79.

———. "Rūmī and Waḥdat al-Wujūd." In *The Heritage of Rumi*, edited by Amin Banani and Georges Sabagh. Cambridge: Cambridge University Press, forthcoming.

———. *The Sufi Path of Love: The Spiritual Teachings of Rumi*. Albany, N.Y.: SUNY Press, 1983.

———. *The Sufi Path of Knowledge: Ibn al-ʿArabī's Metaphysics of Imagination*. Albany, N.Y.: SUNY Press, 1989.

Chittick, W.C., and P.L. Wilson. *Fakhruddin ʿIraqi: Divine Flashes*. New York: Paulist Press, 1982.

Chodkiewicz, M. *Le Sceau des saints: Prophétie et sainteté dans la doctrine d'Ibn ʾArabī*. Paris: Gallimard, 1986.

Chodkiewicz, M., et al. *Les Illuminations de La Mecque/The Meccan Illuminations: Textes Choisis/Selected Texts*. Paris: Sindbad, 1988.

Combs-Schilling, M.E. *Sacred Performances: Islam, Sexuality, and Sacrifice*. New York: Columbia University Press, 1989.

Corbin, Henry. *Creative Imagination in the Ṣūfism of Ibn ʿArabī*. Princeton: Princeton University Press, 1969.

———. *The Man of Light in Iranian Sufism*. Boulder: Shambhala, 1978.

Dārimī, al-. *al-Sunan*. N.p.: Dār Iḥyāʾ al-Sunnat al-Nabawiyya, n.d.

Elias, Jamal J. "Female and Feminine in Islamic Mysticism." *Muslim World* 78 (1988) 209–24.

Ernst, C. *Words of Ecstasy in Sufism*. Albany, N.Y.: SUNY Press, 1985.

Fanārī, al-. See Qūnawī. *Miftāḥ al-ghayb*.

Farghānī, Saʿīd al-Dīn. *Mashāriq al-darārī*. Edited by S.J. Āshtiyānī. Tehran: Anjuman-i Islāmī-yi Ḥikmat wa Falsafa-yi Īrān, 1358/1979.

———. *Muntahā al-madārik*. Cairo: Maktab al-Ṣanāʾiʿ, 1293/1876.

Firdawsī. *Shāhnāma*, vol. I. Edited by Y.A. Bertels. Moscow: Academy of Science, 1963.

Furūzānfar, B. *Aḥādīth-i Mathnawī*. Tehran: Amīr Kabīr, 1347/1968.

Gawharīn, S.S. *Farhang-i lughāt wa taʿbīrāt-i Mathnawī*. Tehran: Dānishgāh, 1337–54/1958–75.

Ghazālī, Muḥammad al-. *Iḥyāʾ ʿulūm al-dīn*. Cairo: Maṭbaʿat al-ʿĀmirat al-Sharafiyya, 1326–27/1908–09.

———. *Kīmiyā-yi saʿādat*. Edited by H. Khadīw-jam. Tehran: Jībī, 1354/1975. Edited by A. Ārām. Tehran: Markazī, 1333/1954.

———. *Mīzān al-ʿamal*. Edited by S. Dunyā. Cairo: Dār al-Maʿārif, 1964.

Gimaret, D. *Les noms divins en Islam: Exégèse lexicographique et théologique*. Paris: Les Editions du Cerf, 1988.

Graham, W. *Divine Word and Prophetic Word in Early Islam*. The Hague: Mouton, 1977.

Gutas, D. *Avicenna and the Aristotelian Tradition*. Leiden: E.J. Brill, 1988.

Ḥāfiẓ. *Dīwān*. Edited by M. Qazwīnī and Q. Ghanī. Tehran: Zuwwār, 1320/1941.

———. *Dīwān*. Translated by H. Wilberforce Clarke as *The Dīvān-i-Ḥāfiẓ*. India, 1891. Reprint. New York: Samuel Weiser, 1970.

Ḥakīm, Suʿād al-. *al-Muʿjam al-ṣūfī*. Beirut: Dandara, 1981.

Hamadānī, ʿAyn al-Quḍāt. *Shakwaʾl-gharīb*. Translated by A.J. Arberry as *A Sufi Martyr*. London: George Allen and Unwin, 1969.

———. *Tamhīdāt*. Edited by ʿA. ʿUsayrān. Tehran: Dānishgāh, 1341/1962.

Hujwīrī. *Kashf al-maḥjūb*. Edited by V. Zhukovsky. Tehran: Amīr Kabīr, 1336/1957. Translated by R. A. Nicholson. *The Kashf al-Mahjúb: The Oldest Persian Treatise on Sufiism*. London: Luzac, 1911.

Ibn Abī Jumhūr. *al-Mujlī*. Tehran: Aḥmad Shīrāzī, 1329/1911.

Ibn al-ʿArabī. *Ayyām al-shaʾn*. In *Rasāʾil Ibn al-ʿArabī*.

———. *Fuṣūṣ al-ḥikam*. Edited by A. ʿAfīfī. Beirut: Dār al-Kutub al-ʿArabī, 1946. Translated by R.W.J. Austin as *Ibn Al'Arabi: The Bezels of Wisdom*. Ramsey, N.J.: Paulist Press, 1981.

———. *al-Futūḥāt al-makkiyya*. Cairo, 1911. Reprint. Beirut: Dār Ṣādir, n.d. (Y refers to the critical edition of Othman Yahya. Cairo: al-Hay'at al-Miṣriyyat al-ʿĀmmat li'l-Kitāb, 1972—.)

———. *Inshā' al-dawā'ir*. In *Kleinere Schriften des Ibn al-ʿArabī*.

———. *Iṣṭilāḥāt al-ṣūfiyya*. In *Rasā'il Ibn al-ʿArabī*. Also in *Futūḥāt* II 128–34.

———. *Kleinere Schriften des Ibn al-ʿArabī*. Edited by H.S. Nyberg. Leiden: E.J. Brill, 1919.

———. "On Majesty and Beauty: The *Kitāb al-Jalāl wa-l-Jamāl* of Muhyiddin Ibn ʿArabi." Translated by R.T. Harris. *Journal of the Muhyiddin Ibn ʿArabi Society* 8 (1989) 5–32.

———. *Rasā'il Ibn al-ʿArabī*. Hyderabad-Deccan: Dāiratu'l-Maʿarifi'l-Osmania, 1948.

———. *ʿUqlat al-mustawfiz*. Edited by H.S. Nyberg in *Kleinere Schriften des Ibn al-ʿArabī*.

Ibn al-Fāriḍ. See Arberry.

Ibn Māja. *al-Sunan*. Edited by M.F. ʿAbd al-Bāqī. Cairo: Dār Iḥyā' al-Kutub al-ʿArabiyya, 1952.

Ibn Sīnā. *Kitāb al-najāh*. Cairo: Muḥyī al-Dīn Ṣabrī al-Kurdī, 1938.

———. *Tarjama-yi risāla-yi aḍḥawiyya*. Edited by H. Khadīw-jam. Tehran: Bunyād-i Farhang, 1350/1971.

Ikhwān al-Ṣafā'. *The Case of the Animals versus Man Before the King of the Jinn*. Translated by L.E. Goodman. Boston: Twayne, 1978.

———[ascribed]. *Jāmiʿat al-jāmiʿa*. Edited by ʿĀrif Tāmir. Beirut: Dār Maktabat al-Ḥayāt, 1970.

———. *Rasā'il Ikhwān al-Ṣafā'*. Beirut: Dār Ṣādir/Dār Bayrūt, 1957.

Izutsu, T. *Sufism and Taoism*. Berkeley and Los Angeles: University of California Press, 1984.

Jāmī, ʿAbd al-Raḥmān. *Lawā'iḥ: A Treatise on Sufism*. Translated by E.H. Whinfield and Mīrzā Muḥammad Ḳazwīnī. London, 1906. Reprint. London: Theosophical Publishing House, 1978.

———. *Naqd al-nuṣūṣ fī sharḥ naqsh al-fuṣūṣ*. Edited by W.C. Chittick. Tehran: Imperial Iranian Academy of Philosophy, 1977.

———. *Sharḥ fuṣūṣ al-ḥikam*. On the margin of al-Nābulsī's *Sharḥ fuṣūṣ al-ḥikam*. Cairo: Maṭbaʿat al-ʿĀmirat al-Sharafiyya, 1304–1323/1886–1905.

———. *Sharḥ-i rubāʿiyyāt*. Edited by Māyil Hirawī. Afghanistan: Anjuman-i Jāmī, 1343/1964.

———. *Silsilat al-dhahab*. In *Mathnawī-yi haft awrang*. Edited by M. Mudarris-i Gīlānī. Tehran: Saʿdī, 1337/1958.

Jandī, Mu'ayyid al-Dīn. *Sharḥ fuṣūṣ al-ḥikam*. Edited by S.J. Āshtiyānī. Mashhad: Dānishgāh-i Mashhad, 1361/1982. Supplemented with the Istanbul ms. Nur Osmaniye 2457.

Kalābādhī, Abū Bakr al-. *al-Taʿarruf li madhhab al-taṣawwuf*. Edited by ʿA.Ḥ. Maḥmūd and Ṭ.ʿA. Surūr. Cairo, 1960. Translated by A.J. Arberry as *The Doctrine of the Sufis*. Lahore: Sh. Muhammad Ashraf, 1966.

Kāshānī, ʿAbd al-Razzāq. *Iṣṭilāḥāt al-ṣūfiyya*. On the margin of Kāshānī's *Sharḥ manāzil al-sā'irīn*. Tehran: Ibrāhīm Lārījānī, 1315/1897–98.

———. *Sharḥ fuṣūṣ al-ḥikam*. Cairo: Muṣṭafā al-Bābī al-Ḥalabī, 1966.

———. *al-Ta'wīlāt* (*Ta'wīl al-Qur'ān*). Published as *Tafsīr al-Qur'ān al-karīm* and wrongly attributed to Ibn al-ʿArabī. Beirut: Dār al-Yaqẓat al-Adabiyya, 1968.

———. *Tuḥfat al-ikhwān fī khaṣā'iṣ al-fityān*. In *Rasā'il-i jawānmardān*. Edited by M. Ṣarrāf. Tehran: Institut Franco-Iranien, 1973.

Kāshānī, Bābā Afḍal. *Muṣannafāt-i Afḍal al-Dīn Muḥammad Maraqī Kāshānī*. Edited by M. Mīnuwī. Tehran: University of Tehran, 1331–37/1952–58.

Kāshānī, ʿIzz al-Dīn. *Miṣbāḥ al-hidāya*. Edited by J. Humā'ī. Tehran: Majlis, 1325/1946.

Kāshānī, Mullā Muḥsin Fayḍ. *Ā'īna-yi shāhī*. Shīrāz: Chāpkhāna-yi Mūsawī, 1320/1941. Translated by W. Chittick in "Two Seventeenth-Century Tracts on Kingship and Rulers." In *Authority and Political Culture in Shiʿism*, edited by Said Amir Arjomand, 267–304. Albany, N.Y.: SUNY Press, 1988.

Kisāʾī, al-. *The Tales of the Prophets of al-Kisaʾi*. Translated by W. Thackston. Boston: Twayne, 1978.

Kubrā, Najm al-Dīn. *Die Fawāʾiḥ al-Ǧamāl wa-Fawātiḥ al-Ǧalāl des Naǧm ad-Dīn Kubrā*. Edition and study by F. Meier. Wiesbaden: Franz Steiner Verlag, 1957.

Kulaynī, al-. *al-Uṣūl min al-kāfī*. Tehran: Maktabat al-Islāmiyya, 1388.

Lāhījī, Muḥammad. *Sharḥ-i Gulshan-i rāz*. Edited by K. Samīʿī. Tehran: Maḥmūdī, 1337/1958.

Lane, E.W. *An Arabic-English Lexicon*. Reprint. Cambridge, England: Islamic Texts Society, 1984.

Majlisī, Muḥammad Bāqir. *Biḥār al-anwār*. 110 vols. Reprint. Beirut: Muʾassasat al-Wafāʾ, 1983.

Makkī, Abū Ṭālib al-. *Qūt al-qulūb*. Cairo: Muṣṭafā al-Bābī al-Ḥalabī, 1961.

Maybudī, Rashīd al-Dīn. *Kashf al-asrār wa ʿuddat al-abrār*. Edited by ʿA. A. Ḥikmat. Tehran: Dānishgāh, 1331–39/1952–60.

McCarthy, R.J. *Freedom and Fulfillment: An Annotated Translation of al-Ghazālī's al-Munqidh min al-Ḍalāl and other Relevant Works of al-Ghazālī*. Boston: Twayne, 1980.

Morewedge, P. "The Internal Sense of Prehension (*Wahm*) in Islamic Philosophy." In *Philosophies of Being and Mind: Ancient and Medieval*. Edited by J.T.H. Martin. Delmar, N.Y.: Caravan Books, forthcoming.

Mufīd, Shaykh al-. *Kitāb al-Irshād: The Book of Guidance*. Translated by I.K.A. Howard. London: Muhammadi Trust, 1981.

Mullā Ṣadrā. *ʿArshiyya*. Edited by Gh. Āhanī. Isfahan: Kitābfurūshī-yi Shahriyār, 1341/1962. Translated by J. W. Morris as *The Wisdom of the Throne*. Princeton: Princeton University Press, 1981.

———. *al-Taʿlīqāt*. On the margin of Quṭb al-Dīn Shīrāzī's *Sharḥ ḥikmat al-ishrāq*. Tehran: Asad Allāh Harātī, 1313/1895–1896.

Murata, S. "Angels." In Nasr. *Islamic Spirituality: Foundations* 324–44.

Musallam, B. *Sex and Society in Islam: Birth Control before the Nineteenth Century*. Cambridge: Cambridge University Press, 1983.

Muslim. *al-Ṣaḥīḥ*. Cairo: Maṭbaʿa Muḥammad ʿAlī Ṣabīḥ, 1334/1915–16.

Nasafī, ʿAzīz al-Dīn. *Insān-i kāmil*. Edited by M. Molé. Tehran: Institut Franco-Iranien, 1962.

———. *Kashf al-ḥaqāʾiq*. Edited by A. Mahdawī-yi Dāmghānī. Tehran: Bungāh-i Tarjama wa Nashr-i Kitāb, 1344/1965.

———. *Zubdat al-ḥaqāʾiq*. Edited by Ḥ. Rabbānī. Appended to Jāmī's *Ashiʿʿat al-lamaʿāt*. Tehran: Kitābkhāna-yi ʿIlmiyya-yi Ḥāmidī, 1352/1973.

Nasāʾī, al-. *al-Sunan*. Beirut: Dār Iḥyāʾ al-Turāth al-ʿArabī, 1348/1929–30.

Nasr, S.H. *An Introduction to Islamic Cosmological Doctrines*. Cambridge: Harvard University Press, 1964.

———, ed. *Islamic Spirituality*. I *Foundations*. II *Manifestations*. New York: Crossroad, 1987–90.

———. "The Male and the Female in the Islamic Perspective." In Nasr. *Traditional Islam in the Modern World*. London: KPI, 1987.

———. "Spiritual Chivalry." In Nasr. *Islamic Spirituality: Manifestations* 304–15.

Nicholson, R.A. *Studies in Islamic Mysticism*. Cambridge: Cambridge University Press, 1967.

Nurbakhsh, J. *Sufi Women*. New York: Khaniqahi-Nimatullahi, 1983.

———. *Sufism* II-IV. New York and London: Khaniqahi-Nimatullahi, 1982–88.

Qayṣarī, Sharaf al-Dīn al-. *Sharḥ fuṣūṣ al-ḥikam*. Tehran: Dār al-Funūn, 1299/1882.

Qūnawī, Ṣadr al-Dīn al-. *Fakk al-khutūm (al-Fukūk)*. On the margin of Kāshānī's *Sharḥ manāzil al-sāʾirīn*. Tehran: Ibrāhīm Lārījānī, 1315/1897–98.

———. *Iʿjāz al-bayān fī taʾwīl umm al-Qurʾān*. Hyderabad-Deccan: Osmania Oriental Publications Bureau, 1949. Also printed as *al-Tafsīr al-ṣūfī li'l-Qur'ān*. Edited by ʿA. Aḥmad ʿAṭā'. Cairo: Dār al-Kutub al-Ḥadītha, 1969.

———. *Miftāḥ al-ghayb*. Printed on the margin of Shams al-Dīn Muḥammad al-Fanārī's *Miṣbāḥ al-ins bayn al-maʿqūl wa'l-manqūl fī sharḥ Miftāḥ ghayb al-jamʿ wa'l-wujūd*. Tehran: Aḥmad Shīrāzī, 1323/1905.

———. *al-Nafaḥāt al-ilāhiyya*. Tehran: Aḥmad Shīrāzī, 1316/1898.

———. *Sharḥ al-ḥadīth* (Istanbul mss.: Şehid Ali Paşa 138/2, 1369/1, 1394/2; Hacı Mahmud Ef. 574; Crh. 2085/7, 2097/6; Ibrahim Ef. 870/1).

———. *Tabṣirat al-mubtadī wa tadhkirat al-muntahī*. Edited by Najafʿalī Ḥabībī. *Maʿārif-i islāmī* I (1364/1985) 69–128.

Qushayrī, Abu'l-Qāsim al-. *Laṭā'if al-ishārāt*. Edited by I. Basyūnī. Cairo: Al-Hay'at al-Miṣriyyat al-ʿĀmmat li'l-Ta'līf wa'l-Nashr, n.d.–1971.

———. *al-Risāla*. Edited by ʿAbd al-Ḥalīm Maḥmūd and Maḥmūd ibn al-Sharīf. Cairo: Dār al-Kutub al-Ḥadītha, 1972.

Rahman, F. *Avicenna's Psychology*. London: Oxford University Press, 1952.

Rāzī, Fakhr al-Dīn al-. *al-Tafsīr al-kabīr*. Istanbul: Dār al-Ṭibāʿat al-ʿĀmira, 1307–08/1889–91.

Rāzī, Najm al-Dīn. *Mirṣād al-ʿibād*. Edited by M. A. Riyāḥī. Tehran: Bungāh-i Tarjama wa Nashr-i Kitāb, 1352/1973. Translated by H. Algar. *The Path of God's Bondsmen from Origin to Return*. Delmar, NY: Caravan Books, 1982.

Renard, J. "Al-Jihād al-Akbar: Notes on a Theme in Islamic Spirituality." *Muslim World* 78 (1988) 225–42.

Robson, J., trans. *Mishkat al-masabih*. Lahore: Sh. Muhammad Ashraf, 1963–65.

Rūmī, Jalāl al-Dīn. *Dīwān-i Shams-i Tabrīzī*. Edited by B. Furūzānfar as *Kulliyyāt-i Shams yā dīwān-i kabīr*. Tehran: Dānishgāh, 1336–46/1957–67.

———. *Fīhi mā fīhi*. Edited by B. Furūzānfar. Tehran: Amīr Kabīr, 1969.

———. *Majālis-i sabʿa*. In the introduction to *Mathnawī-yi maʿnawī*. Edited by M. Ramaḍānī. Tehran: Kulāla-yi Khāwar, 1315–19/1926–30.

———. *The Mathnawī*. Edited and translated by R.A. Nicholson. London: Luzac, 1925–40.

Rūzbihān Baqlī. *ʿAbhar al-ʿāshiqīn*. Edited by H. Corbin and M. Moin. *Les Jasmin des Fidèles d'amour*. Tehran: Institut Franco-Iranien, 1958.

———. *Mashrab al-arwāḥ*. Edited by N. M. Hoca. Istanbul: Edebiyat Fakültesi Matbaası, 1974.

———. *Risālat al-quds*. Edited by J. Nūrbakhsh. Tehran: Khānaqāh-i Niʿmatullāhī, 1351/1972.

Ṣadūq. *al-Tawḥīd*. Edited by Hāshim al-Ḥusaynī. Tehran: Maktabat al-Ṣadūq, 1387/1967.

Samʿānī, Aḥmad. *Rawḥ al-arwāḥ fī sharḥ asmā' al-malik al-fattāḥ*. Edited by N. Māyil Hirawī. Tehran: Intishārāt-i ʿIlmī wa Farhangī, 1368/1989.

Sanā'ī Ghaznawī. *Ḥadīqat al-ḥaqā'iq*. Edited by Mudarris Raḍawī. Tehran: Sipihr, 1329/1950.

Sarrāj, Abū Naṣr al-. *Kitāb al-lumaʿ*. Edited by R.A. Nicholson. Leiden: Brill, 1914.

Sayyid-Marsot, Afaf Lutfi al-, ed. *Society and the Sexes in Medieval Islam*. Malibu: Undena, 1979.

Schimmel, A. *As Through a Veil: Mystical Poetry in Islam*. New York: Columbia University Press, 1982.

———. *Islam in the Indian Subcontinent*. Leiden-Cologne: Brill, 1980.

———. *Mystical Dimensions of Islam*. Chapel Hill: University of North Carolina Press, 1975.

———. *The Triumphal Sun: A Study of the Works of Jalāloddin Rumi*. London: Fine Books, 1978.

———. "Women in Mystical Islam." In *Women and Islam*, edited by Azizah al-Hibri, et al., 145–51. Elmsford, N.Y.: Pergamon Press, 1982.

Smith, J.I. and Y.Y Haddad. "Eve: Islamic Image of Woman." In *Women and Islam*, edited by Azizah al-Hibri, et al., 135–44. Elmsford, N.Y.: Pergamon Press, 1982.

———. "The Virgin Mary in Islamic Tradition and Commentary." *Muslim World* 79 (1989) 161–87.

Shabistarī, Maḥmūd. *Gulshan-i rāz*. See Lāhījī.

Smith, M. *Rabia the Mystic and Her Fellow Saints in Islam* (1928). Reprint. Lahore: Hijra International, 1983.

SPK. See Chittick. *Sufi Path of Knowledge*.

SPL. See Chittick. *Sufi Path of Love*.

Suhrawardī, Shihāb al-Dīn Abū Hafṣ. *ʿAwārif al-maʿārif*. Beirut: Dār al-Kitāb al-ʿArabī, 1966.

Suhrawardī al-Maqtūl, Shihāb al-Dīn. *Majmūʿa-yi āthār-i fārsī*. Edited by S.H. Nasr. Tehran: Imperial Iranian Academy of Philosophy, 1977.

——— *The Mystical and Visionary Treatises of Shihabuddin Yahya Suhrawardi*. Translated by W. Thackston. London: Octagon, 1982.

Sulamī, Abū ʿAbd al-Raḥman al-. *The Book of Sufi Chivalry*. Translated by Tosun Bayrak. New York: Inner Traditions, 1983.

———. *ʿUyūb al-nafs wa mudāwātuhā*. Edited by E. Kohlberg. Jerusalem: Jerusalem Academic Press, 1976.

Suyūṭī, Jalāl al-Dīn al-. *al-Jāmiʿ al-ṣaghīr*. In al-Munāwī. *Fayḍ al-qadīr fī sharḥ al-jāmiʿ al-ṣaghīr*. Beirut: Dār al-Maʿrifa, 1972.

Ṭabrisī, Faḍl al-. *Majmaʿ al-bayān*. Edited by S. Ḥ. al-Rasūlī al-Maḥallātī. Tehran: Maktabat al-ʿIlmiyyat al-Islāmiyya, n.d.

Tabrīzī. *Mishkāt al-maṣābīḥ*. Delhi: Maṭbaʿ al-Mujtabā'ī, 1325/1907.

Tirmidhī, al-. *al-Jāmiʿ al-ṣaḥīḥ, wa huwa sunan al-Tirmidhī*. Edited by A.M. Shākir. Cairo: al-Maktabat al-Islāmiyya, 1938.

Tirmidhī, al-Ḥakīm al-. *Bayān al-farq bayn al-ṣadr wa'l-qalb wa'l-fu'ād wa'l-lubb*. Edited by Nicholas Heer. Cairo: ʿĪsā al-Bābī al-Ḥalabī, 1958. Translated by Heer as "A Ṣūfī Psychological Treatise." *Muslim World* 51 (1961) 25–36, 83–91, 163–72, 244–58.

Wensinck, A.J., et al. *Concordance et indices de la tradition musulmane*. Leiden: Brill, 1936–69.

Wilhelm, R., trans. *I Ching or Book of Changes*. London: Routledge & Kegan Paul, 1951.

Yahya, O. *Histoire et classification de l'oeuvre d'Ibn ʿArabī*. Damascus: Institut Français de Damas, 1964.

INDEX OF KORANIC VERSES

1:4 Thee alone we serve and Thee alone we ask for help. 71, 72–73, 102

2:2 A guidance for the godfearing. 140

2:19 The likeness of [the hypocrites] is . . . as a cloudburst out of heaven. . . . 127

2:22 . . . who assigned to you earth for a bedding, and heaven for a building. . . . 119, 184

2:22 So set not up compeers to God willingly. 244

2:29 It is He who created for you all that is in the earth. . . seven heavens. 120, 246–47

2:30 I am placing in the earth a vicegerent. 44, 65, 308

2:30 What, wilt Thou set therein one who will do corruption . . . while we proclaim Thy praise . . . ? 36, 138, 220, 286

2:30 I know what you know not. 41, 138, 286

2:31 He taught Adam the names. . . . 41, 66, 89, 273, 308

2:32 We know nothing but what Thou hast taught us. 308

2:34 When We said to the angels, "Prostrate yourselves to Adam." So they prostrated themselves, except Iblis. . . . 274

2:35 We said, "Adam, dwell with your wife in the Garden. . . ." 274

2:36 Then Satan caused them to slip therefrom. . . . 274

2:55 "Moses, we will not have faith in you till we see God openly". . . . 337n72

2:59 We sent down upon the wrongdoers punishment out of heaven. . . . 125

2:60 Now the people knew their drinking places. 337n64

2:63 Remember what is in it; haply you will be godfearing. 293

2:74 Then your hearts became hardened. . . . 291

2:97 [Gabriel] it was who brought [the Koran] down upon thy heart. . . . 290

2:107 Do you not know that God's is the kingdom of the heavens and the earth? 124

2:115 Wherever you turn, there is the face of God. 9, 53, 89, 92

2:116 To Him belongs all that is in the heavens and the earth. . . . 124

2:145 If thou followest their caprices. . . . 123

2:164 Surely in the creation of the heavens and the earth. . . . are signs for a people having intelligence. 125, 212, 238, 244

2:168 O people, eat of what is in the earth. . . . 246

2:170 And when it is said to them, "Follow what God has sent down." . . . 238

2:171 Deaf, dumb, blind—they do not understand. 229

2:177 Those who are faithful to their covenants. . . . 71

2:186 When My servants ask you about Me—surely, I am near. . . . 53, 76, 208

2:187 They are a garment for you, and you are a garment for them. 181

2:187 So God explicates His signs to people. . . . 293

2:213 God . . . sent down with them the Book with the Real. . . . 121

2:213 God guides whomsoever He will to a straight path. 113

2:225 God . . . will take you to task for what your hearts have earned. 289, 290

2:228 Divorced women shall wait by themselves for three periods. . . . God is Inaccessible, Wise. 173

2:228 They have [rights over their husbands] similar to those [their husbands have] over them. . . . 174, 176, 177

2:228 The men have a degree above them. 173–74, 177, 179, 180, 181, 183, 195

2:245 God contracts, and He expands. . . . 90

2:255 He is the Alive, the Self-subsistent. 127, 235

2:257 God . . . brings them forth from the darknesses into the light. 253

2:260 Show me how Thou bringest the dead to life. 74

2:267–68 . . . Satan promises you poverty and commands you unto indecency. . . . 257

2:282 Fear God and God will teach you. 260

2:283 And conceal not the testimony; whoso conceals it, his heart is sinful. 291

3:5 From God nothing whatever is hidden in heaven and earth. 118

3:6 It is He who forms you in the wombs as He will. 149

3:8 Our Lord, make not our hearts to swerve after that Thou hast guided us. . . . 290

3:17 And God sees His servants . . . the patient, the truthful, the obedient, the expenders. . . . 172

3:42–45 And when the angels said to Mary "God has chosen you." . . . 313–14

3:59 The likeness of Jesus, in God's sight, is as the likeness of Adam. 178

3:67 Abraham in truth was . . . submitted, unswerving. 261

3:79 Be you lordly. 348n54

3:83 To Him is submitted everyone in the heavens and the earth. 203

3:96 The first house established for the people was that at Mecca, a place blessed. 139

3:97 [God is] independent of the worlds. 51

3:103 . . . He brought your hearts together, so that by His blessing you became brothers. 291

3:106 A day on which some faces shall be whitened and others blackened. 137

3:154 And a party had grieved, thinking of God thoughts that were not the Real. . . . 122

3:159 . . . Hadst thou been harsh and hard of heart, they would have scattered from about thee. 291

3:163 They are degrees with God. 129, 134

4:1 Fear your Lord, who created you from a single soul, and from her He created her spouse, and from the two of them scattered forth many men and women. 197, 309

4:4 Give the women their dowers as a free gift. 175

4:19 Treat them with honor. 174

4:34 Men stand over the women for that God has preferred one of them over the other in bounty. 178, 355n2

4:36 Serve God and associate naught with Him and be good to parents. 313

4:43 Do not approach the ritual prayer while you are drunk. . . . 78

4:135 Be those who stand firmly in justice. 267

4:135 Follow not caprice, lest you swerve. 123

5:13 . . . We cursed them and made their hearts hard. 291

5:17 To God belongs the kingdom of the heavens and of the earth and all that is between them. 131

5:41 Those are they whose hearts God desired not to purify. . . . 291

5:48 Follow not their caprices, leaving the Real that has come to thee. 123

5:54 He loves them, and they love Him. 9, 70

5:58 . . . That is because they are a people who have no intelligence. 238

5:64 His two hands are outspread; He expends how He will. 82

5:77 . . . Go not beyond the bounds in your religion, other than the Real. . . . 122

5:108 Fear God and listen. 260

5:116 Thou knowest what is in my self but I know not what is in Thy self. 237

5:119 God is pleased with them and they are pleased with Him. 71

6:1 Praise belongs to God, who created the heavens and the earth and appointed the darknesses and the light. 121, 124

6:12 . . . has written mercy against Himself. 138

6:59 With Him are the keys to the Unseen. . . . 149

6:59 There is not a thing, fresh or withered, but in a Manifest Book. 164, 167

6:73 It is He who created the heavens and the earth with the Real. . . . 122, 130

6:74 . . . the Knower of the unseen and the visible. 118

6:91 And you were taught what you did not know, neither you nor your fathers. 348n54

6:96 That is the ordaining of the Inaccessible, the Knowing. 306

6:97 It is He who has appointed for you the stars. . . . signs for a people who know. 24

6:99 It is He who sent down out of heaven water. . . . signs for a people who have faith. 125, 245–46

6:112 We have appointed for every prophet an enemy. 239

6:122 Why, is he who was dead, and We gave him life . . . as one who is in the darknesses . . . ? 253

6:141 God does not love the immoderate. 246

6:151 Slay no soul that God has forbidden, except by the Real. 122

6:161 Say: "As for me, . . . the creed of Abraham, unswerving." 261

7:8 The weighing on that day is the Real. 122

7:8 He whose scales are heavy, they are the prosperers. . . . 277

7:12 He said, "What prevented you from prostrating yourself." . . . Said he, "I am better than he. . . ." "You are among the humbled." 269, 274–75. Cf. 38:76.

7:20 Then Satan whispered to them . . . "Your Lord has prohibited you from this tree lest you become two angels. . . ." 275

7:21–23 And he swore to them, "Truly, I am for you two a sincere adviser." . . . 275

7:26 Children of Adam! We have sent down on you a garment to cover your shameful parts. . . . 276

7:54 God . . . created the heavens and the earth in six days. Then He sat Himself upon the Throne. 121, 234

7:54 He makes the night cover the day, which it pursues urgently. . . . 121, 146

7:54 Verily, His are the creation and the command. . . . 88, 234, 308

7:58 And the good land. . . . Even so We turn about the signs for a people who have gratitude. 24

7:100 Did We will, We would smite them because of their sins, sealing their hearts so that they do not listen. 260

7:137 All the east and the west of the land that We had blessed. 139

7:143 Show me, that I might gaze upon Thee. 75

7:143 Thou shalt not see Me. 75

7:145 We wrote on the tablets something of Everything. 166

7:151 . . . Most merciful of those who have mercy. 87

7:155 It is only Thy trial whereby Thou misleadest whom Thou wilt and Thou guidest whom Thou wilt. 200

7:156 My mercy embraces all things, and I shall write it down. . . . 107, 206, 315

7:162 We sent down upon them punishment out of heaven for their wrongdoing. 125

7:172 He made them bear witness. . . . Am I not your Lord? . . . Yes, we give witness. 70, 71, 280

7:176 . . . He inclined toward the earth and followed his own caprice. . . . 306

7:176 The likeness of him is as the likeness of a dog. 280

7:179 We have created for Gehenna many jinn and men. . . . They are like cattle; no, they are even more misguided. . . . 228–29, 290

7:181 Of those We created are a nation who guide by the Real, and by it act with justice. 122

7:189 It is He who created you from one soul and made from it its spouse that he might rest in her. 121, 146, 154, 226, 305, 340n10. Cf. 4:1, 30:21.

7:189 Then, when he covered her, she bore a light burden. . . . 146

7:201 The godfearing, when a visitation from Satan touches them, remember. . . . 129, 293

8:11 He sends down on you water . . . to purify you thereby. 130

8:24 Know that God comes in between a man and his heart. . . . 289–90

8:37 God will distinguish the loathsome from the good . . . and put them in Gehenna. 90

8:63 He has made their hearts familiar. . . . 300–301

9:15 He will remove the rage within their hearts. . . . 291

9:30 The Jews say, "Ezra is the son of God." The Christians say, "The Messiah is the son of God." 345n31

9:45 Those whose hearts are filled with doubt. . . . 290

9:64 The hypocrites are afraid, lest a sura should be sent down against them, telling thee what is in their hearts. 289

9:104 Do they not know that God is He who receives repentance from His servants and takes the free will offerings? 98

9:112 . . . the repenters, the worshipers, the praisers, the fasters. 180, 296

10:2 They have a foot of truthfulness with their Lord. 85–86

10:5 It is He who made the sun a radiance. . . . God created that not save with the Real. . . . 122

10:6 In the alternation of night and day . . . are signs for a godfearing people. 24

10:21 When We let the people taste mercy after hardship. . . . Say: "God is swifter at deception." 276

10:32 That then is God, your Lord, the Real. What is there after the Real save going astray? 121

10:35–36 Say: "Is there any of your associates who guides to the Real?" . . . 121

10:61 Not so much as the weight of an ant in earth or heaven escapes from thy Lord. 119

10:108 O people, the Real has come to you from your Lord. . . . 122

11:7 It is He who created the heavens and the earth in six days. . . . that He might try you. . . . 123

11:40 Carry in it two of every kind. 59, 60, 87

11:69 Our messengers came to Abraham . . . , and he made no delay in bringing a roasted calf. 341n36

11:105–108 . . . Some of them shall be wretched and some felicitous. . . . 230

11:118–19 . . . cease not to differ, except those on whom thy Lord has mercy, and for that He created them. 341n44

11:123 To Him will be returned the whole affair. 87

12:30 Love for him has rent her innermost heart. 297

12:31 This is no mortal man, this is but a noble angel! 280

12:53 The soul commands to evil, except inasmuch as my Lord has mercy. 256, 283, 295

13:1 . . . And that which has been sent down to thee from thy Lord is the Real. . . . 122

13:2 He governs the affair, He differentiates the signs. 12, 63

13:3 It is He who stretched out the earth and set therein firm mountains. . . . 245

13:4 Surely in that there are signs for a people who have intelligence. 238, 245

13:15 To God prostrate themselves all who are in the heavens and the earth as do their shadows. . . . 124

13:17 He sends down out of heaven water, and the wadis flow each in its measure. . . . 128–30

13:19 What, is he who knows that what is sent down to thee from thy Lord is the Real, like him who is blind? . . . 122

13:23–24 And the angels shall enter unto them from every gate. . . . 263

13:28 . . . in God's remembrance are at peace the hearts of those who have faith. . . . 260, 291, 298

13:33 What, is He who stands over every soul through what it earns . . . ? 178, 222

13:39 God obliterates whatsoever He will, and He establishes; and with Him is the Mother of the Book. 154

14:1 . . . that thou mayest bring forth mankind from the darknesses to the light. . . . 253

14:19 Have you not seen that God created the heavens and the earth with the Real? 122

14:27 God misguides the wrongdoers. 113

14:32–34 It is God who created the heavens and the earth and sent down out of heaven water. . . . 125, 245

14:33 And He subjected to you the sun and the moon. . . . 123

14:48 On the day the earth shall be changed to other than the earth. . . . 120

15:8 We send not down the angels, save with the Real. 125

15:21–22 Naught is there, but its treasuries are with Us, and We send it not down but in a known measure. . . . 125

15:26 . . . dry clay, . . . stinking mud. . . . 138, 271–72

15:28 . . . "I am creating a mortal from a clay of molded mud. When I have proportioned him. . . ." 233, 339n53

15:29 I blew into him of My spirit. 43, 190, 212, 235, 237, 284, 287, 307, 347n34

15:42 Surely, My servants. . . . 76

15:85 We created the heavens and the earth and everything between the two only with the Real. 122

16:10 It is He who sends down to you out of heaven water of which you drink. . . . 125

16:13 And that which He has multiplied for you in the earth. . . . a sign for a people who remember. 24

16:22 . . . Their hearts deny, and they have waxed proud. 290

16:40 Our only word to a thing, when We desire it, is to say to it "Be," and it is. 148, 151, 152

16:48 Have they not seen all things that God has created casting their shadows to the right and to the left . . . ? 205

16:49 To God prostrate themselves all who are in the heavens, and every creature crawling on the earth. . . . 124, 205

16:50 They fear their Lord above them and they do what they are commanded. 205

16:60 And God's is the highest likeness. 33

16:78 And God brought you out from the bellies of your mothers. . . . 221, 348n54

16:79 Have they not regarded the birds. . . . signs for a people who have faith. 24

17:1 Glory be to Him who carried His servant by night . . . to the Further Mosque, the precincts of which We have blessed. . . . 139, 302–303

17:2–7 And We gave Moses the Book. . . . And We have made Gehenna a confinement for the unbelievers. 303–304

17:23–24 Thy Lord has decreed that you shall not worship any but Him, and to be good to parents. . . . 147

17:27 Verily the squanderers are brothers of Satan. 246

17:44 . . . There is nothing that does not glorify Him in praise. . . . 124, 126

17:53 Say to My servants. . . . 76

17:55 We preferred some of the prophets over others. 129

17:71 . . . Whoso is given his book in his right hand. . . . 82

17:81 The Real has come and the unreal has vanished away. . . . 110, 121

17:82–84 . . . Your Lord knows very well who is best guided as to the way. 302

17:85 . . . The spirit is from the command of my Lord. . . . 233, 233–34

17:95 Had there been in the earth angels walking at peace. . . . 125

17:105–106 With the Real We have sent [the Koran] down. . . . 122

17:110 Call upon Allah, or call upon the All-merciful. . . . 206

18:13 They were chivalrous youths who had faith in their Lord. 267

18:13–14 And We increased them in guidance, and We strengthened their hearts. 267, 290

18:17 You might have seen the sun, when it rose, inclining from their Cave towards the right. . . . 301

18:28 Obey not him whose heart We have made forgetful of Our remembrance. . . . 123, 290

18:29 But say: "The Real is from your Lord. . . ." 123

18:46 . . . subsisting works, deeds of righteousness. 277

18:57 Surely We have laid coverings upon their hearts. . . . 290

18:109 Say: "If the sea were ink for the Words of my Lord. . . ." 164

18:110 Say: "I am only a mortal like you. . . ." 265

19:17 [Gabriel] became imaginalized to her. . . . 181

19:19 I am but a messenger come from your Lord. . . . 181

19:23 And the pangs of childbirth drove her to the trunk of the palm tree. 313

19:52 . . . right side of the mountain. 82

19:93 None is there in the heavens and the earth that comes not to the All-merciful as a servant. 101, 102, 124, 204

20:4–6 He created the earth and the high heavens. . . . and all that is beneath the soil. 121

20:5 The All-merciful sat upon the Throne. 86, 219, 353n29

20:50 He gave everything its creation, then guided. 104, 196

20:53 He . . . sent down water out of heaven, and therewith We have brought forth pairs of various growing things. 126

20:55 Out of the earth We created you, and We shall restore you into it. 140, 341n49

21:2 . . . their hearts neglectful. 290

21:4 My Lord knows what is said in heaven and earth. 119

21:19–20 Those who are with Him wax not too proud to do Him service. . . . 168

21:30 Have not the unbelievers beheld that the heavens and the earth were a mass all sewn up . . . ? 120, 136, 158

21:32 We set up the heaven as a well-protected roof. 139, 140

21:102 They shall dwell forever with the objects of their souls' appetite. 187

21:104 On the day when We shall roll up heaven as a scroll is rolled for the writings. 83

22:5 We created you of dust, then of a sperm drop. . . . And We establish in the wombs what We will. . . . 216

22:5 It swells and puts forth herbs of every joyous kind. 152

22:6 That is because God is the Real. . . . 121

22:18 Have you not seen how before God prostrate themselves all who are in the heavens . . . and many of mankind? 204

22:32 . . . that is of the godfearing of the hearts. 291

22:46 . . . so that they have hearts to intellect with or ears to hear with? . . . 238, 290

22:52 Satan cast into his wish, when he was wishing. 129

22:61 God makes the nighttime enter into the daytime. . . . 146, 147

22:62 That is because God is the Real. . . . 121

22:63 Hast thou not seen how God has sent down out of heaven water . . . ? 125

22:65 Hast thou not seen that God has subjected to you all that is in the earth . . . ? 120, 123

22:65 He holds back heaven lest it should fall upon the earth. . . . 120

22:70 Did you not know that God knows all that is in heaven and earth? . . . easy for God. 119, 153

23:18 And We sent down out of heaven water in measure and lodged it in the earth. 125

23:71 Had the Real followed their caprices. . . . 110, 122, 284

23:78 It is He who made for you hearing and eyes and hearts. . . . 228

24:25 On that day . . . they shall know that God is the manifest Real. 122

24:35 God is the light of the heavens and the earth . . . even if no fire touched it. 160, 232, 299–300

24:35 Light upon light. God guides to His Light whom He will. 299, 300

24:50 What, is their sickness in their hearts . . . ? 291

25:25 Upon the day that heaven is split asunder . . . and the angels are sent down in majesty. 127

25:43 Have you seen him who has taken his caprice to be his god? 123

25:53 It is He who let forth the two oceans . . . between them a *barzakh*. . . . 160

25:61 Blessed is He who has set in heaven constellations. 139

26:4 If We will, We shall send down on them out of heaven a sign. . . . 125

26:87–89 . . . except for him who comes to God with a faultless heart. 291

26:192–94 . . . brought down by the Faithful Spirit upon thy heart. 290

27:1 . . . the Koran and a Manifest Book. 167

27:60 He who . . . sent down for you out of heaven water. . . . 125

27:75 . . . in a Manifest Book. 119

28:15 This is of Satan's doing; he is surely a blatant misguiding enemy. 239

28:30 [A voice called . . .] in the blessed hollow. 139

28:50 Who is further astray than he who follows his caprice rather than guidance from God? 123

28:88 Everything is perishing but His face. 32, 52, 309

29:22 You are not able to frustrate Him either in the earth or in heaven. 119

29:44 God created the heavens and the earth with the Real. . . . 122

29:64 Surely the abode of the next world—that is life, did they but know. 114, 262

29:69 Those who struggle in Us. . . . 234

30:7 They know an outward dimension of the life of this world. . . . 229

30:8 . . . did not create the heavens and the earth and everything between the two except through the Real. 119

30:20 . . . He created you of dust. . . . 26

30:21 And among His signs is that He created for you, of your own souls, spouses, so that you might rest in them, and He has placed between you love and mercy. . . . 154, 313. Cf. 7:189.

30:24 And of His signs is that He shows you lightning. . . . signs for a people who have intellect. 24

30:25 And of His signs is that the heaven and earth stand firm by His command. 120

31:20 Have you not seen how God has subjected to you everything in the heavens and the earth? 55, 123

32:4 God is He that created the heavens and the earth and everything between the two in six days. 119

32:5 He governs the affair from the heaven to the earth. 193

32:7–9 He originated the creation of man out of clay. . . . and He blew into him of His spirit. 233

32:17 No soul knows what comfort is laid up for them secretly. . . . 219, 262

33:5 . . . only in what your hearts premeditate. 289

33:12 When the hypocrites, and those in whose hearts is sickness. . . . 291

33:33 Display not your beauty as did the pagans of old. 317

33:35 The submitted ones and the submitted ones, the faithful and the faithful . . . a mighty wage. 172, 179–80

33:43 . . . to bring you forth from the darknesses into the light. 253

33:51 God knows what is in your hearts. 289

33:52 Thereafter women are not lawful to thee. . . . 186

33:72 We offered the Trust to the heavens and the earth and the mountains. . . . 123, 287

35:10 To Him good words go up, and the righteous deed—He uplifts it. 262

35:27 Hast thou not seen how God sends down out of heaven water. . . . 125

35:31 What We have revealed to thee of the Book is the Real. . . . 121

36:37 And a sign for them is the nighttime: We draw the daytime out from it. 146

36:69–70 . . . That he may warn whosoever is alive. 212

36:71 Of that which Our own hands wrought. 85, 88

36:82 His only command, when He desires a thing, is to say to it "Be!" and it is. 13, 158

36:83 In His hand is the dominion of each thing. 205

37:11 . . . sticky clay. . . . 137, 138

37:96 He created you and what you do. 204

37:164 None of us there is but has a known station. 104, 287

37:180 Glory be to God, the Lord of Inaccessibility, above everything that they describe. 8

38:17 Remember Our servant David, the man of might. 84

38:26 O David, . . . rule among people with the Real and follow not caprice. 122

38:27 We have not created heaven and earth and everything between the two as vanity. 122

38:35 My Lord, forgive me, and give me a kingdom such as may not come to anyone after me. 352n100

38:37–38 . . . and the satans, every builder and diver, and others also, coupled in fetters. 353n101

38:71 I am about to create a mortal from clay. 39

38:75 What prevented you from prostrating yourself before him whom I created with My own two hands? 81, 88, 89, 90, 91, 101, 138, 308

38:76 I am better than he. . . . 96, 316, 323, 325. Cf. 7:12.

39:6 He created you of a single soul, then from it He appointed its spouse. 121

39:6 He creates you in your mothers' wombs, creation after creation, in threefold shadows. 345n26

39:22 Is he whose breast God has opened up to submission . . . ? 256, 291–92, 297

39:22 But woe to those whose hearts are hardened. . . . 291–92

39:23 . . . their skins and their hearts soften to the remembrance of God. 291

39:42 God takes the souls at the time of their death. . . . signs for a people who reflect. 24

39:53 O My servants who have been immoderate . . . , despair not of God's mercy—surely God forgives all sins. 79, 84

39:67 The earth altogether shall be His handful on the Day of Resurrection, and the heavens shall be rolled up in His right hand. . . . 83, 90, 101, 108, 114, 214

39:73 . . . "Peace be upon you! Well you have fared; enter in, to dwell forever." 262

40:7 Our Lord, Thou embracest all things in mercy and knowledge. 315

40:13 It is He who shows you His signs and sends down to you out of heaven provision. 125

40:16 Whose is the Kingdom today? God's, the One, the Intensely Severe. 333n12

40:57 The creation of the heavens and the earth is greater than the creation of mankind. 179

41:9–10 What, do you disbelieve in Him who created the earth in two days? . . . And He set therein firm mountains over it. . . . 120, 139–40

41:11–12 Then He lifted Himself to heaven when it was smoke. . . . He determined them as seven heavens in two days. 120, 134

41:12 He revealed its command to each heaven. 143

41:31 Therein you shall have all the objects of your souls' appetite. . . . 187

41:53 We shall show them Our signs upon the horizons and within their own souls. . . . 23, 25, 225, 227, 230

42:11 Nothing is like Him. 8, 52, 88, 89, 118

42:11 He is the Hearing, the Seeing. 88

43:10–11 He who appointed the earth to be a cradle for you, . . . even so you shall be brought forth. 125

43:68 O My servants, today no fear is on you. . . . 76

43:71 Therein shall be all the objects of the souls' appetite. . . . 219, 262

43:84 It is He who in heaven is God and in earth is God. 118

44:38–39 We created not the heavens and earth . . . in play. . . . 122

45:5 . . . the provision God sends down from heaven, and therewith brings the earth to life. . . . 125

45:13 He has subjected to you what is in the heavens and what is in the earth. . . . 123, 145, 148

47:24 . . . Or is it that there are locks upon their hearts? 290

48:4 It is He who sent down tranquility into the hearts of the believers. . . . 290

48:26 When the unbelievers set in their hearts fierceness. . . . 291

48:26 He fastened to them the word of godfearing. 138

49:3 Those are they whose hearts God has tested for godfearing. . . . 291

49:7 But God has made you love faith, decking it out fair in your hearts. . . . 291

49:13 O people, We created you from a male and a female. 186

49:14 You do not have faith; rather say, "We submit," for faith has not yet entered your hearts. 290

50:9–11 And We sent down out of heaven water blessed . . . and thereby We brought to life a land that was dead. 125

50:16 We are nearer to the human being than the jugular vein. 9, 53

50:17–18 When the two angels meet together, sitting one on the right, and one on the left. . . . 84

50:22 Today We have lifted thy covering, so thy sight today is piercing. 281

50:30 Are there any more? 86

50:33 Whosoever fears the All-merciful in the Unseen, and comes with a penitent heart. 291

50:37 Surely in that is a reminder for him who has a heart. . . . 185–86, 290, 294, 298

51:20–21 In the earth are signs for those having sure faith, and in your selves/souls—what, do you not see? 24, 61, 125, 140

51:22–23 And in heaven are your provision. . . . It is as surely Real as that you have speech. 125

51:47 And heaven—We built it with might [hands]. . . . 84, 125

51:48 And the earth—We spread it forth. . . . 125–26

51:49 And of everything We created a pair. . . . 12, 14, 117, 126, 152, 171, 293

51:50 So flee unto God. 117, 118

51:56 I created jinn and mankind only to worship/serve Me. 26, 54, 123, 172, 243

53:1 By the star when it falls. 284

53:8–9 He drew near and suspended hung, two bows' length away or nearer. 286

53:11–13 His [inner] heart lies not of what he saw. . . . 290, 297

53:44 He makes to die and makes to live. 87

53:45 God Himself created the pair, male and female. . . . 12, 87, 171

54:50 Our command is but one [word], like the blink of an eye. 88, 166

54:55 . . . in a sitting place of truthfulness, in the presence of a King Omnipotent. 262

55:7–11 And heaven—He raised it up. . . . And earth—He set it down. . . . 120

55:14 . . . like baked clay. 272

55:19–20 He let forth the two oceans that meet together, between them a *barzakh*. . . . 160, 161, 310

55:22 From the two come forth the pearl and the coral. 161

55:27 The face of Thy Lord remains. 85

55:29 All those in the heavens ask from Him; each day He is upon some task. 126, 245

56:27–43 The Companions of the Right. . . . The Companions of the Left. . . . 82

56:89 Then repose, and ease, and a garden of delight. 295

57:1 Everything in the heavens and the earth glorifies God. 203

57:3 . . . the Outward and the Inward. 200

57:4 He is with you wherever you are. 9, 53, 70, 72, 221

57:9 . . . that He may bring you forth from the darknesses into the light. 253

57:12 . . . their light running before them and on their right hands. . . . 83, 137

57:16 Is it not time that the hearts of those who have faith should be humbled. . . . 291

57:27 And We set in the hearts of those who followed him tenderness and mercy. 291

58:22 He has written in their hearts faith and confirmed them with a spirit from Him. 71, 84, 169, 290, 297

59:14 Their valor is great, . . . but their hearts are scattered. . . . 290

59:23 . . . the Invincible, the Magnificent. 252

59:24 . . . the Creator, the Author, the Form-giver. 252

60:13 . . . who have despaired of the world to come. . . . 260

64:1–2 All that is in the heavens and all that is in the earth glorifies God. . . . And God sees the things that you do. 114

64:11 . . . Whosoever has faith in God, He will guide his heart. . . . 290

65:12 He created seven heavens. 120

64:14–15 O believers, you have an enemy in your wives and children . . . your wealth and your children are only a trial. 199–200

66:4 If you two support one another against him, God is his Protector, and Gabriel. . . . 177

66:5 . . . the repenters, the worshipers, the fasters. 180

66:6 . . . disobey God not in what He commands them and do what they are commanded. 230

67:2 He created death and life to test you. . . . 200

68:1 *Nūn*. By the Pen and what they inscribe! 12, 153, 164, 168

69:19–26 Then as for him who is given his book in his right hand. . . . 82

74:31 And none knows the armies of thy Lord save He. 242

75:2 Nay, I swear by the blaming soul! 295

75:22–23 Faces on that day radiant, gazing at their Lord. 71

78:18 On the day the Trumpet is blown, and you shall come in troops. 278

78:38 On the day the Spirit and the angels stand in ranks. 233

79:8 . . . Hearts upon that day shall be athrob. . . . 290

79:27 Are you stronger in creation or the heaven He built? 179

79:40–41 . . . and forbade the soul its caprice. . . . 72

82:6 . . . your generous Lord, who created you, and proportioned you, and balanced you? 293

82:8 In any form He will, He composes. 149

83:7 No indeed, but the book of the ungodly is in Sijjīn. 101

83:14 No indeed, but what they were earning has rusted upon the hearts. 260

83:15 No indeed, but on that Day they shall be veiled from their Lord. . . . 250–51

83:18 No indeed, the book of the lovingly kind is in the high realms/ones. . . . 101, 262

83:22 Surely the lovingly kind shall be in bliss. 262

85:21–22 Nay, but it is a glorious Koran, in a guarded tablet. 12

86:9 Upon the day when secrets are divulged. 138

88:18–20 What, do they not consider how the camel was created, how heaven was raised up. . . ? 120

89:27–28 O soul at peace, return to thy Lord, well pleased, well pleasing. 287, 295

91:1–2 By the sun and her brightness! By the moon who follows her! 252

91:7–8 By the soul and Him who proportioned it and inspired in it its wickedness and its godfearing. 256, 257, 283, 295, 305

91:9–10 Prosperous is he who purifies it. . . . 102, 283

95:4 We created the human being in the most beautiful stature. 40, 95, 293

95:5 Then We drove him down to the lowest of the low. 40

96:1–4 Read out! And thy Lord is the most generous, who taught by the Pen. 12

96:5 He taught the human being what he did not know. 12, 348n54

98:6–7 . . . They are the worst creatures. . . . They are the best creatures. 232

112:3 . . . who did not give birth and was not born. 59

112:4 He has no equal. 180

114:5 . . . he who whispers in people's breasts. 301

INDEX OF HADITHS AND SAYINGS

Among the signs of the last hour will be that . . . women become many. . . . 326

Ask for a pronouncement from your heart. . . . 294

The best among you is the one who acts best toward his wife. . . . 172, 174, 175

Both of God's hands are right and blessed. 82, 83, 108

A branch of the heart of the son of Adam lies in every stream bed. . . . 291

By Him in whose hand is Muhammad's soul. 166, 167

The child belongs to the bedding. 184, 345n46

The client of a people is one of them. 182

The creation of each of you is brought together in his mother's belly for forty days. . . . 348n43

The creatures are God's family. 178

The earth was made for me pleasant, pure, and a mosque. 341n47

. . . Every one whose heart is swept. . . . 291

Everything returns to its root. 161

Fear God in the affair of women, for you have taken them in trust from God. . . . 176

The felicity of the pious is the wretchedness of the saints. 250

A few mouthfuls to firm up his backbone are enough for the son of Adam. 214

The first thing created by God was the Intellect. . . . 165

The first thing God created was my spirit (or "my light"). 166

The first thing God created was the Pen. Then He said, . . . 153, 165

Give to each that has a right its right. 196

Give us ease, Bilāl! 172, 344n12

God brings hearts to life through the light of wisdom. 290

God created a hundred mercies. . . . 207

God created Adam and struck him with His right hand. . . . 83

God created Adam in His own form. 54, 89, 236–37, 308

God created Adam in the form of the All-merciful. 182

God (He) created Adam with His two hands. 95

God created the creatures in darkness. . . . 169, 334n5

God created the creatures. When He finished with them the womb stood up, . . . 215

God created the intellect and said to it, "Stand up." It stood up. . . . 212–13

God created the intellect and said to it, "Turn away from Me" so it looked away. . . . 239

God created the Tablet from a white pearl. . . . 153

God has containers, and they are hearts. 128

God has finished with creation, [character,] provision, and fixed terms. 158, 164

God has seventy thousand veils of light and darkness. 60

God (I) kneaded the clay of Adam with His (My) two hands for forty days. 39, 40, 95, 234

God looks . . . at your hearts. 289, 296, 353n24

God loves everyone who undergoes trials and who turns toward Him. 200

God's (My) mercy precedes His (My) wrath. 9, 55, 77, 78, 83, 84, 92, 108, 156

God's self-disclosure never repeats itself. 11

God's veil is light. . . . 353n41

God was (is), and nothing was (is) with Him. 7, 59, 333n4

God will grasp the heavens in His right hand. . . . 83

God will only chastise the one who is. . . . 215

God would not chastise the heart of His Prophet! By God, the Messenger of God did not die before He made women lawful to him. 186

The good, all of it, is in Thy two hands, while evil does not go back to Thee. 83–84

He poured His light down upon them. 26

He who knows his own soul [or "himself"] knows his Lord. 26, 39, 189, 227, 230, 236, 256, 283, 288, 307

He who makes *tafsīr* according to his own opinion has become an unbeliever. 227

He who meets God not associating anything with Him will enter the Garden. . . . 79

The heart is like a feather in a desert of the earth. . . . 292, 296

The heart of the child of Adam is between two fingers of the Invincible/the All-merciful. He turns it wherever He desires. . . . 85, 292

A human being fills no container worse than his belly. . . . 347n33

I am God and I am the All-merciful. I created the womb and I gave it a name derived from My own name. . . . 215

I am his hearing through which he hears. . . . 253, 288

I am the most knowledgeable of God among you. 290

I am with My servant's opinion of Me. 72

I choose the right hand of the Lord, though both hands of my Lord are right and blessed. 83

I counsel you to be good to your wives. . . . 175

I have a time with God when no angel brought nigh or prophet sent out embraces me. 265

I have returned from the lesser *jihād* to the greater *jihād*. 234

I have seen none who fall shorter in intelligence and religion in the eye of the possessor of insight than you. . . . 174

I love nothing that draws My servant near to Me more than [I love] what I have made obligatory for him. . . . 253

I seek refuge in Thee from the goadings of Satan. 129

I sit with him who remembers Me. 72

I was a hidden treasure and I desired (loved) to be known. . . . 10, 62, 184, 312
I was sent with the all-comprehensive words. 189
I will not observe the right of My servant until My servant observes My right. 175
If any owner of camels does not pay the alms tax that is due on them. . . . 278
If I advance a fingertip, I will be consumed by fire. 287
If the servant commits a sin, a black spot appears in his heart. . . . 260
If you did not sin, God would take you away and bring a people who sin. . . . 334n16
The intellect is a fetter against ignorance. . . . 239
It is newly acquainted with my Lord. 127
It is no concern of Mine. 83, 86, 90, 338n2
This Koran is God's banquet. . . . 291
Let each of you take a tongue that remembers God, a heart that thanks Him, and a wife who has faith. 175
Let the servant of the dinar fall on his face, . . . 255, 350n14
Let them [go on doing good deeds]. 80
The love of the homeland is part of faith. 345n35
Loving kindness is that through which the heart gains peace. . . . 294
The majority of the people of the Fire are women. 345n53
Many have reached perfection among men, but among women only Mary the daughter of ʿImrān and Āsiya the wife of Pharoah. 180
Marriage is my Sunna. . . . 171
Marriage is one-half of religion. 195
Most of the people of the Fire are bachelors. 172
A Muslim man can acquire no benefit after Islam greater than a Muslim wife. . . . 172
My heavens and My earth embrace Me not. . . . 290, 315
No building is built in Islam more beloved to God than marriage. 172
None knows God but God. 50
O God, give my soul its godfearingness and purify it. . . . 102
O God, I ask Thee by every name by which Thou hast named Thyself. . . . 201
O God, wash away from me my offenses with the water of snow and hail. . . . 291
O He who makes hearts fluctuate (turn about). . . . 292
O Moses, thank me with true gratitude. . . . 200
Oh, my community! 74, 337n70
On the day God created mercy, He created it as one hundred mercies. . . . 207
People who are metamorphosized become one of thirteen. . . . 279
A people who give the rule of their affairs to a woman will never prosper. 183
People will be thrown into the Fire continuously and it will keep on saying "Are there any more?" . . . 86
A person who marries achieves half his religion. . . . 171
Prostrated before Thee is my face, my blackness, and my imagination. 206
Put the females behind. 317
Put them behind, since God has put them behind. 354n76
Satan flows in people like blood. . . . 290

The seeker of the Lord is male. . . . 318
Show us the things as they are! 159
Talk with me, O ʿĀ'isha. 173, 226
Ten groups of my community will be gathered separately. . . . 278
. . . That he not hit her in the face and not abuse her. . . . 176
. . . That she obey him and not disobey him. . . . 176
There are four kinds of hearts. . . . 306
There is a group of the People of the Garden from whom the Lord is not hidden or veiled. 222
There is in the body a lump of flesh. . . . 298
There is no child of Adam whose heart does not lie between two of God's fingers. . . . 292
There is no prophet who does not have a counterpart in his community. 252
There is no strength and no power except in God, the High, the Tremendous. 178
There is no sword but Dhu'l-Fiqār, there is no *fatā* but ʿAlī.
There is no verse of the Koran that does not have an outward sense, an inward sense. . . . 227
These are for the Garden, and it is no concern of Mine. These are for the Fire, . . . 90
The thickness of the unbeliever's skin on the Day of Resurrection will be a three-day's journey. 101
Things become distinguished through their opposites. 127, 131, 221, 250, 252
Three things of this world of yours were made lovable to me. . . . 173, 183, 186, 189, 202
Were I to command someone to prostrate himself before another, I would command the woman to prostrate herself before her spouse. . . . 176
What does dust have to do with the Lord of lords? 50
What no eye has seen, what no ear has heard, and what has never passed into the heart of any mortal. 219, 304
When a Muslim man intends to come to his wife, God writes for him 20 good deeds and erases from him 20 evil deeds. . . . 174
When a person has an admonisher within his heart, God has given him a protector. 260
When God created the earth, she began to sway. So He created the mountains and said to them, "Overwhelm her!" . . . 214–15
When God desires good for a servant, he appoints for him an admonisher from within his heart. 260
When something scratches your heart, leave it. . . . 294
When the call to prayer is made, Satan turns away while breaking wind. . . . 290
When [the Koran] falls into the heart and becomes firmly rooted there, it gives benefit. 291
When the child of Adam dies, his works are cut off. 222
Whenever the time of prayer arrives, pray, for the earth is a mosque for you. 341n47
While I was lying down at al-Ḥaṭīm someone came to me and made a split from here to here, . . . then took out my heart. . . . 133
Wipe yourselves with the earth, for it is lovingly kind to you. 213

Who is most deserving of loving kindness? The Prophet answered, "Your mother" three times. . . . 213, 214
The womb is a branch of the All-merciful. . . . 182, 216
The womb is attached to the Throne and says. . . . 216
The womb stood up and seized the All-merciful by the belt. . . . 216
Women are the likes of men. 180, 183, 185
Women fall short in intelligence and religion. 285, 318
Worship God as if you see Him. 89
Your soul has a right upon you, and your eye has a right upon you. 214
Your worst enemy is your soul that is between your two sides. 283

GENERAL INDEX

Aaron, 134
ab, 145
ʿabath muṭlaq, 113
ʿabd, 16, 54, 69, 204
abdāl, 268
ablution, 191
Abraham, 74, 134, 135, 261
absolutes, none in cosmos, 58, 131–33
Abū Bakr, 201, 252
Abū Ḥanīfa, 184
Abū Jahl, 252
Abū Lahab, 252
Abū Sulaymān Dārānī, 175
Abū Yazīd Basṭāmī, 78, 140, 318
activity (*fāʿiliyya*, *fiʿl*), 114; contrasted with receptivity (receiving activity), 66, 68, 92, 94, 98, 99, 100, 101, 105–8, 158, 179, 180, 184–85, 189, 192–93, 196, 197–99, 208, 210, 211, 265, 308, 312, 314
acts (*afʿāl*), God's, 182; names of, 55–56
actuality (*fiʿl*), contrasted with potentiality (*quwwa*), 44, 264–66
adab, 77, 84, 122
adāh, 293; *adawāt*, 209
ʿadāla, 111, 246
Adam, 11, 64, 133, 134; the Great, 307; true, 189, 198; children of, 83; contrasted with angels, 296, 305; contrasted with Iblis (satan), 269–70, 301; creation of, 39–43, 81; created with two hands, 81, 82–85, 88–114; clay/earth of, 40, 95, 138–39, 184, 233, 269–70, 271–72, 284; fall of, 65, 138–39, 249; four kinds of, 159; his being honored, 40, 85, 88–89, 91; intellect as, 281–82; situated between two feminines, 197–98; taught (manifests) all the names, 34, 36, 65–66, 89, 273–74; as vicegerent, 44, 46, 78, 184. *See* human being, Iblis
Adam and Eve, 35, 146; spiritual, 154; as heart and soul, 273–74; as human spirit and animal spirit, 305; correlated with intellect and soul, 168, 238; as intellect and body, 281; as spirit and soul, 309; as World of Spirits and World of Bodies, 343n69; priority of Eve to Adam, 120; creation of Eve from Adam, 163, 178–82, 305; creation of Eve with Adam, 120; Adam's appetite for Eve, 181
ādam, 274
adawāt, 209
Addas, Claude, 345n51
ʿadl, 9, 52, 69, 84, 258
āfāq wa'l-anfus, al-, 23
affliction (*balā'*), 71; divine names of, 90; benefit of, 276
afrād, 340n65
ʿafw, 69
aḥadiyya, 62; *aḥadiyyat al-aḥad*, 58; *aḥadiyyat al-jamʿ*, 67; *aḥadiyyat jamʿ al-jamʿ*, 354n73; *aḥadiyyat al-kathra*, 59
aḥkām al-nujūm, 14
ahl, 156
Aḥmad ibn Khaḍrūya, 318
aḥwāl, 73, 244, 247, 309
ʿā'ila, 178
ʿĀ'isha, 173, 176–77, 186, 201–2, 226
akhfā, 253, 301
ākhira, 120
akhlāq, 257
akmaliyya, 180
ālā', 90
ʿalam, 160
ʿālam, 45, 160; *ʿālam-i akbar*, 334n1; *al-ʿālam al-kabīr*, 23; *al-ʿālam al-ṣaghīr*, 23; *ālam al-tadwīn wa'l-tasṭīr*, 163; *ʿālam al-tawallud*, 156; *asmā' al-ʿālam*, 63
ʿalāma, 45, 160
Alast, 70
alchemy (*kīmiyā'*), 72, 261; of the Sharia, 286
ʿalī, al-, 131
ʿAlī (ibn Abī Ṭālib), 173, 246, 247, 267, 268
ʿAlī al-Riḍā, 84
ʿAlī ibn al-Ḥusayn, 213
ʿAlī ibn Sahl Ṣūfī, 310
ʿalīm, 52
ʿālim, 57
all-comprehensive (*jāmiʿ*), *barzakh*, 36, 189–90, 198, 199; engendered thing, 34, 95, 103, 161; heart, 312; isthmus, 36; name, 34, 103, 250, 314; oneness, 312; reality, 308; self-disclosure, 312; unity, 65, 96, 97, 98, 100; word(s), 45, 199; all-comprehensiveness (*jamʿiyya*), human, 15–17, 33–37, 39, 65, 89, 91, 95–101, 280, 308; divine 191; unitary, 98; of the Real, 110, 308; comprehension of, 96, 316; presence of, 63, 314; station of, 67,

all-comprehensive (*jāmiʿ*) (*cont.*) 68; unity of, 67, 315; contrasted with dispersion, 63–65
All-merciful (*raḥmān*), 206–7, 219–20. *See* Breath
Allah, 34, 44, 55, 57, 150, 165, 187, 206–7, 250–51, 314; form of, 34, 103, 192; as the first father, 148; as name of Being, 68; *mā siwā Allāh*, 8
alphabet, 164
ʿamal, 146
ambiguity, of created things, 132, 185
Ames, Roger T., 10
amr, 88, 118; *al-amr al-taklīfī*, 250; *al-amr al-takwīnī*, 249
amthāl, 127
anā'iyya, 302
anāniyyat al-juz'iyya, al-, 95
ʿanāṣir, 135
Andrae, Tor, 344n1
androgyne, 340n10
angels (*malā'ika*), 127, 137, 154, 167, 205, 281; enraptured, 165; two guardian, 84; of bounty and justice, 84; of the seven heavens, 30–31; contrasted with enemy, 293–94; contrasted with humans, 38, 104, 215, 296; degrees of, 351n80; food of, 155, 231; limited knowledge of, 36, 41, 42, 220; prostration of before Adam, 190, 308; as faculties in the microcosm, 218, 274; as intellects, 263; as one in substance with the spirit, 234; as qualities achieved by humans, 102, 219, 280, 282; as souls, 263; angelic (*malakī*) contrasted with satanic (demonic), 230
anger (*ghaḍab*), 230, 300; and appetite, 258–59; 242–43, 268, 269, 283; and caprice, 284–89; anger and caprice as children of soul, 287; equilibrium of, 285–86
animals (*ḥayawān*), 40, 188, 204; contrasted with humans, 32–33, 37, 38; contrasted with angelic and satanic, 230; animal qualities of soul, 278–83. *See* beasts
annihilation (*fanā'*), 297, 298, 314; contrasted with subsistence, 76, 304
Anṣārī, Khwāja ʿAbd Allāh, 73, 297. *Manāzil al-sā'irīn*, 49, 267–68; *Ṣad maydān*, 267
anthropomorphism, 51
appetite (*shahwa*), 187, 230; 43, 111, 172, 173, 177, 181, 284; as source of love, 195; and anger (*see* anger); imaginalized as a pig, 282; marriage as an animal appetite, 188
ʿaql, 12, 42, 111, 155, 165, 212, 229, 238, 239, 299, 349n32; *al-ʿaql al-ʿamalī*, 301; *al-ʿaql al-faʿʿāl*, 263; *al-ʿaql al-hayūlānī*, 263; *al-ʿaql al-naẓarī*, 301
Aqṣā, al-, 303
arc (*qaws*), 39. *See* Ascent
architecture, 145–46
arḍ, 119, 136, 137
Aristotle, 265
arkān, 135
ʿarsh, 86
ʿarūs, 226
ascent (*ʿurūj*), Arc of, and that of Descent, 39, 64, 155, 263–64, 308; contrasted with descent, 40, 88
aṣḥāb al-qulūb, 292
Ashʿarites, 11
Āsiya, 180, 345n28
asmā' al-ʿālam, 63
association of others with God (*shirk*), 79, 87, 108, 285
astrology, 14, 104
ʿAṭṭār, Farīd al-Dīn. *Tadhkirat al-awliyā'*, 80, 317–18
attributes (*ṣifāt*), 27; names of, 55, 56. *See* names
aṭwār, 251
Avicenna, 263, 273, 350n36, 351n77; *al-Najāh*, 263, 264, 283; *Tarjama-yi risāla-yi aḍ-ḥawiyya*, 282–83
awe (*hayba*) and intimacy, 56, 69, 74–79, 86, 87, 90, 91, 95, 98, 100, 173, 339n43
awlād, 210
awliyā', 44
ʿawrāt, 220
āya, 206, 227; *āyāt*, 10, 23
ʿAyn al-Quḍāt. *See* Hamadānī
Azrael, 31

Babylon, 307
Baghdādī, Majd al-Dīn, 40
bahīma, 230
baḥr, 213
balā', 71, 90
balance (*ʿadāla*), 111, 246, 301
banāt, 63
Baqlī, Rūzbihān, 78, 337n64. *ʿAbhar al-ʿāshiqīn*, 297; *Mashrab al-arwāḥ*, 73, 256, 257, 298; *Risālat al-quds*, 297–98
bāri', al-, 135
barr, 213
barzakh, 160; 15, 107, 111, 132, 159, 163; all-comprehensive, 36, 189–90, 198, 199; supreme, 188; heart as, 310; soul as, 237; *al-barzakhiyyat al-kubrā*, 15; human *barzakh*-reality, 198, 221, 315
basāṭa, 135
bashar, 89; *basharī*, 305
basīṭ, 29
basṭ, 69, 90, 337n71
baʿtha, 180
bāṭil, 121
bāṭin, 299
Bayḍāwī, 85
"Be" (*kun*), 13, 87, 148, 153, 184, 201, 225, 234–35, 249
beasts (*bahīma, sutūr*) and predators, 40, 230–31, 282, 283, 285, 287, 303
beauty (*jamāl*) and majesty, 17, 69–74, 76, 86, 91, 92, 94, 100, 124, 307, 308
Being (*wujūd*), 62–63; Necessary, 106, 117, 135, 169, 189, 219; Nondelimited, 265; Sheer, 62, 66, 67; activity of, 106; full manifestation of, 150; Oneness of (*see* oneness); as a father, 148; as light (*see* light); as yin, 206–7; contrasted with knowledge (*see* oneness); contrasted with finding, 264–65; and existence, 66–68, 206–7, 322
belief (*iʿtiqād*), diversity of, 104
Bilāl, 173, 344n12
birr, 213
birth (*tawallud*), world of, 156
body (*jism, badan*), this-worldly and next-worldly, 137–38; nondelimited, 190; universal, 156–57, 210; connection with Satan, 256; contrasted with soul, 29, 218; contrasted with spirit (heart), 12–13, 14, 17, 38, 43, 56–57, 70–73, 130, 144, 153, 221, 231, 233, 234–36, 242, 245, 262, 300, 311; criticism of, 221–22; mutual love of with spirit, 191; marriage of with spirit, 284; as source of self-

awareness, 221–22; world of bodies contrasted with that of spirits, 118, 124, 131, 205, 300
book (*kitāb*), mother of, 155, 190; universe as, 45–46, 163, 228; worlds as, 164
Bouhdiba, Abdelwahab, 344n2, 346n57
bounty (*faḍl*) and justice, 84, 85
brain (*damāgh*), as place of intellect, 306
breast (*ṣadr*), 256, 295, 297
Breath of the All-merciful (*nafas al-raḥmān*), 93, 105–7, 137, 140, 149, 167, 188, 190, 194, 207–9, 219, 221, 250
brightness (*ḍiyā'*), 31, 132
bu'd, 69
būdan, 264
Bukhārī, Abū Ibrāhīm Mustamlī. *Sharḥ-i ta'arruf*, 74–75, 295
Burāq, 133, 286, 287
buṭlān, 109

caprice (*hawā*), 76, 111, 245, 255, 256, 277; contrasted with god-fearing, 293; contrasted with intellect, 293; contrasted with the Real, 110, 122–23; paired with anger, 284–89; importance of equilibrium of, 285–86
Cave, Companions of, 301
change, 7, 11
character (*khuluq*), rectification of, 262
character traits (*akhlāq*), 102, 244, 245, 257, 277, 286, 302, 315; of satans, 255; of the soul, 255, 313; assumption of divine, 191; development of, 261; imaginalized in appropriate forms, 281–83; and animals, 262, 279–80
cherubim (*karrūbiyyūn*), 168
child (*walad*), loving vs. recalcitrant, 306; heart as, 309–10, 311–12; rational soul as, 305; children (*mawālīd*), of day and night, 147; of the elements [= the three kingdoms], 28, 37–39, 40, 64, 88, 103, 143, 145, 155, 158, 161, 217–18, 308
chilla, 349n18
chivalry (*futuwwa*), 267–69, 337n70
Christ. *See* Jesus.
Chuang Tzu, 11, 16
circle (*dā'ira*), of engendering, 308; of existence, 310; central point of, 140, 150, 301, 314–15
Cloud (*'amā'*), 107, 166
Combs-Schilling, M. E., 346n57, 354n1
command(s) (*amr*), engendering vs. prescriptive, 249–51, 278, 292, 340n76; world of, 232; (world of) contrasted with that of creation, 118, 211, 218, 219, 234, 235, 247, 305, 308, 310; and prohibitions, 88
compound (*murakkab*), composition, compoundness (*tarkīb*), contrasted with simple (simplicity), 38, 39, 108, 119, 135, 161, 164, 235, 265
Confucius, 7, 14, 17; Confucianism contrasted with Taoism, 9, 92, 325
conjunction (*iltiḥām*), sensory and supra-sensory, 148
constitution (*mizāj*), 38, 98, 126, 216
contraction (*qabḍ*), contrasted with expansion, 73, 87, 90, 298
Corbin, Henry, 225, 344n24, 346n59
correlativity, 131. *See* thrall, vassal
cosmology, 7, 15–16, 24–25, 117, 321
cosmos (*'ālam*), 8, 23, 43; as book of God, 45–46; contrasted with God, 51, 58, 97, 117, 191; as identical with existence, 66; as manifesting divine names, 51, 62, 63, 90; names of, 63; necessity of human beings in, 16; as receptive (yin) toward God, 57–58, 123–24, 180, 210
creation (*khalq*), 13; continual, 11, 94–95, 309; contrasted with command. *See* command
cuckold (*dayyūth*), 285

dadagān, 230
ḍa'f, 187
Ḍaḥḥāk, al-, 74, 83
dalīl, 152
Daqqāq, Abū 'Alī, 337n70
daraja, 174; *rafī' al-darajāt*, 334n12; *al-tarāfu' fi'l-darajāt*, 334n12
darkness (*ẓulma*). *See* light
David, 61, 62
dawāt, 153
day(time) (*nahār*) and night(time), 146–47, 245
dayyūth, 285
degree (*daraja*), of man over woman, 173–81; of woman over man, 183
deiformity (*ta'alluh*), 255, 262
delimitation (*taqyīd*), contrasted with nondelimitation, 93–96, 202
Descent (*nuzūl*), five of the Essence, 194, 198. *See* Ascent
desire (*irāda*), God's, 151–53, 165, 177, 194, 210
devils (*dīwān*). *See* satans
dhikr, 72, 74, 76, 123, 168, 260, 290, 293, 295, 312
Dhu'l-Faqār, 267
Dhu'l-Nūn, 74, 75
Dhu'l-Qarnayn, 161
differentiation (*tafṣīl*), and undifferentiation, 34, 41, 45, 62–66, 68, 134, 159, 164, 165, 167, 168, 216, 217, 302
Differentiator (*al-mufaṣṣil*), contrasted with Governor, 12–13, 62–63, 166
dil, 296
dīn, 280; *al-dīn al-ḥanīfī*, 261
dispersion (*farq, tafriqa*). *See* all-comprehensiveness
divinity (*ulūhiyya*), 50, 67, 68; level of, 167. *See* Essence
divorce, 343n38
ḍiyā', 31, 132
dog, 258–59, 270, 281
Dominion (*malakūt*), 247, 276, 277, 284, 286, 293; contrasted with Kingdom, 40, 61, 114, 118, 218, 235, 274–75, 310, 343n69; contrasted with Kingdom and Invincibility, 150, 159–61, 163–64; paired with Invincibility, 36, 205, 303
duality (*ithnayniyya*), 7, 49, 58–60, 94, 95, 117–18, 154, 238
dunyā, 120
Dust (*habā'*), 64, 136, 163, 210; as mother, 156–57

earth (*arḍ, turāb*), 17; blameworthy attributes of, 272; contrasted with heaven (*see* heaven); its being honored, 41; as a mother, 140; priority of to heaven, 13, 120; qualities of as an element, 136–41, 296 (*see also* Adam, clay/earth of); similarity of to soul, 306
east and west, 252, 300
Eden, 88, 352n99

effectivity (*taʿthīr*), 68, 105–7, 145–46
effusion (*fayḍ*), 13, 14, 68, 119–20, 124; holy and most holy, 98–99; of existence, 107
ego (*anāʾiyya, anāniyya*), 95, 302, 304
element(s) (*ʿunṣur*; pl. *ʿanāṣir*), 28–29, 30, 39–40, 98, 135–40, 145; Greatest, 64, 136–37; as mother of soul, 284; qualities of, 272, 284; world of, 101; and the four humors, 217; elemental (*ʿunṣurī*) world, 150
embryo, 30; development of in the womb, 216–18
emerald, 153, 163
enemy (*ʿadū*), contrasted with angel, 293–94
enraptured (*muhayyam*) angels, 165, 168
entification (*taʿayyun*), 134; First, 64, 93–94, 105, 167, 189, 197–98; Second, 64; contrasted with non-entification, 67, 94–96, 198
entity (*ʿayn*), 66; reception of existence by, 63, 184; immutable entities (*al-aʿyān al-thābita*), 33, 86, 98–99, 100, 148, 159, 176, 182, 185, 189, 194, 201, 205
envy (*ḥasad*), 285–86
Ephesus, Seven Sleepers of, 301
equilibrium (*iʿtidāl*), 246; of anger and caprice, 285; of character traits, 258, 260, 315; of divine names, 150; of constitution, 38, 216; of the human state, 95; as perfection, 311, 315–16
Essence (*dhāt*), 34, 67, 68, 114, 124, 151, 152–53, 303; absoluteness of, 131; contrasted with Divinity (God), 49–51, 57, 58, 69, 93, 117, 189; contrasted with names, 81, 165, 190, 195, 300; five descents of, 194; as identical with Being, 66; as inaccessible, 191; marriage of, 149; names of, 55, 66; as Mother, 76; nondelimitation of, 93–94, 265; nonentification of, 198; permeates all, 103
ethics (*akhlāq*), 257–58
Eve, 35, 197; created from Adam's rib, 179, 181, 200; created for Adam's rest, 226; masculine qualities of, 178, 185; and Jesus, 178, 180, 181, 185–86. *See* Adam
evil (*sharr*), 15, 273; necessitated by certain divine names, 66; and good (*see* good)
evolution, 37, 44, 216–17, 335n30
existence (*wujūd*), levels of, 264–65; three directions of, 230; of cosmos contrasted with its non-existence, 68, 157, 182, 210; distinguished from Being, 66–67; engendered existence (*kawn*) contrasted with Being, 109–11
expansion (*basṭ*). *See* contraction
expansiveness, bold (*inbisāṭ*), 74, 77–79, 112, 173, 324, 337n71
Ezra, 180

face (*wajh*), two of First Intellect (Pen), 13, 165–67, 266; two of each thing, 64, 111, 112, 164, 252; of the heart, 301, 310–11
faculties (*quwā*), 245; animal, 244; earthly and heavenly, 205; intellective, 245; spiritual vs. natural, 102; as angels, 218; of heart, 242, 314–15; of soul, 275
faḍāʾil, 261
faḍl, 9, 69, 84
fāʿil, 92; *fāʿiliyya*, 66
faith (*īmān*) and unbelief, 111, 114
familiarity (*ulfa*), 246, 300–1
fanāʾ, 297, 304, 314
Fanārī, al-, 342n19
fard, 151, 195; *afrād*, 340n65
Farghānī, Saʿīd al-Dīn, 64, 339n58; *Mashāriq al-darārī*, 67, 68, 311; *Muntahā al-madārik*, 64–65, 65–66, 66, 88, 105–8, 109–14, 134–35, 136–37, 158, 166–67, 311–12
farīḍa, 186
farq, 63
fatā, 267
fatḥ, 149
father (*ab*), second, 178; God as, 145
father and mother, 145–47; as theological terms, 9; Dominion and Kingdom as, 158, 160; heaven and earth as, 145; Intellect and Soul as, 155, 167; light and darkness as, 161; the Reality as, 197–98; spirits and souls as, 144–47; spirit and Nature as, 212–14. *See* man and woman, parents
Fātiḥa, 71, 199, 228
fāṭir, 120
fayḍ, 119; *al-fayḍ al-aqdas*, 98; *al-fayḍ al-muqaddas*, 98
fear (*khawf*) and hope, 91, 98, 126
felicity (*saʿāda*), 322; of heart, 242; rooted in knowledge, 242, 283
felicity and wretchedness, 230; 90, 101–2, 114, 231, 239, 250–52, 277, 283, 306; connected with names of similarity and incomparability, 250–51
femininity (*unūtha*), 77, 198; divine, 199, 324; priority of in reality, 196–99; as a negative quality, 285, 286. *See* masculinity, woman
fikr, 38, 228, 273, 301
fiʿl, 68, 105, 209, 264, 265
fingers (*anāmil*), of God, 85, 295–96
fiqh, 5, 290; *uṣūl al-fiqh*, 2
Firdawsī, 335n27; *Shāhnāma*, 136
fire (*nār*), qualities of, 95–96, 138, 272; as a quality of soul, 237, 269; the Fire contrasted with the Garden, 86, 111. *See* Iblis
fish, mythical, 153
fiṭra(t), 17, 173, 268
food, of body and soul, 228–29, 261–62; of heart, 274
foot (*qadam*), two feet of God, 85–88
Footstool (*kursī*) and Throne. *See* Throne
forgetfulness (*ghafla*), 249, 254, 262
form (*ṣūra*), divine of human beings, 11, 16, 34, 43, 44, 45, 54, 89, 159, 182, 183, 184, 190, 193, 195, 200–1, 221, 263, 264, 278. *See* matter
frame (*qālib*). *See* body
freedom, 54, 79, 123, 251
friends of God (*awliyāʾ*), 44; types of, 104
fuʾād, 290, 297
furqān, al-, 301–2, 310
futūḥ, 227
futuwwa, 267, 337n70

Gabriel, 31, 133, 134, 154, 181, 270–71, 280, 287, 290; two wings of, 169
Garden (*janna*), 102, 120; of Adam and Eve, 65, 274; of the Attributes, 277. *See* felicity, paradise
gender, grammatical, 196–99
gentleness (*luṭf*) and severity, 11, 61, 92, 187–88, 277
ghaḍab, 9, 69

ghafla, 249, 324, 354n1
gharaḍ, 293
ghayb, 25, 61, 118; *ghayb al-ghayb*, 105
ghayr and *ghayra*, 11, 65, 73, 94, 191, 285
Ghazālī, Abū Ḥāmid Muḥammad, 2, 292; *Iḥyā'*, 258–60, 348n2; *Kīmiyā-yi saʿādat*, 172–73, 173, 230–31, 233–34, 242–43, 282; *Mīzān al-ʿamal*, 280
ghusl, 191
Gimaret, D., 334n7
gnosis (*maʿrifa*), 294–95; gnostic(s) (*ʿārif*), 73, 75; their longing for women, 181; their friendship with women, 266
God, as "no thing," 95; femininity of, 77, 199; predominance of yin or yang in, 77; made a god by the entities, 201; two senses of word, 57. *See* cosmos, Essence, thrall
godfearing (*taqwā*), 260, 276, 285
good (*khayr*) and evil, 109, 205, 293–94, 301; deeds, 84
good pleasure (*riḍā*) and wrath, 91, 94
governing, governance (*tadbīr*), 63, 233, 236
Governor (*al-mudabbir*). *See* Differentiator
Great Ultimate (Tai Chi), 7, 50, 61
guidance (*hudā, hidāya*), contrasted with misguidance, 111, 113, 239–40
gustākhī, 337n71

habā', 136, 163
hādī, al-, 239
ḥadīth qudsī, 61, 219, 290
ḥaḍra, 67; *ḥaḍrat al-jamʿ*, 314
Ḥāfiẓ, 253
Ḥafṣa, 176–77
ḥājib, 168
Ḥallāj, 78, 201, 326
Hamadānī, ʿAyn al-Quḍāt. *Tamhīdāt*, 252, 256
Hamadānī, Sayyid ʿAlī, 326
Ḥamza, 226
hand(s) (*yad*), two, of God, 11, 16, 40, 81–85, 88–114, 167, 169, 208, 239, 250–52, 308–9
handful(s) (*qabḍa*), 214; two, 90, 109–14
ḥanīf, 261
ḥanīn, 181
ḥaqīqat al-muṭlaqa, al-, 18
ḥaqq, 14, 18, 52, 57, 109, 121
ḥaqqiyya, 77, 109
ḥaraka, 11
Hārūt, 307
Ḥasan, al-, 83
hawā, 110, 111, 122, 293, 345n34
hawā', 122, 181, 345n34
ḥawwā', 274
ḥayā', 181
ḥayawān, 188
hayba, 56, 69
hayūlā, 156
ḥayy, 27
He-ness (*huwiyya*), 105, 191, 207, 265, 315; Presence of, 316
heart (*qalb, dil*), 231; 42, 51, 128–29, 130, 232, 233–34, 257, 289–315; true, 310; true vs. relative, 312; universal, 190; of all-comprehensiveness and existence, 314–15; between spirit and soul, 296, 299, 300–1; born of spirit and soul, 304–13; born of spirit and body, 284; combines spirit and earth, 296; connected to intellect, 212; contrasted with body (frame), 71–72, 231; contrasted with soul, 191, 273–74, 277, 284, 302; contrasted with spirit, 155, 191; creation of, 85; derived from love, 310; as the divine form, 292; eye of, 229; faces of, 242, 314–15; fluctuation of, 292, 299, 309; form vs. reality of, 310; hardness of, 277; levels (kinds) of, 296–97, 306, 311–312; lights of, 294–95, 298; as a mirror, 259–60; possessors of, 305; station of, 277, 302, 303; as Throne in microcosm, 310
heat (*ḥarāra*), and cold, 211
heaven (*samā'*), excellence of over human beings, 179; in the microcosm, 243–47; of this world, 155; seven heavens, 30–31, 42, 126, 132, 133–35, 246–47
heaven and earth, 118–20; 12, 13–14, 17, 42, 57, 90, 108, 114, 121–34, 143, 152, 179, 193; as intellect and body, 244; as spirits and bodies, 205; spirit and soul as, 144, 244, 295
hell, as rooted in blameworthy character traits, 285–86; and paradise, 55, 77, 82, 108
hermaphrodite (*khunthā*), 285, 286, 316–17, 318
hermeneutics, esoteric, 226. See *ta'wīl*
Hermeticism, 220
hidāya, 239
Hidden Treasure, 10–11, 14, 16, 33–34, 37, 61–63, 66, 77, 148, 159, 183, 217, 221, 244, 263, 312
hierarchy (*tartīb*), 60, 146, 322; normative of microcosm, 243, 249, 252, 259; of cosmos, 155–56, 157, 168, 196, 237; of qualities, 31–32, 37, 56; and freedom, 79
ḥifẓ al-sirr, 80
high and low, 114, 131–32, 229, 246, 295, 311; worlds, 266; fathers and mothers as, 148; highest of the high (vs. lowest of the low), 40, 124, 286
ḥikma, 111
ḥilm, 239
himma, 194
ḥirṣ, 271
hope (*rajā'*). *See* fear
hudā, 239
Ḥudhayfa, 306
Hujwīrī. *Kashf al-maḥjūb*, 75–76
ḥukm, 88
ḥulūl, 53
human beings (*insān*), true, 315; all-comprehensiveness of (*see* all-comprehensiveness); as children of Nature, 212–14; as combining spirit and Nature, 215; as combining spirit and body, 348n54; contrasted with other creatures, 11, 15–16, 32–33, 37–39, 43–45, 88–90, 102–3, 123, 204–5, 218, 278–81; contrasted with Iblis, 269–70; created for God, 35; created in God's form or image (*see* form); as the fifth marriage, 150; as goal of creation, 145; as the Great Isthmus-Nature, 15; inward tendencies (realities, levels) of, 249, 301, 310–11, 315; as knowing (or manifesting) all divine names, 41, 44, 54, 200–1; as the last creation, 26, 65; as microcosm, 28–29 (*see also* macrocosm); most excellent of, 263; necessary for full self-disclosure of God, 65; normative hierarchy of, 249–

human beings (*insān*) (*cont.*)
52; receptivity of, 232, 314; stages of development of, 44–45, 216–17, 251; three basic kinds of, 104; as vicegerents, 15–16. *See* Adam, angels
perfect human being(s) (*al-insān al-kāmil*), 40, 64–65, 98, 103, 161, 167, 200, 222, 299; Adam as, 88, 159; as a *barzakh*, 315; as bringing together all levels of existence, 265; as combining nondelimitation and delimitation, 202; contrasted with animal human being, 44, 305; dependence upon, 180; as manifesting God's two hands, 91, 103–4; as manifesting Allah, 102–3; as servant, 96. *See* perfection, vicegerency
humanity (*insāniyya*), 179, 185; true, 299
husband and wife, God's acts and soul as, 256–57; heart and soul as, 274; intellect and soul as, 306; spirit and soul as, 238, 308. *See* father and mother, man and woman
ḥūt, 153
huwiyya, 105
hyle (*hayūlā*), 156, 163
hypocrites, 127–28

I Ching, 7, 59
ʿibāda, 71, 173, 204
ibdāʿ, 246
Iblis, 15, 37, 41–42, 46, 89, 139, 140, 296, 319, 323; black light of, 252; as constriction and definition, 96; connection with ego, 95; connection with misguidance, 101, 239, 251–52; fall of, 65; fiery qualities of, 96, 138, 269–70, 274–75; in the microcosm, 42, 273–75; refusal to prostrate before Adam, 81, 91, 95, 98. *See* intuition
iʿāda, 333n12
ibn, 145
Ibn ʿAbbās, 83, 153, 174, 342n34
Ibn al-ʿArabī, 44, 50, 51–52, 53, 114, 307; his original dislike of women, 186; his view of the heart, 299; *Fuṣūṣ al-ḥikam*, 52, 58, 91, 93, 152–53, 188–97, 339n53; *al-Futūḥāt al-makkiyya*, 8, 36, 45, 51, 57–59, 63, 68, 70, 74, 83, 88–90, 111, 119, 122, 132, 140, 143–49, 151–54, 156, 160, 162–63, 168, 178–88, 199–202, 208, 210–11, 213–14, 253, 264, 268, 283, 333n7, 343n38; *Inshāʾ al-dawāʾir*, 16, 45; *Iṣṭilāḥāt al-ṣūfiyya*, 86; *Kitāb al-nikāḥ al-sārī*, 147; *ʿUqlat al-mustawfiz*, 163
Ibn al-Fāriḍ, 64; *al-Tāʾiyya*, 68, 109, 311
Ibn Ḥazm, 345n28
Ibn Sīnā. *See* Avicenna
iʿdām, 333n12
idlāl, 239
Idris, 134
ʿiffa, 268
iftiqār, 348n57
ignorance (*jahl*), contrasted with intellect, 239–41
iḥsān, 147
ījād, 333n12
ijmāl, 62
Ikhwān al-Ṣafāʾ, 24, 220; *Jāmiʿat al-jāmiʿa*, 59, 124, 157–58; *Rasāʾil*, 28–30, 32–33, 38, 59, 60, 161–62, 204–5, 209–10, 216, 218–19, 228–29, 236, 261–63, 279, 348n54
ilāh, 50, 57, 68
ʿilla, 197
ʿilm, 160; *kathrat al-ʿilm*, 67
iltiḥām, 148
imagination (*khayāl*), 89, 206, 350n36; contrasted with intellect, 299; of the cosmos, 155, 194; as locus of afterlife events, 278, 281–83; as a womb, 149; world of, 132, 133, 159, 160, 190, 194, 259, 274, 315; imaginal (*khayālī*, *mithālī*), descents, 194; forms, 64, 257
imām, 63, 145
imkān, 348n57
immutable. *See* entity
inbisāṭ, 74
incomparability (*tanzīh*), of Essence with incomparability, 94
incomparability and similarity, 8–9, 49, 50, 51–55, 69, 88, 91–92, 93, 94, 104, 121, 145, 162, 299, 338n33; correlation with paradise and hell, 108, 250–51; divine names of, 9, 250; priority of similarity over incomparability, 53; as the two hands of God, 89–90; and continual creation, 11, 94–95; and human role in cosmos, 16; and society, 77–80, 172, 325
infāq, 174
infiʿāl, 68, 105, 314; *maḥall infiʿāl*, 179
inḥirāf, 315
inkwell (*dawāt*), 153, 163–64
insān al-ḥayawān, al-, 44, 195, 305; *al-insān al-kabīr*, 23; *al-insān al-kāmil*, 44, 305; *al-insān al-ṣaghīr*, 23; *insāniyya*, 179, 299
intāj, 151, 188
intellect (*ʿaql*), 232, 238–40; 111, 165, 246, 267, 306; Active, 39, 263–64, 265–66, 273, 299–300; First, 39, 131, 159, 160, 189, 212, 238, 264, 266; material, 263; partial, 349n32; practical, 275; as Adam of the microcosm, 281; as angelic faculty, 230; angels as, 263; contrasted with love, 270, 287; contrasted with Pen, 16, 165; contrasted with senses, 245; contrasted with soul, 265, 270, 294; faces of, 164–68, 266; First (Universal) contrasted with (Universal) Soul, 12, 87, 154–58, 162–63, 165–69, 210–11, 228, 305, 308–9; as heaven, 259; as Jesus, 281; Koran as, 302; light of, 304; as microcosmic prophet, 111, 239–40, 242, 258, 276; negative sense of, 349n32; perfection of, 112; place of, 306; as receptive and active, 32; soldiers of, 240–41; as Solomon, 281; as tablet, 155; as vicegerent, 31, 46; world of, 265
interpenetration (*tadākhul*), 148; of Real and creation, 209
inṭibāʿ, 274
intimacy (*uns*). *See* awe
intiqām, 69
intuition, sensory (*wahm*), 273; 46, 244, 274–77, 351n77
invincibility (*jabarūt*). *See* Dominion
ʿiqāl, 212, 239
iqtirān, 32
irāda, 151, 177
ishāra, 352n82; *ishārāt*, 282
islām, 16, 54, 77, 78, 111, 127, 203–4, 251, 264, 272, 291, 297, 324, 337n78
ism, 27, 51; *al-ism al-jāmiʿ*, 34, 103; *asmāʾ al-ʿālam*, 63

Israel, 303
isthmus. See *barzakh*
isti'dād, 43, 107, 245
istifāda, 119
istiḥāla, 11
i'tidāl, 38, 95, 216, 246, 258, 311, 315
ittiḥād, 53
izdiwāj, 235
'izza, 69

jabarūt, 69, 150, 159
jabbār, 86
jadhba, 340n78
Ja'far al-Ṣādiq, 153–54, 168, 227, 239–40, 257, 345n43, 348n7
jahl, 239–40
ja'l, 339n63
jalāl, 9, 69, 70
jam', 63, 151; *aḥadiyyat al-jam'*, 67; *ḥaḍrat al-jam'*, 314; *jam' al-jam'*, 96; *maqām al-jam'*, 67; *jam'iyya*, 15
jamāl, 9, 69, 70
Jāmī, 'Abd al-Raḥmān, *Naqd al-nuṣūṣ*, 33–34; *Sharḥ al-fuṣūṣ*, 193; *Silsilat al-dhahab*, 35–37, 62
jāmi', 151, 152; *al-ism al-jāmi'*, 34, 103; *al-kawn al-jāmi'*, 34, 103
Jamshid, 253
jān, 233
janāba, 174
Jandī, Mu'ayyid al-Dīn, 92, 189, 193; *Sharḥ al-fuṣūṣ*, 94–96, 192, 195, 198–99, 269–70
janna, 65, 120
jawhar al-habā'ī, *al-*, 163
jealousy (*ghayra*) and the others, 11, 65, 73, 94, 191, 285, 287, 333n12, 339n49
Jerusalem, 303
Jesus, 126, 134, 262; spirituality of, 261–62; connection to Eve, 178, 180, 181, 185–86; contrasted with his ass, 270; in the microcosm, 281, 313–14
jihād, 249, 269; lesser and greater, 234, 252
jimā', 152
jinn, 15, 137, 145, 274, 314
jismānī, 61
John, 313
Junayd, 74
Jūnī, Shams al-Dīn Aḥmad, 149
Jupiter, 31
jurisprudence (*fiqh*), 10; stress of on incomparability, 9, 70
justice (*'adl*), 52, 272; in ethics, 258. *See* bounty

Kaaba, 133, 298, 303
Ka'b al-Aḥbār, 337n62
kāfir, 96
Kalābādhī, Abū Bakr. *al-Ta'arruf*, 74–75
Kalām, 3, 10, 18, 51, 322; stress of on incomparability, 8, 9, 51–52, 53, 70, 75, 77–78
Kalīla wa Dimna, 278, 279
kamāl, 44
kān, 333n4
karāma, 85
Kāshānī, 'Abd al-Razzāq, 28, 96, 177; *Iṣṭilāḥāt al-ṣūfiyya*, 299; *Sharḥ al-fuṣūṣ*, 97–99, 189–90, 191, 192, 194, 196–98; *al-Ta'wīlāt*, 118, 124, 126, 130, 131, 147, 155, 205–6, 226–27, 244–47, 273–78, 299–304, 313–14; *Tuḥfat al-ikhwān*, 268
Kāshānī, Bābā Afḍal, 3; *'Arḍ-nāma*, 265; *Rahanjām-nāma*, 264–65
Kāshānī, 'Izz al-Dīn Maḥmūd, 306; *Misbāḥ al-hidāya*, 307–11
Kāshānī, Mullā Muḥsin Fayḍ, 239
kathrat al-'ilm, 67
kawn al-jāmi', *al-*, 34, 103, 334n15
keys (*mafātīḥ*), to the unseen, 149
khabar, 88
khādim, 243
khafā', 247
khāfiḍ, 126
khalīfa, 15, 16
khāliq, 57
khalq, 57, 118, 234
Kharraqānī, Abu'l-Ḥasan, 80, 317
Kharrāz, Abū Sa'īd, 209, 255
khawāṭir, 293
khawf, 69
Khiḍr, 161
khirqa, 317–18
khuluq, 257; *tahdhīb khuluq*, 262
khuṣūṣiyya, 85
khwud, 265
kibla, 103
kibriyā', 69
king (*malik*, *pādshāh*) and soldiers, 29; heart and faculties as, 231, 242–43; intellect and virtues as, 240
Kingdom (*mulk*), lower 274; contrasted with Dominion (*see* Dominion)
knowledge (*'ilm*), as food of soul, 228, 261–62; God's, 166, 168; God's as source of cosmos, 68, 149, 185; of God as felicity, 242; identity of knower and known in, 105; manyness of (*see* Oneness of Being); as transformative, 265; of universals and particulars, 221; object of knowledge (*ma'lūm*), 66, 68, 106–7
Koran, as an intellect, 302; like a bride, 226. *See ta'wīl*
Kubrā, Najm al-Dīn, 298; *Fawā'iḥ al-jamāl*, 73–74, 76, 299
kufr, 95–96, 339n51, 352n81
kull, 264; *kulliyyāt*, 132
kun, 234
kura, 136
kursī, 86

lā shay', 93
lā ta'ayyun, 93
ladhdha, 187
Lāhījī, Muḥammad. *Sharḥ-i Gulshan-i rāz*, 167–68
Lalla of Kashmir, 326
language, 52; at the heart of existence, 45, 225
laṭīfa, 271; *laṭīfa-yi rabbānī*, 310
lawḥ, 12
left (*shimāl*), connected to soul, 256; and right (*see* right). *See also* hand
level (*martaba*), 67
life (*ḥayāt*), as the primary divine attribute, 210, 341n38
light (*nūr*), 33–34, 38–39, 63, 67, 128, 129–30; ascent of in cosmos, 39; contrasted with Nature, 213–14; as a synonym for *wujūd* (Being), 66, 106, 239; and darkness, 31–32, 61, 67, 132, 157, 159–61, 163, 239, 253, 268, 295; and shadow, 205–6
lord (*rabb*), lordship (*rubūbiyya*), contrasted with servant (servanthood), 70, 72, 101, 255, 272; Presence of Lordship, 101, 147; lordly (*rabbānī*) contrasted with satanic, 258–59. *See* vassal
love (*ḥubb*, *maḥabba*), 157, 200–201, 245, 246, 297; non-delimited, 201–2; unqualified,

love (*ḥubb, maḥabba*) (*cont.*)
184; between humans and God, 190; between men and women, 196; between spirit and soul, 310, 313; as the cause of all interrelationship, 191, 196; contrasted with appetite, 195; contrasted with intellect, 270, 287; contrasted with servanthood, 70–73; for God, 8–9, 74, 78–79, 200–1, 333n7; of God for creation, 34–35, 135, 154, 177, 183, 201, 312; as implying intimacy, 76; of a man for a specific woman, 201–2; as the shadow of Oneness, 246, 301; as transformed caprice, 287; of the whole for the part (*see* whole); world of, 217
low, lowest of the, 204. *See* high
luṭf, 9, 69, 187

mā siwā Allāh, 8
maʿād, 39, 229, 272
mabdaʾ, 39
macrocosm and microcosm, 15, 23, 28–31, 33, 34, 42–43, 45, 46, 82, 100, 145, 171, 179, 216, 218, 225, 229, 245, 249–51, 280, 281, 310, 334n1
madhhab, 72, 337n64
maghfira, 69
maḥabba, 69, 177
maḥall infiʿāl, 179
māhiyya, 66; *māhiyyāt*, 159
maʿiyya, 9, 221
majdhūb, 111
majesty (*jalāl*). *See* beauty
majʿūl, ghayr, 339n63
makhlūq, 57
Makkī, Abū Ṭālib, 271; *Qūt al-qulūb*, 255, 293–94
malakūt and *mulk*, 40, 61, 114, 118, 150
malik, al-, 168
Mālik, 85
maʾlūh, 57
maʿlūm, 57, 66
mamlaka, 168
mamsūkh, 279
man (*rajul*), 317; perfect, 195; deluded by natural yang, 177; loved by woman, 196; made two by woman, 190–91
man and woman, 173–82; Divine Command and Nature as, 211; heaven and earth as, 14, 142; intellect and soul as, 317; spirit and soul as, 189. *See* husband and wife
maʿnā, 42
manifest(ion) (*ẓāhir, zuhūr*), as goal of creation, 11, 33–35. *See* Hidden Treasure
manifest(ion) and nonmanifest(ion), 66, 87, 88, 91–92, 94, 97, 103–4, 158, 197–98, 311–12; as dimensions of existence, 220; as dimensions of the human being, 193–94, 235
mankūḥ, 156, 177, 266
manliness (*murūʾa*), 266–69, 275
manyness (*kathra*), true and relative, 106; of the objects of God's knowledge, 64; and oneness, 63, 88, 95, 108, 111, 134, 167, 169; and oneness of the soul, 312. *See* Oneness of Being
maqām: *maqām al-jamʿ*, 67; *maqāmāt*, 72, 239, 244, 247, 249, 309
maqūliyya, 150
marʾ, 183, 266
marʾa, 183, 210
maraḍ, 291
marbūb, 57
maʿrifa, 290
Māristānī, Ibrāhīm, 75
marriage (*nikāḥ*), 143, 145–51, 171–73, 193–95; as an animal appetite, 188; as a dissoluble contract, 343n38; divine, 148, 149, 176–77, 193; five (or four) levels of, 149–50, 193–95; pervading all atoms, 147, 153, 194, 208; for pleasure, 184; as the best supererogatory act, 184; universal, 194; of spirit and soul, 305–6, 308
Mars, 30, 31, 135
martaba, 67
Mary, 180, 345n28; likeness to Adam, 178, 185; masculinity and femininity of, 318; body as, 313; soul as, 313–14
masculinity (*dhukūra*), 198; standing between two feminines, 197; and femininity, 73, 198, 309
mashāʾim, 83
mashrab, 72, 337n64
matriarchy. *See* patriarchy
matter (*mādda*), prime, 156, 163; tablet of, 155; and form, 59, 157, 161–62
mawālīd, 28, 210
mawjūd, 207
mayāmīn, 83
Maybudī, Rashīd al-Dīn, 83, 85; *Kashf al-asrār*, 25–26, 84, 118, 127–28, 140–41, 174–75, 212–13, 244, 296–97
mayl, 181
Maymūn ibn Mahrān, 260
maẓhar, 61
meaning (*maʿnā*), 148; world of meanings, 149, 194, 195
measure, measuring out (*qadar, taqdīr*), 63, 125, 153
Mercury, 30, 135
mercy (*raḥma*), of the All-compassionate, 55, 107–8; of the All-merciful, 55, 107–8, 206; of necessity, 107–8; connected to Throne, 86; identical with *wujūd*, 206–7; and wrath, 11, 55, 61, 79, 85, 138
Messiah, 314
Michael, 31, 134, 154, 280
microcosm. *See* macrocosm
midād, 153
minerals, 37, 204
miʿrāj, 44, 74, 120, 132, 270, 284, 297, 302–3
misguidance (*iḍlāl*). *See* guidance
Misguider (*al-muḍill*), 101, 239, 252
mithālāt, 28
mizāj, 38
moon, 135; and sun, 30
Morewedge, P., 351n77
Moses, 74, 75, 82, 134, 200, 303, 337n62
mother (*umm, mādar*), 197; of the Book, 155, 190; contrasted with father, 55; body as, 284; earth as, 140; elements as, 284; Essence as, 76; Nature as (*see* Nature); rights of, 213; mothers (*ummahāt*) [= elements] 28, 29; of the names, 63
Muʿādh, 79, 173, 176
muʿallim, 154
muʾaththar fīh, 145
muʾaththir, 57, 145
mubāḥī, 112
mubāshara, 89
mudabbir, 62
muḍill, al-, 239
mufaṣṣil, 62
mufrad, 29, 152; *mufradāt*, 160
mukāshif, 259
Muhammad, 188; contrasted with

Iblis, 252; love of for women, 183–86, 196; as most perfect human being, 189–90, 265, 287, 311; way of, 261–62. *See mi*ʿ*rāj*
Muhammadan, form, 65; friend of God, 345n51; light, 166, 252; Presence, 66; Reality, 68, 189; Soul, 166; Spirit, 166, 189
Muḥammad al-Bāqir, 84, 176
muḥyī, 27
mujāhada, 234, 249, 252
Mujāhid, 153
mukhtaṣar, 179
mulk. *See malakūt*
Mullā Ṣadrā, 3, 53; *ʿArshiyya*, 265; *Taʿlīqāt*, 282
mumīt, 27
mumkināt, 68
munāsaba, 190
Munkar, 141
murakkabāt, 29
murū'a, 266
Musallam, B., 348n43
muslim, 261
muta'allihūn, 255
mutaʿallim, 154
mutarawḥinūn, 214
mutashābih, 185
muṭlaq, 93, 201
muṭma'inna, 102, 254
muwallad, 145; *muwalladāt*, 28
mystery, inmost (*sirr*), 247, 253

nafas, 229
nāfila, 183
nafs, 76, 111, 155, 229, 236–37, 256, 265; *al-nafs al-ammāra*, 254; *al-nafs al-lawwāma*, 254; *al-nafs al-mulhama*, 294; *al-nafs al-muṭma'inna*, 254; *nufūs*, 144
nahār, 146
nahy, 88
nākiḥ, 156, 177
Nakīr, 141
name(s) (*ism*), of beauty and majesty (mercy and wrath), 17, 56, 77–79, 81; complementary (contrasting, polar), 55–57, 81, 87, 98; demanded by cosmos, 89; divine, 9, 27–28, 31–35, 36, 40, 51, 97, 103, 113; equilibrium of, 150; of Essence (*see* Essence); as the human kingdom, 182; leaders of, 38, 63; priority among, 68; reflected in signs, 10, 206; rejoicing of, 148; two denotations of, 81, 103; as source of cosmos (*see* cosmos); of yin and yang, 9, 11, 56, 173; and incomparability, 52
naqāwa, 179
nāqiṣ, 180
Nasafī, ʿAzīz al-Dīn, 13, 14, 168; *Insān-i kāmil*, 30–31, 45–46, 158–61, 217–18, 281; *Kashf al-ḥaqā'iq*, 119–20, 231–32, 235–36; *Zubdat al-haqā'iq*, 38–39
Nature (*ṭabīʿa*, *ṭabʿ*), 39, 150, 169, 209–11, 220, 274, 275; as Breath of All-merciful, 196, 210; as child, 156; contrasted with spirits, 103, 145, 210–15; as darkness, 163; as father, 156–57; four, 30, 42, 210, 216; as mother, 145, 156, 197, 210, 212, 213–14; pillars of, 136–37, 221; receptivity of, 194, 260; reproduction in, 152; two active principles of, 87; universal, 194; as wife, 210; as womb, 219–22
natural (*ṭabīʿī*), world, 158; contrasted with spiritual, 102, 104
nāz, 72
naẓar, 228, 307
necessary (*wājib*), necessity (*wujūb*), contrasted with possible, possibility, 97, 106–8, 117, 134–35, 149, 168, 169, 182, 189, 210, 221, 312
Neoplatonism, 220, 335n30
next world (*ākhira*) and this world, 61
niche (*mishkāt*), 159–61, 299–300
Nicholson, R.A., 335
night (*layl*), 303. *See* day(time)
nikāḥ, 143, 152
niʿma, 84
nisba, 8, 51
niyāz, 72
Noah, 303
nondelimitation (*iṭlāq*). *See* delimitation
nonentification (*lā taʿayyun*), 93. *See* entification
nonexistence (*ʿadam*). *See* existence
nonmanifest (*bāṭin*). *See* manifest
nubuwwa, 180
nufūs, 144
numbers, 59–60
nūn, 153–54, 168
nuqṭa-yi ṣafā', 296
nūr, 31, 132
nuskha, 45
nuṭq, 38

ocean (*baḥr*), two, 160–61
oddness (*fardiyya*). *See* singularity
One/Many (*al-wāḥid al-kathīr*), 62, 67, 92
oneness (*waḥda*), 300–1; correlated with activity and receptivity, 66, 106; true and relative, 64, 105–7; and severity, 333n12
Oneness of Being (*waḥdat al-wujūd*), 124; contrasted with manyness of knowledge, 67–68, 99, 106, 109–10, 112–113, 149, 158, 165, 312, 336n49. *See* manyness
opposites (*aḍdād*), 32, 70, 81, 131, 156, 209
Origin (*mabda'*). *See* Return
orthodoxy, 3, 8
other(s) (*ghayr*), 31, 77, 109. *See* jealousy

pair(s) (*zawj*), 117–18, 120, 126; love between, 154
paradise (*bihisht*), 231; limitations of, 250. *See* hell, Garden
parda, 296
parents (*wālidān*), 147, 152, 182; spirit and nature as, 212–14; spirit and soul as, 313
patriarchy contrasted with matriarchy, 79, 208, 322
Pen (*qalam*), as a *barzakh*, 165; faces of, 13, 164–68; Supreme, 188; and the Tablet, 12–13, 64, 153–57, 158, 162–67
perfection (*kamāl*), of the cosmos, 38–39; as equilibrium of attributes, 95, 150–51, 258; God's name-derived, 65; human, 18, 35, 44, 150–51, 218–19, 254, 264, 265, 269, 301, 302, 303, 311–12; of the (rational) soul, 263–64, 268, 275–76, 300; true vs. relative, 108. *See* human being (perfect)
Pharoah, 74, 180
philosophy, philosophers, 222, 261, 286, 336n47
pig, 258–59, 270, 281
pillars (*arkān*), (=elements) 28, 29–30, 38, 64, 135–39, 155; activity and receptivity of, 208 (*see also* elements); (= four primary divine names), 37, 45–46, 210

placenta (*mashīma*), soul as, 311–12; spirit as, 312
planets, 30, 132, 133, 135, 216
plants, 37, 38, 40, 204
Plato, 282
Plenum, Higher (*al-mala' al-aʿlā*), 134, 219, 308
Pole (*quṭb*), 65, 183, 187, 195
possible things (*mumkināt*), 68; possibility (*imkān*), 348n57; presence of, 148. *See* necessity
power (*qudra*), 32; God's, 152, 210
predators (*sibāʿ*, *dadagān*), 258, 279. *See* beasts
predestination, 72, 125, 153
premises (*muqaddimāt*), 148, 152, 194, 195
preparedness (*istiʿdād*), 107; 68, 103, 130, 211, 245, 275, 300, 302, 303
presence (*ḥaḍra*), 67, 101; of Being, 106; Divine, 89, 96, 103, 113, 147, 200, 221, 231, 243; Five Divine, 342n20; of Knowledge, 106; of lordship, 101, 147; of Necessity, 106; of Possibility, 106; of servanthood, 101
prophecy (*nubuwwa*), 263; exclusive to men, 309; shared by men and women, 180; function of, 77
prophets (*anbiyā'*), 27, 33, 37, 111; in the heavens, 133–34; as perfect human beings, 44, 64; connected with intellect. *See* intellect
psychology, spiritual, 69
Pythagoras, 28; Pythagoreans, 59

qabḍ, 69, 73, 90, 337n71
qabḍa, 83
qābil, 92; *qābiliyya*, 66
qabūl, 68, 105
qaḍā', 154
qadam Ṣidq, 85
qadar, 125, 153, 155, 339n63
qadīm, 234
qahr, 9, 69, 187; *qahr al-ladhdha*, 187
qā'im, 178
qalam, 12,
qalb, 229, 232, 289, 296, 297, 301; *aṣḥāb al-qulūb*, 292; *muṣarrif al-qulūb*, 292
qawī, *al-*, 176, 209
qaws, 39
Qayṣarī, Sharaf al-Dīn Dāwūd, 99, 189; *Sharḥ al-fuṣūṣ*, 99–101, 190–95
Qazwīnī, 233
qualities, of elements, 135–41; of heaven and earth, 136; of the human self, 229–30; of spirit and body, 236; qualitative ambiguity, 132; qualitative correspondences (analogy), 28, 104, 128, 210, 280–81; qualitative evaluation of things, 8, 14, 15, 17, 24–25, 27–28, 31–32, 37, 257–58
qudra, 84, 197
qudus, 69
quiddity (*māhiyya*), 66, 159, 205
Qūnawī, Ṣadr al-Dīn, 64, 83, 92, 149, 159, 339n58, 342n20; *Fakk al-khutūm*, 134, 315; *Iʿjāz al-bayān*, 103–4, 165–66, 206, 251, 315–16; *Miftāḥ al-ghayb*, 149–51, 314; *al-Nafaḥāt al-ilāhiyya*, 107; *Sharḥ al-ḥadīth*, 84, 101–2, 219–22; *Tabṣirat al-mubtadi'*, 206
qur'ān, *al-*, 301–2, 310
qurb, 69
Qurṭubī, al-, 345n28
Qushayrī, Abu'l-Qāsim. *Laṭā'if al-ishārāt*, 84–85, 128, 177; *Risāla*, 256, 267
quṭb, 183, 187, 340n65
quwwa, 84, 209, 264

rabb, 57; *rabbānī*, 258; *rabbāniyyūn*, 255, 262
Rabīʿ, al-, 83
Rābiʿa, 250
rāfiʿ, 126
rafīq, 266
raḥim, 182, 215
raḥīm, 55
raḥma, 9, 69, 182, 206, 215
raḥmān, 55, 182, 206
rain, 127
rajā', 69
rajʿa, 174
rajul, 210, 268
Rāzī, Fakhr al-Dīn, 83, 85, 127; *al-Tafsīr*, 139–40, 153
Rāzī, Najm al-Dīn. *Mirṣād al-ʿibād*, 39–43, 61, 137–38, 234–35, 272–73, 283–88, 326
real (*ḥaqq*), 121–22; absolutely vs. relatively, 50, 54, 64, 67, 77–78, 92
reality (*ḥaqīqa*), 179; 66; as both father and mother, 197; engendered vs. divine, 101; Muhammadan, 188; of realities, 188–89
realness (*ḥaqqiyya*) and unrealness, 109–11
reception (*qabūl*), receptivity (*qābiliyya*), receiving activity (*infiʿāl*), 68; of God, 53, 207–8; of the soul (*see* soul). *See* activity
relationships (*nisba*), 8, 49–51, 57, 321–22; changing, 12, 106–7; as making God a God, 50, 68; as sole means to knowledge, 132–33
relativity of all things, 32–33, 132–33
religions (*adyān*), diversity of, 104; unity of, 112
remembrance (*dhikr*) of God, 75, 129, 254, 298. *See* dhikr
reports (*khabar*) and rulings, 88
reproduction (*tawālud*), 147, 151–52, 157; love for, 184
resolve (*himma*), 194
resurrection (*qiyāma*), kinds of, 159
Return (*maʿād*), 218, 229, 283; compulsory and voluntary, 272; and Origin, 39, 158
revelation (*waḥy*), 88
riḍā, 69, 91
Riḍwān, 85, 141
right (*yamīn*) and left, 82–84, 101, 107–8, 167, 168, 214–15, 239–40; Companions of, 82, 83, 101–2, 108, 109, 301; as good and evil, 205
rīḥ, 229
risāla, 180
rizq, 58
rubūbiyya, 255; *tanāzuʿ maʿ al-rubūbiyya*, 272
rūḥ, 229, 232, 236, 237, 301; *al-rūḥ al-iḍāfī*, 212; *al-rūḥ al-ilāhī*, 232; *al-rūḥ al-rūḥānī*, 312; *rūḥānī*, 61; *rūḥāniyyūn*, 240
rujūliyya, 268
rulings (*ḥukm*), 88
Rūmī, 70, 192, 342n5; spiritual psychology of, 270; *Dīwān*, 131, 178, 221, 229, 233, 238, 250, 270; *Fīhi mā fīhi*, 62, 226, 280, 287, 313; *Majālis-i sabʿa*, 62; *Mathnawī*, 11, 14, 42, 45, 50, 51, 55, 72, 126, 131, 185, 206, 219, 226, 253, 270,

282, 287–88, 305, 317, 318
rushd, 239
Rustam, 226, 318
Rūzbihān. *See* Baqlī

saʿa, 34
saʿāda, 230
sābiḥ, 132
ṣabr, 271
ṣadr, 296
ṣafā', 296
ṣāḥiba, 180
Saʿīd ibn al-Musayyib, 174
sakhṭ, 69
ṣalāḥ, 295
ṣalāt, 52
samʿ, 228
samā', 119
Samʿānī, Aḥmad. *Rawḥ al-arwāḥ*, 35, 52, 61–62, 65, 71–73, 138–39, 280, 296, 316, 333n12, 334n1
Sanā'ī, 155, 161
Sarrāj, Abū Nasr. *Kitāb al-lumaʿ*, 255
Satan (*shayṭān*), 15, 129, 245, 258, 276–77, 290; differentiated from Iblis, 281; satans (devils), 230–31; becoming a satan in the afterlife, 282. *See* Iblis
satanic, contrasted with All-merciful, 256; contrasted with angelic, 230; contrasted with lordly, 258–59; satanity, 272, 277
Saturn, 31, 135
scales (*mīzān*), 277
Schimmel, Annemarie, 70, 337n81, 342n5
self-disclosure (*tajallī*), first, 166
senses (*ḥawāss*), sense perception (*ḥiss*), 242–43; world of, 194; contrasted with world of intellect, 277
separation (*farq*, *firāq*) and union, 70, 72, 76
Seraphiel, 31, 134, 141, 154
servant (*ʿabd*), 252; connected with incomparability, 16, 54–55, 77–78; contrasted with lord (*see* lord); paired with vicegerent, 16–17, 54–55, 56, 69–70, 98, 100, 177, 204, 246, 251; of one's wife, 255
servanthood (*ʿubūdiyya*), of the Pole, 187; as the highest human station, 264, 302–3. *See* worship
severity (*qahr*), of enjoyment, 187; connection with soul, 256–57. *See* gentleness
Shabistarī, Maḥmūd. *Gulshan-i rāz*, 167, 227–28
shadow (*ẓill*), contrasted with light, 205–6
shafʿ, 59
shaghāf, 297
shahāda, 25, 61, 118; the Shahāda, 52, 322
shāhid, 75
shahwa, 111, 177, 187, 284
shajana, 182
shame (*ḥayā'*), 181
shaqā', *shaqāwa*, 230
sharah, 271
Sharia, 2–3, 35–36, 60, 109, 111–112, 172, 174, 187, 246, 284, 303, 317, 322; as establishing love for God, 333n7; light of, 244; as means of keeping attributes in equilibrium, 285; as rectifying character, 276, 286; stress of on incomparability and distance, 53–54, 77–79, 325
sharīk, 126
shaṭḥiyyāt, 78
shay', 66
shaykh, 76; *al-shaykh al-ra'īs*, 263
shayṭānī, 258
Shiblī, 75, 76
shimāl, 82
shirk, 87, 108, 285
shu'ūn, 347n8
sibāʿ, 230
ṣiddīq, 295
ṣifa, 27, 51, 197
sifāḥ, 152
signs (*āyāt*), 10, 14, 23–28, 97, 127, 206, 209
Sijjīn, 101
similarity (*tashbīh*). *See* incomparability
simple things (*mufradāt*), 160; the twenty-eight, 343n69; simplicity (*basāṭa*) (*see* compound)
singularity (*fardiyya*), 151, 152, 188–89; prime, 194
sirr, 247, 253, 301, 311; *ḥifẓ al-sirr*, 80
sitr, 96
society, and natural laws, 121; and attributes of incomparability, 77–80, 172, 325; relationships in, 54, 174
Socrates, 261–62
Solitary (*fard*; pl. *afrād*), 104, 195
Solomon, 281
soul (*nafs*), 144, 236–38, 283–84, 307; achieving actuality of, 282; animal, 278, 299, 312; animal qualities of, 278–83; ascent of, 264–65; appetitive, 314; as a *barzakh*, 237; blaming, 254, 271, 295; as Burāq of the spirit, 287; as a child of spirit and body, 284, 287; as a child of human and animal spirits, 305; commanding to evil, 42, 78, 254–56, 257, 269–71, 273, 283, 286, 295, 306, 316; connected with fire, 237, 269; connected with severity, 256–57; darkness of, 256; as an enemy, 283, 293–94; femininity of, 266; food of, 228–29, 261; heavenly, 155; inspired, 294–95; levels (stages, tendencies) of, 236–37, 254, 255, 294–95, 306–7; as Mary, 313–14; as a mother, 306; as mother of caprice and anger, 287; as negative, 271–72; negative yin and yang tendencies of, 284; as opponent of religion, 280; at peace, 78, 102, 254, 269, 271, 283, 286, 295, 299, 306, 316; perfection of, 218–19; as positive, 271; purification of, 283; rational, 155, 194, 212, 263, 310; receptivity of, 238, 260–66, 269, 313; as satanic, 256, 270; two faces of, 252; Universal, 209 (*see* Intellect); as wife of First Intellect, 156; as wife of God's activity, 256–57; as wife of spirit, 238, 308, 310; contrasted with spirit, 12, 40, 57, 76, 130, 144, 189, 229, 235–37, 255–56, 269, 273, 295, 298; contrasted with body (*see* body); contrasted with heart (*see* heart); contrasted with intellect (*see* intellect)
speech (*kalām*, *nuṭq*), as human attribute, 45; as a marriage, 145–46
sperm drop (*nuṭfa*), 30, 216–17, 284
sphere (*falak*), first, 158, 159, 160
spirit (*rūḥ*), 38, 232–36; angelic, 232; animal, 38, 231, 234, 276, 283, 305, 310, 312; attributed, 212, 307, 308; of the Command, 232; disengaged, 194; divine,

spirit (*rūḥ*) (*cont.*)
214, 232; greatest, 158, 307, 308; heavenly, 305; high, 305–6; holy, 232; human, 212, 218, 231–32, 235, 305–6; levels of, 31, 218, 231–32, 236–37; luminous, 194; masculinity of, 309; spiritual, 312; universal, 190; two visions of, 308; contrasted with body (*see* body); contrasted with Nature (*see* Nature); contrasted with soul (*see* soul); ascent of animal spirit, 38–39; World of Spirit(s), 39–40, 194, 195, 274, 287
spiritual (*rūḥānī*), contrasted with corporeal, 157 (*see also* body)
stages (*aṭwār*), 251
states (*aḥwāl*), contrasted with stations, 73, 244, 247, 309–10
station(s) (*maqām*), 239, 249, 303, 315–16; known, 287; of no station, 95–96, 105, 150, 315; contrasted with states (*see* states)
strength (*quwwa*), of woman, 177; and weakness, 209
struggle (*jihād, mujāhada*), 234, 249, 252–53
submission (*islām*), 70, 77–78, 294–95; of all things to the Real, 203–4; paired with struggle, 252; prerequisite for vicegerency, 323; to the wife, 226. See *islām*
subsistence (*baqā'*), 76, 283–84
substance (*jawhar*), First, 343n69; four genera of, 282; and accident, 157
Substitutes (*abdāl*), 65, 268
Sufis(m), 3; antinomianism of, 78–79; connection with Christ, 261–62; contrasted with Kalām, 51–53, 70, 78; Sufi practices, 261, 262
Sufyān al-Thawrī, 153–54
Suhrawardī, Shihāb al-Dīn ʿUmar. *ʿAwārif al-maʿārif*, 271–72, 305–6
Suhrawardī al-Maqtūl, Shihāb al-Dīn, 3, 132, 282; *Majmūʿa*, 169
Sulamī, Abū ʿAbd al-Raḥmān. *ʿUyūb al-nafs*, 255–56
sulūk, 340n78
sun, 30, 31, 135, 216
Sunna, 82, 297
supererogatory acts (*nāfila*), 183–84
supra-sensory (*maʿnawī*), contrasted with sensory (*ḥissī*), 148
ṣūra, 34, 42
suṭūr, 230
syllogism, 148, 152. *See* premises

ta'addub, 122
ta'alluh, 262
taʿayyun, 134
ṭabʿ, 209, 210, 211, 260, 274
ṭabīʿa, 209, 260
tablet (*lawḥ*), as emerald, 163; four kinds of, 155; Guarded, 190, 303; as a pen, 163; contrasted with Supreme Pen (*see* Pen)
Ṭabrisī, Faḍl al-, 85; *Majmaʿ al-bayān*, 176
tadākhul, 148, 209
tadbīr, 216, 233
tadhkīr, 249, 354n1
tafāḍul, 334n12
tafriqa, 63
tafṣīl, 62
tafsīr, 226, 227, 244
taghashshā, 146
taḥaqquq, 299
tahdhīb khuluq, 262
tajallī, 11, 64, 192, 227
taklīf, 180
takwīn, 246
tamaththul, 137
tanāsukh, 278
tanāsul, 147
tanāzuʿ maʿ al-rubūbiyya, 272
tanzīh, 8, 49
Tao, 7–8, 61; as *ḥaqq*, 121; as *islām*, 203; the nameable and unnameable, 50, 58, 93; Taoism, 9–10, 50, 92, 196, 325
taqdīr, 63, 234
taqlīb, 292
taqwā, 260
al-tarāfuʿ fi'l-darajāt, 334n12
Ṭarīqa, 208, 317, 325
taṣarruf, 302
taṣawwuf, 261
tashabbuh, 261
tashbīh, 9; *tashbīhāt*, 28
tashrīf, 89
taswiya, 339n53
ta'thīr, 68, 105
tathlīth, 151
taʿṭīl, 53
tawallud, 156
tawālud, 147
tawāluj, 147, 209
tawfīq, 212
tawḥīd, 7, 10, 18, 49, 50, 71, 77, 108, 130, 147, 178, 225, 238, 239, 253, 285, 294, 295, 298, 304, 314, 321–22
ta'wīl, 14–15, 28, 159, 205, 225–28, 244, 313, 316, 343n57, 348n7, 352n82
tayammum, 213
ṭaysh, 271
tazawwuj, 154
Ten Thousand Things, 7, 8, 59, 61, 119
thany, 154
theodicy, 35–36
theology, negative vs. positive, 8–9
thing (*shay'*), 66; immutable, 159; thingness (*shay'iyya*), 148
thoughts, incoming (*khawāṭir*), 293–94, 298, 312
thrall, divine (*ma'lūh*), 57, 61, 131, 191, 208
Throne (*ʿarsh*), 236, 311; parents of, 156; connected with mercy, 86–87, 156, 219; and Footstool, 31, 64, 86, 156, 246
thubūt, 86
time (*zamān*), and space, 157
Tirmidhī, al-Ḥakīm al-, 294–95
traits. *See* character
transcription (*nuskha*), of Spirit and Soul, 309; microcosm as, 16, 36, 45, 280
transmigration (*tanāsukh*), 278, 283
triplicity (*tathlīth*), 151–53, 189, 191; in God, 151
Trust (*amāna*), 33, 40, 54, 123, 219, 287, 310
Ṭūbā, 88
turāb, 136, 137
Two Bows' Length, 286

ʿubūdiyya, 177
Uhud, 267
ulfa, 246
ulūhiyya, 50
ʿUmar (ibn al-Khaṭṭāb), 79, 175, 252, 348n2
umm, 197, 210
undifferentiation (*ijmāl*). *See* differentiation
union (*waṣl, wiṣāl*), 253–54, 261. *See* separation
unity (*aḥadiyya*), Inclusive, 64; Exclusive vs. Inclusive, 62, 190; of Essence, 59; of Oneness vs. that of manyness, 58–59
unrealness (*buṭlān*). *See* realness
uns, 56, 69, 173
unseen (*ghayb*), keys to, 149; of the Unseen, 105; and visible, 13,

25, 33, 61, 87–88, 97, 103–4, 118
unūtha, 285
ʿuqalāʾ al-majānīn, 112
ustādh, 154
uṣūl al-fiqh, 2
ʿuyūb, 255

vassal (*marbūb*) and lord, 57–58, 59, 61, 131, 177, 182, 191, 208
veil (*ḥijāb*), 96, 109, 111, 276, 297, 298
Venus, 31, 135
vicegerent (*khalīfa*), 33, 40, 64–65, 100, 272–73, 281; Adam as, 44, 46, 78, 184; the First, 307; first and second, 217; first and last, 308; intellect as, 31, 46; perfect human being as, 98; connected with similarity, 15, 54–55; connected with cosmos, 91, 123. *See* servant
virtues (*faḍāʾil*), 218, 245, 261, 302, 303–4
visible (*shahāda*), world of, 194. *See* unseen

wadd, al-wadūd, 343n38
waḥdat al-wujūd, 67
wāḥid al-kathīr, al-, 62, 92; *wāḥidiyya*, 62
wahm, 46, 273, 351n77
waḥsha, 75
wajh, 64, 152
walāya, 104, 268
walī, 104; *awliyāʾ*, 44
waraʿ, 297
water (*māʾ, āb*), of life, 161; qualities of, 138, 208
whole (*kull*), its love for the part, 181, 182, 190, 200
wife. *See* husband
wisdom (*ḥikma*), 111, 261, 262, 307, 333n12
withness (*maʿiyya*), 221
witness (*shāhid*), 75
witnessing (*shuhūd*) God, 74, 75–76, 297; through the body, 222; through woman, 192–93
woman (*marʾa*), women (*nisāʾ*), attributes as, 73–74, 337n67; as falling short in intelligence and religion, 174, 179, 285, 318; as a "Platonic" friend, 266; as the root, 197; rulership of, 183; similar to Nature, 179, 197; the soul (that commands to evil) as, 266, 285, 314, 316–17; strength of, 177; as a trial, 199–201; weakness of, 177; witnessing God in, 192–93, 195–96; and the house, 233. *See* feminine, man, mother, husband
womb (*raḥim*), 29, 30, 44, 153, 179, 215–22, 232; analogy of with this world, 218–19; as a branch of the All-merciful, 182, 220; imagination as, 149
word (*kalima*), active vs. verbal, 344n73; creative, 13, 151–52; creatures as, 207–8, 335n37; divine spirit as, 214; division of the One Word into two, 88, 156
world (*ʿālam*), 160; three vs. two, 132; of writing and inscription, 163, 165, 168; this world (*dunyā*) contrasted with next world (*ākhira*), 120, 137, 157
worship (*ʿibāda*), 71, 203–6; as a yin reality, 204
wrath (*ghaḍab*), destroys "others," 333n12. *See* good pleasure, mercy
wretchedness (*shaqāʾ, shaqāwa*). *See* felicity
wuḍūʾ, 191
wujūd, 32, 66, 109, 206–7, 264, 265; *al-wujūd al-maḥḍ*, 62; *waḥdat al-wujūd*, 67; *wujūdī*, 178
wuṣūl, 159

yad, 82
yāftan, 264
yaḥyā, 313
yamīn, 82
yang. *See* yin
yawm, 146
yin and yang, 6–8, 50, 57–58, 177–78, 185; their interpenetration, 208–9; predominance of yin over yang, 9; relation of with similarity and incomparability, 54–55; and the divine names, 53

ẓālimūn, 274
zawj(ān), 117, 121, 154, 190, 340n10
zindīq, 112
ẓuhūr, 11
ẓulm, 274
ẓulma, 31, 132, 274, 352n83